*"I'm the 82ND Airborne Division!"*

# *"I'm the 82ND Airborne Division!"*

## A History of the All American Division
## in World War II After Action Reports

### *Robert P. Anzuoni*

**Schiffer Military History**
Atglen, PA

*Acknowledgements*

I would like to thank my wife, Sara, for her patience, understanding, and support and my daughters, Lily and Eden, for being themselves. Special thanks to Alexander S. "Big Al" Nemeth, C Company, 307th Airborne Engineer Battalion World War II for his contributions and support, and to my editor, Bob Biondi, for his hard work and support.

*Dedication*

In memory of Fred DiCesare, E Company, 505th Parachute Infantry Regiment World War II and all those who served.

Book design by Robert Biondi.

Printed in China.
ISBN: 0-7643-2347-4

We are always looking for people to write books on new and related subjects. If you have an idea for a book, please contact us at the address below.

Published by Schiffer Publishing Ltd.
4880 Lower Valley Road
Atglen, PA 19310
Phone: (610) 593-1777
FAX: (610) 593-2002
E-mail: Info@schifferbooks.com.
Visit our web site at: www.schifferbooks.com
Please write for a free catalog.
This book may be purchased from the publisher.
Please include $3.95 postage.
Try your bookstore first.

In Europe, Schiffer books are distributed by:
Bushwood Books
6 Marksbury Ave.
Kew Gardens
Surrey TW9 4JF
England
Phone: 44 (0)20 8392-8585
FAX: 44 (0)20 8392-9876
E-mail: Bushwd@aol.com.
Free postage in the UK. Europe: air mail at cost.
Try your bookstore first.

# Contents

# Preface

This book is based upon a series of after action reports, combat narratives, documents, charts, maps, and photographs describing the campaigns of the 82nd Airborne Division, the "All American", in World War II. The campaigns described herein are those in which the Division, or major elements of the Division, fought. They are officially titled, SICILY, NAPLES-FOGGIA (Salerno), ANZIO, NORMANDY, RHINELAND (Holland, 1944), ARDENNES-ALSACE (Battle of the Bulge), RHINELAND (Belgium and Germany, 1945), and CENTRAL EUROPE (Germany). This is the story of the 82nd in its own words, so to speak. The documents used for this text were created as a historical record of the Division by the Division staff members themselves. The story was recorded by those who were there shortly after the events happened. It has been sixty years since these documents were published. They have been edited for consistency and accuracy.

In the course of its operations the 82nd Airborne Division became the first American Airborne Division in action and the only Airborne Division to fight in two Theaters of Operations (the Mediterranean, and the European Theaters). The 82nd conducted four airborne operations (Sicily, Salerno, Normandy, and Holland). The first two operations involved only the parachute forces of the Division. Normandy and Holland saw the incorporation of gliders into large-scale airborne operations involving the whole Division. General Officers who served in the 82nd Airborne Division became commanders of every American airborne division which saw action in World War II (11th, 17th and 101st), and one became commander of the only American airborne corps formed during the war.

Not only did the 82nd pave the way for other airborne divisions and an airborne corps, but it also contributed significantly to victory wherever it was assigned. Whether in the airborne, amphibious, or light infantry role, the 82nd was successful. In the face of a determined enemy and suffering heavy casualties, the mission was accomplished. It has always been a combination of intense training, discipline, and esprit-de-corps that has made the 82nd Airborne Division successful. I hope this book reveals what individuals, working together from squads to regiments, contributed to make the 82nd a Division. A Division only comes to life when it is filled with individuals who have a sense of *esprit de corps* that bonds them to their fellow soldiers and commits them to the higher mission at hand.

Robert P. Anzuoni
Aiken, South Carolina
2005

# Introduction

The 82nd Division, a unit which spent more consecutive days under fire than any other American Division in World War I and which suffered a total of 1,035 men killed and 6,387 other casualties, became more than a file card in the War Department on 25 March 1942 when it was reactivated at Camp Claiborne, Louisiana. With the 77th and 90th Divisions, the 82nd became one of the first three "reserve" divisions to be reactivated for service in World War II.

In World War I, the 82nd Division had participated in the Lorraine 1918, St. Mihiel and Meuse-Argonne campaigns. Its officer ranks had included Major Jonathan M. Wainwright, in World War II a full general and the hero of Bataan; Lieutenant Colonel John C.H. Lee, in World War II a Lieutenant General and commander of the Communications Zone in the European Theater; and Colonel Gordon Johnston, Chief of Staff, who received the Medal of Honor for action in the Philippines in 1906. Its enlisted ranks included Sergeant Alvin C. York, recipient of the Congressional Medal of Honor and classed by General Pershing as the outstanding American soldier of World War I.

Reorganized as a triangular division in the reserves, the 82nd on 25 March included the Division Headquarters, Division Headquarters Company, 325th, 326th and 327th Infantry Regiments; Headquarters and Headquarters Battery, 82nd Division Artillery; the 319th, 320th, 321st and 907th Field Artillery Battalions; and the 307th Engineer Battalion, 307th Medical Battalion, 407th Quartermaster Battalion, 82nd Reconnaissance Troop, 82nd Signal Company, and the 82nd Military Police Platoon.

Among officers assigned to the 82nd Infantry Division upon activation were Major General Omar N. Bradley, Commanding General, who later became a full General and, in succession, Commander of II Corps, First United States Army, and Twelfth United States Army Group; Brigadier General Matthew B. Ridgway, Assistant Division Commander, who succeeded General Bradley as Division Commander on 26 June 1942 and later Commanded XVIII Corps (Airborne) and was promoted to Lieutenant General; Brigadier General Joseph M. Swing, Division Artillery Commander and later commander of the 11th Airborne and Assistant Division Commander of the 86th Infantry Division; Colonel Claudius S. Easley, Commander of the 325th Infantry, who later became a Brigadier General and was killed in action in the Pacific Theater, Colonel Stuart Cutler, Commander of the 326th Infantry, later promoted to Brigadier General and serving on the Staff of the First Allied Airborne Army; Lieutenant Colonel Ralph Eaton, Adjutant General, later promoted to the rank of Brigadier General after service as Chief of Staff of both the Division and XVIII Corps (Airborne); and Lieutenant Colonel Francis A. March, 320th Field Artillery Battalion Commander and later commander of the 82nd Airborne Division Artillery.

The Division, setting a new record for speed in its plan of classifying and assigning recruits to units, underwent training appropriate for the various arms of a normal infantry division during the first few months after activation. When General Ridgway succeeded General Bradley as Division commander, Colonel Maxwell D. Taylor became Chief of Staff. Colonel Taylor later became a general officer, commanding first the 82nd Airborne Division Artillery and later the 101st Airborne Division.

During the early summer word was received that the 82nd was to become a motorized division and was to move in the fall to Camp Atterbury, Indiana. This plan however was canceled and on 15 August 1942 the 82nd Infantry Division became the 82nd Airborne Division. The 82nd Infantry Division of World War II held its first and only parade on that date.

The change to the airborne saw the 82nd split practically in half, one half becoming the 82d Airborne Division and the other half the 101st Airborne Division. In the process the 82nd lost the 327th Infantry and two artillery battalions (321st and 907th).

The 325th and 326th regiments each contributed a battalion to form a new regiment for the 101st and most other units contributed approximately one-half of their strength to the 101st. (One of the "lost" battalions, the 2nd Battalion, 401st was attached to the Division in early 1944 and eventually was incorporated permanently as the 3rd Battalion, 325th.)

Following the conversion, the 82nd Airborne Division's order of battle included Division Headquarters; Division Headquarters Company; 325th and 326th Glider Infantry Regiments (each reduced to a two-battalion basis); 504th Parachute Infantry Regiment which had been activated only a few months earlier at Fort Benning, Georgia; Headquarters and Headquarters Battery, 82nd Airborne Division Artillery; 319th and 320th Glider Field Artillery Battalions; the newly-activated 376th Parachute Field Artillery Battalion; the 307th Airborne Engineer Battalion with two lettered glider companies (A and B) and one lettered parachute company (C); the 307th Airborne Medical Company; 407th Airborne Quartermaster Company; 82nd Airborne Signal Company; and 82nd Airborne Military Police Platoon. The new Table of Organization did not provide for a Division reconnaissance element, but personnel remaining with the Division from the former 82nd Reconnaissance Troop were formed into a provisional platoon.

The 80th Airborne Anti-Aircraft Battalion was activated on 3 September 1942 and the 782nd Airborne Ordnance Maintenance Company was activated on 6 October 1942.

Ground training of the Division proceeded at Camp Claiborne, Louisiana, until 1 October 1942, when the 82nd moved to Fort Bragg, North Carolina, for more advanced ground training in alternation with airborne training. A feature of the move saw both the 82nd and 101st Airborne Divisions send advance parties of approximately 250 men and officers each to Fort Bragg by air, the largest movement of American military personnel by air up to that time.

A further change in the organization of the Division was effected on 12 February 1943, when the 326th Glider Infantry was withdrawn from the Division, and the 505th Parachute Infantry and 456th Parachute Field Artillery Battalion were assigned. To complete this change to two-thirds parachute combat strength, Company B of the 307th Airborne Engineer Battalion was converted from a glider into a parachute unit.

Meanwhile Brigadier General Joseph M. Swing left his post as Division Artillery Commander to become Commanding General of the 11th Airborne Division. Colonel Maxwell D. Taylor was promoted to Brigadier General and became Division Artillery Commander. Brigadier General William M. Miley was relieved as Assistant Division Commander of the 82nd and became Commanding General of the 17th Airborne Division. Colonel Charles L. Keerans, Jr. Chief of Staff of the 101st Airborne Division, was promoted to Brigadier General and became Assistant Division Commander of the 82nd Airborne Division. (General Keerans later was listed as missing in action when his plane did not return from a flight to observe the 504th Parachute Combat Team's drop into Sicily.)

All parachute maintenance personnel were combined into the provisional 82nd Parachute Maintenance Company.

On 29 March 1943, Colonel James M. Gavin led his 505th Parachute Infantry Regiment on a parachute assault near Camden, South Carolina. This was the first regimental-size parachute exercise. The troops quickly assembled and seized the objective, a bridge over the Wateree River. Three paratroopers (Sergeant Major Howard R. Calahan, Private Arthur W. Elliott, and Private Carroll A. Hedlind) were killed during the jump when one aircraft lost power and cut through their parachute canopies.

Alerted for overseas movement, the 82nd Airborne Division began its departure from Fort Bragg, North Carolina, on 17 April 1943. The Division staged at Camp Edwards, Massachusetts, from 21 to 27 April 1943 and departed for the New York Port of Embarkation. The 82nd Airborne Division sailed from Staten Island early on the morning of 29 April 1943, thus becoming the first American Airborne Division to sail overseas.

The Division landed at Casablanca on 10 May 1943, marshaled at Camp Don B. Passage near that city, and began a move to the vicinity of Oudja, French Morocco and Marnia, Algeria, on 13 May 1943. Here the Division bivouacked as combat teams with the 325th Glider Combat Team, 80th Airborne Anti-aircraft Battalion, and 320th Glider Field Artillery Battalion stationed at Marnia and the remainder of the Division stationed near the Oudja airport.

A Division planning room was established in the gendarmerie building of Oudja (popularly known as the "Pentagon" building), and here plans were worked out for the Division's first combat mission, Operation "HUSKY" or the Invasion of Sicily (Code name: HORRIFIED).

In the Oudja area Division parades were given for Lieutenant General Mark Clark, Fifth Army Commander; Lieutenant General George S. Patton, Commander of I Armored Corps; and Major General Omar Bradley, Commander of II Infantry Corps. The Division's first airborne review, which included a ground parade, a battalion parachute drop and an exhibition glider landing, also was given for the Governor of Spanish Morocco.

Proceeded by small advance parties, the Division on 24 June 1943, began movement by truck, train, plane and glider from its dusty camps amid the wheat fields of French Morocco, to the cactus-hedged areas of Tunisia in the vicinity of Kairouan. Troops were camped near their proposed takeoff airfields. As a result, regiments and other units were scattered, each regiment having headquarters approximately 25 miles from Division Headquarters and some regiments being some 50 road miles apart. Division Headquarters and Headquarters of the 52nd Troop Carrier Wing were established in adjacent almond orchards. Ten takeoff fields were to be used.

The invasion of Sicily began on the windy night of 9 July 1943, when Colonel James M. Gavin, later to become Assistant Division Commander and Division Commander, led his 505th Parachute Combat Team in its drop into Sicily.

Unit Commanders and staff officers at this time were as follows:

Commanding General ........................................ Major General MATTHEW B. RIDGWAY

Assistant Commanding General ........................ Brigadier General CHARLES L. KEERANS, JR.

Division Artillery Commander ......................... Brigadier General MAXWELL D. TAYLOR

Chief of Staff .................................................... Colonel RALPH P. EATON

G-1 .................................................................... Lieutenant Colonel FREDERICK M. SCHELLHAMMER

G-2 .................................................................... Lieutenant Colonel GEORGE E. LYNCH

G-3 .................................................................... Lieutenant Colonel RICHARD K. BOYD

G-4 .................................................................... Lieutenant Colonel ROBERT H. WIENECKE

Adjutant General .............................................. Lieutenant Colonel RAYMOND M. BRITTON

Chemical Officer .............................................. Lieutenant Colonel JOHN P. GEIGER

Chaplain ........................................................... Lieutenant Colonel GEORGE L. RIDDLE

Finance Officer ................................................ Lieutenant Colonel WILLIAM E. JOHNSON

Headquarters Commandant .............................. Captain WILLIAM C. SHREVE

Inspector General ............................................. Lieutenant Colonel CHARLES BARRETT

Judge Advocate General ................................... Lieutenant Colonel CASIMIR D. MOSS

Ordnance Officer ............................................. Lieutenant Colonel JOSHUA FINKEL

Provost Marshall .............................................. Major WILLIAM P. BOWDEN

Quartermaster .................................................. Lieutenant Colonel JOHN W. MOHRMAN

Signal Officer .................................................. Lieutenant Colonel FRANK MOORMAN

Surgeon ............................................................ Lieutenant Colonel WOOLCOTT L. ETIENNE

Special Service Officer .................................... Major FREDERICK G. MCCOLLUM

CO, 325th Glider Infantry ................................ Colonel HARRY L. LEWIS

CO, 504th Parachute Infantry .......................... Colonel REUBEN H. TUCKER

CO, 505th Parachute Infantry .......................... Colonel JAMES M. GAVIN

Executive Officer, Division Artillery ................ Colonel FRANCIS A. MARCH

CO, 319th Glider FA Battalion ......................... Lieutenant Colonel WILLIAM H. BERTSCH, JR.

CO, 320th Glider FA Battalion ......................... Lieutenant Colonel PAUL E. WRIGHT

CO, 80th Airborne Anti-Aircraft Battalion ........ Lieutenant Colonel WHITFIELD JACK

   (on DS with Div HQ as Asst G-3) ................... Major RAYMOND E. SINGLETON (Acting)

CO, 376th Parachute FA Battalion ..................... Lieutenant Colonel WILBUR M. GRIFFITH

CO, 456th Parachute FA Battalion ..................... Lieutenant Colonel HARRISON HARDEN

CO, 307th Airborne Engineer Battalion ............. Lieutenant Colonel ROBERT S. PALMER

CO, 82nd Airborne Signal Company ................. Captain ROBERT E. FURMAN

CO, 307th Airborne Medical Company .............. Major WILLIAM H. HOUSTON

CO, 407th Airborne Quartermaster Company .... Captain SAMUEL L. MAYS

CO, 782nd Airborne Ordnance Company .......... Captain JEFF DAVIS, JR.

CO, 82nd Parachute Maintenance Company ...... Captain ALBERT C. MARIN

   (Provisional)

CO, Division Headquarters Company ............... Captain WILLIAM C. SHREVE

CO, Headquarters Battery Division Artillery ..... Captain TONY J. RAIBL

CO, 82nd Airborne Military Police Platoon ....... Major WILLIAM P. BOWDEN

CO, Division Reconnaissance Platoon .............. 1st Lieutenant ROLAND M. HUDSON

   (Provisional)

# CHAPTER ONE

# Operation Husky:
# The 82nd Airborne Division in Sicily

## Section 1: Division Report
(Numbers In Parentheses Refer To Footnotes At End Of Narrative)

**The Plan**

The plan for the Invasion of Sicily provided for landings to be made on the southeastern extremity of the island, with British and Canadian forces on the east coast and American forces on the south coast. The American assault forces were to consist of the 3rd, 1st and 45th Infantry Divisions, with attached units, which were to land in the LICATA, GELA, and SAMPIERE vicinities, respectively, and parachute troops from the 82nd Airborne Division, which were to land inland from GELA. The remainder of the 82nd Airborne Division and the 2nd Armored Division, in Army reserve, were to be brought in as quickly as possible.

The assaulting paratroopers were of the 505th Combat Team, reinforced, commanded by Colonel James M. Gavin, and their mission was thus stated in Field Order #6 issued by the II Corps:

(1) Land during night D-1/D in area N and E of GELA, capture and secure high ground in that area.
(2) Disrupt communications and movement of reserves during night.
(3) Be attached to 1st Infantry Division effective H+1 hours on D-Day.
(4) Assist 1st Infantry Division in capturing and securing landing field at PONTE OLIVO."

The elements to be employed as part of the 505th Combat Team, with their commanding officers, were as follows:

| | |
| --- | --- |
| 505th Parachute Infantry[1] | Col. James M. Gavin |
| 3rd Bn., 504th Prcht. Inf. | Lt. Col. Charles Koune |
| 456th Prcht. Field Artillery Bn. | Lt. Col. Harrison Harden |
| Co. B., 307th Abn. Engineer Bn. | Capt. William H. Johnson |
| Det. 82nd Abn. Signal Co. | 2nd Lt. Edward Kacyainski |
| Det. 307th Abn. Medical Co. | S/Sgt. Kenneth I. Knott |
| Air Support Party | Capt. Jack M. Batley |
| PWI Personnel | 1st Lt. Louis P. Testa |

The 505th plan, as embodied in its first field order, directed that Regimental Headquarters, the 1st Battalion, and the 2nd Battalion, 505th, and Batteries A and B of the 456th, should drop just north of an important road junction about seven miles east of GELA, attack and overcome an enemy strong point commanding the junction, and defend the junction against attack. The 3rd Battalion, 505th, and Battery C, 456th, should drop south of the same junction, and occupy the high ground overlooking it. The 3rd Battalion, 504th, should drop south of NISCEMI and establish and defend road blocks on the road from NISCEMI to the south. Each of these elements was to be prepared to assist the 1st Infantry Division in seizing the PONTE OLIVO Airdrome. Three planes of troops, including the Demolition Section, were to drop about five miles further east and prepare the demolition of rail and road crossings of the ACATE River.

The mission assigned the Division less the 505th Combat Team was outlined in Field Order #1 of Force 343 (Seventh Army):

"(a) 82nd Airborne Division (-Dets) concentrate rapidly by successive airlifts in SICILY, by D+7, in either or both the DIME (45th Infantry Division) or JOSS (3rd Infantry Division) areas, as directed."

"(b) 2nd Battalion, 509th Parachute Infantry, remain in North Africa, in Force 343 reserve, available for drop missions as directed."

In compliance with this order, the Division devised a Movement Table (Annex 2 to Field Order #1), under which the 504th Combat Team, as a second lift, was alerted for movement the evening of D-Day; or, in the event of negative instructions at that time, the evening of D+1, or of any day thereafter. Division Headquarters was to constitute a third lift, ready for movement in gliders the evening of D+1, or thereafter. The 325th Combat Team and the 80th Airborne Anti-Aircraft Battalion were to follow by planes and gliders in designated order.

The 504th Combat Team, under the command of Colonel Reuben H. Tucker, included the following units, under the command of the officers named:

| | |
|---|---|
| 504th Prcht. Inf. (less 3rd Bn.)[2] | Col. Reuben H. Tucker |
| 376th Prcht. FA Bn. | Lt. Col. Wilbur M. Griffith |
| Co. C, 307th Abn. Engineer Bn. | Capt. Thomas M. Wight |

The Division Headquarters serial was to include members of the general and special staff sections and of the following units: Hq. and Hq. Btry., Div. Arty.; Div. Hq. Co.; 82nd Abn. Signal Co.; 407th QM Co.; 307th Med. Co.; 782nd Ord. Maint. Co.; and the 307th Abn. Engineer Bn., all under the command of Lt. Col. Robert Palmer, Division Engineer.

The Commanding General of the Division, Major General M.B. Ridgway, with a special command party, boarded the Monrovia, Seventh Army Command Vessel, at ALGIERS, July 4, from which he and the party would land at GELA on D-Day. The Commanding General's party included Colonel R.P. Eaton, Chief of Staff; Lt. Col. G.E. Lynch, G-2; Lt. Col. R.K. Boyd, G-3; Lt. Col. R.H. Wienecke, G-4; Lt. Col. Frank Moorman, Signal Officer; Major E.S. Adams, Liaison Officer; Capt. Don C. Faith, Aide-de camp; and eleven enlisted men from the staff sections.

## The Three Lifts

D-1, the day of the first lift, was, as usual for the time of year in North Africa, hot and clear. The men of the 505th Combat Team, stationed near KAIROUAN, TUNISIA, lounged in their bivouac area, made last preparations of arms and equipment, ate supper at 1600 hours, and went to the ten airdromes from which they were to take off. The 226 Army transport planes, type C-47, in which they were flown, cleared the fields between 2010 and 2116 hours, July 9th.

The route was by way of Juriate Island and Malta, thence directly to the Sicilian Coast east of GELA and over the various drop zones; and the flight was expected to require, including time for air rendezvous, about three hours and twenty minutes.

Late in the afternoon the wind off the south coast of Sicily was of gale intensity. Although it diminished as the evening progressed, the weather continued sufficiently rough that an unusually large proportion of the men were ill in the planes, and much worse, that the plane formations were badly scattered. The difficulty in avoiding that consequence was, of course much enhanced by the darkness after 2130 hours, by the absence of inter-plane communication, and by the extremely low flying, dictated by tactical reasons. It is also testified[3] that there were some tracer fire on the planes, which, although not heavy, was the cause of the destruction of at least one plane which was seen to fall in flames. Many of the men stated that they were standing, hooked up, for 30 to 50 minutes while their planes searched for the drop zone. In any event, the formations were broken, and not only were the drop zones missed by most of the planes, but also the Combat Team as a whole was badly scattered from the vicinity of GELA to points east of MODICA.[4]

Although eight planes failed to return, the parachutists had cleared them before they were lost. Three planes returned with full loads, including one officer and fifteen men of Company A, 505th, and 17 men of Batteries B and C, 456th. All these men, having been completely cleared of responsibility for the failure to drop were allowed to participate in the Second Lift.

The 504th Combat Team, alerted throughout D-Day for the Second Lift, at the fields and loaded in the planes, waited while a negative message from General Ridgway was delayed in delivery, but was finally released at 1840, when Colonel Clark of the 52nd Wing decided that it was too late for the mission to be undertaken. The next day, D+1, at 1100 hours, orders were received that the Second Lift would be flown that evening.

This lift comprised 144 planes, and was to proceed to MALTA, thence to the southeastern coast of Sicily at SAMPIERE, thence along the coast to Lake BIVIERE southeast of GELA, thence inland to the FARELLO Airport.

The air was considerably quieter than two days before; the night was lighted by a quarter moon; and the drop zone was behind the 1st Division line. The highest hope for a safe crossing seemed justified. Nevertheless, full instructions were issued to the commanders of friendly troops and naval units relating to the flight, including the route, the time and the objective.[5]

The hope was realized until the first planes neared the drop zone. How trouble began is best described in a statement name by Captain Willard E. Harrison, Company A, 504th Parachute Infantry:

> "On the night of July 11-12, 1943, I flew in the leading plane of the first serial and reached the coast of SICILY near PUNTA SOCCA at approximately 2230 hours, thence flew in a northwesterly direction along the coast toward GELA. The left wing plane flew just over the water line, and the squadron of 9 planes continued perfect formation up to the coast at an altitude of approximately 900 feet. We encountered no fire of any kind until the lead plane reached the lake at H30-25 (Lake BIVIERE), when one .50 caliber machine gun, situated in the sand dunes several hundred yards from the shore, opened fire. As soon as this firing began, guns along the coast as far as we could see toward PUNTA SOCCA, opened fire and the naval craft lying off the shore, both towards PUNTA SOCCA and toward GELA, began firing anti-aircraft guns."

The squadron mentioned by Captain Harrison was not hit, nor were any of his men fired on in the descent, but the anti-aircraft fire, particularly from naval units, grew more intense, and to it was added fire from machine gunners and riflemen on descending parachutists, and anti-aircraft units of the Army and Navy later declared that bombers had been overhead simultaneously with our own planes, one of which could not be distinguished from the other. In passing through this fire many planes were badly damaged and twenty-three of the 144 were destroyed. The entire formation was badly scattered. The pilot of one of the planes which did return told of his difficulties:

> "A few minutes before reaching the drop point with the paratroopers, a shell smashed into the starboard side of the fuselage and knocked out a hole four by six feet while a fragment from the shell slit the aluminum and every rib from hole to rudder. Passing through the plane the fragment ripped off a door as a second ack-ack blast carried away a portion of the left stabilizer. The explosion also blew away a large piece of equipment, and the impact was so great that it felt like a motor crash in the pilot's cabin.
>
> "The airplane spun at a right angle and nearly pulled the controls from my grasp. For a second I didn't realize what had happened, then finding myself out of formation I began a violent evasive action. I saw three planes burning on the ground and red tracers everywhere as machine gunners sprayed us as if potting a flight of ducks.
>
> "Meanwhile I had cut into a less dangerous spot to give the parachutists a fighting chance to reach ground. But I've got to hand it to those boys; one, who had been pretty badly hit by shrapnel, insisted on leaping with the others although he had been ordered to remain in the plane."

One of the more harrowing reports was that of 1st Lieutenant C.A. Drew, Company F, 504th. His statement shows that some men were lost because warning of the flight had not been conveyed to the men of one unit, and others because each division then had its own password[6]:

"I was jump-master in Plane 531. This plane was leading a formation of three planes and was No.7 in our Company. The pilot of my plane gave me the warning 20 minutes out from the DZ. After the red light came on he had to give me the green light in about 1 minute, due to the plane being on fire.

"We jumped into a steady stream of AA fire, and not knowing that they were friendly troops. There was 4 men killed and 4 wounded from my Platoon. Three of these men were hit coming down and one was killed on the ground because he had the wrong password. After landing we found out this had been changed to "Think" – "Quickly".

"The AA we jumped into was the 180th Infantry of the 45th Division. They also were not told we were coming. Later we found out that the 45th Division had been told we were coming but word never had got to the 180th Infantry of the 45th Division."

"We tried to reorganize but found we didn't have but 44 men including three officers. We searched all night for the rest of the men. After accounting for them we took care of the dead and wounded and started towards our objective. We arrived at the 504th CP at 2 o'clock July 12, 1943."

"About 75 yards from where I landed, Plane No.915 was hit and burned. To my knowledge, only the pilot and three men got out. The pilot was thrown through the window."

"Another plane was shot down on the beach and another plane was down burning about 1,000 yards to my front. Altogether there were three planes I know of being shot down."

Of the twenty-three destroyed planes, fortunately only six were shot down before the parachutists had jumped. One of the six carried five officers and fifteen men of Headquarters and Headquarters Company, 504th; one carried three officers and fifteen men of Headquarters Company, 2nd Battalion, 504th; and four carried one officer and thirty-two men of Battery C, 376th; a total of nine officers and sixty-two men. Miraculously, some of these survived. Lieutenant Colonel L.G. Freeman, Executive Officer 504th, two other officers and twelve men survived – eleven of them wounded when their plane crash-landed. 1st Lieutenant M.C. Shelly, Headquarters Company, 2nd Battalion, 504th, was thrown clear of his plane when it crashed, all other occupants being killed. One of the Battery C planes was shot down at sea, carrying all its nine parachutists down with it, but from the other three there were five men saved by their reserve chutes; two struggled out of their plane after it had been twice hit and was afire; three were actually blown clear as their planes were demolished by ack-ack.

One of the planes lost on its return flight, and of which no remains have been found, carried as an official observer Brigadier General Charles L. Keerans, Jr., Assistant Division Commander.

In the returning planes were four dead and six wounded parachutists, and eight full loads which had not been given an opportunity to jump. These included ten officers, two warrant officers and ninety-five men.[7]

The dispersion was as great as that of the 505th, men being dropped practically as far east, and others being dropped west of GELA.

The following day, D+2, gliders were loaded and men of the Division Headquarters serial ready to embark, when an order was received from Force 141 (15th Army Group) canceling all projected movements by air.[8] The possibility was left open of a movement by sea, but no decision was made known until Division Headquarters notified the 52nd Wing at 1000 July 16, that the Third Lift would be carried to Sicily by plane and landed at PONTE OLIVO Airdrome, taking off at 1315 hours that same day. It cleared the fields on schedule, in a flight of fifty-one planes, escorted by fighters, and flew direct to Sicily by way of PANTELLARIA. All planes arrived safely, about 1515 hours.

## Guerilla Warfare

The scattered fashion in which Combat Team 505 was dropped made fully organized combat impossible. Of all its elements only "I" Company, less one plane, jumped on an assigned drop zone; but "I' Company is credited with having accomplished its mission, with reducing a blockhouse and several pillboxes and taking a great many prisoners.

Most of the men upon landing found themselves alone or near only one other or a few of their comrades. Those who were not already pinned down by fire immediately set out to find others; and during the remainder of the night, the great majority succeeded in grouping themselves into three or fours at least (although frequently members of such groups were from different units), and sometimes into groups of platoon size or larger. Indeed, the 2nd Battalion Serial was almost entirely assembled within twelve hours of landing.

Thus the fighting was begun and continued by groups of all sizes and compositions, and against a variety of objectives. On one occasion on the 11th at BIAZZO Ridge between GELA and VITTORIA an important engagement was fought against a substantial force of the Hermann Goering Division by 200-300 paratroopers led by Colonel Gavin. At several points, groups of platoon size made planned attacks on strong points or ambushed enemy columns. On many more occasions, individuals or small groups, seeking at once to avoid capture, to find their units, and to do as much damage to the enemy as possible, chanced onto pillboxes, couriers, vehicles, and small garrisons, killed or captured the enemy, or fought him off and retired. Such action can be described only in its individual instances, as it occurred.

One case of two paratroopers isolated in enemy territory is so vividly told by a principal that it is here reproduced in his own words.[9]

"We first received the order to stand up and hook up just off the coast. Just over the beach we ran into AA fire. Our plane kept diving and banking. The pilot passed the word down the line to jump on the red light. At the time the word reached Lieutenant Mills[10] the red light flashed on. We started out. Just as I got to the door our plane was hit. I was knocked back against the opposite side of the ship. I finally got out. Where we landed there were a couple of pillboxes burning from the bombing raid.

"We started to assemble in an orchard when the artillery opened up on us. That didn't last long. We assembled and found out that we had one man, Cpl. Len, [who] had broken his leg. We wrapped him in a chute and hid him in a vine patch. We left him with two riggers.

"Lieutenant Mills got his bearings and told us what the score was. We had dropped 15 miles from the right DZ in enemy territory. We got our weapons and marched down the road. We heard somebody yelling and a whirring sound like an auto stuck in the mud. I don't know why but we marched right into them. We walked across a bridge. As we reached the end we heard someone yell halt. It was the Hienies. Lieutenant Mills said, "Ground equipment and jump over the bridge." He no sooner said that than they opened fire on us. We ran into a vine patch and hid. They shot flares in the air and tried to pick us off. They tossed grenades and fired their guns into the patch. Privates Boggs, Wright and I were cut off from the rest. We started to run and were chased and fired on. We lost Wright somewhere. Boggs and I hid in a cane break for an hour or two.

"We got disgusted and decided to work our way back to the DZ about three miles away. We started and changed our minds again and headed due north the way we were ambushed. I had a compass and we started towards what we thought was GELA. About noon we seen a German patrol. Just two men. We were afraid to fire on them because the range was too great for a carbine. We ducked them and later came across a gun set upon a hill. We looked it over but couldn't make it out so we avoided it and started up the RR tracks."

"I seen someone on the skyline and started up the hill. I seen it was an American G.I. He had me covered with a .50 caliber so I started yelling. It was a 1st Division man. They took us to the assembly area."

In another case, two plane loads of Company "B", 307th Airborne Engineer Battalion, landed 15 miles northeast of the drop zone, and were joined by one plane load of Company "A", 505th. They spent the remainder of the night searching for the drop zones and cutting telegraph wires, and just before dawn, dug in at a road intersection. The rest of their story is told as follows:

"At 0530, a German motorcycle containing three passengers pulled up to the crossroads and stopped. The passengers were killed. Another motorcycle arrived fifteen minutes later and likewise caught under fire and the occupants killed. The men were then assembled and moved out in the general direction of the DZ. Five of this group were separated when they went to pick up two equipment chutes which were spotted a half mile away. The remainder continued on and took up a position on ground commanding the two valleys. Here contact was made with elements of Company "G", and defensive positions were set up. During the afternoon, 2nd Battalion 180th Infantry, 45th Division, arrived at the hill. The men attached themselves to it and remained with it for three nights and two days. During this period of time additional parachutist drifted in and became part of their organization."

One of the most substantial victories was accomplished by 1st Lieutenant F. E. Thomas, Company "I", 504th, without blood shed. While with several men under his command being served a meal by friendly civilians, he was surprised and covered by the weapons of a small German force which had three disabled tanks in the vicinity, including one Mark VI. Lieutenant Thomas resorted to reason with his captor, pointing out the inevitability of Allied victory and the futility of his captors efforts. It turned out that among the Germans there was one severely wounded man for whom the leader desired the excellent medical aid that he knew the Americans could afford. Consequently an understanding was reached. The Americans being released and given custody of the wounded man, promised to secure his immediate medical treatment. The Germans put their tanks out of commission, abandoned them, and departed in the opposite direction.

A vastly different sort of action involving a 1st Battalion group is narrated by Jack Thompson, Chicago Tribune correspondent who jumped with the First Lift:

"One group of the 1st Battalion, including Lieutenant Colonel Arthur Gorham, landed 4 miles south of NISCEMI, about 2 1/2 miles from the scheduled DZ. They were just east of a very sturdy, thick-walled farmhouse which had been converted into a military fort held by sixty men with heavy machine guns and six lights. It was well wired in with trench defenses. Colonel Gorham ordered an assault on the house and it was organized and led by Captain Edwin Sayre[11] and twenty-two men. Their first attack was launched at two o'clock in the morning. They held up then until they attacked again just before dawn, with rifles, grenades, one 60mm mortar and a bazooka. They forced the Italians back out of the trenches and into the house and attacked the house with grenades. Sayre led the assault, carrying one hand grenade in his teeth and another in his left hand, and with his carbine in his right hand. It wasn't until after they had taken the farmhouse that he discovered the man who was covering him with a trench knife and not a Tommy gun as he had thought. A rifle grenade fired at about ten feet blew open the door; but the door swung shut again. Sayre walked up, threw open the door, and pitched a hand grenade inside. They found a total of fifteen dead and took forty-five prisoners, some of whom were Germans. Four paratroops were wounded, one of whom later died. The house soon came under fire from an 88 and Col. Gorham withdrew his men back to another hill and it wasn't until two days later that they were able to recapture the farmhouse."

This group later made contact with the 1st Division, and joined the 2nd Battalion, 16th Infantry, with which they fought two days until relieved. In resisting an enemy attack while with the 16th Infantry, paratroopers succeeded with their rocket-launchers in stopping several tanks. It was in such an act at this time that Lieutenant Colonel Arthur Gorham, Commanding Officer, 1st Battalion, was killed. This episode is also related by Mr. Thompson:

"The position where Gorham's men were at that time acting as assault troops with the 16th Infantry, with whom they had made contact, came under heavy attack by Mark VI and Mark IV tanks and enemy artillery, as well as extremely heavy machine gun fire. [Lt.] Col. Gorham was killed by a shell from a Mark VI while firing a bazooka at the tanks on the nearby road. Captain Comstock[12], Medical Officer, ran to his aid and was wounded by the next shell burst. Lt. Dean McCandless[13], who was nearby, ran up to help the wounded doctor and called for Corporal Thomas Higgins[14], to get a jeep and evacuate him. Higgins ran a quarter of a mile through a concentration of machine gun fire until he found a jeep. The driver was reluctant to go into this fire so Higgins was joined by a paratroop cook, Private Bernard Williams.[15] The two of them drove the jeep under fire back to the hill and with the aid of Lt. McCandless evacuated Captain Comstock and the body of [Lt.] Col. Gorham."

Another 1st Battalion group, dropped about fifty miles east of GELA, occupied and held the town of NOTO; and a third group, consisting of twelve men from the 1st Battalion, participated in the capture of RAGUSA.

A group of about forty men of the Headquarters Serial, including men from two platoons of Engineers, under the command of 1st Lieutenant H.H. Swingler, Headquarters Commandant, occupied early in the morning of the 10th an area of high ground commanding the road net leading inland from the 45th Division beaches, and is credited with greatly facilitating the landing of that Division. They destroyed one armored vehicle as it approached the beach, cut off advance elements seeking to retire before the 45th's attack, reduced several pillboxes, and themselves captured 5 officers and 96 men. This same group joined Colonel Gavin on the 11th in time to participate in the action at BIAZZO Ridge.

Although the 2nd Battalion serial landed south of RAGUSA, twenty-five miles from its drop zone, and was attacked before reaching the ground, a large part of the Serial was assembled under its CO, Major Alexander, by noon the 10th. Even during that morning, it was engaged in attacking enemy positions near S. CROCE-CAMERINA, where it took forty-five prisoners. Thence, it advanced on the town itself, occupied it after a short but hard fight, and captured 144 more prisoners and a great deal of equipment. After a third victorious skirmish east of the city, it bivouacked, reorganized the next day, and marched west on the 12th to join CT Headquarters.

Two and one-half miles southeast of NISCEMI a group of men from the 3rd Battalion 504th, under Lieutenant Willis J. Ferrill, Company "I", ambushed a force of 350 Germans from the Hermann Goering Division, who were retreating up the road.

The paratroopers, who by the end of the afternoon of D Day numbered 110, had taken up a defensive position on a hill. They had already shot up a German patrol, and one small group had demolished an Italian patrol, killing fourteen. Eleven of these Italians were killed by two privates, Shelby R. Hord[16] and Thomas E. Lane.[17] On the following day after Ferrill's force had begun to increase, it was in position on a hill at noon when an enemy column was observed coming up the road from the south. With the Germans were several American prisoners. Lieutenant Ferrill withheld fire until the Germans were almost opposite his position. Then at noon the Germans suddenly halted for a ten-minute break. The Americans waited until the Germans started to get up and put on their packs, and then fired on them with devastating effect. The battle lasted all afternoon. It was joined by two enemy tanks which shelled the Americans from the far-off hills. Late in the afternoon a German Lieutenant came up the hill with a white flag to arrange a surrender but when he saw the Americans were parachutists he refused to surrender and went down the hill again. Then the battle was resumed and lasted until dusk, when the Germans withdrew, leaving fifty dead. The cost to the Americans was five killed and fifteen wounded. The hill from which the Americans fought was identified on the map as CASTLE NOCERA.

Of the 3rd Battalion Serial, 505th, forty-five men under 1st Lieutenant F. Willis, Battery C. 456th, joined forward elements of the 180th Infantry, and served with them as assault troops; and sixty others, with three guns of the 456th, were the first troops to enter VITTORIA. It was on this occasion that 1st Lieutenant William J. Earris, 3rd Battalion Headquarters Company, taken prisoner by the Italians, persuaded the garrison commander of the futility of resistance, and induced him to surrender himself and his command of eighty men on the spot.

The largest part of the 3rd Battalion, 180 men under Major Krause, were the backbone of the force which fought a battalion of the Hermann Goering Division at BIAZZO Ridge.

BIAZZO Ridge is a prominence about twelve miles west of VITTORIA on the GELA Highway. Colonel Gavin, approaching it the morning of the 11th from the direction of VITTORIA with the 3rd Battalion force mentioned above, was warned of the presence of Germans. He succeeded in compelling them to retire from the ridge and in occupying the crest of it, but after an attempt to continue his advance, decided to organize the high ground and to be prepared to defend it against counter-attack. During the day three 75mm pack howitzers, two 57mm anti-tank guns from the 45th Division, and a few rocket launchers were assembled.

The expected enemy counter-attack with tanks – Mark IV's and Mark VI's was made shortly after noon, and surged within fifty yards of the detachment's CP. One tank was knocked out by a 75mm pack howitzer, and much aid was rendered by 155mm guns of the 45th Division and Navy 5 inchers. A last-ditch defense finally forced the enemy to withdraw for a reorganization.

In the meantime, about 1900, Lieutenant Swingler and his group arrived, and also eleven General Shermans (M-4 medium tanks), making possible an American attack at 2030 which completely routed the Germans and gave the detachment undisputed possession of the ridge.

American losses in this action were forty-three killed and one hundred wounded. At least fifty enemy dead were left on the field, and fifty prisoners taken. Two German armored cars and one tank were knocked out; twelve 6-inch mortars, and many machine guns, small arms and vehicles taken. A caliber .50 crew of Battery D, 456th, was credited with the destruction of three ME-109's, which attacked the position.

After burying the dead the morning of the 12th, the force proceeded toward GELA.[18]

## Reorganization

The beach assault had begun at 0245 July 10th. At 0730 General Ridgway and Captain Faith went ashore to seek the drop zones and elements of the 505th, but succeeded in finding only Company "I", 505th, and in learning that Company

"A" was in contact with the CP of the 2nd Battalion, 16th Infantry. This CP, and also that of the 1st Division, was visited later in the day by Lieutenant Colonels Lynch and Boyd, who debarked at 1700, just after General Ridgway's return.

Contact with the 505th Command Post was not made on the 10th or 11th, nor was any substantial progress made in reassembly of the combat team on those days. At 0830 on the 11th an order was sent Division Rear that the 504th should be flown across that evening, and during the remainder of the day the MONROVIA party was occupied preparing for the arrival. A message was sent Seventh Army requesting notification of all friendly troops, and one to Division Rear to apprise the Wing of the great dispersion of the 505th. Arrangements were made for rations and water from the 1st Division, and immediate medical treatment at the drop zone by the 51st Medical Battalion. A Division CP was set up ashore at 1500 hours, about three miles southeast of GELA and one mile from the coast.

While General Ridgway and staff waited on the FARELLO landing field, the first elements of the 504th came down at 2250, July 11th, and by 0715 the next morning Colonel Tucker had arrived at the CP. In the meantime, word came indirectly that a number of members of the 505th were in the vicinity of RAGUSA. Nevertheless at 0755 on the 12th, General Ridgway was compelled to report to the Seventh Army:

> "No formed element of Combat Team 505 under my control. Expect some today based on 1st Division reports. Elements of Combat Team 504 dribbling in. At present one battery 75 pack howitzer and equivalent of one infantry company available for use … Am concentrating all efforts on reorganization."

His expectations in regard to the 505th were not realized that day, however; and the 504th "dribbled in" only enough that the first G-1 Report to Seventh Army at 1730 could list present for the 504th thirty-seven officers and 518 men.

Colonel Gavin reached the Division CP July 13 at 0900, and confirmed the location of 1200 troops under his command. Henceforth, reassembly proceeded more rapidly, so that at 1800 hours, Captain Alfred W. Ireland, S-1 of the 505th, could report a total strength of 1648. Information from other units, particularly 1st Division Artillery and the 45th Division, facilitated the location of troops and a G-1 Report to the Seventh Army showed Division strength in Sicily as 3024 at midnight July 13. This figure grew to 3790 at midnight July 14, almost completing the reassembly of forward personnel which had not become casualties. With the acquisition of 426 officers and men of the Third Lift, the total Division strength in Sicily was only 4309 at 2400 July 17, and 4390 at 2400 July 27.

Thus, out of 5307 men on the first two lifts, 3024 represented the total strength July 13th, 3790 on July 14th. Out of 5733 in the three lifts, 4309 represented the total strength July 17th, and 4390 on July 27. Subtracting the 436 brought in the Third Lift from the strength for the 17th, there had been an increase in strength of the two combat teams of only ninety-three men in three days from July 13th-17th.

As the reassembly progressed, preparations for action were being made. The 3rd Battalion, 504th, rejoined the 504th Combat Team. The Division CP was moved on July 13th two miles north to a point near Highway 115, and the 504th and 505th assembly areas were maintained close at hand. A request was made July 15th for the movement of the Third Lift with fighter escort, which bore fruit the following day. The great problem of transportation for a Division which had been able to bring almost none of its own[19] was met by the procurement July 16 from Provisional Corps of twenty-four 2 1/2 ton trucks and seven 1/4 ton trucks, which were retained throughout the following operations, and from the 39th Combat Team of eighty-three 2 1/2 and 3/4 ton trucks which were retained only for the movement from GELA to PALMA.[20] A basic load of ammunition, acquired before leaving the GELA area, sufficed for the entire campaign on which the Division was about to embark.

These preparations had proceeded under Seventh Army orders to reassemble and reorganize in Army reserve. At noon the 15th, a directive was received from Seventh Army, ordering the 82nd Airborne Division to assemble with attached troops in the PALMA DI MONTECHIARO area, to relieve elements of the 3d Division in that area by dark, July 19th, and to be prepared to advance west. The projected zone of action of the Division was a coastal strip including Highway 115 and extending 5-10 miles inland, until, in the vicinity of the VERDURA River, west of RIBERA, the right boundary, shared with the 3rd Division, turned north to PALERMO. The left boundary was the sea.

The movement west from the assembly area near GELA began by truck shuttle at 0600 July 17th and carried that evening to a new area about 5 miles west of PALMA, with the 504th Combat Team and most of Division Headquarters moving in the first serial, the 505th and the remainder of Division Headquarters in the second. On the 17th, at 1100 hours, Provisional Corps directed immediate relief of the 3rd Division in the 82nd Division zone, pursuant to which the 39th Combat Team was moved the evening of the 17th onto the high ground east of AGRIGENTO, from which it advanced at dawn the 18th through AGRIGENTO and PORTO EMPEDOCLE, where the 3rd Division had been engaged the day before. Early in the morning of the 18th, elements of the 39th were astride Highway 115 at REALMONTE. This position they secured, occupying the high ground in that vicinity and patrolling to the CANNE River. Behind the 39th Combat Team, the Division CP was moved two miles west of PORTO EMPEDOCLE on the afternoon of the 18th and the 504th moved to an area near REALMONTE, immediately behind the line of the 39th, from which it could undertake an advance the next day.

Although the 3rd Division had met some resistance and taken a great many prisoners in AGRIGENTO, not even the 39th Combat Team patrols ever gained contact with the enemy, and the 82nd moved forward during the 17th and 18th entirely without molestation.

## The Campaign

The orders under which the 82nd's campaign to the west were about to begin were the Provisional Corps Field Order #1, issued at 1500 July 18, directing the Division to advance by 0800 the 19th from the Realmonte Line, and the Division Field Order #2 of the same day, directing Combat Team 504 to relieve Combat Team 39 by 0800 the 19th, secure crossings over the Canne River by daylight and continue westward. Battery A of the 82nd Armored Field Artillery Battalion and Battery A & B of the 83rd Chemical Battalion were attached to Combat Team 504 for this mission.

Prospects of resistance were assessed in the Intelligence Annex of the Division Field Order in these words: "At this time no known organized fighting forces are located to the immediate west on the route of advance of this Division."

Actually, some elements of Combat Team 504 were at REALMONTE by noon the 18th, before the formal orders were issued. The entire Combat Team, moving by marching and truck shuttle, assembled there during the day, and secured before dark the CANNE crossings and the high ground to the west. At 0300 the 19th, troops of the 2nd Battalion, 504th, were in MONTALLEGRO; at 0900 at the PLATANI River; at 1015 at the MAGGAZOLO River; and at 1200 had occupied RIBERA. Before 2100, they had reached and were stopped by the Corps phase line halfway between RIBERA and SCIACCA. Every phase of the advance, and of subsequent advances as well, was led in person by General Ridgway, who kept himself in personal touch with the reconnaissance elements, the point, and the advance guard command.

This headlong progress had almost been retarded by enemy destruction the previous day of the highway bridge across the CANNE River, in what was reported by the Commanding Officer, 3rd Battalion, 39th Infantry, as "the best job of demolition seen in a long time. Requires a major engineering job." But a by-pass for heavy vehicles around the demolished bridge was completed by a 307th Airborne Engineer Battalion detachment under Lieutenant Colonel Palmer at 0400 the 19th, aided by a detachment of the 17th Engineer Battalion, Armored, of the 2nd Armored Division.

Active enemy resistance during the entire day was extremely light. The only exceptions were brief machine gun fire just east of RIBERA and machine gun and light artillery fire at the VERDURA River, encountered by detachments of the Division Reconnaissance Platoon under 1st Lieutenant Roland Hudson, and of the 82nd Armored Reconnaissance Battalion, operating on our front under Corps order. No casualties were suffered in either case, and in the former the enemy surrendered almost as soon as the fire was returned.

The latter resistance was somewhat more determined. It began about 1400 hours, when HE shells fell near the Reconnaissance vehicles. The vehicles deployed off the highway, the 75mm and for 37mm guns of the 82nd Armored detachment undertaking counter-battery fire and the .50 calibre machine guns of the Division Platoon moving toward the railroad line to the south to engage machine gun emplacements. As accurate fire was brought to bear on them, the personnel of one enemy gun after another raised a white flag; and at the end of an hour all resistance had ceased. In the course of it, ten Italians had been killed and 250 captured, along with four 75mm and six 40mm guns, and a much larger number of machine guns.

The point of the 2nd Battalion, 504th, came under light arms fire for a few minutes just west of RIBERA, but without being caused delay or casualties. The reconnaissance elements discovered a minefield just east of RIBERA in conjunction with a roadblock, and another just west of the town at a railroad crossing, all of which were removed without mishap. The only Division casualties during the day resulted from a general strafing of the entire column on three different occasions by two to five ME-110's. Five men of Company E, 505th, and two men of the 2nd Battalion, 504th, were wounded.

At the end of the day, Combat Team 504 had secured the phase line halfway from RIBERA to SCIACCA. The artillery, all then under Division control, which had moved into the PLATANI VALLEY in the afternoon, was in position west of RIBERA and registered. Combat Team 505 was assembled just northeast of RIBERA; and Combat Team 39 at SICULIANA.[21] An advance of twenty-five miles had been made and 500 prisoners taken at a cost of seven casualties.

Substantially, all the circumstances of the advance on the 19th, the promptness and rapidity of it, the token resistance and voluntary surrender of isolated enemy garrisons were repeated on the 20th, with a few minor variations.

At 0450 the 20th, the Division relayed to Combat Team 504 the Corps order to proceed at 0600 to the next phase line. The advance began on schedule, and leading elements entered SCIACCA at 0925, but the preparation of a difficult by-pass around a demolished bridge on the western outskirts of SCIACCA and the removal of mines in that vicinity so delayed the main body that it did not pass through the city until about noon. There the 2nd Battalion, then leading, was turned north on the SAN MARGHERITA Road with TUMMINELLO as the night's objective, and Combat Team 504 (-2nd Battalion) continued west on Highway 115 toward MENFI, which was entered at 1800. By nightfall the 2nd Battalion reached a point about 8 miles north of SCIACCA. Both sides were somewhat delayed during the afternoon by small minefields in road-beds, and the 1st Battalion, 504th, leading from SCIACCA to MENFI, was fired on briefly by a battery of 75mm guns, which were quickly captured.

Combat Team 505 had spent the day securing the right flank and rear by patrolling the roads north from RIBERA. Batteries of the 376th, 34th and 62nd Field Artillery[22] had been called into action briefly on enemy batteries, pillboxes, and personnel east of SCIACCA; and the 307th Airborne Engineer Battalion had prepared the by-pass at SCIACCA, and removed the minefields on three sides of the city.

The advance during the day was fifteen to twenty miles; the number of prisoners taken approximately 1,000; and our own casualties, two.[23] North of SCIACCA was discovered an abandoned German bivouac area and anti-aircraft position, and a large Italian quartermaster dump.

The order of the day, July 21, was to proceed to and secure a line on the BELLICE River in the Division's zone, there to protect the right flank of the 2nd Armored Division as it moved north along the west bank of the BELLICE to PALERMO.

The 2nd Battalion, 504th, which had stopped about five miles short of TUMMINELLO the night before, resumed its advance the morning of the 21st and reached TUMMINELLO at 0800. The enemy, prepared at this point in a strong natural position, resisted with the fire of a battery of 75mm guns, two 90mm guns and small arms for a period of fifteen to thirty minutes, killing six and wounding eight men of Company F. But by 0830, as soon as a flanking party approached the position, it was captured with all its personnel and equipment. Two abandoned light Renault tanks, apparently in good condition, were discovered by the Division Reconnaissance Platoon north of TUMMINELLO.

The responsibility for continuing the advance from this point to the BELLICE had been assigned Combat Team 505. With the 2nd Battalion leading, it had set out at 0300 from a bivouac area one mile east of SCIACCA, and it marched continuously that day without food or resupply of water until the objective was attained – a distance of twenty-three miles. The 2nd Battalion passed through the 2nd Battalion, 504th, at TUMMINELLO at 0930; occupied SAN MARGHERITA at 1140; and was organizing its positions on the BELLICE at 1500. Company I was diverted eastward at SAN MARGHERITA to occupy SAMBUCA, and one platoon of Company G, westward to occupy MONTEVAGO. In carrying out this last mission, the platoon came under very brief machine gun fire; but except for this and the engagement at TUMMINELLO no resistance was encountered by the Division throughout the day; nor was any contact whatsoever established north of SAN MARGHERITA. At 1350 the Combat Team 505 occupied the SCIACCA Airdrome about ten miles north of the city, where it captured 175 prisoners and took possession of thirty airplanes and several field pieces, most of which were badly damaged.

At the end of the day the 2nd Battalion, 504th, was occupying SAMBUCA; the 2nd and 3rd Battalions, 505th, were protecting the highway bridges over the BELLICE near MONTEVAGO and north of SAN MARGHERITA, and securing the general area to the north and northwest; the 1st Battalion, 504th, was established just north of SAN MARGHERITA; and Combat Team 504 was being moved into the same area from MENFI. The Reconnaissance Platoon had entered SALAPARUTA and GIBELLINA without resistance, and the Division was prepared to move on an hour's notice either in support of the 2nd Armored Division's PALERMO drive, or to the westward extremity of the island.

The day's advance had netted fifteen miles at a cost of fourteen casualties. Prisoners taken totaled 1515 and much stores and equipment in addition to that already mentioned.

The Division being in Corps reserve, the same positions were maintained throughout the 22nd, with no activity except uneventful patrolling to the north and east[24], but all preparations were made for immediate resumption of the advance.

Corps orders were received at 0830 July 23 to "move without delay to seize TRAPANI and the above mentioned held portion of Sicily, (that west of line CASTELLAMARE-MAZZARA)," and for that purpose attaching to the Division, Task Force X, consisting of Combat Team 39, the 77th Field Artillery Battalion, and the 1st, 3rd, and 4th Reconnaissance Battalions.

Task Force X, which was separated between CASTELVETRANO and MAZZARO, was ordered north along the coast road from MAZZARO to seize MARSALA, and north from there to a point about six miles south of TRAPANI. Combat Team 505, with the 376th, and 34th Field Artillery Battalions and the 20th Engineer Battalion, was to be moved by truck to TRAPANI; and Combat Team 504, using the same vehicles, shuttled back from TRAPANI to SAN MARGHERITA, was to be moved to CASTELLAMMARE and ALCAMO.

The 3rd Battalion, 505th, departed MONTEVAGO at 1130, proceeded by way of PARTAANNA, SANTA NINTA, and SALENI to Highway 113, and thence west toward TRAPANI. All along the route, which west of SANTA NINTA had been traversed by no other Allied troops, the local population competed with each other in their expressions of good will. In the towns the roads were lined with people who not only shouted their approval and showed in one place a prepared sign: "Welcome Liberators", but who also showered the vehicles with fruit, bread and chocolate, much of which had been pilfered from abandoned Italian military stores.

In spite of these popular greetings, at about 1600 hours when shortly east of TRAPANI, the Division encountered a strong position of defense. On the outskirts of the city the reconnaissance vehicles found roadblocks and mine fields and immediately thereafter were met with machine gun fire. By the time the advance guard had fanned out to return the fire effectively, the enemy here began an artillery barrage from the mountain north of the city and a hill southwest of it onto the highway, which he maintained almost constantly for two to three hours.[25] The 34th and 376th Field Artillery Battalions and the 83rd Chemical (4.2 Mortar) Battalion returned the fire; and the 3rd Battalion, 505th, advanced on the gun positions, which surrendered before dark. In spite of this impressive artillery duel, the only Division casualty of the afternoon was a bazooka operator who sustained a burn from his own weapon.

A treaty of surrender was immediately dictated by General Ridgway to Admiral Manfredi, Commander of the TRAPANI district, requiring cessation of resistance, preservation of stores, and the posting of a guard on all military and naval property. In addition to Admiral Manfredi, Brigadier General Antonio Sodero, who was to have succeeded the Admiral in the command of the district, and 2639 other prisoners were taken during the evening of the 23rd and the day of the 24th, in and around the city of TRAPANI. An uncounted amount of guns and other military and naval material and stores were also taken.

During the afternoon of the 23rd, Colonel Tucker and a reconnaissance party from Combat Team 504 entered CASTELLAMARE, and the main body followed the next day on the return of the transportation from TRAPANI. On the morning of the 24th Combat Team 504 proceeded to the occupation of ALCAMO; and Company A and the 2nd Battalion, 505th, to that of SAN VITO, and 505th patrols contacted Task Force X patrols at PACECO; all without enemy resistance. Meanwhile Task Force X had occupied MARSALA, and had taken 6856 prisoners in the CASTELVETRANO-MARSALA area.

Nothing remained but to police the occupied area and garrison it against the possibility of enemy counterattack, assemble captured stores, and gather in straggling prisoners; but this was to be the work of many days. Prisoners were still being picked up and drifting in from isolated outposts weeks later.[26] Enemy barracks and stores, which were being looted even as the Division entered the area, were first put under guard and the food stores later appropriated to feed prisoners. Among the food stores taken were 28,000 hard rations from one warehouse, 700 pounds of beef, 2,000 pounds of sugar, 500 pounds coffee, and 400 gallons of tomato paste.[27]

Of the vehicles taken, sixty-two were in suitable condition to use.[28] Weapons and ammunition were dumped, and passed through the proper ordnance channels.

The EGADI ISLANDS-FAVIGNANA, LEVANZO, and MARETTINO situated ten to twenty miles off TRAPANI, which had been out of communication with the mainland since the 23rd, surrendered July 29th to Captain Richard Gerard of the G-3 section and 1st Lieutenant Louis P. Testa, P.W.I., who approached FAVIGNANA in a sail boat and negotiated the surrender with Lieutenant Colonel Silvio Serralunga. The population of the Islands is about 6000; their garrison was nearly 1000.

In each of the two phases of its participation in the Sicilian Campaign the Division had served effectively. In the first, it was prevented from achieving its specifically assigned mission; but at the cost of many casualties[29] it engaged elements of the Hermann Goering, 15th Panzer, 4th Livorno and 54th Napoli Divisions, and of the 206th Coastal Division. Major General J.M. Swing, Commanding General, 11th Airborne Division and airborne advisor to General Eisenhower, declared that the work of the airborne troops advanced the progress of the beach assault by two days.

In the second phase, both the opposition and the Division's own casualties were incomparably lighter. The only elements of divisional strength encountered were the 202nd, 207th, and 208th Coastal Divisions, although there were a large number of supporting units. The Division lost one officer and six men killed, and sixteen men wounded. In five days of campaigning during the course of this phase, it advanced more than one hundred miles through enemy territory, and took prisoner or occupied the territory in which it later rounded up a total of 23,191 officers and men.

In recognition of this service General Ridgway received the following letter from Major General Geofrrey Keyes, commanding the Provisional Corps, of which the 82nd Airborne Division had served as a part:

SEVENTH UNITED STATES ARMY
HEADQUARTERS PROVISIONAL CORPS
A.P.O. 758

24 July 1943

Major General M. B. Ridgway
Commanding 82nd Airborne Division
A.P.O. 469

My dear General Ridgway:

With the remarkably rapid and successful conclusion of the mission assigned the Provisional Corps of the Seventh Army in the operation to capture Palermo and the Western portion of the island of Sicily, I wish to express to you and your splendid division, together with the attached units, my admiration for feats accomplished.

The rapid assembly and organization of your force of mixed units, and their more rapid advance on each objective to include the important city and locality of Trapani, reflects great credit upon you, your staff and your men.

It is an honor for me to be privileged to command the Provisional Corps composed of such fine divisions and it is with extreme regret that I learn that the 82nd is to be withdrawn for other important missions.

With best wishes to you and your command for continued success, I am,

Sincerely yours,

/S/ Geoffrey Keyes
GEOFFREY KEYES
Major General, U.S.A.,
Commanding

**Footnotes**

[1] Battalion Commanding Officers of the 505th Parachute Infantry were: 1st Bn. – Lt. Col. Arthur Gorham; 2nd Bn. – Major Mark Alexander; 3rd Bn. – Major Edward C. Krause.

[2] Battalion Commanding Officers were: 1st Bn. – Lt. Co. Warren Williams; 2nd Bn. – Lt. Col. William Yarborough.

[3] Lt. Louis Testa, PWI Officer

[4] The difficulty of navigating and controlling the planes as a group was revealed by the fact that Gen. Taylor could get and send to Gen. Ridgway the following: "Incomplete information from Wing indicated all drops approximately on DZ except 2nd Bn 505 which is west of Gela ..."

[5] At 110845 Seventh Army sent the following message to the II Corps and the 45th, 1st, 3rd, and 2nd Armored Divisions: "Notify all units especially AA that parachutists 82nd Airborne Division will drop at about 2330 tonight July 11-12 on Farello Landing Field."

[6] 1st Lt. Z. C. Lutcavage, Co. F, 504th Parachute Infantry, declared two of his men were killed when they gave the wrong password.

[7] The personnel in these eight planes were from the following units: two planes – Hq. Co., 504th; one plane, Co. F, 504th; two planes, Btry C, 376th; two planes, Btry D, 376th; one plane, Hq. Btry., Div Arty.

[8] Rec'd 121237. "TWX from Force 141 to Seventh army, TCC, 82nd Airborne Division. View of unfortunate incident last night no further repeat no further movement by air except assault will take place."

[9] Pvt. Keith K. Scott, 1st Bn. Hq. Co., 504th Parachute Infantry, was a member of the Second Lift; but as the experiences of many of the members of the Second Lift were identical in nature to those of the First, they will be related here without discrimination.

[10] 1st Lt. Richard Mills, 1st Bn. Hq. co., 504th.

[11] Co. A, 505th Prcht. Inf.

[12] Capt. Carl R. Comstock, Med. Det., 505th Prcht. Inf.

[13] 1st Lt. Dean McCandless, Hq. Co. 1st Bn., 505th Prcht. Inf.

[14] Hq. Co. 1st Bn., 505th Prcht. Inf.

[15] Hq. Co. 1st Bn., 505th Prcht. Inf.

[16] Pfc Shelby R. Hord, Co. H, 504th Prcht. Inf.

[17] Pvt. Thomas E. Lane, Co. H, 504th Prcht. Inf.

[18] The strength and casualties of each lift by units during the entire campaign is shown in a table printed at a later stage of this history. Casualties later in the campaign were so extremely light that figures in this table give a fair picture of lessons in the first so-called Guerilla Warfare.

[19] The Command Party brought on the Monrovia one 3/4 ton Command and Reconnaissance Car, four 1/4 ton trucks and two 1/4 ton trailers; and the third lift brought in the planes with it twenty-two 1/4 ton trucks, all being a part of the Division's organic transportation.

[20] A note will be added here to complete a statement of the transportation available to the Division on its movement from Gela to Trapani. In addition to the Transportation brought by the Command Party and the Third Lift, the 505th CT, then situated west of Ribera, received on July 19th at Licata eighteen 1/4 ton trucks of its organic transportation. On July 19, Co. E, 47th QM Truck Bn., was attached to the Division, making available forty-six 2-1/2 ton trucks for transportation and supply. From time to time during the periods of their attachment, other transportation was obtained from the 62nd Armored, 34th and 77th FA Bns.

[21] CT 39 and 83rd Chem. Bn. had been attached to the Division July 17. The 34th FA Bn., the Armored FA Bn., the 1st Bn., 77th FA., and a detachment of the 56th Medical Bn. were attached July 18th.

[22] During the day CT 39, 1st Bn. 77th FA, the 62nd Armored FA Bn., and the 3rd Rn. Bn. were relieved from attachment to the Division. CT 39 followed CT 504 into Menfi, whence it advanced on Casstelvetrano the next day and occupied it at noon.

[23] 2nd Lt. Vernon P. Ellis, Co. C, 307th A/B Engr. Bn., was killed and Pvt. George C. Phillips of the same organization wounded while removing mines near Santa Ninfa.

[24] On the 21st and 22nd, Co. E, 47 QM Truck Bn. and the 20th Engineer Bn were attached to the Division.

[25] A battery of four 75mm guns was found after the surrender at one of the firing positions with 155 empty shell cases nearby; a battery of six 90mm guns was found at another position with about 12 cases; and a 149mm Battery, fired several salvos from the position southwest of the city. There is some dispute as to the reason for the inaccuracy of the enemy fire. It was without effect, except to force a halt and deployment, although his observation was perfect and his targets at short range.

[26] See the accompanying table for a day-by-day count on the registration of prisoners.

[27] Until the occupation of Trapani, the fare had been extremely limited in kind, and even that obtained only by the greatest effort – the morning's rations often not arriving until late in the evening. Prior to the reorganization of the Division, members of the first two lifts had only one K and one D ration, plus what they could forage, or what was given some individuals by members of other units. At Gela, fortunately, C rations were obtained, and C and K Rations constituted the sole fare from there to Trapani. Thereafter, U Rations were obtained, and supplemented by captured supplies.

[28] See the accompanying table for a list of vehicles captured and their assignment to units.

[29] See table below.

## List of Prisoners

The number of prisoners, officers and men, taken day by day during the western campaign and rounded up from the Trapani and nearby garrisons during the three successive days were as follows:

| DATE | NO. PRISONERS |
|------|---------------|
| July 19 | 848 |
| 20 | 745 |
| 21 | 1515 |
| 22 | 19 |
| 23 | 898 |
| 24 | 1741 |
| 25 | 3268 |
| 26 | 2231 |
| **Total** | **11,265** |

The number rounded up during the period July 27 to August 15, in the course of a general reconnaissance of western Sicily, were eighty-three officers and 4,127 enlisted men, or a total of 4,210. Adding this to the sum of the figures above, it is shown that a grand total of 15,475 prisoners were taken during the campaign, by organic elements of the Division alone.

**Captured Vehicles**

List of captured motor vehicles, and their distribution to units:

| Unit | M/C | 1/4-3/4 | 1-1 1/2 | 2-3 | Amb. | Total |
|------|-----|---------|---------|-----|------|-------|
| 307 Engrs | 3 | 2 | | 7 | | 12 |
| Hq. Co. | | | 2 | | | 2 |
| MP Plat. | 1 | 1 | | | | 2 |
| 782d Ord | 1 | 3 | | 1 | | 5 |
| 505 CT | 6 | 3 | 3 | 3 | 2 | 17 |
| 504 CT | 15 | 3 | 4 | 1 | 1 | 24 |
| Total | 26 | 12 | 9 | 12 | 3 | 62 |

# Section 2: 505th Parachute Infantry Reports
### HEADQUARTERS 505TH PARACHUTE INFANTRY
### A.P.O. #469, U.S. ARMY,

In Field

August 14, 1943

SUBJECT: AIRBORNE ASSAULT OPERATIONS.

TO: Commanding General, 82nd Airborne Division.

I. <u>GENERAL</u>:

1. All units departed from take-off airdromes in North Africa in accordance with plans scheduled.

2. <u>The Headquarters and Command Serial</u> dropped approximately ten miles South of VITTORIA, thirty miles from its assigned Drop Zone. Small groups of fighters were organized during the night, and at daylight, enemy strong-points and pill-boxes were attacked wherever found. Some small groups worked South to the beaches and rendered direct assistance in the landing of the 45th Division. One group consisting of the Combat Team Commander, Colonel Gavin; the S-3, Major Vandevoort; the Adjutant, Captain Ireland, and three enlisted men captured one prisoner who later escaped. They then moved west, and after a brief engagement in which one parachutist was killed, and four casualties inflicted on the enemy, succeeded in joining the 45th Division at 0240, D plus one, at which time the reorganization of the Combat Team was initiated by the Combat Team Commander. A group of approximately forty men of the Headquarters Serial, under the command of Headquarters Commandant (Lt. H.H. Swingler), occupied high key terrain commanding the main road net leading inland from the 45th Division. This group destroyed one armored vehicle which was attempting to move to the beach and prevented the retirement of the enemy forces inland from the beach after the assault had been begun by the 45th Division. They captured five officers and ninety-six men who were attempting to retire inland from the beach defense. Also, it reduced several pill-boxes and captured a large amount of enemy material, including machine guns. This group rejoined the Combat Team on D plus one (11 July), in time to participate in the attack on enemy positions on BIAZZO RIDGE.

3. <u>The First Battalion Serial</u> landed approximately four miles South of NISCEMI, and was immediately engaged by the enemy. Captain Sayre [A Co.] and forty-five men attacked and captured an Italian garrison, taking twenty-two prisoners. During this attack four parachutists were killed. An advance was continued until the 1st Division was joined. Upon joining the 2nd Battalion, 16th Infantry, the attack was resumed with them. The enemy counter-attacked with tanks at 1130, causing a withdrawal of some of the troops participating. The parachute troops held their ground and succeeded in knocking out several of the attacking tanks. Lt. Colonel Arthur F. Gorham personally manned an anti-tank [rocket]launcher in this defense and knocked out a tank before he was killed. The attack was later resumed and the First Battalion continued to fight with the 16th Infantry until relieved to join its own Combat Team. A portion of the First Battalion Serial landed approximately fifty miles East of GELA, occupied and held the town of NOTO. A detachment of twelve men assisted in the capture of RAGUSA. Further estimate of their combat activities is not known at the present. Major Winton, the Battalion Executive Officer, was outstanding in assisting the organization of the Battalion while under fire, refusing to be evacuated despite a wrenched knee received on landing.

4. The Second Battalion Serial landed South of RAGUSA, approximately forty kilometers from the scheduled Drop Zone. At the time of the jump the entire serial was being harrassed by small arms fire, several men being killed in their chutes. Immediately upon landing, reorganization was started. With the aid of patrols searching for small isolated groups the complete Serial was intact by 1200 hour, D day. At 0900 on D day, the Battalion began to clean up the strong-point and the area near S. CRUCE-CAMERINA. During this action, two officers and six enlisted men were killed. Forty-five Italians, a quantity of small arms and ammunition were captured. As soon as this strong concentration had been completely wiped out the Battalion worked toward the South and set up a defensive position on the outskirts of S. CROCE-CAMERINA overlooking the sea. "E" Company, acting as an advance guard in this action, encountered fire from the city. They immediately went into an organized attack. The city was taken after a short but hard fight. The company captured 144 Italians, one 47mm anti-tank gun, 13,600 rounds of machine gun ammunition, 330 grenades and enough rifles and carbines and equipment to equip an Italian Battalion. This Battalion also captured a strongly held point East of S. CROCE-CAMERINA. The Battalion was under the command of Major Alexander. July 11 was spent in more complete reorganization, and contact was made with Regimental Headquarters. The evening of the 11th they left the area, marched through CAMERINA PASS, and came in contact with men of the 45th Division, outside of the town along the coast. They passed through VITTORIA and moved into bivouac about 1500 hour on the 12th, joining the rest of the 505th Combat Team.

5. The Third Battalion Serial upon approaching the coast to turn inland over its drop zone, was turned by the Air Corps out to sea again, less "I" Company. "I" Company, less one plane landed on its drop zone and fully accomplished its mission in addition to reducing pill-boxes and a blockhouse, and taking prisoners. The remainder of the 3rd Battalion Serial, on its second pass was dropped at 0025, well scattered in an area about 3 1/2 miles Southeast of ACATE RIVER. Eighty-five men of "G" Company were assembled within an hour, under their Company Commander; and with little resistance reached a point of high ground where the coastal highway crosses the ACATE RIVER. Forty-five men of the Serial under Lt. Willis joined forward elements of the 180th Infantry and were employed as assault troops, and succeeded in reducing strong enemy positions in front of the 45th Division. Lt. Willis and two men were killed. Sixty men of the Serial with the aid of three guns, "C" Battery, 456th Field Artillery, were the first troops into VITTORIA. They reduced an Italian garrison, approximately eight prisoners were taken besides numerous vehicles, small arms, and other stores. In this action Lt. Harris was captured and held prisoner in the Italian curatel for a period of several hours. During this time he succeeded in convincing the defenders of the ineffectiveness of their defense and their inability to cope with the advancing troops of the 45th Division. As a result of this, the Italian Commanding Officer raised the white flag and surrendered approximately eighty men and numerous small arms and other stores. After local night fighting and patrolling the remainder of the 3rd Battalion Serial was assembled and reorganized and equipment gathered during the hours of daylight on D day. Efforts to make contact with the rest of the 505th Combat Team were made to no avail. At 1900 hours, D day, the Serial Commander with 180 men and officers, set out toward VITTORIA for the purpose of orientation. Upon reaching the GELA-VITTORIA highway, about five miles Northeast of VITTORIA, the unit was halted. Colonel Gavin appeared in the area about 0600, D plus one, and ordered the unit to move toward GELA. They then participated in the action on BIAZZO RIDGE.

6. Company "B", 307th Engineer Battalion:

a. The first plane load, first platoon, Company "B", 307th Engineers, was forced down in North Africa, and took off alone later on. They jumped at 0022, July 10, and landed six kilometers south of COMISO. There they assembled and started in a southerly direction at 0400. They traveled three kilometers and encountered shell fire from the sea and dug in. They met a group from the 3rd Battalion, going north, and joined them and traveled until 1400. They left the 3rd Battalion and headed west where they met the 160th Infantry and dug in for the night along highway 115 at a point about five miles Northwest of VITTORIA. The Combat Team Commander moved the men from that point at 0600, July 11, and they were joined by "G" Company, 505th Parachute Infantry. They started fighting under Major Hagan at 1030, in which engagement Lt. Wexler and several enlisted men were wounded. They remained under the 3rd Battalion until rejoining the Engineer Company at 1930, July 11. The second and third plane loads, first platoon, Company "B", 307th Engineers, landed at 0025, July 10, fifteen miles northeast of drop zone. Assembling on the ground, one planeload from Company "A", 505th Parachute Infantry, was met and forces joined. From time of assembly until 0430, a search was made for the assigned drop zone and accomplishment of their mission. During the search, telegraph and telephone wires were cut, but they were unable to locate themselves in relation to the drop zone. It was decided to dig in at a crossroad and wait for morning. At 0530, a German motorcycle containing three passengers pulled up to the crossroads and stopped. The passengers were killed. Another motorcycle arrived 15 minutes later and was likewise caught under fire and the occupants were killed. The men were then assembled and moved out in the general direction of the drop zone. Five of this group were separated when they went to pick up two equipment chutes which were spotted a half mile away. The remainder continued on and took up a position on ground commanding the two valleys. Here contact was made with elements of "G" Company, 505th Parachute Infantry, and defensive positions were set up. During the afternoon, 2nd Battalion, 180th Infantry, 45th Division arrived at the hill. The men from "B" Company, 307th Engineers, and men from "A" Company, 505th Parachute Infantry attached themselves to 2nd Battalion, 180th Infantry, and remained with them for three nights and two days. During this period of time additional parachutists drifted in and became part of their organization. On the 13th, contact was made through patrols with the 505th Combat Team Headquarters and a march was made to that position, where they again came under control of their Company Commander.

b. The second and third platoons jumped at 0026 on July 10, approximately five kilometers South of COMISO. Platoons were ordered to assemble and move toward objective. The Company Commander and one sergeant left Drop Zone immediately and proceeded Northwest, assembling all men encountered. They joined Lt. Swingler and a group of Headquarters personnel at dawn, about four miles northwest of the drop zone. Leaving the bulk of the men at a farmhouse, Captain Johnson and eight men went on patrol, where they encountered opposition consisting of three pill-boxes at a crossroads. During the encounter with the pill-boxes they wrecked a German personnel carrier, towing a tank. One German was killed and three were captured. After also killing a German motorcyclist and a dispatch carrier, the eight men were forced to retire by three tanks. One man was wounded during the encounter. They withdrew to a position in a field and gathered the remainder of their forces which had been left under Lt. Swingler. The group set up a position on top of two small hills, with an all around defense. It was planned to move the entire force to the beach that night. At about 1530 one battery of the 288th Italian Field Artillery Battalion approached the hill on which the defensive position was located. The entire battery was captured, consisting of four officers and approximately one hundred enlisted men. They then set up prisoner of war straggler posts. They sent out patrols to locate a radio with which to contact all their forces at their Drop Zone and did so at 2000, July 10, turning their prisoners over to the 45th Division. They bivouacked at the Drop Zone until 1700, on July 11. They joined the 3rd Battalion, 505th Parachute Infantry, for an attack on enemy Northwest of VITTORIA. Lt. RIFFLE and three enlisted men were killed and several enlisted men were wounded in this encounter.

7. The action at BIAZZO RIDGE: A prolonged engagement took place on the BIAZZO RIDGE on the VITTORIA-GELA highway about two miles East of the ACATE RIVER on D plus one. This affair, judging by the intensity of the fighting and the results accomplished, appears to be the only engagement of magnitude participated in by the Combat Team during the landings.

a. At 0600 the morning of D plus one the Combat Team Commander and S-3 proceeded West on the GELA road from VITTORIA to obtain control of any parachute troops that might be found, determine what, if any, enemy troops were between VITTORIA and GELA, and move all available parachute troops West to join the 1st Division as per plan. About two hundred men of the 3rd Battalion under the command of Major Kraus were located near the road about eight to ten miles west of VITTORIA. About two miles west of their bivouac a group of forty men of "L" Company, 180th Infantry and twenty parachutists were found. At this point individual soldiers stopped the Combat Team Commander and informed him that enemy troops were to the West and astride the road. Continued questioning of those who professed to know the enemy situation failed to disclose any specific information of his location, strength or dispositions.

b. The Commanding Officer and S-3 continued West to the railroad station about one mile East of BIAZZO RIDGE where a point reconnaissance was made. At this point a German Officer and private suddenly came around the corner in a motorcycle and were captured. They made no effort to resist capture and appeared to be quite disgusted with the lack of resistance being offered by the Italian troops, but refused to give any information regarding their own troops. The twenty nearby parachutists under the command of Lt. Wexler were ordered forward at once and the Combat Team S-3 was sent to the rear to bring Major Kraus and his men and to go to the 45th Division Command Post. Here he was to send a message to the 1st Division and the 82nd Division informing them of the Combat Team plan to advance west along the GELA highway.

c. The twenty parachutists under the command of Lt. Wexler arrived promptly and after being given the situation were moved in the direction of BIAZZO RIDGE. They were ordered to proceed west to the ACATE RIVER and short of the Ridge they came under small arms fire coming from the Ridge. They continued to advance driving the enemy to the West. Upon reaching the top of the Ridge they had intense small arms and mortar fire that stopped their advance. Here they were ordered to dig in and hold until the arrival of the Battalion.

d. At approximately 1000 the 3rd Battalion group, consisting of about 200 men, arrived at the railroad station under the command of Major Hagan. The Combat Team Commanding Officer outlined the situation to Major Hagan and directed him to proceed West along the GELA Road to the ACATE RIVER, here to reorganize and move forward on Combat Team order. Rolls were dropped, orders issued, and the battalion moved out. By this time it was established through contact with the 180th Infantry that the regiment was held up on a line generally parallel to the GELA highway and South of that road. They had been unable to advance. Upon the departure of the battalion a small combat team reserve of about three squads was made up. Later in the day the forty men from "L" Company, 180th Infantry, joined this unit.

e. The attack of the 3rd Battalion continued west with some losses from small arms fire until about noon. At this time it had advanced, about one mile. Only German troops were encountered and a number were wounded, killed and captured early in the fight. From there it was determined that the enemy force consisted of one battalion of the Herman Goering Division. It was evidently within supporting distance of another battalion and a large number of tanks. About noon the Germans counterattacked with tanks inflicting heavy losses on our attacking infantry. Major Hagan was wounded and evacuated and Major Krause who had arrived took command of the battalion. Orders were issued by the Combat Team Commanding Officer to the reserve to dig in on BIAZZO RIDGE. It appeared evident that the Ridge dominated the area between the ACATE River and VITTORIA and its loss would seriously jeopardize the landings of the 45th Division. It was decided to hold the Ridge at all cost and if the tanks entered the defense to destroy the infantry accompanying them. Because of the loss of equipment during the drop there were few rocket launchers present. By noon one 75mm howitzer had arrived, about an hour later another arrived and by the end of the day there were three present.

f. Shortly after noon Captain Ireland of the Combat Team Staff was sent up as liaison party for a 155mm Battalion and Navy 5 inch liaison party. They did splendid work and about three o'clock were firing upon the known German assembly areas and positions. By this time all of the launchers except three had been destroyed and the tanks were within fifty yards of the Combat Team Command Post. The 45th Division also sent up two 57mm anti-tank guns. One 75mm gun from the 456th Field Artillery Battalion engaged and destroyed one of the attacking tanks. The attacking force withdrew and appeared to be regrouping and reorganizing about 1000 yards to a mile in front of the ridge.

g. Information was received at 1800 that Regimental Headquarters Company, 505th Parachute Infantry, under the command of Lieutenant Swingler, with some Engineers of "B" Company, had been located and would arrive by 2000. At about the same time a company of tanks (11) arrived. Orders were then issued for a counter-attack to be made at 8:30 (2030) employing Regimental Headquarters Company, the available engineers and the tank company supported by all available artillery fire. The mission given the attacking force was to attack and destroy all enemy to the front, advancing far enough to permit evacuation of our dead and wounded, and then to organize a further defense around BIAZZO Ridge.

h. The attack jumped off at about 8:45. Very heavy mortar and artillery fire was brought to bear on the attacking troops and on the Ridge. The attack was continued through the enemy position, inflicting heavy losses in men and equipment upon him. Twenty-two dead bodies and many wounded were recovered. The Germans withdrew in apparent confusion, leaving many dead and wounded and considerable equipment of all types. Four tanks were believed to have been knocked out, although all but one were recovered by the Germans during the night.

i. The following day the dead were buried and those not yet found removed from the battlefield. All abandoned enemy equipment was taken up. Our losses were forty-three killed and 100 wounded. No equipment was lost. Enemy losses abandoned on the battlefield amounted to about fifty killed. Fifty prisoners were taken, all German. Two armored cars were knocked out, twelve six-inch Russian mortars captured, besides many machine guns, small arms, vehicles, and ammunition dumps. A caliber .50 gun crew of Battery "D", 456th Field Artillery, is credited with knocking down three ME 109's which strafed and bombed our positions on the Ridge. The Battalion Commanding Officer confirms the fact that one was shot down.

j. One section of Battery "C", 456th Field Artillery, under command of Lieutenant Loren and Sergeant Thomas, particularly distinguished by taking positions in the open at the top of BIAZZO Ridge and engaging openly tanks in range. Despite small arms fire of all types and four rounds of direct fire from an 88mm cannon on a Mark VI tank which the gun disabled, this crew held their gun in position even after members of the crew were knocked down by shell concussion. They succeeded in delaying the tanks in the attack until sufficient reinforcements arrived to permit continuation of the attack.

k. Third Battalion Medical Section under Captain McElroy, and elements of the Regimental Aid Station under the Regimental Surgeon, Captain Smith, and the Assistant Regimental Surgeon, Lieutenant Suer, were outstanding in their intense and devoted performance of their first aid tasks under fire of all types. Wounded were removed from the battlefield promptly at all times, allowing the maximum number of combat troops to be kept in the engagement.

/s/t/ JAMES M. GAVIN
Colonel, Infantry,
Commanding.

## 505th Parachute Infantry
## After-Action Report

**The Plan**

The planning for this unit's part of the "HUSKY" Operation began in the middle of May, 1943 while it was stationed at OUJDA, Fench Morocco. The 82nd Airborne Division was given the mission of securing the amphibious landing of the 1st Division in Sicily by establishing an airborne bridgehead. The 1st Division was to land between GELA and SCOGLITTI at 0255 hours on July 10th, 1943. The greatest threat to the success of this landing was a German Panzer Division concentrated near CALTAGIRONE, a small town about fifteen miles inland.

It was determined that the best method of accomplishing this mission was to drop a parachute combat team to seize and hold the road net and surrounding terrain running from CALTAGIRONE to the sea. The object was to prevent the enemy from intercepting the landing of the 1st Infantry Division. The center of this defense was to be the intersection where the minor road running south from CALTAGIRONE met the main coast road running between GELA and VITTORIA.

The combat team was made up to include the 505th Parachute Infantry, the 3rd Battalion of the 504th Parachute Infantry, the 456th Field Artillery, and Company "B", 307th Airborne Engineers. The time set for the drop was 2346 hours on July 9th, 1943.

With the mission assigned, a training program was drawn up for specialized work to be done during the period prior to the jump to better prepare us for the fight to come. This schedule provided for both day and night training in all necessary basic subjects such as bayonet fighting, scouting and patrolling, and hand to hand fighting. As the period progressed, small unit tactics were reviewed with emphasis placed on setting up defensive positions at night. Ranges were made available for final zeroing of all weapons.

The regimental plans and training section developed a standard plane loading plan for both equipment and personnel which was tried and accepted.

Battalion combat teams were organized and began training as such. Each one executed a practice parachute jump with their full combat loads, stressing the method of assembly and the tactics of defense. The entire combat team participated in a dry run of the actual operation during the latter part of June. In this problem only jumpmasters jumped working from jump patterns already on the ground. Sand table replicas of the operational terrain were made and studied in conjunction with aerial photographs.

The training areas were in the wind swept, dusty valley eight miles north of OUJDA. The terrain was generally flat and rocky with little or no vegetation. There was some hilly ground to the west and this was utilized as much as possible. The temperature was the greatest training obstacle, often reaching 120 degrees.

The first days of July, the combat team moved by plane to the vicinity of KAIROUAN, Tunisia. Here each battalion combat team was bivouacked near the airfield where its planes were based. The week just prior to the actual operation was spent clearing up supply and administrative details. The operation was gone over in more detail with the help of better aerial photographs and maps. Equipment and weapons were given the final touches. The Air Corps provided training in the use of their rubber life rafts and other safety devices.

The morning of the 9th of July was spent in loading the equipment bundles in the para-racks and the drop testing of them. During the afternoon the men rested and dressed for combat. After the evening mail the Company Commanders gathered their men around them and gave them final instructions and the password. Everyone, less the rear echelon, then moved by truck to their planes. Last minute conferences were held between jumpmasters and pilots and the take off started at 2020 hours.

## The Air Corps Angle

The combat team was flown in the planes of the 52nd Wing, which was broken down into five serials. The Third Battalion Serial was flown by the 314th Group, the 504th Battalion Serial by the 64th Group, the First Battalion Serial by the 313th Group, the Headquarters Serial by the 316th Group and the Second Battalion Serial by the 61st Group. Each serial was to fly as an individual unit on a definite planned time schedule. The flight plan consisted of a rendezvous over Tunisia, then east to the island of MALTA, then northwest to Sicily and along its southern coast to the point east of GELA where each group turned north over the LAGO DI BIVARRE to their drop zones. Here the parachutists were to jump when the pilots turned on the green jump light.

This drop plan however did not materialize for several reasons. A strong west wind developed ranging between twenty and thirty miles per hour and literally blew the planes off their course whereupon the pilots lost their direction. Strong anti-aircraft fire was encountered along the coast and at the crossroads in the drop area that also drove the planes off the course. As a result the Combat Team was spread over an area sixty-five miles wide.

Stone fences, rock piles, and olive trees covered the area in which most men landed. A large number consequently were seriously injured on the jump. Leg and ankle injuries were the most common, however one soldier broke his back on landing. The rugged nature of the terrain also made the assembly plan more difficult.

## The First Five Days

The First Battalion Serial which was supposed to be dropped just northwest of the crossroads above GELA was well scattered. A group of three hundred and twenty were dropped three miles northwest of the city of AVOLA on the eastern coast of the Island. Small groups were organized, found their equipment, and became involved in several small skirmishes with the Italians. The individual groups were assembled at daylight and attacked the town of AVOLA. After some short skirmishes with the enemy, contact was made with the British. This group then moved to the outskirts of the city and set up a defensive position. The next day was spent in reorganization and the evacuation of the wounded. On July 12th this group started marching toward GELA in an effort to rejoin the Combat Team. Upon their arrival in NOTO they received word that the British were ordered by Allied Force Headquarters to evacuate all parachutists in that area that had been cut off from their unit. This was done from embarkation points south of AVOLA. While en route the parachutists acted as guards for Prisoners of War who were also being evacuated. Debarkation of this group was made at SOUSSE, Tunisia, and they were then sent overland to KAIROUAN. Another group of this same serial was dropped about two miles northeast of their actual drop zone and landed in a well fortified area. Several skirmishes developed immediately and before the group could become oriented they were pinned down by fire. The next night parts of this group were started moving south. On July 11th, the main body was attacked by several German tanks. A stiff fight developed and the Battalion Commander, Lieutenant Colonel Gorham, was killed. Parts of the 16th Infantry joined this group at this time and took up the fight with anti-tank weapons. On the 13th the Battalion Executive Officer, Major Winton, assembled the group and awaited the arrival of the Combat Team on the 14th. One plane of this serial searched for their drop zone and finally returned without dropping for lack of gasoline. Another plane dropped their parachutists near MARINA DI RAGUSA.

The Third Battalion Serial was dropped at 0030 hours in between SCOGLITTI and VITTORIA. The men assembled in small groups and due to the unfamiliar terrain were unable to orient themselves. The early hours of the morning were spent in searching for equipment bundles. A provisional battalion command post was set up about two miles north of SCOGLITTI at 0345 hours. Patrols were sent out in an effort to contact the other battalions. A defensive position was organized and the salvage of equipment began. At 1900 hours a group of one hundred and sixty men started marching toward VITTORIA leaving a salvage crew of twenty men behind. After marching two miles the Battalion Commander, Major Krause, contacted the Regimental Executive Officer who directed the Battalion to bivouac for the night about four miles west of VITTORIA on the GELA road. Another group of this same Battalion consisting of about sixty men moved west during the first night and set up a defense on a hill eleven miles west of VITTORIA. Here they remained until they joined the combat team on July 13th. Several other groups contacted the enemy along the road to VITTORIA from SCOGLITTI but only small skirmishes developed. Eventually these men found their way to Hill 125 where the Combat Team assembled.

## The Biazzo Ridge Battle

At 0615 hours on July 11th, the Combat Team Commander ordered the Third Battalion group and all others that had assembled to march west on the GELA-VITTORIA COAST Road in an effort to reach the assigned defensive area. About 0830 hours at a position approximately eight miles west of VITTORIA the point of the column was fired upon. Under command of the Third Battalion Executive Officer the Battalion deployed and moved on to Hill 125 on their right. Already on the hill were about twenty parachutists from the airborne engineers. The Battalion machine gun platoon was brought forward and a section placed on each flank. An attack was made immediately and by 0915 hours the enemy had been driven out of the valley to the west. The 81mm mortar observation post then moved forward, and, with a [SCR] 536 radio, the mortar platoon leader directed effective fire on enemy positions in building 400 yards to the northwest. One mortar shell lit on top of what was thought to be a pillbox and turned out to be a tank (Mark VI). This tank then pulled out and started down the road to the enemy's rear. In a few minutes it returned with three other tanks that worked their way forward into our positions in the vineyard. Bazookas were sent forward but were unable to place effective fire. Both tanks and ground guns then laid down heavy machine gun fire that covered our entire position. At this time the assistant mortar platoon leader was killed, the executive officer seriously wounded. Casualties were increasing. The tanks advanced to the base of Hill 125 under cover of the enemy machine gun fire but our lines held on the crest. The bazookas held their fire until the tanks were within seventy-five yards and scored two hits. This apparently caused the enemy to be uncertain of our strength and to withdraw. As one tank turned a direct hit was made on the rear of the tank which caused it to catch fire.

One and one half sections of the parachute artillery (75mm howitzer) Battalion then moved into position behind Hill 125 and delivered fire on the enemy positions. One gun was moved to the crest of the hill and then ensued a duel of heavy caliber fire in which two enemy tanks were knocked out. Fire was requested from the 45th Division Artillery and an observer was brought forward.

After adjustment by radio, effective fire was placed on enemy positions. Tank support was requested and it arrived at 1745 hours along with seventy-five more members of the combat team. An attack was made around sundown in an effort to recover our dead and wounded. Company L of the 180th Infantry supported the attack from the right flank.

A request was made through a Navy Liaison Officer for supporting Naval fire. The coordinates were radioed in and within three minutes, fire was placed on the target without adjustment. It appeared as though the enemy was attempting an attack at the same time. 120mm mortar fire covered the hill we held and many casualties were inflicted. This was the most harassing fire yet received. The tanks completed their mission which was a circuit through the valley to our front. Two enemy tanks were knocked out. Our tanks returned to the rear in their original position. This attack drove the enemy completely from the valley. The wounded were taken to the aid station and equipment lost in the valley during the morning was recovered. The position on the hill was then consolidated and outposts placed for the night, and so ended the 11th of July 1943.

The Second Battalion Serial was dropped in an area about six miles northwest of the small town of MARINA DI RAGUSA. Complete assembly was not achieved until the noon of the 10th. In the meantime small skirmishes were fought with pillboxes and machine gun nests and several casualties resulted. At 1400 hours, the battalion moved out toward the beach. Scattered sniper fire was encountered during the march from behind the many stone walls which covered the countryside. The Battalion was held up at one point en route and a Company was sent around the right to flank the enemy position. This Company ran into an Italian Garrison located about a mile north of MARINA DI RAGUSA. The garrison was composed of two barracks and six pillboxes which were all taken after a short fire fight. In this instance no casualties were sustained. Information was gained as the whereabouts of the Combat Team and the Battalion proceeded to march in that direction through the ST. CROCE CAMERINA and VITTORIA. The unit reached the crossroads six miles west of VITTORIA by the morning of the twelfth and rejoined the Combat Team.

The Headquarters Serial (less the demolition section) was dropped between ST. CROCE CAMERINA and VITTORIA. The main body of this serial worked their way in small groups toward VITTORIA and eventually to Hill 125. Several skirmishes developed involving pillboxes and roadblocks along the way. The group which was supposed to be dropped near the railroad bridge three miles east of GELA was dropped sixty miles away, just south of SYRACUSA on the eastern coast of the island. They set up a defensive position around a highway bridge which the British later took over. On July 20th, this demolition section was evacuated to SOUSSE, Tunisia, from SYRACUSA.

The Third Battalion of the 504th was scattered from their assigned drop zone north and west to NISCEMI. A large number were taken prisoner by the Germans in this area. Small groups formed and slowly fought their way back to their assigned drop zone and dug in awaiting their regiment.

Company I was dropped on their assigned drop zone at 2349 hours and proceeded to accomplish their missions. A part of the Company set up a defensive position adjacent to their drop zone but no enemy was encountered. One platoon of the Company proceeded to the beach to contact the 16th Infantry but met stiff resistance from an Italian garrison. A patrol reached the west end of the LAGO DI BIVARRE and lit the beacon fire to guide the 16th Infantry on their landing. With these missions accomplished the parts of the Company withdrew to the defensive position and awaited the arrival of the combat team. One plane of the Company dropped their load near NISCEMI and was then shot down by anti-aircraft fire. This group rejoined the Company on July 13th.

July 12th and 13th were spent in the burial of the dead and salvaging of enemy and our own equipment and reorganization.

## The Road To Trapani

On July 14th, the Combat Team, after collecting of remnants, moved to a bivouac area five miles east of GELA. The next three days were spent in the care, cleaning, and inspection of equipment. On July 18th, the Combat Team started moving as part of the Division through LICATA to AGRIGENTO, SCIACCA, MENFI, and SAN MARGHERITA.

On July 23rd, the Third Battalion Commander received orders to alert his command for a movement as advance guard for the Regimental Combat Team. At 1000 hour, orders came to move by truck on Highway 113 via PARTANIA, SANTA NINFA, SALEMI, and CALTAFINI into the province and city of TRAPANI, a distance of 45 miles. The Battalion entrucked and with attachments crossed IP at 1130 hour. Order of march: "H" Company, "G" Company "Headquarters" Company, Company "B" 83rd Chemical Mortar Battalion, "I" Company, and Battery "C" 456th Parachute Field Artillery Battalion. Nine demolitionists from Regimental Headquarters Company were attached to Headquarters Company. The third Platoon of Company "B", 307th Airborne Engineers, was attached to the point for the purpose of detecting and reducing mine fields and demolitions, thus securing the uninterrupted advance of the main body.

Mined roads were encountered at two points north and northwest of SANTA NINFA. Engineer crews quickly cleared these hazards during short halts. Thence the advance was without incident to a point ten kilometers east of TRAPANI. Here a group was dispatched to capture some Italian soldiers who were seen taking cover in a nearby railroad tunnel. After the preparations for an attack were made, the enemy surrendered. As the column advanced, a party was left to take control of the prisoners and to investigate a radio station which was situated several hundred yards to the north of the highway at this point. Investigation showed the station to be abandoned and the equipment destroyed. After a further advance of about three kilometers, the point was fired upon by small arms and machine gun fire originating from trenches and small pillboxes on the right and left of the road, the heaviest portion of fire came from the stronger points on the right. The resistance appeared reluctant to carry the fight and the forward elements of the advance party rapidly closed in. Seizure was made without casualties and 110 Italian officers and men were taken prisoners. As the Advance Guard proceeded, the point was halted by artillery fire about three kilometers, east of the city of TRAPANI at about 1500 hours. The artillery fire appeared to be coming from the high ground approximately 1,000 yards north of the road. The point displaced forward to feel out and reconnoiter the enemy positions and strength. After determining the enemy to be emplaced in strong fortified positions on the road and high ground to the right, orders were issued to detruck, deploy and move forward to ready positions in preparation for a coordinated attack against the enemy positions. This movement continued rapidly with the point displacing forward.

At approximately 1545 the Company Commanders were given their missions with imperative instructions that the advance be rapid and all covered approaches be utilized. The disposition of the Battalion Combat Team was as follows: "H" Company to move forward on the left of the road with the road as a right boundary; "I" Company on the right; Headquarters Company in support of "G" Company in reserve. The plan was to seize and destroy enemy installations on the high ground and thereafter to move forward on TRAPANI. Line of departure was a northeast-southwest line through the hangars at MILO AIRPORT. Jump off was immediate and advance was swift. Supporting fires were called for from 105's, 75's and chemical mortars which were received after some delay. Enemy artillery from positions mentioned above increased and was joined by heavy caliber, flat trajectory explosive fire which seemed to originate at a point southwest of the airport.

The advance of the assault companies was swift and well controlled and essentially aided by the dominating accurate fire laid down by the light machine gun platoon, harassing the enemy to the extent that this return fire was ineffective. Actions of the LMG Platoon in this operation was superior. Good alternate gun positions were used.

Friendly counter-battery fire could be heard from the 75mm and chemical mortar positions in an orchard about 1 km to the rear. First supporting fires were registered by the 456th Field Artillery Battalion and continued throughout the assault. Though necessarily in close proximity throughout to our forward elements, the fire fell with great accuracy on enemy targets.

At 1605, the Company Commander of Headquarters Company was summoned by the Battalion Commander, then at an observation post, to be given the mission for the 81mm Mortar Platoon. As the forward movement continued rapidly, it assumed a northwesterly direction toward the gun emplacements on the high ground to the north of the road. A group moving west on the highway encountered a roadblock and pillbox manned by twenty of the enemy. The group fired several rounds and the enemy surrendered. Fire was immediately placed from the captured guns against the positions on the hill. This fire was maintained until it was masked a short time later by "I" Company closing with the enemy.

The attack continued, "I" Company gaining their objective. Enemy resistance then ceased and the Battalion quickly reorganized. Company "I" was assigned the mission of mopping up enemy installations and securing garrisons and stores on the hill. This mission yielded 525 prisoners including one Naval garrison containing large stores of naval explosives, torpedoes, etc. (partly wrecked by the enemy); twelve 90mm field pieces, ammunition, small arms, etc.

No enemy inflicted casualties were sustained by this unit due to the inability of the enemy artillery to follow its rapid covered approach. Throughout the movement artillery fire fell in and near the rear elements.

The approach march formation continued its movement on Highway 113 into TRAPANI; order of march: "H", Headquarters and "G" Companies. After advancing about one kilometer into the city, the Division Commanding Officer halted the column and the Division G-2 went forward and received the official surrender of the city.

At 2000 the Battalion Combat Team was ordered to a bivouac area two kilometers east of the city on Highway 113. One platoon, given the mission of outposting the entrance to the city, was left to maintain order in compliance with the terms of the surrender.

After the capture of TRAPANI, the Combat Team patrolled the city and surrounding areas. Training was conducted whenever it could be done in conjunction with the guard work. A Battalion problem was held on the terrain to the east and proved profitable. On August 20th the Combat Team moved back by plane to Africa and so ended the Campaign in Sicily.

# Section 3: 504th Parachute Infantry Reports

Headquarters 504th Parachute Infantry

A.P.O. #469, U. S. Army

August 21, 1943

SUBJECT: AIRBORNE ASSAULT OPERATIONS 9-14 July 1943.

TO: Commanding General, 82nd Airborne Division.

## I. General

1. This is an informal report on the activities of the 3rd Battalion, 504th Parachute Infantry, participating with Combat Team 505 in the initial airborne assault operations in SICILY during the period 9-14 July 1943.

2. The first plane-loads of elements of the 3rd Battalion, 504th Parachute Infantry, operating with Combat Team 505, were dropped in SICILY about 1130 on the night of 9 July 1943, scattered over an area approximately sixty miles wide, southeast and east of NISCEMI to PACHINO in the southeast tip of the island. Six plane-loads were not accounted for, and from another ten planes, only one to five men were located during initial operations. Groups assembled and organized as best they could, and attempted to contact other groups and move toward scheduled drop zones or reach the Battalion Command Post.

3. Many isolated elements, scattered in the British area of operations, attached themselves to Canadian forces, worked and fought with them, and some were evacuated by the British to the coast and picked up by Major Beall on 10 and 11 July. In the American sector, isolated men and groups attached themselves to Seventh Army Units and fought with them until able to contact the Battalion. The size of groups assembled, ranged from six to 107 men, the latter number being reached after several days of action.

4. Generally, it appeared that the TC planes had become widely dispersed, either as the result of poor navigation or by separation from formations in the face of heavy Ack-Ack. Plane-loads were dropped everywhere. Some were engaged while landing, most within an hour or so later as the men located or were located by the enemy. Very little decisive fighting occurred during darkness of night 9-10 July, but early on the 10th, as officers were able to assemble men, each group did what it could, endeavoring to reach Battalion objectives or the Command Post, knocking out whatever enemy resistance was found en route, or consolidating with other groups for offensive action at vital points.

5. It is noteworthy that operations of the many Battalions groups were conducted in spite of severe loss of key personnel during the night landings. It was later determined that initial losses included all Company Commanders, all First Sergeants, except one, all the Battalion Staff except Major Beall, all communication except four runners and one [SCR] 511 operator, and all supply section NCO's except one artificer. Many of these missing men may have been evacuated and may possibly turn up later.

## II. Action Vicinity Niscemi

1. <u>Lieutenant James C. Ott</u>: The group with Lieutenant Ott landed nearest of all to scheduled Drop Zone, approximately one and a half miles away from it, falling near an orchard. After landing, he managed to assemble approximately fifteen men, some injured, and set out with them to accomplish his mission, that of covering right flank of the Battalion, which he thought was in position as scheduled. He moved north toward a house, found that occupants were friendly, and left 4 injured troopers there. Lieutenant Ott then oriented himself in relation to NISCEMI by questioning the Italians. From about 0200 of 10 July, he patrolled the area to the east and got exact bearing for road to NISCEMI.

2. <u>Lieutenant Colonel Charles W. Kouns</u>: About 1 mile from east-west secondary road to NISCEMI and some three miles southeast of NISCEMI, Lieutenant Colonel Kouns, with nine men, was in position on a hill. Early on the morning of 10 July, Lieutenant Ott working east, joined his group to that of Lieutenant Colonel Kouns. In position, they saw a column of German Infantry, estimated as one regiment of the Hermann Goering Division, moving along the road toward NISCEMI and turning left on the by-pass toward GELA. Lieutenant Colonel Kouns asked Lieutenant Ott to go to the road and observe. Lieutenant Ott, with nine enlisted men, including a rocket-launcher team, proceeded toward the road, a distance of 500-700 yards, covered by the rifles of Lieutenant Colonel Kouns and the remaining men. This was accomplished without observation by the enemy, although they had machine guns in position dominating the zone. Lieutenant Ott reached a cactus hedge and through an opening observed that the enemy was taking a break and their men were somewhat scattered.

Lieutenant Ott was seen by a German officer, so he shot him and took a rocket-launcher from one of his men and blew a German car to bits, killing three officers and the driver. German trucks and riflemen opened fire. Colonel Kouns and his men directed a covering fire against the enemy as Lieutenant Ott's group withdrew by taking quick cover in bamboo and running or crawling back through a vineyard, getting to a house with three of his men.

3. Lieutenant Willis J. Ferrill: Landing approximately six miles southeast of NISCEMI, Lieutenant Ferrill and two men marched north and, by 0900, 10 July, had assembled twenty-four enlisted men. A strong offensive position was set up on the high ground at CASTLE NOCERA, three miles southeast of NISCEMI. A patrol sent out to contact the rest of the Battalion encountered a company of German anti-aircraft. In the engagement two Germans were killed and two captured, but the patrol was forced to withdraw to the defensive position. About 1400, 10 July, about twenty Italians attacked the position and were repulsed, losing fourteen of their force killed and two captured. In this engagement Private Shelby R. Hord killed seven Italians while attacking hostile machine gun positions, enabling his men to use captured machine gun fire on rest of enemy. At the same time Private Lane killed four Italian riflemen who were protecting the machine guns. This engagement lasted approximately four hours, then the remaining Italians fled, leaving behind machine guns, rifles, pistols, ammunition, and transportation. During the night, hostile patrols were driven off with a few shots by the listening posts which had been established by Lieutenant Ferrill. During the morning of the 11th there was no action. At 1300 Lieutenant Watts contacted Lieutenant Willis J. Ferrill and that afternoon Lieutenant Watts' group joined Lieutenant Ferrill.

4. Lieutenant George J. Watts: About one and a half miles southeast of NISCEMI, 1st Lieutenant George J. Watts had assembled another group of about fifteen men by 0830, and had moved to a strategic hill and set up all round defensive positions which were maintained July 10-11. About 1300 on Sunday, 11 July, this group contacted Lieutenant Ferrill's group by radio and moved over to join them. About 1330, 13 July, the group fired on a column of German Infantry moving northeast toward NISCEMI with two tanks. A fierce fight ensued with the paratroopers repulsing the Germans, killing about seventy-five and losing five of their own men.

In this engagement maps were captured which proved of great value to the 16th Infantry, as well as mortars and other equipment. Private Lane, under exposure of heavy enemy machine gun and rifle fire, carried water to 103 of his companions. The group had mined roads surrounding their position (HAWKINS mines) and fought with three machine guns, two mortars, rifles and two rocket launchers, plus machine guns which Lieutenant Ferrill's men had captured, and had plenty of ammunition. On 14 July, Lieutenant Watt's group contacted a motorized patrol of the 16th Infantry who asked that he hold the position to protect the right flank. Wounded and enemy prisoners were turned over to the 16th Infantry. On 14 July, he located the Battalion Command Post and reported there with remaining 104 men. Captured material included German recon cars, valuable medical supplies, three 240mm Russian mortars, eight German machine guns, and a large quantity of ammunition.

5. Lieutenant Fred E. Thomas: About five miles southeast of NISCEMI, 1st Lieutenant Fred E. Thomas landed, and at 0200 on 10 July, he and five enlisted men advanced towards NISCEMI reaching the outskirts of the city about 0330. No troops were located there and the group worked their way west looking for the rest of the Battalion. About 1000, 10 July, they encountered a strong force of Germans which was under fire. Lieutenant Thomas and his group attacked the left rear of the Germans, killing seven Germans, losing two dead and one wounded of this group. The unidentified friendly force which had been firing on the Germans had withdrawn, and Lieutenant Thomas was forced to withdraw with his two remaining men. Later that day eight men from "H" Company, under command of Private Ferrari, joined Lieutenant Thomas. The group of eleven worked its way to the southeast, several times being subjected to the fire of artillery and automatic weapons. On the 14th July, Lieutenant Thomas came upon a large winery, about ten miles east of GELA, in which were two seriously injured and three uninjured men of the 16th Infantry. While treating the injured, three German tank-men entered the winery and were captured. However, the winery was covered by two Mark VI Tanks. The Germans also had a wounded man, and an agreement was reached whereby neither force would take prisoners, but would attempt to procure a doctor to treat the wounded. An American Medical Officer reached the group and attended the injured. Because their two Mark VI Tanks were too slow to evade the advancing Americans, the Germans burned them and about thirty in number withdrew on foot towards VITTORIA. Lieutenant Thomas and his group joined the 504th Combat Team in the GELA area about 1700 on 14 July.

### III. Action Northwest of Biscari – (Lieutenant Peter J. Eaton)

1. Approximately two miles northwest of BISCARI, at 2355 on 9 July, 1st Lieutenant Peter J. Eaton, "Headquarters Company", 3rd Battalion Mortar Platoon, took charge of three planeloads that landed intact. On the morning of 10 July, he rounded up all equipment and men he could find and proceeded west toward NISCEMI.

2. At 1200, 10 July, scouts encountered two Italian cars towing 47mm anti-tanks guns. They killed the occupants and took the guns. With this added equipment, positions were set up, mined, and manned, with guns covering roads toward BISCARI. Sergeant Suggs of Headquarters Company, and seven other men of that Company manned these guns of which they had no knowledge. Bore-sighting them, they fired them like veterans.

3. About 1230, a column of Italian motorized infantry, with an 11-ton Italian tankette in lead (estimated at a battalion because it occupied about 2200 yards on Highway NISCEMI-BISCARI). Sergeant Suggs and his men knocked out the tankette with their Italian 47mm anti-tank guns and so disorganized the foe with their fire, backed by their own 81mm mortars that they retreated in confusion.

4. Lieutenant Eaton, believing that the enemy force after reorganization, would be too large and possess too much fire power for his own weapons, which were carbines, destroyed the enemy equipment and withdrew to the south.

5. On 11 July, Lieutenant Eaton's group contacted a Battalion of 180th Infantry and continued to fight with this force to 12 July, when he learned the location of the Battalion Command Post and joined it in the vicinity of GELA. It is noteworthy that through all this fighting, Lieutenant Eaton displayed superior leadership and utilization of his men and firepower, and that he brought his group out without loss of a man killed or wounded. On one occasion the fight was so hot that he destroyed his 81mm mortars and withdrew. Worked with 180th Infantry for twodays.

### IV. Action Vicinity Pachino – (Major William R. Beall)

1. Major Beall found himself with one (1) Medical Officer (Captain William W. Kitchin) after jumping beside an Italian garrison. Surrounded by enemy, who were hunting them in the dark, they withdrew to a vineyard to figure their location and attempt to round up more men. About 0200, 10 July, they heard machine gun fire about 200 yards away and carbine return fire intermittently for 1 hour, and knew other troopers were in the vicinity. About 0730, 10 July, an advance patrol of Canadians came up. They gave Major Beall their positions, he asked help to attack garrison, but was not able to secure it, because Canadians had another mission, that of establishing and protecting beach-heads in another zone. He worked back to the beach and got assistance. The garrison was taken with Canadian assistance a little later. One Italian Officer and twenty enlisted men were captured, and six paratroopers were released, having been imprisoned by Italians. The results were one United States and one Canadian killed and buried, and one United States Officer and one United States enlisted man evacuated to Canadian Hospital. Major Beall continued his search for more men, and with what he rounded up, went back to the beach on the night of 10 July, staying there all night.

2. On the morning of 11 July, went out to 1st Canadian Division Headquarters on boat, met General Simmons, who promised transportation by boat to enable Americans to rejoin unit.

3. July, 12, Tuesday, Major Beall, Captain Kitchin, and eighteen enlisted men left by RAF crash boat to rejoin unit, and stopped en route at coast towns to pick up United States paratroopers, landed at SCOGLITTI on 13 July, and reported to bivouac area west of VITTORIA (505th Combat Team CP) with Captain Kitchin, one other officer, and forty-eight enlisted men from various organizations. At VITTORIA, Major Beall was told that Battalion Commanding Officer had been captured and he was in command. He proceeded to organize the remainder of the Battalion preparatory to continuing operations. Assembled a total of four officers and ninety enlisted men. Their reorganization was affected and Battalion continued its mission with Combat Team 504.

### Authentication:

1. It is indicated that this report does not cover in full detail every action in which sections of the 3rd Battalion were engaged. It does, however, present a general picture, which will be supplemented by such further data as will become available.

**Excerpt From 504th Parachute Infantry History Book**
**The Devils in Baggy Pants**

## Sicily History

The African sun, like a bloody curious eye, hung on the rim of the world as hundred of airplane engines coughed into life, spewing miniature dust storms across the flat wastes of a desert airfield.

Thin aluminum skins of C-47s vibrated like drawn snare drums and as paratroopers heaved themselves up into the planes and sought their pre-designated seats, they wrinkled their noses at the smell of gasoline and lacquer that flooded the planes' interiors.

Spearheading the airborne invasion of Sicily, the 3rd Battalion, 504th Parachute Infantry, crossed the North African coast as the sun flared briefly, then plummeted into the Mediterranean. Flak rose thinly into the dusky sky ahead – probably Malta, the paratroopers grimly thought.

Detached from the regiment for tactical requirements, the 3rd Battalion crossed over the Sicilian coast on schedule and jumped on its assigned drop zone, July 9, 1943.

For two days the men of the 3rd Battalion fought an enemy superior in numbers and equipment. By D+3 it had achieved its initial mission and was returned to regimental control.

The remainder of the regiment, led by Colonel R. H. Tucker, loaded planes and took off from the dusty airstrips around Kairouan, Tunisia, on July 11, 1943. As the planes cruised over the churning sea, all was quiet; some closed their eyes and prayed that it would remain quiet, while others anxiously craned their necks to peer ahead or to look down at the white-capped waves which tossed fifteen feet below the planes.

Nearing the Sicilian coast, the formation of C-47s was fired upon by a naval vessel. Immediately, as though upon a prearranged signal, other vessels fired. Planes dropped out of formation and crashed into the sea. Others, like clumsy whales, wheeled and attempted to get beyond the flak, which rose in fountains of fire, lighting the stricken faces of men as they stared through the windows.

More planes dived into the sea and those that escaped broke formation and raced like a covey of quail for what they thought was the protection of the beach. But they were wrong. Over the beach they were hit again – this time by American ground units, who, having seen the naval barrage, believed the planes to be German. More planes fell and from some of them, men jumped and escaped alive; the less fortunate were riddled by flak before reaching the ground.

Fired upon by our own Navy and shore troops, in one of the greatest tragedies of World War II, the 504th Parachute Infantry, less the 3d Battalion, was scattered like chaff in the wind over the length and breadth of Sicily Island. Colonel Tucker's plane, after twice flying the length of the Sicilian coast and with over 2000 flak holes through the fuselage, reached the DZ near GELA; however, few others were as fortunate and by morning, only 400 of the regiment's 1600 men (excluding the 3rd Battalion) had reached the regimental area.

Other plane loads of 504 men dropped in isolated groups on all parts of the island, and although unable to join the regiment, carried out demolitions, cut lines of communications, established inland road-blocks, ambushed German and Italian motorized columns, and caused confusion over such extensive areas behind the enemy lines that initial German radio reports estimated the number of American parachutists dropped to be over ten time the number actually participating!

On the 13th of July, with the 3rd Battalion returned to regimental control and with about half of the remainder of the regiment assembled in the vicinity of AGRIGENTO, the 504 moved out in the attack, spearheading the coastal drive of the 82nd Airborne Division. With Italian light tanks, motorcycles, horses, bicycles, mules, trucks, and even wheelbarrows for transportation, the regiment pressed forward; a cocky, spirited bunch of "mechanized" paratroopers heading into battle.

Resistance, for the most part, was light; the Germans had withdrawn to the north and east, leaving behind garrisons of Italian soldiers who would fire a few shots, and having "saved face" (and other portions of their respective anatomies) would raise the white flag of their surrender. The grueling Mediterranean sun, however, told on the foot-weary paratroopers; it was march, march, march, day and night – they prayed for the enemy to make a stand so that they could stop and fight – and rest. For five days and nights this continued, and in an outstanding tribute to the physical stamina of parachute troops, men of the 504 walked and fought their way from AGRIGENTO to ST. MARGUERITA – a distance of 150 miles.

Having reached ST. MARGÚERITA, the regiment again parted from Division and turned north toward ALCAMO and CASTELLAMARE DEL GOLFO. These towns were taken successfully and at CASTELLAMARE the regiment assumed the duties of a policing force, which activity they continued for ten days. On the tenth day, the 504 was shuttled by plane back to its base at KAIROUAN, North Africa.

Although the Sicilian operation was costly, both in lives and equipment, valuable experience was gained by those who survived, untold damage was inflicted behind enemy lines, many prisoners were captured (the 82nd Division was credited with 22,000), and Nazi and Fascist forces were given their first dose of a medicine that proved to be fatal – and one that they understandably feared. It was with this experience that the now-veteran 504 returned to Africa to prepare for the invasion of the Italian mainland.

# Section 4: Casualties in Sicilian Campaign
(Corrected Through 5 May 1945)

Entire Division

|  | Officers | Enlisted Men | Total |
|---|---|---|---|
| Killed in Action | 25 | 165 | 190 |
| Died of Wounds | 0 | 6 | 6 |
| Prisoners of War | 8 | 164 | 172 |
| Missing in Action | 5 | 43 | 48 |
| Missing in Action to Return to Duty | 2 | 71 | 73 |
| Wounded | 16 | 121 | 137 |
| Wounded to Duty | 24 | 314 | 438 |
|  | 80 | 884 | 964 |

**Casualties by Type and Unit**

|  | Officers | Enlisted Men | Total |
|---|---|---|---|
| Division Headquarters |  |  |  |
| Missing in Action | 1 | - | 1 |
| TOTAL | 1 | - | 1 |
| | | | |
| 504th Parachute Infantry Regiment | | | |
| Killed in action | 11 | 69 | 80 |
| Died of Wounds | - | 1 | 1 |
| Prisoners of War | 6 | 104 | 110 |
| Missing in Action | 4 | 29 | 33 |
| Missing in Action to Return to Duty | - | 6 | 6 |
| Wounded | 7 | 50 | 57 |
| Wounded to Return to Duty | 5 | 96 | 101 |
| TOTAL | 33 | 355 | 388 |
| | | | |
| 505th Parachute Infantry Regiment | | | |
| Killed in action | 8 | 56 | 64 |
| Died of Wounds | - | 4 | 4 |
| Prisoners of War | 2 | 56 | 58 |
| Missing in Action | - | 5 | 5 |
| Missing in Action to Return to Duty | 2 | 57 | 59 |
| Wounded | 7 | 57 | 64 |
| Wounded to Return to Duty | 14 | 156 | 170 |
| TOTAL | 33 | 391 | 424 |

<u>307th Airborne Engineer Battalion</u>

| | | | |
|---|---|---|---|
| Killed in action | 2 | 5 | 7 |
| Prisoners of War | - | 3 | 3 |
| Missing in Action | - | 1 | 1 |
| Missing in Action to Return to Duty | - | 3 | 3 |
| Wounded | 1 | 5 | 6 |
| Wounded to Return to Duty | <u>2</u> | <u>17</u> | <u>19</u> |
| TOTAL | 5 | 34 | 39 |

<u>376th Parachute Field Artillery Battalion</u>

| | | | |
|---|---|---|---|
| Killed in action | 2 | 26 | 28 |
| Prisoners of War | - | - | - |
| Missing in Action | - | 7 | 7 |
| Missing in Action to Return to Duty | - | 1 | 1 |
| Wounded | - | 5 | 5 |
| Wounded to Return to Duty | <u>-</u> | <u>16</u> | <u>16</u> |
| TOTAL | 2 | 55 | 57 |

<u>456th Parachute Field Artillery Battalion</u>

| | | | |
|---|---|---|---|
| Killed in action | 2 | 9 | 11 |
| Died of Wounds | - | 1 | 1 |
| Prisoners of War | - | 1 | 1 |
| Missing in Action | - | 1 | 1 |
| Missing in Action to Return to Duty | - | 4 | 4 |
| Wounded | 1 | 4 | 5 |
| Wounded to Return to Duty | <u>3</u> | <u>29</u> | <u>32</u> |
| TOTAL | 6 | 49 | 55 |

| **TOTAL DIVISION CASUALTIES** | **80** | **884** | **964** |
|---|---|---|---|

*A grenadier from the 505th PIR in Kairouan, Tunisia, July 1943.*

*Opposite*
*Top: Equipment of a grenadier: T-5 main parachute and reserve; M-1903 rifle and grenades; M-1936 suspenders with M-1923 cartridge belt. Note the .45 cal. Pistol and M-1918 trench knife. Kairouan, Tunisia, July 1943.*

*Bottom: Troops of the 505th PIR load an A-5 parabundle onto a C-47 for a demonstration drop in Oujda, French Morocco, in North Africa, 3 June 1943.*

*Above: The 505th PIR conducts a demonstration jump at Oujda, French Morocco, in North Africa, 3 June 1943.*

*Airborne training being conducted in North Africa, 1943, in preparation for the invasion of Sicily.*

*Soldiers of the 80th Anti-Aircraft Battalion practice loading a jeep into the CG-4A Glider prior to the invasion of Sicily. The jeep was the prime mover for the 37mm and 57mm antitank guns used by the 80th. North Africa, 1943.*

*The 82nd Band entertains troops in North Africa, 1943.*

*Major General Matthew B. Ridgway, CG, 82nd Airborne Division (left) with Colonel Reuben H. Tucker, Commander, 504th PIR, in North Africa, 1943.*

*Colonel James M. Gavin, Commander, 505th PIR, inspects his troops prior to the invasion of Sicily. North Africa, July 1943.*

*Colonel James M. "Slim Jim" Gavin, Commander, 505th Parachute Infantry Regiment, in North Africa, July 1943.*

*Paratroopers from E Company, 505th PIR practice parachute landings in Oujda, French Morocco, on 5 June 1943 in preparation for the invasion of Sicily. PVT John Cages is on the left.*

Troops of Headquarters Company, 505th PIR in North Africa, 1943. Charles "Pop" Burt is second from the right. He was called "Pop" because he was in his fifties when he began jumping.

Brigadier General Charles L. Keerans, Jr., Assistant Division Commander, wishes Colonel James M. Gavin, 505th PIR Commander, good luck prior to take off for Sicily. Keerans was reported as missing in action with the 504th PIR on 11 July 1943. Tunisia, North Africa, July 1943

*Opposite*
Top: *Colonel James M. Gavin briefs paratroopers of the 505th PIR prior to the parachute assault into Sicily on 9 July 1943.*

Bottom: *Paratroopers rigging for the jump into Sicily. Kairouan, Tunisia, 9 July 1943.*

Above: *Preparing to board a C-47 in Kairouan, Tunisia, 9 July 1943.*

*Opposite*
*Top: Paratroopers bound for Sicily, 9 July 1943.*

*Bottom: Preparing to jump into Sicily, 9 July 1943.*

*Right: One of the many stone pillboxes encountered by the 82nd in Sicily, July 1943.*

*Below: Paratroopers of the 505th PIR advance on Biazzo Ridge, Sicily, 10 July 1943.*

*Bottom: The 505th PIR on Biazzo Ridge, Sicily, 10 July 1943.*

*Paratroopers on the road to Gela, Sicily, July 1943.*

*Advancing through Sicily, 11 July 1943.*

*Paratroopers assembled in a town wait to move out. Sicily, 11 July 1943.*

*Chicago Tribune reporter Jack "Beaver" Thompson (left) with Colonel James M. Gavin, Commander of the 505th Combat Team, in Sicily near Biazzo Ridge, 11 July 1943.*

*An 81mm mortar team sighting its weapon in a Sicilian olive grove, July 1943.*

*Paratroopers of the 3rd Platoon, E Company, 505th PIR in Sicily, July 1943. (L to R) Bill Embery, Rudy Oppeliger, Bill Eppler, Tony Demayo, Ken Peirel, and William Tomsen.*

Above: Paratroopers take a break near Ponte Olivo Airfield, Sicily, July 1943.

Left: MG Matthew B. Ridgway with Colonel Reuben H. Tucker in Sicily, July 1943.

Opposite
Top: MG Matthew B. Ridgway with some of his staff in Sicily, July 1943.

Bottom: MG Matthew B. Ridgway in his jeep in Sicily, July 1943. Note his M-1903 rifle in the leather scabbard.

*82nd troopers with some helpful Sicilian civilians, July 1943.*

*Paratroopers laden with combat equipment advance through Sicily, July 1943. The paratrooper on the right carries the SCR-511 radio. Although designed for the cavalry, it was widely used by the infantry and airborne because of its lightweight.*

*Above: Paratroopers advance through a Sicilian town, July 1943.*

*Right: Airborne Cavalry – A paratrooper on a mule. Transportation was scarce and anything was better than walking. Sicily, July 1943.*

*Below: Mules were useful pack animals in the rough terrain of Sicily.*

*Bottom right: Paratroopers examine a captured German truck from the Herman Goering Division, Sicily, July 1943.*

*Paratroopers advance on carts towed by a captured Italian tankette in Sicily, July 1943.*

*Paratroopers examine a captured Italian tankette in Sicily, July 1943.*

*Paratroopers move through a town in a captured German Opel Blitz truck of the Herman Goering Division, Sicily, July 1943.*

*Paratroopers move through a Sicilian town. Some ride in captured carts. July 1943.*

*Paratroopers move by truck through a Sicilian town, July 1943.*

*Paratroopers advance west by truck, Sicily, July 1943.*

*Paratroopers mount a truck for an advance in Sicily, July 1943.*

*Paratroopers of the 504th Combat Team lead the way into Sciacca, Sicily, 20 July 1943.*

*(L to R) Private D. Rice, Corporal J. Fowler, and Private F.S. Cole eat ice cream in Palermo, Sicily, July 1943.*
*Rice wears the bazooka patch on his left sleeve and carries an M-1918 Trench Knife.*

*An 81mm mortar team after operations in Sicily.*

*Division Staff in Trapani, Sicily, July 1943. (L to R) LTC Schellhammer, G-1; LTC Lynch, G-2; Colonel Ralph "Doc" Eaton, Chief of Staff; LTC Boyd, G-3; and LTC Weinecke, G 4.*

*Glider training in Sicily, August 1943.*

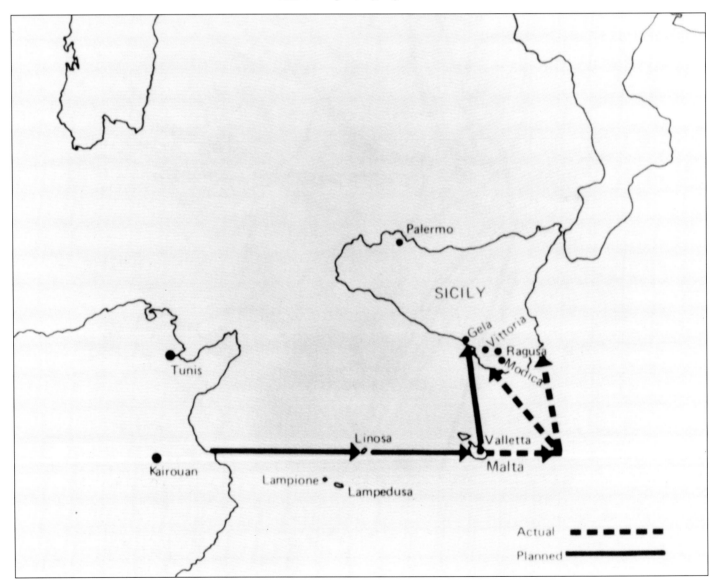

*Flight routes to Sicily, 9 July 1943.*

# CHAPTER TWO

# Operation Avalanche:
# The 82nd Airborne Division in Italy

## Section 1: "Contact Imminent"
(A narrative of pre-campaign activities of the 82nd Airborne Division,
July-September 1943)

### Foreword

The combat operations of the 82nd Airborne Division on the Italian Campaign are recorded elsewhere. The following account is concerned only with the remarkable series of orders, counter orders, plans, changes in plans, marches and counter-marches; missions and remissions, by air, water and land, endured by the Division prior to entry in combat. This record might be termed, "A Saga of Change." It is a monument to the spirit and mental flexibility of the men and officers of the Division.

### The Story

On July 29, 1943, the parachute elements of the 82nd Airborne Division, together with a minimum of Headquarters and Special Troops, some 5,000 officers and men in all, were disposed in and around TRAPANI, CASTELVETRANO, MARSALA, MAZAR, CASTELLAMARE and ALCAMO, Sicily.

These troops had just completed a whirlwind conquest of Western Sicily; commencing on July 9 when the first parachutist dropped and ending with the assault and reduction of the fortified city of TRAPANI on July 23, 1943. Now, without rest from the arduous campaign, they were fully occupied with the impressive task of evacuating some 28,000 prisoners of war, restoring order, and assisting in rehabilitating the country. The complexity of this work was tremendously increased by the fact that spread throughout the western third of the Island, the Division had only fifty-two jeeps and forty-eight 2 1/2 ton trucks.

Air Corps supplies, personal clothing and equipment, in fact all items of issue, were sadly depleted. Personnel had parachuted or airlanded with one combat uniform and in most instances without blankets or tentage. However, the troops were in fine condition and in excellent morale.

The remainder of the Division restively awaited combat orders at their departure airfields in the vicinity of KAIROUAN, TUNISIA, some 275 miles across the MEDITERRANEAN.

It was under these circumstances that the Division Commander, on July 29, 1943, received his initial instructions for the participation of the Division in the coming Italian campaign. Profiting from the lessons learned in Sicily, he repeatedly and vigorously urged a minimum of three weeks combined air-ground training with the Troop Carrier Command. He urgently recommended that the 82nd Airborne Division be immediately concentrated in the KAIROUAN area for the purpose of reorganization, reequipping and training.

On August 2, a portion of the Division staff reported to Fifth Army Headquarters at ALGIERS, where plans were formulated for the employment of the Division, worked out in detail, and then changed many times. The Fifth Army ground force assault plan was definitely fixed from the beginning. In substance it was to land on the SALERNO beaches, fight northwest, capture NAPLES, push on to ROME and eventually overrun all of northern ITALY. How best to exploit the Airborne Division was a problem of considerable concern and much speculation.

By now it had become apparent that higher headquarters would move the Troop Carrier Command from the KAIROUAN area to Sicily a few days prior to the Italian Campaign. This at once presented a serious obstacle to combined training. Further it was impossible to obtain a release so that the troops in Sicily could return to KAIROUAN. Permission for the return was withheld until other forces became available in SICILY to replace the 82nd Airborne Division.

While the Division proper, both in Sicily and in NORTH AFRICA, went about its training and its duties, operational projects for the Airborne invasion of Italy were born, matured and died, one after another, at Fifth Army Headquarters, ALGIERS.

The original of six missions for the 82nd Airborne Division, all planned in detail, called for the seizure by an airborne task force of the towns of NOCERA and SARNO at the exits to the passes leading northwest from SALERNO. Every available transport plane and every available glider, 318 of each, were earmarked for the operation. The early capture of these passes, on the night of D-1 Day, was held to be vital to the debouchment of the X British Corps onto the Plain of NAPLES. A small seaborne task force from the Division was designated to land in the AMALFI-MAIORI Area. Plans were developed to the last detail. Excellent serial photographs were obtained, drop zones and landing fields carefully selected and minutely located. The air approach to the drop zones and landing fields presented many difficulties. One approach would carry the transport planes over intense enemy flak. The other approach required passage over the high mountains of the SORRENTINE Peninsula. The most suitable drop zones were far from satisfactory. The most suitable glider landing zones consisted of widely scattered small fields. In order for parachutists to drop in force from a suitable altitude, the flight would have been in from the sea and across the coast northwest of CASTELLAMARE. The only suitable glider release point was some 4,500-6,000 feet above the SORRENTINE Mountains, with a resultant glide of several miles. After a great deal of study and planning, the NOCERA-SARNO operation was rejected.

It was now August 12, only twenty-seven days before D-Day, September 9th. One-half of the Division was still scattered over the western end of SICILY, not yet re-clothed or reequipped. There had been no combined air-ground training. There was no plan for the employment of the Division, other than the very definite understanding that the Division would be employed somehow somewhere. All of this despite the continued efforts of the Division Commander to concentrate, reorganize and train the Division in the KAIROUAN Area, from which the Troop Carrier Command had not as yet moved.

It was on August 18 that the Division Commander received his first intimation of a brand new plan for the employment of the Division. On that date he was told that a decision had been made to conduct an airborne operation on the VOLTURNO River, northwest of NAPLES and some forty miles from the nearest Allied beach landings in the vicinity of SALERNO. Relief of the airborne troops by ground elements of the Fifth Army could not be expected for many days. Re-supply by air became a critical item. Again the airborne machinery shifted into high gear. Now, only nineteen days remained before D-Day.

Gone was the expectation for any substantial air-ground training with the Troop Carrier Command. It was too late. Every effort had to be concentrated on getting the troops back from Sicily and reequipping them. It was imperative that the planning stage be cut to a minimum in order that the Division might have an opportunity to acquaint itself with its mission. Better than a thousand replacements must be absorbed into the two parachute combat teams.

The junior officers and the enlisted men of the Division did not know, but they sensed a coming operation. The Division Commander flew almost in circles, again and again, from his Division Command Post at TRAPANI, 600 odd miles to his planning staff at Fifth Army Headquarters, ALGIERS, thence over 400 miles to his Division Command Post at KAIROUAN, thence almost 300 miles to his Division Command Post at TRAPANI. He and his staff labored ceaselessly with the concurrent problems of the coming operations and those of reassembly and re-equipping the Division. Unit commanders were practically helpless, in so far as preparations were concerned, because of the absence of definite plans. No supplies or replacements could be shipped into Sicily in the time available; that would have to be done upon return to NORTH AFRICA. The long distances separating the various headquarters greatly hampered communications when time was of the essence.

After many requests to have the Division relieved from the Sicilian Army of Occupation and returned to its base in KAIROUAN, orders were received to send staff representatives to Seventh Army Headquarters in PALERMO to formulate plans to move the Division by truck to PALERMO, thence by sea to BIZERTE and thence by truck to KAIROUAN. The G-3 and asst. G-3 departed from TRAPANI on August 17 on this mission. The Division Commander was in ALGIERS when these orders were received.

At 1500 August 18 a radio from the Division Commander at ALGIERS was received at TRAPANI directing the Chief of Staff and the two parachute combat team commanders to meet him at 1600 on CASTELVETRANO airfield. At CASTELVETRANO the Division Commander informed these officers that all arrangements had been made and that, commencing the next morning, the troops in Sicily would be prepared for air movement back to KAIROUAN.

During the night units scattered over the western end of Sicily were alerted by radio, telephone and courier. The Division had only twenty-four trucks to move personnel and equipment to the airfields, which were as much as forty-five miles away. All jeeps were accounted for and impounded. At 0200 hours the orders were confirmed and the troops moved out. On that day, August 19, and until dark on August 20, C-47 planes droned singly and in groups in and out of BORIZZO and CASTELVETRANO airfields, loading airborne troops and equipment. Thus better than half of the strength of the Division, with all but the heaviest of equipment, was air-transported by shuttle to the KAIROUAN Area on August 19 and 20. Speed was essential, and it is well indeed that the movement was executed by air without red tape and complicated "coordination". The troops and equipment simply loaded up and took off for North Africa. The Staff officers who had been in Army Headquarters at PALERMO, formulating the move by sea to Africa arrived with approved but complicated plans for a rail-water-rail journey just in time to board the last transport plane for Africa. The official confirmatory orders for the truck and sea movement arrived three days later after the Division closed in the KAIROUAN area. Only sixteen days until D-Day.

The now red hot operational plan for the VOLTURNO mission involved simultaneous airborne and seaborne landings by the Division. It was planned that the seaborne task force would take in essential ammunition and supplies for the airborne task force, with which it was to make contact within twenty-four hours after landing. Again, all available airplanes and gliders were to participate. That portion of the Division not involved in the air assault was to land on the beaches at the mouth of the VOLTURNO during the night of D-1 Day. This mission was denominated as the GIANT operation. It underwent several changes within the few days immediately following August 18. Finally, it was broadened to include the destruction of all crossings over the VOLTURNO from TRIFLISCO (northeast of CAPUA) to the sea.

Not one individual in the entire Division, officer or man, had ever had any experience or instruction in amphibious operations. Yet, a full-fledged beach assault was scheduled to be undertaken within two weeks. A limited number of officers was selected and rushed off to PORTE POULE, North Africa for amphibious training.

On August 20 the composition of the seaborne task force could not be settled, because the number and composition of the assault boats was not definite. Plans were made for amphibious training of the troops at BIZERTE, but there were no craft yet available at the port. Shuttle of the troops to BIZERTE was nevertheless commenced. They began to arrive at BIZERTE on August 25. There were no craft available for training. Only eleven days remained before embarkation. The number of assault craft to be made available was suddenly increased and more units were sent to BIZERTE. The assault craft finally arrived and intensive training was immediately commenced. Training efforts were pointed to the elements being loaded and prepared for the invasion by midnight September 5.

The amphibious operation had been planned on the sketchiest of beach studies. While the amphibious training was in progress at BIZERTE, it became doubtful that the beaches at the mouth of the VOLTURNO River were suitable for landing. Nevertheless, the amphibious training continued apace with the beach study. As the beach study progressed, it became increasingly obvious that there would be great difficulty attendant upon a landing.

Then, in the midst of frantic efforts to pass on a minimum of training to all units, orders were received on September 1 directing that loading must be completed by September 3. Water-proofing of the vehicles was conducted concurrently with amphibious training, and, by 1600 on September 3, all troops vehicles, supplies, ammunition and equipment were loaded on the assault craft and ready to sail.

Turn now to Army Headquarters at ALGIERS. There, unknown to the Seaborne Task Force Commander, the beach assault, because of the reefs and shoals, was successively reduced, first to one battalion of infantry; then to one company of infantry, and finally to a naval bombardment without troop landings. This left approximately half of the combat strength of the Division stranded at BIZERTE without a mission. It now became imperative that the airborne task force in the VOLTURNO River be re-supplied by air and plans therefore were fully developed with the greatest possible haste.

The Troop Carrier Command was ordered to permanent change of station in SICILY, on nine separate departure airfields, stretching more than 100 miles across the island. The 82nd Division obviously had to make the same change of station. This in the midst of assault plans that changed almost daily. Unimaginable communications difficulties arose. The dispersion of the Division at KAIROUAN itself was over an area of approximately 600 square miles.

Gone was the opportunity for any real air-ground training. It was impossible to parachute, rescue parachutes and repack them in time for the impending operation. However, because of its vital necessity, a week of such training was scheduled and some four days of same executed to a fairly satisfactory degree. The Division was only able to place the jumpmaster in each plane and have the "sticks" of parachutists represented by a few replacements who had not had a night jump. Whether the units at BIZERTE would participate in the Italian campaign at all, and, if so, when and how, was now an important question. Army Headquarters solved this by directing that to the extent that shipping became available the units at BIZERTE would be embarked as a floating reserve.

All of this time, the 2nd Battalion, 509th Parachute Infantry, was attached to the Division. About August 23, orders were received to the effect that it was contemplated using the 509th for a drop mission on call in any of the areas around the NOCERA, SARNO, MINTURNO, BATTAPAGLIA, etc. Studies and plans for such a call had to be at once instituted and carried to a practical degree of conclusion.

Concurrently, arrangements were being hastily made with the Air Forces and with the Navy for the routing of the air columns, placing of ships with radio and lights to mark points along the route, etc.

Alternative plans and studies were undertaken for the use of the divisional units to be embarked at BIZERTE in floating Army Reserve. For re-supply of the airborne task force scheduled to drop in the VOLTURNO Valley, a daily automatic ninety-plane re-supply program was worked out.

It was agreed with the Troop Carrier Command that upon termination of the one week's joint air-ground training on August 31, the Troop Carrier Command would move to Sicily, get itself settled, and then return to the KAIROUAN area to pick up the airborne assault troops who were to be already combat-loaded. The airborne assault troops would then be landed at the proper fields in Sicily, from which they would take off for combat a few days later.

It should be borne in mind that all of these plans and changes, orders and counter-orders, were issued from and communicated to widely separated Command Posts. Fifth Army Main Headquarters were at MOSTOGANEM, 680 miles by air from KAIROUAN. Army Advance Headquarters were at ALGIERS, 600 miles from SICILY and over 400 miles from Division Headquarters at KAIROUAN. Troop Carrier Command was at SOUSSE, thirty miles from KAIROUAN, until it moved over 200 miles, into Sicily.

Re-supply by air for the VOLTURNO River air assault force was, of course, utterly essential. Hindsight shows that re-supply by ground forces could not have been effected for several weeks. Beach landings could not be made. So, when the Air Forces determined on August 26 that re-supply by air was deemed impracticable, the VOLTURNO River mission had to be drastically altered. The Commander-in-Chief directed a new plan reducing the size of the airborne task force to a parachute regimental combat team, less one infantry battalion, carrying enough supplies and ammunition to last four or five days. At the time of these instructions it was apparently thought by higher headquarters that ground relief would be effected within that period. Notice of this major change was dispatched by officer courier from ALGIERS, and the next day, September 1, began all of the multitudinous cancellations and revisions down to smaller units. Only seven days remained.

The Division Commander, Assistant Division Commander, Chief of Staff, G-2, 3 and 4 remained in KAIROUAN assisting the regimental combat team commander affect his plans and checking the air movement of the combat team and the remainder of Division (less amphibious force) to departure fields in Sicily. They were to sail with the amphibious force on September 3. They planned to leave KAIROUAN at 1300 September 2, baggage and personnel was to be loaded on ships by 1600 that day. At 1130 a message was received that the Commanding General, North African Air Forces, desired to see the Division Commander at his headquarters in LAMARSA. When the Division Commander and his staff arrived at LAMARSA they were informed that an airborne operation was contemplated in the ROME Area. The Division Commander was to report to the Commanding General, Fifteenth Army Group, at SYRACUSA, Sicily, without delay. The importance of the mission overweighed any objections as to lack of time to properly brief troops of any other serious defect that might arise. The Division Commander and his staff departed for SYRACUSA by air and arrived at dusk on September 2 and immediately went into conference.

The ROME operation became known as GIANT II. It called for the placing of the strongest airborne task force which available aircraft would carry, on and near three airfields immediately east and northeast of ROME on the night of D-1 Day, September 8, 1943, with the mission of defending that city in conjunction with Italian forces in the area.

Turn back now to KAIROUAN. There the Division continued its preparations for the VOLTURNO and for the seaborne floating reserve, wholly unaware of the fast-developing radical change. The ROME mission had not become definite enough and plans had not reached a sufficiently advanced stage to justify changing the course of preparation in which the Division was already engaged.

At SYRACUSA conversations with the Italian Army representatives continued over the next thirty-six-hour period. It finally developed that the Italian Army representatives could make no guarantee that their forces could silence the coastal anti-aircraft over which the troop transport planes would have to fly to arrive at ROME, nor to guarantee that airfield necessary for air landing would be controlled by them. To have attempted the mission under these circumstances would have been disastrous. Meanwhile, time ticked on.

But American troops had to land in ROME. The Armistice had been signed, sealed and delivered with that understanding. Only the most unlooked for complications could justify the non-performance of an airborne mission to ROME. It was determined to jump and air-land a small airborne task force of one parachute regimental combat team, less one infantry battalion, with air-landed reinforcements, and an advance echelon of Division Headquarters, at two airfields, FURBARA and CERVETERI, some twenty-five miles northwest of ROME. Then, if everything went well, it was planned to jump and air-land other elements of the Division on successive nights.

The Troop Carrier Command was busily engaged in moving to SICILY. Upon contemplation of that move the airborne troops at KAIROUAN had to be transported to SICILY and immediately thereafter troops would have to take off from Sicilian departure airfields for ROME, or whatever other mission might be determined upon.

With the ROME mission definitely ordered, the Division Commander released his staff planning group on September 3. They returned by air to KAIROUAN and BIZERTE and late that evening the Division troops at BIZERTE received their first notice of this most recent change. Only four full days remained. Two of these would have to be used for air movement from KAIROUAN and BIZERTE to Sicily.

Meanwhile, on that same day, September 3, at about 1300 the Commanding Officer of the amphibious task force, Colonel Lewis, received radio instructions to meet the Fifth Army Commander personally at BIZERTE Airfield at 1400. There, Colonel Lewis was instructed that this amphibious mission had been canceled, that all of the assault craft were urgently needed for another mission involving other troops, and that all of his troops, supplies, vehicles, etc., now being loaded must be cleared off the craft not later than 1900 that afternoon. Back to the amphibious loading area went Colonel Lewis as fast as his jeep would take him. It was a bitter disappointment to all of the officers and men, but in the best traditions of the Division all hands turned to and unloaded and cleared all craft in record time. By 1730 that evening every craft had been released. Water-proofing on vehicles was removed. Units, vehicles, etc., returned to bivouac on the beach ten miles from BIZERTE. Further instructions were awaited.

An interesting sidelight on the cancellation of the amphibious task force orders was the fact that so close was the time element that it was necessary for the Army Commander at SYRACUSA to take the message to Colonel Lewis personally. When the Army Commander made the decision, his was the only plane available and the order could only be transported by plane in time to reach Colonel Lewis before his forces would have sailed.

Late on the afternoon of September 3, Colonel Lewis received instructions from the Division Commander to prepare for movement to Sicily by plane at once. The designated departure field was at MATEUR, a two and a half hour truck trip from the bivouac. Some trucks as could be procured were immediately put into operation and shuttling of troops, equipment, and supplies was commenced.

The next morning, September 4, the Division Commander returned by air to BIZERTE to disseminate the GIANT II plan and speed both planning and movement. On September 5 the Division Commander and his staff at BIZERTE continued to supervise planning for those elements which the day before had been aboard assault craft and were now scheduled for commitment to action by air landing in the ROME Area. A complicated juggling of available aircraft was worked out whereby the troops at BIZERTE could be flown to Sicily and then on successive days to reinforce the troops which would have already dropped on D-1 in the ROME Area.

On the night of September 4 representatives of the Division Staff and the Troop Carrier Command worked until late in the night planning the troop movement by air from KAIROUAN and BIZERTE to Sicilian departure airfields. The next morning September 5, troop movement by air from KAIROUAN was commenced. Two days were required for the shuttling of the troops at KAIROUAN and BIZERTE into Sicily.

Meanwhile, at BIZERTE the Division Commander and his staff were preparing to leave for SICILY. At about 0800 that day, September 5, radio instructions were received to the effect that shipping would be made available that day for a small seaborne task force of one artillery battalion, three anti-aircraft batteries and a company of infantry. Also, the same radio instruction attached three platoons of the 813th Tank Destroyer Battalion to the Division and directed that these three platoons would be included in the newly set up seaborne task force. The mission of this seaborne task force was to support the ROME operation.

The Division Commander designated the 319th Glider Field Artillery Battalion, plus the anti-aircraft batteries of the 80th Airborne Anti-Aircraft Battalion and one company of the 504th Parachute Infantry, together with the tank destroyer elements. Lt. Col. Bertsch was placed in command of this sea expedition. The Division Commander and his staff left by plane for Sicily. Colonel Lewis assumed full responsibility for the water-borne project.

No one knew the whereabouts of the 813th Tank Destroyer Battalion. None of the port authorities had received any orders at all concerning the existence of any such amphibious force as had been directed. The 319th Field Artillery Battalion and the 80th Anti-Aircraft Battalion were diverted from movement by air just in time. Late that night the Tank Destroyer Battalion was located some forty miles from BIZERTE. All units commenced movement into the dock area. Vehicles and weapons were again waterproofed.

Actually, it was not until the next morning, September 6, that Colonel Bertsch received definite orders and it was ascertained that two LCTs and two LCIs were available for the sea expedition. Additional vessels had been assigned but their whereabouts were not known. These additional vessels were British and it was finally determined that they might not be available at all. In this emergency the American admiral in the harbor came to the rescue and provided additional craft. Loading commenced on September 7. No one knew when the expedition would up-anchor and away. Many changes had been made in vessel assignments, so that the final composition of the little armada was three LCIs and only on LST. However, all of the above troops were crowded aboard.

Under secret orders the three LCIs sailed September 8. The LST sailed September 9.

When the little flotilla pulled away from the BIZERTE docks, its commander knew only that his destination was "FF", and that if no one met him at "FF" he was to sail on to "GG". He strongly suspected that "FF" and "GG" were in the ROME area. (Later information disclosed that the point "FF" was on the beach just north of the mouth of the TIBER River and that the point "GG" was up the TIBER River halfway from its mouth to the City of ROME.)

Colonel Bertsch, on the LST, knew not where his three LCIs were and could only depend on fate and fortune for a rendezvous. Nor would the naval officers in command of the vessels know any more than he did.

Once at sea, radio instructions were received directing that the seaborne force report to the Commanding General, Fifth Army, aboard U.S. ANCON, in the Gulf of SALERNO, for orders. Fortunately, these rendezvous instructions were received by all craft and on September 10 Colonel Bertsch reported to the Fifth Army Commander aboard the U.S. ANCON. The Fifth Army Commander directed that the seaborne force land on the beaches at MAIORI, where they would go into action as a part of the Ranger Force operating through the passes across the SORRENTINE Peninsula.

With destination and mission changed, the flotilla landed on the beaches of MAIORI on September 11 and joined the Ranger Force.

As soon as the seaborne task force had been set up at BIZERTE, Colonel Lewis proceeded with the movement of the remainder of his force, principally the 325th Glider Infantry and the 3rd Bn., 504th Parachute Infantry, on to departure fields in Sicily.

Meanwhile, in Sicily, every member of both the Division and the Troop Carrier Command worked day and night making final preparations for the ROME mission. Twenty-four hours prior to take-off time, Brigadier General Taylor, Division Artillery Commander, was moved secretly by Italian Army authorities into the City of ROME. He was accompanied by a representative of the Troop Carrier Command.

It was not until 1400 on D-1 Day, when Brigadier General Lemmnitzer, Fifteenth Army Group, arrived at the Division Command Post at LICATA by plane, that the Division Commander first knew of the possibility of the ROME mission being called off.

The Italian Armistice had been signed. It was to be announced by the Allied Commander-in-Chief in a radio broadcast scheduled for approximately 1730 on D-1 (September 8). Marshal Badoglio, broadcasting from Radio ROME, was scheduled to follow the Commander-in-Chief on the air. By the use of a code word inserted into his speech, Badoglio was to signify whether or not the Italian authorities were still prepared to support the 82nd Airborne assault.

The Division Commander and several members of his staff drove to Troop Carrier Command Headquarters, LICATA, late on the afternoon of September 8 to listen in on a special receiving set. This set failed to function at the appointed time. Had the Armistice been announced or not? Fortunately, the Division Chief of Staff discovered a small portable commercial set in time to hear the concluding remarks of the Commander-in-Chief, which included an announcement of the Armistice. For some unknown reason Marshal Badoglio did not immediately follow General Eisenhower. In fact his radio address came on the air about 1900.

The Division Commander and his staff immediately returned to the Division Command Post, believing that the mission would be flown as prepared. Meanwhile, General Taylor had returned from ROME with the strong recommendation that the mission be canceled because the Germans had full knowledge of the plan and the Italians would be unable to support the assault. Based on this recommendation, the Commander-in Chief directed the postponement of the mission for twenty-four hours. His instructions were received by the Division Commander through Air Force channels only five minutes before the scheduled departure of the first planes, which were loaded with personnel and the motors being warmed up.

The next afternoon, as take-off time neared, all was in readiness again. So ready were men and equipment that the units on one field got into their planes, started the motors, and would have taken off had it not been for the arrival there of the Division Chief of Staff. That evening the ROME mission was definitely canceled and abandoned.

The next instructions for employment of the Division were to be prepared to move as many troops as possible by nine LCIs from LICATA, Sicily, into the Italian operations.

Less vehicles and heavy weapons, the 325th Glider Infantry and the 3rd Battalion of the 504th Parachute Infantry were assembled by plane at LICATA, Sicily, on September 13. At 2000 that night it sailed from the harbor and landed near SALERNO, Italy, late on the night of September 15. The 3rd Battalion of the 504th was sent to join its regiment near ALBANELLA. The 325th was moved shortly thereafter into the operations on the SORRENTINE Peninsula.

On the afternoon of September 13th, at about 1330 hours, a tired, begrimed pilot landed in an A-36 at LICATA Field having just flown down from the SALERNO front. He had an urgent message for the Division Commander and refused to give it to anyone else. In the meantime, the Division Commander, G-2 and G-4, had taken off from LICATA for TERMINI to report to the Commanding General, Fifth Army, in Italy. The Chief of Staff of the Division had the LICATA Field Control tower call the Division Commander's plane and bring him back. The message brought by the pilot was a personal letter from the Commanding General, Fifth Army, containing an appeal for immediate help, and requesting specifically that one parachute RCT [regimental combat team] be dropped on the beach south of the SELE River to reinforce the VI Corps that same night. The Army Commander also directed that the 509th Parachute Battalion drop on the mountain village of AVELLINO, far behind the German lines, on the night of September 14.

Reallocation of departure fields, re-shuffling of troops, air routes, coordination with friendly anti-aircraft fire, etc., were arranged within eight hours.

On the night of September 13, the 504th Parachute Infantry, with Company "C" [minus 1st Platoon], 307th Airborne Engineer Battalion attached, dropped on the SELE River beaches. The drop zone was well lighted and from its reflection the paratroops could be seen for miles by both friend and foe. A dramatic meeting ensued. The reinforcements had been badly needed. The enemy was dangerously near a breakthrough to the beaches, which would have separated the VI and X Corps. The VI Corps had suffered heavy casualties. With his troops assembled in the dark less than an hour after landing, Col. Tucker, commanding, reported to the Army Commander. The Army Commander directed, "As soon as assembled you are to be placed in the front lines." Col. Tucker replied, "Sir, we are assembled and ready now." The 504th RCT moved, within a matter of minutes, into a front line position and shouldered its battle responsibility.

The AVELLINO drop was made as planned on the night of September 14. The drop zone was high in a mountain valley. Navigational obstacles were tremendous. While only a portion of the troops were dropped on the proper drop zones, the operation was successful in delaying and harassing enemy concentrations in the vicinity of AVELLINO. Many of the troops were not contacted by ground elements for a period of three weeks.

On the same night, September 14, CT [combat team] 505, likewise parachute, repeated the drop on the SELE River beaches and also went into action.

There is little doubt but that these most timely air reinforcements turned the tide of battle in the VI Corps sector.

On 15 September gliders on departure fields were loaded and the troops stood in readiness to climb in. However, reconnaissance in the SELE River area failed to disclose suitable glider landing areas and on 16 September further glider operations were suspended.

On the afternoon of 17 September orders were received at LICATA to move the remainder of the combat troops by motor vehicle to TERMINI for sea movement to Italy on the 19th. By jeep, truck and air the movement was commenced immediately. An advance party was dispatched by plane to TERMINI. No sooner had the motor movement to TERMINI been commenced than instructions were received to air-land fifty planeloads of Division Headquarters and Special Troops in the PAESTUM area, Italy, on September 18, twenty-five planes to depart at 1000 and twenty-five planes to depart at 1300. The troops to be moved by air included detachments of the Quartermaster and Ordnance Companies, who were scheduled for 1000 departure. These detachments had already left by motor vehicle for TERMINI. Both jeeps and cub planes were dispatched to overtake them. They were not overtaken until they were entering the outskirts of TERMINI. They immediately turned back and reached the departure field at LICATA the next morning at 0950 and by 0958 disappeared into C-47s. At 0600 a garbled radio [message] was received stating it was most imperative 3,000 rounds of M-2 artillery ammunition be transported to Italy. This ammunition displaced seven planeloads of personnel and equipment and caused a hasty reallocation of planes.

These serials landed on a newly constructed landing strip at PAESTUM ruins. The runway was so short and rough that ten planes crashed on landing. Fortunately only one person was slightly injured.

The remainder of the Division, less the 456th Parachute Field Artillery Battalion and certain base echelon personnel poured into TERMINI on organic and borrowed vehicles to meet the embarkation deadline. But there were no craft to be boarded. A last minute priority change allocated all available shipping to other units. For many days the troops were at TERMINI. Finally shipping was made available and they were landed on the SALERNO beaches.

In such fashion did the airborne, seaborne, truckborne, railborne, All American 82nd Division go to the war in Italy.

## Section 2: A. DESCRIPTION OF OPERATION FROM PLANNING PHASE TO EXECUTION

1. On about July 28, 1943, Brigadier General Taylor, Division Artillery Commander, reported at Fifth Army Headquarters as planning representative for the Division Commander. On August 7 three Division Staff Officers joined General Taylor and remained with him until approximately August 15, 1943. Thereafter the Division was represented by General Taylor alone.

2. Between July 28 and September 13, a total of six missions were prepared in detail. They are briefly as follows:

    A. NOCERA and SARNO Passes.
    B. VOLTURNO River (subsequently known as Giant I).
    C. ROME (subsequently known as Giant II).
    D. AVELLINO (subsequently known as Giant III)
    E. Area northeast of NAPLES and vicinity of CAPUA.
    F. Reinforcement of VI Corps on beaches south of SELE River.

3. The development, changes, and details of the several planned operations is best followed chronologically, as shown below.

4. When planning commenced at Headquarters, Fifth Army, the combat parachute elements of the Division were in Sicily. The remainder of the Division and the 2nd Battalion, 509th Parachute Infantry, then attached, were in North Africa.

5. D-Day for the Italian Campaign having been tentatively set for September 9, the Division Commander strongly urged the necessity of at least three weeks combined training to include a detailed dress rehearsal, in compliance with Paragraph 4, Training Memorandum No. 43, Allied Force Headquarters, 2 August 1943. Because of considerable depletion both in personnel and material, the Division Commander likewise urgently and repeatedly recommended that the Division be immediately moved to North Africa for reorganization.

6. The original mission assigned the Division was to seize the towns of NOCERA and SARNO, situated at the exits to passes leading northwest from SALERNO, and cover the debouchment of X Corps (British) onto the plains of NAPLES. At that time it was considered vital that these passes be seized on D-1 Day and held at all cost. Due to enemy flak, necessity for dropping paratroopers and releasing gliders at high altitudes, and further due to the lack of suitable glider landing zones, this mission presented considerable difficulties. Air coverage was secured and drop zones and landing zones selected. It was tentatively planned to drop paratroopers from height of from 1,500 to 2,000 feet and to release gliders along the SORRENTO Ridge at altitudes of from 4,500 to 6,000 feet. This was to be a night operation with the benefit of moonlight.

7. On about August 12 the NOCERA-SARNO mission was abandoned and the VOLTURNO River mission (later known as Giant I) was assigned. The VOLTURNO River mission called for simultaneous air and sea landings on D-1 Day. Specifically, the mission as originally approved was as follows:

> "To land from sea and air under the cover of darkness on the night of D-1/D Day south of the VOLTURNO River, seize, organize and defend Hill Mass B (just outside of CAPUA) and prevent movement of hostile forces south across the VOLTURNO towards the NAPLES area, in order to assist the Fifth Army's attack of the NAPLES area from the Southeast."

8. Meanwhile, on August 19-21, the Division closed in the KAIROUAN area.

9. On August 22 the mission was changed to "seize, organize and defend a bridgehead to include the CANCELLO area." (One parachute battalion with attached engineers to demolish the river crossing near CAPUA.)

10. The original combined air and sea assault in the VOLTURNO Area contemplated the employment of four (4) LSTs and twenty (20) LCIs and 310 planes and 130 gliders. The airborne force consisted of two parachute RCTs (reinforced), and one glider field artillery battalion. The seaborne force consisted of one glider infantry RCT.

11. On August 23 the VOLTURNO mission was broadened to include the destruction of the crossings over the VOLTURNO from CAPUA to the sea. At the same time it was ascertained that the beaches in the vicinity of the mouth of the VOLTURNO were not suitable for landings. The seaborne effort was thereupon reduced to one battalionn of infantry, to one company of infantry, and then limited solely to a naval bombardment.

12. The Division Commander was informed on August 24 that these elements of the Division not to be employed in the air assault would be embarked and used as a floating reserve for the Army Commander.

13. About August 24 the Division Commander was informed that it was contemplated using the 2nd Battalion, 509th Parachute Infantry in army reserve for drop missions on call. Studies were made for the employment of this battalion in the NOCERA, SARNO, MINTURNO, and BATTIPAGLIA areas. Resupply by air for the VOLTURNO mission was to be daily, automatic, ninety planes per day, until relieved by X Corps.

14. Meanwhile, all arrangements were made with the Navy for route, visual lights from ships to be stationed along the route, radio directional beams, etc. As planned, the air assault would have the benefit of sufficient moonlight, both in and out, insofar as the transport planes were concerned.

15. The allocation of craft to the seaborne portion of the Division remained the same. On August 27, Fifth Army directed that loading be completed at BIZERTE by D-5.

16. One week of joint training with TCC [Troop Carrier Command] was scheduled. However, due to a number of factors, including (a) TCC's movement to new bases in Sicily, (b) lack of facilities for return of gliders after landings, necessity for overhaul of planes and equipment prior to departure mission, etc., the training was neither particularly realistic nor satisfactory. The main accomplishment was the demonstration of the value of the pathfinder radio homing device.

17. Complete and detailed air support, commencing on D-3 Day, was arranged for jointly with the Troop Carrier Command.

18. Plans for coordination with respect to routes, timings, navigational aids, naval, and ground forces, use of pathfinder aircraft, establishment of airborne corridors, altitude for flight, use of downward recognition lights etc.

19. On September 1 the size of the force for the VOLTURNO mission was reduced to two parachute infantry battalions, a company of parachute engineers, and a battery of glider AT [ antitank] guns. The mission was restricted to the destruction of the crossings at CAPUA.

20. On September 2 the Division Commander was orally informed that the VOLTURNO mission was canceled and that, instead, the Division would air land in the ROME area (known as Operation Giant II), commencing on D-1 Day. The waterborne force, which had meantime substantially completed loading at BIZERTE, was ordered to disembark. The air operation in the ROME area was ordered for parachute and air landings on successive nights, on airfields adjacent to the city.

21. On September 5, Fifth Army directed that the 2nd Battalion, 509th, be prepared to drop missions on call at EBOLI, AVELLINO or BENEVENTO.

22. On September 6 one LST and three LCIs were assigned to the Division for loading at BIZERTE. A battalion of field artillery, one company of infantry, three Anti-Aircraft batteries, a detachment of engineers, and four TD [tank destroyer] guns were loaded. These troops, along with three LCIs loaded with ammunition, sailing from separate points, were to join the air assault at the mouth of the TIBER River. The air route, navigational aids, etc., were rapidly readjusted with the Navy to fit the new mission.

23. On September 6 the Division CP opened at LICATA, Sicily, and on September 8 all air combat elements of the Division closed in Sicily. Take-off ROME was set for 1745 September 8.

24. On September 8, at 1650, orders were received postponing the ROME mission.

25. On September 9 the ROME mission was canceled and orders issued to be prepared for Giant I, or a similar operation, on short notice.

26. Meanwhile, the one LST and the three LCIs had sailed from BIZERTE. On Army Group order they were diverted to the SORRENTO Peninsula.

27. The Division passed to Fifth Army control on September 9. On September 12 orders were received directing that 2nd Battalion, 509th, drop in the AVELLINO area and that Giant I be executed in the area northeast of NAPLES, both

missions to be executed on the night of September 12/13. To this, reply was made that the AVELLINO mission could be executed on the night of September 15/16 and the Giant I mission in the CAPUA Area on September 14/15, there being no suitable drop zones northeast of NAPLES.

28. On September 13 the Division Commander was directed to execute Giant I in the CAPUA Area on call on or after September 14/15, and to drop one parachute RCT near the beach south of the SELE River in the zone of the VI Corps on the night of the 13th.

29. On September 13 the 325th Glider Infantry, with one battalion of 504th Parachute Infantry [third], less transportation, cleared LICATA in nine LCIs, destination SORRENTO Peninsula.

30. On September 13 Army directed the execution of the AVELLINO drop on the night of September 14/15.

31. On the night of September 13 the 504th Parachute Infantry, with one company of parachute engineers [C Co., 307th] attached, dropped near the beaches approximately six miles south of the SELE River in support of VI Corps.

32. At 1400 on September 14 orders were received that the AVELLINO mission (Giant III) and a repeat of the SELE River mission would be executed on that night.

33. On the night of September 14 the 2nd Battalion, 509th [with 1st Platoon, C Company, 307th Engineer Battalion] dropped on AVELLINO in forty planes and the 505th Parachute Infantry, with one company of parachute engineers [B Co., 307th] attached, dropped near the beach six miles south of the SELE River as reinforcement to the VI Corps.

34. For these missions, routes, timing, use of pathfinder aircraft, establishment of airborne corridors, altitudes, use of downward recognition lights etc., were planned as set forth subsequently, in the report.

35. In all three of the last-mentioned drops, routes, timings, coordination with ground troops, navy, etc., were quickly and effectively arranged on short notice.

36. On September 15 plans were set up for a movement of glider troops and Division Headquarters and Division Special troops into the SELE River area. Gliders were allotted and loaded. However, on September 16 orders were received suspending all glider operations. On September 17 orders were received directing that substantially all of the remaining combat troops be moved to TERMINI for sea movement to Italy. The movement to TERMINI was commenced.

37. On September 18 Division Headquarters and detachments of Division Special Troops air landed in the PAESTUM area, Italy. There were no further air movements. The remainder of the Division, less 456th Parachute FA, was brought by sea to Italy

## B. SPECIFIC MEASURES TAKEN TO COORDINATE WITH AIR, NAVAL AND GROUND FORCES

As set forth in Annex No.1, measures for coordination with air, naval and ground forces for the VOLTURNO River mission were prescribed by MAAF. However the provisions of this plan were inapplicable to the SELE River mission, and since time was of the essence, Lt Gen Clark summoned Admiral Hewitt, Naval Commander and Maj. Gen Lucas, VI Corps Commander and personally informed them that troop carrying planes would fly a prescribed course at a certain time and directed that from 2100 until contrary orders were given by him, all anti aircraft guns on the SALERNO would be silenced, and barrage balloons taken down.

Lt Gen Clark directed Major Geyer of TCC and Lt Col Yarborough, then Fifth Army, to make a spot check to determine whether crews of AA guns on the SALERNO Beachhead had been informed of the bar on firing. Every gun crew checked by these officers had received orders to suspend firing until further orders.

## C. ESTABLISHMENT OF AIRBORNE CORRIDORS AND USE OF GUIDE SHIPS

There was no airborne corridor prescribed for this operation and no guide ships were used to mark the route.

In planning the VOLTURNO River mission, airborne corridors were set forth and guide ships were to be stationed to mark the lane. These plans are set forth in detail in ANNEX No. 1. While the VOLTURNO mission was still pending, a rehearsal was held in which a lane was marked as set forth in ANNEX No. 1 and flown by TCC units. The test run was highly successful.

## D. MEANS EMPLOYED TO GUIDE AIRCRAFT TO DROP ZONE

This phase of the operation was greatly facilitated by the fact that the drop was made behind friendly lines.

The letter from Lt Gen Clark which was delivered to General Ridgway directing the jumps to be made set forth that the drop zone would be marked with a white T. A penciled note indicated how it would be done. The marking was actually accomplished by formation of a T, each leg a half mile long, and of issue gas cans, cut in half and filled with sand permeated with gasoline. These gas cans were laid out during the daylight and one man stood by each. At a prearranged signal all flares were lit, and upon completion of the drop they were extinguished by dousing.

In addition to these smudge pots, very signals were fired for the benefit of planes at the tail of the formations. These were of material assistance to some pilots.

## E. USE OF DOWNWARD RECOGNITION LIGHTS

For downward recognition, amber lights on belly and wing tips of each flight leaders' plane have been employed by TCC since midsummer. They were employed while flying over water on this mission.

## F. ALTITUDES DURING FLIGHTS

Troop Carrier crews were briefed to fly below 1000 ft to DZ. Departure from these orders was necessary because of low cloud formations encountered enroute and due to hill masses just south of drop zones. Aircraft returned to bases at altitudes of not less than 6,000 ft.

# Section 3

9 September 1943
MEMORANDUM FOR: A.C. of S., G-3, Allied Force Headquarters.

**SUBJECT : Mission to ROME.**

1. In compliance with verbal orders from AFHQ and the Fifteen Army Group, Brigadier General Maxwell D. Taylor and Colonel W. T. Gardener, A.C., left Palermo for Rome at 0200 September 7 for the purpose of completing arrangements in Italy for the execution of Operation GIANT TWO. Transportation was by a British P.T. boat to Ustica Island where the party was transferred to a waiting Italian corvette. Rear admiral Maugeri, Chief of Naval Intelligence received the American officers on board and remained with them until their arrival in Rome. The corvette put into GAETA at 1950 where the party was quickly put in a Navy sedan, taken to the outskirts of town and transferred to a Red Cross ambulance. The trip up the Appian Way to Rome was uneventful. Few German troops were seen and the visible defenses along the route were unimpressive. The party entered Rome just at nightfall and was taken to the Palazzo Caprara opposite the War Office (intersection of V. Firenze and V. 20 Sottombro) where accomodations had been prepared.

2. Colonel Salbi, Chief of Staff to General Carboni, the General's Aide, Lt. Lanza and Major Marchesi received the officers. No conferences had been scheduled for that evening but, at the insistence of the Americans, interviews were

hastily arranged with General Carboni, Commanding the Army Corps about Rome (concurrently Chief of Intelligence since August 20) and General Rossi, Deputy Chief of the Supreme General Staff. For reasons shown subsequently the interview with Rossi did not take place.

### 3. <u>Interview with General Carboni.</u>

General Carboni arrived at 2130. He immediately launched upon an expose of his views of the military situation in the Rome area. Since the fall of Mussolini (he said), the Germans had been bringing in men and supplies thru the Brenner Pass and also thru Resia and Tarvisio, with the result that their forces near Rome had greatly increased. There were now 12,000 Germans principally parachutists in the valley of the Tiber who have heavy equipment including 100 pieces of artillery, principally 88mm. The panzer Grenadier Division had been raised to an effective strength of 24,000 men with 50 light and 150 heavy tanks. In the meantime the Germans had ceased to supply the Italians with gas and munitions so that their divisions were virtually immobilized and had only enough ammunition for a few hours of combat. General Carboni's estimate of the situation was as follows:

If the Italians declare an armistice, the Germans will occupy Rome, and the Italians can do little to prevent it. The simultaneous arrival of U.S. airborne troops would only provoke the Germans to more drastic action. Furthermore the Italians would be unable to secure the airfields, cover the assembly and provide the desired logistical aid to the airborne troops. If it must be assumed that an Allied seaborne landing is impossible North of Rome, then the only hope of saving the capital is to avoid overt acts against the Germans and await the effect of the Allied attacks in the South. He stated that he knew that the Allied landings would be at Salerno, which was too far away to aid directly in the defense of Rome. He stated that General Roatta shared his views.

It was apparent to the American officers that regardless of the soundness of General Carboni's information and views, he displayed an alarming pessimism certain to affect his conduct of operations in connection with GIANT TWO. General Taylor proposed that they request an immediate interview with Marshal Badoglio to permit General Carboni to present his recommendations and receive the decision of the Head of State. The interview was requested and granted.

5. The delegation reached Marshal Badoglio's private villa at about midnight, where the household was awake as the result of an air alarm. General Carboni was received at once by the Marshal while the American officers waited in the antichamber. After about fifteen minutes they were admitted and greeted cordially by the Marshal. Throughout the ensuing interview he made frequent expressions of his friendship for the Allies and his desire to enter into effective cooperation.

6. Interview with Marshal Badoglio.

General Taylor explained the late visit, saying that General Carboni had raised questions so grave that the immediate decision of the Head of the State was required. Was Marshal Badoglio in accord with General Carboni in considering an immediate armistice and the reception of airborne troops impossible of execution? The Marshal replied that he agreed with Carboni and repeated much the same arguments. General Taylor asked if he realized how deeply his government was committed by the agreements entered into by the Castellano mission. He replied that the situation had changed and that General Castellano had not known all the facts. The only result of an immediate armistice would be a German supported Fascist government in Rome. He was asked if he feared the possible occupation of Rome by the Germans more than the renewed attacks of the Allied Air Forces which would certainly come if he rejected the armistice. He answered with considerable emotion that he hoped the Allies would not attack their friends who were only awaiting the right moment to join forces. If any bombing is to be done let it be on the Northern rail centers serving the German troops.

In reply to the question as to how he expected the Allied Chiefs to react to these charges he expressed the hope that General Taylor would return and explain the situation. The latter declined to accept any responsibility for the Italian interpretation of the situation but offered to act as a messenger if so instructed by the Allied authorities. The urgent business was to send to Algiers a definite statement of the Italian views over Badoglio's own signature.

7. The Marshal accepted this proposal and drafted the message which is appended as Enclosure 1. General Taylor prepared another message at the same time (Enclosure 2) recommending the cancellation of GIANT TWO and

requesting instructions for himself and Colonel Gardiner. The visitors withdrew and returned to the Palazzo Caprara where the two messages were turned over to General Carboni for transmission. At 0800 the next morning, word was received of their reception in Algiers.

8. In order to present a clearer picture of the local situation, General Taylor with the concurrence of General Carboni and Colonel Gardiner sent off the message attached as Enclosure 3. At 1135, as no acknowledgment of the message recommending the cancellation of GIANT TWO had been received, the code phrase "Situation Innocuous" (Enclosure 4) was sent off. This had not been sent initially as its use had been reserved for the case of an Italian refusal to transmit a request for cancellation. It was used in this instance to save time as the encoding of longer messages was taking as much as three hours.

9. The Italians showed great concern over the possible reaction of the Allied Chiefs to their reversal of position on the armistice. The American officers reinforced their apprehension by emphasizing the gravity of the situation in which the Badoglio government found itself. The Italians repeatedly urged the American officers to return and plead their cases whereas the latter declined to be anything other than messengers. It was then decided that some senior officers should return with the Americans. The name of General Roatta was first proposed then withdrawn as he was considered indispensable in dealing with the Germans. (He had been military attaché to Germany.) General Rossi, Deputy Chief of the Supreme General Staff, was eventually selected and message No.4 (Enclosure 5) was dispatched.

10. The American officers expressed a desire to see General Ambrosio, Chief of the Supreme General Staff who was reported to be out of the city. This interview was arranged eventually for 1830 but never took place as the officers were ordered back to Tunis by a message arriving about 1500. Although no authorization for their visit had been received, General Rossi and Lt. Tagliavia (interpreter) joined the American officers who were again put in an ambulance and driven to the Centocelle airfield. The party took off at 1705 in a tri-motor Savoia-Marchetti bomber which flew straight to El Aloina, Tunis, arriving at 1905. The officers were driven from here to "Fairfield" where the Americans reported to the Commander in Chief.

Conclusion.

While the Castellano mission was committing the Badoglio government to active military cooperation, the Germans were building up their strength in the Rome area and throttling the flow of munitions and gasoline to the Italian troops. Although their fear of the Germans was mounting daily, the Italian leaders allowed themselves to become deeply committed to the Allies in the belief (so they said) that the major landings would be near Rome. By the time General Taylor and Colonel Gardiner arrived, this illusion was dispelled and the Italians knew for certain that AVALANCHE would strike in the Salerno area. While this produced a profound pessimism and a realization of their over commitments, they were allowing matters to drag without redefining clearly their position to the Allies. The arrival of the American officers, their insistence on the imminence of events and the importance of action brought matters to a head and stopped an operation (GIANT TWO) which was near being launched into a situation which invited disaster.

Maxwell D. Taylor
Brigadier General,
U.S. Army.
W.T. Gardiner,
Colonel, Army Air Forces.

**Enclosure 1**

**Message of Marshal Badoglio to Allied Commander in Chief**

Dati Mutamenti di situazione determinatesi in dislocazions et entita' forze Germaniche zona Roma non e'piu possible accettazione immediata armistizion poiche' essa provocherebbe occupazione capitale ed assunzione violenta governo perparte tedesca. Operazione Giant Two no piu possible perche mancano forze per garantire campi anazione. Il generale Taylor disponibile per rientrare in Sicilia per presentare vedute del governo ed attende ordini.

Badoglio.

**Translation**

Due to changes in the situation brought about by the disposition and strength of the German forces in the Rome area, it is no longer possible to accept an immediate armistice as this could provoke the occupation of the capital and the violent assumption of the government by the Germans. Operation GIANT TWO is no longer possible because of lack of forces to guarantee the airfields. General Taylor is available to return to Sicily to present the views of the government and await orders.

## Enclosure 2

Message No.1
8 September
In view of the statement of Marshal Badoglio as to inability to declare armistice and to guarantee fields GIANT TWO is impossible. Reasons given for change are irreplaceable lack of gasoline and munitions and new German dispositions. Badoglio requests Taylor return to present government views. Taylor and Gardiner awaiting instructions. Acknowledge.

Taylor          Time signed 0121

## Enclosure 3

Message No.2
8 September
Summary of situation as stated by Italian authorities. Germans have 12,000 troops in Tiber Valley. Panzer Grenadier Division increased by attachments to 24,000. Germans have stopped supply gasoline and munitions so that Italian Divisions virtually immobilized and have munitions only for a few hours of combat. Shortages make impossible the successful defense of Rome and the provision of logistical aid promised airborne troops. Latter not wanted to present as their arrival would bring an immediate attack on Rome. Source of these views Marshal Badoglio and General Carboni.

Taylor          Time signed 0820

## Enclosure 4

Message No.3
8 September
Situation innocuous.

Taylor          Time signed 1135

## Enclosure 5

In case Taylor is ordered to return to Sicily, authorities at Rome desire to send with him the Deputy Chief of the Supreme General Staff, General Rossi, to clarify issues. Is this visit authorized?

Taylor          Time signed 1140

# Section 4
## Division After Action Report, September – November 1943

1. Preparatory to the operations undertaken by the Division and its component units during the month of September, 1943, six different missions were prepared in detail by the Division Staff, only two of which were destined to be put in execution. These two were a jump by the 509th Parachute Infantry Battalion in the vicinity of AVELLINO on the night of September 14 and jumps by the 504th and 505th Combat Teams on the nights of September 13 and 14 on the beaches south of the SELE River as reinforcement for the VI Corps. Although the Division Staff participated in the planning of these operations, the combat teams undertaking them passed to Army or VI Corps control on their take-off and the history of their subsequent maneuvers is therefore the history of the units themselves and of the Army or Corps of which they were at that time a part. Likewise the 325th Combat Team (including 3rd Battalion, 504th Parachute Infantry), which cleared LICATA, Sicily September 13 for a seaborne movement to AVALANCHE began its Italian operations under control other than that of the 82nd Airborne Division Command.

2. Division Headquarters and detachments of Division Special Troops air-landed in the PAESTUM Area September 18 and the 504th and 505th Combat Teams were brought under Division control after they were withdrawn from actual combat operations in the vicinity of ALBANELLA and ALTAVILLA, Italy. Thereafter, for several days the Division Command, through these two combat teams, undertook patrol activities in the vicinity of ROCCADASPIDE and CASTELCIVATA, while the 325th Combat Team was being actively engaged on the SORRENTO Peninsula as an element of the Ranger Force.

3. Movement of the main body of the Division from the vicinity of CASTELCIVATA to the SORRENTO Peninsula was begun September 26 and the Division CP opened at MAORI on that date and immediately took command of a task force on the peninsula, consisting principally of what had been the Ranger Force already operating there and the divisional parachute element newly brought from CASTELCIVATA. Lt. Col. Darby was placed in command of the East Force under the Division Commander, with headquarters at MAORI, and Col. James M. Gavin, in command of West Force, in the AGEROLA area. The Division CP was moved to AMALFI September 27. That night a general advance was begun, with the main effort through CHIUNZI Pass in the East, and a supporting effort through the AGEROLA-GRAGNANO tunnel in the West. The advance was lightly opposed and entirely successful, the first troops debouching into the SARNO Plain early the following morning. From the 28th to the 30th the entire force converged on CASTELLAMARE and concentrated in that vicinity. On the 30th the 3rd Battalion, 505th Parachute Infantry, led the advance along the main highway routes as far as TORRE ANNUNXIATA, and the entire division proceeded into the city of NAPLES the following day.

4. Leading elements of the 82nd Airborne Division, with the 3rd Battalion, 505th Parachute Infantry, serving as advance guard, entered the city of NAPLES about noon October 1, 1943, on the main highway leading into the city from the South. The Division was preceded as far as the southern extremity of the city suburbs by reconnaissance elements of the 23rd Armored Brigade (British), which at that point diverged to the Northeast and by-passed the city itself. The entire city was occupied and put under patrol before nightfall.

5. Except for elements of the Division detached from it to serve under other commands, the Division remained throughout the month in the city of NAPLES, charged with the responsibility for maintaining order, and saw no further combat services, sailing for Northern Ireland on 19 November 1943.

Headquarters Fifth Army
A. P. O. #464, U.S. Army

In the field,
1 October 1943.

SUBJECT: Division of Responsibility between CG, 82d Airborne Division and CG, Fifth Army Base Section.
TO : CG, 82nd Airborne Division
CG, Fifth Army Base Section
                    CG, 10th Corps (Br.)
                    CG, VI Corps (U.S.)

1. The CG, 82nd Airborne Division, utilizing Allied troops under his command, is charged with the maintenance of peace and good order in the City of Naples and the guarding of all military installations, public works and other public property. He will act directly under the Commanding General, Fifth Army, pursuant to Operation Instruction No.3, 22 September 1943. He will also utilize the services of the Carabinieri and other Italian civilian police which he will control through Allied Military Government channels. He will also be responsible for local defense, and the disciplinary control of all Allied Military personnel within the city.

2. The CG, Fifth Army Base Section (Brig. Gen. Ponce) will be charged with the general administrative control of Naples, except for the function allotted to CG, 82nd Airborne Division under Par. 1. Among his functions will be:

A. Control of Allied Military Government within the area, except for its policing functions. This will include supervision of the provision of food and medical supplies for the civilian population.
B. Maintenance of utilities of all sorts to the extent necessary for military purposes.
C. Establishment of supply dumps in coordination with chiefs of section, Fifth Army.
D. Reconstruction and operations of the port area.
E. Acquisition of real estate and matters of quartering, billeting and similar activities, as prescribed in Administrative Instruction No. 11.
F. Signal communications within the Fifth Army Base Section.
G. Transportation insofar as it pertains to base section activities.
H. PAD, fire fighting, traffic control and sanitation.

By command of Lieutenant General CLARK:

/s/t/ M. F. GRANT
Colonel, AGD,
Adjutant General

# Section 5:
## a. The 325th Glider Infantry

On September first, 1943, the 325th Combat Team, consisting of the 325th Glider Infantry, with an attached parachute infantry battalion [3/504th], field and coast artillery, combat and shore engineers, and medical personnel, was undergoing intensive training near Bizerte, Tunisia, for the shore landing operation known as "Avalanche". On September 3rd, while the Combat Team was engaged in loading its heavy equipment on LST's [Landing Ship, Tank], the mission was canceled.

Planning was commenced on September 4th to move the Combat Team to Sicily by plane, and on the 5th, the 1st Battalion, 325th Glider Infantry, Company "A", 307th Airborne Engineers, and the advance party of the Combat Team moved to Airport No. 2, Mateur, Tunisia. The advance detail boarded planes at 1700 and landed at Licata,

Sicily, at 1915 on September 6th. On the same date the 3rd Battalion of the 504th moved to Airport No.2, Mateur. Both the 1st and 2nd Battalions boarded planes on the 7th. The 1st Battalion landed at Gela, Sicily. The battalion headquarters and part of Company "F" of 2nd Battalion landed at the Trapani-Mico airfield, Sicily, and the rest of 2nd Battalion landed at Comiso, Sicily. On the same date the 3rd Battalion, 504th Parachute Infantry, attached, moved by plane from Africa to Comiso. Also on September 7th, the 319th Glider Field Artillery Battalion and the 2nd Platoon, [A Company], 307th Airborne Engineer Battalion attached left by water for Maiori, Italy, from which point the 319th was used in support of the Ranger Task Force. The Engineer platoon was also used in action north of Maiori.

Regimental Headquarters Company, Service Company and the Regimental Medical Detachment of the 325th, together with Battery "A" of the 80th Airborne Antiaircraft Battalion and Company "A", 307th Airborne Engineers less the 2nd Platoon, moved by plane to Castelvetrano, Sicily, on September 8th. The advance echelon of the Combat Team had already moved from Licata to Castelvetrano by truck on September 7th. The dispersion of the 325th Combat Team, less detachments, among various Sicilian airfields was dictated by the possibility of a mission involving air landings in the vicinity of Rome.

The next few days were spent standing by in case the airborne mission materialized. On the 9th, reconnaissance was made for a possible bivouac area to be used in case of concentration of the Combat Team near the Trapani-Milo airport. On September 10th, the Regimental Personnel Section arrived at Castelvetrano from Bizerte by plane.

The Combat Team, less the elements previously sent on a separate mission on the 8th, and less the two antitank platoons of Regimental Headquarters Company, moved by plane to Licata on September 13th and was loaded on LCI's [Landing Craft, Infantry], which left the port at 2000 the same date. At 1430 the following day, the LCI's arrived at Palermo, Sicily. The troops remained aboard overnight, and at 0500 on the 15th, the LCI's left for a destination near Salerno, Italy. At 2300 that night the Combat Team landed on the beach eighteen kilometers south of Salerno and remained there until morning.

On the 16th, the 3rd Battalion, 504th Parachute Infantry, left on an unknown mission. The 2nd Battalion, 325th Glider Infantry, less Company "G", which was attached to Headquarters, Fifth Army, departed by LCI's to work with the Rangers on a beach head north of Salerno. For the next five days the 2nd Battalion held positions on Mt. San Angelo di Cava against enemy action which culminated in an eight-hour attack on September 20th. The Battalion held its ground.

The remainder of the Combat Team marched five miles to a bivouac area near Staz di Cappuccio, Italy. At 0700 on September 17th, Company "G", 325th Glider Infantry, left by LCI's to occupy the Island of Ischia, southwest of the harbor of Naples. The 3rd Battalion of the 504th was relieved from attachment at 0001 the same date, and the rest of the Combat team was alerted to go to the front at 2130.

At 0300 the following morning, the 1st Battalion, 325th Glider Infantry, moved out and took up positions northeast of Albanella, Italy, in support of the 3rd Battalion, 504th Parachute Infantry. Regimental Headquarters Company, Service Company, and the Regimental Medical Detachment, 325th, with Company Headquarters of Company "A" of the 307th Airborne Engineers, moved to a bivouac area about one mile southeast of Albanella. The Regimental CP was also established at this point. At 0630 on the same date (September 18th), the 1st Platoon of Company "A", 307th Engineers, joined the 1st Battalion.

The Intelligence and Reconnaissance Platoon of Regimental Headquarters Company, 325th Glider Infantry, established an observation post northeast of Albanella during the morning of the 18th. During the afternoon there was more or less shelling from German 88's, and during the night there was some artillery fire. At 1622 on the 18th, Company "C" of the 1st Battalion furnished a thirty man reconnaissance detail to a tank destroyer unit. During the 19th, the 1st Battalion remained in a defensive position. At 0935 a patrol from Company "C" reported that it was west of Altavilla and that there was no enemy opposition. At 1700 it was reported that the thirty man detail with the tank destroyer unit was at Altavilla.

On September 20th, the Combat Team was withdrawn from its position and moved by truck to Beach No.1 near Paestum, Italy, remaining there overnight. At 1500 on the 21st the Combat Team personnel moved by LCI and LST to Maiori, Italy. Equipment was sent over land by truck. The Combat Team arrived at Maiori at 1830 and was attached to the Ranger Force. The 1st Battalion, 325th, moved up to positions at Mt. San Angelo di Cava to relieve the 2nd Battalion, which moved back and took up positions behind the 1st Battalion. The 3rd Battalion, 504th Parachute Infantry, less Company "H", was again attached to the 325th Glider Infantry and took up positions on Mt. di Chiunzi. The 319th Glider Field Artillery Battalion was relieved from attachment and was attached to the 1st Ranger Battalion.

The Regimental CP was temporarily established at Maiori, and Major Zinn, Regimental S-3, with Captain Berkut, Regimental S-2, went forward to the front to give the field order for the following day's operations.

On the 23rd, the 1st Platoon, 307th Airborne Engineers moved up to work with the 1st Battalion of the 325th. The Intelligence and Reconnaissance Platoon of Regimental Headquarters Company was also sent to the front, where it was extensively used in patrol work. Lt. Col. Sitler, Regimental Executive officer, and Major Zinn, S-3, established a forward CP on the road to Chiunzi Pass. A report was received that the 1st Battalion was in position by 1500. Meanwhile, the general attack, in which the 325th's mission was a defensive one, had started at 0330 on the 23rd. Allied naval vessels shelled the mountains north of Maiori during the day.

The Regimental CP was moved from Maiori into the mountains on the Chiunzi Pass road on the morning of the 24th, and the forward CP personnel moved to the Regimental CP location at 1200. At 2000 Colonel Lewis, Commanding officer of the 325th Glider Infantry, directed a machine gun platoon of 1st Battalion with rifle protection to occupy high ground at Fornace and strafe the road toward Camerelle. By 0900 the following day, however, these troops were forced to withdraw, having suffered several casualties.

On the 25th the 1st Battalion positions were the same as on the preceding day, strong enemy opposition being reported in front of Company "B" from 0530 to 0600. On this day, information was relayed back from the Regiment's observation post which enabled British artillery and naval guns to shell an enemy truck column south of Camerelle, destroying seventeen trucks.

Major General Ridgway, Commanding General, 82nd Airborne Division, was placed in command of all the area west of Salerno on September 26th. The area was divided into east and west sectors, Lt. Col. Darby of the Rangers remaining in command of the east sector, in which the 325th was operating. The 26th was a day of patrol activity, the British being reported out of contact with the enemy. The 1st Battalion of the 325th sent patrols toward Caremelle, the 2nd Battalion, toward Nocena. The 3rd Battalion, 504th Parachute Infantry, patrolled toward Pagani, and other units, to the south of Sala. On this date the 3rd Battalion of the 504th reverted to regimental control, and the 325th returned to Division control at 2400.

On orders from the Commanding Officer of Force Headquarters, a battalion of the 325th attacked the road southwest of highway 18 to establish contact with the 46th Division on the right. This operation was part of the Force plan to seize positions in the valley in the east sector. On the 28th of September this operation was successfully completed as far as units of the 325th Combat Team were concerned, and units held the positions established on the previous day.

On September 29th, the 325th Combat Team moved to San Egidio and bivouacked there overnight. On September 30th, the Combat Team moved to an assembly area east of Castellamare, where the antitank platoons of Regimental Headquarters Company rejoined the Regiment, having arrived by boat from Termini, Sicily. On this day the officers of the Combat Team were informed of plans for the occupation of Naples by the 82nd Airborne Division to restore order and prevent rioting.

### Headquarters 325th Glider Infantry
### APO #469, U. S. Army

October 20, 1943

ANNEX #1:

To "The 325th Glider Infantry in Action", dated October 19, 1943.

The 1st Battalion, 325th, in execution of orders to attack the road southeast of their position and establish contact with the British 46th Division, sent Company "B", with one platoon of Company "A", against enemy strong point at 1330 on September 27th. After a four hour fight, in the course of which Lieutenant Gibson, commanding Company "B", was wounded and Captain Bishop of Company "A" took over the direction of the attack, the strong point was captured, together with four prisoners, a German radio and considerable other enemy material. Our losses were eight wounded against thirty Germans killed. This strong point had been protecting an artillery observation post, and had been holding up the advance of the British 15th Armored Brigade and the British 46th Division.

## b. The 504th Parachute Infantry
## (Excerpts From "DEVILS WITH BAGGY PANTS"
## The Combat Record of the 504th)

Most men of the 504 were reluctant to leave their new-found home in Sicily; grapes were ripe for one thing, the language was much easier than the thousand and one Arab dialects encountered in Africa, and then the Sicilians, who were firmly convinced that their homeland was now an "American Island", were quite willing to show their new bosses a good time.

An order from Fifth Army headquarters, however, returned the regiment to Kairouan, North Africa, where it became immediately evident that another parachute mission was in the wind. Replacements were absorbed by the companies, training was resumed, and the 3rd Battalion was once again detached from the regiment – this time they were sent to Bizerte for special beach assault training with the Rangers and the 325th Glider Infantry.

Orders soon came for the 504 to return to Sicily: a more suitable jumping-off place for the invasion of Italy. They again boarded planes in Africa and flew, this time undisturbed by enemy and friendly flak, to Comiso and Trapani, Sicily.

Weeks of preparation for a jump at Capua, briefings, tiny scale models of the proposed drop zone expertly carved by former German toy makers – were forgotten. The mission to Capua had been canceled; the enemy had been warned and was waiting on the DZ.

Then there was the mission where men of the regiment were to jump on Rome and with the help of Italian partisans, occupy the city. That, too, had been canceled – and only three minutes before the scheduled take off. The men of the 504 were disgusted at the time, but subsequently felt differently when they learned the full story of General Taylor's negotiations with Marshal Badoglio in Rome, and of his resultant decision to stop the 504 men from jumping into what his eleventh hour information disclosed to be a trap.

The 3rd Battalion then moved to Licata and rejoined the 325th and the Rangers. Here they boarded LCI's and set out to sea; they knew they were going to Italy, but other than that, information was vague. H Company's boats left the convoy, and on September 9, with a group of Rangers, made the initial landings on the Italian coast at Maiori. Opposition on the beach was slight, and the parachutists quickly advanced into the mountains overlooking the coast where they captured the now famous Chiunzi Pass and a vital railroad tunnel.

Headquarters, G, and I Companies, with the remainder of the 325th Combat Team, swerved south and on September 11, landed on the bloody Salerno beach. The Luftwaffe and the American and British Air Forces provided an overhead show that ran twenty-four hours a day. That the military situation at Salerno was not as it should have been became more evident with each passing hour; German tanks and strong infantry forces were pressing relentlessly toward the beach, and the word was passed around that it would be fight or swim. No paratrooper on that beach was in the mood for a twelve mile swim, and with the prospects of a last-ditch stand staring them in the face, men of the 3rd Battalion settled down and awaited developments.

The remainder of the 504 was restlessly waiting at airfields in Comiso, and Trapani, Sicily, for the parachute mission they had been told to expect. On September 13, they were again alerted. "Another dry run", was the cynical comment of most men. Nevertheless each man gave his equipment a last minute check – just in case. Early chow was eaten and immediately afterward the troops fell in at their bivouac areas in the appointed plane loading formations; then marched to the battered and roofless hangars where they picked up their chutes.

It was not until the men were seated in the planes that the mission was disclosed. In probably the briefest briefing of any comparable operation of the war, men of the 504 were informed that the Fifth Army beachhead in Italy was in grave danger of being beached; that the 504 was to jump behind friendly lines in the vicinity of the threatened breakthrough in order to stem the German advance. A pathfinder group was going in ahead with special equipment to guide the planes onto the DZ, the center of which the Fifth army was to indicate with a large flaming "T". That was all; no one knew specifically what was to be required of him – nothing more than the fact that the Fifth Army was endangered and that the 504 was needed badly. Each man felt an inward surge of pride in his importance. Morale climbed.

As the planes sped down the air strip and lifted into the night sky, these men felt that they had a big assignment ahead of them; the rescuing of the Fifth Army. Though some may have had misgivings about what the morrow would bring, they were confident in their strength and happy to be on the way.

Shortly after midnight the planes, flying in a column of battalions, passed over the clearly marked DZ and unloaded their human cargoes. With the exception of eight planes which failed to navigate properly to the DZ, but whose plane loads were subsequently accounted for, there was little difficulty of confusion experienced in completing the operation. Assembly was made in the designated areas with a minimum loss of time and a later check revealed than only 75 men had suffered injuries as a result of the jump. This mission is still regarded as history's greatest example of the mobility of airborne troops – in exactly eight hours the 504 had been notified of its mission, briefed, loaded onto planes, jumped on its assigned drop zone, and committed against the enemy.

On the DZ, situated a few hundred yards from the beach and two miles South of Paestum, the boom of cannon and the flash of gunfire were distinctly evident a short distance to the North. Assembled, organized, and entrucked, the regiment was within the hour moving slowly along the road that led in the direction from whence the sounds of battle came.

By dawn the regiment, less the 3rd Battalion, was firmly emplaced in a defensive sector three miles from Paestum and Southwest of Albanella. The days of the 14th and 15th of September, were spent in anticipation of a tank attack that threatened from the Calore River region to the North. The 2nd Battalion assisted in the repulsing of one tank attack across the Sele River while E Company on a reconnaissance in force of the same area, encountered scattered and small elements of the enemy. The regimental recon platoon patrolled the area several miles to the front and battalions also sent out reconnaissance and combat patrols of their own with particular emphasis on the Altavilla sector.

Hostile artillery fire was spasmodic and largely interdictory in character. Air activity was confined principally to friendly craft, though the enemy ingroups of two and three would occasionally make an appearance over 504 positions only to be driven off by intense fire from supporting anti-aircraft units.

On the morning of the 16th, the regiment marched four miles to occupy the town of Albanella, where at noon, Colonel Tucker issued to the battalion commanders the order to seize and hold the high ground surmounting Altavilla.

The days following were, in the words of General Mark W. Clark, commander of the Fifth Army, "responsible for saving the Salerno beachhead." Men of the 1st and 2nd Battalion advanced across the flat valley floor, subjected to intense enemy artillery and small arms fire; contact between the battalion and the CP group were lost, but all units pressed relentlessly forward and in spite of overwhelming enemy superiority in numbers, took their assigned objectives. The enemy counter-attacked stubbornly, and on the night of the 17th, it became evident that help had to be secured if the 504, now completely cut off from friendly forces, was to hold those key positions so necessary for security of the beachhead.

General Dawley, commander of the Sixth Corps, was contacted by radio, and suggested that the regiment withdraw and attempt to establish a line nearer to the beach. It was then that Col. Tucker uttered the statement that epitomized the saga of Altavilla – "Retreat Hell! – Send me my other battalion." The third Battalion was then sent to rejoin the regiment. They moved into position of Hill 344, the 1st and 2nd Battalions repulsed strong counter-attacks, contact between the units was made, and the Salerno beachhead was saved. The next day the 504 was relieved.

This, the first contact with the enemy for men of the 504 since Sicily and the first time that the regiment had been committed as a unit in any single tactical operation, was a battle that turned the tide of the German onslaught on the Salerno beachhead and frustrated the attempts to contain the Fifth Army within the confines of the coastal plain reaching as far as Altavilla. With its flanks secured, the Fifth Army was at liberty to extend itself northward in the direction of Salerno, and ultimately to Naples.

The area in the region of Altavilla for several years had been a firing range for a German artillery school; consequently there was no problem of range, deflection, or prepared concentrations that the enemy had not solved long before the advent of the Americans. Needless to say, hostile artillery and mortar fire was extremely accurate and capable of pin-pointing with lethal concentrations such vital features as walls, trails, and draws. During the three days that the 504th occupied the several hills behind Altavilla, approximately thirty paratroopers died, 150 were wounded, and one man was missing in action.

The majority of these casualties were caused by the enemy's artillery fire. Enemy casualties were, judging from the number of dead left on the field of battle and from information divulged by prisoners, several times those of the regiment. Four separate and distinct attacks by the enemy launched from the north, east, and west of 504th positions were driven back with heavy casualties resulting for the Germans.

On the morning of September 20, the 504th, less the 3rd Battalion, moved back into a reserve position. The 3rd Battalion moved directly from Hill 344 to Blue Beach in the vicinity of Paestum where they boarded LCI's and headed toward Maiori to join "H" Company, still holding out with the Rangers at Chiunzi Pass.

For the remainder of the regiment, the period 20-25 September, was for the most part one of rest and resupply. However, road patrols were maintained by the regimental recon platoon which at the same time kept in constant touch with the British Eigth Army on the right flank. The enemy had apparently withdrawn to the north, and the report of the villagers was always the same – that the Germans had passed through in trucks a day or two before headed north.

Before noon on the 25th, the regiment was ordered to join the 3rd Battalion and boarded LCI's at Red Beach where they skirted the coast to Maiori.

Terrain in this sector was precipitous and hilly with plenty of concealment provided by underbrush and trees. All evidence of the enemy was confined to the valley which stretched like a vast carpet below – the valley of Naples. Even in the valley there was little, aside from an occasional truck movement or a gun flash, to be seen of the Germans. Positions were occasionally shelled, particularly that portion of the road that wound around the mountain and came out in full view of the German guns located at the base of Mount Vesuvius some ten miles to the front. This outlet was known as Chiunzi Pass – but because of trigger happy German artillerymen, was promptly renamed "88" Pass by 504 men.

On September 28, the regiment contacted the British 10th Corps, and moved out in the attack, spearheading the drive for the great port of Naples. British tanks skirted around the base of Mount Vesuvius to the east, bypassing the city, while 504 men turned west, captured Castellamare. The 504th entered Naples on October 1st.

The city was a scene of ruin, starvation, and general wretchedness. Bombed buildings were to be seen everywhere and the streets were littered with an accumulation of rubble piled by months of bombing. The public utilities – water, gas, and electricity – had been carefully and systematically destroyed by the enemy on the eve of his departure from the city. Business was at a standstill, with the exception of an occasional barber who did, needless to say, a great trade.

Looting was common, riots were in constant occurrence, and everywhere the American soldier was called upon by civilians to arbitrate and judge their street differences. For most Americans this was a difficult and most irksome task, inasmuch as the language was foreign and the simultaneous pleadings and cajoling of the conflicting parties for a judgment would increase in intensity and dramatic quality until the confused soldier in his inability to understand the accusations, or even have the faintest idea of the bone of contention, would throw up his hands in dismay to wash himself of the whole affair. Then the Italians would smile gently and mutter with a little nod in the direction of the American, "No capisco".

These were happy days; duty was light, wine, women, and song were the order of the day, and with each passing week Naples could be seen to progress another degree toward business and life as usual. Shops and cafes opened gradually in spite of the scars of war. Then came inflation – everything doubled, then tripled, in price; champagne, wine, and cognac disappeared in favor of a new and more deadly beverage – "Ten minute" cognac. Pure medicinal alcohol, with sugar and water added, and primed with a few drops of the essence of cognac, was bottled, labeled, aged, and sold on the streets within a matter of minutes.

Naples and its dubious pleasures had begun to pall on most men and it was with a certain amount of enthusiasm that the news of a forthcoming mission was received. Advance information indicated that the mission involved the assaulting of precipitous mountain positions. A group of thirty men was dispatched to the Fifth Army Mountain Climbing School near Naples to receive specialized training in cliff scaling and mountain climbing.

On October 27, 1943, the 504 Combat Team moved by truck to a bivouac area in the vicinity of Castello d'Alife. It became apparent at that time that the objective would not be the assault of any particular mountain position, but instead to make a general advance toward Isernia, about 25 miles due north from Alife. Two days later, the 504 launched an epic attack through the mountains of central Italy that was to carry them 22 miles ahead of the Fifth Army on their left and the Eight Army on their right. Driving North toward Gallo, in a battle that proved for the most part to be one of physical stamina interspersed with sharp patrol engagements, the 504 crossed the Volturno, entered the rail and road center of Isernia, cleared Colli, Macchia, Fornelli, Cerro, and Rochetta, and fifteen men from H and I Companies doggedly fought their way through mine fields to reach the summit of Hill 1017 – the Fifth Army objective and key point of the entire sector.

All supplies in this advance were of necessity carried by men and mules, since jeepable roads were non-existent. Communications were extremely difficult to maintain because the front was wide, the distance between the regimental

CP and the battalions great, and inclusive of rough and rocky mountains. Because of the constant forward movement and redisposition of the unit's elements, it was necessary for the wire team to work night and day in their efforts to provide even the barest minimum of communication required for the efficient functioning of the Combat Team.

Probably the most valuable asset possessed by the 504 in this phase of the Italian campaign was dogged stamina and the initiative and will to overcome or circumvent all obstacles in their pursuance of the part they were ordered to play in this operation.

On this mission, almost without exception; combat was restricted to small local engagements between patrols over a broad front. The terrain was such that no distinct front line, either enemy or friendly, could be designated. German patrols operated behind our "lines" and the same thing was true of the American patrols to an even greater extent. It is in this type of warfare that the 504 proved itself to be the unequivocal master of the enemy; there were few encounters, even when the Germans had the advantage of numerical superiority, that the enemy didn't come out second best. Trained to fight in small independent groups, in the technique of scouting and stealth, and for stamina and perseverance, the paratroopers proved the value of their specialized preparation for combat.

With the enemy falling back for a stand along a line running from Cardito to Alfedena, the 504 Combat Team was warned to stand by for a displacement forward to Scapoli. However, before any such movement began, the CT was ordered into Corps reserve, its positions to be exchanged with the 133rd Infantry.

The 3rd Battalion moved to the rear on November 23, followed by the remainder of the Combat Team on successive days thereafter. At Ciorlano, Thanksgiving was celebrated with a sumptuous repast transported in special containers to the regiment from Naples, and arrived in such quantities that mess kits were foregone in favor of the greater volume of tin helmets.

After a dull and somewhat uncomfortable two weeks spent in bivouac in a reserve position near Ciorlano, the Combat Team received orders to move forward for an assault on Mt. Summucro and the adjacent hills beyond Venafro – positions that dominated the gateway to the German stronghold of Cassino.

On the rainy cold evening of December 10, 1943, the regimental CP was established at Venafro, and the 1st and 2nd Battalions closed in on their respective bivouac areas at the base of the high ground overlooking the Volturno Valley and Venafro. Companies G and I of the 3rd Battalion moved immediately forward to relieve elements of the 3rd Ranger Battalion who were in position on Hill 950. While advancing to relieve the Rangers, I Company became subjected to enemy small arms fire, and in the midst of a German counter-attack, managed to take up their assigned positions. The next twelve hours found the Germans counter-attacking seven times in force and although I Company had suffered forty-six casualties by noon of the following day, they still held the position.

The following morning the 2nd Battalion completed the difficult climb up Mt. Sammucro (1205) to take up positions formerly occupied by the 143rd Infantry. The remainder of the 3rd Battalion joined G and I Companies and continued to repel repeated enemy counter-attacks. The 307th Airborne Engineers laid a mine field in the draw between Hills 1205 and 950. Enemy artillery increased in intensity to a degree unprecedented in the Italian campaign – it became quite evident that the Germans were determined to regain these heights at all costs.

The 1st Battalion, supposedly in reserve, was used for litter-bearing details, and to carry food, water, and ammunition up the rocky, heavily-shelled trails to the troops clinging stubbornly to positions on the heights.

During the succeeding several days the 2nd Battalion launched an attack on the enemy-held Hill 687, but was repulsed and withdrew to a defensive position in front of Hill 1205. The 1st Battalion moved out of reserve and, with the exception of Company B which occupied Hill 710, moved up to Hill 1205 in support of the 2nd Battalion's attack. The 3rd Battalion sent out patrols toward the enemy lines, and although meeting little resistance, discovered extensive mine fields, and defensive positions that had recently been vacated.

By this time the 376th Parachute Field Artillery Battalion was well emplaced and giving the direct support to the 504 Combat Team that was of exceptional accuracy and efficiency. The wire section established and maintained communications with various units of the CT – an endless and fatiguing job frequently necessitating work under artillery fire, which usually knocked out the wire as fast as it could be replaced.

By December 20, the 504 CT was holding Hills 1205, 950, 954, 710, and 687, with patrols operating on Hills 877 and 610. The fighting of this operation consisted of the assaulting of one hill after another. It was an uphill fight all the way characterized by rock and tree, bare, forty-five degree slopes, and unusually stubborn resistance by the enemy. Supply and evacuation of the wounded was a matter of back-breaking work. The medic's task, at best a difficult one, was increased ten-fold on the high, craggy, windswept, and shelter-less hill tops. Medical supplies were short when they were needed most and there was no quick way of obtaining more. Casualties had to be carried on stretchers down to the road – a painful six hour journey. Mule trains were able to carry supplies to a certain point, after which it became necessary because of the increased angle of ascent, for all supplies and ammunition to be transported up to the summits by carrying parties of men. This work was carried out over heavily-shelled trails, with supplies always reaching the units engaged just in time.

During the nineteen days that the 504th was in action near Venafro they suffered a total of fifty-four dead, 226 wounded, and two men missing in action. These figures are exclusive of the 376th FA Battalion and Company C, 307th Engineers, each of whom suffered dead and wounded. Most of the casualties were the result of enemy artillery fire, which was, as has been mentioned, intense.

However high the number of casualties may seem, compared to those of the enemy they must be considered light. Only the very roughest of estimates can be made of the enemy casualties, however information revealed by prisoner (51 were taken) indicated German dead and wounded to be at least five times greater than those suffered by the 504. On December 27, the regiment was relieved of duty in the Venafro sector and was moved to new bivouac areas in the vicinity of Pignatoro.

Small, much bombed Pignatoro, located in the heart of the lower Volturno Valley in the shadow of Hill 620, which five months before had been designated as the objectives for the 504 on their much-briefed Capua mission, had now become a scene of rest for men of the regiment. A belated Christmas was celebrated, New Year's Day dinner eaten under the hungry gaze of the town's population, and finally the long-awaited Christmas packages were received and opened. The regiment was paid and for the next several days the Italian courtyards of Pignatoro echoed with the almost forgotten of rippling dice, and the strident coaxing of "Waup, seven – do it!"

Shower baths were made available, movies were shown nightly in a tiny renovated picture house, orange trees groaned under the weight of fresh fruit (all off limits), and "tough guy" Humphrey Bogart, wife, and company put on a few skits for the regiment from the back of a six-by-six parked in a nearby soccer field.

Still, these were simple pleasures and the paratroopers longed for Naples gaiety and relaxation of another sort, so it was with cheery hearts that the Combat Team moved again on January 4, 1944, to the suburbs of Naples.

Officially, Naples was off limits to the 504, but then who were they – the victors of Alta Villa, the assaulters of Mt. Sammucro, and the participants of a hundred other engagements – to suddenly impotent at the flicker of a PBS directive; besides hadn't they taken the town four months before? Naples was retaken by mass infiltration.

The city had changed in some ways for the better and in some ways for the worse. The lights had come on, water rain in the toilets, and the opera and the movies were playing to packed houses, the streets were cleared of the wreckage of bombed buildings, stores were well stocked with everything but good "vino", and the enlisted men's Red Cross was a structure of grandeur that topped anything from the United States to the UK.

Naples had assumed the cosmopolitan and multi-colored atmosphere of Casablanca, Algiers, and Cairo. The streets were iridescent with the uniforms of sailors and soldiers of half a dozen different nationalities. In a manner of speaking, Naples had become the property of the world. There were those who said with a nostalgic sigh, "I liked it better before", but then such statements are merely human and not necessarily to be taken seriously, for Naples, though it had changed, was still the mother of fun and Maria was still as friendly as ever, even though her ideas had changed too.

However, all was not play. There was training, inspections, re-equipping, and it soon became evident that the rumors of, "We're going home", or "England is next", were doomed to go the way of all rumors; another mission was forthcoming – this time a parachute mission.

Sand tables were constructed, recognition crews sent out to nearby units and finally came the briefing – on January 20, the 504 was ready to take off. The operation was called "Shingle" and involved a vertical envelopment of the enemy in a sector behind the coastal town of Anzio, twenty-eight miles South of Rome. The S-2's estimate of the enemy's capabilities did not appear encouraging, to say nothing of the fact that in spite of all efforts to maintain secrecy of the impending operation, it seemed that every Italian Joe in Naples and vicinity had a least vague idea of what was going on. Consequently, there was a certain amount of "sweating" on the part of paratroopers, for most felt certain that the Germans, aware of the plans, would be waiting on the DZ with upturned bayonets – a situation, that to say the least, would have been embarrassing. However, subsequent events on the beachhead proved that their fears were unfounded, for that particular sector of the Italian coast was lightly defended and the jump would probably have gone off without a hitch.

Nevertheless, on the morning of January 20, orders were received from the Fifth Army to the effect that the 504 would not jump in the "Shingle" operation, but would go in on the beach assault in LCI's. Movement orders and boat lists were issued to all elements of the Combat Team and the following morning found the 504 loading on boats at the tiny fishing port of Possuoli, North of Naples.

That afternoon the regiment's small convoy of LCI's swung out from the port to become part of the huge northbound invasion fleet that stretched in both directions as far as the eye could see. The afternoon was quiet and as the sun submerged into the sea, men became impressed with the magnitude of the operation – an endless string of ships moving on their pre-designated course like the hand of fate across the sea.

Dawn of the 22nd found the 504 standing out from the beach upon which they were to later debark. There was an LST sinking off the port bow of the lead 504 craft, but aside from this there seemed to be amazingly little evidence of the enemy that had been expected – everything seemed quiet, too quiet.

Reports had been received that five waves had been landed when through the loudspeaker of a neighboring boat Col. Tucker was ordered to land the Combat Team on Red Beach. Immediately the thirteen LCI's that contained the members of the regiment commenced to move toward the shore. There was no confusion; everything was proceeding with the regularity and order of clockwork. The lead boats were grinding into the sand. Already the ramps had slammed down into the water and men were splashing their way toward the shore. It was perfect. The operation couldn't have gone more smoothly. The only thing that was lacking to make this a perfect movie operation was the enemy.

At that precise moment the tense stillness was shattered by a whining roar that left no doubt in anyone's mind as to its source. Straight out of the sun the enemy planes came – their machine guns blasting. For a few brief seconds the world became one great kaleidoscope of raging sound, then the planes were gone and in the water where they had passed over lay several boiling circles where bombs had struck. One LCI, its nose disgorging men, settled in the shallow water. Its aft section was a mass of twisted metal and oily black smoke. Men could be seen hanging from the bits of twisted steel. That had been LCI number 20 – C Company's craft.

The landing craft continued to come, unload their personnel, and back out into the water, while the German dive bombers returned again and again. The paratroopers ran down the ramps and jumped into the surf. Some went in to their knees, some to their waists, and some went in over their heads and swam for the shore. And all the while the German planes continued to roar in from the sun to bomb and strafe. The ship borne anti-aircraft units sent up a terrific barrage, but nobody in the 504 was watching for hits – they were too busy getting ashore and seeking cover.

Two days later, the regiment was ordered to the right flank of the beachhead where German elements had forced the withdrawal of 3rd Division reconnaissance units in the vicinity of bridges number Two and number Five over the Mussolini Canal.

Near bridge number Five, Lt. Col. W. R. Williams, commanding the 1st Battalion, ordered B Company to attack the Germans in the vicinity. After an unsuccessful attempt to take the bridge, a platoon of A Company was committed along with a platoon of tanks. Four hours later, with the aid of tanks and 75mm guns manned by the 376, the enemy was pushed across the canal and bridge number Five was secured.

In the vicinity of bridge number Two, Lt. Col. L.G. Freeman, commanding the 3rd Battalion, committed I Company to clear the sector. The company was ambushed, however, and forced to take up defensive positions. At dawn of the 24th, I Company, now reinforced by a platoon of tanks and naval gunfire from the sea, counter-attacked frontally while G and H Companies brought the enemy under cross fire from the flanks. Two hours later the enemy, after suffering sixty-nine killed, twenty-four wounded, thirty-three prisoners, two halftracks knocked out and one captured, was driven back to the other side of the canal. Casualties in the 504 were two men killed, three wounded, and none missing.

Following days found the regiment patrolling actively and consolidating its line along the Mussolini Canal. It was then decided to attack the town of Berge Piave, an important road center that came to be known as the "spider" because of the five main roads that joined in the city.

At 1330 on January 25, all three battalions moved out in the attack. The 1st Battalion attacked Sessano, the 3rd Battalion Borge Sabatino, and the 2nd Battalion made the main drive for Berge Piave. The 3rd Battalion attained its objective and pushed strong combat patrols to the North and East supported by naval gunfire. The 1st Battalion encountered stiff opposition and heavy enemy artillery fire; nevertheless, a small group of C Company men did reach the objective – Sessano. The 2nd Battalion, supported by a rolling barrage, reached Berge Piave and D Company pushed 200 yards east of town. However, the enemy counter-attacked with an armored force of about five tanks and eight flak wagons and isolated D Company from the remainder of the battalion. Upon order from the Third Division, the 2nd Battalion withdrew to the Mussolini Canal leaving behind a strong combat outpost and several tank-hunting teams. D Company, after suffering heavy losses, subsequently infiltrated through the enemy's encirclement and regained their own lines.

As a result of those operations, the regiment had gained outpost positions on the other side of the canal, but generally speaking had not advanced any appreciable distance – the MLR still remaining along the Mussolini Canal.

After a week of holding and attacking along a front extending from bridge number Five south to the sea, the 504 was relieved in this sector by the 179th Infantry. The 3rd Battalion was attached to the First Armored Division and sent to the northern (British) flank of the beachhead, while the remainder of the Combat Team was sent North of bridge number Five to participate in an attack scheduled to take place in the Third Division sector.

The 3rd Battalion, after several days in reserve with the First Armored Division, was committed with the British First (Guards) Division in the Carrecoto sector. German artillery fire in this area was unusually intense and it was here that the enemy launched his main drive to push the beachhead into the sea. After one of the heaviest artillery barrages ever experienced by 504 men, the Germans began their attack in the early hours of February 5, 1944. On successive days British Units were cut off from the 3rd Battalion, which was forced to withdraw to the famous "factory" in Mussolini's wonder-town of Aprilia. Enemy railroad guns and dive bombers then concentrated their efforts on the 3rd Battalion garrison. The paratroopers suffered severe casualties, and by the time enemy infantry moved in, the companies had been reduced in strength to between twenty and thirty men.

Fierce hand-to-hand fighting ensued, in which the paratroopers by sheer determination and courage, were able to repel repeated German onslaughts. Rather than remain in the exposed positions in which they now found themselves, they withdrew to a railroad underpass several hundred yards behind the "factory" and established defensive positions. H Company was ordered to attack and attempt the rescue of a British general who had been captured. After bloody fighting, they recaptured the general, only to find themselves cut off from friendly forces. I Company was then ordered to attack and make contact with H Company. The sixteen men remaining in the company carried out this mission successfully and a semblance of order was restored to this sector – the backbone of the German attack had been broken. It was for this outstanding performance in the period 8-12 February, that the 3rd Battalion was given one of the first Presidential Citations in the European Theater of Operations.

The remainder of the Combat Team, meanwhile, had been engaged in heavy fighting in the Third Division sector. On January 30, the 1st and 2nd Battalions jumped off in an attack that was to take them to Cisterna River. The 1st Battalion led the way and encountered only light resistance as they passed through the German outpost line. Soon after, however, as they neared their first bridge objective over the Mussolini Canal, they were engaged by strong enemy forces. The reserve company was committed and the enemy driven back across the stream, first blowing the bridge behind him and thus saving the paratroopers the trouble.

While the 1st Battalion was consolidating its gains, the 2nd Battalion advanced along the left flank of the 1st Battalion and under similar circumstances, were engaged by the enemy in the vicinity of a bridge farther upstream. Here again, the enemy was forced to retreat across the canal after blowing the bridge behind them. The 2nd Battalion continued to attack to the north on the heels of the retreating Germans, who proceeded to blow another bridge – this time it was the bridge crossing the Cisterna River. The loss of this bridge denied the paratroopers any further support from friendly tanks, a factor which caused the 2nd Battalion to halt its advance and dig in on the far side of the river.

Much enemy material in the form of halftracks, 75mm howitzers, small arms, and vehicles was either captured or destroyed in this attack. Eighty prisoners were taken with very heavy casualties inflicted upon the enemy. The 504 losses were comparatively light.

For the remainder of their eight-week stay on the Anzio beachhead 504 men found themselves confronted with a defensive situation, rather than offensive for which they had been trained. With the exception of the first week of fighting on the beachhead, no appreciable advance was made by our forces. It was strictly trench-type warfare characteristic of the First World War. For the first time, 504 men were digging dugouts and living in them for weeks at a time; barbed wire entanglements and mine fields in unusual depth covered all areas where the enemy might conceivably tread; alternate positions were prepared for any eventuality, and there were times when such an eventuality did not seem too remote. All in all, this was not the type of combat for which the 504 was psychologically suited. In fact, it was absolutely contrary to the way that paratroopers had always been taught to fight, and so it was with something more than the usual enthusiasm that the men of the 504 received the order to embark from Anzio on March 23, for the trip to Naples.

As the LST's loaded with paratroopers got under way, the Germans were dropping shells into the harbor, as though in some final frantic gesture to keep the 504 from leaving; like a murderer's last stab at his executioner. This had been a costly campaign for the 504 – but ten times as costly for the enemy. During the eight-week period, 120 paratroopers were killed, 410 wounded, and sixty missing in action. Many lessons had been learned at Anzio, and many men had been lost. It was a good place to bid farewell.

After one uneventful night on the water, the small convoy turned in toward the coast and before long the port of Pozzuoli, from which the regiment had sailed on the mission to Anzio, came into sight. The big LST's nudged their noses up to the beach, dropped their ramps, and the already entrucked troops rolled out onto land again.

Bagneli, the bivouac area, was but fifteen minutes from the heart of Naples by way of local railway system and was the site of the projected Italian World's Fair. Many fine buildings, statues, and other architectural features typical of this type of exhibition were in evidence. The 504 was quartered in the modern, and only recently constructed Italian University for the education of Ethiopian students. The buildings of the university were spacious and an excellent example of modern Italian designing.

Once firmly ensconced in their quarters at the university, the regiment fell into a daily routine which for the most part, consisted of very light training, turning in equipment, and taking off for Naples at every opportunity. General Clark reviewed the regiment at a ceremony held in honor of the 3rd Battalion and presented Col. Freeman, the battalion commander, with a Presidential Unit Citation for the battalion's outstanding performance at Carrecoto.

It had been generally assumed that the 504 would leave Italy and sail to England to rejoin the 82nd Airborne Division; however, up until the last moment the hopeful, rumor that the regiment was on the way back to the States could still be heard. On April 10, 1944, the Combat Team moved by train into Naples where they alighted at Garibaldi Station, marched down the Via Umberto to the water front, and boarded the Capetown Castle – a large British ship of streamlined appearance.

The following morning 504 men awoke to feel the throb of the ship's engines beneath them and with the knowledge that Italy now obscured by a mist that hung against the horizon its battles, its moments of sorrow and happiness, had become another chapter in the history of courage of the 504th Parachute Infantry.

### c. The 505th Parachute Infantry Regiment

1. After many various plans had been made to jump the Combat Team, first near the VOLTURNO River, then on ROME, a final mission was received 141500B Sept., 1943. This mission as planned and executed involved jumping on the night of Sept. 14 and 15 behind the lines of friendly troops, the VI Corps, then engaged to the North and East of PAESTUM, Italy. In describing this operation in succeeding paragraphs the following points will be discussed:
A. Plans and operation of 505 Combat Team
B. a. Organization of a Pathfinder Group
   b. Equipment of Pathfinder Group
C. Plans for employment of personnel and equipment
D. Actual execution of plan
E. Results achieved

2. Plans and operation of 505 Combat Team:
Fortunately the Combat Team had been on air alert status for a seven (7) day period and all the physical labor that remained to be done prior to taking off was to load equipment bundles, which were already packed, and draw personnel chutes. Plane assignments and take off airdromes had previously been designated, however, a time schedule remained to be worked out. It was decided to take off and jump according to the following plan:

| UNIT | AIRPLANES | DEPARTURE AIRDROME | DEPARTURE |
|------|-----------|--------------------|-----------|
| Pathfinder Group | 3 | AGRIGENTO | 2100 |
| 3rd Bn | 36 | CASTELVETRANO | 2130 |
| Hq Co 505 CT | 9 | CASTELVETRANO | 2145 |
| Co "B", 307 Engr Bn | 9 | BARIZZO | 2130 |
| 2nd Bn | 36 | COMISO | 2145 |
| 1st Bn | 36 | BARIZZO | 2200 |

Drop times were in general to follow same sequence as units are listed above. It was realized at that time that considerable difficulty would arise in regrouping planes following the jump of the 504th CT the night before.

Battalion and separate unit commanders were assembled at 1600 hr., given the situation and plan to be executed. The DZ located just N of the SOLOFRONE River (S 785699) was to be marked by a "T" of white lights. The horizontal line was to represent the "Go" line.

Units were to assemble as follows:

| | |
|---|---|
| Pathfinder Group | Center of Lights |
| 3rd Bn | N edge of DZ on red flare |
| Hq Co | NW edge of DZ |
| 2nd Bn | S edge of DZ on green flare |
| Engineers | S edge of DZ |
| 1st Bn | SW edge of DZ on white flashlight |

**RESULTS OF THE OPERATION:**

| UNIT | DEPARTURE TIME | DROP TIME | PLANES MISSING |
|------|----------------|-----------|----------------|
| Pathfinder Group | 2100 | 2338 | 0 |
| 3rd Bn | 2240 | 0110 | 4 |
| Hq Co | 2240 | 0120 | 1 |
| Co "B", 307 Engr Bn | 2330 | 0140 | 0 |
| 2nd Bn | 2320 | 0130 | 0 |
| 3rd Bn | 0100 | 0255 | 2 |

Jumping Altitude: 600-900 feet

Moonlight: æ Moon

Course: Just in side N coast of Sicily, passed immediately N of MT ETNA, then NE to coast of Italy, the N along coastline to point opposite SOLO-FRONE River, then E to DZ.

As a unit the CT loaded and jumped without incident. The battalion jump patterns were extremely small and with exceptions as noted, all personnel and equipment were assembled in a remarkably short period of time (No Battalion taking more than 60 minutes to assemble). Jump casualties were extremely light. Of the seven (7) missing planes four (4) had turned back due to faulty navigation, two (2) never got off the ground, and one (1) dropped its load near EBOLI. This plane load later joined the CT in NAPLES on Oct. 1.

The use of radar equipment was definitely proven as most successful. A more detailed description follows:

The marking of the DZ was satisfactory from the standpoint of results achieved and the situation of jumping behind our own lines. It is believed, however, that under normal circumstances Krypton Lights or Aldis Lamps would be more practical from the security viewpoint. Smoke Pots as used consisted of gasoline and sand, and threw off a considerable flame.

Plane reception was accomplished with Amber Lights on the underside of the wings. The lights were easily visible from the ground. Plane formations flew directly over friendly ships in harbor at PAESTUM, and also over shore installations. Previous instructions to shore and naval gun crews had been given – not to fire on transport aircraft. These instructions with the additional aid of Amber Recognition Lights were most necessary and no doubt helped prevent a reoccurrence of the disaster, which met the 2nd Lift in the SICILIAN Operation two (2) months previous.

The use of flares by the 2nd and 3rd Battalions for assembling off the DZ was most instrumental in the rapid assembly of their personnel, however, it is believed that ten (10) to twelve (12) flares are excessive and should be reduced to two (2) at a maximum. Furthermore, if plane loads are sufficiently close to DZ, a complete assembly by use of flash light is preferred. We later found that our ground signals were easily visible to enemy observation fifteen (15) to twenty (20) miles away where enemy gun installations were reported in position at the time.

3. a. Organization of a Pathfinder Group
(1) When and Where Organized: One week prior to combat jump at AGRIGENTO, Sicily.
(2) Personnel: Lt. Col. Billingslea and two (2) radar teams

(See para C below for Organization)
(3) Training:
(a)Large proportion of personnel, i.e., same Radar Operators had made a previous test of equipment in a practice operation (302100B Aug., '43) at ENFIDAVILLE, N Africa (Known as "SNOWBALL"). In this operation the two (2) sets of radar were both ready for operation within five (5) minutes after drop time.
(b) One (1) week at AGRIGENTO was spent with further familiarizing teams with equipment; nomenclature, operation method of wearing same. Men actually became proficient at setting up equipment blindfolded in a few minutes
(c) Lt. Col. Billingslea accompanied 504 CT for their jump the night previous.

b. EQUIPMENT OF PATHFINDER GROUP
(1) 2 sets of radar equipment, each consisted of four (4) parts:
    (a) Battery 12 Volt, wet cell
    (b) Power Converter
    (c) Receiver and transmitter group with detonator device. [AN/PPN-1]
    (d) Aerial

Each set weighed about 51 lbs. fitted into a compact container known as a leg pack, jumped on one man. Two (2) men were were required to work each set; one (1) to jump with equipment, and the other to assist in setting up and provide a safety factor for operation. Both men knew how to operate the equipment well.

(2) One (1) beacon or radio compass device was packed in an A-5 container together with one (1) Aldis Lamp. The original idea was to check the beacon and the radar, one against the other, and test the usefulness of the lights. At the last minute the above container and contents were left behind since the 509th Parachute Battalion was executing a combat jump the same night using a beacon and interference was probable.

(3) Twelve (12) Flash Lights, Government Issue.
c. PLANS FOR EMPLOYMENT OF PERSONNEL AND EQUIPMENT.
Planes to be loaded as follows:
First Plane: Piloted by Lt. Col. Crouch – Jump Master Col. Gavin
Lt. Kenar, with one (1) radar set to be put into operation immediately.
Lt. Col. Billingslea, with one (1) SCR-536 to notify plane No.2 in case of accident.
Cpl. Houston, to assist Lt. Kenar
Cpl. Fitzgerald, with team of two (2) men equipped with flash lights to augment DZ markings if necessary.
Two (2) rifle men from 307 Engineer Bn to provide security
Second Plane: Pilot unknown – Jump master, Major Mulcahy with SCR-536 to provide communication with plane No.1
Cpl. Kuth, with one (1) radar set to be ready for operation pending mishap to team in plane No. 1.
Cpl. Girodo, to assist Cpl. Kuth
Same light and security teams as plane No.1.
Third Plane: Piloted by Major Brown – Jump master, Captain Norton; Capt. Wight
Lt. Cooperider, in charge of light crews (crews to assemble on center of DZ or center of "T" of lights)
Same light and security teams as plane No.1.

d. ACTUAL EXECUTION OF PLANS.

This Pathfinder group loaded at AGRIGENTO, Sicily at 2100 hr. after a brief conference concerning the DZ location and a final review of each drop. It was evident at the time that the navigation of the lead plane would largely govern the results of the Pathfinder work. Our planes flew in a close "V" formation at an altitude of 6000 to 7000 ft. from AGRIGENTO along a prescribed course until a few miles off the coast of Italy. We crossed the coastline at about 1000 ft. and jumped at 700 ft. There wasn't any wind. The chutes came straight down near the center of the DZ. Groups assembled as planned without difficulty and without casualty. In three minutes Lt. Kenar's radar set was in operation. Cpl. Kuth (standing by) had his set ready for operation. The flash lights were not needed as the gasoline sand fire signals were operating in good order.

e. RESULTS ACHIEVED:

From observation from the DZ and later conversation with pilots and men, the radar was the chief reason for such a successful jump, and without a doubt it was the most successful jump the 505 CT has ever made. In numerous cases squadrons and groups approached from varied directions further indicating that the radar was instrumental in their locating the DZ. In almost every instance, however, the formation of the planes split the DZ and dropped their loads within 500 yards of its center.

I would further like to emphasize that only the ability of the lead pilot of the Pathfinder Planes to hit the DZ plus the efficient operation of radar made possible such a successful jump.

/s/t/                                                   JOHN NORTON
                                                        Captain, Infantry
                                                        S-3


## 2nd Bn., 505 Inf. Combat Report


### October 4, 1943

The 2nd Battalion was alerted at 0650 hour on October 4, 1943, and at 0930 hour all of the details were received from higher headquarters. The movement order was issued at 0845 hour and at 1000 hour the battalion moved north from its present bivouac area. At a point opposite the Naples Airport the battalion entrucked on thirty British lorries at 1130 hour. At 1315 hour the battalion detrucked 1000 yards west of GIUGLIANO IN CAMPANIA and moved by foot one and a half miles west into a forward assembly area. D Company mounted British tanks and the balance of the battalion moved out on foot at 1450 hour.

The battalion continued the march toward Villa Literno until 2030 hour when a CP was set up in a farm house on south edge of Villa Literno. F Company sent one platoon at 2045 hour to secure bridge at the canal, and also a road block to the east and west of the village. These patrols made first contact with the enemy at 2116 hour in village square, but after firing several thousand rounds of automatic small arms fire the enemy withdrew to the north and F Company continued on mission. E Company bypassed the village and moved into defensive position on north edge. Harassing enemy small arms fire continued through most of the night. During the night D Company returned to battalion control.


### October 5, 1943

At 0530 battalion continued attack; D, E, and F were 1/4 mile north of VILLA LITERNO; D Company made contact. They continued attack but were held up after 300 yards by strong enemy forces to the left of Street. E Company was committed on left flank, cleaned up situation and suffered light casualties from numerous booby traps placed in open fields and around buildings, and advance continued to bridge which was reached at 0830 hour. One section of a three section bridge was blown in spite of stubborn resistance from the platoon of F Company which had the previous night been given the mission to seize the bridge. The platoon did prevent the enemy from completely destroying the remaining two sections of the bridge.

With E on the right, D on the left, and F in reserve the battalion pushed aggressively forward never losing contact with the enemy and at 1000 hour, the canal was reached where orders from higher command stopped our advance; Battalion moved into defensive position.

At 1830 hour platoons from D, E, and F companies were sent on patrol to reconnoiter routes to the river, possible river crossings and any enemy information. Patrols reported to Battalion CP.

East patrol reported route passable, river approximately 25 yards wide, depth unknown and easy to bridge. They encountered small groups of enemy. Center patrol was unable to reach river due to enemy activity. West patrol reported route passable, river approximately sixty yards wide, depth unknown, and difficult to bridge. They also encountered small groups of the enemy.

### October 6, 1943

At 0230 hour another platoon patrol from F Company was sent out to capture prisoners but returned at 0530 hour after being unable to contact enemy.

At 0900 hour a platoon from F Company was sent into Arnone to seize and secure the village and with the exception of artillery fire they encountered no enemy resistance.

At 1130 hour the balance of F Company plus the 81mm mortar platoon was ordered into the village.

At 1430 hour the 1st platoon of E Company was committed north along railroad to protect F Company's left flank.

At 1530 hour a very heavy enemy artillery concentration began to fall on ARNONE and at 1540 hour F Company reported the enemy counter-attacking. Prisoners later volunteered information that one company was to attack the village from the west and they were to be reinforced by a battalion which was to cross the river.

The balance of E Company was committed north along railroad at 1540 hour. At 1600 hour the 1st platoon of E Company hit the enemy's right flank along the railroad tracks in the vicinity of the railway station and at the same time the platoon of F Company covering the company's withdrawal struck back at the enemy crossing the river. Our artillery opened up all along the river and the enemy was stopped in his tracks. By 1700 hour E and F Companies had withdrawn to road running east and west 1000 yards south of ARNONE and a defensive position established.

At 1847 hour A Company of the 1st Battalion moved into E Company's former position on the canal.

Outposts were placed and with the exception of harassing enemy artillery fire the night was quiet.

### October 7, 1943

At 0957 hour E Company reported an enemy patrol crossing the river on the remains of the railroad bridge but our artillery stopped any further action on the enemy's part. During the day our patrols were active to the river and no enemy were encountered.

At 2130 hour the battalion was relieved by the 46th British Division and the battalion moved into bivouac æ of a mile to the east of Villa Liturno. The night was quiet.

### October 8, 1943

At 0630 hour the battalion entrucked on British lorries and returned to the City of Naples. The convoy arrived at 0930 hour. The balance of the day was spent cleaning equipment.

**Headquarters First Battalion**
**505th Parachute Infantry**
APO 469 % POSTMASTER, NEW YORK, N. Y.

11 October 1943

Subject: Combat Action First Battalion October 4-9, 1943, Inclusive.
To : S-3, 505 Parachute Infantry

1. Following are the accounts of activities of 1st Bn. during the above mentioned period.

At 0900 hour the battalion moved by foot to Capuccini Airdrome in preparation for movement by motor to the vicinity of Villa Literno where the 2nd Battalion had relieved a battalion of the 143rd Infantry. The effort was toward the Volturno River along the Villa Literno-Arnone highway and the 1st Battalion was in regimental reserve.

At 0600 Oct. 5 the Bn. moved out and at 0830 reached Villa Literno set up the Bn. CP in the eastern outskirts of town and set up a defense straddling the road north just out of town about 200 yards. All day the Bn. received artillery fire, three casualties resulted, none fatal.

At 1700 hour Bn. moved forward again and set up a defense to cover rear and flanks of the 2nd Bn. Center of the defense was RJ 049706, right flank 067700, left flank 032691. Bn. CP in a farmhouse 054704. On the way to this position two casualties resulted from trip wires.

Oct. 6 – 0800 hour Capt. Sayer was seriously wounded by and "S" mine.

"C" Co. Patrols, composed of one platoon, left early to reconnoiter the coast road south of Castle Volturno, the town itself and the area between the Villa Literno-Arnone road and the coast road. No enemy was contacted except for a few snipers in Castlevolturno. Both bridges over canal immediately south of Castlevolturno were blown. At 2000 hour "A" Co. attached to 2nd Bn. and moved out to join them at approximately 043717.

Oct. 7 – two patrols were sent to reconnoiter as follows – one to reconnoiter Grazzanise and the main roads between our own positions and Grazzanise. The other to reconnoiter Castlevolturno and the area between our own positions and Castlevolturno. Patrol that went to Grazzanise reported on air field with wrecked planes at 075745. In Grazzanise British Recon units were contacted. A German patrol was encountered at La Socia. A short fire fight ensued, two Germans killed. The other patrol reported heavy shelling of Castlevolturno but no other enemy activities. Civilians report North bank of Volturno River heavily mined.

Continuous patrolling by "B" Co. During the night protected both flanks of the 2nd Bn. on Sept. 7-8. Sept. 8 the Bn. was relieved at 2030 hours by British. Bn. marched to Villa Literno, bivouacked East South East of there about 600 yards until 0630 hours when the Bn. departed in trucks for Naples. Arrived in Naples approximately 1000 hours.

/s/t/

DALE A. ROYSDON

Capt. 505 Inf.

S-3

**Headquarters Third Battalion**
**505th Parachute Infantry**
A. P. O. 469

**31 October 1943**

Battalion Historical Record
OCTOBER 1943

On October 1st, 1943 the Third Battalion left forward assembly area at Torre-Del Annunziata at 0730 hour aboard British motor lorries and moved North toward Naples, on highway No.18, behind the 7th Armored Corps, reconnaissance units. At a temporary assembly area at Portici this battalion (less "I" Company) was given the mission at 1200 hour of escorting the Fifth Army Commander into the city of Naples. The battalion was employed as follows: One (1) platoon of "G" Company assigned as Army Commander's personal guard, balance of battalion to follow in convoy to the first stopping point, Piazzi Garibaldi, and deploy immediately around perimeter of square as a civilian mob control cordon.

The above mission was expedited on schedule and elicited the Army Commander's commendation.

The battalion C.P. was established on Northwest Island of Piazzi Garibaldi. The battalion (less "I" Company attached to the Scottish Grays of the 10th Armored Corps in the vicinity of San Giorgio, Southeast of Naples) was then dispatched to patrol previously assigned area of responsibility, this being accomplished by 1600 hour. "I" Company was relieved of assignment and closed the battalion area at 0330 hour 2 October 1943.

One platoon of "H" Company and one (1) section of 81mm mortar platoon was withheld from patrols and assigned a mission by the Battalion Commander; S-3 report concerning this mission quoted herewith: (other than stated herein no contact was made with the enemy).

Following is the account of the action of Third Platoon Company "H", on an assigned mission to secure a reservoir that supplied the water for the city of Napoli.

At 1400 hours October 1st, Major Krause ordered Lt. Ziegler to take a platoon of men and accompany him on a mission to secure a water reservoir that was alleged to be in German hands. The platoon with the Mortar platoon of Headquarters Company attached, moved from the Railway station at 1400 hours.

With the aid of a civilian guide they arrived on trucks at 213509. The men detrucked and Major Krause gave Lt. Ziegler the order to take his men to 212515 and determine if there were any Germans in the area. It was found that the Germans had left after blowing up the reservoir.

An investigation by Major Krause disclosed another important reservoir in the nearby vicinity that was also alleged to be in German hands. Major Krause then ordered Lt. Ziegler to take his platoon and investigate reservoir and prevent its destruction if it were possible. The platoon moved out at 1525 hours. They arrived at 193518 at 1630 hours. Lt. Ziegler took a six man patrol and moved to 197518.

The reservoir was found to be intact and civilians stated the Germans had left a few hours earlier. The reservoir was left guarded and the remainder of the platoon was assembled at 193518. At 1800 hours a civilian reported that the Germans had prepared a bridge for demolition, and were returning to blow it that night. Lt. Ziegler took four men and with the civilian as a guide went to investigate the Bridge. Upon arrival there he found the charges. He arranged for a guard at the Bridge all night, and returned to his platoon C.P. At 020800 the 7th Armored Force arrived and the demolition charges were removed. Lt. Ziegler with two men as scouts moved out ahead of the British Reconnaissance unit and at 196531 came in contact with a German Mark IV tank. The tank fired a few bursts with its Machine Guns and departed. Neither scouts nor the officer were harmed by the shots. Lt. Ziegler stayed with the Reconnaissance unit until he returned to his company area at 021400.

# Section 6: Casualties in Italy

(Corrected to 5 May 1945)

### DIVISION TOTAL

| Enlisted | Officers | Men | TOTAL |
|---|---|---|---|
| Killed in Action | 30 | 230 | 260 |
| Died of Wounds | 4 | 47 | 51 |
| Prisoner of War | 1 | 18 | 19 |
| Missing in Action | – | 71 | 71 |
| Missing in Action to Returned to duty | 2 | 62 | 64 |
| Wounded | 24 | 316 | 340 |
| Wounded to Returned to Duty | <u>61</u> | <u>739</u> | <u>800</u> |
| TOTALS | 122 | 1483 | 1605 |

## UNIT TOTALS

### 504th Parachute Infantry Regiment

| | Officers | Men | TOTAL |
|---|---|---|---|
| Killed in Action | 19 | 160 | 179 |
| Died of Wounds | 1 | 33 | 34 |
| Prisoner of War | 1 | 13 | 14 |
| Missing in Action | – | 61 | 61 |
| Missing in Action to Returned to duty | – | 10 | 10 |
| Wounded | 13 | 223 | 236 |
| Wounded to Returned to Duty | <u>51</u> | <u>521</u> | <u>572</u> |
| TOTALS | 85 | 1021 | 1106 |

### 505th Parachute Infantry Regiment

| | Officers | Men | TOTAL |
|---|---|---|---|
| Killed in Action | 4 | 8 | 12 |
| Died of Wounds | – | 4 | 4 |

| | | | |
|---|---|---|---|
| Missing in Action | – | 1 | 1 |
| Missing in Action to Returned to duty | 1 | 22 | 23 |
| Wounded | 3 | 21 | 24 |
| Wounded to Returned to Duty | <u>3</u> | <u>108</u> | <u>111</u> |
| TOTALS | 11 | 164 | 175 |

**325th Glider Infantry Regiment**

| | | | |
|---|---|---|---|
| Killed in Action | 1 | 15 | 16 |
| Died of Wounds | 1 | 3 | 4 |
| Prisoner of War | – | 5 | 5 |
| Missing in Action | – | 4 | 4 |
| Missing in Action to Returned to duty | – | 1 | 1 |
| Wounded | 1 | 18 | 19 |
| Wounded to Returned to Duty | <u>1</u> | <u>25</u> | <u>26</u> |
| TOTALS | 4 | 71 | 75 |

| | Officers | EM | TOTAL |
|---|---|---|---|

**307th Airborne Engineer Battalion**

| | | | |
|---|---|---|---|
| Killed in Action | 1 | 30 | 31 |
| Died of Wounds | – | 1 | 1 |
| Missing in Action | – | 5 | 5 |
| Missing in Action to Returned to duty | 1 | 29 | 30 |
| Wounded | 1 | 17 | 18 |
| Wounded to Returned to Duty | <u>4</u> | <u>39</u> | <u>43</u> |
| TOTALS | 7 | 121 | 128 |

**376th Parachute Field Artillery Battalion**

| | | | |
|---|---|---|---|
| Killed in Action | 2 | 8 | 10 |
| Died of Wounds | 1 | 5 | 6 |
| Wounded | 5 | 16 | 21 |
| Wounded to Returned to Duty | – | <u>29</u> | <u>29</u> |
| TOTALS | 8 | 58 | 66 |

**456th Parachute Field Artillery Battalion**

| | | | |
|---|---|---|---|
| Killed in Action | 2 | – | 2 |
| Died of Wounds | 1 | 1 | 2 |
| Wounded | 1 | 7 | 8 |
| Wounded to Returned to Duty | – | <u>1</u> | <u>1</u> |
| TOTALS | 4 | 9 | 13 |

**319th Glider Field Artillery Battalion**

| | | | |
|---|---|---|---|
| Killed in Action | 1 | 3 | 4 |
| Wounded | – | 7 | 7 |
| Wounded to Returned to Duty | <u>2</u> | <u>8</u> | <u>10</u> |
| TOTALS | 3 | 18 | 21 |

**320th Glider Field Artillery Battalion**

| | | | |
|---|---|---|---|
| Killed in Action | – | 4 | 4 |
| Wounded to Returned to Duty | – | <u>2</u> | <u>2</u> |
| TOTALS | – | 6 | 6 |

<u>80th Airborne Anti-Aircraft Battalion</u>

| | | | |
|---|---|---|---|
| Killed in Action | – | 1 | 1 |
| Wounded to Returned to Duty | – | <u>1</u> | <u>1</u> |
| TOTALS | – | 2 | 2 |

<u>407th Airborne Quartermaster Company</u>

| | | | |
|---|---|---|---|
| Wounded | – | 6 | 6 |
| Wounded to Returned to Duty | – | <u>3</u> | <u>3</u> |
| TOTALS | – | 9 | 9 |

<u>Headquarters Company 82nd Airborne Division</u>

| | | | |
|---|---|---|---|
| Killed in Action | – | 1 | 2 |
| Wounded to Returned to Duty | – | <u>1</u> | <u>2</u> |
| TOTALS | – | 2 | 2 |

<u>307th Airborne Medical Company</u>

| | | | |
|---|---|---|---|
| Wounded | – | 1 | 1 |

<u>82nd Airborne Military Police Platoon</u>

| | | | |
|---|---|---|---|
| Wounded and Returned to Duty | – | 1 | 1 |

| | | | |
|---|---|---|---|
| **Total Division Casualties** | **122** | **1483** | **1605** |

*Waiting for orders to go into Salerno. Sicily, September 1943.*

*C-47s on a Sicilian airstrip ready for the jump into Salerno, September 1943.*

*Colonel Harry L. Lewis, Commander, 325th GIR, briefs his troops prior to sailing to the Salerno Beachhead, September 1943.*

*Major General Matthew B. Ridgway in Salerno, Italy, September 1943.*

*LTG Mark Clark, Fifth Army Commander, addresses the 325th GIR after their operation in Salerno. Salerno, Italy, 23 September 1943.*

*(L to R) LTC Krause, Lt. Patterson, and Colonel Gavin at the 505th Command Post one mile south of the Volturno River, Italy, October 1943.*

*A 60mm mortar in action in Italy, 1943.*

*Paratroopers of the 504th PIR move through the mountainous terrain of Italy, 1943.*

*Engineers from C Company, 307th Airborne Engineer Battalion repair a bridge in Italy, 1943.*

*Troopers of the 504th PIR near San Pietro, Italy, December 1943.*

*An 81mm mortar team from the 504th in the Anzio Beachhead, January 1944. Mules were often used to carry equipment in Italy.*

*Opposite*
*Top: Engineers clear mines at Anzio, Italy, January 1944.*
*Bottom: The 504th Combat Team comes ashore on the Anzio Beachhead near Nettuno, Italy, during operation SHINGLE on 22 January 1944.*

*Above: Operation Shingle begins as troops of the 504th Combat Team disembark from their LCI on 22 January 1944 near Nettuno, Italy.*

*Paratroopers wring out their equipment after landing at the Anzio Beachhead on 22 January 1944.*

*Paratroopers assemble on the Anzio Beachhead after landing on 22 January 1944.*

*The 2nd Battalion, 504th PIR crosses the Mussolini Canal in the Anzio Beachhead on 26 January 1944.*

*Fighting positions of the 504th along the Mussolini Canal, Anzio Beachhead, 19 February 1944.*

# CHAPTER THREE

# Operation Neptune:
# The 82nd Airborne Division in Normandy

Section 1: Preface

Section 2: Narrative

Section 3: Distribution

Section 4: Annexes

33 Days of action without relief, without replacements.

Every mission accomplished. No ground gained ever relinquished.

(Report of Major General RIDGWAY.)

COMBAT EFFICIENCY: Excellent, short 60% Infantry, 90% Artillery.

(From G-3 report as of 062400 June 1944.)

MAPS: GSGS 4347, FRANCE, 1/25,000, Sheets 31/20 SE, 31/18 NE, SE, SW,NW; GSGS 4249, FRANCE, 1/ 100,000, Sheets 5E, 6E, 5F, 6F.

## Section 1: Preface

The 82nd Airborne Division arrived in the European Theater of Operations on 9 December, 1943, bronzed by the summer suns of North Africa and Sicily and bled and battle-tested in campaigns in Sicily and the Italian mainland. One Regimental Combat Team, the 504th, had been left behind when the Division sailed from Naples, Italy, on 19 November, 1943.

The 504th Regimental Combat Team, (consisting of the 504th Parachute Infantry, the 376th Parachute Field Artillery Battalion, and Company C, 307th Airborne Engineer Battalion) was detached from the Division and was fighting in the mountains north of the Volturno River when the 82nd sailed from NAPLES. Later it was to spend more than sixty days of grueling warfare on the famous Anzio Beachhead before rejoining the Division in May in England.

The Division disembarked at Belfast, North Ireland, and occupied an area northwest of that city. Division Headquarters was established at Castle Dawson, which was approximately thirty miles from Belfast. The Division was attached to XV Corps.

A shortage of adequate training facilities, the short days and long nights, and no facilities at all for airborne maneuvers, handicapped training. The need for such facilities and training became increasingly important with the attachment to the Division on 14 January, 1944, of the 2nd Airborne Brigade, which included the Brigade Headquarters and Headquarters Company and the 507th and 508th Parachute Infantry Regiments, and preparations were made for the 82nd to move to the Nottingham-Leicester-Market Harboro area in the English Midlands. Brigadier General Maxwell B. Taylor, Division Artillery Commander, rejoined the Division after duty with the North African Theater of Operations.

The move to the midlands was made in mid-February, 1944, and an intensive program of airborne and other types of training was begun. A parachute school was opened to train reinforcements, and a series of parachute problems was mapped out to begin with battalion drops and to culminate with a drop of three regiments. Glider personnel trained with the British Horsa gliders as well as with the CG-4A (Waco) gliders, took training rides of more than two hours duration.

Division Headquarters was established in a hutted camp in Braunstone Park, Leicester. The telephone code names of "Leader" and "Keystone", employed by the Division in North Africa, Sicily, and Italy, were dropped and the Division became known as "Champion". The 456th Parachute Field Artillery Battalion, which had seen much of its personnel detached and left in Italy, was reorganized. The 2nd Battalion, 401st Glider Infantry, 101st Airborne Division, was attached to the 325th Glider Infantry. This move gave the 325th a total of three battalions. Brigadier General Taylor left the Division to become Commanding General of the 101st Airborne Division. The Division was attached to VIII Corps.

Meanwhile, preparations were being made for the Division's participation in the invasion of the Normandy, France, peninsula by Allied forces in Operation NEPTUNE. Brigadier General James M. Gavin, the assistant Division Commander, had preceded the Division on its move from Italy and had been a member of the airborne planning staff established by the Allies in London. The Division Staff began preliminary planning work in January and started intensive planning in February when the Division Situation Room was opened at Camp Braunstone. The Division Commander, Major General Matthew B. Ridgway, was the senior American Airborne Representative on an inter-Allied airborne planning committee.

"Y-Day", the day by which all plans were to be completed, had been set by Supreme Headquarters, Allied Expeditionary Force, as 1 June. Regimental staffs were "briefed" on Y-60 and battalion staffs on Y-30 in accordance with instructions received from the First United States Army and VII Corps to which the Division would be attached upon landing.

## Section 2: Narrative

By 26 May 1944 all plans and preparations were completed for the Division to carry out the mission assigned it by the First United States Army. Field and administrative orders had been published and distributed. In a series of map maneuvers on a special 1/5,000 map regimental and battalion commanders had outlined their plans in order that all commanders might be briefed thoroughly on the prospective Division operations. Divisional seaborne echelons already had departed for the marshaling yards and were assembled in camps scattered along the Welsh and southern English coasts. The Division mission was to be as follows:

"Land by parachute and glider before and after dawn of D-Day west of ST. SAUVEUR LE VICOMTE: seize, clear and secure the general area ST. JACQUES DE NEHOU (136985) – BESNEVILLE (137928) (both inclusive) – ST. SAUVEUR LE VICOMTE (exclusive) – BLANDAMOUR (167982) (inclusive), and reorganize; seize and destroy the crossings of the PRAIRIES MARECAGEUSES north of LA SANGSURIERE (188898), at ST. SAVEUR DE PIERRE PONT (145890); destroy the crossings of the OLLONONDE River in the vicinity of ST. LO D'OURVILLE (090894) and block crossroads vicinity LE CHEMIN (102902); prevent enemy forces moving north between ST. LO D'OURVILLE and junction of DOUVE River with PRAIRIE MARECAGEUSES (228921); and protect the south flank of VII Corps north of the same line."

The mission, however, was changed by the First Army Commander on 26 May due to confirmed intelligence reports the enemy had strengthened his forces on the COTENTIN (CHERBOURG) Peninsula with the addition of the 91st Infantry Division in the general area of ST. SAVEUR LE VICOMTE. The revised mission of the 82nd Airborne Division was to be:

"Land by parachute and glider before and after dawn of D-Day astride the MERDERET River, seize, clear and secure the general area: CR (261938) – CR (265958) – CR (269975) – RJ (274982) – RJ (283992) – Bridge (308987) – NEUVILLE AU PLAIN (340985) – BANDIENVILLE (360987) within its zone; capture ST. MERE EGLISE (349965); seize and secure the crossings of the MERDERET River at (315957) and (321930), and a bridgehead covering them, with MLR along the general line: CR (261938) – CR (265953) – CR (269975) – RJ (274982) – RJ (283992); seize and destroy the crossings of the DOUVE River at BEUZEVILLE LA BASTILLE (309911) and ETIENVILLE (also known as PONT L'ABBE) (269927); protect the northwest flank of VIII Corps within the Division zone; and be prepared to advance west on Corps order to the line of the DOUVE north of its junction with the PRAIRIES MARECAGEUSES."

New orders and other administrative details made necessary by the new mission were worked out quickly and disseminated within four days. The change did not effect the basic plan for movement in three echelons which had been worked out as follows:

Force "A" – commanded by Brigadier General James M. Gavin, assistant Division Commander, to be committed by parachute before dawn of D-Day and to include:

|  | Planes |
|---|---|
| Det Hq & Hq Co, 82nd Abn Div | 4 |
| Pathfinders | 9 |
| Det Hq 82nd Div Arty | 2 |
| Det 82nd Abn Sig Co | 3 |
| Det 456 Prcht FA Bn (atchd 505 Prcht Inf) | |
| Air Support Party (atchd Hq 82nd Abn Div) | |
| 505 Prcht Inf | 117 |
| 507 Prcht Inf | 117 |
| 508 Prcht Inf | 117 |
| Co. B, 307 Abn. Engineer Battalion | 9 |
| Naval Shore Fire Control Party (atchd 505 Prcht Inf) | |
|  | ____ |
| TOTAL | 378 |

Force "B" – Commanded by Major General MATTHEW B. RIDGWAY, Division Commander, to be committed by glider before and after dawn of D-Day and to include:

|  | Gliders |
|---|---|
| Hq & Hq Co 82nd Abn Div (-) | 22 |
| Hq & Hq Btry, 82nd Abn Div Arty (-) | 11 |
| 82nd Abn Sig Co (-) | 13 |
| 325 Glider Inf. | 172 |
| 319 Glider FA Bn. | 40 |
| 320 Glider FA Bn. | 54 |
| Btrys A, B & C, 80 Abn AA Bn (AT)[57mm] | 57 |
| Co A, 307 Abn Engr Bn | 10 |
| 307 Abn Med Co (-) | 20 |
| 82nd Abn Rcn Plat (-) | 13 |
| Air Support Party | 4 |
| Command vehicles – Parachute Regts | 12 |
| TOTAL | 428 |

Force "C" – Commanded by Brigadier General GEORGE P. HOWELL, Commanding General of 2nd Airborne Infantry Brigade, to be committed by sea, to land between D plus 2 and D plus 7 and to include:

| | |
|---|---|
| 456 FA Bn (-) | 87 Armd FA Bn, atchd |
| 80 Abn AA Bn (-) | 899 TD Bn, atchd |
| 307 Abn Engr Bn (-) | Tr B, 4 Cav Sqdn, atchd |
| 782 Abn Ord Maint Co | Co C, 746 Tk Bn (M), atchd |
| 407 Abn QM Co | 3809 QM Trk Co, atchd |
| 82nd Abn MP Plat | 3810 QM Trk Co, atchd |
| Corps Med Dets | 1st Plat, 603 QM (GR) Co, atchd |
| Seaborne elements of units in Forces "A" and "B" | |

Under the plan Force "A in its entirety was to approach the CHERBOURG (COTENTIN) Peninsula from the west and to drop between 0100 and 0315 hours on the night of D-1/D-Day on three drop zones. The 505th Parachute Infantry Regiment and its attachments were to land east of the MERDERET River about 1,000 yards northwest of STE. MERE EGLISE (3397). The 507th Parachute Infantry Regiment was to land west of the MERDERET River about 1,000 yards north of AMFREVILLE (3098). The 508th Parachute Infantry Regiment and Force "A" Headquarters were to land west of the MERDERET River about 1,000 yards north of PICAUVILLE (2995).

Fifty-two gliders of Force "B" were to approach the CHERBOURG Peninsula from the west prior to H-Hour and land on the 505th drop zone. The remainder of Force "B" was to approach the peninsula from the east and was to land late on D-Day and early on D plus one on landing zones astride the STE. MERE EGLISE-BLOSVILLE Road (3694). In a last-minute change of plan General Ridgway parachuted with Force "A".

Aerial resupply missions were scheduled automatically for the morning of D plus one and on call thereafter if needed. The automatic mission was the only parachute mission ultimately flown but a small amount of equipment and supplies were received later by glider.

All airborne elements of the Division had closed and were sealed in special camps at the take-off fields by twenty-four hours before the scheduled take-off time. Parachute elements were located at seven airfields in the GRANTHAM-COTTESMORE-LANGAR area of the British Midlands, and glider elements were at seven airfields in the ALDERMASTON-RAMSBURY-MERRYFIELD area. (See Annex No.3A)

All men were briefed thoroughly on their missions, a recheck was made of all equipment and personnel, and planes and gliders were loaded with equipment. The Allied D-Day was postponed twenty-four hours because of weather conditions, and the first planes of Force "A" took off at 052315 June 1944.

The main flight was preceded by the three regimental pathfinder teams which dropped one-half hour prior to the first group. The pathfinders sustained many casualties and had difficulty in using lights, but they accomplished their mission and set up beacons to guide the incoming planes to the three designated drop zones.

The flight over the English Channel was in good formation and without incident, but between the west coast and the drop zones a heavy fog bank tended to break up the formation of the planes. Flak and some enemy night fighters activity caused some of the troop carrier planes to take up evasive action, and by the time the drop zones were reached many planes were scattered, and were flying at excessive speeds and at altitudes higher than those ideal for jumping.

The 505th Parachute Infantry Regiment landed generally in the vicinity of its drop zone. The 507th Parachute Infantry was scattered, one element dropping in the vicinity of MONTEBOURG, another south of CARENTAN and the remainder astride the MERDERET River east of the drop zone. The 508th Parachute Infantry Regiment was likewise scattered widely, the bulk of its parachutists dropping east of the Drop Zone and some personnel landing as far away as nine kilometers south of CHERBOURG.

The fifty-two gliders containing batteries of the 80th Airborne Antiaircraft Battalion and detachments and forward parties of artillery, signal and Division Headquarters groups followed the main body of paratroopers and began landing at 0404 hours. The gliders also encountered fog and flak. They too were scattered, and many of them were damaged upon crashing into the small fields and high hedgerows.

Enemy reaction to the landing of the 82nd Airborne Division in the NORMANDY area was prompt and severe, but from the time the first member landed until thirty-three days later, when the Division was finally relieved, every mission was accomplished and no ground gained was ever relinquished.

A day-by-day account of the Division's activities follows:

## D-DAY, 6 JUNE 1944 (See Annexes 5 and 6)

The first element of the main body of the Division jumped at 0151 hours, having been preceded 30 minutes by the Pathfinder teams. By 0312 hours all paratroopers had landed, and at 0404 hours the first of fifty-two gliders in the initial glider serial crash landed. Both parachutists and gliders were scattered.

Small groups and some units attacked to secure the Division zone. Groups of men and individuals who had been scattered in the landings rejoined their units throughout the day, and by nightfall approximately thirty per cent of the Division's forces were under control.

At 2100 hours one hundred gliders landed with artillery, engineers, and special troops. Seaborne elements set sail at 0645 from BRISTOL except for a task Force consisting of Company C, 746th Tank Battalion; the 1st Platoon, Troop B, 4th Cavalry Squadron; and elements of Company F, 3rd Battalion (originally 2nd Battalion, 401st Glider

Infantry), 325th Glider Infantry. This task Force landed on Utah Red Beach at 1400 hours and preceded inland with the mission of contacting the Division near STE. MERE EGLISE.

At the close of the day, the Division was in the midst of severe fighting. It had captured STE. MERE EGLISE and held a general line along the MERDERET River from LA FIERE (319963) south to include the eastern end of the causeway over the MERDERET River at 321930.

### Headquarters & Headquarters Company, 82nd Airborne Division

Parachute elements, part of Force "A", dropped at 0214 hours near the west bank of the MERDERET River, and glider elements, leading echelon of Force "B", landed at 0205 hours. The Force "A" Command Post was set up initially at 305965, west of the MERDERET River, but at 0730 the group waded across the River to the east bank and assembled at LA FIERE (319963). A new Force "A" Command Post was established at a railroad crossing at 326944.

The Division Commander, who jumped with the 505th Parachute Infantry, established his Command Post in a hedgerow west of STE. MERE EGLISE at 332965. Elements of Headquarters and of the Defense Platoon moved south to secure the bridge west of CHEF DU PONT (321930) where it encountered severe enemy fire. This group returned to the Command Post at 1700, but part of the Defense Platoon moved to a new Force "A" Command Post at a railroad pass at 323960.

The Division Headquarters initial glider serial, which landed in the dark at approximately 0415 hours, was scattered, and the G-2 and G-3 did not reach the command post until late afternoon. The Chief of Staff was injured in a glider crash and later evacuated. The G-1 did not reach the command post for two days.

### 505th Parachute Infantry Regiment

The first element, the 2nd Battalion, dropped at 0151 hours and the entire regiment landed by 0202 hours. Most of the troops landed on or near the drop zone, but a few were widely dispersed over the countryside. Assembly was rapid, and the battalion moved off toward their objectives. The 3rd Battalion entered STE. MERE EGLISE at 0400 hours, and the town was securely held and out posted within an hour. The American Flag was raised over STE. MERE EGLISE, the first French town to be liberated by the Allies. After assembling the 2nd Battalion started to move out to take NEUVILLE AU PLAIN, but orders were received from the regiment to stand by. At 0600 hours the 2nd Battalion moved into position north of STE. MERE EGLISE and assisted the 3rd Battalion in holding the town. The 1st Battalion moved toward its objective, the bridge over the MERDERET River (314956) at LA FIERE at 0630 hours and by 0830 held the eastern end of this bridge against heavy enemy fire from the western approaches.

### 507th Parachute Infantry Regiment

The first element, the 1st Battalion, jumped at 0232 hours, and by 0312 hours the entire regiment was on the ground generally east of the MERDERET River and was fairly dispersed. Small groups assembled to form small task forces until such time as the regiment could assemble completely. One such force on the west bank of the MERDERET River attacked AMFREVILLE but was forced back by overwhelming superiority in enemy strength to FLAUX (303955). A patrol was sent to the western end of LA FIERE Bridge and contact was made with elements of the 505th Parachute Infantry on the eastern end at 1430 hours. The enemy recaptured FLAUX and drove this patrol from the western end of the LA FIERE Bridge. Another Force of the regiment joined with Force "A" Headquarters and at 1130 attacked to secure the CHEF DU PONT Bridge (321930), meeting extremely severe resistance. The eastern end of the bridge was finally secured by nightfall. Leaving one company to hold the bridge, the remainder of this second Force moved to an assembly area at 1715 hours in the vicinity of the railroad overpass at 323960. Still another group, led by the regimental commander, landed on or near the scheduled drop zone but had no contact with other elements of the Division during the day.

### 508th Parachute Infantry Regiment

The 3rd Battalion jumped at 0208 hours and the entire regiment was on the ground by 0220 hours. Four separate groups were assembled. One group was in the vicinity of LA FIERE, fought along the railway and attacked the LA FIERE Bridge. This group was later relieved by the 1st Battalion, 505th Parachute Infantry and moved to an assembly area in the vicinity of the railroad overpass (323960) to organize a defensive position. Two other groups joined forces west of the MERDERET River in the vicinity of PICAUVILLE after taking part in heavy fighting around

GUETTEVILLE (300948) and north of PICAUVILLE. An officer of this group shot and killed the commanding general of the German 91st Division [Lt. Malcolm D. Brannen, HQ Co., 3/508th, shot MG Wilhelm Falley]. The combined group then seized the high ground west of the MERDERET River south of GUETTEVILLE at 310940 during the night of June 6-7. A fourth group dropped in the vicinity of STE. MERE EGLISE, fought with the 507th Parachute Infantry to take the CHEF DU PONT Bridge (321930) and later organized a defensive position covering this bridge.

### 325th Glider Infantry Regiment

Company F, 3rd Battalion, supporting Company C, 746th Tank Battalion, landed on Utah Red BEACH at 1400, de-waterproofed vehicles and moved inland at 1600 to make contact with the Division. Heavy artillery, mortar and small arms fire held up this task Force at crossroads 363933. Two tanks were knocked out. The remainder of the regiment prepared to take off from airports in England.

### 82nd Airborne Division Artillery

Parachute elements jumped at 0210 hours, joined a group from the 508th Parachute Infantry and assisted in the attack on the LA FIERE Bridge. At 1330 hours this element joined the glider element at the Division CP at 332965. Glider elements landed at 0500 hours and moved directly to the Division CP. At 2305 hours Headquarters and Headquarters Battery of Division Artillery, the 319th Glider Field Artillery Battalion and the 320th Glider Field Artillery Battalion glided into NORMANDY and encountered severe enemy small arms and mortar fire. Reorganization commenced immediately but was handicapped by intense enemy fire. The section of the 456th Parachute Field Artillery Battalion attached to 505th Parachute Infantry jumped with the 3rd Battalion, but was able to assemble only one of the two 75mm howitzers which had been dropped.

### 80th Airborne Antiaircraft Battalion (AT)

Batteries A and B landed by glider at 0405 hours. Six 57mm antitank guns had been recovered and were in position by 1730 hours. Battery C glided into the area at 2100 hours and began assembly and reorganization. The remainder of the Battalion sailed from BRISTOL, ENGLAND, at 0645 hours.

### 307th Airborne Engineer Battalion

Company B (less one platoon attached to the 505th Parachute Infantry) jumped with the 508th Parachute Infantry at 0210 hours. Some Engineer personnel took up defensive positions at LA FIERE in support of one group of the 508th, and other personnel joined the 508th group west of the MERDERET River. One "stick", which included the Battalion Commander, was dropped over ST. SAUVEUR LE VICOMTE, and only a few escaped. Part of Headquarters and Company A landed by glider at 2300 hours and started to assemble under heavy enemy artillery and small arms fire. The remainder of the battalion prepared to take off from airports to ENGLAND.

### 307th Airborne Medical Company

Elements of the company landed by glider about 2100 and immediately began assembly, recovering by use of life rafts much equipment from gliders that had landed in shallow water near the banks of the MERDERET River. A clearing station was set up at a crossroad north of BLOSVILLE.

### 82nd Airborne Signal Company

Parachute and glider elements of the company which landed prior to H-Hour were scattered and assembled with difficulty. Much equipment was lost. Only one of the three SCR 193 radios landed during D-Day was operative, and it was not until the night of June 6-7 that radio contact was established with the 4th Infantry Division and with the Division base in ENGLAND.

## D Plus 1, 7 June 1944

The Division continued to assemble, reorganize, and secure its area against extremely severe enemy resistance which included armor. Enemy troops, identified as the 91st Infantry Division, were held along the MERDERET River to the west and were driven back to the north and northwest. Contact was established with the 4th Infantry Division during the day, and the VII Corps Commander visited the Division Command Post late in the day. The 325th Glider Infantry arrived by glider during the morning. Additional personnel which had been scattered in the original landings continued to report back to their units.

During the afternoon garbled radio messages signed "CO 507" were received at the Division Command Post, and it was finally determined that they originated with the Regimental Commander who was isolated with a group of about 300 men west of AMFREVILLE.

### 325th Glider Infantry Regiment

The first glider elements began landing at 0700 hours about 2,500 yards southeast of STE. MERE EGLISE. There were many crash landings, and casualties totaled approximately 7.5 per cent. Assembly was rapid, however, and by 1015 hours all battalions were reported. The 3rd Battalion moved out toward CARQUEBUT at 1415 hours and reached LE PORT (328918) without encountering opposition. The remainder of the regiment proceeded to move into an assembly area northeast of CHEF DU PONT. At 1600 hours the 2nd Battalion was ordered to move into an assembly area east of LA FIERE in the vicinity of 325962 and later was attached to the 505th Parachute Infantry at 2100 hours. The 1st and 3rd Battalions were ordered to move into and to outpost the regimental assembly area. Company F, 3rd Battalion in support of Company C, 746th Tank Battalion, and the 1st Platoon, Troop B, 4th Cavalry Reconnaissance Squadron, assisted the 8th Infantry in its attack towards STE. MERE EGLISE from the west at 0630 hours and made contact with gliderborne elements of the 325th by 0900. The 325th's regimental strength at the close of the day was approximately 85 per cent.

### 505th Parachute Infantry Regiment

The 2nd and 3rd Battalions continued to hold STE. MERE EGLISE against severe attacks from the north and south. The 2nd Battalion patrols contacted elements of the 8th Infantry Regiment of the 4th Infantry Division at STE. MARTINE (384973) at 1000 hours and attacked north to clear the outskirts of STE. MERE EGLISE. The 1st Battalion withstood several counterattacks and pushed the enemy back to the eastern bank of the MERDERET River in the vicinity of the LA FIERE Bridge. They were supported late in the day by one platoon of tanks from Company C, 746th Tank Battalion. At the close of the period the 2nd and 3rd Battalions prepared to attack north toward NEUVILLE AU PLAIN in conjunction with the 4th Infantry Division's drive on the right. The 2nd Battalion, 325th Glider Infantry, was attached at 2100 to assist in this attack.

### 507th Parachute Infantry Regiment

The regiment moved into an area west of STE. MERE EGLISE in the vicinity of 335960, rested and reorganized. At 1600 hours the regiment moved into positions south of the LA FIERE-STE. MERE EGLISE Road west of the railroad to assist the 1st Battalion, 505th Parachute Infantry, against a threatened counterattack at the LA FIERE Bridge. At 1900 hours the 507th, at approximately 25 per cent strength, successfully pushed the enemy back to the west bank of the MERDERET River in its sector.

### 508th Parachute Infantry Regiment

One group near the railroad overpass (323960) moved into positions in the vicinity of the road junction 334972 to protect the Division's north flank against enemy penetration. This group was in position by 0630 hours, but it later moved to join another group of the regiment in position defending the CHEF DU PONT Bridge. It mopped up numerous enemy strong points surrounding CHEF DU PONT and established patrol contact with elements of the regiment west of the MERDERET River on the high ground in the vicinity of 310940. The group on the high ground, now recognized as the 2nd Battalion, had completed organization of its position by 1300 hours, wiping out a number of enemy mortar and artillery positions. A road block was set up on the western approaches to the CHEF DU PONT Bridge and contact was established with forces in CHEF DU PONT. Regimental strength at the close of the day was approximately 25 per cent.

### 82nd Airborne Division Artillery

Various groups of the artillery were involved in individual skirmishes with the enemy as they found their way back to their parent units. The 319th Glider Field Artillery Battalion assembled east of STE. MERE EGLISE in the vicinity of 371974 with six 75mm pack howitzers. The 320th Glider Field Artillery Battalion was placed in direct support of the

505th Parachute Infantry. After salvaging two 105mm M3 howitzers and taking over the 75mm pack howitzer of the 456th Parachute Field Artillery Battalion detachment with the 505th, the 320th went into position 400 yards west of STE. MERE EGLISE. The first round was fired at 0911 hours. The seaborne echelon of the 456th Parachute Field Artillery Battalion arrived off Utah Beach but did not land.

### 80th Airborne Antiaircraft Battalion

Batteries A, B, and C continued to reorganize and by 1800 hours six 57mm antitank guns of Battery C and three guns each from Batteries A and B were in position covering the two bridges over the MERDERET River. The remainder of the Battalion remained on board ships preparing to disembark on Utah Beach.

### 307th Airborne Engineer Battalion

The remainder of Company A landed by glider at 0700 hours and moved to join the 325th Infantry in the vicinity of CHEF DU PONT at 0930 hours. Bridges and culverts south of LE PORT (328918) and near LIESVILLE (331905) were blown.

### Aerial Resupply

An aerial resupply mission, including 148 of the 248 C-47 planes which had taken off, arrived over the area at 0620. They dropped 155.5 tons of ordnance, quartermaster and medical supplies, 74% of the originally scheduled load. The drop pattern was poor and bundles were scattered, many of them falling into enemy hands or being covered by enemy fire. Limited recovery was effected initially.

### D PLUS 2, 8 JUNE 1944

The Division continued to attack along its north flank, maintained its positions along the MERDERET River, and cleared the southern flank area to establish contact with the 101st Airborne Division.

During the night of 7-8 June a messenger from the isolated group east of AMFREVILLE crossed the MERDERET River on a sunken bridge northwest of LA FIERE and reported to the Division Command Post. It was now evident that there were three isolated groups west of the MERDERET River, as follows:

a. A strong force of 2nd Battalion, 508th Parachute Infantry, on high ground in the vicinity of 310949 south of GEUTTEVILLE (300948).

b. The 2nd Battalion, 507th Parachute Infantry, located north of FLAUX in the vicinity of 305968.

c. A force of approximately 425 men, most of them from the 507th Parachute Infantry, located west of AMFREVILLE.

As the above situation became clear, the Division Commander developed a plan to relieve the isolated groups west of the MERDERET and also establish a clear-cut bridgehead over the river. The 1st Battalion, 325th Glider Infantry, was to cross the MERDERET River on the sunken bridge northwest of LA FIERE, establish contact with the 2nd Battalion, 507th Parachute Infantry, and swing south to capture the western approaches to the LA FIERE Bridge. The 507th Force west of AMFREVILLE was to attack to the east to contact the 1st Battalion 325th, and 2nd Battalion, 507th. The 2nd Battalion, 508th Parachute Infantry, was to remain in place.

### 325th Glider Infantry Regiment

At 2330 the 1st Battalion crossed the MERDERET River northwest of LA FIERE by means of a sunken road and a railroad embankment against little enemy opposition to establish a bridgehead and contact the isolated forces of the 507th Parachute Infantry. At the close of the period the 1st Battalion had crossed the river successfully and was marching towards the western approaches to the LA FIERE Bridge.

### 505th Parachute Infantry Regiment

The 1st Battalion initially remained in position north of LA FIERE assisting the 507th Parachute Infantry in guarding the MERDERET River crossing at that point. The 2nd and 3rd Battalions attacked abreast to the north and seized NEUVILLE AU PLAIN by 0430 hours against slight opposition. Supported by the 2nd Platoon, Company C, 746th Tank Battalion, these two battalions continued their attack to the north and seized GRAINVILLE by 2300 hours. The 1st Battalion relieved the 3rd Battalion, the 3rd then taking up a reverse position southwest of GRAINVILLE in the vicinity of 308993. Attached to the 505th, the 2nd Battalion, 325th Glider Infantry, assumed defensive positions west of the town and prepared to attack to the north toward FRESVILLE on the Division's north flank at the close of the period.

**507th Parachute Infantry Regiment**
One Force of 175 men isolated since D-Day on the west bank of the MERDERET River north of FLAUX in the vicinity of 305968 was still intact but suffered from heavy enemy artillery, mortar, and small arms fire. It attempted unsuccessfully to cross the River to the east to rejoin the regiment. Part of the 507th Force west of AMFREVILLE succeeded in joining the group east of the town, but another portion of the group, including the regimental commander, was ambushed and taken prisoner. The portion of the 507th east of the MERDERET continued to hold a line between 322945 and 313978, maintaining contact with adjacent regiments.

**508th Parachute Infantry Regiment**
Attacking with two reinforced companies, the regiment cleared the area on the Division's south flank to include the towns of LE PORT, CARQUEBUT, and ETURVILLE by 1920 hours and established contact with the 101st Airborne Division at Road Junction 363930 north of BLOSVILLE. Resistance was severe, but 160 prisoners were taken. The 2nd Battalion on the west bank of the MERDERET River repulsed several sharp enemy tank counterattacks directed at the western causeway to the CHEF DU PONT Bridge. Contact with the regiment on the east bank could not be maintained because of excessive enemy activity and observation.

**82nd Airborne Division Artillery**
The 319th Glider Field Artillery Battalion moved seven 75mm howitzers into position east of CHEF DU PONT in support of the 507th and 508th Parachute Infantry Regiments. The 320th Glider Field Artillery Battalion moved eight 105mm M3 howitzers into position west of STE. MERE EGLISE in direct support of the 505th Parachute and 325th Glider Infantry Regiments. The 87th Field Artillery Battalion was relieved of attachment to the Division before it was in position to fire a shot in support of our operations.

**Seaborne Echelon**
The seaborne echelon, Force "C", began landing at 1500 hours and moved into a bivouac area preparatory to joining the rest of the Division. Troops included the 456th Parachute Field Artillery Battalion, Batteries D, E and F of the 80th Airborne Antiaircraft Battalion, Headquarters Company of the 307th Airborne Engineer Battalion, some attached troops and seaborne elements of units that had arrived by parachute and glider.

**D PLUS 3 – 9 JUNE 1944**
The Division gained a clear-cut bridgehead over the MERDERET River, relieved two of the three isolated groups and some members of the third, and continued its attack to the northwest in the LE HAM sector.

**325th Glider Infantry Regiment**
The 1st Battalion continued to press forward to reach the western approaches of the LA FIERE Bridge but at 0400 hours was pinned down by heavy fire of all types in the vicinity of CAUQUIGNY (309959). Following a 15-minute artillery preparation, the 3rd Battalion attacked across the LA FIERE Bridge at 1030 hours with two companies of the 507th Parachute Infantry and supported by Company C, 746th Tank Battalion. A bridgehead was established despite heavy losses. CAUQUIGNY was secured by 1530 hours and the 3rd Battalion was linked up with the 1st Battalion, 325th, on the left and with the 2nd Battalion, 507th on the right. Only a small portion of the group west of AMFREVILLE succeeded in reaching our lines. An enemy counterattack lasting from 1900 to 2100 was repulsed successively by the 3rd Battalion and the 507th Parachute Infantry.

**505th Parachute Infantry Regiment**
GRAINVILLE and the bridge over the MERDERET River at the town were seized by 0100. The regiment attacked again at 0530 with the 2nd Battalion on the left, 2nd Battalion, 325th Glider Infantry, attached, on the right, and 1st Battalion following. The regiment reached a line 300 yards south of the canal, 300008 to 302007, by 1200. The 2nd Battalion then moved through positions of 2nd Battalion, 325th and continued the attack with the 1st Battalion.

**507th Parachute Infantry Regiment**

Two companies attacked across the LA FIERE Bridge with the 325th Glider Infantry at 1030 to establish a firm bridgehead in a fierce and savage attack. These two companies captured LE MOTEY (299962) despite heavy fire of all types. Contact was made with the 2nd Battalion, 507, and the two companies moved into a reserve position 500 yards east of LE MOTEY. The regiment again assisted the 325th, at 2000 hours, in repelling a strong enemy counterattack, the repulse of which assured a firm hold on the MERDERET Bridgehead.

**508th Parachute Infantry Regiment**

The 3rd Battalion crossed over LA FIERE Bridgehead at 1200 hours and attacked south to clear the area between GUETTEVILLE (300948) and the high ground at 310940. Contact was established with the 2nd Battalion, and the MERDERET Bridgehead was thus extended to include both the causeways at LA FIERE and southwest of CHEF DU PONT. A sharp enemy counterattack from the direction of AMFREVILLE was repulsed successfully between 1930 and 2100 hours. The remainder of the regiment maintained position holding the CHEF DU PONT Bridge. It received spasmodic artillery fire during the evening.

**82nd Airborne Division Artillery**

The 456th Parachute Field Artillery Battalion and seaborne elements of the remainder of Division Artillery units arrived. Grouping was made of the 456th Parachute and 320th Glider Field Artillery Battalions in direct support of the 325th Glider and 505th Parachute Infantry Regiments. The 456th went into positions west of NEUVILLE AU PLAIN with seven 75mm howitzers and fired its first rounds at 2130 hours. The 90th Division Artillery and one battalion of the 4th Division Artillery were in general support.

**307th Airborne Engineer Battalion**

The 1st Platoon, Company A, crossed the MERDERET River with 1st Battalion, 325th Glider Infantry north of LA FIERE. The remainder of Company A supported the attack across LA FIERE Bridge. The remainder of the Battalion salvaged equipment and resupply bundles, set up water points and assembled one mile west of STE. MERE EGLISE.

**Seaborne Echelon**

Force "C", under command of Brigadier General George P. Howell, closed into the STE. MERE EGLISE area at 1330.

**Resupply**

Two CG-4A gliders landed near STE. MERE EGLISE carrying greatly needed signal equipment. This constituted the second air resupply mission flown.

**D PLUS 4 – 10 JUNE 1944**

The Division was relieved within the bridgehead across the MERDERET River by the 90th Infantry Division, which passed through the 82nd and continued the attack to the west. Despite the scattered parachute drops and isolation of some Battalions, the Division within four days secured the NEUVILLE AU PLAIN-STE. MERE EGLISE-CHEF DU PONT area and established a firm bridgehead across the MERDERET River from its junction with the DOUVE River to and including the railway bridge 1,500 yards north of LA FIERE. Resistance had been stubborn and severe. Although it suffered heavy losses in the battle of the MERDERET, the Division virtually destroyed the German 91st Infantry Division and prevented it from contacting the Beach assault forces of the First U.S. Army.

Although relieved in the MERDERET Bridgehead, Division troops continued the attack in the north.

**325th Glider Infantry Regiment**

The 357th Infantry, 90th Division, passed through the 325th front line at 0540 hours. The 1st and 3rd Battalions remained in position throughout the day and night as a reserve.

**505th Parachute Infantry Regiment**

Supported by artillery, the 1st and 2nd Battalions jumped off across the canal at 1400 hours to seize LE HAM (280013) and MONTEBURG STATION (289024). The 1st Battalion by-passed LE HAM and seized the station by 1800 hours in the face of stiff resistance throughout the advance. Elements of the 2nd Battalion were forced to withdraw from the outskirts of LE HAM at 2310 hours. Attempts to retake the town during the night were contested savagely. The 3rd Battalion remained in reserve, and the 2nd Battalion, 325th Glider Infantry, attached, protected the regiment's southwestern flank.

**507th Parachute Infantry Regiment**

The 357th Infantry, 90th Division, passed through the 507th lines at 0540 hours. The regiment assembled east of the MERDERET River in the vicinity of LA FIERE and reorganized and rested.

**508th Parachute Infantry Regiment**

The 358th Infantry, 90th Division, passed through the 508th lines at 0510 hours. The regiment, less one company still at LE PORT, assembled on high ground west of the MERDERET River in the vicinity of 310940 and reorganized.

**82nd Airborne Division Artillery**

The 320th Glider and 456th Parachute Field Artillery Battalions, reinforced by the 915th Field Artillery Battalion, 90th Division, continued to fire harassing and interdiction missions in support of the 505th Parachute Infantry.

**Resupply**

Two CG-4A gliders landed at STE. MERE EGLISE carrying signal equipment.

**D PLUS 5 and D PLUS 6 – 11-12 JUNE 1944**

The Division secured the area north of STE. MERE EGLISE after fierce fighting on the part of the 505th Parachute Infantry, with 2nd Battalion, 325th Glider Infantry attached, seized LE HAM and drove the enemy north and northwest. By this action the 82nd Airborne Division delayed considerably the German 243rd Infantry Division from contacting the Beach assault forces of the First U.S. Army.

**325th Glider Infantry Regiment**

After being passed through by the 359th Infantry, 90th Infantry Division, the regiment closed in an assembly area in the vicinity of GUETTEVILLE (303948), and rested and reorganized. The 2nd Battalion remained attached to the 505th Parachute Infantry.

**505th Parachute Infantry Regiment**

The 2nd Battalion with the 2nd Battalion, 325th Glider Infantry, attached, on the left, attacked at 111130 hours to capture LE HAM. Overcoming severe opposition in wet and difficult terrain, the 2nd Battalion, 325th, seized LE HAM at 2025 hours. By 2300 hours positions were consolidated along the entire MERDERET River up to and including the MONTEBURG railroad station at 289024. Contact with the 8th Infantry, 4th Infantry Division, was made by the 1st Battalion at MONTEBURG station. The bridge over the MERDERET River at 277015 was blown by our troops at 2145. The regiment remained in position, patrolling west across the river until relieved by the 357th Infantry, 90th Infantry Division, during the night of 12-13 June.

**507th Parachute Infantry Regiment**

The regiment continued to rest and reorganize in the vicinity of LA FIERE.

**508th Parachute Infantry Regiment**

The regiment continued to rest and reorganize in the vicinity of the high ground west of the MERDERET River at 310940. Contact was maintained with the 101st Airborne Division on the left. Preparations were completed on 12 June for an attack to establish a bridgehead over the DOUVE River at BEUZEVILLE LA BASTILLE on the night of 12-13 June.

**82nd Airborne Division Artillery**

The 456th Parachute Field Artillery Battalion remained in direct support of the 505th Parachute Infantry. The 320th Glider Field Artillery Battalion prepared to reinforce fires of the 319th Glider Field Artillery Battalion and moved south of PICAUVILLE. The 319th, in direct support of the 508th Parachute Infantry, moved west across the DOUVE River into positions north of BEUZEVILLE LA BASTILLE. The 915th Field Artillery Battalion, attached from 90th Infantry Division, was relieved at 110600. The 188th Field artillery Battalion (105mm howitzer) was attached at 121800 and moved into positions to reinforce the fires of the 319th.

### 307th Airborne Engineer Battalion
The Battalion continued to salvage resupply bundles and operate water points in the area. Extensive surveys of the DOUVE River were conducted during this period, and bridging material, assault boats and other river crossing equipment were obtained.

### Attached Units
Company C, 746th Tank Battalion, was relieved from attachment to the Division at 110800 June.

### D PLUS 7 – 13 JUNE 1944
The Division, using the 508th Parachute Infantry, extended its right flank by establishing a bridgehead across the DOUVE River at BEUZEVILLE LA BASTILLE and contacted the 101st Airborne Division again at BAUPTE. Other elements of the Division continued to reorganize and regroup preparatory to passing through the 90th Infantry Division and attacking to the west in conjunction with the 9th Infantry Division. The Division Command Post moved to a point near PICAUVILLE at coordinates 294928.

### 325th Glider Infantry Regiment
The 2nd Battalion rejoined the regiment at 1000 hours. The regiment closed in a new assembly area south of PICAUVILLE at 1630 hours. Preparations were made to attack to the west the following day.

### 505th Parachute Infantry Regiment
The 2nd Battalion, 325th Infantry, was relieved from attachment. The regiment moved from LE HAM area to an assembly area east of PICAUVILLE, rested and reorganized.

### 507th Parachute Infantry Regiment
The regiment moved from the LA FIERE area to an assembly area north of PICAUVILLE. Preparations were made to attack to the west the following day.

### 508th Parachute Infantry Regiment
A combat team composed of the regiment, the 319th Glider Field Artillery Battalion, Battery A, 80th Airborne Antiaircraft Battalion, a detachment from the 307th Airborne Engineer Battalion and one platoon of Troop B, 4th Cavalry Reconnaissance Squadron, attacked south across the DOUVE River. Company F crossed the DOUVE by assault boats at 0001 hours and seized BEUZEVILLE LA BASTILLE. The remainder of the troops crossed the river on a footbridge, constructed by engineers, beginning at 0400 hours. The 1st Battalion cleared CRETTEVILLE by 0745 hours, destroyed considerable enemy equipment, including twelve light tanks, and occupied defensive positions at ODIGNY. The 2nd Battalion met determined resistance outside of BAUPTE but occupied the town by 1800 and established contact with the 101st Airborne Division to the south. The 3rd Battalion secured the area between PONT AUNY and HOTOT. During the entire action fourteen light tanks were knocked out and sizeable quantities of enemy equipment captured or destroyed.

### 82nd Airborne Division Artillery
The 319th and 320th Glider and 188th Field Artillery Battalion fired in support of the 508th Parachute Infantry's crossing of the DOUVE River at BEUZEVILLE LA BASTILLE. These three battalions expended 1,880 rounds in fifty minutes, and their fires were reinforced as well by the 90th Division Artillery. The 319th Glider Field Artillery Battalion displaced south of the DOUVE River at 1800 hours. The 456th Parachute Field Artillery Battalion moved from the LE HAM sector into positions north of PICAUVILLE at 1800 hours.

**80th Airborne Antiaircraft Battalion**

Battery A knocked out five enemy light tanks in conjunction with the 1st Battalion, 508th Parachute Infantry's attack south of the DOUVE River.

**307th Airborne Engineer Battalion**

Company A operated assault boats across the DOUVE River at BEUZEVILLE LA BASTILLE beginning at 0001 hours in support of the 508th Parachute Infantry. A footbridge was constructed first, and, with the assistance of VII Corps Engineers, a Bailey bridge was completed by 0830 hours. The 3rd Platoon of Company B was attached to the 508th Parachute Infantry and prepared the bridge south of BAUPTE for demolition.

**Attached Troops**

Company A, 746th Tank Battalion, was attached to the Division at 1700 hours.

**Resupply**

Eleven gliders carrying ordnance and signal equipment landed at STE. MERE EGLISE.

**D PLUS 8 – 14 JUNE 1944**

The Division continued to mop up in the BAUPTE area and also passed through the 90th Division to attack west toward ST. SAVEUR LE VICOMTE.

The attack, with the 82nd Airborne Division on the left and the 9th Infantry Division on the right, originally was scheduled to begin shortly after dawn but was delayed until 1000 to permit units being relieved additional opportunity to seize the contemplated line of departure. The attack began at 1000 even though the line of departure had not been seized. The fighting was bitter, hedgerow-to hedgerow onslaught, but considerable progress was made.

**325th Glider Infantry Regiment**

The regiment attacked at 1000 in column of battalions with the 3rd Battalion leading. The 507th Parachute Infantry was to the regiment's right. As the scheduled line of departure had not been seized, the 325th attacked to the right of the 358th Infantry, 90th Division, instead of through it, but later swung in front of that regiment. The main highway due west of ETIENVILLE was strongly defended by the enemy, but he was driven off the road by 1830 hours after exceptionally hard fighting and repeated thrusts by both the 3rd and 1st Battalions supported by one platoon of Company A, 746th Tank Battalion. The 1st Battalion continued to attack and advanced west 400 yards. The regiment consolidated its positions at 2100 hours, established firm contact with the 507th Infantry on the right and prepared to continue the attack to the west.

**505th Parachute Infantry Regiment**

The regiment remained in Division reserve. Company I moved to secure the bridge south of ETIENVILLE (PONT L'ABBE), holding positions at the north end of the bridge. Company H was attached to the 325th Glider Infantry Regiment at 1400 hours to act as Infantry escort for a platoon of Company A, 746th Tank Battalion through and beyond ETIENVILLE, but the company reverted to regimental control at 1940 hours. The regiment was ordered at 2100 hours to move into position 1,000 yards north of ETIENVILLE. Company I remained at the ETIENVILLE Bridge and established patrol contact with the 508th Parachute Infantry in the BEUZEVILLE LA BASTILLE Bridgehead.

**507th Parachute Infantry Regiment**

Attacking in column of battalions with the 3rd Battalion leading, the regiment crossed the creek between RETOUF and ETIENVILLE at 1000 hours, passing through the 90th Division. The 325th Glider Infantry was on the left and the 60th Infantry, 9th Division was on the right. Encountering heavy pounding of enemy artillery, the 3rd Battalion turned north to block RENOUF and protect the north flank of the Division while the 9th Division spent the better part of the day seizing the town. Enemy resistance was severe. Counter-attacks in the evening were repulsed with the assistance of one platoon of tanks from Company A, 746th Tank Battalion. The 2nd and 1st Battalions in that order, followed the 3rd Battalion and continued the attack to the west, reaching the outskirts of LA BONNEVILLE by 2200 hours. After consolidating positions and reorganizing, all Battalions prepared to continue the attack the next day.

## 508th Parachute Infantry Regiment

The 1st Battalion moved from the vicinity of COIGNY to assist the 2nd Battalion clear BAUPTE at 0130 hours. The 3rd Battalion repelled a sharp counterattack at 0700 hours in the vicinity of HOTOT. The enemy attempted to break through the 3rd Battalion positions again at 1005 hours, but the attack failed after the enemy sustained heavy casualties. The highway and railroad bridges southwest of HOTOT were blown by attached elements of the 307th Airborne Engineer Battalion moved from BAUPTE to the northwest at 1030 and attacked PONT AUNY to dislodge an enemy concentration building up in that area. After a sharp fire fight the 1st Battalion broke contact at 1600 hours and withdrew toward BAUPTE, assembling in a reserve position in the vicinity of FRACQUETOT. The 2nd Battalion left Company D at BAUPTE and moved at 2300 hours to a position in the vicinity of COIGNY.

## 82nd Airborne Division Artillery

The 319th Glider Field Artillery Battalion remained in direct support of the 508th Parachute Infantry and fired 600 rounds against enemy buildups in the HOTOT area. The 320th Glider and 456th Parachute Field Artillery Battalions were placed in direct support of the attacking 325th Glider and 507th Parachute Infantry Regiments, respectively. The 188th Field Artillery Battalion was in direct support. More than 2,200 rounds were fired in support of the attack toward the west. The 87th Armored Field Artillery Battalion was attached to the Division at 0900 hours and moved into position north of ETIENVILLE.

## 80th Airborne Antiaircraft Battalion

Batteries A and B remained attached to the 508th Parachute Infantry Regiment. Battery C was attached to the 507th Parachute Infantry. The remainder of the Battalion remained in reserve.

## 307th Airborne Engineer Battalion

One platoon of Company B, was attached to the 508th Parachute Infantry and blew the culvert and the railroad bridge southwest of HOTOT at 1800 hours. The bridge at CRETTEVILLE was blown by 508th Parachute Infantry. The Platoon reverted to Company control at 2300 hours. Company A continued to provide security for bridges at BEUZEVILLE LA BASTILLE and performed reconnaissance work along the 508th Parachute and 325th Glider Infantry fronts.

## Attached Troops

Company A, 746th Tank Battalion, supported the Division's attack to the west, with one platoon each attached to the 325th glider and 507th Parachute Infantry Regiments. Tanks were withdrawn at nightfall into an assembly area north of PICAUVILLE.

## Resupply

Four 75mm pack howitzers were flown by C-47 to STE. MERE EGLISE.

## D PLUS 9 – 15 JUNE 1944

The Division continued the hedgerow-to-hedgerow attack, but shortly after nightfall it became apparent that the crust of the enemy resistance west of the DOUVE River had been broken. The 505th Parachute Infantry relieved the 507th Parachute Infantry after a strong enemy counterattack in the flank, supported by tanks, halted the 507th advance. The Division Command Post moved to coordinates 255934 west of ETIENVILLE.

## 325th Glider Infantry Regiment

In the order 1st, 2nd and 3rd Battalions, the regiment attacked at 0500 hours and reached the creek southwest of LA BONNEVILLE by 0810 hours, meeting only moderate resistance. Tanks from Company A, 746th Tank Battalion, supported the attack.

## 505th Parachute Infantry Regiment

The regiment attacked to the west, passing through the 507th Parachute Infantry in the latter's zone at 1500. Battery C, 80th Airborne Antiaircraft Battalion and one Platoon of Company A, 746th Tank Battalion, were attached. Moderately strong enemy opposition was encountered and by nightfall the regiment had advanced to the creek line north of

CROSVILLE (228948). Company I, guarding the bridge at ETIENVILLE, was relieved by the 507th Parachute Infantry and reverted to regimental control.

### 507th Parachute Infantry Regiment

The regiment attacked at 0500 hours and advanced 600 yards, meeting little opposition up to 0630 hours. One Platoon of Company A, 746th Tank Battalion, moved up to forward positions at 0615 to support the regiment. A heavy counterattack supported by tanks, launched by the enemy at 0930 hours from the right flank, halted the advance of the regiment. However, the 507th, recovering from the heavy artillery and mortar fire, ejected the enemy Force which had penetrated its lines and reestablished its front by 1500 hours, at which time the 505th Parachute Infantry passed through the 507th. The regiment then assembled, moved to ETIENVILLE, and later crossed the DOUVE River into the CRETTEVILLE-BAUPTE area preparatory to relieving the 508th Parachute Infantry Regiment. Company B relieved Company I, 505th Parachute Infantry, at the bridge at ETIENVILLE.

### 508th Parachute Infantry Regiment

The regiment continued active defense of the CRETTEVILLE-BAUPTE sector, repulsing enemy attempts to break through in vicinity of HOTOT and BAUPTE. The 2nd Battalion relieved the 3rd Battalion near PONT AUNY. The 3rd Battalion assembled and moved north of the DOUVE River into Division reserve one-half mile west of LA BONNEVILLE. The remainder of the regiment prepared to join the 3rd Battalion upon completion of relief by the 507th Parachute Infantry during the night of 15-16 June.

### 82nd Airborne Division Artillery

The 319th Glider Field Artillery Battalion remained in position and prepared to support the 507th Parachute Infantry moving into the BEUZEVILLE LA BASTILLE Bridgehead. The 456th Parachute Field Artillery Battalion changed to support the 505th Parachute Infantry when the latter relieved the 507th, and with the 320th Glider Field Artillery Battalion displaced to positions north and west of ETIENVILLE. Division Artillery, with the 87th Armored Field Artillery Battalion (105mm howitzers) and the 188th Field Artillery Battalion (155mm howitzers), in general support of the Division's attack to the west, fired more than 4,800 rounds in all types of missions. Company B, 87th Chemical Mortar Battalion (4.2 inch mortars) was attached in the vicinity of ETIENVILLE at 1130 hours.

### 80th Airborne Antiaircraft Battalion

Battery A was relieved from attachment to the 508th Parachute Infantry. Batteries B and C were attached to the 507th and 508th Parachute Infantry Regiments, respectively.

### Attached Troops

In the attack to the west the following troops were attached to the Division and assisted materially in the accomplishment of the mission:

> Company A, 746th Tank Battalion (One platoon was attached to the 325th Glider Infantry Regiment and one was attached first to the 507th and later to the 505th Parachute Infantry.)
> Troop B, 4th Cavalry Reconnaissance Squadron
> 87th Armored Field Artillery Battalion
> 188th Field Artillery Battalion
> Company C, 899th Tank Destroyer Battalion (In Division reserve).
> Company B, 87th Chemical Mortar Battalion (Attached to Division Artillery).

### D PLUS 10 – 16 JUNE 1944

The Division, attacking to the west and protecting the southern flank of VII Corps during the Corp's operations to seize CHERBOURG, forged ahead against the German 77th Infantry Division. The Division routed the enemy in its sector, drove across the DOUVE River and established a firm bridgehead around ST. SAUVEUR LE VICOMTE.

The orders from Corps were to "seize the line of the DOUVE and prepare to continue the attack to the west", however, upon arriving on the east bank of the DOUVE it was quite obvious that the German forces were in a state of complete confusion. The Division Commander immediately requested Corps authority to cross, but because of difficulties in communication, an immediate answer was not obtained. Seizing the initiative, after personal reconnaissance, General Ridgway ordered the 2nd Battalion, 505th Parachute Infantry to cross without delay. By the time clearance had been obtained from Corps two battalions had crossed the river and had established a secure bridgehead for further operations.

In three days of fierce hedgerow-to-hedgerow fighting the Division pushed the enemy steadily westwards and made it possible for the 9th Infantry Division to drive to the sea and cut the CHERBOURG Peninsula in two. A forward Division Command Post was established in a chateau just east of ST. SAUVEUR LE VICOMTE and the DOUVE River. A new Force "A" was formed to include the 505th and 508th Parachute Infantry Regiments and established its Headquarters in ST. SAUVEUR LE VICOMTE.

### 325th Glider Infantry Regiment
The 325th continued the attack and reached its assigned objectives on the east bank of the DOUVE River overlooking ST. SAUVEUR LE VICOMTE at 0950 hours. The regiment consolidated positions and patrolled aggressively across the DOUVE River.

### 505th Parachute Infantry Regiment
The regiment continued the attack to the west and reached its objectives on high ground east of the DOUVE River, overlooking ST. SAUVEUR LE VICOMTE, by 1130 hours. Finding the enemy in a high state of confusion, the 2nd Battalion crossed the river and seized ST. SAUVEUR LE VICOMTE. The 1st Battalion followed and pressed on to secure an area 2,000 yards in depth. The 3rd Battalion was relieved by the 3rd Battalion, 508th Parachute Infantry at 1540 of its mission to protect the right flank of the Division. This Battalion then crossed the river and attacked to the north of ST. SAUVEUR LE VICOMTE to seize and hold the crossroads at 189958. By 2230 the bridgehead was secure and approximately 2,000 and 3,000 yards in depth.

### 507th Parachute Infantry Regiment
The regiment completed relief of the 508th Parachute Infantry at 0415 in the CRETTEVILLE-BAUPTE area. The 2nd Battalion took up positions between BAUPTE and COIGNY, and the 3rd Battalion defended a line from COIGNY to FRANCEQUETOT. The 1st Battalion was in reserve in FRANCQUETOT. The entire area was subjected to heavy enemy artillery and mortar fire.

### 508th Parachute Infantry Regiment
After relief by the 507th Parachute Infantry, the regiment closed into reserve positions northwest of ETIENVILLE at 0900 hours. The 3rd Battalion relieved the 3rd Battalion, 505th Parachute Infantry, in the vicinity of CROSVILLE with the mission of protecting the Division's north flank. The 1st and 2nd Battalions moved into position north of RAUVILLE and at 2200 hours moved into the ST. SAUVEUR LE VICOMTE Bridgehead and took up positions south of the town and along the ST. SAUVEUR LE VICOMTE-LA HAYE DU PUITS Highway.

### 82nd Airborne Division Artillery
Until troops crossed the DOUVE River fires were massed on routed enemy columns and convoys in and around ST. SAUVEUR LE VICOMTE. All battalions except the 319th Glider Field Artillery Battalion in the CRETTEVILLE-BAUPTE sector displaced forward. At 1830 hours the 172nd Field Artillery Battalion (4.5 inch guns) was attached and went into position immediately to the east of ST. SAUVEUR LE VICOMTE. Artillery liaison planes arrived from base in ENGLAND.

### 80th Airborne Antiaircraft Battalion
Battery A remained in reserve. Battery B was attached to the 507th Parachute Infantry, and Battery C supported the attack of the 505th Parachute Infantry. The remainder of the Battalion was in reserve.

### 307th Airborne Engineer Battalion
The Battalion continued extensive reconnaissance of the DOUVE River and supported the attack against ST. SAUVEUR LE VICOMTE.

**Attached Troops**

Company A, 746th Tank Battalion, supported the attack of the Division, attaching one platoon each of the two assault regiments. Tanks crossed the DOUVE River into the ST. SAUVEUR LE VICOMTE Bridgehead. One platoon from Company C, 899th Tank Destroyer Battalion, was attached to the 3rd Battalion, 508th Parachute Infantry and another to the 505th Parachute Infantry. Company B, 87th Chemical Mortar Battalion, was relieved from support of the 325th Glider Infantry and was placed in support of the 505th Parachute Infantry. It remained, however, attached to Division Artillery.

**D PLUS 11 AND 12 – 17-18 JUNE 1944**

During this period the Division secured the bridgehead at ST. SAUVEUR LE VICOMTE, reorganized and prepared to attack south of ETIENVILLE to extend its southern boundary. The 9th Infantry Division passed through the bridgehead and attacked to the west coast of the peninsula.

**325th Glider Infantry Regiment**

The regiment moved to an assembly area southeast of ETIENVILLE on 17 June and made plans to cross the DOUVE River south of ETIENVILLE.

**505th Parachute Infantry Regiment**

The 505th cleared the ST. SAUVEUR LE VICOMTE Bridgehead to a depth of 3,000 yards of all enemy pockets of resistance, consolidated defensive positions north and west of ST. SAUVEUR LE VICOMTE, and effected passage of the 47th Infantry, 9th Infantry Division, through its lines to continue the attack to the west. The regiment patrolled extensively, rested and reorganized.

**507th Parachute Infantry Regiment**

The regiment continued to hold defensive positions in the CRETTEVILLE-BAUPTE area and patrolled extensively, concentrating its efforts along the western front. Contact was maintained with adjacent units.

**508th Parachute Infantry Regiment**

The 1st and 2nd Battalions cleared the bridgehead of all enemy resistance south and west of ST. SAUVEUR LE VICOMTE. Company C established a road block and blew the bridge on the ST. SAUVEUR LE VICOMTE-LA HAYE DU PUITS Highway across the PRAIRIES MARECAGEUSES. Company A reinforced Company C on 18 June. The 3rd Battalion remained in position protecting the north flank of the Division until 18 June when it moved to the bank of the DOUVE River west of ETIENVILLE.

**82nd Airborne Division Artillery**

The 456th Parachute Field Artillery Battalion, reinforced by the 172nd Field Artillery Battalion, continued to support the 505th and 508th Parachute Infantry Regiments in the ST. SAUVEUR LE VICOMTE Bridgehead. The remainder of Division Artillery, less the 319th Glider Field Artillery Battalion which supported the 507th Parachute Infantry in the CRETTEVILLE-BAUPTE area, moved back into position north of ETIENVILLE and made preparations to support the attack south of ETIENVILLE across the DOUVE River.

**80th Airborne Antiaircraft Battalion**

Battery A was attached to the 3rd Battalion, 508th Parachute Infantry, and Battery D (.50 caliber machinegun) moved into position protecting the bridge at ST. SAUVEUR LE VICOMTE. Battery E made preparations to support the attack of the Division south of ETIENVILLE across the DOUVE River.

**307th Airborne Engineer Battalion**

Company A procured river crossing material and prepared to assist the crossing of the DOUVE River south of ETIENVILLE. The Battalion continued to reconnoiter the DOUVE River.

**Attached Troops**

Tanks of Company A, 746th Tank Battalion, and armored cars of Company C, 899th Tank Destroyer Battalion, moved into reserve positions and prepared to revert to parent units. Troop B, 4th Cavalry Reconnaissance Squadron, patrolled extensively to the west and north and south, reporting valuable information on enemy movements and dispositions.

**Resupply**

The last air resupply mission was flown on 18 June when 5,000 Gammon Grenades were landed by C-47 at STE. MERE EGLISE.

**D PLUS 13 – 19 JUNE 1944**

The Division crossed the DOUVE River south of ETIENVILLE and established a firm bridgehead extending south to PRETOT. Contact was made with the troops on the CRETTEVILLE-BAUPTE area and the entire Division area south of the DOUVE was cleared of enemy. The 90th Infantry Division relieved the 82nd of the responsibility of guarding ST. SAUVEUR LE VICOMTE. The Division was attached to VIII Corps which had the mission of protecting the south flank of VII Corps in the VII Corps assault to the north of CHERBOURG.

**325th Glider Infantry Regiment**

The 2nd Battalion crossed the DOUVE River southeast of ETIENVILLE and west of MONTESSY by assault boats at 2350 hours the night of 18-19 June. The crossing was accomplished without incident. A feint by one squad distracted the enemy's attention to the area west of ETIENVILLE. Supported by an artillery barrage, the 1st Battalion, followed by the 3rd Battalion, crossed over an engineer foot-bridge beginning at 0215 hours and attacked against slight opposition to the south to join forces with the 2nd Battalion which was attacking from the rear the enemy Force defending the bridgehead area. By 0730 hours the 2nd Battalion had been passed through by the 1st and 3rd Battalions and the regiment held an area extending from LE HAU DE HAUT (242920) along the edge of the BOIS DE LIMORS, thence north of LA DANGUERIE to VINDEFONTAINE. The 3rd Battalion, 508th Parachute Infantry, was attached to the 325th and crossed at the same point as the 2nd Battalion. It attacked on the regiment's left flank to pass through the 1st Battalion, 507th Parachute Infantry, in VINDEFONTAINE and to seize PRETOT. Enemy resistance increased but the regiment finally broke through and extended its lines securely to a depth of 3,000 yards south of the DOUVE River by 2000 hours. The engineers completed a bridge south of ETIENVILLE by 1730, permitting supporting artillery and vehicles to join the regiment.

**505th Parachute Infantry Regiment**

Late in the evening the regiment moved by truck from the ST. SAUVEUR LE VICOMTE area to an assembly area south of LES MOITIERS EN BAUPTOIS (269920) in the bridgehead established during the day by the 325th Glider Infantry.

**507th Parachute Infantry Regiment**

The 1st Battalion attacked across the bridge west of CRETTEVILLE at 0015 hours to seize VINDEFONTAINE in conjunction with the attack by the 325th Glider Infantry to establish a bridgehead south of ETIENVILLE. After bitter fighting and considerable sniping the Battalion reached its objective by 0740 hours and spent the remainder of the day clearing the town of snipers and pockets of enemy resistance. At 1405 hours the 3rd Battalion, 508th Parachute Infantry, passed through the 3rd Battalion lines. The remainder of the 507th stayed in position in the CRETTEVILLE-BAUPTE sector.

**508th Parachute Infantry Regiment**

The regiment was relieved of responsibility of guarding the ST. SAUVEUR LE VICOMTE area at 1440 and assembled prior to moving to join the remainder of the Division. The 3rd Battalion, attached to the 325th Glider Infantry, crossed the DOUVE River in assault boats southeast of ETIENVILLE and west of MONTESSY at 280915 at 0700 hours. The crossing was made without incident and the battalion proceeded south, meeting increasing resistance. At 1405 hours this battalion passed through the 507th Parachute Infantry positions at VINDEFONTAINE and pushed on to the outskirts of PRETOT. Here an enemy strongpoint held up the advance temporarily.

## 82nd Airborne Division Artillery

The 320th Glider, 87th Armored and 188th Field Artillery Battalions, supported the attack of the 325th Glider Infantry and crossed the river into the bridgehead area during the late afternoon and night. The 172nd Field Artillery Battalion was relieved from attachment to the Division. The 319th Glider Field Artillery Battalion moved into the bridgehead area and was placed in direct support of the 325th Glider Infantry. The 320th Glider Field Artillery Battalion was placed in direct support of the 505th Parachute Infantry.

## 80th Airborne Antiaircraft Battalion

Battery B supported the attack of the 1st Battalion, 507th Parachute Infantry. Two 57mm guns were ferried across the river with the 2nd Battalion, 325th Glider Infantry. At least three enemy light tanks were knocked out in the sector in the bridgehead. Battery C crossed into the bridgehead late in the afternoon. Batteries D and E went into position to provide antiaircraft protection to the ETIENVILLE Bridge.

## 307th Airborne Engineer Battalion

Company A used twenty-five assault boats to ferry attacking troops across the DOUVE River southeast of ETIENVILLE and west of MONTESSY at 280915. Company B erected footbridges at ETIENVILLE and VINDEFONTAINE for the infantry and later, under enemy shellfire, erected a vehicular bridge at VINDEFONTAINE by 0400 hours and a class 40 bridge by 2210 hours. Assistance was given to Corps engineers in repairing the bridge and causeway south of ETIENVILLE.

## Attached Troops

Company C, 899th Tank Destroyer Battalion, was relieved from attachment to the Division at 1400 hours, and Company A, 607th Tank Destroyer Battalion was attached at 1800 hours. Company B, 87th Chemical Mortar Battalion, supported the 325th Glider Infantry from positions in the vicinity of the 2nd Battalion crossing. Company A, 746th Tank Battalion, was attached to the 325th Glider Infantry. Troop B, 4th Cavalry Reconnaissance Squadron, continued patrolling activities. The 87th Armored and 188th Field Artillery Battalions remained attached to the Division, but the 172nd Field Artillery Battalion was relieved at 1100 hours.

## D PLUS 14 – 20 JUNE 1944

The Division Command Post moved south of ETIENVILLE and south of the DOUVE River and was established at coordinates 286912.

## 325th Glider Infantry Regiment

The regiment consolidated positions, strengthened the defenses of the bridgehead and patrolled into enemy lines.

## 505th Parachute Infantry Regiment

The 3rd Battalion moved into the BOIS DE LIMORS and occupied positions along the western edge after encountering only slight enemy opposition initially. Later it came under intense mortar and artillery fire. The rest of the regiment remained in an assembly area south of LES MOITIERS EN BAUTOIS, having closed into the area at 0150 hours.

## 507th Parachute Infantry Regiment

The 1st Battalion remained in position around VINDEFONTAINE until 2330 hours when it relieved the 3rd Battalion. Other elements of the regiment remained in the CRETTEVILLE-BAUPTE sector, preparing to be relieved by the 90th Infantry Division.

## 508th Parachute Infantry Regiment

The regiment was passed through by 90th Infantry Division troops west of ST. SAUVEUR LE VICOMTE and moved south of the DOUVE River, closing into an assembly area southwest of LES MOITIERS EN BAUPTOIS by 1330 hours. The 3rd Battalion launched a determined attack against PRETOT at 0600 hours and seized the town and took up defensive positions after a sharp, short battle. The Battalion was subjected to heavy artillery and mortar shelling throughout the day. At 1600 hours the Battalion moved to positions west of PRETOT and was relieved in place at 2330 hours by the 1st Battalion, 507th Parachute Infantry.

**D PLUS 15 TO D PLUS 24 – 21-30 JUNE 1944**

During this period, which was marked by sharp local actions, the Division secured and held its area with a front generally that of D plus 14. An VIII Corps attack had been planned for late on 22 June in which the Division was to seize the high ground overlooking LA HAYE DU PUITS while the 90th Infantry Division, thrusting from both flanks, would pinch the Division out and seize the town. This attack was postponed until 3 July because of a very severe storm in the English Channel which interrupted lines of communication and supply and necessitated restriction of ammunition and ordnance lines. The First U.S. Army placed priority on its attack to seize the vital port of CHERBOURG, which fell to VII Corps on 26 June. Meanwhile, the Division reorganized, regrouped and patrolled aggressively and extensively. On 26 June the Division participated in a simulated Corps attack, firing all possible weapons between 0730 and 0800.

**325th Glider Infantry Regiment**

The 2nd Battalion was relieved on 24 June by 3rd Battalion, 508th Parachute Infantry, and the regiment then held a line between the 508th Parachute Infantry on the right and the 507th Parachute Infantry on the left. The 1st Battalion was on the right of the regimental sector, 2nd Battalion on the left and 3rd Battalion in reserve. During the entire period the regiment remained in position, patrolled extensively and made preparations for attack to the west.

**505th Parachute Infantry Regiment**

The 3rd Battalion remained in position in the western sector of the BOIS DE LIMORS until relieved by 1st Battalion on 22 June. The 2nd Battalion took over defense of the eastern sector at the same time. On 26 June the 3rd Battalion relieved 2nd Battalion, and, in turn, the 3rd Battalion was relieved by the 1st Battalion, 508th Parachute Infantry, attached, on 29 June. During the entire period it occupied the BOIS DE LIMORS the regiment suffered losses from heavy enemy mortar and artillery concentrations. Extensive patrolling was carried out, contact with adjacent units was established firmly, and firing was held to a minimum in order that friendly positions would not be disclosed.

**507th Parachute Infantry Regiment**

The 1st Battalion remained in position on the high ground west of PRETOT. The 2nd and 3rd Battalions in the CRETTEVILLE-BAUPTE sector was relieved by the 359th Infantry, 90th Infantry Division, at 240130 June and moved into reserve positions backing up the 1st Battalion to the north of PRETOT. The 2nd Battalion relieved the 3rd Battalion, 508th Parachute Infantry, in the latter's sector on 30 June and became attached to the 508th Parachute Infantry. During the entire period the regiment patrolled aggressively into enemy lines.

**508 Parachute Infantry Regiment**

The 1st Battalion occupied defensive positions northeast of VINDEFONTAINE on 22 June and remained there until relieved by the 507th Parachute Infantry on 24 June. On the same day the 3rd Battalion relieved the 2nd Battalion, 325th Glider Infantry southeast of BOIS DE LIMORS and established contact with the 505th Parachute Infantry on the right and 325th Glider Infantry on the left. The 2nd Battalion moved into reserve positions behind the 3rd Battalion, and the 1st Battalion took up positions in the rear of the 2nd. On 29 June the 1st Battalion relieved the 3rd Battalion, 505th Parachute Infantry and became attached to the 505th. The 3rd Battalion was relieved by the 2nd Battalion, 507th Parachute Infantry, attached, and moved into the 1st Battalion's former position on 30 July. The regiment patrolled actively along the front during the entire period.

**82nd Airborne Division Artillery**

The 319th Glider Field Artillery Battalion was in direct support of the 507th Parachute Infantry, 320th Glider Field Artillery Battalion in direct support of the 325th Glider Infantry, 456th Parachute Field Artillery Battalion in direct support of the 505th and 508th Parachute Infantry Regiments. The 87th Armored and 188th Field Artillery Battalions, attached, were in general support. The 319th Glider Field Artillery Battalion was placed in direct support of the 508th Parachute Infantry on 24 June and the 456th Parachute Field Artillery Battalion was placed in direct support of the 505th Parachute Infantry. During the remainder of the period support missions of the battalions were not changed and Division Artillery continued to harass and interdict enemy troops and lines of communication.

**80th Airborne Antiaircraft Battalion**

Battery A was placed in support of the 505th Parachute Infantry. Battery B supported the 507th Parachute Infantry and Battery C supported the 508th Parachute Infantry. The machine gun batteries, D, E, and F, provided antiaircraft protection for the ETIENVILLE and VINDEFONTAINE Bridges.

**307th Airborne Engineer Battalion**

The Battalion during this period built roads through the BOIS DE LIMORS, checked the Division area for mines and booby traps, operated water points, made ground engineer reconnaissance, and screened the ETIENVILLE-ST. JORES Road to guard against observation from Hill 131 (195875). The bridges at ETIENVILLE and VINDEFONTAINE were guarded by squads from Company A.

**Attached Troops**

The 87th Armored and 188th Field Artillery Battalions remained attached to Division Artillery. Troop B, 4th Cavalry Reconnaissance Squadron, was relieved from attachment to the Division at 231435 June. Company A, 746th Tank Battalion, was relieved from attachment on 21 June. The 801st Tank Destroyer Battalion was attached on 30 June, and Company A, 607th Tank Destroyer Battalion, remained attached during the period. Company B, 87th Chemical Mortar Battalion, was relieved in the early part of the period.

**D PLUS 25 TO D PLUS 26 – 1-2 JULY 1944**

The Division continued to maintain positions in the ETIENVILLE Bridgehead with a front generally along the line as of D plus 14. Preparations were completed, reorganization effected, and new troops attached for the attack to the west on 3 July. The Division was firmly in contact with the 79th Infantry Division on the right and the 90th Infantry Division on the left. An advance Division Command Post was opened at 260895 at 022330 hours.

**325th Glider Infantry Regiment**

The regiment continued to hold positions southwest of LA DRANGUERIE (257875), maintaining contact with the 508th Parachute Infantry on the right and 507th Parachute Infantry on the left. The 1st Battalion remained on the right, 2nd Battalion on the left and 3rd Battalion in reserve.

**505th Parachute Infantry Regiment**

The regiment continued to hold positions in the BOIS DE LIMORS, with the 1st Battalion, 508th Parachute Infantry, attached, on the left, the 1st Battalion on the right. Patrolling continued. Contact was maintained with the 79th Infantry Division on the right and the 508th Parachute Infantry on the left.

**507th Parachute Infantry Regiment**

The regiment continued to hold positions in the vicinity of PRETOT, maintaining contact with the 90th Infantry Division on the left and the 325th Glider Infantry on the right. The 1st Battalion held front line positions with the 3rd Battalion in reserve. The 2nd Battalion remained attached to the 508th Parachute Infantry.

**82nd Airborne Division Artillery**

Preparations were made to displace and support the attack of the Division on 3 July. The 319th Glider Field Artillery Battalion remained in direct support of the 508th Parachute Infantry, the 320th Glider Field Artillery Battalion in direct support of the 325th Glider and 507th Parachute Infantry Regiments, the 456th Parachute Field Artillery Battalion in direct support of the 505th Parachute Infantry. The 87th Armored Field Artillery Battalion, less Battery B, which reinforced the fires of the 320th, and the 188th Field Artillery Battalions were in general support. Company D, 86th Chemical Mortar Battalion (4.2 inch mortars), was placed under Division Artillery control and attached to the 505th Parachute Infantry at 011600 July.

**80th Airborne Antiaircraft Battalion**

Batteries A and E were attached to the 505th Parachute Infantry, Battery B to the 507th Parachute Infantry and Battery C to the 508th Parachute Infantry for the 3 July attack.

## 307th Airborne Engineer Battalion

Two platoons of Company A were attached to the 325th Glider Infantry. One squad of Company B was attached to the 507th Parachute Infantry, and two squads from Company B were attached to each of the 505 and 508 Parachute Infantry Regiments. Squads of Company A guarding the bridges at ETIENVILLE and VINDEFONTAINE were relieved by Corps engineers on 2 July.

## Attached Troops

Company A, 712th Tank Battalion, attached to the Division 011150 July, moved into the bridgehead area late on 2 July. The 1st Platoon was attached to the 507th Parachute Infantry and the 2nd Platoon to the 325th Glider Infantry. The 801st Tank Destroyer Battalion was relieved from attachment on 1 July, and the 803rd Tank Destroyer Battalion was attached on 010100 July. Company A, 607th Tank Destroyer Battalion, remained attached. Company D, 86th Chemical Mortar Battalion was attached at 011600 July, placed under control of 82nd Division Artillery and later attached to the 505th Parachute Infantry.

## D PLUS 27 – 3 JULY 1944

The Division attacked despite heavy rainfall at 0630 hours after days of waiting, reorganization and preparation. The Division's mission was to attack, seize and secure Hills 131 (195875) and 95 (188855) and the high ground northeast of LA HAYE DU PUITS known as the LA POTERIE RIDGE. Flanked by the 79th Infantry Division on the right and the 90th Infantry Division on the left, the 82nd was to be pinched out of the VIII Corps attack and was to assemble and await further orders. The Division attacked according to plan, with the 505th Parachute Infantry on the right, 508th Parachute Infantry in the center, and 325th Glider Infantry on the left. The 2nd Battalion 507th Parachute Infantry, initially covered a small draw between the 325th and 508th. Stubborn resistance was offered initially by the 265th and 353rd German Infantry Divisions reinforced by OST Battalions. The enemy had made good use of the eleven day delay to organize an elaborate defense. However, by aggressive action the Division moved ahead to seize Hill 131 by noon and to secure the eastern edge of the LA POTERIE Ridge, exclusive of the town of LA POTERIE (221857) by dark. Fighting was sharp and severe and enemy defensive positions were heavily mined and booby trapped. Many casualties were inflicted on the enemy. The Forward Division Command Post moved to AUVRAIRIE (209887).

## 325th Glider Infantry Regiment

With the 1st Battalion on the left and the 2nd Battalion on the right, the regiment jumped off at 0630 hours, meeting considerable small arms and mortar fire. In the vicinity of LA DRANGUIRIE the 3rd Battalion was committed temporarily to close a gap that had developed between the 2nd and 1st Battalions at 1000 hours. The 90th Infantry Division on the left flank was held up, leaving the flank exposed and under pressure. By 1600 hours the 325th had reached the town of FAUDEMER (240868). At 1550 hours the regimental objective was changed from Hill 95 to the eastern edge of the LA POTERIE Ridge to include the town of LA POTERIE. The 2nd and 1st Battalions continued to attack towards the town, but increasing enemy opposition prevented the capture of the town by nightfall. The 3rd Battalion was again placed in the line, and the regiment dug in preparatory to attacking and seizing LA POTERIE the following day.

## 505th Parachute Infantry Regiment

The regiment attacked at 0630 hours initially with the 1st and 2nd Battalions in column, the 2nd Battalion leading. Passing the creek line at VARENGUEBEC, the 2nd Battalion seized DUPINERIE Ridge (north of Hill 131) by 0830 hours and resumed the attack at 1015 hours with the 1st Battalion abreast and on the right. These two battalions, by bold advances, secured the north slope of Hill 131 and the ST. SAUVEUR LE VICOMTE-LA HAYE DU PUITS Highway by 1225 hours despite heavy enemy artillery fire, mines, and booby traps. The 3rd Battalion followed the assault battalions to mop up by-passed pockets of resistance. The regimental zone was enlarged at 1550 hours to include all of Hill 131. The 3rd Battalion moved into position through the 2nd and into the 508th Parachute Infantry's area on the southern slope of Hill 131. The regiment dug in by the end of the day along a line from LA SANGSURIERE south to LES ROULAND and then to a junction with the 508th Parachute Infantry at BLANCHELANDE. Preparations were made to continue the attack on 4 July.

**507th Parachute Infantry Regiment**

The 2nd Battalion, under regimental control, attacked at 0630 hours, flanked on the left and right by the 325th Glider and 508th Parachute Infantry Regiments, respectively. The Battalion cleared all enemy from its area and reached its objective, LA FAUVERIE (223869), by 1700. Preparations were then made to attack to the south the next day. Other units of the regiment remained in Division reserve south of VINDEFONTAINE and prepared to follow the advance of the 325th Glider Infantry on Division order. The regiment moved to the vicinity of LA DRANGUERIE at 1650. The 1st Battalion followed and maintained contact with the 325th Glider Infantry, and the 3rd Battalion protected the Division left flank to the left rear of the 1st Battalion.

**508th Parachute Infantry Regiment**

With the 2nd Battalion on the right and the 3rd Battalion on the left, the regiment attacked at 0630 hours, passing through the 1st Battalion's positions. The high ground between VARENGUEBEC and LA DAUDERIE was secured by 0900 hours, and the 1st Battalion moved into reserve in the vicinity of LA COTELLERIE. The 2nd Battalion reached the southern slope of Hill 131 by 1145 hours and was joined by the 3rd Battalion by 1600 hours. The regiment moved south at 2000 hours to occupy a zone in the vicinity of BLANCHELANDE, dug in and prepared to attack south towards the LA POTERIE Ridge. Enemy opposition was moderate heavy during the action. Extensive minefields were encountered.

**82nd Airborne Division Artillery**

All battalions fired a preparation to precede the Division's attack, and during the entire action the battalions fired harassing, interdiction and counter-battery fires with telling effect despite inclement weather which precluded accurate observation. Reconnaissance was made to displace battalions into more favorable positions closer to the advancing infantry. A total of 7,727 rounds were fired during the period.

**Attached Troops**

One platoon of Company A, 712th Tank Battalion, supported the 325th Glider Infantry during its attack near LA DRANGUERIE and another Platoon supported the 2nd Battalion, 507th Parachute Infantry in clearing its zone and then went into positions near LA FAUVERIE commanding observation of the LA POTERIE-PRETOT Highway. At 1315 one Platoon of Company A, 803d Tank Destroyer Battalion, moved to support the 2nd Battalion, 508th Parachute Infantry. Company D, 86th Chemical Mortar Battalion, was relieved from attachment to the 505th Parachute Infantry at 1920 hours and was attached to the 325th Glider Infantry.

**D PLUS 28 – 4 JULY 1944**

The Division resumed its attack at 0800 and by the end of the day had secured Hill 95 and the LA POTERIE Ridge against a determined enemy. Many severe counterattacks were driven back and any ground lost as a result of the counter thrusts was retaken. More than 500 enemy killed and more than 700 taken prisoner in the bitter fighting.

**325th Glider Infantry Regiment**

The 1st and 3rd Battalions resumed the attack against the town of LA POTERIE at 0800 hours and secured it by 1250 hours. The 2nd Battalion remained in reserve. After passing through LA POTERIE the regiment occupied defensive positions within its sector and established contact with the 90th Infantry Division on the 82nd Airborne Division's left flank.

**505th Parachute Infantry Regiment**

The 1st and 3rd Battalions attacked at 0800 to seize the northern slope of Hill 95 and secured this objective by 1150 hours. Firm contact was made with adjacent units. Contact with the 3rd Battalion, 314th Infantry, 79th Infantry Division, on the right, was made at 2100 hours.

**507th Parachute Infantry Regiment**

The 2nd Battalion reverted to regimental control and moved at noon to the breakthrough position in the vicinity of BLANCHELAND. The 3rd Battalion moved into an assembly area north of LA POTERIE and attacked at 2015 hours through the 508th Parachute Infantry to seize the western hill mass at 210350 on LA POTERIE Ridge. The 3rd

Battalion reached the hill and was consolidating positions and establishing contact with adjacent units by 2400 hours. The 2nd Battalion attacked at 2200 hours between the 2nd and 3rd Battalions, 508th Parachute Infantry, and pushed up to the center hill mass of LA POTERIE Ridge directly east of Hill 95. This Battalion circled the hill in the darkness against considerable small arms and artillery fire and prepared to seize it completely before daylight. The 1st Battalion, meanwhile, remained in position to the rear of the 325th Glider Infantry along the Division's right flank.

**508th Parachute Infantry Regiment**
At 0800 the Regiment attacked south against Hill 95 and the LA POTERIE Ridge. The 2nd Battalion, passing through elements of the 505th Parachute Infantry, seized Hill 95 at 1220. Enemy resistance was particularly strong and losses were heavy on both sides. An enemy counterattack at 1400 hours forced the 2nd Battalion back but it retook the position by 2400 hours despite considerable artillery and small arms fire. The 3rd and 1st Battalions attacked at 0800 on the left of the regimental zone. Heavy concentrations of mortar, artillery and small arms fire pinned the units down along the general line running due west from the town of LA POTERIE and all attempts to reach the objective were repulsed during the day. The 2nd Battalion, 507th Parachute Infantry, moved into positions between the 2nd and 3rd Battalions and launched an attack against the 3rd Battalion's objective at 2200. The 3rd Battalion, 507th, passed through elements of the 1st and 3rd Battalions in its attack at 2015 hours on the eastern edge and northern slopes of LA POTERIE Ridge.

**82nd Airborne Division Artillery**
Reinforced by eight battalions of VIII Corps artillery, the battalions of Division Artillery fired numerous concentrations in support of the infantry advance and succeeded in breaking up enemy counterattacks in the vicinity of Hill 95 and along the LA POTERIE Ridge.

**Attached Troops**
Company D, 86th Chemical Battalion, was relieved from attachment to the Division at 2300 hours. Company A, 607th Tank Destroyer Battalion, was relieved at 1115 hours. One platoon of tanks from Company A, 712th Tank Battalion, was relieved from the 325th Glider Infantry and supported the 508th Parachute Infantry in repulsing counterattacks in that sector. Guns from the 803rd Tank Destroyer Battalion were placed on the south slope of Hill 131 to maintain fire on the woods south and west of the 508th Parachute Infantry front.

**D PLUS 29 – 5 JULY 1944**
The Division secured all of the area within its zone of action, mopping up all remaining pockets of enemy resistance, consolidating defensive positions and maintaining contact with the adjacent units in their advance to pinch off the Division. Corps orders restrained the Division from further advances. Defensive positions were established along the general line from Hill 131 south along the ST. SAUVEUR LE VICOMTE-LA HAYE DU PUITS Highway to the southern slopes of Hill 95 and thence along the southern slope of the LA POTERIE Ridge.

**325th Glider Infantry**
The regiment established a defensive line on the forward slopes of the LA POTERIE Ridge with the 3rd Battalion, 507th Parachute Infantry, attached, on the regiment's right flank. Contact was maintained with the advancing 90th Infantry Division on the left.

**505th Parachute Infantry Regiment**
The regiment maintained defensive positions on the reverse slope of Hill 95 and from that point north to the base of Hill 131. Contact was maintained with the 79th Infantry Division on the right and the 508th Parachute Infantry.

**507th Parachute Infantry Regiment**
The 2nd Battalion continued fighting to secure the westernmost hill of the LA POTERIE Ridge due east from Hill 95. This ridge was under control at 0700 hours. During the remainder of the day this battalion killed or destroyed all enemy within its area, established contact with adjacent units and strengthened positions. The 3rd Battalion secured the easternmost hill of the LA POTERIE Ridge and was attached to the 325th Glider Infantry after having established contact. The 1st Battalion remained in reserve.

**508th Parachute Infantry Regiment**

The 1st Battalion moved into reserve positions in the vicinity of BLANCHELANDE. The 2nd Battalion cleared enemy from the forward slopes of Hill 131 and maintained contact with the 505th Parachute Infantry. The 3rd Battalion, in the center of LA POTERIE Ridge, established defensive positions between the 2nd Battalion, 507th, and the 2nd Battalion on Hill 131. The regiment suffered from enemy concentrations of artillery fire. All enemy were cleared from the regimental sector.

**82nd Airborne Division Artillery**

All battalions assisted in breaking up enemy counterattacks, particularly in the 507th Parachute Infantry area. The 456th Parachute Field Artillery Battalion was ordered to reinforce fires of the 319th Glider Field Artillery Battalion which was still in direct support of the 508th Parachute Infantry. Ammunition expended during the day totaled 2,733 rounds.

**D PLUS 30 TO D PLUS 31 – 6-7 JULY 1944**

The Division maintained and strengthened defensive positions, drove out all attempts by the enemy to infiltrate patrols through the sector, and maintained contact with the 79th Infantry Division on the right and the 90th Infantry Division on the left. The 2nd Battalion, 325th Glider Infantry, moved into position between the 2nd and 3rd Battalions, 507th Parachute Infantry. The 505th Parachute Infantry sector was enlarged to include the eastern slopes of Hill 95, and, with the 2nd Battalion, 508th Parachute Infantry, attached, cleared the area of infiltrating enemy patrols. At 070800 July the Division regrouped its forces, placing 325th Glider and 508th Parachute Infantry Regiments in reserve and making 505th and 507th Parachute Infantry Regiments responsible for the right and left portions respectively, of the Division's front lines.

**D PLUS 32 TO D PLUS 35 – 8-11 JULY 1944**

The Division reverted to Corps reserve and was relieved of all attachments. The 8th Infantry Division passed through the Division's positions to continue the attack to the south on 8 July, D plus 32. The Division assembled and on 11 July withdrew into First Army reserve. It then moved to Utah Beach preparatory to its return to base camps in ENGLAND.

Upon returning to base camps the Division immediately began an intensive training program. The Division had not received reinforcements in France and the Infantry losses were particularly heavy, one company coming out of the lines with a strength of only sixteen officers and enlisted men.

Refitting also occupied much of the time; however, by mid-August this phase had been accomplished and training dominated the activities. One phase of the training included tests to determine the possibilities of employing heavy bombers in air landing operations. Both the B-17 and B-24 were used in these tests.

Major General Matthew B. Ridgway left the Division to become Commanding General of XVIII Corps (Airborne), and Brigadier General James M. Gavin assumed command of the 82nd Airborne Division.

As the month of August ended the Division was moving to takeoff airfields in the British Midlands in preparation for a mission in Belgium [Linnett] that was canceled less than twenty-four hours prior to scheduled takeoff time. The Division's next mission began 17 September when it jumped and glided into the NIJMEGEN-GRAVE-GROESBEEK area of the Netherlands.

**SECTION 4: ANNEXES**

1. Personnel
    a. Command and Staff
    b. Troop List
        (1) Organic
        (2) Attached
    c. Consolidated list of Aircraft, Personnel and Vehicles of Forces "A", "B" and "C"
    d. Casualties
        (1) Casualties resulting from Parachute drops and Glider landings.
        (2) Consolidated casualty reports by units.
        (3) Analysis of officer casualties.
        (4) Analysis of casualties by branch.
2. Air Resupply
3. Air Movement Table
    a. Chart: Departure Airfields
4. Drop and Landing Patterns
    a. Parachute Drops
    b. Glider Landings
5. Statistical Study of Glider Landings
6. Chart: D-Day to D+2
7. Chart: D+3 to D+6 (MERDERET River Crossing)
8. Chart: D+7 (CRETTEVILLE-BAUPTE)
9. Chart: D+8 to D+12 (ST. SAUVEUR LE VICOMTE)
10. Chart: D+13 to D+18 (ETIENVILLE BRIDGEHEAD)
11. Chart: D+25 to D+33 (Hills 131 and 95 – LA POTERIE RIDGE)


**ANNEX NO. 1 A TO**
**ACCOMPANY HISTORICAL**
**NARRATIVE FOR NORMANDY**

<u>COMMAND AND STAFF DURING THE 82ND AIRBORNE DIVISION'S</u>
<u>PARTICIPATION IN THE NORMANDY CAMPAIGN</u>

| | |
|---|---|
| Commanding General | Major General MATTHEW B. RIDGWAY |
| Assistant Commanding General | Brigadier General JAMES M. GAVIN |
| Assistant Commanding General | Brigadier General GEORGE P. HOWELL |
| | |
| 325 Glider Infantry Regiment | Colonel HARRY B. LEWIS |
| 504 Parachute Infantry Regiment* | Colonel REUBEN H. TUCKER |
| 505 Parachute Infantry Regiment | Colonel WILLIAM E. EKMAN |
| 507 Parachute Infantry Regiment | (Colonel GEORGE V. MILLET (Captured by enemy on or about 8 June 1944) |
| | (Lieutenant Colonel ARTHUR A. MALONEY (From on or about 8 June) |
| | (Colonel EDSON B. RAFF (From 15 June 1944) |
| 508 Parachute Infantry Regiment | Colonel ROY E. LINDQUIST |
| 82d Airborne Division Artillery | Colonel FRANCIS A. MARCH |
| 319 Glider Field Artillery Battalion | Lieutenant Colonel JAMES C. TODD |
| 320 Glider Field Artillery Battalion | Lieutenant Colonel PAUL E. WRIGHT |
| 376 Parachute Field Artillery Battalion* | Lieutenant Colonel WILBUR M. GRIFFITH |

| | |
|---|---|
| 456 Parachute Field Artillery Battalion | Lieutenant Colonel WAGNER J. D'ALESSIO |
| 80 Airborne Antiaircraft Battalion | Lieutenant Colonel RAYMOND E. SINGLETON |
| 307 Airborne Engineer Battalion | Lieutenant Colonel ROBERT S. PALMER (Less C Company)* |
| | (Captured by enemy on or about 6 June 1944) |
| | Major EDWIN A. BEDELL (From 8 June 1944) |
| 307 Airborne Medical Company | Major WILLIAM H. HOUSTON |
| | (Killed 6 June 1944) |
| | Major JERRY J. BELDEN (From 6 June 1944) |
| 407 Airborne Quartermaster Company | Captainn SAMUEL H. MAYS |
| 782 Airborne Ordnance Maintenance Co. | Captain JEFF DAVIS, JR. |
| 82nd Airborne Division Headquarters Co. | Captain GEORGE J. CLAUSSEN |
| 82nd Airborne Signal Company | First Lieutenant ROBERT B. NERF |
| 82nd Airborne Reconnaissance Platoon | First Lieutenant JOSEPH V. DEMASI |
| 82nd Airborne Military Police Platoon | Major FREDERICK G. MC COLLUM |
| 82nd Parachute Maintenance Company (Provisional) | Captain JAMES E. GRIFFIN |

STAFF

| | |
|---|---|
| Chief of Staff | (Colonel RALPH P. EATON (Injured in glider crash 6 June 1944) |
| | (Colonel EDSON D. RAFF (Acting 8-15 June) |
| | (Lieutenant Colonel ROBERT H. WIENECKE |
| | (Acting 15 June – 11 July) |
| AC of S, G-1 | Lieutenant Colonel FREDERICK M. SCHELLHAMMER |
| AC of S, G-2 | Lieutenant Colonel WHITFIELD JACK |
| AC of S, G-3 | Lieutenant Colonel ROBERT H. WIENECKE |
| | Lieutenant Colonel WALTER F. WINTON (Acting 15-19 June, 5-11 July) |
| | Lieutenant Colonel HENRY E. ADAMS (Acting 19 June – 5 July) |
| AC of S, G-4 | Lieutenant Colonel BENNIE A. ZINN (Wounded 7 June 1944) |
| | Lieutenant Colonel FRANK W. MOORMAN (From 7 June 1944) |
| Inspector General | Lieutenant Colonel CHARLES M. BARRETT |
| Signal Officer | Lieutenant Colonel FRANK W. MOORMAN |
| | Captain ROBERT E. FURMAN (Acting from 7 June 1944) |
| Adjutant General | Lieutenant Colonel RAYMOND M. BRITTON |
| Judge Advocate | Lieutenant Colonel CASIMIR D. MOSS |
| Surgeon | Lieutenant Colonel WOLCOTT L. ETIENNE (Wounded 6 June 1944) |
| | Major WILLIAM C. LINDSTROM (Acting from 6 June 1944) |
| Finance Officer | Lieutenant Colonel WILLIAM E. JOHNSON |
| Chaplain | Lieutenant Colonel GEORGE L. RIDDLE |
| Ordnance Officer | Lieutenant Colonel JOSHUA A. FINKLE (Wounded 7 June 1944) |
| Quartermaster Officer | Lieutenant Colonel JOHN M. MOHRMAN |
| Headquarters Commandant | Major DON C. FAITH |
| Provost Marshall | Major FREDERICK G. MC COLLUM |
| Special Service Officer | Captain RUDRICK R. OTTO |
| Military Government Officer | Captain PETER SHOUVALOFF |

**ANNEX NO. 1 B TO**
**ACCOMPANY HISTORICAL**
**NARRATIVE FOR NORMANDY**
<u>**TROOP LIST**</u>
<u>**ORGANIC***</u>

Headquarters and Headquarters Company, 82nd Airborne Division
Headquarters and Headquarters Company, 2nd Airborne Brigade
Headquarters and Headquarters Battery, 82nd Airborne Division Artillery
325th Glider Infantry Regiment
504th Parachute Infantry Regiment*
505th Parachute Infantry Regiment
507th Parachute Infantry Regiment
508th Parachute Infantry Regiment
319th Glider Field Artillery Battalion
320th Glider Field Artillery Battalion
376th Parachute Field Artillery Battalion*
456th Parachute Field Artillery Battalion
80th Airborne Anti-Aircraft Battalion
307th Airborne Engineer Battalion
307th Airborne Medical Battalion
407th Airborne Quartermaster Company
782nd Airborne Ordnance Maintenance Company
82nd Airborne Signal Company
82nd Airborne Military Police Platoon
82nd Airborne Reconnaissance Platoon (Provisional)
82nd Airborne Parachute Maintenance Company (Provisional)

<u>UNIT</u>
<u>ATTACHED</u> <u>DATES</u>

| | |
|---|---|
| C Company, 746 Tank Battalion | 1 June – 11 June |
| A Company, 746 Tank Battalion | 13 June – 21 June |
| A Company, 712 Tank Battalion | 1 July – 8 July |
| C Company, 889 Tank Destroyer Battalion | 1 June – 19 June |
| A Company, 607 Tank Destroyer Battalion | 19 June – 4 July |
| 801 Tank Destroyer Battalion | 30 June – 1 July |
| 803 Tank Destroyer Battalion | 1 July – 8 July |
| B Troop, 4 Cavalry Reconnaissance Squadron | 1 June – 23 June |
| 87 Armored Field Artillery Battalion | 1 June – 8 June, 14 June – 8 July |
| 188 Field Artillery Battalion | 12 June – 8 July |
| 172 Field Artillery Battalion | 16 June – 19 June |
| D Company, 86 Chemical Mortar Battalion | 1 July – 4 July |
| B Company, 87 Chemical Mortar Battalion | 15 June – 21 June |
| 3809 Quartermaster Truck Company | |
| 3810 Quartermaster Truck Company | |
| 1 Platoon, 464 Ambulance Company, 31 Medical Group | |
| 493 Collecting Company, 179 Medical Battalion | |
| 374 Collecting Company, 50 Medical Battalion | |
| 429 Litter Bearer Platoon | |
| 591 Collecting Company | |
| 1st Platoon, 603 Quartermaster Graves Registration Company | |

NOTE: *504th Parachute Infantry Regiment, 376th Parachute Field Artillery Battalion, and C Company, 307th Airborne Engineer Battalion remained in base camps, United Kingdom after returning from ANZIO, ITALY.

## ANNEX 1 C TO
## ACCOMPANY HISTORICAL
## NARRATIVE FOR NORMANDY

### CONSOLIDATED LIST OF AIRCRAFT, PERSONNEL AND MAJOR
### EQUIPMENT OF FORCES "A", "B" AND "C"

### FORCE "A" (PARACHUTE)

| UNIT | A/C | PERSONNEL | GUNS |
|------|-----|-----------|------|
| Div Hq, 82nd Abn | 9 | 105 | |
| 508th Prcht Inf | 117 | 1994 | |
| 507th Prcht Inf | 117 | 2004 | |
| 505th Prcht Inf | 117 | 2095 | 2 75mm Pack How |
| 307th Abn Engr Bn | 9 | 144 | |
| 82nd Abn P/F Grps. | 9 | 54 | |
| TOTAL | 378 | 6396 | |

### FORCE "B" (GLIDER)

| UNIT | A/C | PERSONNEL | GUNS | TRKS 1/4T | TLRS | M/C |
|------|-----|-----------|------|-----------|------|-----|
| Div Hq, 82nd Abn Div | 19 | 185 | | 12 | 9 | 4 |
| 82nd Abn Rcn Plt | 13 | 49 | | 9 | | 4 |
| 82nd Abn Div Arty | 11 | 50 | | 4 | 3 | |
| 82nd Abn Sig Co | 13 | 82 | | 7 | 4 | 5 |
| 80th Abn AA Bn | 57 | 228 | 24 57mm AT | 27 | 15 | |
| 307th Abn Med Co | 20 | 144 | | 18 | 14 | |
| 307th Abn Engr Bn | 10 | 99 | | 5 | 3 | |
| 319th GI FA Bn | 40 | 362 | 12 75mm How | 32 | 17 | |
| 320th GI FA Bn | 54 | 343 | 12 105mm How | 30 | 20 | |
| 325th GI Inf | 129 | 1841 | 9 57mm AT | 28 | 15 | |
| 2nd Bn, 401st GI Inf | 43 | 459 | | 6 | 5 | |
| Comd Vehs, 505, 507, 508 Prchts Infs | 15 | 24 | | 13 | | |
| ASP | 4 | 5 | | 2 | | |
| TOTAL | 428 | 3871 | | 193 | 105 | 13 |

**FORCE "C" (SEABORNE)**

| UNIT | PERS ONNEL | 2 1/2T TRK | 1T TLR | 1 1/2T TRK | 3/4T W/C | 2 1/2T DUMP | 75mm HOW | 3/4T AMB | 1/4T TRK | 1/4T TRL |
|---|---|---|---|---|---|---|---|---|---|---|
| 82nd Abn Div Hq | 70 | 1 | 6 | 7 | 1 | | | | | |
| 505th Prcht Inf | | 83 | | | | | | | | |
| 507th Prcht Inf | | 78 | | | | | | | | |
| 508th Prcht Inf | | 64 | | | | | | | | |
| 325th GI Inf | 77 | | | 9 | | | | | 2 | |
| Hq & Hq Btry, 82nd Abn Div Arty | 19 | 3 | 3 | | 1 | | | | | |
| 319th GI FA Bn | 47 | 3 | 3 | | 13 | | | | | |
| 320th GI FA Bn | 50 | 3 | 3 | 12 | 1 | | | | | |
| 456th Prcht FA Bn | 471 | 15 | 15 | | 18 | | 10 | | 27 | 18 |
| 80th Abn AA Bn, Bn Hq & Med Det | 258 | | | 24 (36 50-cal. AA mg) | | | | | 12 | 6 |
| 307th Abn Engr Bn | 65 | 2 | 2 | | | 4 | | | | |
| 82nd Abn Sig Co | 17 | 1 | 1 | 1 | | | | | | |
| 307th Abn Med Co | 26 | 1(H2O) | | 5 | | | | 8 | | |
| 82nd Abn Ord Maint Co. | 68 | 6 | 3 | | | | | | 3 | 3 |
| 407th Abn QM Co | 59 | | | 1 | | | | | 3 | 3 |
| 82nd Abn MP Plat | 30 | | | 1 | | | | | 3 | 3 |
| 3809 QM Trk Co | 115 | 53 | | | | | | | 3 | |
| 3810* QM Trk Co | 115 | 53 | | | | | | | 3 | |
| TOTALS | 1712 | 140 | 37 | 60 | 34 | 4 | 10 | 8 | 56 | 33 |

FORCE "B" 3871

FORCE "A" 6396

TOTAL 11,979

* Remained attached during operation

# ANNEX 1 D TO
# ACCOMPANY HISTORICAL
# NARRATIVE FOR NORMANDY

*CASUALTIES*

1. 82ND AIRBORNE DIVISION CASUALTIES:

a. Recapitulation —

| | NUMBER | PER CENT |
|---|---|---|
| *Committed Strength | 11,770 | 100.00 |
| Total Casualties | 5,436 | 46.18 |
| illed in action or died of wounds | 1,142 | 9.70 |
| Wounded | 2,373 | 20.16 |
| Missing or known captured | 840 | 7.13 |
| Evacuated Sick | 377 | 3.20 |
| Evacuated Injured | 704 | 5.98 |

*Organic Troops Only

b. Casualties from parachute drops and glider landings: See Annex No. 1 D(1)

c. Consolidated casualty reports by units: See Annex No. 1 D (2)

d. Analysis of Officer Casualties: See Annex No. 1 D (3).

NOTE: The tabulation shown in this annex was prepared on information available as of 26 July 1944 and therefore is somewhat incomplete in respect to final adjusted figures. It does, however, give a reliable indication of casualties among officers of the Division.

e. Analysis of casualties by branch: See Annex No. 1 D (4)

NOTE: The tabulation shown in this annex was prepared on information available as of 26 July 1944 and therefore is somewhat incomplete in respect to final adjusted figures. It does, however, give a reliable indication of casualties by branch of service.


**2. ENEMY CASUALTIES:**

a. Personnel —

(1) Estimated killed in major battles only – 1,500

(2) Captured – 2, 159

(3) During its campaign in NORMANDY the 82nd Airborne Division was engaged with all or major portions of five different enemy divisions, including the 91st, 243rd, 77th, 265th and 353rd. It is estimated that the 91st and 265th Divisions were virtually destroyed as effective fighting units.


b. Material: The return of the Division to the United Kingdom prevented a thorough search of territory gained during the period 3-8 July 1944. However, a summary of enemy material known captured or destroyed by the 82nd Airborne Division in NORMANDY is as follows:

| | |
|---|---|
| Tanks, all types | 62 |
| Light, Reconnaissance Vehicles | 2 |
| Anti-tank guns (all calibers) | 24 |
| Anti-aircraft guns (all calibers) | 14 |
| Self-propelled guns (all calibers) | 3 |
| Artillery field pieces (all types) | 3 |


**ANNEX NO. 1 D (1) TO
ACCOMPANY HISTORICAL
NARRATIVE FOR NORMANDY**


CASUALTIES RESULTING FROM PARACHUTE DROPS AND GLIDER LANDINGS

Following is a report of an official investigation conducted by the Division Inspector General and submitted to the Division Commander on 25 July 1944:

In compliance with your directive dated 13 July 1944 the following data is submitted for your information:

a. Dispersion: See Annexes 4 and 5

b. Landing: 6396 paratroopers dropped.

(1) Casualties:

| | NO. | % |
|---|---|---|
| Known drowned as a result of the drop | 36 | .56 |
| Paratroopers abandoned to the enemy as a result of jump injuries | 63 | .98 |
| Injured in jumping and evacuated by friendly forces | 173 | 2.7 |

(2) One complete stick from the 507th is still missing.

(3) No sticks were destroyed completely by loss of aircraft before jumping.

(4) Out of 237 CG-4A's and 187 Horsas used, five (5) CG-4A's are still unaccounted for. These five (5) CG-4A's were cut loose shortly after making a landfall on the west coast of the peninsula and are all from the 80th AA Battalion. Two are reported to have been the result of tow ropes severed by AA fire.

(5) Casualties in glider serials:

|  | DAYLIGHT | | DARKNESS | |
| --- | --- | --- | --- | --- |
| Total carried | 2796 | | 957 | |
|  | NO. | % | NO. | % |
| KIA | 38 | 1.35 | 23 | 2.4 |
| WIA | 204 | 7.29 | 118 | 12.2 |
| MIA | 0 | 0.0 | 14 | 1.46 |

(6) The percentage chance of becoming a casualty:

|  | DAYLIGHT | DARKNESS |
| --- | --- | --- |
| Horsas | 10.5% | 16.2% |
| CG-4A | 5.8% | 10.7% |

(7) The following equipment was unserviceable due to landing:

| | JEEPS | | | TRAILERS | | | GUNS | | |
| --- | --- | --- | --- | --- | --- | --- | --- | --- | --- |
| | NO. | % NO. | CARRIED | NO. | % NO. | CARRIED | NO. | % NO. | CARRIED |
| **Daylight** | | | | | | | | | |
| Horsas | 5 | 12.1 | 41 | 3 | 9.3 | 32 | 2 | 25 | 8 |
| CG-4A | 14 | 20. | 70 | 5 | 20.0 | 25 | 2 | 22.2 | 9 |

| | JEEPS | | | TRAILERS | | | GUNS | | |
| --- | --- | --- | --- | --- | --- | --- | --- | --- | --- |
| | NO. | % NO. | CARRIED | NO. | % NO. | CARRIED | NO. | % NO. | CARRIED |
| **Darkness** | | | | | | | | | |
| Horsas | 19 | 31.6 | 60 | 11 | 28.0 | 39 | 7 | 58.0 | 12 |
| CG-4A | 11 | 47.8 | 23 | 1 | 20.0 | 5 | 7 | 25.0 | 28 |

(8) There was one known case occurred of tow rope breaking during flight. This was a CG-4A.

(9) There are no known cases of gliders pulling loose in flight during or after take-off.

/s/t/ C.F. BARRETT, JR.,

Lt. Col., IGD,
Inspector General.

NOTE: There are minor discrepancies between this report and Annexes 1 C and 3 in respect to the number of gliders and number of vehicles.

**ANNEX 1 D (2) TO
ACCOMPANY HISTORICAL
NARRATIVE FOR NORMANDY**

CONSOLIDATED CASUALTY REPORT
NORMANDY CAMPAIGN
(Adjusted to 12 December 1944)

| | Missing In Action | Wounded In Action | RTD | Injured In Action | RTD | Killed In Action & Died | Captured |
|---|---|---|---|---|---|---|---|
| Hq 82d Abn Div | 3 | 7 | 7 | 4 | 2 | 1 | |
| Hq Co 82d Abn Div | 1 | 10 | 8 | 4 | 4 | 12 | |
| 82d Abn MP Plat | 1 | 1 | | | | | |
| 504th Prcht Inf | | | | | | | |
| 505th Prcht Inf | 60 | 492 | 353 | 164 | 129 | 186 | 51 |
| 325th Gli Inf | 24 | 488 | 351 | 162 | 108 | 200 | 12 |
| 82d Abn Div Arty | 3 | 2 | 1 | | | | |
| 319th Gli FA Bn | 1 | 40 | 24 | 41 | 32 | 27 | |
| 320th Gli FA Bn | 29 | 21 | 27 | 17 | 22 | | |
| 376th Prcht FA Bn | | | | | | | |
| 456th Prcht FA Bn | 14 | 10 | 5 | 4 | 8 | | |
| 80th Abn AA Bn | 8 | 28 | 22 | 22 | 18 | 14 | 3 |
| 307th Abn Engr Bn | 19 | 30 | 18 | 3 | 2 | 17 | 15 |
| 407th Abn QM Co | | | | | | | |
| 82d Abn Sig Co | 9 | 4 | 2 | 17 | 12 | 11 | 1 |
| 307th Abn Med Co | 1 | 3 | 2 | 3 | 2 | 4 | |
| 782d Abn Ord Maint Co | 1 | 1 | 1 1 | | | | |
| 401st Gli Inf | 6 | 210 | 149 | 37 | 32 | 74 | |
| 508th Prcht Inf | 192 | 487 | 313 | 118 | 83 | 315 | 93 |
| 507th Prcht Inf | 337 | 526 | 270 | 96 | 56 | 251 | 4 |
| | | | | | | | |
| **TOTAL** | **661** | **2373** | **1554** | **704** | **502** | **1142** | **179** |

Net Personnel Loss To Division — 3003

**ANNEX NO. 1 D (3) TO**
**ACCOMPANY HISTORICAL**
**NARRATIVE FOR NORMANDY**

OPERATION NEPTUNE
82ND AIRBORNE DIVISION
ANALYSIS OF OFFICER CASUALTIES
(Adjusted July 26, 1944)

| | COMMITTED STRENGTH | | TOTAL CASUALTIES | | TOTAL % CASUALTIES | | KIA | |
|---|---|---|---|---|---|---|---|---|
| | INF | OTH | INF | OTH | INF | OTH | INF | OTH |
| GENERAL OFFICERS | | 3 | | 1 | | | | |
| COLONELS | 3 | 3 | 1 | 1 | 33.3 | 33.3 | | |
| LT COLS. | 15 | 20 | 9 | 5 | 60.0 | 25.0 | 1 | |
| MAJORS | 24 | 16 | 10 | 1 | 41.6 | 6.3 | 4 | 1 |
| CAPTAINS | 123 | 78 | 41 | 22 | 33.3 | 28.4 | 14 | 1 |
| 1ST LTS | 238 | 89 | 168 | 18 | 70.5 | 20.2 | 39 | 6 |
| 2D LTS | 178 | 77 | 115 | 16 | 64.6 | 20.7 | 34 | 8 |
| WARRANT OFFICERS | 10 | 8 | | 4 | | 50.0 | | |
| TOTAL: | 591 | 294 | 344 | 67 | 58.2 | 22.8 | 92 | 16 |
| AGGREGATE | 885 | | 441 | | 46.4 | | 108 | |

| | WOUNDED INJURED | | SICK IN HOSPITAL | | MIA | | CAPTURED | | RETURNED TO DUTY | |
|---|---|---|---|---|---|---|---|---|---|---|
| | INF | OTH | INF | OTH | INF | OTH | INF | OTH | INF | OTH |
| GENERAL OFFICERS | | | | | | | | | | |
| COLONELS | | 1 | | | 1 | | | | | 1 |
| LT COLS | 7 | 4 | | | 1 | 1 | | | 3 | 3 |
| MAJORS | 5 | | | | 1 | | | | 1 | |
| CAPTAINS | 22 | 14 | 1 | 1 | 3 | 6 | 1 | | 4 | 7 |
| 1ST LTS | 98 | 9 | 2 | 1 | 26 | 2 | 3 | | 36 | 1 |
| 2D LTS | 56 | 4 | 3 | | 22 | 4 | | | 12 | 1 |
| WARRANT OFFICERS | | 3 | | 1 | | | | | | |
| TOTAL: | 188 | 35 | 6 | 3 | 54 | 13 | 4 | | 56 | 13 |
| AGGREGATE | 223 | 9 | 67 | 4 | 69 | | | | | |

**ANNEX NO. 1 D (4) TO
ACCOMPANY HISTORICAL
NARRATIVE FOR NORMANDY**

ANALYSIS OF CASUALTIES BY BRANCH
OPERATION NEPTUNE
82ND AIRBORNE DIVISION
(Adjusted as of 26 July 1944)

| | COMMITTED STRENGTH | | TOTAL CASUALTIES | | TOTAL % CASUALTIES | | KILLED | |
|---|---|---|---|---|---|---|---|---|
| | O | EM | O | EM | O | EM | O | EM |
| DIV TROOPS | 44 | 1282 | 33 | 239 | 22.9 | 18.7 | 5 | 37 |
| GLIDER INF | 104 | 2177 | 68 | 1263 | 65.3 | 58.0 | 21 | 185 |
| PRCHT INF | 452 | 5622 | 268 | 3166 | 59.5 | 56.3 | 70 | 534 |
| DIV ARTY | 121 | 1256 | 23 | 194 | 19.0 | 15.4 | 11 | 40 |
| MEDICAL | 64 | 548 | 19 | 156 | 29.6 | 28.4 | 1 | 17 |
| TOTAL | 885 | 10885 | 411 | 5018 | 46.4 | 46.1 | 108 | 813 |
| AGGREGATE | 11770 | | 5429 | | 46.1 | | 921 | |

| | MISSING | | CAPTURED | | -EVACUATED- Sick | | Injured | | Wounded | |
|---|---|---|---|---|---|---|---|---|---|---|
| | O | EM | O | EM | O | EM | O | EM | O | EM |
| DIV TROOPS | 8 | 61 | | | 3 | 23 | 7 | 37 | 10 | 81 |
| GLIDER INF | 1 | 70 | | | 4 | 149 | 13 | 176 | 29 | 683 |
| PRCHT INF | 54 | 738 | 4 | | 5 | 164 | 21 | 338 | 114 | 1392 |
| DIV ARTY | | 2 | | | 1 | 6 | 4 | 71 | 7 | 75 |
| MEDICAL | 4 | 32 | | | 2 | 20 | | 3 | 12 | 84 |
| TOTAL: | 67 | 903 | 4 | | 15 | 362 | 45 | 625 | 172 | 2315 |
| AGGREGATE | 970 | | 4 | | 377 | | 670 | | 2487 | |

**ANNEX NO. 2 TO
ACCOMPANY HISTORICAL
NARRATIVE FOR NORMANDY**

AIR RESUPPLY

Following is a report submitted by the Assistant Chief of Staff, G-4 on 25 July 1944.

1. Resupply during Operation NEPTUNE breaks down into two phases.

Phase I. Automatic resupply dropped by parachute the morning of D plus 1.

Phase II. Resupply on call delivered by glider at various times after break through occurred and beachhead was sufficiently organized to permit gliders to land on the Beach or large fields without opposition.

2. Phase I. This was a pre-arranged delivery of about 250 tons of all types of expendable supplies – mainly ammunition. Of the 250 tons, only about 200 tons left the UK due to non-availability of equipment in UK. This was dropped in and around the Division area. About 50% was picked up at once – some items reaching small groups who were still isolated west of the MERDERET River. Some undoubtedly fell in German hands. A continuing search was made for these bundles and it is believed that we eventually found about 70% or 140 tons of this equipment.

3. Phase II. Deliveries during this period were in response to our requests for signal equipment, crew-served weapons, including artillery pieces, and GAMMON grenades. All of this equipment arrived safely and reached this Division except for 6000 GAMMON grenades lost due to our not sending a representative to follow this property through to this Division. A list of major items of these shipments follows:

| | |
|---|---|
| 4 – 57mm, AT guns | 3 – 105 mm, M3 Hows |
| 19 – 81mm mortars | 11,000 – GAMMON grenades |
| 20 – 60mm mortars | 4 – SCR-193 |
| 10 – LMG | 4 – SCR-284 |
| 20 – HMG | 3 – SCR-300 |
| 50 – ATRL | 45 miles wire, W-130 |
| 4 – 75mm, Pack Howitzers | 1 ton batteries |

**ANNEX NO. 3 TO**
**ACCOMPANY HISTORICAL**
**NARRATIVE FOR NORMANDY**

AIR MOVEMENT TABLES

Extracted from official air movement tables published in Field Orders of the 82d Airborne Division and the 52d and 33d Troop Carrier Wings. Code names were those assigned by Supreme Headquarters, Allied Expeditionary Force.

AIR MOVEMENT TABLE – PARACHUTE

| Ser-ial | Airborne Unit | USTCC Unit | No. A/C | Takeoff Airfield | DZ | DZ Time |
|---|---|---|---|---|---|---|
| 4 | 82d Pathfinders | 1st P/F | 3 | N. Witham | O | 0121 |
| 5 | 82d Pathfinders | 1st P/F | 3 | N. Witham | N | 0138 |
| 6 | 82d Pathfinders | 1st P/F | 3 | N. Witham | T | 0202 |

MISSION "BOSTON"
(D-DAY)

| Ser-ial | Airborne Unit | USTCC Unit | No. A/C | Takeoff Airfield | DZ | DZ Time |
|---|---|---|---|---|---|---|
| 17 | 2 Bn 505 Prcht Inf | 316 Gp | 36 | Cottesmore | O | 0151 |
| 18 | 3 Bn 505 Prcht Inf | 316 Gp | 36 | Cottesmore | O | 0157 |
| | 2 Secs. 456 Prcht FA | | | | | |
| 19 | 1 Bn 505 Prcht Inf | 315 Gp | 36) | | | |
| | Hq & Hq Co. 505 | | 9) 48 | Spanhoe | O | 0203 |
| | Plat 307 Abn Engr Bn | | 3) | | | |
| | Det. Hq 82 Abn Div | | | | | |
| 20 | 2 Bn 508 Prcht Inf | 314 Gp | 36 | Saltby | N | 0208 |
| 21 | Hq & Hq Co 508 | 314 Gp | 9) | | | |
| | Co B (-) 307 Engr | | 6) 24 | Saltby | N | 0214 |
| | Force "A" Hq | | 9) | | | |
| 22 | 1 Bn 508 Prcht Inf | 313 Gp | 36 | Folkingham | N | 0220 |
| 23 | 3 Bn 508 Prcht Inf | 313 Gp | 36 | Folkingham | N | 0226 |
| 24 | 2 Bn 507 Prcht Inf | 67 Gp | 36 | Barkston Heath | T | 0232 |
| 25 | 3 Bn 507 Prcht Inf | 61 Gp | 36 | Barkston Heath | T | 0238 |
| 26 | 1 Bn 507 Prcht Inf | 442 Gp | 36) | | | |
| | Hq & Hq Co 507 | | 9) 45 | Fulbock | T | 0244 |

MISSION "FREEPORT"
(D PLUS ONE)
(RESUPPLY)

| Ser-ial | Airborne Unit | USTCC Unit | No. A/C | Takeoff Airfield | DZ | DZ Time |
|---|---|---|---|---|---|---|
| 38 | Resupply | 61 Gp | 47 | Barkston Heath | O | 0611 |
| 39 | Resupply | 313 Gp | 46 | Folkingham | O | 0617 |
| 40 | Resupply | 314 Gp | 46 | Saltby | O | 0623 |
| 41 | Resupply | 316 Gp | 46 | Cottesmore | O | 0629 |

TOTAL AIRCRAFT – 378

## AIR MOVEMENT TABLE – GLIDER

| Serial | Airborne Unit | USTCC Unit | No. A/C | Gliders CG 4A | Hor sa | Takeoff Airfield | LZ | LZ Time |
|---|---|---|---|---|---|---|---|---|
| | | | | | | | | |

### MISSION "DETROIT"
### (D-DAY)

| Serial | Airborne Unit | USTCC Unit | No. A/C | Gliders CG 4A | Hor sa | Takeoff Airfield | LZ | LZ Time |
|---|---|---|---|---|---|---|---|---|
| 28 | Btrys A & B 80 437 Gp Abn AA Bn | | 52 | 42 | | Ramsbury | O | 0400 |
| | Hq 82 Abn Div (-) | | 6 | | | | | |
| | ASP (Glider) | | 1 | | | | | |
| | 82 Abn Div Arty | | 1 | | | | | |
| | 82 Abn Sig Co | | 2 | | | | | |

### MISSION "ELMIRA"
### (D-DAY)

| Serial | Airborne Unit | USTCC Unit | No. A/C | Gliders CG 4A | Hor sa | Takeoff Airfield | LZ | LZ Time |
|---|---|---|---|---|---|---|---|---|
| 30 | Btry C 80 Abn AA Bn | 437 Gp | 26 | 13 | | Ramsbury | W | 2110 |
| | Hq 82 Abn Div | | | 4 | | | | |
| | Cmd Veh, Div Hq | | 3 | | | | | |
| | 82 Abn Sig Co | | 1 | | | | | |
| | ASP (Glider) | | 1 | | | | | |
| | 82 Abn Div Arty | | 1 | 1 | | | | |
| | Hq 80 Abn AA Bn | | 2 | | | | | |
| 31 | 307 Abn Med Co | 438 Gp | 50 | 18 | | Greenham | W | 2120 |
| | 82 Rcn Plat | | | 11 | | Commons | | |
| | 82 Abn Sig Co | | | 1 9 | | | | |
| | Hq 82 Abn Div | | | | 9 | | | |
| | ASP Vehicles (Prcht) | | 2 | | | | | |
| 32 | 319 Gli FA Bn | 436 Gp | 50 | 40 | | Membury | W | 2300 |
| | 320 Gli FA Bn | | | | | | 4 | |
| | 82 Abn Div Arty | | | 1 2 | | | | |
| | 307 Abn Med Co | | | 1 1 | | | | |
| | Co A 307 Abn Engr Bn (-) | | | 1 | | | | |
| 33 | 320 Gli FA Bn | 435 Gp | 50 | 12 38 | | Welford | W | 2310 |

### MISSION "GALVESTON"
### (D PLUS ONE)

| Serial | Airborne Unit | USTCC Unit | No. A/C | Gliders CG 4A | Hor sa | Takeoff Airfield | LZ | LZ Time |
|---|---|---|---|---|---|---|---|---|
| 34 | 1 Bn 325 Gli Inf | 437 Gp | 50 | 28 15 | | Ramsbury | W | 0700 |
| | Co A 307 Abn Engr Bn | | | 4 3 | | | | |

| Serial | Airborne Unit | USTCC Unit | No. A/C | Gliders CG 4A | Hor sa | Takeoff Airfield | LZ | LZ Time |
|---|---|---|---|---|---|---|---|---|
| 35 | Hq & Hq Co 325 Gli Inf | 434 Gp | 50 | 40 | | Aldermaston | W | 0710 |
| | 82 Abn Div Arty | | | 5 | | | | |

| | | | | | | |
|---|---|---|---|---|---|---|
| Co A 307 Abn Engr Bn | | | 2 | | | |
| 82 Abn Rcn Plat | | 2 | | | | |
| Cmd Veh 508 Prcht Inf | | | 1 | | | |

## MISSION "HACKENSACK"
### (D PLUS ONE)

| | | | | | | | |
|---|---|---|---|---|---|---|---|
| 36 | 2 Bn 325 Gli Inf 439 Gp | 50 | | 10 15 Uppotery | | W | 0900 |
| | 2 Bn 401 Gli Inf | | | 10 15 | | | |
| | | | | | | | |
| 37 | 2 Bn 325 Gli Inf Sply 441 Gp | | | 50 18 | | | 0910 |
| | 2 Bn 401 Gli Inf Sply | | | 18 | | | |
| | Serv Co 325 Gli Inf 3 | | | | | | |
| | Cmd Veh 505, 507, 508 | | 11 | | | | |
| | Prcht Infs | | | | | | |
| TOTALS | | | 428 | 240  188 | | | |

NOTE: Figures for Headquarters, 82nd Airborne Division include Division Headquarters Company and 82nd Airborne MP Platoon.

*Brigadier General James M. Gavin (L) and Colonel Reuben Tucker (R) confer as the 504th PIR rejoins the 82nd in England, May 1944.*

*Opposite*
*Top: Colonel Harry Lewis, MG J.L. Collins, Commander of VII Corps, and MG Matthew B. Ridgway inspect a 57mm antitank gun of the 325th GIR in England on 16 May 1944. The 57mm gun was used by the 325th and the 80th AA Bn. It was the most powerful antitank weapon in the Division.*

*Bottom: A 57mm antitank gun and crew in front of a CG-4A Glider in England prior to Normandy, 1944.*

*Above: MG J.L. Collins, VII Corps Commander, inspecting 82nd Airborne Division mortar men prior to the invasion of Normandy. England, 16 May 1944.*

*Above: Rigging for the invasion of Normandy. England, 5 June 1944.*

*Opposite: Pathfinder teams of the 505th PIR: 1st Bn. (top), 3rd Bn. (center), and 2nd Bn. (bottom). They would be among the first to land in Normandy. England, 5 June 1944.*

*Above: Rigging for the invasion of Normandy. England, 5 June 1944.*

*Opposite*
*Top: A stick of paratroopers in front of their C-47. England, 5 June 1944.*

*Bottom: A stick of paratroopers before boarding their C-47 for Normandy. England, 5 June 1944.*

*Boarding aircraft for Normandy. England, 5 June 1944.*

Above: C-47 airplanes and CG-4A gliders ready for Normandy. England, June 1944.

Below: Glider troops wait to board a Horsa glider bound for Normandy. England, 4 June 1944.

*Above: Glider troops in a Horsa en route to Normandy, France, 6 June 1944.*

*Opposite*
*Top: Horsa gliders lined up on an airfield ready for Normandy. England, 6 June 1944.*

*Bottom: A Horsa glider taking off for Normandy. England, 6 June 1944.*

*Glider troops disembark from their Horsa glider in Normandy, France, 6 June 1944.*

*A Piper L-4A Grasshopper observation aircraft of Division Artillery sits beneath the wing of a Horsa Glider in Normandy, June 1944.*

*A WACO CG-4A glider painted with Allied aircraft recognition (invasion) stripes, England, July 1944.*

*A WACO CG-4A Glider lands in Normandy, France, June 1944.*

*A rifleman in the hedgerows of Normandy, France, June 1944.*

*An airborne medic in Normandy, June 1944.*

*Opposite*
*Top: Paratroopers on horseback and motorcycle in Ste. Mere Eglise, Normandy, France, June 1944.*

*Bottom: COL Lewis, 325th GIR, looks over a map with an 81mm mortar crew in Normandy, France, June 1944.*

*Right: James Schaffner, left, and Gerald Arnold, right, 325th GIR, in front of the Church in Cauquigny, Normandy, France, 9 June 1944.*

*A machinegun crew of the 325th GIR in Normandy, France, June 1944.*

*Chaplain George B. Wood (R) 505th PIR, at the aid station in Ste. Mere Eglise, Normandy, France. June 1944. Chaplain Wood made four combat jumps in World War II.*

*Gerald Arnold, left, and James Schaffner, right, 325th GIR, at Cauquigny, Normandy, France, 9 June 1944, after crossing the Merderet River.*

*James Schaffner, 325th GIR, in front of Church at Cauquigny, Normandy, France, 9 June 1944. Note German positions to the left.*

*MG Matthew B. Ridgway, 82nd Airborne Division Commander, in Ste. Mere Eglise, Normandy, France, June 1944.*

*MG Matthew B. Ridgway and BG James M. Gavin with other American commanders in Ste. Mere Eglise, Normandy, France, June 1944.*

*Right: Gavin and Ridgway on the road to St. Saveur, Normandy, France, 16 June 1944.*

*A mounted patrol in Normandy, June 1944. The soldier in the back of the jeep carries an M-1903A4 sniper rifle.*

*Lt. Briand N. Beaudin, battalion surgeon, 3/508th PIR and Lt. Paul E. Lehman, also of 3/508th PIR, celebrate their liberation on 17 June 1944 in Orglandes, Normandy, France.*

*Below: An SCR-300A radio at a 505th PIR command post in Normandy, 26 June 1944.*

*Opposite*
Top: *A paratrooper takes time to talk with two French children in Normandy, June 1944.*

Bottom: *A parachute field artillery 75mm pack howitzer in Normandy, June 1944.*

Above: *2LT Jack E. Gavin, HQ, 3rd Battalion, 505th PIR, outside 3rd Bn. Command Post in Normandy, France, June 1944.*

*LTC Strom Thurmond, 325th GIR, driving a captured German kettenkrad in Normandy, June 1944. Mobility was often provided by captured vehicles.*

*A testimony to intense fighting – an abandoned 57mm antitank gun sits next to a knocked out German assault gun. Normandy, France, June 1944.*

*Paratroopers gather along the side of a road in Normandy, France, June 1944.*

*A 1 1/2 ton truck with gun crew and 57mm antitank gun in Normandy, France, June 1944.*

*Chaplain George B. Wood, 505th PIR, back in England after operations in Normandy. July 1944.*

*General Eisenhower addresses the 82nd Airborne Division after the campaign in Normandy. England, 8 August 1944.*

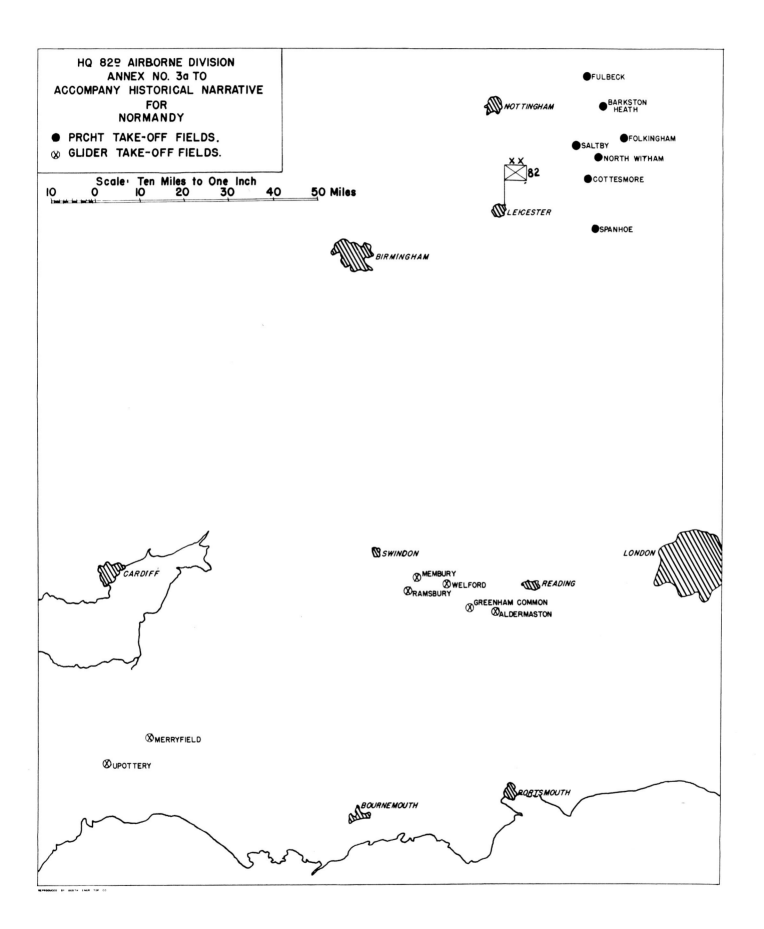

HQ 82ᴰ AIRBORNE DIVISION
ANNEX NO. 3a TO
ACCOMPANY HISTORICAL NARRATIVE
FOR
NORMANDY

● PRCHT TAKE-OFF FIELDS.
⊗ GLIDER TAKE-OFF FIELDS.

Scale: Ten Miles to One Inch
10    0    10    20    30    40    50 Miles

● FULBECK

⊗ NOTTINGHAM

● BARKSTON HEATH

● FOLKINGHAM

● SALTBY

● NORTH WITHAM

XX
82

● COTTESMORE

⊗ LEICESTER

● SPANHOE

BIRMINGHAM

SWINDON
⊗ MEMBURY
⊗ WELFORD
⊗ RAMSBURY
⊗ GREENHAM COMMON
⊗ ALDERMASTON

READING

LONDON

CARDIFF

⊗ MERRYFIELD

⊗ UPOTTERY

BOURNEMOUTH

PORTSMOUTH

82º AIRBORNE DIVISION
ANNEX NO. 5 TO
ACCOMPANY HISTORICAL NARRATIVE
FOR
NORMANDY

# HQ. 82° AIRBORNE DIVISION

APO 469 U.S. ARMY

29 JULY 1944

STATISTICAL STUDY, BASED ON REPORTS OF DIVISION PERSONNEL, OF GLIDER LANDINGS OF 82° A/B DIVISION TROOPS IN OPERATION 'NEPTUNE' 6-7 JUNE 1944

RIDGWAY
COMMANDING

## HORSA

SERIAL 30 TIME OF DROP · 2110 FIELD · RAMSBURY LZ · W ROUTE · W GROUP Nº 437

| ORGANIZATION | TAIL | GLIDER | | | | PERSONNEL | | | | JEEP | | TRAILER | | GUN | | DISTANCE |
|---|---|---|---|---|---|---|---|---|---|---|---|---|---|---|---|---|
| | NUMBER | INTACT | DAM | DES | MISS | Nº | KIA | EVAC | MISS | SERV | UNSER | SERV | UNSER | SERV | UNSER | FROM LZ |
| BTRY C, 80 AABN | DP-616 | | | X | | 7 | | | | X | | X | | | | 300 YDS. |
| " | IG-721 | | X | | | 13 | | | | | | X | | | | 200 " |
| " | DP-671 | | X | | | 13 | | | | | | X | | | | 1500 " |
| " | LG-881 | | | X | | 13 | | | | | | X | | | | 1½ MI. |
| " | LH-125 | | X | | | 13 | | 1 | | | | X | | | | 500 YDS. |
| " | HG-770 | | | X | | 2 | | | | X | | | | X | | 800 " |
| " | IG-887 | | X | | | 2 | | | | X | | | | X | | 1500 " |
| " | IF-923 | | | X | | 2 | | | | | X | | | | X | 1½ MI. |
| " | LJ-161 | | | X | | 2 | | | | | X | | | | X | " " |
| " | LF-898 | | | X | | 2 | | 1 | | X | | | | X | | 400 YDS. |
| " | LG-980 | | X | | | 2 | | | | X | | | | X | | 2½ MI. |
| " | HG-922 | | X | | | 2 | | 2 | | X | | | | X | | 1400 YDS |
| " | HG-935 | X | | | | 2 | | | | X | | | | X | | ? |
| " | LJ-230 | X | | | | 6 | | | | X | | | | | | ½ MI. |
| 82° DIV ARTY | DP-809 | | X | | | 3 | | | | X | | | | | | 1½ " |
| 82° A/B DIV | LJ-182 | X | | | | 6 | | | | | | X | | | | 1000 YDS |
| " | LJ-216 | | | X | | 7 | | 1 | | X | | | | | | |
| " | LH-954 | | | X | | 7 | | | | | X | | X | | | 1 MI. |
| TOTAL | 18 | 3 | 7 | 8 | | 104 | | 5 | | 10 | 3 | 6 | 1 | 6 | 2 | |
| PERCENTAGE | | 17 | 39 | 44 | | | | 4.8 | | 76 | 24 | 86 | 14 | 75 | 25 | |

SERIAL 31 TIME OF DROP · 2120 FIELD · GREENHAM COMMONS LZ · W ROUTE · E GROUP Nº 438

| ORGANIZATION | TAIL | GLIDER | | | | PERSONNEL | | | | JEEP | | TRAILER | | GUN | | DISTANCE |
|---|---|---|---|---|---|---|---|---|---|---|---|---|---|---|---|---|
| | NUMBER | INTACT | DAM | DES | MISS | Nº | KIA | EVAC | MISS | SERV | UNSER | SERV | UNSER | SERV | UNSER | FROM LZ |
| 82° MP PLAT. | DP-675 | | | X | | 5 | | 1 | | X | | X | | | | 3½ MI. |
| " | DP-607 | | | X | | 7 | | | | X | | | | | | 2 " |
| HQ 82° A/B DIV. | LF-899 | | X | | | 19 | | | | | | | | | | ¾ " |
| " | LH-945 | X | | | | 6 | | | | X | | X | | | | ON LZ |
| " | HG-877 | | | X | | 7 | | | | X | | X | | | | 500 YDS E |
| " | HS-125 | | X | | | 7 | | 1 | | X | | X | | | | 2000 " |
| " | LH-121 | | | X | | 9 | | | | X | | X | | | | ½ MI NE |
| " | LH-573 | | X | | | 7 | | | | X | | X | | | | ON LZ |
| " | DP-645 | | | X | | 7 | | 1 | | X | | X | | | | 100 YDS E |
| 307 MED. CO. | LJ-238 | X | | | | 7 | | | | X | | X | | | | ON LZ |
| " | LJ-304 | | X | | | 7 | | | | X | | X | | | | " " |
| " | LG-678 | | | X | | 3 | | 1 | | | X | | | | | " " |
| " | ?-239 | | | X | | 7 | | | | X | | X | | | | " " |
| " | LG-728 | X | | | | 7 | | | | X | | X | | | | " " |
| " | LG-973 | | X | | | 7 | | | | X | | X | | | | 2 MI E |
| " | ? | | X | | | 7 | | | | X | | X | | | | ON LZ |
| " | LG-687 | | X | | | 7 | | | | X | | | X | | | 2 MI NE |
| " | DP-602 | X | | | | 9 | | | | | | | | | | 2 " E |
| " | LN-960 | X | | | | 9 | | | | | | | | | | 2 " E |
| " | DP-596 | | | X | | 9 | | | | | | | | | | 2 " E |
| " | LN-969 | | X | | | 7 | | | | X | | X | | | | 2 " E |
| " | LH-951 | X | | | | 7 | | | | X | | X | | | | 2 " E |
| " | LF-915 | X | | | | 7 | | | | X | | X | | | | 2 " E |
| " | HG-860 | | X | | | 7 | | | | X | | X | | | | 2 " E |
| " | HG-932 | | X | | | 7 | | | | X | | X | | | | 2 " E |
| " | LG-114 | X | | | | 3 | | | | X | | | | | | 2 " E |
| " | HG-870 | | X | | | 7 | | | | X | | X | | | | 2 " E |
| 82° SIG. CO. | LG-496 | | | X | | 14 | | 1 | | | | X | | | | 300 YDS. |
| " | HG-768 | | | X | | 3 | | | | X | | X | | | | ON LZ |
| " | LG-677 | | | X | | 3 | | 3 | | | X | | X | | | 2 MI. |
| " | DP-436 | | | X | | 15 | 2 | 9 | | | | | | | | 1 " |
| " | LJ-160 | | X | | | 3 | | | | X | | X | | | | 3 " |
| " | LJ-257 | | X | | | 3 | | | | X | | X | | | | 2 " |
| " | HG-907 | | | X | | 11 | | 2 | | | | | | | | 3 " |
| " | DP-712 | | X | | | 12 | | | | | | | | | | 3 " |
| TOTAL | 35 | 8 | 14 | 13 | | 262 | 2 | 19 | | 26 | 2 | 23 | 2 | | | |
| PERCENTAGE | | 23 | 40 | 37 | | | .76 | 7.2 | | 93 | 7 | 92 | 8 | | | |

SERIAL 32 TIME OF DROP · 2300 FIELD · MEMBURY LZ · W ROUTE · E GROUP Nº 436

| ORGANIZATION | TAIL | GLIDER | | | | PERSONNEL | | | | JEEP | | TRAILER | | GUN | | DISTANCE |
|---|---|---|---|---|---|---|---|---|---|---|---|---|---|---|---|---|
| | NUMBER | INTACT | DAM | DES | MISS | Nº | KIA | EVAC | MISS | SERV | UNSER | SERV | UNSER | SERV | UNSER | FROM LZ |
| 319 FA. BN. | | | X | | | 7 | | | | X | | | | | | 4½ MI. NE |
| " | | | X | | | 13 | | | | | X | | | | | 5200 YDS |
| " | | | | X | | 13 | | 7 | | | X | | | | | 4400 " |
| " | | X | | | | 6 | | | | X | | X | | | | 5000 " |
| " | | X | | | | 6 | | | | X | | X | | | | " " |
| " | | | | X | | 6 | 1 | 5 | | | X | | X | | | " " |
| " | | | X | | | 6 | | | | X | | X | | | | 4000 " |
| " | | | | X | | 6 | | | | X | | X | | | | 6000 " |
| " | | X | | | | 22 | | | | | | | | | | 6 MI. |
| " | | | | X | | 7 | 1 | 2 | | | X | | X | | | 2½ MI. |
| " | | | | X | | 9 | | | | X | | X | | | | 5000 YDS. |
| " | | | | X | | 14 | | | | | | | | | | 4000 " |
| " | | | | X | | 14 | | | | | | | | | | 4000 " |
| " | | | | X | | 5 | | | | X | | | | X | | 4½-5 MI. |
| " | | | | X | | 5 | | 2 | | | X | | | | X | 6000 YDS. |
| " | | | | X | | 5 | | 1 | | | X | | | | X | 3000 " |
| " | | | X | | | 5 | 3 | 2 | | | X | | | | X | 6000 " |
| " | | | | X | | 5 | | 2 | | | X | | | X | | 3 MI. |
| " | | | | X | | 5 | | 2 | | X | | | | | X | 4½-5 MI. |
| " | | | | X | | 6 | | | | X | | X | | | | 3½ MI. |
| " | | | | X | | 7 | | 5 | | | X | | X | | | 1000 YDS. |
| " | | | | X | | 14 | | | | | | | | | | 4½ MI. |
| " | | | | X | | 14 | | 6 | | | | | | | | 4000 YDS |
| " | | X | | | | 6 | | | | X | | X | | | | 3 MI. |
| " | | | X | | | 7 | | 1 | | | X | | X | | | 2 MI. |
| " | | | | X | | 7 | | 1 | | | X | | X | | | 4000 YDS |
| " | | X | | | | 9 | | | | X | | X | | | | 2 MI. |
| " | | | | X | | 14 | 2 | 2 | | | | | | | | 3 MI. |
| " | | | X | | | 14 | | | | | | | | | | 5000 YDS |
| " | | | | X | | 5 | | 3 | | | | | | | X | 4½ MI. |
| " | | | | X | | 5 | 2 | 3 | | | | | | | X | " " |
| " | | | | X | | 5 | | | | X | | | | | X | 2 MI NE |
| " | | | X | | | 5 | | | | X | | | | X | | 3 " |
| " | | X | | | | 5 | | | | X | | | | X | | 4 " |
| " | | | | X | | 5 | | | | X | | | | X | | 4½ MI. |
| " | | | | X | | 7 | | 5 | | X | | X | | | | 5 MI. |
| " | | | | X | | 14 | 3 | 10 | | | | | | | | 4½ " |
| " | | | | X | | 14 | 2 | 3 | | | | | | | | 4 " |
| " | | | | X | | 7 | | 1 | | | X | X | | | | 2 " |
| " | | | X | | | 7 | | | | X | | X | | | | 2 " |
| " | | | | | | | | | | | | X | | | | 3 MI NE |
| HQ.BTRY. DIV. ARTY. | | X | | | | 13 | | | | | | X | | | | 5000 YDS |
| " | | X | | | | 13 | | | | | | | | | | 3500 " |
| 307 A/B ENGR | | | X | | | 13 | | | | | | | | | | 1 MI. |
| 320 FA BN | | | X | | | 5 | | | | | | | | | | |
| " | | | X | | | 6 | | | | | | X | | | | 1½ MI. |
| " | | | | X | | 4 | | | | | X | | X | | | 3000 YDS. |
| " | | | | X | | 5 | | 1 | | | X | | X | | | 2 MI. |
| 307 A/B MED | | X | | | | 7 | | | | X | | X | | | | 2 MI. |
| TOTAL | 48 | 9 | 11 | 28 | | 402 | 14 | 64 | | 18 | 14 | 15 | 7 | 5 | 7 | |
| PERCENTAGE | | 19 | 23 | 58 | | | 3.4 | 15.9 | | 56 | 44 | 66.7 | 33.3 | 41.6 | 58.4 | |

SERIAL 33 TIME OF DROP 2310 FIELD · WELFORD LZ · W ROUTE · E GROUP Nº 435

| ORGANIZATION | TAIL | GLIDER | | | | PERSONNEL | | | | JEEP | | TRAILER | | GUN | | DISTANCE |
|---|---|---|---|---|---|---|---|---|---|---|---|---|---|---|---|---|
| | NUMBER | INTACT | DAM | DES | MISS | Nº | KIA | EVAC | MISS | SERV | UNSER | SERV | UNSER | SERV | UNSER | FROM LZ |
| 320 FA BN. | HG-897 | | | X | | 8 | 2 | 1 | | X | | X | | | | 3000 YDS NW |
| " | DP-521 | | | X | | 8 | | | | X | | X | | | | " " |
| " | DP-767 | | | X | | 8 | | | | X | | X | | | | 2 MI |
| " | HG-863 | | X | | | 7 | | | | X | | X | | | | ON LZ |
| " | LJ-108 | | | X | | 7 | | | | X | | X | | | | 900 YDS SE |
| " | LJ-120 | | X | | | 8 | | | | X | | X | | | | 2800 " NW |
| " | DP-624 | | | X | | 23 | | 8 | | | | | | | | 2 MI |
| " | LG-949 | | | X | | 7 | | | | X | | X | | | | 3500 YDS NW |
| " | LH-976 | | | X | | 7 | 2 | 5 | | | X | | X | | | 2000 METERS |
| " | DP-627 | | | X | | 7 | 1 | 1 | | X | | X | | | | 2½ MI NW |
| " | H-337 | | | X | | 6 | | | | X | | X | | | | " " |
| " | LG-844 | | | X | | 4 | | 1 | | | X | | X | | | 2 MI NE |
| " | HG-834 | X | | | | 6 | | | | X | | X | | | | " " NW |
| " | LJ-316 | | | X | | 3 | | 2 | | | X | | X | | | 3½ " SW |
| " | HG-842 | | X | | | 4 | | | | X | | X | | | | 2½ " NW |
| " | DP-819 | | | X | | 4 | | | | | | | | | | 2 MI N |
| " | LG-884 | | | X | | 10 | | 4 | | X | | | | | | 3 " |
| " | DP-568 | | X | | | 10 | | | | X | | | | | | 3 " |
| " | HS-125 | | X | | | 4 | | | | | | | | | | 2000 YDS NE |
| " | HG-784 | | | X | | 4 | | 3 | | | | | | | | |
| " | LJ-208 | | | X | | 10 | | | | X | | | | | | 5 MI W |
| " | HG-854 | | | X | | 4 | | 3 | | | | | | | | ON LZ |
| " | DP-674 | | | X | | 10 | | 1 | | | X | | | | | 3 MI NW |
| " | HG-745 | | | X | | 10 | | | | X | | X | | | | 2 " E |
| " | DP-746 | X | | | | 8 | | | | X | | | | | | 2 " " |
| " | HS-138 | | X | | | 10 | | | | X | | | | | | 250 YDS |
| " | HG-767 | | | X | | 10 | | | | X | | | | | | 4 MI N |
| " | LJ-320 | | | X | | 6 | | | | | | | | | | 2½ " N |
| " | LJ-164 | | | X | | 5 | | | | | | | | | | " " " |
| " | LJ-291 | | | X | | 9 | | | | X | | | | | | 2 MI |
| " | DP-702 | | | X | | 10 | | | | X | | | | | | 3000 YDS NW |
| " | LH-169 | | | X | | 5 | | | | | | | | | | 3 MI |
| " | LJ-232 | | | X | | 10 | | | | X | | | | | | 2500 YDS |
| " | LJ-191 | X | | | | 3 | | | | X | | X | | | | 3 MI |
| " | HG-800 | | | X | | 10 | | | | X | | | | | | " " NW |
| " | LH-963 | | | X | | 3 | | | | | | | | | | ON LZ |
| " | LG-720 | X | | | | 24 | | | | | | | | | | " " |
| " | HG-966 | | | X | | 4 | | | | | X | | X | | | 2 MI NW |
| TOTAL | 38 | 4 | 6 | 28 | | 296 | 5 | 30 | | 23 | 5 | 13 | 4 | | | |
| PERCENTAGE | | 10 | 16 | 74 | | | 1.6 | 10.2 | | 82 | 18 | 76 | 24 | | | |

SERIAL 34 TIME OF DROP · 0700 FIELD · RAMSBURY LZ · W ROUTE · E GROUP Nº 437

| ORGANIZATION | TAIL | GLIDER | | | | PERSONNEL | | | | JEEP | | GUN | | TRAILER | | DISTANCE |
|---|---|---|---|---|---|---|---|---|---|---|---|---|---|---|---|---|
| | NUMBER | INTACT | DAM | DES | MISS | Nº | KIA | EVAC | MISS | SERV | UNSER | SERV | UNSER | SERV | UNSER | FROM LZ |
| CO A, 325 | LJ-135 | | | X | | 29 | 14 | 15 | | | | | | | | 2000 YDS SE |
| " | LJ-219 | | X | | | 27 | | 2 | | | | | | | | " " " |
| " | HS-131 | | X | | | 27 | | | | | | | | | | 3000 " E |
| " | LG-998 | | X | | | 29 | | 12 | | | | | | | | 2000 " SE |
| " | (LG-889) | | | | | (28) | | | (NEVER LEFT AIRPORT) | | | | | | | |
| CO C, 325 | LG-845 | | | X | | 29 | | | | | | | | | | 5 MI E |
| " | HG-790 | | X | | | 29 | | | | | | | | | | 5 " " |
| " | HG-940 | | X | | | 28 | | | | | | | | | | 5 " " |
| " | HG-865 | | | X | | 29 | | | | | | | | | | 5 " |
| " | LG-931 | | | X | | 29 | | | | | | | | | | 5 " |
| CO B, 325 | HG-924 | | | X | | 29 | | | | | | | | | | 4½ " |
| " | LG-872 | X | | | | 29 | | | | | | | | | | 4 " E |
| " | LJ-136 | | | X | | 29 | | | | | | | | | | 4 " E |
| " | LJ-186 | | | X | | 29 | | | | | | | | | | 2-3 MI. |
| " | LG-871 | | | X | | 29 | | | | | | | | | | 3-4 " |
| CO C, 325 | | | | X | | 29 | | | | | | | | | | 5 MI. |
| " | | | | X | | 29 | 1 | 10 | | | | | | | | 5 MI |
| CO A, 307 ENGRS | DP-435 | | X | | | 21 | | | | | | | | | | 6000 YDS E |
| BN HQ " " | LH-246 | | X | | | 22 | | | | | | | | | | " " |
| CO A, 307 ENGRS | LF-941 | X | | | | 22 | | | | | | | | | | " " |
| TOTAL | 19 | 2 | 7 | 10 | | 524 | 15 | 63 | | | | | | | | |
| PERCENTAGE | | 10 | 37 | 53 | | | 2.86 | 12. | | | | | | | | |

SERIAL 36 TIME OF DROP 0900 FIELD · UPPOTERY LZ · W ROUTE · E GROUP Nº 539

| ORGANIZATION | TAIL | GLIDER | | | | PERSONNEL | | | | JEEP | | TRAILER | | GUN | | DISTANCE |
|---|---|---|---|---|---|---|---|---|---|---|---|---|---|---|---|---|
| | NUMBER | INTACT | DAM | DES | MISS | Nº | KIA | EVAC | MISS | SERV | UNSER | SERV | UNSER | SERV | UNSER | FROM LZ |
| CO G - 401 ST | B-1 | | | X | | 29 | | | | | | | | | | 2800 YDS |
| " " | B-2 | | X | | | 27 | | | | | | | | | | 2500 " |
| " " | B-3 | | | X | | 29 | | 18 | | | | | | | | 2000 " |
| " " | B-4 | | | X | | 27 | | | | | | | | | | 2500 " |
| " " | B-5 | | | X | | 28 | | | | | | | | | | 4500 " |
| CO F " | B-6 | | | X | | 21 | | 4 | | | | | | | | 2 MI |
| " " | B-7 | X | | | | 18 | | | | | | | | | | " " |
| " " | B-8 | | X | | | 21 | | | | | | | | | | 4 " |
| CO E " | B-9 | | X | | | 29 | | | | | | | | | | 2½ " |
| " " | B-10 | | X | | | 29 | | | | | | | | | | " " |
| " " | B-11 | | X | | | 29 | | | | | | | | | | " " NE |
| " " | B-12 | | X | | | 28 | | | | | | | | | | 7000 YDS |
| " " | B-13 | | | X | | 29 | | | | | | | | | | 9 MI |
| HQ CO " | H-14 | | | X | | 25 | | 4 | | | | | | | | 3 " |
| CO F 325 | W-25 | X | | | | 28 | | | | | | | | | | 1 " |
| " " | W-26 | | | X | | 29 | 4 | 6 | | | | | | | | 300 YDS |
| " " | W-27 | | X | | | 29 | | | | | | | | | | 1 MI |
| " " | W-28 | | | X | | 29 | | | | | | | | | | " " |
| " " | W-29 | X | | | | 29 | | | | | | | | | | " " |
| CO E " | W-30 | | X | | | 29 | | | | | | | | | | ¼ " |
| " " | W-31 | | | X | | 29 | | | | | | | | | | " " |
| " " | W-32 | | | X | | 29 | 6 | 6 | | | | | | | | 2 " |
| " " | W-33 | | X | | | 29 | | | | | | | | | | 4 " |
| " " | W-34 | | | X | | 29 | | | | | | | | | | 2½ " |
| CO G " | W-35 | | | X | | 29 | 3 | 17 | | | | | | | | 1000 YDS |
| " " | W-36 | | X | | | 29 | | | | | | | | | | 1500 " |
| " " | W-37 | | | X | | 29 | | | | | | | | | | ½ MI |
| " " | W-38 | | | X | | 29 | | 2 | | | | | | | | 1300 YDS |
| " " | W-39 | | | X | | 29 | 2 | 2 | | | | | | | | 1300 " |
| TOTAL | 29 | 3 | 10 | 16 | | 803 | 15 | 59 | | | | | | | | |
| PERCENTAGE | | 10 | 35 | 55 | | | 1.8 | 7.3 | | | | | | | | |

SHEET 2 ON 2, STATISTICAL STUDY

# CG4A

SERIAL Nº 28 — TIME OF DROP 0407 — FIELD: RAMSBURY LZ: O — ROUTE: W — Gl Nº 437

SERIAL Nº 30 — TIME OF DROP: 2110 — FIELD: RAMSBURY LZ: W — ROUTE: E — GP Nº 437

SERIAL Nº 31 — TIME OF DROP: 2120 — FIELD: GREENHAM COMMONS LZ: W — ROUTE E — GP Nº 438

SERIAL Nº 32 — TIME OF DROP: 2300 — FIELD: MEMBURY LZ: W — ROUTE: E — GP Nº 436

SERIAL Nº 33 — TIME OF DROP: 2310 — FIELD: WELFORD LZ: W — ROUTE: E — GP Nº 435

SERIAL Nº 34 — TIME OF DROP: 0700 — FIELD: RAMSBURY LZ: W — ROUTE: E — GP Nº 437

SERIAL Nº 35 — TIME OF DROP 0710 — FIELD: ALDERMASTON LZ: W — ROUTE: E — GP Nº 441

SERIAL Nº 36 — TIME OF DROP: 0900 — FIELD: UPPOTERY LZ: W — ROUTE E — GP Nº 439

SERIAL Nº 37 — TIME OF DROP: 0910 — FIELD: MERRYFIELD LZ: W — ROUTE: E — GP Nº 441

| | Nº | GLIDER | | | | PERSONNEL | | | JEEP | | TRAILER | | GUN | |
|---|---|---|---|---|---|---|---|---|---|---|---|---|---|---|
| | | INTACT | DAM | DEG | MISS | Nº | SER | UNSER | SER | UNSER | SER | UNSER | SER | UNSER |
| GRAND TOTAL CG4A | 237 | 53 | 112 | 67 | 5 | 1363 | 10 | 82 | 12 | 68 | 25 | 24 | 6 | 28 | 9 |
| PERCENTAGE | | 22.3 | 47.2 | 28.3 | 2.2 | | .73 | 6.01 | .88 | 73.1 | 26.9 | 80 | 20 | 75.7 | 24.3 |
| GRAND TOTAL HORSA | 187 | 29 | 55 | 103 | 0 | 2390 | 51 | 240 | 0 | 77 | 24 | 57 | 14 | 11 | 9 |
| PERCENTAGE | | 15.5 | 29.4 | 55.1 | | | 2.1 | 10 | - | 76.3 | 23.7 | 80.3 | 19.7 | 55 | 45 |
| AGGREGATE | 424 | 82 | 167 | 170 | 5 | 3753 | 61 | 322 | 12 | 145 | 49 | 81 | 20 | 39 | 18 |
| PERCENTAGE | | 19.4 | 39.4 | 40.1 | 1.1 | | 1.62 | 8.57 | .32 | 74.7 | 25.3 | 80.2 | 19.8 | 68.4 | 31.6 |

# CHAPTER FOUR

# Operation Market:
# The 82nd Airborne Division in Holland

## Narrative

Upon its return from Normandy on 19 July 1944 this Division was located in the Nottingham-Leicester-Market Harboro Area. There it remained and trained until its participation in operation MARKET on 17 September 1944. Twenty-four hours prior to take-off, all airborne elements of the Division were closed at seven airfields in the Grantham-Cottesmore-Langar area. Briefings were conducted, loading plans formulated, all final checks made, and the Division took off for the Netherlands commencing at 170950 September 1944.

The mission of the Division in this operation was as follows:

"Land by parachute and glider commencing D Day South of Nijmegen; seize and hold the highway bridges across the Maas River at Grave and the Waal River at Nijmegen; seize, organize, and hold the high ground between Nijmegen and Groesbeek; deny the roads in the Division area to the enemy; and dominate the area bounded North by line running from Beek West through Hatert thence Southwest to Eindschestraat, South by River Mass and the Nook-Riethorst highway, East by Cleve-Nijmegen highway and Forest Reichswald, and West by line running North and South through Eindschestraat."

The first lift consisted of:

|  | Prcht | Glider |
|---|---|---|
| Hq & Hq Co 82nd A/B Div | 9 | 20 |
| Hq & Hq Btry Div Arty | 3 | 2 |
| 82nd A/B Sig Co |  | 6 |
| Btry A 80th A/B AA Bn |  | 22 |
| 307 A/B Engr Bn | 27 |  |
| 504 Prcht Inf | 137 |  |
| 505 Prcht Inf | 126 |  |
| 508 Prcht Inf | 130 |  |
| 325 Glider Inf | 2 |  |
| 376 Prcht FA Bn | <u>48</u> |  |
| TOTAL | 482 | 50 |

All units dropped as planned except two serials of the 505 Parachute Infantry. A mixup in marshalling caused the 2nd Battalion serial to drop before the 3rd Battalion serial, and as a consequence the 2d Battalion serial was dropped two thousand yards Northeast of its scheduled drop zone.

The entire flight was preceded by a pathfinder team, which landed on DZ "O" ten minutes prior to the arrival of the first elements of the main body. With the exception in the 505 Parachute Infantry indicated above, all units landed on the drop zones, or in the immediate vicinity thereof, on schedule. Flak en route was spotty and light. Flak coming from DZ "O" was initially heavy but inaccurate. The first parachutists to land destroyed all flak crews and took over their weapons. Enemy dispositions along the Maas-Waal Canal in the vicinity of all bridges and in the wooded country around the Nijmegen heights and in the Reichswald were, as anticipated, well organized and of about a strength of eight battalions. Harassing fire continued to come from the edges of the drop zones throughout all of the landings until overcome. Enemy reaction was prompt and appeared to follow in piece meal fashion. Nearby "homeguard" type troops were thrown in as quickly as they could be rushed to the operational area. This piece meal build up increased until a coordinated attack was made by the German 6th Para Division on D+4.

Local enemy units were initially overcome and destroyed or, except for those in the city of Nijmegen proper, they dispersed in the first several hours after landing.

A day by day summary of the activities of each unit of the Division follows:

### D Day, 17 September

Division parachute elements in four hundred and eighty-two C-47's and a serial of fifty gliders left airports in the area of Grantham, England, between 0950 and 1040. All serials except those of 504 Parachute Infantry landed North, East, and South of Groesbeek, Holland, between 1250 and 1400. The 504 Parachute Infantry landed West of the Maas-Waal Canal and North of the Maas River. All drop patterns were excellent. Personnel and equipment losses en route and during the drop were light, and assembly was the best in the history of the Division.

### Headquarters and Headquarters Company 82nd A/B Division

Parachute elements dropped 1306; glider elements landed 1350 on zone South of Groesbeek, moved North through woods, and established Division Command Post at predesignated location 1000 yards West of Groesbeek at 1700.

### 505 Parachute Infantry

Dropped after the Pathfinders at 1300, seized Groesbeek, occupied its area of defensive responsibility from Kamp Southeast to Mook, cleared its area of enemy, and contacted 504 Parachute Infantry at the Maas-Waal Canal bridge near Heuman. All initial missions were accomplished by 2000.

### 504 Parachute Infantry

Dropped beginning 1313 West of the Maas-Waal Canal on three drop zones, two North and one South of the Maas River. One battalion dropped North-east of Overasselt and at 1600, after overcoming strong enemy resistance, captured intact the Maas-Waal Canal bridge at Heuman. The sites of the Canal bridges near Blankenberg and Hatert, both of which had been destroyed by the enemy upon the approach of the battalion, were captured before dark. One battalion dropped West of Overasselt, blocked all Southward movement along the Grave-Nijmegen highway, and cleared the enemy from the Western portion of the Division area. One battalion dropped one rifle company South of the Maas at Grave and the balance of the battalion North of the river and West of Overasselt. Both forces moved against the bridge at Grave immediately. Surprise was complete and the bridge captured at 1430. The town of Grave was occupied at 2300 after having been abandoned by 400 enemy. All initial missions of 504 were accomplished by 1930.

### 508 Parachute Infantry

Dropped Northeast of Groesbeek at 1328. Based on a report from the Dutch that the town and bridges were lightly held, immediately moved into Nijmegen to take the Waal River bridges. At 2000 the attack met heavy enemy resistance about 400 yards from the highway bridge and was stopped. The regiment occupied the area immediately East of the Maas-Waal Canal and established road blocks to prevent enemy movement South of a line running East and West through Hatert. One company moved to clear the glider landing zone Northeast of Groesbeek and met considerable enemy resistance. One battalion, less a company, occupied the important high ground in the vicinity of Berg en Dal without too heavy an opposition. One company advanced on the Nijmegen Bridges from the Southeast and at 2400 had reached Hill 64.4 Northeast of Ubbergen. All initial missions of the 508 were accomplished by 2030.

### 376 Parachute Field Artillery Battalion
Dropped 1335 on drop zone South of Groesbeek, assembled the battalion with ten howitzers, and displaced 1000 yards to the position area. The battalion, initially in support of 505 Parachute Infantry, fired its mission on call from the regiment at 1800.

### 307 A/B Engineer Battalion
Companies B, C, and D, all parachute, dropped South of Groesbeek at 1320. Companies B and D furnished cover on route march to elements of Division Headquarters and protected Division Command Post when it was established at 1715. Company C moved out to contact 504 Parachute Infantry West of Maas-Waal Canal.

### Battery A, 80th A/B Antiaircraft Battalion
Eight 57mm AT guns allotted as follows: Two, 505 Parachute Infantry; Two, 508 Parachute Infantry; Two, 504 Parachute Infantry upon making contact; Two, Division Reserve in vicinity of Division Command Post.

## D Plus 1, 18 September

### 504 Parachute Infantry
Continued to hold the Maas River bridge at Grave and the Maas-Waal Canal bridge at Heuman. Vigorous patrolling was continued on the West and Northwest of the regimental area along the Grave-Nijmegen highway. At 1200 one platoon moved North along the West bank of the Maas-Waal Canal and assisted in the capture of the bridge on the Grave-Nijmegen highway near Honinghutie.

### 505 Parachute Infantry
Maintained its area of defensive responsibility; repelled enemy attacks at Horst, Grafwegen, and Riethorst; captured an enemy patrol trying to work its way North to the Maas-Waal bridge at Heuman, and captured a train attempting to escape into Germany. At 1240 the regiment attacked and cleared the glider landing zone South and Southeast of Groesbeek.

### 508 Parachute Infantry
Withdrew battalion in Nijmegen and attacked to clear the glider landing zone Northeast and East of Groesbeek. The attack crossed the scheduled line of departure at 1310, completely surprised the enemy, and the landing area was swept by 1400. Sixteen antiaircraft guns and 149 prisoners of war were captured. Maintained its defensive sector throughout the 18th. At 181200 a platoon, with the assistance of 504 Parachute Infantry which advanced up the Maas-Waal Canal from the West, captured the Maas-Waal Canal bridge at Honinghutie. Regiment held the high ground vicinity Berg en Dal through the 18th against enemy patrols and sporadic enemy artillery action. One company moved into Nijmegen at 0900, advanced to the same spot to which the regiment had reached on the 17th, fought against a strong enemy force through the entire day, and at 1500 was withdrawn into the sector near Berg en Dal.

### Glider Elements
Between 1000 and 1100 a lift of 450 gliders carrying an antitank battery of the 80th A/B Antiaircraft Battalion, 319 Glider Field Artillery Battalion, 320 Glider Field Artillery Battalion, 456 Parachute Field Artillery Battalion, and 307 Airborne Medical Company departed from fields in the United Kingdom and flew the same route as the lift of the previous day. Gliders landed in zones cleared by the 505 Parachute Infantry and 508 Parachute Infantry in the vicinity of Groesbeek. Several gliders overshot the landing zone and landed beyond the Dutch-German border, but a substantial number of personnel made their way back to the Division area. The overall glider recovery was very satisfactory. After landing and assembling, 319 Glider Field Artillery Battalion was put in direct support of 508 Parachute Infantry, 456 Parachute Field Artillery Battalion in direct support of 505 Parachute Infantry, and 320 Glider Field Artillery Battalion in general support of the Division.

## Resupply

Following the glider lift by 20 minutes, a flight of 135 B-24 bombers dropped resupply on drop zone South of Groesbeek. Drop pattern was good. Recovery was estimated to be at 80%.

## D Plus 2, 19 September

Guards Armored Division reached Grave and the 504 Parachute Infantry at 0820.

## 504 Parachute Infantry

Regiment, less one company left to guard the bridge at Grave, one company left to guard each of the Maas-Waal Canal bridges at Heuman and Honighutie, and one company left to patrol and guard the highway from Grave to the Honinghutie bridge, was moved East of the Maas-Waal Canal, relieved 2nd battalion 508 Parachute Infantry, and occupied the Jonker Bosch Woods, 3rd Battalion was moved to vicinity Malden as Division Reserve.

## 505 Parachute Infantry

Regiment, less 2nd Battalion, maintained its sector of responsibility on the South of the Division area throughout the 19th.

## 2nd Battalion 505 Parachute Infantry

Attached to Guards Armored Division 191100 and moved North to assault the Nijmegen bridges. The battalion reached the edge of Nijmegen without incident and, in moving through the outskirts of the town, received only artillery fire. When the battalion reached the center of the town, one company supported by seven tanks turned Northwest and moved against the railroad bridge. The balance of the battalion, the remainder of the tanks of the 2nd Battalion Grenadier Guards, and one company of British Armored Infantry advanced against the highway bridge. The assault was stopped at the Maria Plein, about 400 yards South of the bridge. A violent engagement lasting throughout the evening and night of the 19th failed to break the strong enemy defensive arc, and at midnight activity consisted of patrolling into the strong point and mortaring it from the cemetery South of the friendly positions.

## 508 Parachute Infantry

Held landing zone East of Groesbeek until 1800. Cleared enemy from and occupied high ground along Nijmegen-Cleve highway between Ubbergen and Wyler. Established road blocks at Wyler, Beek, and Im Thal. Relieved by 504 Parachute Infantry in Jonker Bosch and occupied sector between Kamp and Voxhill. Reinforced Beek road block with platoon of Company D, 307 A/B Engineer Battalion; repelled counterattacks against Toufels Berg throughout entire day.

## Attached Units

1st Coldstream Guards, Armored, and 5th Coldstream Guards, Infantry attached to Division and moved to Dekkerswald in Division Reserve.

## Resupply

Dropped at 1500, approximately 30 C-47's from excessively high altitude, recovery negligible.

## D Plus 3, 20 September

## 504 Parachute Infantry

With 2nd Irish Guards attached, cleared area between Jonker Bosch and Waal River. 3rd Battalion relieved as Division Reserve. Regiment at 1500 effected crossing of Waal River East of Maas; at 1800 captured North end of railroad bridge over the Waal River, seized and cleared bridgehead North of Waal insuring passage of Guards Armored Division. Mopped up Western outskirts of Nijmegen and area South of railroad bridge.

## 505 Parachute Infantry

Regiment, less 2nd Battalion, repelled sharp enemy attack at Horst and Heikant during morning. From 1300 to 2000 repelled at Mook enemy attack of an infantry regiment strongly supported by artillery after attack had penetrated

Division perimeter to depth of 1000 yards on a 1000 yard front. Division perimeter restored at 2000. Regiment reinforced with attachment of 185 glider pilots.

## 2d Battalion 505 Parachute Infantry

Attacked enemy strong points at Southern ends of Nijmegen bridges during morning. At 1400 stormed strong point South of highway bridge, cleared area of enemy, and reached bridge by 1700. First tank of Grenadier Guards crossed 1830.

## 508 Parachute Infantry

Attacked at 1000 at Wyler by one company of enemy infantry moving North and two companies of enemy infantry moving South, all supported by artillery and armor. Forced to withdraw to high ground to West. Enemy immediately occupied Im Thal and Lagewald. Attacked at Beek at 1200 by 2 battalions of enemy parachutists supported by armored vehicles, and forced to withdraw 1000 yards to high ground to Southwest. By counterattack drove enemy from and reoccupied Beek at 2140. Attacked again at Beek 2300 by enemy now reinforced and compelled to withdraw, leaving a detachment surrounded by the enemy in the town. Captured document from prisoner of war which revealed that enemy attacks at Mook, Beek, and Wyler were part of a coordinated Division attack intended to split Division area and sever the Grave-Nijmegen highway.

## Attached Units

Sherwood Rangers Yeomanry and one squadron of the Royals, its reconnaissance unit, attached to Division at 1700 and moved into Dekkerswald.

## D Plus 4, 21 September

## 504 Parachute Infantry

Continued defense of bridgehead over Waal and on mission of mopping up South bank of Waal from outskirts of Nijmegen to Maas-Waal Canal.

## 505 Parachute Infantry (less 2nd Battalion)

Continued to hold defensive sector on South of Division area from Kamp to Mook.

## 2nd Battalion 505 Parachute Infantry

Relieved of mission of close in defense of Nijmegen Bridges and assumed defense of line from Eastern exits of Nijmegen to Ubbergen.

## 508 Parachute Infantry

Counterattacked Beek at first light from Northeast, East and Southeast. Initial attack failed, and enemy, pressing his temporary advantage, penetrated to within 200 yards of Berg en Dal, but was held there. Attack renewed at 1300, and at 1800 Beek cleared of enemy and all defenses reestablished.

## Resupply

At 1300 supplies dropped from approximately 400 C-47's on drop zone West of the Maas-Waal Canal. Drop pattern was six miles in length by two miles in width. Recovery estimated at 60% was accomplished with assistance of Dutch civilians.

## D Plus 5, 22 September

## 504 Parachute Infantry (less 2nd Battalion)

Relieved of mission to Nijmegen bridgehead and displaced to Dekkerswald as Division Reserve.

## 2nd Battalion 504 Parachute Infantry

Relieved 2nd Battalion 505 Parachute Infantry in sector between Nijmegen and Ubbergen and, upon Division order, with Royals, cleared by 1700 area between Nijmegen-Cleve highway and Waal River East to line Ubbergen-Pals.

## 505 Parachute Infantry (less 2nd Battalion)

Reestablished road block at Mook. With Royals, reconnoitered to Rietherst and found road clear of enemy.

## 2nd Battalion 505 Parachute Infantry

Relieved in Nijmegen-Ubbergen sector by 2nd Battalion 504 Parachute Infantry, reverted to regimental control, and relieved Coldstream Guards at Heuman Bridge.

## 508 Parachute Infantry

Held Wyler Berg throughout day and night against persistent enemy counterattacks. With one company Royals attached, effected a reconnaissance in force to Wercheren and high ground West of Erlekom. Met strong resistance and withdrew to high ground vicinity Berg en Dal.

## Attached Units

Coldstream Guards relieved from attachment to this Division and moved South to Vegel to restore line of communication of Second British Army.

## D Plus 6, 23 September

On this date the third glider lift of the Division took off from six airfields in the Grantham-Cottesmore-Langar area bearing 325 Glider Infantry; 80th A/B Antiaircraft Battalion, less Batteries A and B; Company A 307 A/B Engineer Battalion; and elements of Division Special Troops, and landed on and in the vicinity of LZ "O". A number of gliders did not land on the proper landing zone; two landed in England, and forty-three were released between the coast and the LZ. Ten gliders are still unaccounted for. Immediately upon landing, the 325 Glider Infantry was closed in the woods West of Groesbeek preparatory to taking up a sector on the front. [Poles parachuted into DZ "O"]

## D Plus 7 To D Plus 30

The Division continued on its mission assigned by 30 Corps of holding the area between the Waal River and the Maas River, with its front generally that of D plus 6. The 325 Glider Infantry cleaned out the larger portion of the Kiekberg Woods and advanced the right flank of the Division.

## Summary of Period 17 September to 16 October

| a. Parachute Lift | Number | Percent |
|---|---|---|
| Planes committed | 482 | |
| Dropped on or within 1000 yards of DZ | 430 | 89.2 |
| Failed to drop on or within 1000 yards of DZ | 52 | 10.8 |
| Unaccounted for | 0 | 0 |

| b. Glider Lifts | Number | Percent |
|---|---|---|
| Gliders committed | 902 | |
| Landed on or within 1000 yards of LZ | 763 | 84.6 |
| Failed to land on or within 1000 yards of LZ | 102 | 11.3 |
| Unaccounted for | 37 | 4.1 |

| c. Our Losses | Number | Percent |
|---|---|---|
| Killed | 469 | 3.4 |
| Wounded | 1933 | 14.0 |
| Missing | 640 | 4.7 |

d. <u>Enemy Losses</u>
Killed                                                                    2490
Prisoners of War                                                          2977


e. <u>Results of Operations</u>
All missions accomplished

*Brigadier General James M. Gavin took command of the 82nd in August 1944 in England.*

*BG James M. Gavin, commander of the 82nd Airborne Division, briefs his staff and regimental commanders in England before the airborne invasion of Holland on 17 September 1944.*

*Checking maps before loading for the jump into Holland, 17 September 1944.*

*Above: BG James M. Gavin, commander of the 82nd, rigs for the jump into Holland. England, 17 September 1944.*

*Opposite*
*Top: Paratroopers sit under the wing of a C-47 waiting to load for Operation MARKET. England, 17 September 1944.*

*Bottom: Fully rigged paratroopers waiting for orders to load their C-47 that will carry them to Holland. England, 17 September 1944.*

*Above: En route to Holland, 17 September 1944.*

*Opposite*
*Top: Paratroopers rigging for the jump into Holland. England, 17 September 1944. The 82nd used the T-5 parachute for all four combat jumps in World War II.*

*Bottom: Loading C-47s in England for the jump into Holland, 17 September 1944.*

*C Company, 307th Airborne Engineer battalion parachuting into DZ "O" north of Grave, Holland, 17 September 1944.*

*Paratroopers descending into Holland, 17 September 1944.*

*Operation MARKET begins – Paratroopers of the 82nd Airborne Division land near Nijmegen, Holland on 17 September 1944.*

*Two troopers of the 504th PIR view the recently captured bridge over the Maas River at Grave, Holland, September 1944. This was the first objective seized by the 82nd Airborne Division in Operation MARKET.*

*A captain prepares his equipment before putting on his parachute. England, 17 September 1944.*

*CG-4A gliders bring in more troops and equipment to Holland, 17 September 1944.*

*Left: Staff Sergeant Egidio Lemme, 307th Airborne Medical Company, in his CG-4A glider after landing in Holland, September 1944.*

*Armored jeeps of the 82nd Airborne Division Recon Platoon in Holland, 1944.*

*Below: People of Holland greet their liberators, 17 September 1944.*

*Left: Sign in front of the 82nd command post in Holland, September 1944.*

*Below: Fighting in the streets of Nijmegen, Holland, September 1944.*

*Opposite*
*Top: Sketch by Lieutenant John Holabird, C Company 307th Airborne Engineer Battalion, showing positions of tanks and boats for the assault crossing of the Waal River at Nijmegen, Holland, on 20 September 1944.*

*Bottom: View of the road bridge at Nijmegen from the north, 20 September 1944.*

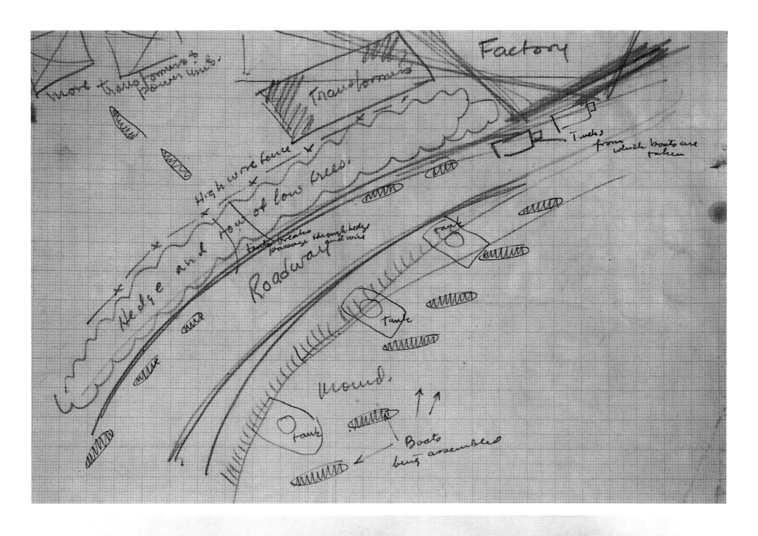

*Vehicles cross the Waal River via the road bridge at Nijmegen, 20 September 1944.*

*Troops cross the road bridge over the Waal River at Nijmegen, 20 September 1944.*

*The railroad bridge facing north. Note the 20mm flak gun on the left that fired upon the troops crossing the Waal on 20 September 1944.*

*The railroad bridge over the Waal River at Nijmegen was captured on 20 September 1944.*

*Aerial view of the railroad bridge (bottom) and pontoon bridge (top) over the Waal River at Nijmegen, Holland, September 1944.*

*Lieutenants (L to R) McLeod, Sabia, and Holabird of C Company, 307th Airborne Engineer Battalion. These officers helped organize and lead the Waal crossing. Holland, September 1944. (Courtesy Al Nemeth)*

*The 3/504th PIR after returning from the Waal crossing, 20 September 1944.*

*Paratroopers of the Polish Parachute Brigade parachute into DZ "O" north of Grave, Holland, 23 September 1944.*

*BG James M. Gavin having a message sent at his field command post in Holland, September 1944.*

*BG James M. Gavin (far right) speaking with several officers including Captain Arie Bestebreurtje (center background) who was Gavin's liaison with the Dutch Interior Forces. Holland, September 1944.*

*BG James M. Gavin, 82nd Commander, in a jeep in Holland, September 1944.*

*A 57mm antitank gun of the 80th Airborne Antiaircraft Artillery Battalion in Holland, 1944. The 80th provided antiaircraft and antitank capabilities for the 82nd.*

*A paratrooper in Holland, 1944.*

*John P. Bouffard, E Company, 505th PIR in Nijmegen, Holland, September 1944.*

# The „All American" ★★ PARAGLIDE

**NIJMEGEN, NETHERLANDS**
**TUESDAY, OCT. 17 1944**

AMERIKA — HOLLAND

## SOUVENIR-BROCHURE NEDERLAND

*PRINTED BY: DE GELDERLANDER-PRESS, NIJMEGEN · HOLLAND*

AIRBORNE

# Invades Holland!

## 17 SEPTEMBER

By Vernon L. Havener.

With „All-American" Airborne Division in Holland. Paratroopers and glidermen of the 82nd Airborne Division — battle-seasoned veterans of Sicily, Italy and Normandy — dropped out of the peaceful Sunday afternoon skies over Holland September 17 to liberate the key Nijmegen sector and pave the way for the sweep of powerful British units northward from Belgium through Holland to the threshold of Germany itself.

The landings — intricately co-ordinated with those of other American, British and Polish units — were a part of the greatest airborne operation in history, and on an incomparably larger scale than any other all-daylight airborne invasion ever attempted.

Wave upon wave of 82nd Division sky troops from English airfields passed over the North Sea and the flooded lowlands of western Holland and dropped on the Nijmegen sector.

Brigadier General James M. Gavin, commander of the 82nd, was the first to jump in his serial.

The 82nd troops quickly swept aside German ground opposition, had accomplished a substantial portion of their mission and entered the outskirts of Nijmegen by dusk.

Landing of the airborne troops was the signal for the uprising of Dutch partisan forces—including an organised underground army 400 strong. The partisans were credited by General Gavin with giving „extremely valuable" assistance to the Allies. They played a vital role in preventing the Germans from blowing the Nijmegen bridges and gave the Allies much valuable information.

The paratroopers fought for nearly 48 hours without contact with ground forces against hastily-committed German troops who put up a stiff fight as the campaign progressed. The Americans linked with leading elements of the advancing British Second Army on D Plus Two.

Additional glider landings in force were made on D Plus Six, when the 325th Glider Infantry, which had been held up by bad weather, landed with re-enforcing troops, anti-tank guns, jeeps, medical and other supplies.

Supplies for the airborne troops were dropped by parachute, and flown in by transports and bombers until contact was made with British forces.

Despite growing enemy aggressiveness after the initial landings, the division accomplished its mission completely. With supporting British armor, the division seized and held the vital highway and railway bridges over the Waal River (a continuation of the Rhine) in Nijmegen, thus holding open a communications corridor to the north and enabling British units to relieve beleaguered British airborne troops who dropped in the Arnhem area.

The division took strategic commanding ground south of Nijmegen and played an important part in the final freeing of the city after fierce fighting in the river area. The division took the Grave bridge over the Maas River and two bridges over the Maas-Waal Canal south and southwest of Nijmegen and freed several villages.

Elements of the division penetrated into and held a portion of Germany northwest of Wyler.

Despite several severe German counter-attacks on narrow fronts, the division never relinquished any ground which it covered in force. It inflicted severe casualties on the Nazis and took many (2889 as of 5 October) prisoners.

## Orange Above

Dutch Patriots give brochure to „All American" Liberators. This paper is made available to troops of the 82nd „All American" Airborne Division and their families through the generosity of the citizens in Nijmegen, Netherlands. As far as we know it's the only paper of its kind in Holland. We express our gratitude and thanks to the Dutch people whose assistance in this campaign has been immeasurable.

-The 82nd Div.

The famous Nijmegen Bridge, one of the main objectives of the Dutch Invasion (Photo, 1936).

## 82ND CAPTURES VITAL NIJMEGEN BRIDGE IN HISTORIC 3 DAY BATTLE

### 504 MAKES HISTORIC RIVER CROSSING

By David H. Whittier.

The 504th Parachute Infantry dropped near Grave early on the afternoon of September 17 after encountering only light flak during its flight over enemy-occupied territory.

The paratroopers, battle-wise from an airborne invasion of Sicily and hard ground fighting near Anzio in Italy, organized speedily, and had accomplished almost their entire mission before dusk of the first day.

Principal objective of the unit was the Grave road bridge over the Maas River, which was taken after a sharp fire fight lasting several hours.

The parachute regiment also captured a strategically-important bridge over the Maas-Waal Canal and seized commanding ground overlooking another Maas-Waal bridge which the Germans had destroyed.

Like other airborne elements, the 504th was re-supplied by air during the early phases of the campaign. The unit made contact with the advance elements of strong British forces on September 19.

With the 307th Engineers, the 504th played a vital role in seizing and holding the railway and highway bridges over the Waal River in Nijmegen. Under the supporting muzzles of British tanks, the 504th crossed the river downstream from the railroad bridge under heavy fire and knocked out stubborn German defenses on the north bank and on the bridges. The engineers, carrying on heroically in the face of withering fire, moved wave after wave of paratroopers across the river in canvas assault boats.

Once across the river, the troopers flanked the Nijmegen bridges and assaulted and took medieval Fort Lent. Three hours later, members of the 504th were fighting 1000 yards north of the river. Hundreds of prisoners had been taken and hundreds more Germans had been killed. Two hundred and sixty-seven German dead were counted on the railway bridge alone. Capture of the bridges permitted British units to pass northward to relieve hard-pressed British airborne forces near Arnhem.

Since these assaults, the 504th has held a wide front against frequent vigorous German counter-attacks and conducted numerous strong combat reconnaissance patrols.

### 505 CRACKS THROUGH NIJMEGEN TO REACH NEAR SIDE

By Robert M. Piper.

On 17 September 1944, the 505th Parachute Infantry jumped in the initial attacking force into German occupied Holland. The unit then stormed the town of Groesbeek and aided in seizing the important crossings of the Maas-Waal Canal. Upon completion of their initial missions two battalions of the Regiment organized the south-eastern defense of the Airborne Sector, which was some 11,000 yards in length.

The reserve battalion of this Regiment moved North with British Armored forces toward the important Nijmegen Bridge, focal point of all roads leading north into Germany. This battalion, the only infantry unit with this armored column, smashed its way into the city of Nijmegen in bitter house to house and hand to hand combat. It drove a numerically superior German force out of pillboxes, fox-holes and prepared trenches. They sought out snipers in houses and soldiers hiding in cellars, clearing the town as they moved on despite the fact they were constantly under heavy artillery fire. This force seized and held the south end of the railroad bridge and the all-important Nijmegen road bridge.

German armor and infantry forces attempting to break through the southern defenses, launched fierce attacks at both Reithorst and Mook, Holland. In bitter hand-to-hand fighting, and with bullets, and cold steel, these combat-seasoned men drove the enemy force back, capturing many and leaving the town strewn with burned vehicles and dead Germans. A captured German parachute officer said, „That is the worst hell I've ever been in." On other parts of this broad front the enemy attempted to seek out front lines in search of a weak sector through which he could attack. He shelled the defenses day and night, attempting to discourage and weaken our forces, but the defenses were held intact, screening the Allied move north.

The Regiment was relieved in the Groesbeek area on the 24th of September, 1944, and moved to Nijmegen. Here they assumed the responsibility of protecting both bridges over the Waal river and protecting the north bank bridgehead. Although under constant shelling and repeated enemy air attacks, the enemy was unable to regain the vital crossing.

## Division Artillery makes history in Holland on D-Day

The 82d A/B "All-American" Division Artillery made airborne history on September 17-18, when the gunners dropped by parachute and landed by glider near Nijmegen, Holland, on D and D plus 1-Day, successfully getting 41 of their 48 howitzers into action. Leading the way, the 376th Parachute F.A. Battalion dropped howitzers on the tail of the parachute infantry, having its first piece assembled and ready to fire in twenty minutes after the green light. Eight howitzers were in position and firing four hours after the drop, the other four having been lost during the flight or damaged in the drop. The battalion supported the attack on Groesbeek on D-Day, and covered the glider landing fields on D plus one, one battery being moved by hand 1000 yards and another over two miles to accomplish their missions. Elements of the Division Artillery Headquarters, the 319th Glider F.A. Battalion, the 320th Glider F.A. Battalion, and the 456th Parachute F.A. Battalion, under the direction of Colonel Francis A. March, Division Artillery Commander, also came in by parachute and glider on D-Day, the remainder landing by glider on D plus 1. By the afternoon of D plus one, the forty-one howitzers had been recovered and were in position supporting the infantry. It was several days before loads, landed in German territory and pinned down by hostile fire, could fight their way to our lines, but fight they did, to join their batteries and assist in pumping thousands of high explosive shells back at the surprised Germans.

With the division entirely surrounded by German troops, the 376th Parachute Battalion set up a perimeter front of 360 degrees, which was strengthened on D plus 1 by the arrival of the 319th, 320th and 456th. Moving from position to position, as the infantry moved to capture bridges, towns, and controlling heights, continuous artillery support was provided for every mission. With little or no sleep during the first 72 hours of action, the gunners brought in ammunition from parachute containers, and gliders, only to fire it as fast as possible as the Germans attacked our front. Due to their tireless efforts and alertness several counter attacks were stopped before they reached the outpost lines. The veterans of Sicily, Maiori, Volturno, Anzio, and Normandy, accustomed to arriving in battle with only the clothing on their back, and the necessity of hauling howitzers and ammunition into position by hand, only worked harder, as they fulfilled a long awaited desire to see their shells leave for Germany. It was only with the arrival of the British armor and artillery from the South that they permitted themselves to rest.

As is usual with artillery, observation and communications were a problem. However, heroic action by forward observers, radio operators, telephone operators and linemen kept our communications in almost continual operation. In many cases, forward observers with their parties were actually surrounded in their positions, but continued to adjust the artillery fire on the Germans. Wires

Continued pag. 4

*Holland issue of the PARAGLIDE, 82nd Airborne Division newspaper.*

*The price we paid – An American cemetery in Holland. In the foreground is the grave of 2nd Lieutenant Jack E. Gavin of Headquarters Company, 3rd Battalion, 505th PIR.*

*Major General James M. Gavin is decorated with the Order of Orange-Nassau for his actions in Holland in 1944.*

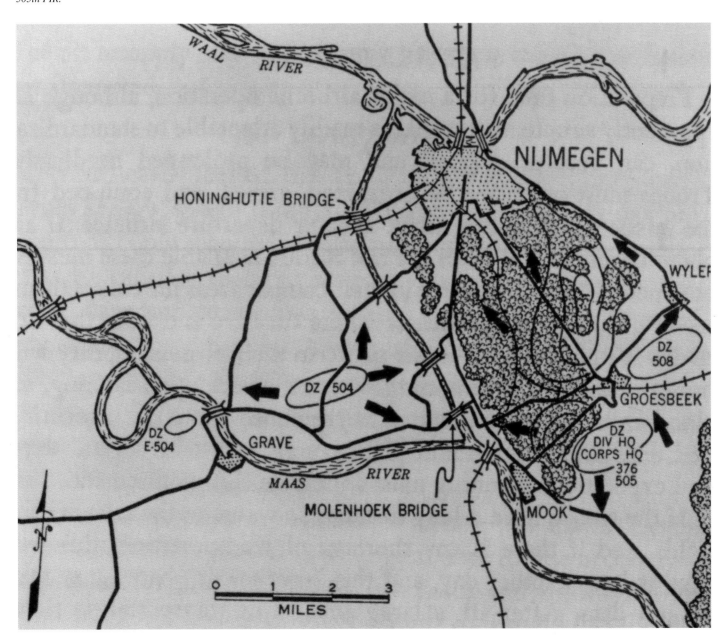

SECRET

# HQ.82º AIRBORNE DIVISION

APO 469 U.S. ARMY

31 OCTOBER 1944

## STATISTICAL STUDY, BASED ON REPORTS OF DIVISION PERSONNEL, ON PARACHUTE LANDINGS OF 82º A/B DIVISION TROOPS IN OPERATION "MARKET" 17 SEPTEMBER 1944

GAVIN
COMMANDING

SERIAL Nº A-2 TIME OF DROP · 1250 DZ · O ROUTE · N FIELD · NORTH WITHAM GP Nº IX TCC

| ORGANIZATION | TAIL NUMBER | PERSONNEL OK | KIA | WIA | MISS | DISTANCE FROM DZ |
|---|---|---|---|---|---|---|
| PF 504 Prcht Inf | 43-15163 | 12 | | | | DZ |
| " | 42-92700 | 12 | | | | DZ |
| TOTAL | | 24 | | | | |
| PERCENTAGE | | 100 | | | | |

SERIAL Nº A-7 TIME OF DROP · 1300 DZ · N ROUTE · N FIELD · FOLKINGHAM GP Nº 313TH

| ORGANIZATION | TAIL NUMBER | PERSONNEL OK | KIA | WIA | MISS | DISTANCE FROM DZ |
|---|---|---|---|---|---|---|
| Hq & Hq Co 505 | 315650 | 19 | | | | 3 mi NE |
| " | 223649 | 20 | | | | 2 mi NE |
| " | 232921 | 21 | | | | " |
| " | 293714 | 20 | | | | " |
| " | 43-48394 | 15 | | | | " |
| " | 42-92880 | 19 | | | | " |
| Hq Co 3rd Bn 505 | 42-5682 | 19 | | | | 3 mi NE |
| " | 43-15198 | 18 | | | | DZ |
| " | 41-18487 | 16 | | 1 | | " |
| " | 42-32863 | 18 | | | | " |
| " | 43-15267 | 19 | | | | " |
| " | 42-23474 | 16 | | | | " |
| " | 42-23647 | 18 | | | | " |
| " | 43-15145 | 19 | | 1 | | " |
| " | 42-68766 | 14 | | | | " |
| " | 42-100514 | 12 | | | | " |
| Co "G" 505 | 42-30648 | 18 | | 3 | | " |
| " | 42-23386 | 18 | | | 1 | " |
| " | 43-15075 | 18 | | | | " |
| " | 42-93814 | 14 | | | | " |
| " | 4[illegible] 30723 | 18 | | | | " |
| " | 42-92970 | 18 | | | | " |
| " | 43-16265 | 16 | | | | " |
| " | 42-93519 | 17 | | | | " |
| " | 42-93027 | 15 | | | | " |
| " | 43-15176 | 13 | | 1 | | " |
| Co "H" 505 | 43-15066 | 20 | | | | " |
| " | 42-32867 | 19 | | | | " |
| " | 315619 | 16 | | | | " |
| " | 42-32923 | 17 | | | 2 | " |
| " | 42-32877 | 18 | | | | " |
| " | 42-23529 | 13 | | | 3 | " |
| " | 42-5702 | 18 | | | | " |
| " | 42-92726 | 16 | | | | " |
| " | 42-93511 | 18 | | | | " |
| " | 42-24211 | 11 | | | | " |
| Co "I" 505 | 43-15709 | 18 | | | | " |
| " | 42-23636 | 18 | | | | " |
| " | 42-32916 | 18 | | | | " |
| " | 43-15260 | 20 | | | | " |
| " | 43-23383 | 19 | | | | " |
| " | 42-32911 | 19 | | | | " |
| " | 43-16122 | 18 | | | | " |
| " | 41-18633 | 18 | | | | " |
| " | 42-32873 | 16 | | | | " |
| TOTAL | | 778 | | 6 | 6 | |
| PERCENTAGE | | 98.4 | | .8 | .8 | |

SERIAL Nº A-8 TIME OF DROP · 1304 DZ · N ROUTE · N FIELD · FOLKINGHAM GP Nº 313TH

| ORGANIZATION | TAIL NUMBER | PERSONNEL OK | KIA | WIA | MISS | DISTANCE FROM DZ |
|---|---|---|---|---|---|---|
| Hq & Hq Co 505 | 42-92870 | 18 | | | | DZ |
| " | 42-32827 | 16 | | | | " |
| " | 42-32920 | 17 | | 1 | | " |
| " | 43-16266 | 14 | | | 1 | " |
| Hq Co 2nd Bn 505 | 347933 | 19 | | | | 3 mi NE |
| Hq Co 2nd Bn 505 | 108991 | 18 | | | | " |
| " | 315082 | 16 | | | | " |
| " | 268705 | 21 | | | | " |
| " | 292064 | 16 | | | | " |
| " | 208979 | 16 | | | | " |
| " | 42-93076 | 18 | | | | " |
| " | 43-16049 | 17 | | | 1 | " |
| " | 43-15323 | 20 | | | | " |
| Co "D" 505 | 315506 | 17 | | | | " |
| " | 293507 | 14 | | | | " |
| " | 315191 | 18 | | | | " |
| " | 43-15662 | 17 | | | | " |
| " | 224177 | 16 | | | | " |
| " | 425690 | 14 | | | | " |
| " | 293521 | 16 | | | | " |
| " | 268758 | 17 | | | | " |
| " | 425700 | 16 | | | | " |
| " | 348415 | 15 | | | | " |
| Co "E" 505 | 348403 | 15 | | | | 2 mi NE |
| " | 293712 | 17 | | | | " |
| " | 4138449 | 13 | | | | 1500 Yds NE |
| " | 43-15202 | 14 | | | | 2000 Yds NE |
| " | 293518 | 15 | | | | " |
| " | 293715 | 16 | | | | " |
| " | 42-24198 | 14 | | | | " |
| " | 292718 | 17 | | | | " |
| " | 42-24184 | 17 | | 1 | | " |
| " | 43-15294 | 19 | | | | " |
| Co "F" 505 | 42-24373 | 18 | | | | 2 mi NE |
| " | 43-15345 | 18 | | | | " |
| " | 43-15160 | 17 | | | | " |
| " | 100878 | 13 | | | | " |
| " | 42-24270 | 13 | | | | " |
| " | 42-93793 | 16 | | | | " |
| " | 42-93005 | 14 | | | | " |
| " | 41-18632 | 15 | | 1 | | " |
| " | 43-15110 | 15 | | | | " |
| " | 232870 | 14 | | | | " |
| Sig Co 82nd A/B Div | 648 | 12 | | | | DZ |
| " | 703 | 12 | | | | " |
| TOTAL | | 710 | | 3 | 2 | |
| PERCENTAGE | | 99.3 | | .4 | .3 | |

| GRAND TOTAL | PERSONNEL OK | KIA | WIA | MISS | TOTAL |
|---|---|---|---|---|---|
| TOTAL | 7127 | 2 | 122 | 26 | 7277 |
| PERCENTAGE | 97.94 | .03 | 1.67 | .36 | 100 |

NOTE:
ON THIS CHART, DROPS WITHIN 1000 Yds OF DZ ARE SHOWN AS BEING ON DZ.

SERIAL Nº A-9 TIME OF DROP · 1308 DZ · N ROUTE · N FIELD · COTTESMORE GP Nº 316TH

| ORGANIZATION | TAIL NUMBER | PERSONNEL OK | KIA | WIA | MISS | DISTANCE FROM DZ |
|---|---|---|---|---|---|---|
| Hq Co 1st Bn 505 | 42-93755 | 17 | | | 1 | DZ |
| " | 43-15513 | 20 | | | | " |
| " | 42-23505 | 18 | | | | " |
| " | 43-15095 | 19 | | 1 | | " |
| " | 42-93815 | 17 | | 1 | | " |
| " | 42-24189 | 20 | | | | " |
| " | 42-92777 | 17 | | | | " |
| " | 43-48390 | 15 | | | | " |
| " | 42-100516 | 16 | | | | " |
| Co "A" 505 | 43-15292 | 22 | | | | " |
| " | 43-15171 | 22 | | | | " |
| " | 43-15295 | 21 | | | | " |
| " | 42-92774 | 19 | | | | " |
| " | 43-15509 | 19 | | | | " |
| " | 43-15510 | 19 | | | | " |
| " | 42-92725 | 20 | | | | " |
| " | 43-15498 | 20 | | | | " |
| " | 43-15212 | 19 | | | | " |
| Co "B" 505 | 42-92884 | 17 | | | | " |
| " | 42-100875 | 18 | | | | " |
| " | 43-15093 | 18 | | | | " |
| " | 42-92846 | 18 | | | | " |
| " | 42-24392 | 19 | | | | " |
| " | 42-100502 | 16 | | 1 | | " |
| " | 43-93100 | 19 | | | | " |
| " | 42-24328 | 18 | | | | " |
| " | 43-30721 | 18 | | | | " |
| Co "C" 505 | 43-15617 | 17 | | 1 | | " |
| " | 42-68772 | 20 | | | | " |
| " | 42-92755 | 17 | | 1 | | " |
| " | 43-48414 | 20 | | | | " |
| " | 42-93734 | 21 | | | | " |
| " | 43-48293 | 17 | | | | " |
| " | 315671 | 18 | | | | " |
| " | 43-15317 | 15 | | | 1 | " |
| " | 42-92886 | 19 | | | | " |
| Hq 82nd A/B Div | | 16 | | | | " |
| " | | 16 | | | | " |
| " | | 15 | | | | " |
| " | | 14 | | | | " |
| " | | 15 | | | | " |
| " | | 16 | | | | " |
| " | | 14 | | | | " |
| TOTAL | | 769 | | 5 | 2 | |
| PERCENTAGE | | 99.1 | | .6 | .3 | |

SERIAL Nº A-10 TIME OF DROP · 1313 DZ · O ROUTE · N FIELD · COTTESMORE GP Nº 316TH

| ORGANIZATION | TAIL NUMBER | PERSONNEL OK | KIA | WIA | MISS | DISTANCE FROM DZ |
|---|---|---|---|---|---|---|
| Hq & Hq 504 | 42-23931 | 18 | | 2 | | DZ |
| " | 43-30652 | 18 | | | | " |
| " | 43-15300 | 15 | | 1 | | " |
| Hq Co 1st Bn 504 | 43-15497 | 17 | | | | " |
| " | 43-15641 | 17 | | 1 | | " |
| " | 43-15207 | 18 | | | | " |
| " | 42-92056 | 18 | | | | " |
| " | 43-15305 | 15 | | 2 | | " |
| " | 42-93075 | 12 | | 2 | | " |
| " | 43-15225 | 18 | | | | " |
| " | 42-24181 | 17 | | | | " |
| " | 42-23935 | 18 | | | | " |
| Co "A" 504 | 43-41972 | 15 | | | | " |
| " | 43-15334 | 16 | | | | " |
| " | 43-15659 | 13 | | | | " |
| " | 43-15194 | 12 | | | | " |
| " | 42-92861 | 13 | | 1 | | " |
| " | 42-93512 | 16 | | 1 | | " |
| " | 43-15633 | 15 | | | | " |
| " | 42-100499 | 14 | | | | " |
| " | 42-23639 | 13 | | | | " |
| " | 43-15265 | 14 | | | | " |
| " | 43-15638 | 15 | 1 | | | " |
| Co "B" 504 | 43-15227 | 14 | | | | " |
| " | 43-15185 | 19 | | | | " |
| " | 43-15643 | 15 | | | | " |
| " | 43-15634 | 12 | | | | " |
| " | 42-100973 | 13 | | 1 | | " |
| " | 43-15179 | 9 | | 1 | | " |
| " | 42-108902 | 17 | | | | " |
| " | 43-15258 | 13 | | | | " |
| " | 42-100517 | 12 | | | | " |
| " | 43-15205 | 9 | | | | " |
| " | 42-24389 | 16 | | | | " |
| Co "C" 504 | 42-23503 | 14 | | 1 | | " |
| " | 42-68769 | 15 | | | | " |
| " | 42-108909 | 14 | | | | " |
| " | 42-687660 | 12 | | | | " |
| " | 42-93780 | 17 | | | | " |
| " | 42-93754 | 13 | | | | " |
| " | 42-23623 | 15 | | | | " |
| " | 43-15106 | 12 | | | | " |
| " | 42-100883 | *14 | | | | " |
| " | 43-15495 | 11 | | | | " |
| " | 42-68765 | 11 | | | | " |
| TOTAL | | 663 | 1 | 13 | | |
| PERCENTAGE | | 97.8 | .3 | 1.9 | | |

SERIAL Nº A-11 TIME OF DROP · 1317 DZ · O ROUTE · N FIELD · SPANHOE GP Nº 315TH

| ORGANIZATION | TAIL NUMBER | PERSONNEL OK | KIA | WIA | MISS | DISTANCE FROM DZ |
|---|---|---|---|---|---|---|
| Hq Co 504 | 42-93064 | 18 | | | | DZ |
| " | 42-100872 | 17 | | 1 | | " |
| " | 43-30652 | 15 | | 1 | | " |
| Hq Co 3rd Bn 504 | 43-15266 | 17 | | 1 | | " |
| " | 43-15255 | 15 | | 1 | | " |
| " | 42-93704 | 16 | | 1 | | " |
| " | 43-24175 | 17 | | 1 | | " |
| " | 43-108871 | 14 | | 4 | | " |
| " | 43-15256 | 15 | | | | " |
| " | 43-15164 | 19 | | | | " |
| " | 42-93031 | 17 | | | | " |
| " | 42-23412 | 18 | | 1 | | " |
| Co "G" 504 | 42-92849 | 15 | | 1 | | " |
| " | 42-108905 | 14 | | 1 | | " |
| " | 42-92138 | 12 | | | | " |
| " | 42-23509 | 16 | | | | " |
| " | 42-92734 | 16 | | | | " |
| " | 42-92737 | 13 | | 1 | | " |
| " | 43-16032 | 9 | | 4 | | " |
| " | 42-108969 | 16 | | 1 | | " |
| " | 43-15289 | 16 | | 1 | | " |
| " | 43-15293 | 16 | | | | " |
| " | 43-15206 | 16 | | 1 | | " |
| Co "H" 504 | 42-93063 | 14 | | | | " |
| " | 43-15308 | | | | 15 | SHOT DOWN HOLLAND |
| " | 43-16022 | 16 | | | | DZ |
| " | 43-15224 | 11 | | 3 | | " |
| " | 43-15173 | 11 | | | | " |
| " | 42-93697 | 12 | | | | " |
| " | 42-24174 | 15 | | | | " |
| " | 43-15321 | 13 | | | | " |
| " | 42-92736 | 12 | | | | " |
| " | 43-15175 | 11 | | 1 | | " |
| " | 43-16023 | 15 | | | | " |
| Co "I" 504 | 42-92682 | 18 | | | | " |
| " | 43-15058 | 12 | | | | " |
| " | 42-93037 | 11 | | | | " |
| " | 43-16263 | 10 | | | | " |
| " | 43-15251 | 13 | | | | " |
| " | 42-93698 | 12 | | | | " |
| " | 43-15071 | 11 | | | | " |
| " | 43-16281 | 13 | | | | " |
| " | 43-15188 | 11 | | | | " |
| " | 42-24172 | 11 | | | | " |
| " | 42-93179 | 14 | | | | " |
| TOTAL | | 624 | | 25 | 15 | |
| PERCENTAGE | | 94 | | 3.8 | 2.2 | |

SERIAL Nº A-12 TIME OF DROP · 1320 DZ · O ROUTE · N FIELD · SPANHOE GP Nº 315TH

| ORGANIZATION | TAIL NUMBER | PERSONNEL OK | KIA | WIA | MISS | DISTANCE FROM DZ |
|---|---|---|---|---|---|---|
| Hq & Hq Co 504 | 42-68811 | 17 | | | | DZ |
| " | 43-15314 | 15 | | 1 | | " |
| " | 43-15157 | 17 | | | | " |
| Hq Co 2nd Bn 504 | 42-93520 | 17 | | | | " |
| " | 42-108883 | 17 | | | | " |
| " | 42-48399 | 17 | | 1 | | " |
| " | 43-48404 | 19 | | | | " |
| " | 42-15199 | 17 | | | | " |
| " | 42-92895 | 10 | | | | " |
| " | 42-108906 | 18 | | | | " |
| " | 42-23303 | 16 | | | | " |
| " | 42-92902 | 13 | | 1 | | " |
| Co "D" 504 | 42-108977 | 14 | | 1 | | " |
| " | 43-15208 | 13 | | 1 | | " |
| " | 43-15346 | 15 | | | | " |
| " | 42-92780 | 13 | | 1 | | " |
| " | 42-92833 | 14 | | | | " |
| " | 43-93701 | 14 | | 1 | | " |
| " | 42-92779 | 15 | | | | " |
| " | 42-93515 | 15 | | 1 | | " |
| " | 43-48402 | 14 | | 1 | | " |
| " | 43-15193 | 16 | | | | " |
| " | 42-92864 | 13 | | | | " |
| Co "E" 504 | 42-23609 | 16 | | 1 | | " |
| " | 43-15325 | 14 | 1 | | | " |
| " | 43-93029 | 13 | | | | " |
| " | 42-92742 | 18 | | | | " |
| " | 43-15339 | 16 | | | | " |
| " | 42-68811 | 16 | | 1 | | " |
| " | 42-93707 | 13 | | | | " |
| " | 43-15187 | 16 | | | | " |
| " | 42-93061 | 16 | | | | " |
| " | 42-93032 | 15 | | | | " |
| " | 43-15204 | 12 | | | | " |
| Co "F" 504 | 42-92733 | 16 | | | | " |
| " | 43-15333 | 13 | | 1 | | " |
| " | 42-93702 | 11 | | 1 | | " |
| " | 42-93799 | 16 | | | | " |
| " | 42-93706 | 15 | | | | " |
| " | 42-108960 | 17 | | | | " |
| " | 42-92890 | 13 | | 3 | | " |
| " | 43-15253 | 16 | | | | " |
| " | 42-92877 | 9 | | | | " |
| " | 43-15612 | 15 | | | | " |
| " | 42-93085 | 15 | | | | " |
| TOTAL | | 673 | 1 | 16 | | |
| PERCENTAGE | | 97.5 | .2 | 2.3 | | |

SERIAL Nº A-13 TIME OF DROP · 1324 DZ · N ROUTE · N FIELD · BALDERTON GP Nº 439TH

| ORGANIZATION | TAIL NUMBER | PERSONNEL OK | KIA | WIA | MISS | DISTANCE FROM DZ |
|---|---|---|---|---|---|---|
| Hq & Hq Btry Div Arty | 42-100858 | 14 | | | | DZ |
| " | 42-100860 | 16 | | | | " |
| " | 42-100862 | 17 | | | | " |
| Co "B" 307 Engr | 651 | 13 | | | | " |
| " | 604 | 14 | | | | " |
| " | 652 | 13 | | 1 | | " |
| " | 650 | 13 | | | | " |
| " | 827 | 14 | | | | " |
| " | 825 | 13 | | | | " |
| " | 824 | 13 | | 1 | | " |
| " | 830 | 15 | | | | " |
| " | 828 | 13 | | | | " |
| Co "C" 307 Engr | 43-15049 | 15 | | | | " |
| " | 42-100847 | 14 | | | | " |
| " | 42-100823 | 13 | | 1 | | " |
| " | 42-92912 | 12 | | | | " |
| " | 42-100833 | 14 | | 1 | | " |
| " | 42-100889 | 13 | | | | " |
| " | 42-100818 | 15 | | | | " |
| " | 43-15169 | 16 | | | | " |
| Co "D" 307 Engr | 316549 | 14 | | | | " |
| " | 42-100846 | 12 | | 1 | | " |
| " | 43-92908 | 15 | | 1 | | " |
| " | 43-15649 | 12 | | 1 | | " |
| " | 42-23601 | 13 | | | | " |
| " | 42-100872 | 15 | | | | " |
| " | 42-93069 | 14 | | | | " |
| " | 42-100842 | 15 | | | | " |
| " | 42-100858 | 14 | | | | " |
| " | 42-100644 | | | | | |
| TOTAL | | 428 | | 7 | | |
| PERCENTAGE | | 98.4 | | 1.6 | | |

SERIAL Nº A-20 TIME OF DROP · 1328 DZ · T ROUTE · N FIELD · LANGAR GP Nº 441

| ORGANIZATION | TAIL NUMBER | PERSONNEL OK | KIA | WIA | MISS | DISTANCE FROM DZ |
|---|---|---|---|---|---|---|
| Hq & Hq Co 508 | 42-32835 | 18 | | | | DZ |
| " | 42-93078 | 19 | | | | " |
| Hq Co 1st Bn 508 | 42-92719 | 17 | | | | " |
| " | 42-101003 | 19 | | | | " |
| " | 42-92905 | 16 | | | | " |
| " | 42-101007 | 18 | | | | " |
| " | 42-101008 | 16 | | | | " |
| " | 42-101009 | 16 | | | | " |
| " | 42-101010 | 18 | | | | " |
| " | 42-101011 | 16 | | | | " |
| " | 42-101013 | 17 | | | | " |
| Co "A" 508 | 43-5355 | 12 | | | | " |
| " | 43-15218 | 13 | | | | " |
| " | 43-16348 | 15 | | | | " |
| " | 42-101005 | 16 | | | | " |
| " | 42-92731 | 16 | | | | " |
| " | 42-93028 | 14 | | | | " |
| " | 42-101004 | 10 | | | | 2000 Yds E |
| " | 43-15216 | 12 | | 1 | | " |
| " | 43-48256 | 16 | | | | DZ |
| " | 42-101012 | 12 | | | | " |
| " | 42-100863 | 14 | | | | " |
| Co "B" 508 | 2100864 | 13 | | | | " |
| " | 223331 | 14 | | | | " |
| " | 42-68843 | 17 | | | | " |
| " | 42-15102 | 15 | | | | " |
| " | 42-101016 | 14 | | 2 | | " |
| " | 43-15646 | 14 | | | | " |
| " | 2101018 | 12 | | | | " |
| " | 42-101034 | 12 | | | | " |
| " | 42-93041 | 15 | | | | " |
| " | 42-92741 | 12 | | | | " |
| Co "C" 508 | 42-101020 | 13 | | | | " |
| " | 42-92681 | 12 | | | | " |
| " | 42-101021 | 17 | | | | " |
| " | 42-101015 | 11 | | | | " |
| " | 42-101014 | 12 | | 1 | | " |
| " | 42-10107 | 12 | | 1 | | " |
| " | 43-15086 | 12 | | | | " |
| " | 42-101023 | 14 | | | | " |
| " | 42-92845 | 15 | | 1 | | " |
| " | 42-101024 | 15 | | | | " |
| " | 42-100865 | 14 | | | | " |
| 325th PF | | 20 | | | | " |
| " | | 20 | | | | " |
| TOTAL | | 665 | | 6 | | |
| PERCENTAGE | | 99.1 | | .8 | | |

SERIAL Nº A-21 TIME OF DROP · 1332 DZ · T ROUTE · N FIELD · LANGAR GP Nº 441

| ORGANIZATION | TAIL NUMBER | PERSONNEL OK | KIA | WIA | MISS | DISTANCE FROM DZ |
|---|---|---|---|---|---|---|
| Hq & Hq Co 508 | 42-32870 | 19 | | | | DZ |
| " | 42-5693 | 18 | | 1 | | " |
| " | 42-68843 | 16 | | | | " |
| " | 42-101035 | 17 | | | | " |
| " | 315644 | 16 | | 1 | | " |
| " | 43-15041 | 20 | | | | " |
| Hq Co 2nd Bn 508 | 42-100866 | 18 | | | | 2000 Yds W |
| " | 42-293810 | 16 | | | | DZ |
| " | 2101030 | 14 | | | | " |
| " | 2100867 | 19 | | | | " |
| " | 42-101029 | 16 | | 1 | | " |
| " | 393709 | 15 | | | | " |
| " | 42-100868 | 17 | | | | " |
| " | 43-15035 | 12 | | | | " |
| " | 43-15353 | 18 | | | | " |
| Co "D" 508 | 43-15033 | 16 | | 1 | | " |
| " | 43-15043 | 16 | | | | " |
| " | 43-15135 | 17 | | | | " |
| " | 43-48260 | 12 | | | | " |
| " | 43-15189 | 14 | | | | " |
| " | 42-92904 | 15 | | | | " |
| " | 43-15034 | 13 | | | | " |
| " | 43-15152 | 16 | | | | " |
| " | 43-15042 | 16 | | | | " |
| " | 43-16378 | 15 | | | | " |
| Co "E" 508 | 43-15038 | 16 | | | | " |
| " | 43-15041 | 13 | | | | " |
| " | 42-93082 | 16 | | | | " |
| " | 42-92921 | 13 | | | | " |
| " | 43-16361 | 12 | | | | " |
| " | 42-100870 | 17 | | | | " |
| " | 42-100869 | 12 | | | | " |
| " | 315036 | 15 | | | | " |
| " | 43-15037 | 15 | | | | " |
| " | 42-93068 | 17 | | | | " |
| Co "F" 508 | 42-101026 | 17 | | | | " |
| " | 42-101033 | 12 | | | | " |
| " | 42-92911 | 13 | | | | " |
| " | 43-16045 | 12 | | | | 5 mi W |
| " | 316042 | 13 | | | | DZ |
| " | 43-15219 | 17 | | | | " |
| " | 42-101032 | 14 | | | | " |
| " | 42-93720 | 11 | | | | " |
| " | 42-101027 | 15 | | | | " |
| " | 42-101028 | 11 | | | | " |
| TOTAL | | 671 | | 4 | | |
| PERCENTAGE | | 99.5 | | .5 | | |

SERIAL Nº A-22 TIME OF DROP · 1336 DZ · T ROUTE · N FIELD · FULBECK GP Nº 440TH

| ORGANIZATION | TAIL NUMBER | PERSONNEL OK | KIA | WIA | MISS | DISTANCE FROM DZ |
|---|---|---|---|---|---|---|
| Hq & Hq Co 3rd Bn 508 | 42-100730 | 17 | | | | DZ |
| " | 42-100904 | 17 | | 1 | | " |
| " | 42-92914 | 16 | | | | " |
| " | 42-93705 | 17 | | | | " |
| " | 42-100908 | 15 | | | 1 | " |
| " | 42-100900 | 18 | | | | " |
| " | 43-15087 | 16 | | | | " |
| " | 43-48400 | 17 | | | | " |
| " | 42-100913 | 15 | | 2 | | " |
| " | 293081 | 16 | | 1 | | " |
| Co "G" 508 | 42-100965 | 14 | | | | " |
| " | 315669 | 14 | | | | " |
| " | 42-118886 | 16 | | 1 | | " |
| " | 42-100906 | 12 | | | | " |
| " | 315503 | 13 | | | | " |
| " | 43-15656 | 16 | | | | " |
| " | 2100917 | 11 | | 1 | | " |
| " | 42-68695 | 12 | | | | " |
| " | 268700 | 15 | | | | " |
| " | 42-100961 | 11 | | | | " |
| " | 43-48468 | 16 | | | | " |
| Co "H" 508 | 43-15069 | 14 | | | | " |
| " | 43-15636 | 13 | | | | " |
| " | 42-100931 | 18 | | | | " |
| " | 108891 | 16 | | | | " |
| " | 42-100922 | 11 | | 3 | | " |
| " | 42-100932 | 15 | | | | " |
| " | 2100939 | 17 | | | | " |
| " | 43-48408 | 14 | | | | 5 mi W |
| " | 42-100933 | 17 | | | | DZ |
| " | 292775 | 10 | | | | " |
| " | 43-15168 | 13 | | | | " |
| Co "I" 508 | 42-108911 | 12 | | 2 | | " |
| " | 2100642 | 14 | | 1 | | " |
| " | 2100915 | 14 | | 1 | | " |
| " | 2100919 | 16 | | | | " |
| " | 2100732 | 14 | | | | " |
| " | 42-100918 | 17 | | | | " |
| " | 42-100921 | 14 | | | | " |
| " | 425673 | 12 | | | | " |
| " | 315654 | 13 | | | | " |
| " | 42-100928 | 14 | | | | " |
| TOTAL | | 602 | | 13 | 1 | |
| PERCENTAGE | | 97.7 | | 2.1 | .1 | |

SERIAL Nº A-23 TIME OF DROP · 1340 DZ · N ROUTE · N FIELD · FULBECK GP Nº 440TH

| ORGANIZATION | TAIL NUMBER | PERSONNEL OK | KIA | WIA | MISS | DISTANCE FROM DZ |
|---|---|---|---|---|---|---|
| 376th FA Bn | 43-15217 | 16 | | 2 | | DZ |
| Hq Btry " | 42-100929 | 16 | | 2 | | " |
| " | 42-100937 | 18 | | 2 | | " |
| " | 42-100925 | 17 | | 4 | | " |
| " | 43-32803 | 16 | | 2 | | " |
| " | 43-15626 | 17 | | 2 | | " |
| Btry "A" " | 42-100909 | 9 | | | | " |
| " | 42-100903 | 12 | | | | " |
| " | 42-100509 | 10 | | | | " |
| " | 42-100839 | 10 | | | | " |
| " | 43-15073 | 12 | | 1 | | " |
| " | 42-92872 | 10 | | | | " |
| " | 42-100731 | 10 | | | | " |
| " | 43-15658 | 11 | | 2 | | " |
| " | 43-15084 | 9 | | | | " |
| " | 42-100912 | 9 | | | | " |
| " | 42-100910 | 11 | | 1 | | " |
| " | 42-100920 | 8 | | | | " |
| " | 42-92728 | 10 | | 1 | | " |
| Btry "B" " | 42-93130 | 9 | | | | " |
| " | 42-100880 | 10 | | | | " |
| " | 43-47960 | 10 | | 1 | | " |
| " | 42-100916 | 10 | | 1 | | " |
| " | 42-100997 | 6 | | | | " |
| " | 43-48392 | 11 | | | | " |
| " | 42-92771 | 9 | | | | " |
| " | 43-15672 | 13 | | | | " |
| " | 42-100927 | 14 | | | | " |
| " | 42-100926 | 10 | | 1 | | " |
| " | 42-93034 | 9 | | | | " |
| " | 42-92729 | 13 | | | | " |
| " | 42-100734 | 10 | | | | " |
| Btry "C" " | 43-15076 | 8 | | | | " |
| " | 43-16043 | 9 | | | | " |
| " | 43-48410 | 9 | | | | " |
| " | 42-108910 | 8 | | | | " |
| " | 42-100737 | 9 | | | | " |
| " | 42-100940 | 9 | | | | " |
| " | 42-100941 | 10 | | | | " |
| " | 42-92920 | 10 | | | | " |
| " | 42-92900 | 11 | | | | " |
| " | 42-100934 | 9 | | | | " |
| " | 42-100938 | 9 | | | | " |
| " | 43-15083 | 9 | | | | " |
| Btry "D" " | 42-100942 | 14 | | 1 | | " |
| " | 42-100736 | 14 | | | | " |
| " | 43-15182 | 15 | | | | " |
| " | 42-100935 | 16 | | 1 | | " |
| TOTAL | | 520 | | 24 | | |
| PERCENTAGE | | 95.6 | | 4.4 | | |

SECRET

# HQ 82° AIRBORNE DIVISION

APO 469    31 OCTOBER 1944    U.S. ARMY

STATISTICAL STUDY, BASED ON REPORTS OF
DIVISION PERSONNEL, OF GLIDER LANDINGS OF
82° A/B DIVISION TROOPS IN OPERATION
"MARKET"  17, 18 & 23 SEPTEMBER 1944

GAVIN
COMMANDING

**SERIAL N° A-1  TIME OF DROP-1350  FIELD-BALDERTON  LZ-N  ROUTE-N  GP N° 439**

| ORGANIZATION | TAIL NUMBER | GLIDER |  |  |  | PERSONNEL |  |  |  | JEEP |  | TRAILER |  | GUN |  | DISTANCE FROM LZ |
|---|---|---|---|---|---|---|---|---|---|---|---|---|---|---|---|---|
| | | INTACT | DAM | DES | MISS | OK | KIA | EVAC | MISS | SER | UNSER | SER | UNSER | SER | UNSER | |
| TOTAL | | 34 | 14 | 2 | | 209 | 7 | | | 24 | 4 | 7 | | 8 | | |
| PERCENTAGE | | 68 | 28 | 4 | | 96.7 | 3.3 | | | 85.7 | 14.3 | 100 | | 100 | | |

**SERIAL N° A-2  TIME OF DROP-1400  FIELD-BALDERTON  LZ-N  ROUTE-N  GP N° 432**

| TOTAL | | 20 | 28 | 1 | 1 | 168 | 6 | 3 | | 25 | 2 | 11 | | 8 | | |
| PERCENTAGE | | 40 | 56 | 2 | 2 | 94.6 | 3.6 | 1.8 | | 92.7 | 7.3 | 100 | | 100 | | |

**SERIAL N° A-3  TIME OF DROP-1407  FIELD-FOLKINGHAM  LZ-N  ROUTE-N  GP N° 313**

| TOTAL | | 11 | 27 | 2 | | 167 | 2 | | | 14 | | 20 | 3 | | | |
| PERCENTAGE | | 27.5 | 67.5 | 5 | | 98.8 | 1.2 | | | 100 | | 86.8 | 13.2 | | | |

**SERIAL N° A-4  TIME OF DROP-1414  FIELD-BARKSTON HEATH  LZ-T  ROUTE-N  GP N° 6137**

| TOTAL | | 26 | 10 | 2 | 2 | 183 | 1 | 7 | 9 | 42 | 15.8 | 85.7 | 14.3 | | 6 | |
| PERCENTAGE | | 6.5 | 25 | | | | | | | | | | | 100 | | |

**SERIAL N° A-5  TIME OF DROP-1421  FIELD-COTTESMORE  LZ-T  ROUTE-N  GP N° 316**

| TOTAL | | 21 | 9 | 2 | 8 | 129 | 2 | 46 | 15 | 7 | 10 | 6 | | | | |
| PERCENTAGE | | 52.5 | 22.5 | 5 | 20 | 73.2 | 1.3 | 25.5 | 68.1 | 31.9 | 83.3 | 16.7 | | | | |

**SERIAL N° A-6  TIME OF DROP-1428  FIELD-FULBECK  LZ-T  ROUTE-N  GP N° 440**

| TOTAL | | 31 | 8 | | 1 | 168 | 3 | 3 | 17 | 1 | 9 | | 6 | | | |
| PERCENTAGE | | 77.5 | 20 | | 2.5 | 96.6 | 1.7 | 1.7 | 94.5 | 5.5 | 100 | | 100 | | | |

# SHEET Nº 2

SERIAL Nº A-7 TIME OF DROP·1435 FIELD·LANGAR LZ·N ROUTE·N GP Nº 441

| ORGANIZATION | TAIL | GLIDER | | | | PERSONNEL | | | | JEEP | | TRAILER | | GUN | | DISTANCE |
|---|---|---|---|---|---|---|---|---|---|---|---|---|---|---|---|---|
| | NUMBER | INTACT | DAM | DES | MISS | OK | KIA | EVAC | MISS | SER | UNSER | SER | UNSER | SER | UNSER | FROM LZ |
| 82º A/B Sig Co | 253146 | X | | | | 3 | | | | X | | | | | | LZ |
| " | 345121 | | X | | | 2 | | | | X | | | | | | " |
| " | 339968 | X | | | | 2 | | | | X | | | | | | " |
| " | 43-10086 | | X | | | 1 | | | | X | | | | | | " |
| " | 277536 | | X | | | 3 | | | | X | | | | | | " |
| " | 340186 | | X | | | 5 | | | | | | X | | | | " |
| " | 277606 | | | X | | 2 | | | | X | | | | | | " |
| " | 340803 | | X | | | 5 | | | | | | X | | | | " |
| " | 342036 | X | | | | 5 | | | | | | X | | | | " |
| " | 42-92843 | | X | | | 3 | | | | X | | | | | | " |
| " | 42-100644 | | | X | | 4 | | | | | | X | | | | " |
| " | 341530 | | X | | | 3 | | | | X | | | | | | " |
| " | 277414 | | | X | | 1 | | 2 | | X | | | | | | 4 mi W |
| " | 336633 | X | | | | 5 | | | | | | X | | | | 2 mi W |
| " | 327430 | | X | | | 3 | | | | X | | | | | | LZ |
| " | 21-01083 | | X | | | 4 | | | | X | | | | | | " |
| " | 42-100865 | | X | | | 2 | | | | X | | | | | | " |
| " | 43-15203 | X | | | | 4 | | | | | | X | | | | " |
| " | 42-101014 | X | | | | 5 | | | | | | X | | | | " |
| " | 341700 | | X | | | 4 | | 1 | | | | X | | | | " |
| " | 342119 | X | | | | 2 | | | | X | | | | | | " |
| 307 A/B Med Co | 277758 | X | | | | 2 | | | | X | | | | | | " |
| " | 273892 | | X | | | 6 | | | | | | X | | | | " |
| " | 319806 | | X | | | 2 | | | | X | | | | | | " |
| " | 336649 | X | | | | 6 | | | | | | X | | | | " |
| " | 327413 | X | | | | 2 | | | | X | | | | | | " |
| " | 339721 | | X | | | 4 | | 2 | | | | X | | | | " |
| " | 319755 | | X | | | 8 | | | | | | | | | | " |
| " | 279268 | | X | | | 2 | | | | X | | | | | | " |
| " | 379157 | | X | | | 6 | | | | | | X | | | | " |
| " | 258091 | | X | | | 2 | | | | X | | | | | | ENGLAND |
| " | 277599 | | X | | | 2 | | | | X | | | | | | LZ |
| " | 336647 | | X | | | 3 | | | | | | X | | | | " |
| " | 340080 | | X | | | 2 | | | | X | | | | | | " |
| " | 42-217398 | | X | | | 9 | | | | | | X | | | | " |
| " | 42-77741 | | X | | | 6 | | | | | | | | | | " |
| 505 Comd Veh | 42-10922 | X | | | | 2 | | | | X | | | | | | " |
| " | 43-15224 | X | | | | 2 | | | | X | | | | | | " |
| " | 43-15076 | X | | | | 2 | | | | X | | | | | | " |
| " | 43-15199 | | X | | | 2 | | | | X | | | | | | " |
| | | | | | | | | | | | | | | | | |
| TOTAL | | 13 | 24 | 3 | | 140 | | 5 | | 24 | | 14 | | | | " |
| PERCENTAGE | | 32.5 | 60 | 7.5 | | 96.5 | | 3.5 | | 100 | | 100 | | | | " |

SERIAL Nº A-8 TIME OF DROP·1442 FIELD·FOLKINGHAM LZ·N ROUTE·N GP Nº 313TH

| ORGANIZATION | TAIL | GLIDER | | | | PERSONNEL | | | | JEEP | | TRAILER | | GUN | | DISTANCE |
|---|---|---|---|---|---|---|---|---|---|---|---|---|---|---|---|---|
| | NUMBER | INTACT | DAM | DES | MISS | OK | EVAC | KIA | MISS | SER | UNSER | SER | UNSER | SER | UNSER | FROM LZ |
| Btry "B" 320 FA Bn | 43-41489 | | | X | | 3 | | | | | X | | | | | 3 mi NE |
| " | 43-41683 | | | X | | 3 | | | | | X | | | | | 4 mi NE |
| " | 43-41089 | | | X | | 7 | | | | | | | | | | " |
| " | 43-41421 | | | X | | 13 | | | | | | | | | | " |
| " | 43-41502 | | | X | | 2 | | | 1 | | X | | | | | " |
| " | 43-41940 | | | | X | | | | 2 | | | | | | X | |
| " | 43-40439 | | | X | | | | | 2 | | X | | | | | 3 mi NE |
| " | 43-141158 | | | X | | 1 | 1 | | | | | | | | X | 4 mi NE |
| " | 42-77890 | | | X | | 1 | | | 1 | | X | | | | | 3 mi NE |
| " | 42-77818 | | | | X | | | | 2 | | | | | | X | |
| " | 43-20131 | | | X | | 2 | | | | | X | | | | | 3 mi NE |
| " | 43-19801 | | | | X | | | | 2 | | | | | | X | |
| " | 43-40093 | X | | | | 2 | | | | X | | | | | | LZ |
| " | 43-40546 | X | | | | 2 | | | | | | | | X | | " |
| " | 43-41379 | X | | | | 2 | | | | X | | | | | | " |
| " | 43-36937 | | X | | | 2 | | | | | | | | X | | " |
| " | 43-41374 | X | | | | 2 | | | | X | | | | | | " |
| " | 43-41459 | | X | | | 3 | | | | X | | | | | | " |
| " | 43-40212 | | X | | | 4 | | | | | | X | | | | " |
| " | 43-42154 | X | | | | 4 | | | | | | X | | | | " |
| " | 43-41905 | | | | X | | | | 4 | | | | X | | | |
| " | 43-42127 | | | | X | | | | 4 | | | | X | | | |
| " | 43-41684 | | | | X | | | | 4 | | | | X | | | |
| " | 43-42110 | | | | X | | | | 4 | | | | X | | | |
| " | 43-41677 | | | | X | | | | 4 | | | | X | | | |
| " | 43-40219 | | | | X | | | | 2 | | X | | | | | |
| " | 43-42007 | | | | X | | | | 2 | | X | | | | | |
| " | 43-40162 | | | | X | | | | 2 | | X | | | | | |
| " | 43-40085 | | | | X | | | | 2 | | X | | | | | |
| " | 43-41629 | | | | X | | | | 2 | | X | | | | | |
| " | 43-41146 | X | | | | 5 | | | | | | | | | | LZ |
| " | 43-40447 | | X | | | 5 | | | | | | | | | | " |
| " | 43-40213 | X | | | | 5 | | | | | | | | | | " |
| " | 43-40461 | X | | | | 5 | | | | | | | | | | " |
| " | 43-37390 | X | | | | 5 | | | | | | | | | | " |
| " | 43-41964 | | X | | | 5 | | | | | | | | | | " |
| " | 43-41994 | X | | | | 5 | | | | | | | | | | " |
| " | 43-36791 | | X | | | 3 | 1 | 1 | | | | | | | | " |
| " | 43-40554 | | X | | | 4 | | | | | | | | | | " |
| " | 43-41607 | | X | | | 4 | | | | | | | | | | " |
| | | | | | | | | | | | | | | | | |
| TOTAL | | 10 | 8 | 9 | 13 | 99 | 2 | 1 | 40 | 4 | 11 | 2 | 5 | 2 | 4 | |
| PERCENTAGE | | 25 | 20 | 22.5 | 32.5 | 69.7 | 1.3 | .9 | 28.1 | 26.6 | 73.4 | 28.5 | 71.5 | 33.4 | 66.6 | |

SERIAL Nº A-9 TIME OF DROP·1449 FIELD·BARKSTON HEATH ROUTE·N LZ·T GP Nº 61ST

| ORGANIZATION | TAIL | GLIDER | | | | PERSONNEL | | | | JEEP | | TRAILER | | GUN | | DISTANCE |
|---|---|---|---|---|---|---|---|---|---|---|---|---|---|---|---|---|
| | NUMBER | INTACT | DAM | DES | MISS | OK | KIA | EVAC | MISS | SER | UNSER | SER | UNSER | SER | UNSER | FROM LZ |
| Btry "A" 320 FA Bn | 43-40442 | | X | | | 3 | | | | X | | | | | | LZ |
| " | 43-41376 | X | | | | 3 | | | | X | | | | | | " |
| " | 43-37436 | X | | | | 3 | | | | X | | | | | | " |
| " | 43-41464 | X | | | | 3 | | | | X | | | | | | " |
| " | 43-40161 | | | X | | 2 | 1 | | | | X | | | | | " |
| " | 43-42084 | X | | | | 3 | | | | X | | | | | | " |
| " | 43-40207 | | X | | | 3 | | | | X | | | | | | " |
| " | 43-37302 | X | | | | 3 | | | | X | | | | | | " |
| " | 43-40557 | X | | | | 2 | | | | X | | | | | | " |
| " | 43-41952 | X | | | | 2 | | | | X | | | | | | " |
| " | 43-87294 | | X | | | 2 | | | | X | | | | | | " |
| | 43-27467 | X | | | | 2 | | | | X | | | | | | " |
| " | 43-37338 | | X | | | 1 | | 1 | | | | | | X | | " |
| " | 43-40536 | | X | | | 2 | | | | | | | | X | | " |
| " | 43-40371 | | X | | | 2 | | | | | | | | X | | " |
| " | 43-37332 | X | | | | 2 | | | | | | | | X | | " |
| " | 42-74039 | | X | | | 2 | | | | X | | | | | | " |
| " | 42-46448 | | X | | | 3 | | | | X | | | | | | " |
| " | 43-39908 | | X | | | 2 | | | | | | | | X | | " |
| " | 43-39909 | | X | | | 2 | | | | | | | | X | | " |
| " | 43-37283 | X | | | | 4 | | 1 | | X | | | | | | " |
| " | 43-39889 | X | | | | 5 | | | | X | | | | | | " |
| " | 43-40059 | X | | | | 5 | | | | | | X | | | | " |
| " | 43-40187 | | X | | | 5 | | | | | | X | | | | " |
| " | 43-39696 | | X | | | 5 | | | | | | X | | | | " |
| " | 43-41491 | | X | | | 4 | | | | | | X | | | | " |
| " | 43-39809 | | X | | | 4 | | | | | | X | | | | " |
| " | 43-42076 | | X | | | 5 | | | | | | | | | | " |
| " | 43-37277 | | X | | | 5 | | | | | | | | | | " |
| " | 43-41087 | | X | | | 5 | | | | | | | | | | " |
| " | 43-36929 | | X | | | 5 | | | | | | | | | | " |
| " | 42-77653 | | X | | | 4 | | | | | | | | | | " |
| " | 43-41170 | | X | | | 5 | | | | | | | | | | " |
| " | 43-40047 | | X | | | 5 | | | | | | | | | | " |
| " | 43-37404 | | | X | | 5 | | | | | | | | | | " |
| " | 43-40307 | | X | | | 5 | | | | | | | | | | " |
| " | 43-42068 | X | | | | 3 | | | | | | | | | | " |
| " | 43-41446 | | X | | | 5 | | | | | | | | | | " |
| " | 42-74016 | X | | | | 4 | | | | | | | | | | " |
| " | 342058 | | X | | | 2 | | | | | | | | | | " |
| | | | | | | | | | | | | | | | | |
| TOTAL | | 14 | 24 | 2 | | 137 | 1 | 2 | | 16 | 1 | 5 | | 6 | | |
| PERCENTAGE | | 35 | 60 | 5 | | 97.8 | .8 | 1.4 | | 94.1 | 5.9 | 100 | | 100 | | |

SERIAL Nº A-10 TIME OF DROP·1456 FIELD·COTTESMORE LZ·T ROUTE·N GP Nº 316TH

| ORGANIZATION | TAIL | GLIDER | | | | PERSONNEL | | | | JEEP | | TRAILER | | GUN | | DISTANCE |
|---|---|---|---|---|---|---|---|---|---|---|---|---|---|---|---|---|
| | NUMBER | INTACT | DAM | DES | MISS | OK | KIA | EVAC | MISS | SER | UNSER | SER | UNSER | SER | UNSER | FROM LZ |
| Hq Btry 320 FA Bn | 43-340119 | | X | | | 7 | | | | | | | X | | | 1 mi East |
| " | 43-40042 | | | | X | | | | 2 | | X | | | | | |
| " | 43-39944 | | | X | | 2 | | | | | X | | | | | 3 mi SE |
| " | 43-40119 | | | X | | 6 | | | 1 | | | X | | | | " |
| " | 43-37399 | X | | | | 2 | | | | | X | | | | | 2 mi E |
| " | 43-41889 | | X | | | 6 | | | | | | | X | | | LZ |
| " | 43-41898 | X | | | | 2 | | | | X | | | | | | 1 mi E |
| " | 42-77895 | | X | | | 6 | | | | | | | X | | | 2 mi SE |
| " | 43-42117 | X | | | | 2 | | | | X | | | | | | " |
| " | 43-41701 | X | | | | 6 | | | | | | X | | | | " |
| " | 43-36756 | | X | | | 2 | | | | X | | | | | | " |
| " | 42-79465 | | | X | | 6 | | | | | | X | | | | 8 mi SW |
| " | 43-40357 | X | | | | 2 | | | | X | | | | | | 2 mi SE |
| " | 43-27632 | | X | | | 5 | | | | | | X | | | | " |
| " | 43-40055 | X | | | | 2 | | | | X | | | | | | " |
| " | 43-41960 | | | | X | | | | 6 | | | | X | | | " |
| " | 43-41095 | | X | | | 13 | | | | | | | | | | " |
| " | 42-56507 | X | | | | 13 | | | | | | | | | | " |
| " | 43-40535 | | | X | | 12 | | 1 | | | | | | | | " |
| H&S Btry 456 FA Bn | 746529 | X | | | | 2 | | | | X | | | | | | LZ |
| " | 748529 | X | | | | 7 | | | | | | X | | | | " |
| " | 43-41035 | X | | | | 14 | | | | | | | | | | " |
| " | 746530 | X | | | | 2 | | | | X | | | | | | " |
| " | 747528 | | X | | | 2 | | 3 | | | | X | | | | " |
| " | 748530 | X | | | | 2 | | | | X | | | | | | " |
| " | 764521 | X | | | | 2 | | | | X | | | | | | " |
| " | 745527 | X | | | | 6 | | | | | | X | | | | " |
| " | 749525 | X | | | | 5 | | | | | | X | | | | " |
| " | 764522 | | X | | | 2 | | | | X | | | | | | " |
| " | 745525 | X | | | | 7 | | | | | | X | | | | " |
| " | 764513 | X | | | | 2 | | | | X | | | | | | " |
| " | 746526 | X | | | | 6 | | | | | | X | | | | " |
| " | 754530 | X | | | | 2 | | | | X | | | | | | " |
| " | 755530 | X | | | | 5 | | | | | | X | | | | " |
| " | 764521 | | X | | | 3 | | | | X | | | | | | " |
| " | 737521 | X | | | | 7 | | | | | | X | | | | " |
| Btry "A" 456 FA Bn | 43-27416 | | | X | | 2 | | | | X | | | | | | " |
| " | 43-41577 | | X | | | 9 | | | | | | | | X | | " |
| " | 43-19914 | X | | | | 2 | | | | X | | | | | | " |
| " | 43-19915 | X | | | | 5 | | | | | | | | X | | " |
| | | | | | | | | | | | | | | | | |
| TOTAL | | 23 | 10 | 5 | 2 | 188 | | 4 | 9 | 15 | 3 | 12 | 4 | 2 | | |
| PERCENTAGE | | 57.5 | 25 | 12.4 | 5.1 | 93.6 | | 1.9 | 4.5 | 83.9 | 16.1 | 75 | 25 | 100 | | |

SERIAL Nº A-11 TIME OF DROP·1503 FIELD·FULBECK LZ·T ROUTE·N GP Nº 440TH

| ORGANIZATION | TAIL | GLIDER | | | | PERSONNEL | | | | JEEP | | TRAILER | | GUN | | DISTANCE |
|---|---|---|---|---|---|---|---|---|---|---|---|---|---|---|---|---|
| | NUMBER | INTACT | DAM | DES | MISS | OK | KIA | EVAC | MISS | SER | UNSER | SER | UNSER | SER | UNSER | FROM LZ |
| Hq&Hq Btry Div Arty | 43-40150 | X | | | | 2 | | 1 | | X | | | | | | LZ |
| " | 43-40153 | | X | | | 4 | | 1 | | | | X | | | | " |
| " | 43-40376 | X | | | | 2 | | | | X | | | | | | " |
| " | 43-40138 | X | | | | 4 | | | | | | X | | | | " |
| " | 43-19831 | | X | | | 3 | | | | X | | | | | | " |
| " | 43-41705 | | X | | | 3 | | | 2 | | | | | | | 60 mi SW |
| " | 43-37304 | X | | | | 3 | | | | X | | | | | | LZ |
| " | 43-40141 | X | | | | 3 | | | | | | X | | | | " |
| " | 43-40393 | | X | | | 3 | | | | X | | | | | | " |
| " | 43-40523 | | X | | | 2 | | | | X | | | | | | " |
| " | 43-40220 | | X | | | 5 | | | | | | X | | | | " |
| " | 341340 | | | X | | 2 | | 1 | | X | | | | | | " |
| " | 40139 | | X | | | 5 | | | | | | X | | | | " |
| Btry "B" 456 FA Bn | 42-77900 | X | | | | 2 | | | | X | | | | | | " |
| " | 43-42094 | X | | | | 5 | | | | | | X | | | | " |
| " | 42-7499 | X | | | | 4 | | | | | | | | X | | " |
| Btry "C" 456 FA Bn | 43-41157 | X | | | | 2 | | | | X | | | | | | " |
| " | 43-41389 | X | | | | 8 | | | | | | | | X | | " |
| " | 43-27375 | X | | | | 9 | | | | | | | | X | | " |
| " | 43-36726 | X | | | | 2 | | | | X | | | | | | " |
| " | 43-41191 | X | | | | 5 | | | | | | | | X | | " |
| " | 43-39738 | X | | | | 9 | | | | | | | | X | | " |
| " | 42-77660 | X | | | | 2 | | | | X | | | | | | " |
| " | 43-41398 | X | | | | 5 | | | | | | | | X | | " |
| " | 43-41181 | X | | | | 10 | | | | | | | | X | | " |
| " | 43-40240 | X | | | | 3 | | | | X | | | | | | " |
| " | 43-36946 | X | | | | 9 | | | | | | X | | | | " |
| " | 42-79454 | X | | | | 2 | | | | X | | | | | | " |
| " | 42-56358 | X | | | | 2 | | | | X | | | | | | " |
| " | 43-40236 | X | | | | 5 | | | | | | | | X | | " |
| " | 43-40241 | X | | | | 10 | | | | | | | | X | | " |
| " | 43-41520 | X | | | | 2 | | | | X | | | | | | " |
| " | 42-56120 | X | | | | 6 | | | | | | | | X | | " |
| " | 43-40429 | X | | | | 7 | | | | | | X | | | | " |
| " | 42-56226 | X | | | | 2 | | | | X | | | | | | 3 mi SW |
| " | 43-43090 | | X | | | 4 | | 2 | | | | X | | | | LZ |
| " | 43-41969 | X | | | | 5 | | | | X | | | | | | " |
| " | 43-39233 | X | | | | 2 | | | | | | X | | | | " |
| " | 43-36917 | X | | | | 4 | | | | | | | | X | | " |
| " | 43-41863 | X | | | | 3 | | | | | | | | | | " |
| | | | | | | | | | | | | | | | | |
| TOTAL | | 31 | 8 | 1 | | 171 | | 5 | 2 | 17 | | 10 | | 11 | | |
| PERCENTAGE | | 77.5 | 20 | 2.5 | | 96 | | 2.2 | 1.8 | 100 | | 100 | | 100 | | |

SERIAL Nº A-12 TIME OF DROP·1510 FIELD·LANGAR LZ·N ROUTE·N GP Nº 441ST

| ORGANIZATION | TAIL | GLIDER | | | | PERSONNEL | | | | JEEP | | TRAILER | | GUN | | DISTANCE |
|---|---|---|---|---|---|---|---|---|---|---|---|---|---|---|---|---|
| | NUMBER | INTACT | DAM | DES | MISS | OK | KIA | EVAC | MISS | SER | UNSER | SER | UNSER | SER | UNSER | FROM LZ |
| Btry "A" 456 FA Bn | 43-41346 | X | | | | 10 | | | | | | | | | | LZ |
| " | 43-19950 | X | | | | 2 | | | | X | | | | | | " |
| " | 42-74008 | | X | | | 5 | | | | | | | | X | | " |
| " | 43-40412 | | X | | | 10 | | 1 | | | | | | | | " |
| " | 43-39740 | X | | | | 2 | | | | X | | | | | | " |
| " | 43-27428 | | X | | | 8 | | | | | | X | | | | " |
| " | 43-27748 | X | | | | 9 | | | | | | | | | | " |
| " | 43-40235 | | X | | | 2 | | | | X | | | | | | " |
| " | 43-40215 | X | | | | 2 | | | | X | | | | | | " |
| " | 43-41044 | | X | | | 5 | | | | | | | | X | | " |
| " | 43-41873 | | X | | | 10 | | | | | | | | X | | " |
| " | 43-41877 | X | | | | | | 2 | | X | | | | | | " |
| " | 43-40351 | | | X | | 4 | | 1 | | | | | | X | | " |
| " | 43-40407 | | X | | | 6 | | | | | | X | | | | " |
| " | 43-40136 | X | | | | 2 | | | | X | | | | | | " |
| " | 43-41575 | | X | | | 5 | | | | | | X | | | | 2 mi SW |
| " | 43-41875 | | | X | | 5 | | | | | | X | | | | LZ |
| " | 43-41873 | X | | | | 2 | | | | X | | | | | | " |
| " | 42-7395 | X | | | | 3 | | | | | | | | X | | " |
| Btry "B" 456 FA Bn | 43-41678 | | X | | | 2 | | | | X | | | | | | " |
| " | 43-41207 | X | | | | 8 | | | | | | | | X | | " |
| " | 43-40532 | | X | | | 2 | | | | X | | | | | | " |
| " | 43-40063 | | X | | | 5 | | | | | | | | | X | 32 mi SW |
| " | 43-37290 | X | | | | 9 | | | | | | | | X | | LZ |
| " | 43-41675 | X | | | | 10 | | | | | | | | X | | " |
| " | 43-39807 | | X | | | 2 | | | | X | | | | | | " |
| " | 43-40552 | X | | | | 5 | | | | | | | | X | | " |
| " | 43-42055 | X | | | | 2 | | | | X | | | | | | " |
| " | 43-39802 | X | | | | 8 | | | | | | X | | | | " |
| " | 43-36915 | X | | | | 6 | | | | | | X | | | | " |
| " | 43-42118 | X | | | | 3 | | | | X | | | | | | " |
| " | 43-40424 | | X | | | 6 | | | | | | X | | | | " |
| " | 43-19851 | | X | | | 4 | | | | | | | | | | " |
| " | 42-77900 | | X | | | 2 | | | | X | | | | | | " |
| " | 43-39707 | X | | | | 5 | | | | | | | | X | | " |
| " | 43-77627 | X | | | | 3 | | | | | X | | | | | " |
| " | 43-36915 | | | | X | | | | 6 | | | | X | | | |
| " | 43-42118 | | X | | | 3 | | | | X | | | | | | LZ |
| " | 43-40424 | X | | | | 6 | | | | | | | X | | | " |
| " | 43-19851 | X | | | | 4 | | | | | | | | | | " |
| | | | | | | | | | | | | | | | | |
| TOTAL | | 21 | 16 | 2 | 1 | 187 | | 4 | 6 | 14 | 1 | 7 | 2 | 10 | 1 | |
| PERCENTAGE | | 52.5 | 40 | 5 | 2.5 | 94.9 | | 2 | 3.1 | 93.3 | 6.7 | 77.7 | 22.3 | 90.9 | 9.1 | |

# SHEET N° 3

**SERIAL N° A-13  TIME OF DROP · 1610  FIELD · FOLKINGHAM  LZ · O  ROUTE · S  GP N° 313 TH**

| ORGANIZATION | TAIL | GLIDER | | | | PERSONNEL | | | | JEEP | | TRAILER | | GUN | | DISTANCE |
|---|---|---|---|---|---|---|---|---|---|---|---|---|---|---|---|---|
| | NUMBER | INTACT | DAM | DES | MISS | OK | KIA | EVAC | MISS | SER | UNSER | SER | UNSER | SER | UNSER | FROM LZ |
| Hq & Hq Co 325 | 43-41577 | X | | | | 6 | | | | | X | | | | | LZ |
| " | 43-41388 | X | | | | 4 | | | | X | | | | | | " |
| " | 43-77677 | X | | | | 4 | | | | X | | | | | | " |
| " | 43-40277 | X | | | | 5 | | | | | | X | | | | 9 mi SW |
| " | 43-41673 | X | | | | 7 | | | | | | X | | | | 14 mi SW |
| " | 43-56316 | X | | | | 4 | | | | X | | | | | | LZ |
| " | 43-41381 | X | | | | 8 | | | | X | | | | | | LZ |
| " | 43-41442 | X | | | | 4 | | | | | | | | | | " |
| " | 43-40046 | | X | | | 4 | | | | X | | | | | | 14 mi SW |
| " | 43-41230 | X | | | | 14 | | | | | | | | | | " |
| Hq & Hq Co 401 | 43-41588 | X | | | | 7 | | | | | | | | | | LZ |
| " | 43-40728 | X | | | | 10 | | | | | | | | | | 14 mi SW |
| Hq & Hq Co 2ᴺᴰ Bn 325 | 337211 | X | | | | 4 | | | | X | | | | | | LZ |
| " | 43-41895 | X | | | | 13 | | | | | | | | | | " |
| " | 43-41722 | X | | | | 5 | | | | X | | | | | | " |
| " | 43-40566 | X | | | | 5 | | | | | X | | | | | " |
| " | 43-41927 | X | | | | 5 | | | | | | X | | | | " |
| " | 43-41356 | X | | | | 5 | | | | X | | | | | | " |
| " | 43-27330 | | X | | | 10 | | 3 | | | | | | | | " |
| " | 43-37278 | X | | | | 4 | | | | X | | | | | | " |
| " | 43-42033 | | X | | | 4 | | | | X | | | | | | " |
| " | 43-40051 | X | | | | 12 | | | | | | | | | | 14 mi SW |
| " | 43-41516 | X | | | | 5 | | | | | | X | | | | LZ |
| " | 43-27311 | X | | | | 4 | | | | X | | | | | | " |
| " | 43-79102 | X | | | | 6 | | | | | | X | | | | " |
| Co "G" 325 "Gli Inf | 43-19849 | X | | | | 13 | | | | | | | | | | " |
| " | 43-40537 | X | | | | 13 | | | | | | | | | | " |
| " | 42-79254 | X | | | | 13 | | | | | | | | | | " |
| " | 42-77459 | X | | | | 13 | | | | | | | | | | " |
| " | 43-79114 | | X | | | 13 | | | | | | | | | | 19 mi SW |
| " | 42-56400 | X | | | | 13 | | | | | | | | | | LZ |
| " | 336919 | X | | | | 12 | | | | | | | | | | " |
| " | 42-77553 | | X | | | 11 | | | | | | | | | | " |
| " | 42-56254 | X | | | | 13 | | | | | | | | | | " |
| " | 43-19849 | X | | | | 13 | | | | | | | | | | " |
| " | 43-39811 | X | | | | 13 | | | | | | | | | | " |
| " | 43-40576 | X | | | | 13 | | | | | | | | | | " |
| " | 43-4610 | X | | | | 13 | | | | | | | | | | " |
| " | 42-77555 | X | | | | 13 | | | | | | | | | | " |
| " | 42-56510 | X | | | | 13 | | | | | | | | | | " |
| Hq & Hq Co 2ᴺᴰ Bn 401 | 367720 | | X | | | 13 | | | | | | | | | | 5 mi SW |
| " | 43-77706 | X | | | | 13 | | | | | | | | | | " |
| " | 43-41299 | | X | | | 4 | | | | | | | | | | " |
| " | 369691 | X | | | | 4 | | | | X | | | | | | " |
| " | 42-77647 | X | | | | 4 | | | | X | | | | | | " |
| " | 43-40105 | X | | | | 4 | | | | X | | | | | | " |
| " | 43-41883 | X | | | | 4 | | | | X | | | | | | " |
| " | 43-40040 | | X | | | 4 | | | | | | X | | | | " |
| " | 43-41568 | X | | | | 6 | | | | | | X | | | | LZ |
| **TOTAL** | | **39** | **7** | | **3** | **400** | | **3** | | **14** | **1** | **12** | | | | |
| **PERCENTAGE** | | **79.6** | **14.2** | | **6.2** | **99.9** | | **.09** | | **93.4** | **6.6** | **100** | | | | |

**SERIAL N° A-14  TIME OF DROP · 1617  FIELD · BARKSTON HEATH  LZ · O  ROUTE · S  GP N° 61 TH**

| ORGANIZATION | TAIL | GLIDER | | | | PERSONNEL | | | | JEEP | | TRAILER | | GUN | | DISTANCE |
|---|---|---|---|---|---|---|---|---|---|---|---|---|---|---|---|---|
| | NUMBER | INTACT | DAM | DES | MISS | OK | KIA | EVAC | MISS | SER | UNSER | SER | UNSER | SER | UNSER | FROM LZ |
| Co "B" 325 Gli Inf | 43-42630 | X | | | | 14 | | | | | | | | | | LZ |
| " | 43-59941 | X | | | | 14 | | | | | | | | | | " |
| " | 43-40510 | | X | | | 14 | | | | | | | | | | LZ |
| " | 43-41466 | X | | | | 14 | | | | | | | | | | " |
| " | 42-56514 | X | | | | 14 | | | | | | | | | | " |
| " | 43-26947 | X | | | | 14 | | | | | | | | | | " |
| " | 43-41074 | | X | | | 14 | | | | | | | | | | " |
| " | 43-54043 | X | | | | 14 | | | | | | | | | | " |
| " | 341591 | X | | | | 14 | | | | | | | | | | " |
| " | 43-40562 | X | | | | 12 | | 1 | | | | | | | | " |
| " | 43-42108 | X | | | | 13 | | | | | | | | | | 19 mi SW |
| " | 341536 | | X | | | 14 | | | | | | | | | | LZ |
| " | 43-41539 | X | | | | 14 | | | | | | | | | | " |
| " | 43-37988 | X | | | | 13 | | | | | | | | | | " |
| " | 43-41710 | X | | | | 13 | | | | | | | | | | " |
| Co "A" 325 Gli Inf | 327282 | X | | | | 14 | | | | | | | | | | " |
| " | 43-41821 | X | | | | 14 | | | | | | | | | | " |
| " | 336703 | X | | | | 14 | | | | | | | | | | " |
| " | 519879 | X | | | | 14 | | | | | | | | | | " |
| " | 339657 | X | | | | 15 | | | | | | | | | | " |
| " | 285083 | | X | | | 15 | | | | | | | | | | " |
| " | 43-41408 | X | | | | 13 | | | | | | | | | | " |
| " | 279393 | X | | | | 13 | | | | | | | | | | " |
| " | 341942 | X | | | | 14 | | | | | | | | | | " |
| " | 379032 | X | | | | 14 | | | | | | | | | | " |
| " | 341593 | X | | | | 15 | | | | | | | | | | " |
| " | 519865 | X | | | | 15 | | | | | | | | | | " |
| " | 340390 | X | | | | 15 | | | | | | | | | | " |
| " | 298651 | X | | | | 14 | | | | | | | | | | " |
| " | 256374 | X | | | | 14 | | | | | | | | | | " |
| " | 42-43657 | | X | | | 15 | | | | | | | | | | " |
| " | 43-19105 | | X | | | 15 | | | | | | | | | | " |
| " | 43-75566 | X | | | | 15 | | | | | | | | | | " |
| " | 43-19741 | X | | | | 15 | | | | | | | | | | " |
| " | 43-40389 | X | | | | 14 | | | | | | | | | | " |
| " | 43-77545 | X | | | | 14 | | | | | | | | | | " |
| " | 43-19871 | X | | | | 14 | | | | | | | | | | " |
| " | 43-40446 | | X | | | 14 | | | | | | | | | | 19 mi SW |
| " | 341395 | X | | | | 14 | | | | | | | | | | " |
| " | 256344 | X | | | | 14 | | | | | | | | | | LZ |
| **TOTAL** | | **51** | **9** | | | **550** | | | | **1** | | | | | | |
| **PERCENTAGE** | | **77.5** | **22.5** | | | **99.8** | | | | **.18** | | | | | | |

**SERIAL N° A-15  TIME OF DROP · 1624  FIELD · COTTESMORE  LZ · O  ROUTE · S  GP N° 314 TH**

| ORGANIZATION | TAIL | GLIDER | | | | PERSONNEL | | | | JEEP | | TRAILER | | GUN | | DISTANCE |
|---|---|---|---|---|---|---|---|---|---|---|---|---|---|---|---|---|
| | NUMBER | INTACT | DAM | DES | MISS | OK | KIA | EVAC | MISS | SER | UNSER | SER | UNSER | SER | UNSER | FROM LZ |
| Hq & Hq Co 2ᴺᴰ Bn 325 | 43-41206 | X | | | | 13 | | | | | | | | | | LZ |
| " | 43-40051 | X | | | | 13 | | | | | | | | | | " |
| " | 42-42049 | | X | | | 13 | | | | | | | | | | " |
| " | 43-40421 | X | | | | 13 | | | | | | | | | | " |
| " | 43-73587 | | X | | | 14 | | | | | | | | | | " |
| " | 43-40795 | X | | | | 13 | | | | | | | | | | " |
| " | 43-59679 | | X | | | 13 | | | | | | | | | | " |
| " | 43-39805 | X | | | | 13 | | | | | | | | | | " |
| " | 43-13733 | X | | | | 13 | | | | | | | | | | " |
| " | 42-77653 | | X | | | 13 | | | | | | | | | | " |
| Co "E" 325 Gli Inf | 43-39815 | X | | | | 13 | | | | | | | | | | " |
| " | 43-39270 | X | | | | 13 | | | | | | | | | | " |
| " | 339721 | X | | | | 13 | | | | | | | | | | " |
| " | 43-42035 | X | | | | 13 | | | | | | | | | | " |
| " | 43-41741 | X | | | | 14 | | | | | | | | | | " |
| " | 43-40021 | X | | | | 13 | | | | | | | | | | " |
| " | 43-42030 | X | | | | 13 | | | | | | | | | | " |
| " | 43-41506 | X | | | | 12 | | | | | | | | | | " |
| " | 43-19210 | X | | | | 13 | | | | | | | | | | " |
| " | 43-37410 | X | | | | 13 | | | | | | | | | | " |
| " | 42-75864 | X | | | | 13 | | | | | | | | | | " |
| " | 43-40449 | X | | | | 13 | | | | | | | | | | " |
| " | 43-40521 | X | | | | 13 | | | | | | | | | | " |
| " | 43-37582 | X | | | | 13 | | | | | | | | | | " |
| " | 43-40788 | | X | | | 13 | | | | | | | | | | " |
| Co "F" 325 Gli Inf | 337237 | X | | | | 13 | | | | | | | | | | " |
| " | 340180 | X | | | | 13 | | | | | | | | | | 13 mi SW |
| " | 339994 | X | | | | 13 | | | | | | | | | | LZ |
| " | 337391 | X | | | | 12 | | | | | | | | | | " |
| " | 340544 | X | | | | 12 | | | | | | | | | | " |
| " | 43-41123 | X | | | | 12 | | | | | | | | | | " |
| " | 43-56275 | X | | | | 12 | | | | | | | | | | " |
| " | 43-41064 | X | | | | 13 | | | | | | | | | | 13 mi SW |
| " | 43-73643 | X | | | | 13 | | | | | | | | | | LZ |
| " | 42-74044 | X | | | | 13 | | | | | | | | | | " |
| " | 43-37403 | X | | | | 13 | | | | | | | | | | 13 mi SW |
| " | 43-40569 | X | | | | 12 | | | | | | | | | | LZ |
| " | 341180 | X | | | | 12 | | | | | | | | | | " |
| " | 43-41210 | | X | | | 12 | | | | | | | | | | " |
| **TOTAL** | | **33** | **5** | | **2** | **514** | | | | **1** | | | | | | |
| **PERCENTAGE** | | **82.5** | **12.5** | | **5** | **99.8** | | | | **.19** | | | | | | |

**SERIAL N° A-16  TIME OF DROP · 1631  FIELD · FULBECK  LZ · O  ROUTE · S  GP N° 440 TH**

| ORGANIZATION | TAIL | GLIDER | | | | PERSONNEL | | | | JEEP | | TRAILER | | GUN | | DISTANCE |
|---|---|---|---|---|---|---|---|---|---|---|---|---|---|---|---|---|
| | NUMBER | INTACT | DAM | DES | MISS | OK | KIA | EVAC | MISS | SER | UNSER | SER | UNSER | SER | UNSER | FROM LZ |
| Hq & Hq Co 325 | 339987 | X | | | | 7 | | | | | X | | | | | 17 mi SW |
| " | 336728 | | X | | | 13 | | | | | | | | | | 19 mi SW |
| " | 42-77594 | X | | | | 5 | | | | X | | | | | | 30 mi SW |
| " | 339625 | X | | | | 9 | | | | | | X | | | | 28 mi SW |
| " | 274065 | | X | | | | | 3 | | | | X | | | | LZ |
| " | 341903 | X | | | | 4 | | | | X | | | | | | " |
| " | 540094 | X | | | | 4 | | | | X | | | | | | " |
| " | 339661 | | X | | | | | 11 | | | | | | | | " |
| " | 342631 | | X | | | 5 | | 1 | | X | | | | | | 28 mi SW |
| " | 42-77762 | | X | | | 5 | | 1 | | X | | | | | | LZ |
| Co "C" 325 Gli Inf | 341202 | X | | | | 16 | | | | | | | | | | " |
| " | 339729 | X | | | | 13 | | | | | | | | | | " |
| " | 336428 | X | | | | 14 | | | | | | | | | | " |
| " | 342173 | | X | | | 14 | | | | | | | | | | " |
| " | 277611 | X | | | | 12 | | | | | | | | | | " |
| " | 372285 | X | | | | 13 | | 1 | | | | | | | | " |
| " | 274085 | X | | | | 13 | | | | | | | | | | " |
| " | 279161 | X | | | | 13 | | | | | | | | | | " |
| " | 256277 | | X | | | 13 | | | | | | | | | | " |
| " | 373070 | X | | | | 11 | | | | | | | | | | " |
| " | 340430 | X | | | | 13 | | | | | | | | | | " |
| " | 277564 | | X | | | 13 | | | | | | | | | | " |
| " | 327466 | X | | | | 13 | | | | | | | | | | ENGLAND |
| " | 277495 | | X | | | 13 | | 1 | | | | | | | | LZ |
| " | 336958 | X | | | | 13 | | | | | | | | | | " |
| Hq & Hq Co 1ˢᵀ Bn 325 | 42-77760 | X | | | | 15 | | | | | | | | | | 12 mi SW |
| " | 341063 | | X | | | 13 | | | | | | | | | | 13 mi SW |
| " | 279181 | X | | | | 11 | | | | | | | | | | ENGLAND |
| " | 277599 | X | | | | 11 | | | | | | | | | | LZ |
| " | 274061 | X | | | | 7 | | 1 | | X | | | | | | 13 mi SW |
| " | 341095 | X | | | | 7 | | | | X | | | | | | 19 mi SW |
| " | 346492 | | X | | | | | 4 | | X | | | | | | " |
| " | 542141 | | X | | | | | 3 | | X | | | | | | " |
| " | 277959 | X | | | | 4 | | | | X | | | | | | 19 mi SW |
| " | 341419 | | X | | | 2 | | 1 | | X | | | | | | " |
| " | 341864 | | X | | | | | 5 | | | | X | | | | " |
| " | 359914 | | X | | | | | 6 | | | | X | | | | " |
| " | 277449 | X | | | | 5 | | | | | | X | | | | 19 mi SW |
| " | 341496 | X | | | | 7 | | | | | | X | | | | " |
| " | 341059 | X | | | | 3 | | | | | | | | | | " |
| **TOTAL** | | **26** | **12** | **5** | **3** | **383** | | **43** | | **6** | **4** | **5** | | **2** | | |
| **PERCENTAGE** | | **65** | **12.5** | **7.5** | **15** | **89.7** | | **1.1** | | **9.2** | **60** | **40** | | | | |

**SERIAL N° A-17  TIME OF DROP · 1638  FIELD · LANGAR  LZ · O  ROUTE · S  GP N° 441 ST**

| ORGANIZATION | TAIL | GLIDER | | | | PERSONNEL | | | | JEEP | | TRAILER | | GUN | | DISTANCE |
|---|---|---|---|---|---|---|---|---|---|---|---|---|---|---|---|---|
| | NUMBER | INTACT | DAM | DES | MISS | OK | KIA | EVAC | MISS | SER | UNSER | SER | UNSER | SER | UNSER | FROM LZ |
| Service Co 325 | 42-77592 | X | | | | 7 | | | | X | | | | | | LZ |
| " | 42-59994 | X | | | | 1 | | | | | | X | | | | " |
| " | 42-56121 | X | | | | 5 | | | | | | X | | | | " |
| " | 43-19832 | X | | | | 7 | | | | X | | | | | | " |
| " | 43-36475 | X | | | | 9 | | | | | | | | | | " |
| AT Co 325 Gli Inf | 42-56349 | | X | | | 12 | | 2 | | | | | | | | " |
| " | 42-77468 | X | | | | 4 | | | | | | | | X | | " |
| " | 43-47410 | X | | | | 5 | | | | X | | | | | | " |
| " | 43-19873 | X | | | | 5 | | | | | | | | X | | " |
| " | 43-56400 | X | | | | 3 | | | | X | | | | | | " |
| " | 42-77751 | X | | | | 2 | | | | X | | | | | | " |
| " | 43-19875 | X | | | | 2 | | | | X | | | | | | " |
| " | 43-40070 | | X | | | 5 | | | | | | | | X | | " |
| " | 42-77352 | X | | | | 2 | | | | | | | | | | " |
| " | 43-40018 | X | | | | 11 | | | | | | | | | | " |
| " | 43-27604 | X | | | | 5 | | | | | | | | X | | " |
| " | 43-27338 | X | | | | 2 | | | | X | | | | | | " |
| " | 43-19772 | X | | | | 4 | | | | X | | | | | | " |
| " | 42-77725 | X | | | | 5 | | | | | | | | | | " |
| " | 43-19864 | X | | | | 5 | | | | | | | | X | | 40 mi SW |
| " | 42-77581 | X | | | | 5 | | | | | | | | X | | LZ |
| " | 43-77306 | X | | | | 2 | | | | X | | | | | | " |
| " | 42-77335 | X | | | | 5 | | | | | | | | X | | " |
| " | 43-27330 | X | | | | 2 | | | | X | | | | | | " |
| " | 42-74080 | X | | | | 5 | | | | | | | | X | | " |
| " | 42-79257 | X | | | | 2 | | | | X | | | | | | " |
| " | 42-77757 | X | | | | 2 | | | | X | | | | | | " |
| Hq & Hq Co 2ᴺᴰ Bn 401 | 43-27425 | | X | | | 14 | | | | | | | | | | " |
| " | 42-74325 | X | | | | 12 | | | | | | | | | | " |
| " | 43-41039 | X | | | | 12 | | | | | | | | | | " |
| " | 42-74080 | X | | | | | | | | | | | | | | " |
| " | 43-40455 | | X | | | | | 12 | | | | | | | | 23 mi SW |
| " | 43-40101 | X | | | | 13 | | | | | | | | | | LZ |
| " | 43-41613 | X | | | | 13 | | | | | | | | | | " |
| " | 43-41478 | X | | | | 14 | | | | | | | | | | " |
| " | 43-41239 | X | | | | 10 | | | | | | | | | | LZ |
| " | 43-40216 | X | | | | | | 3 | | | | | | | | " |
| " | 43-4463 | X | | | | | | 14 | | | | | | | | " |
| " | 43-41932 | X | | | | 11 | | 10 | | | | | | | | " |
| **TOTAL** | | **27** | **8** | **5** | **3** | **240** | | **5** | | **36** | **12** | | | **2** | | |
| **PERCENTAGE** | | **67.5** | **20** | **5** | **7.5** | **85.4** | | **1.8** | | **12.8** | **100** | | | **100** | | |

**SERIAL N° A-18  TIME OF DROP · 1645  FIELD · FOLKINGHAM  LZ · O  ROUTE · S  GP N° 313 TH**

| ORGANIZATION | TAIL | GLIDER | | | | PERSONNEL | | | | JEEP | | TRAILER | | GUN | | DISTANCE |
|---|---|---|---|---|---|---|---|---|---|---|---|---|---|---|---|---|
| | NUMBER | INTACT | DAM | DES | MISS | OK | KIA | EVAC | MISS | SER | UNSER | SER | UNSER | SER | UNSER | FROM LZ |
| Co "E" 401 Gli Inf | 277425 | X | | | | 12 | | | | | | | | | | LZ |
| " | 341578 | | X | | | 13 | | | | | | | | | | " |
| " | 339717 | X | | | | 14 | | | | | | | | | | " |
| " | 340061 | X | | | | 13 | | | | | | | | | | " |
| " | 527344 | X | | | | 14 | | | | | | | | | | " |
| " | 342062 | X | | | | 13 | | | | | | | | | | " |
| " | 341595 | X | | | | 13 | | | | | | | | | | " |
| " | 341448 | X | | | | 13 | | | | | | | | | | 13 mi SW |
| " | 337292 | X | | | | 13 | | | | | | | | | | LZ |
| " | 43-36784 | X | | | | 14 | | | | | | | | | | " |
| " | 340185 | X | | | | 13 | | | | | | | | | | " |
| " | 43-41358 | X | | | | 14 | | | | | | | | | | " |
| " | 341449 | X | | | | 14 | | | | | | | | | | " |
| " | 43-37408 | X | | | | 13 | | | | | | | | | | " |
| " | 43-40052 | X | | | | 13 | | 1 | | | | | | | | " |
| Co "F" 401 Gli Inf | 341628 | X | | | | 13 | | | | | | | | | | " |
| " | 340184 | X | | | | 14 | | | | | | | | | | " |
| " | 43-41637 | X | | | | 14 | | | | | | | | | | " |
| " | 379658 | X | | | | 14 | | | | | | | | | | " |
| " | 43-40073 | X | | | | 14 | | | | | | | | | | " |
| " | 279390 | X | | | | 12 | | | | | | | | | | " |
| " | 340444 | X | | | | 15 | | | | | | | | | | " |
| " | 340435 | X | | | | 15 | | | | | | | | | | " |
| " | 340861 | X | | | | 15 | | | | | | | | | | " |
| " | 327374 | X | | | | 15 | | | | | | | | | | " |
| " | 339082 | X | | | | 13 | | | | | | | | | | " |
| " | 341362 | X | | | | 13 | | | | | | | | | | " |
| " | 255686 | X | | | | 13 | | | | | | | | | | " |
| " | 273529 | X | | | | 13 | | | | | | | | | | " |
| " | 342069 | X | | | | 13 | | | | | | | | | | " |
| Co "G" 401 Gli Inf | 279903 | X | | | | 14 | | | | | | | | | | " |
| " | 42-77636 | X | | | | 14 | | | | | | | | | | " |
| " | 542065 | X | | | | 15 | | | | | | | | | | " |
| " | 341015 | | X | | | 14 | | | | | | | | | | " |
| " | 43-40062 | X | | | | 14 | | | | | | | | | | " |
| " | 279106 | X | | | | 14 | | | | | | | | | | " |
| " | 341570 | X | | | | 14 | | | | | | | | | | 15 mi SW |
| " | 335290 | X | | | | 14 | | | | | | | | | | LZ |
| " | 256271 | X | | | | 14 | | | | | | | | | | " |
| " | 336783 | X | | | | 15 | | | | | | | | | | " |
| " | 340482 | X | | | | 13 | | | | | | | | | | " |
| " | 247453 | | X | | | 15 | | | | | | | | | | " |
| " | 341647 | X | | | | 14 | | | | | | | | | | " |
| " | 342116 | X | | | | 14 | | | | | | | | | | LZ |
| Hq & Hq Co 401 Gli Inf | 339809 | X | | | | 5 | | | | X | | | | | | 12 mi SW |
| " | 341885 | X | | | | 4 | | | | X | | | | | | 12 mi SW |
| " | 379131 | | X | | | 4 | | | | X | | | | | | " |
| " | 342060 | X | | | | 6 | | | | X | | | | | | " |
| **TOTAL** | | **33** | **12** | **4** | | **618** | | | | **2** | | | | | | |
| **PERCENTAGE** | | **67.3** | **24.5** | **8.2** | | **99.84** | | | | **.0016** | | | | **100** | | |

# SHEET Nº 4

## SERIAL Nº A-19 TIME OF DROP·1659 FIELD·COTTESMORE LZ·O ROUTE·S GP Nº 316th

| ORGANIZATION | TAIL | GLIDER | | | | PERSONNEL | | | | JEEP | | TRAILER | | GUN | | DISTANCE |
|---|---|---|---|---|---|---|---|---|---|---|---|---|---|---|---|---|
| | NUMBER | INTACT | DAM | DES | MISS | OK | KIA | EVAC | MISS | SER | UNSER | SER | UNSER | SER | UNSER | FROM LZ |
| Btry"C" 80th AABn | 43-41026 | | X | | | 2 | | | | | X | | | | | LZ |
| " | 42-56279 | | X | | | 7 | | | | | | | | | | " |
| " | 43-27546 | X | | | | 7 | | | | X | | | | | | " |
| " | 43-37710 | | X | | | 11 | | | | | | | | | | " |
| " | 42-74029 | X | | | | 11 | | | | | | | | | | " |
| " | 43-27844 | X | | | | 11 | | | | | | | | | | " |
| " | 43-41065 | | X | | | 2 | | | | | | X | | | | " |
| " | 43-75880 | X | | | | 8 | | | X | | | | | | | " |
| " | 43-79457 | | X | | | 8 | | | | | | X | | | | " |
| " | 42-40549 | X | | | | 8 | | | X | | | | | | | " |
| " | 42-62733 | X | | | | 8 | | | | | | X | | | | " |
| " | 43-19948 | | X | | | 2 | | | X | | | | | | | " |
| " | 42-56855 | | X | | | 2 | | | | | | X | | | | " |
| " | 42-56219 | | X | | | 2 | | | X | | | | | | | " |
| " | 43-39120 | X | | | | 2 | | | | | | X | | | | " |
| " | 43-39804 | | X | | | 2 | | | X | | | | | | | " |
| " | 43-19024 | | X | | | 2 | | | | | | X | | | | " |
| " | 43-40386 | | X | | | 2 | | | X | | | | | | | " |
| " | 42-73917 | X | | | | 2 | | | | | | X | | | | " |
| " | 42-36642 | X | | | | 2 | | | X | | | | | | | " |
| " | 43-39555 | | X | | | 2 | | | | | | X | | | | " |
| " | 43-40934 | X | | | | 2 | | | X | | | | | | | " |
| Btry"D" 80th AA | 274065 | X | | | | 13 | | | | | | | | | | " |
| " | 341439 | | X | | | 11 | | / | | | | | | | | " |
| " | 272385 | X | | | | 12 | | | | | | | | | | " |
| " | 274014 | | X | | | 5 | | | | X | | | | | | " |
| " | 256232 | | X | | | 5 | | | X | | | | | | | " |
| " | 272387 | | X | | | 5 | | | | X | | | | | | " |
| " | 277345 | X | | | | 2 | | | X | | | | | | | " |
| " | 256522 | | | X | | 2 | | | | X | | | | | | " |
| " | 256289 | | X | | | 2 | | | X | | | | | | | " |
| " | 279134 | X | | | | 2 | | | | X | | | | | | " |
| " | 277448 | | X | | | 2 | | | X | | | | | | | " |
| " | 256206 | X | | | | 2 | | | | X | | | | | | " |
| " | 425687 | | X | | | 2 | | | X | | | | | | | " |
| " | 341409 | | X | | | 2 | | | | X | | | | | | " |
| " | 42-17238 | X | | | | 2 | | | X | | | | | | | " |
| " | 43-13868 | X | | | | 2 | | | X | | | | | | | " |
| " | 41-39692 | | X | | | 5 | | | | X | | | | | | " |
| Div Rcn Plat | 42-56826 | X | | | | 2 | | | X | | | | | | | " |
| " | 42-39125 | X | | | | / | | | X | | | | | | | " |
| " | 42-77330 | X | | | | / | | | | X | | | | | | " |
| " | 42-75081 | | X | | | / | | / | X | | | | | | | " |
| 508 CompTch | 43-41961 | X | | | | 2 | | | X | | | | | | | " |
| " | 42-37196 | X | | | | 2 | | | X | | | | | | | " |
| " | 42-56194 | X | | | | 2 | | | X | | | | | | | " |
| " | 34068 | X | | | | 2 | | | X | | | | | | | " |
| **TOTAL** | | 25 | 22 | | | 178 | | 2 | | 24 | 10 | | | 8 | | |
| **PERCENTAGE** | | 52 | 45.8 | 2.2 | | 98.8 | | 1.2 | | 100 | 100 | | | 100 | | |

## SERIAL Nº A-20 TIME OF DROP·1706 FIELD·FULBECK LZ·O ROUTE·S GP Nº 316th

| ORGANIZATION | TAIL | GLIDER | | | | PERSONNEL | | | | JEEP | | TRAILER | | GUN | | DISTANCE |
|---|---|---|---|---|---|---|---|---|---|---|---|---|---|---|---|---|
| | NUMBER | INTACT | DAM | DES | MISS | OK | KIA | EVAC | MISS | SER | UNSER | SER | UNSER | SER | UNSER | FROM LZ |
| Btry"E" 80th AA Bn | 42-77451 | X | | | | 5 | | | | X | | | | | | LZ |
| " | 42-77620 | | X | | | 2 | | | X | | | | | | | " |
| " | 43-40318 | | X | | | 2 | | | | X | | | | | | " |
| " | 43-41143 | X | | | | 3 | | | X | | | | | | | " |
| " | 43-27351 | X | | | | 3 | | | X | | | | | | | " |
| " | 43-40353 | X | | | | 3 | | | X | | | | | | | " |
| " | 43-41791 | X | | | | 3 | | | | X | | | | | | " |
| " | 43-19191 | X | | | | 2 | | | X | | | | | | | " |
| " | 43-39800 | X | | | | 3 | | | | | | X | | | | " |
| " | 42-47934 | | X | | | 2 | | | X | | | | | | | " |
| " | 42-77673 | | X | | | 3 | | | | X | | | | | | " |
| " | 42-47427 | | X | | | 2 | | | X | | | | | | | " |
| " | 43-36629 | | X | | | 3 | | | | X | | | | | | " |
| " | 42-56504 | | X | | | 2 | | | X | | | | | | | " |
| " | 43-19735 | | X | | | 3 | | | | X | | | | | | " |
| " | 43-41588 | X | | | | 3 | | | | | | | | | | " |
| " | 43-40456 | X | | | | 11 | | | | | | | | | | " |
| " | 42-29733 | X | | | | 11 | | | | | | | | | | " |
| " | 42-75915 | X | | | | 10 | | | | | | | | | | " |
| " | 42-79417 | | X | | | 2 | | | X | | | | | | | " |
| " | 43-40800 | | X | | | 3 | | | | | | X | | | | " |
| Btry"F" 80th AA Bn | 277100 | | X | | | 12 | | | | | | | | | | 1MI N |
| " | 274004 | X | | | | 2 | | | X | | | | | | | 8 MI SW |
| " | 255628 | X | | | | 2 | | | | X | | | | | | LZ |
| " | 319861 | X | | | | 5 | | | X | | | | | | | " |
| " | 340149 | X | | | | 2 | | | X | | | | | | | " |
| " | 277590 | | X | | | 2 | | | | X | | | | | | " |
| " | 255217 | | X | | | 2 | | | X | | | | | | | " |
| " | 277152 | X | | | | 5 | | | | X | | | | | | " |
| " | 339139 | X | | | | 2 | | | | X | | | | | | " |
| " | 341911 | X | | | | 2 | | | X | | | | | | | " |
| " | 256328 | X | | | | 5 | | | X | | | | | | | " |
| " | 256131 | X | | | | 2 | | | X | | | | | | | " |
| " | 277724 | | X | | | 12 | | | | | | | | | | " |
| " | 341330 | X | | | | 2 | | | | | | | | | | 8 MI N |
| " | 277745 | X | | | | 13 | | | | | | | | | | LZ |
| Div Rcn Plat | 317368 | | X | | | 2 | | | X | | | | | | | 150 MI SW |
| " | 100922 | X | | | | 2 | | | X | | | | | | | LZ |
| " | 341724 | X | | | | 2 | | | X | | | | | | | " |
| " | 277716 | X | | | | 2 | | | X | | | | | | | " |
| " | 256218 | | | X | | 5 | | | | | | | | | | 35 MI SW |
| " | 219694 | | | X | | 10 | | | | | | | | | | 10 MI SW |
| " | 256193 | X | | | | 10 | | | | | | | | | | 8 MI SW |
| Div MP Plat | 274040 | X | | | | / | | | | | | | | | | ENGLAND LZ |
| " | 273996 | X | | | | 3 | | | X | | | | | | | " |
| " | 274048 | X | | | | 2 | | | | X | | | | | | " |
| " | 277793 | X | | | | 2 | | | | | | X | | | | " |
| " | 339695 | | X | | | 7 | | | | | | | | | | " |
| **TOTAL** | | 28 | 18 | 2 | | 222 | | | | 27 | 9 | | | 8 | | |
| **PERCENTAGE** | | 58.3 | 37.5 | 4.2 | | 100 | | | | 100 | 100 | | | 100 | | |

## SERIAL Nº A-21 TIME OF DROP·1652 FIELD·LANGAR LZ·O ROUTE·S GP Nº 441/t

| ORGANIZATION | TAIL | GLIDER | | | | PERSONNEL | | | | JEEP | | TRAILER | | GUN | | DISTANCE |
|---|---|---|---|---|---|---|---|---|---|---|---|---|---|---|---|---|
| | NUMBER | INTACT | DAM | DES | MISS | OK | KIA | EVAC | MISS | SER | UNSER | SER | UNSER | SER | UNSER | FROM LZ |
| Hq Det 80th AA Bn | 277668 | X | | | | 12 | | | | | | | | | | LZ |
| " | 256740 | | X | | | 12 | | | | X | | | | | | " |
| " | 256375 | | X | | | 6 | | | | | | X | | | | " |
| " | 256284 | X | | | | 2 | | | | | | | | | | " |
| " | 319732 | | X | | | 2 | | | X | | | | | | | 1MI SE |
| " | 277371 | X | | | | 2 | | | X | | | | | | | LZ |
| Co"A" 307th Engr | 42-58104 | | X | | | 5 | | | X | | | | | | | " |
| " | 42-62349 | X | | | | 5 | | | | X | | | | | | " |
| " | 279449 | X | | | | 11 | | | | | | | | | | " |
| " | 43-41465 | | X | | | 12 | | | | | | | | | | " |
| " | 43-41526 | X | | | | 2 | | | | | | | | | | " |
| " | 43-39956 | X | | | | 2 | | | X | | | | | | | " |
| " | 42-77340 | | X | | | 2 | | | | X | | | | | | " |
| " | 43-27421 | | X | | | 12 | | | | | | | | | | " |
| " | 42-21893 | | X | | | 12 | | | | | | | | | | ENGLAND LZ |
| " | 43-41453 | X | | | | 2 | | | X | | | | | | | " |
| " | 43-41461 | | X | | | 2 | | | X | | | | | | | " |
| " | 41-41659 | X | | | | 2 | | | X | | X | | | | | " |
| " | 42-19703 | X | | | | 2 | | | X | | | | | | | " |
| " | 43-19827 | X | | | | 2 | | | X | | | | | | | " |
| " | 43-4116 | | X | | | 2 | | | | | | | | | | " |
| " | 42-56240 | | X | | | 2 | | | X | | | | | | | " |
| " | 43-37607 | X | | | | 2 | | | X | | | | | | | " |
| " | 42-58102 | X | | | | 5 | | | X | | | | | | | " |
| " | 42-37408 | | | | | 11 | | | X | | | | | | | " |
| " | 42-77451 | | | | | 11 | | | | | | | | | | " |
| H&S 307th Engr | 43-41048 | X | | | | 2 | | | X | | | | | | | " |
| " | 43-39938 | X | | | | 2 | | | | X | | | | | | " |
| " | 43-36759 | | | | | 2 | | | X | | | | | | | " |
| " | 43-39476 | | | | | 2 | | | X | | | | | | | " |
| " | 43-40167 | | X | | | 2 | | | X | | | | | | | " |
| " | 43-56533 | | X | | | 2 | | | X | | | | | | | " |
| " | 43-77766 | | X | | | 2 | | | X | | | | | | | " |
| " | 42-56341 | | X | | | 2 | | | X | | | | | | | " |
| " | 341054 | | X | | | 2 | | | X | | | | | | | " |
| " | 43-27386 | X | | | | 3 | | | X | | | | | | | " |
| " | 42-62748 | | X | | | 3 | | | X | | | | | | | " |
| " | 42-79037 | | X | | | 3 | | | X | | | | | | | " |
| " | 43-37617 | | X | | | 3 | | | X | | | | | | | " |
| " | 43-27415 | | X | | | 3 | | | X | | | | | | | " |
| " | 42-77639 | X | | | | 2 | | | | X | | | | | | " |
| Div MP Plat | 274043 | | X | | | 7 | | | | X | | | | | | " |
| " | 42-73951 | | X | | | 14 | | | | | | | | | | " |
| " | 43-39176 | X | | | | 3 | | | X | | | | | | | " |
| " | 42-34019 | X | | | | 2 | | | X | | | | | | | " |
| " | 43-39690 | X | | | | 2 | | | X | | | | | | | " |
| " | 42-73535 | X | | | | 2 | | | X | | | | | | | " |
| **TOTAL** | | 22 | 25 | | | 244 | | | | 20 | | 17 | | | | |
| **PERCENTAGE** | | 47.9 | 52.1 | | | 100 | | | | 100 | | 100 | | | | |

| | Nº | GLIDER | | | | PERSONNEL | | | | JEEP | | TRAILER | | GUN | |
|---|---|---|---|---|---|---|---|---|---|---|---|---|---|---|---|
| | | INTACT | DAM | DES | MISS | OK | KIA | EVAC | MISS | SER | UNSER | SER | UNSER | SER | UNSER |
| GRAND TOTAL | 902 | 519 | 298 | 48 | 37 | 5233 | 4 | 65 | 186 | 300 | 38 | 170 | 19 | 83 | 6 |
| PERCENTAGE | | 57.5 | 33.0 | 5.3 | 4.2 | 95.3 | .1 | 1.2 | 3.4 | 88.8 | 11.2 | 89.9 | 10.1 | 93.3 | 6.7 |

# CHAPTER FIVE

# Battle of the Bulge:
# The 82nd Airborne Division in the Ardennes

## Section I – Preface

Presented herewith is a written and graphic report of operations carried out by the 82nd Airborne Division in the celebrated battles of "The Belgian Bulge" in Belgium and Germany during December, 1944, and January and February, 1945.

This record, written as it is in the terse, military language employed in such reports, can merely hint at the almost indescribable difficulties faced – and mastered – by both the combat and service echelons of the Division.

In brief, the 82nd Airborne Division, still awaiting reinforcements and much re-supply at its base camps in the general area of RHEIMS, France, moved 150 miles with its first combat elements going into position in less than twenty-four hours and the entire Division closing in a new combat area in less than forty hours from the times of the initial alert. It fought, stopped, and held against the best divisions the German leader, Field Marshal Von Runstedt, could pit against it, protecting the North shoulder of the Allied line, preventing the German break-through from turning North to LIEGE, Belgium, and providing a safe area through which trapped Allied units could withdraw from the break-through area. This it did despite the fact that its lines at times stretched more than 25,000 yards. Then, turning to the offense, the Division set the pace for other units, forcing the enemy back through his famed Siegfried Line.

Men fought, at times, with only rifles, grenades and knives against German armor. They fought with only light weapons in waist-deep snow, in blizzards, in near zero temperatures and in areas where heavy forestation and the almost total lack of roads presented problems that only men of stout hearts and iron determination could overcome.

The battles of "The Bulge", ranking on a par with the brightest victories in the Division's history, also proved again that plans and materiel are important but the most important essential of all is a fighting heart, a will-to-win. To the officers and men of the line goes full credit for the brilliant record they made in the name of the 82nd Airborne Division.

JAMES M. GAVIN,
Major General, USA,
Commanding.

## Section II – Division Commander's Report

The 82nd Airborne Division was located at Camps Suippes and Sissonne, France undertaking normal ground divisional training when, on December 17, 1944, first orders were received to move to the east. At about 1930 hours, while at dinner with the Staff, I received a phone call from Colonel Eaton, Chief of Staff, XVIII Corps (Airborne). He stated that he had just received a call from SHAEF to the effect that the situation on the front to the east appeared to be critical; that the airborne divisions were to be prepared to move twenty-four hours after daylight the following day; that the Corps Commander, General Ridgway, was in England and could not be contacted immediately. I instructed Colonel Eaton to issue orders to the Commanding General of the 101st Airborne Division, Brigadier General McAuliffe, to prepare immediately for movement in accordance with the SHAEF estimate, twenty-four hours after daylight. I assembled my Staff in the Division War Room at 2000 hours. I had listened to a radio news broadcast at 1800 hours and was aware of the fact that a German penetration was being made in the direction of St. Vith.

The Division was ready for a quick move, since, because of our past and usual quick commitments, we have maintained a high degree of readiness as a standard operating procedure. A basic load of ammunition was in the hands of each regiment, complete in all respects. Two "K" and two "D" rations for the Division were at hand and could be distributed in a matter of hours. All weapons, uniform and equipment were up to an operating standard. The Staff assembled at 2000 hours when the initial directive was issued that started their planning.

I called General March at Camp Suippes at about 1945 hours, giving him the situation and alerting him for the move. Unit Commanders at Camp Sissonne were assembled with the Staff in the War Room at 2100 hours when the situation was outlined to them and a tentative plan for the movement to Bastogne issued. At about 2130 hours I received a call from the Chief of Staff, XVIII Corps (Airborne), who said that Corps had orders to move without delay in the direction of Bastogne where further orders would be received. He also said that Corps was to be attached to the First United States Army. After further discussion I decided that the 82nd Airborne Division would move approximately one hour after daylight and move in the direction of Bastogne. The 101st Airborne Division was to move at 1400 hours, 18 December, also in the direction of Bastogne. At that time Oise Base Section was devoting all its efforts to pulling in all transportation off the roads to provide the necessary lift for both divisions.

At 2330 I left with my G-1, Lt. Col. Alfred W. Ireland, and my Aide, Captain Hugo V. Olson, for the command post of the First United States Army at Spa. The drive was very difficult due to the general condition of the roads, rain and fog, and the absence of bridges on a number of important highways. I reported to General Hodges in person at about 0900 hours 18 December. At that time the situation appeared rather vague. The first reports of enemy contact at Stavelot were just coming in. It was reported that an enemy force at Stavelot had driven our troops across the river and had succeeded in capturing and destroying a large map supply. They apparently blew the bridge upon driving out our forces. The situation south and west of Stavelot was unknown except that the enemy had evidently overrun our front positions. There appeared to be a large force of U.S. troops centered on St. Vith. There also appeared to be a large pocket of the 106th Division surrounded in the Eifel.

After some staff discussion, the Commanding General, First U.S. Army decided to attach the 82nd Airborne Division to V Corps. It was to close in an area in the vicinity of Werbomont. The 101st Airborne Division was to be attached to VIII Corps and would assemble in the vicinity of Bastogne. I placed a request with the First U.S. Army for tanks, TD's [tank destroyers], 4.2's [mortars]and medium artillery, and left the CP for Werbomont. At this time there was considerable movement west of service and command installations in and around Spa. It was apparently being evacuated.

I arrived at Werbomont at approximately mid-afternoon and immediately made a reconnaissance of the entire area. It offered excellent defensive possibilities, being the dominant terrain for many miles from the crossroads at Werbomont. At about 1600 hours I contacted an engineer platoon at the bridge at Hablemont. The bridge was prepared for demolition and they reported the Germans were in the immediate vicinity, coming over the main highway from Trois-Ponts. At that time a number of civilians were very excitedly moving west on the Trois-Ponts – Werbomont road. They all stated that the Germans had passed Trois-Ponts and were "coming this way". I made a reconnaissance down the valley from Hablemont to the Ambleve River but encountered no enemy or any indication of his whereabouts. One bridge was still intact at Forge and was not prepared for demolition. Upon returning to Hablemont I asked the Lieutenant at that bridge about it, but he appeared to be fully occupied with the means at his disposal of blowing the bridge at Hablemont. At about 1630 hours I left for Bastogne to meet General McAuliffe.

I reported to the VIII Corps CP in Bastogne and had a short conversation with General Middleton and talked to his G-2 and G-3. At that time the Corps CP was preparing to move. The situation was very vague. The 28th Division officers present seemed to feel that their division had been overrun, although they were uncertain of its whereabouts. I met General McAuliffe, gave him his orders that he was to assemble in Bastogne, reporting to the Corps Commander of the VIII Corps, and I left, moving north and passing through Houffalize shortly after dark. I arrived in Werbomont at approximately 2000 hours and about that time the first large group of 82nd vehicles started arriving.

A command post was established and troops disposed as rapidly as they arrived. Drivers and troops were very tired, having by this time been up for two nights. All during the night the staff worked on closing the vehicles into Werbomont area. About two hours after daylight December 19th the division closed in that area.

In the meantime the first enemy contact was made at Hablemont. A road block of the 30th Division was contacted by a German armored reconnaissance party at about 1900 hours the 18th. I visited the locality at daylight December 19th and found about five armored vehicles, armored cars and SP's, knocked out, with several German dead lying about the road. About a platoon of 2nd Battalion, 119th Infantry was present. They reported that all of their road block party proper, despite having knocked out the German reconnaissance party, had either been killed or captured or had moved east. It appeared quite clear that this was a reconnaissance party of a German armored column that had been endeavoring to move from Trois-Ponts to Werbomont and had succeeded in crossing the river at Forge. The Hablemont bridge was blown. At daylight, December 19, it was learned that the north-south road from Bastogne to Werbomont, had been cut by the Germans in the vicinity of Houffalize. The depth of this penetration was unknown, but there were rumors from truck drivers that the Germans were on the road in the vicinity of Hotton.

At 1100 hours, December 19, orders were received to dispatch one infantry battalion and one platoon of TD's [tank destroyers] to the area north of Hotton to block and clear all approaches from Hotton to the north, northwest and northeast. Permission was later obtained from the Corps Commander to send this battalion to Barvaux.

During the afternoon of December 19 information and orders were received from Headquarters XVIII Corps (Airborne), which had been established about one mile north of Werbomont, that First Army was to hold along the general line Stoumont-Stavelot-Malmady and counterattack in the direction of Trois-Ponts to halt the enemy's advance to the northwest. The XVIII Corps (Airborne) assumed command of the sector generally south of the Ambleve River to include Houffalize.

In compliance with instructions received from Corps Headquarters, the 504th Parachute Infantry advanced and seized the high ground northwest of Rahier and the 505th Parachute Infantry advanced and seized the high ground in the vicinity of Haut-Bodeux. The 508th Parachute Infantry sent one company to the crossroads one mile east of Bra. The regiment, less one company, occupied the high ground in the vicinity of Chevron. The 325th Glider Infantry remained at Werbomont, having sent the third battalion to the vicinity of Barvaux and one company to the crossroads at Manhay. These dispositions were consolidated during the night of December 19-20 and patrols pushed to the front to gain contact with the enemy.

Shortly after daylight, December 20, I met Colonel Reuben Tucker, 504th Commanding officer, in the town of Rahier at which time he had just received intelligence from civilians to the effect that approximately 125 vehicles, including approximately 30 tanks, had moved through the town the afternoon before, moving in the direction of Cheneux.

The information appeared to be reliable. It posed some interesting problems, It appeared that the Germans had given up hope of crossing the creek obstacle at Hablemont with their heavy armor and had turned to the main road through Stoumont-LaGlieze. If this were the case, the seizure of the bridge over the Ambleve River at Cheneux was imperative if their further movement was to be blocked.

I ordered Colonel Tucker to move into the town of Cheneux without delay and, conditions permitting, to seize the bridge. It was imperative that the bridge be seized. If 125 armored vehicles engaged the 504th in the country around Rahier we were in for some anxious moments, but we had come a long way to find the German and we had beaten in the past better units than these appeared to be, even with our limited means, so there was but one thing to do and that was to close with the enemy as rapidly as possible and destroy him by any means possible. But the seizure of the bridge was imperative.

Initial contact was made at the western exit of Cheneux by a patrol which had been sent from Rahier by the first battalion of the 504th. They fired on a German motorcyclist who was accompanied by a small patrol. Contact was first made on the ridge one-half mile west of Cheneux. This small patrol was followed by approximately a company of Germans moving along the ridge. They were engaged at once and a heavy fight took place, lasting all day long. This German force, we know now, was the advance guard of a reinforcement battalion of the 1st SS Panzer Division. The 1st battalion of the 504th drove them back into Cheneux , the battalion commander setting up his command post in a building in the western limits of Cheneux on the main road during the hours of darkness of the first night. During the day firing could be heard and some vehicular movement could be observed in the direction of LaGlieze.

I went to the 505th Parachute Infantry where I found that they had contacted some engineers who remained in Trois-Ponts. They had occasionally been under fire but no major German force had moved through the town. All civilians in these northern regimental areas reported that many Germans and much armor had passed through. The situation south of the 505th in the direction of Vielsalm was vague. Reconnaissance was pushed in that direction.

On the afternoon of December 20 at about 1600 hours I was called to Headquarters XVIII Corps (Airborne) to receive orders for an advance to the Vielsalm-Hebronval line. In the meantime contact had been established with a German SS force later identified as the 1st Panzer Division at Cheneux. First contacts indicated that they were well equipped and reasonably trained troops who would give us a good fight. It was with some difficulty that our first prisoners were taken. At about 1630, prior to leaving the division advance CP, which was now established at Hablemont, I had all unit commanders assembled, including the battalion commanders of the 508th. It was felt that speed was vital and if we were to move to Vielsalm with the mission to be assigned us by XVIII Corps (Airborne), we had to move without delay, regardless of conditions of light or darkness.

At Corps Headquarters I received information that they were advancing to the southeast and establishing an active defense along the line Vielsalm-Hebronval-Laroche; that this division, 82nd Airborne, would establish a defensive line from contact with the 30th Division, in the vicinity of LaGleize, to Cheneux-Trois-Ponts-Grand Halleux-Vielsalm-Salmchateau-Hebronval. Contact was to be immediately established with units reportedly cut off in the area of Vielsalm-St. Vith. The 3rd Armored Division was on our right and was to hold the sector from Hebronval west.

Orders to accomplish this were issued at the division CP at Hablemont shortly before dark, December 20. Units moved promptly and by daylight were on their objectives, well organized and prepared to defend. Regiments were in the line in the order, left to right: 504, 505, 508, 325. One battalion of the 325 was held in division reserve in the vicinity of LaVaux. The division forward CP was established in the town of Lierneux at the railroad crossing on the northern edge of the town.

In Vielsalm contact was made with General Hasbrouck who had established the CP of the 7th Armored Division in the town. The division was then fighting around St. Vith. West of Vielsalm, General Jones had established the CP of the 106th Division at Reneveaux. From a visit to both of these officers I learned that the 7th Armored Division, except for battle losses, was intact and fighting with unit integrity. The 106th Division appeared to be rather badly chewed up and had but one regiment, the 424th Infantry, remaining, with some division artillery and divisional units. There were also present a regiment of the 28th Division, the 112th Infantry, in addition to a number of Corps and larger units such as medium artillery.

On the left of the division very heavy fighting was taking place in the vicinity of Cheneux where the German 1st SS Panzer Division was making a desperate and all-out effort to drive out the first battalion of the 504th. Further south at Trois-Ponts, and extending down to Grand Halleux, determined, apparently well planned and executed attacks were being made with increasing strength against the very thinly held front of the 505th. On the south, the 508th and the 325 had no contact with the enemy. The Division Reconnaissance Platoon was pushed south. Information available indicated that the Germans were moving in great strength to the west, having passed Houffalize, and were moving towards the Meuse River. The 3rd Armored Division, which was supposed to be on the division's right, could not be contacted. I believe that on this date a reconnaissance party may have established contact.

On December 21 I visited the CP's of the 7th Armored and 106th Divisions with the Corps Commander of XVIII Corps (Airborne), General Ridgway. The situation in the vicinity of St. Vith appeared to be critical. The town was being overwhelmingly attacked in several directions and there appeared to be little prospect of preventing its being cut off. The Corps Commander informed me that his original plan was for the 30th Division to attack south from Stavelot to relieve the situation at St. Vith and for the 3rd Armored to attack on the right of the 82nd so as to drive in the Germans moving to the west. On this date, December 21, however, only the narrow neck of land from Vielsalm to Salmchateau, held by the 82nd Airborne Division, connected the St. Vith forces with remaining forces of the First Army. Its retention would be decisive.

The fighting at Cheneux was increasing in bitterness. On this date the first battalion of the 504th, assisted by a company of the third battalion of that regiment, made a final, all-out assault on the Germans in that town and in close hand-to-hand fighting, many of the parachute troops jumping aboard the German half-tracks and knifing the Germans at their posts, the Germans were driven back across the Ambleve River and our troops seized the bridge. In this attack we destroyed a considerable amount of armor and killed and captured many Germans from the 1st SS Panzer Division.

Farther to the south and east, the 505th Parachute Infantry was having very hard fighting with the remainder of the 1st SS Panzer Division. The 505th had initially sent a covering force east of the Salm River in the vicinity of Trois-Ponts. Through sheer weight of numbers this small force was finally driven to the river line where it held. Being very much overextended, the regiment managed to hold by diagnosing or estimating the point of German main effort from time to time and then marshaling all available infantry as quickly as possible and beating off the attack at that point.

This process was repeated, where necessary, day and night until finally the German attacks waned in their intensity about December 23.

The 508th Parachute Infantry on the Vielsalm-Salmcheteau front was without enemy contact except for patrols. The 325th Glider Infantry, aided by the Division Reconnaissance Platoon, had established contact with enemy forces several miles south of their front line.

On December 21 I was instructed by the Corps Commander to make a reconnaissance of the divisional area with a view to withdrawing after the extrication of the St. Vith forces to a suitable defensive position that would tie in with the divisions on my right and left. To date no firm contact had been established with the 3rd Armored Division. The merits of the present defensive position were discussed and it was agreed that the Thier-du-Mont line offered splendid defensive possibilities provided it could be continued on our right. As well as I could determine, however, there were no friendly troops except light reconnaissance elements west of Hebronval.

I objected to the withdrawal but the Corps Commander explained that regardless of my wishes in the matter it might be necessary to require the division to withdraw. It was quite evident at this time that if a major German attack developed from the south, threatening the right of the division, its continued occupation of the salient extending out to Vielsalm would be costly in life and to no advantage after the extrication of the St. Vith forces. It was emphasized by the Corps Commander that it was absolutely necessary to secure properly the withdrawal of the St. Vith forces by holding and defending our present positions.

A reconnaissance was undertaken and at its completion it was quite clear that there was but one reasonably good defensive position and that was Trois-Ponts-Basse-Bodeux-Bra-Manhay line. At the direction of the Corps Commander a reconnaissance was also made of a position farther to the rear, generally along the Cheneux-Rahier-Chevron-Werbomont line. On December 22 I went to Manhay where I met General Rose, commanding the 3rd Armored Division. He stated that he was covering a concentration of other forces and that his front was so extended that he could not occupy and hold in strength the terrain west of Hebronval.

From my viewpoint, it was obvious that the loss of Regne-Lierneux ridge would result in the complete neutralization of the defensive capabilities of the right portion of the division sector. This ridge dominated the entire road north from Vielsalm to Bra. This was the only road not south of the Trois-Ponts-Werbomont road. In addition, all of the division's installations and division artillery were located in the Lierneux-Goronne-Vielsalm valley. Accordingly, orders were issued to the 325th Glider Infantry to extend its right flank and seize and hold Rogne and the ridge extending north therefrom. This ridge had to be held at any cost.

On the afternoon of December 22 an enemy force of approximately 100 vehicles of all types preceded by about twenty-five tanks advanced north through Ottre. The tanks entered Joubieval. They were permitted to close up, then brought under devastating artillery fire. Artillery observers who remained on the outpost line on the ridge immediately north of Ottre kept the column under close observation and put very effective artillery fire on it. This unit was later identified as a portion of the 2nd SS Panzer Division. At 1700, December 22, the outpost of the 325 was forced to withdraw. The enemy build-up was increasing in intensity on our southern front.

At the direction of the Division Commander, the Division Engineer conducted a thorough study and reconnaissance of the southern portion of the division sector. It became clearly evident that the German could not bring armor to bear against the sector anywhere between Salmchateau and the Fraiture crossroads except by bringing it up the Petite-Langlir road, and if the Petit-Langlir bridge could be blown he would be incapable of bringing armor to bear anywhere within this 10,000 yard gap without approaching up the main road towards Salmchateau, which was well covered.

The possibility of canalizing his armored attack was obvious and steps were taken to take advantage of this. Early on December 22 orders were issued to the Engineer Battalion to move without delay and prepare the Petite-Langlir Bridge for demolition and to destroy it upon hostile threat. Thorough and detailed preparations were made, possibly too thorough, because as the demolition party moved south from Ottre it encountered a large group of German vehicles coming northward. The Germans had the bridge. This was at about 1400 hours. Evidently thoroughness in preparation had cost us the bridge.

During the night of December 22-23 an engineer patrol, lead by Major J.C.H. Lee, Jr., made its way behind the enemy lines to the bridge over the creek south of Petite-Langlir and destroyed the bridge while it was actually being used by German vehicles. They displayed unusual gallantry and perseverance in the performance of their task.

In the following twenty-four hours enemy pressure built up in intensity all along the southern front. It was easily handled south of Thier-du-Mont. The enemy, however, showed promise of getting entirely out of hand on the right, apparently wide open beyond Regne. Returning to the left flank, the German forces appeared to be cut off in the vicinity of La Glieze but were fighting a very intense engagement with the 30th Division on our left. Their occasional isolated efforts to cross the Ambleve River were easily dealt with by small patrols from the 504th Parachute Infantry.

I therefore ordered the release of the Division reserve battalion of the 325 to the Regimental Commander of that regiment and ordered one battalion of the 504, the 2nd Battalion, to move at once to the ridge 5,000 yards southwest of Lierneux. These troops went into position during daylight of December 23. On this date the enemy attacked in considerable strength and overran the town of Regne. The 325 was ordered to counterattack and retake the town. The retention of this ridge was most vital if the Division was to accomplish its mission of extricating the St. Vith forces. Supported by attached armor and with unusual gallantry and elan, the 325 attacked and retook the town and held it until later ordered to withdraw.

It was on this occasion that the Regimental Adjutant of a regiment of the 2nd SS Panzer Division was captured with the orders for the advance of the following day. In the confusion incident to the retaking of the town by the 325, he had been sent forward by his Regimental Commander to learn the true situation. During his reconnaissance he found himself aboard a motorcycle side car in the outskirts of Regne when our troops were retaking the town. He was captured with the town and had the orders on his person. They proved to be of great value, since they gave us definite information of the enemy's intentions for the following several days.

It was becoming increasingly evident that the German was determined to ultimately reach Werbomont and move north towards Aywaille and Leige. Colonel Billingslea, Commanding Officer of the 325th Glider Infantry, was ordered to extend his right flank to include the Fraiture ridge. No firm contact with the 3rd Armored Division on our right appeared possible.

The Fraiture crossroads began to assume increasing importance. Inquiry was made on several occasions of the Commanding General of XVIII Corps (Airborne) as to what was being done to insure its retention. On December 22 I made a personal reconnaissance from Ievigne to Fond de la Justice to Manhay. Quite a number of armored vehicles were in the vicinity of Manhay and some were on the ridge 1 1/2 miles south thereof. The 3rd Armored Division CP was in Manhay. A conversation with the Division Commander made it apparent that they were incapable of committing sufficient strength to the crossroads to guarantee its retention by our troops.

From my view point, its loss would mean that German armor which we had successfully turned back from Trois-Ponts to Regne, with the aid of both terrain and a very active defense, would bypass the Division and occupy the Lierneux-Regne ridge mass, thus preventing us from accomplishing our present mission of covering the withdrawal of the St. Vith troops. I accordingly ordered Colonel Billingslea to again extend his right flank and to include in his defensive organization the cross-roads southwest of Fraiture. This he did by sending Company F, under the command of Captain Woodruff to the area. The situation all along the southern front was becoming critical when I visited the battalion commanders of the 325th several times during the period December 22-24. On the afternoon of December 23, at about 1700 hours, I checked the dispositions along the Fraiture ridge. At this time riflemen were scattered 100 to 200 yards apart. There was a little antitank defense, and the possibility of defending the ridge against a major German attack appeared nothing less than fantastic. On the other hand, nothing could be spared from the other fronts, since the situation was much the same in other sectors, although the threat was not as great. The attacks of the 1st SS Panzer Division on our left began to wane.

On the afternoon of December 23, at about 1730 hours, I arrived at the CP of Captain Gibson in the town of Fraiture. It was then under heavy mortar fire. A considerable volume of small arms fire could be heard to the south and west. SCR-300 [radio] contact was made with Captain Woodruff at the crossroads. He stated that he was under terrific attack which was completely engulfing his small unit. I moved on foot from Fraiture towards the crossroads and managed to reach the edge of the woods several hundred yards beyond the town.

It was clearly evident that the attack at the crossroads was an all-out affair of great magnitude. As it developed, it was the attack of a regiment of the 2nd SS Panzer Division supported by attached armor, attacking with the mission of driving up the main highway to Werbomont. The one company was soon completely overrun. During the hours of darkness, in desperate, close-quarters fighting, Captain Woodruff managed to extricate about 40 men. They accounted for many Germans in fighting their way out, and rejoined their battalion commander in the vicinity of Fraiture.

At this point it was evident that there was nothing to prevent the German forces from entering the rear of the Division area, which was now closely engaged along its entire 25,000-yard front.

I moved to the CP of the reserve battalion in the region southwest of Lierneux, arriving there at about dark. I issued verbal orders to the battalion commander, Major Wellems, outlining the situation to him and directing him to secure the right flank as far west as Malempre. I then moved without delay via Tri-le-Chesliang to Manhay, the CP of the 3rd Armored Division. Here I found one MP on duty at the crossroads and the town completely abandoned. I then moved without delay to Corps Headquarters to explain the situation to them and obtain further assistance in holding the main highway which was out of my sector, but the retention of which was necessary to the accomplishment of my mission.

By telephone Colonel Tucker was told to be prepared to move the 504 Regimental Headquarters and one battalion to the vicinity of Lansivel where he would take over the sector on the right of the Division. Two TD's were moved southwest of the Division CP at Bra at approximately 2200. Upon my arrival there I learned by telephone from [XVIII Airborne] Corps that Manhay had fallen to the German attacking forces. There seemed to be some doubt about this, however, and due to the darkness and confusion it was impossible to determine exactly where anyone was. All units were informed of the situation and efforts made to get units under control and have the situation in hand so as to be able to engage the German forces on reasonably favorable terms at daylight.

At about daylight XVIII Corps (Airborne) made available to me Combat Command B of the 9th Armored Division under the command of General Hoge, which had been withdrawn from the St. Vith area. General Hoge reported to my CP at about 0700. At about 0545, December 24, Colonel Tucker was ordered to leave the smallest possible force in the northern sector and to move south to Bra by motor without delay. He had been given a warning order about 24 hours earlier. At 0645 the 505 was ordered to regroup one battalion, the 2nd, and have it prepared to move in Division reserve without delay, warning orders having been given them to prepare for this prior to this time.

At 0820 verbal orders were issued to General Hoge to hold Malempre until further orders, to contact the 504 on his left and the 7th Armored on his right. The 7th Armored had been recommitted by XVIII Corps (Airborne) down the main road towards Manhay. Combat Command B, 9th Armored Division, and the 7th Armored Division were practically exhausted from the past week's fighting. They were very short of infantry, and in the opinion of General Hoge Combat Command B was incapable of a sustained defense or offense. However, Malempre had to be held and appropriate orders were issued.

At 1315 hours General Hoge reported to me that he was holding Malempre. The situation in that sector, however, still appeared confused. This was further added to by the presence in the area of German troops wearing American uniforms and using American armor. It would appear certain that the Germans were fighting in Manhay, that they held the ridge south and east of Manhay, that we held Malempre and that we held Fraiture. Between Malempre and Fraiture the 2nd Battalion of the 504th Parachute Infantry was fighting in the woods. This battalion a veteran, experienced outfit, had as clear a picture as could be expected of the situation. Numerous Germans were endeavoring to attack through the woods to the northeast between Malempre and Fraiture. There was much close, bitter fighting and the Germans were very roughly handled by Major Wellem's battalion. He finally succeeded in stabilizing his position and containing the Germans, although his frontage was very great, particularly for the wooded sector in which he was fighting. The Germans were well equipped and armed and were fighting with unusual esprit. They were from the 2nd SS Panzer Division.

During the day of December 24 Colonel Tucker brought up his full regiment less one battalion which he had left at Cheneux to contain the forces north of the river. That battalion was charged with holding the Ambleve River line from immediately north of Trois-Ponts to where contact was established with the 30th Division in the vicinity of La Gleize, a frontage of approximately 12,000-15,000 yards, much of it closely wooded country and broken up terrain. However, since the situation was so critical on the right, and the German attack had apparently been beaten off on the left, no other course of action appeared practicable at the moment. The 505 appeared to have all it could do to continue to hold the Trois-Ponts-Grand Helleux line and the 508 was becoming heavily engaged on the Veilsalm-Salmchateau-Joubieval line.

In accordance with the warning order given me by the Corps Commander, similar warning orders were given to unit commanders to be prepared to withdraw if necessary to the Trois-Ponts-Erria-Manhay line. Early on December 24, therefore, they directed to make small unit reconnaissance of the defensive position and sectors were allotted and missions assigned. A conference was held at Headquarters XVIII Corps (Airborne) at about 1330 hours, December 24th, at which time orders were issued for the voluntary withdrawal to the Corps defensive position. Division plans were completed and orders issued during the afternoon to effect the withdrawal starting after darkness.

I was greatly concerned with the attitude of the troops toward the withdrawal, the Division having never made a withdrawal in its combat history. The German was using every artifice conceivable to create doubt and confusion in the minds of American fighting units. He was using our arms, equipment and vehicles, frequently leaving their own abandoned and disabled at bottlenecks on the roads. False messages were being used and Germans in American officers' uniforms were known to be in the rear areas. One trooper, who later was recaptured, was captured by Germans in American uniforms in the vicinity of Tri-le-Chesliang. All of these factors made the prospects of a withdrawal most unpleasant. On the 24th I published a memorandum to be read to the troops, emphasizing the dangers in the operation with which we were confronted, and I spent from early evening until after midnight visiting the troops of all battalions.

In all of the operations in which we have participated in our two years of combat and they have been many of multitudinous types, I have never seen a better executed operation than the withdrawal on Christmas Eve. The troops willingly and promptly carried into execution all the withdrawal plans, although they openly and frankly criticized it and failed to understand the necessity for it. But everybody pitched in and the withdrawal went smoothly.

Christmas Eve was a very cold, bright moonlight night. The enemy was closely engaged with us on the entire front from Trois-Ponts to Malempre, but there was in no locality any feeling of unusual pressure being exerted against us. All Unit Commanders, down to Platoon Leaders I believe, felt that they had the situation well under control. The rear area, except for some medium artillery which had been abandoned in fields off the main roads, was completely cleared of the St. Vith pocket forces.

The withdrawal started shortly after dark. Covering shells were to be withdrawn at four A.M. The 307th Airborne Engineer Battalion supported the withdrawal by blowing bridges over the Salm River, laying minefields and establishing roadblocks. This worked very well on the right with the 504 and the 325. The 508 was attacked in great forces and had some close and intense fighting at the bridges over the Salm River before it finally withdrew. Its shell on Thier-du-mont was apparently cut off, but finally made its way back under the command of Major Taylor without the loss of a single man. All the troops, except for the shell, were in the valley in the vicinity of Gorronne where I saw them about 2200 hours, and everything was going smoothly.

At about 2300 hours I passed through St. Jacques on the way to the 505th Parachute Infantry Command Post, which was at Dairomont. At St. Jacques I met a platoon in a deployed formation moving north. They said they believed that there was a large force of Germans in the area and that they were looking for them. I went to the regimental CP. Here an unusual situation was becoming apparent. Earlier in the night a report was received from vehicle drivers that while driving their jeeps on a road in the vicinity of Basse-Bodeux they observed troops wearing full field equipment walking in the woods toward the east. These troops hit the ground and took cover, generally acting very evasive. Later in the night a lineman, checking his lines, had his jeep shot up by what he guessed were German troops in the rear area. This accounted for the platoon that I had met at St. Jacques being on its mission of clearing Germans from the rear area.

I talked to the regimental commander about the situation and he believed that at this time a force of approximately 500 Germans were somewhere in the regimental rear area moving to the east. Their presence could hardly be accounted for unless they had escaped from the La Glieze-Stoumont pocket. At first we did not believe that there were German troops in the area, but piecing together all available intelligence seemed to establish the fact unmistakably. At this time the regiment was under some pressure along the river line and had left a company in three platoon positions at the most likely crossing sites as a shell to cover the withdrawal of the regiment, which was now taking place. After discussing the situation for some time with the regimental commander, it was decided that the withdrawal would continue as planned; that by daylight the 505 would be on its defensive position with the area to its front wired and mined, and that it would be prepared to defend that position at all costs in coordination with the units on its right and left. This made it impractical for the regimental commander to divert any of his forces to a task of searching for the Germans. Orders were issued to proceed to new positions as previously planned and to be on the alert for loose German forces.

Several hours before daylight one platoon positioned north of Grand Halleux was attacked by a German force of great strength. A heavy fight ensued. A number of Germans were killed and wounded, as well as troopers of the Division. Among those captured was an American major of the U.S. 30th Infantry Division. He had been captured in earlier fighting at La Gleize and the force that was accompanying him when captured was a force of approximately 500-800 Germans endeavoring to withdraw to their own lines east of the Salm River. During their withdrawal they were rather well chewed up but they nevertheless succeeded in reaching their lines except for several killed and captured. On December 25th we realized that we had just succeeded in withdrawing through a hostile withdrawing force, which was a rather novel maneuver.

At daylight, December 25th, all regiments were on their positions, mining and wiring were under way and all troops were dug in. Communications were being laid under great difficulty because of the mountainous terrain, particularly in the 504 and 508 sectors. At daylight I joined Major Gerard, commanding a battalion of the 325, in the town of Tri-le-Chesliang on our right flank. Its occupation, in which contact was established with infantry of the 7th Armored Division on our right, finally buttoned up our defense. Contact was already established with the 30th Division on our left.

About two days after occupying this position an attack was made be the 62nd Volks-Grenadier Division on our left and the 9th SS Panzer Division on our center. The 62d V.G. Division in all of its operations proved to be of very poor quality and not well trained. They consistently lost patrols by having them destroyed by our outposts and they appeared to be very vulnerable to our own patrols.

The 9th SS Panzer Division appeared to be much better equipped and better trained. They launched an attack up the main axis from Lierneux to Hablemont, hitting the 508 and 504 in a coordinated effort that was characterized by great dash and courage. The 3rd Battalion of the 508 was completely overrun. The men remained, however, manning their positions in the houses and foxholes. The battalion commander, Lt Colonel Mendez, obtained the use of the reserve company of the 2nd Battalion of the 508 on his left, counter-attacked with great gallantry and determination, and drove the 9th SS Panzers from his positions, restoring his MLR [main line of resistance]. The Storm Troopers' losses were extremely heavy. From one field alone sixty-two bodies were later removed.

On interrogation some of the Storm Troopers stated that they had been accustomed to attacking with such dash and elan, yelling and firing their weapons, and the usual reaction of the enemy was to break and run as the Storm Troopers closed with them. They were frankly surprised to find troops who would man their positions after being overrun. The unit of the 9th SS attacking the 504 after overrunning the outpost of the 2nd Battalion of that regiment, were stopped and driven back. They told an identical story of their attack technique.

This ended all offensive efforts of the German forces in the Battle of the Bulge. About a week later the division attacked, completely overrunning the 62nd V.G. Division and the 9th SS Panzer Division, and capturing 2500 prisoners, including five battalion commanders. It regained its former position on the Thier-du-mont heights.

From here the Division withdrew to a rest area from which it was later committed to the attack east of St. Vith, attacking through deep snow over thickly wooded mountains and overrunning a considerable group of German defensive forces in a constant day and night attack lasting for six days. Ultimately they drove into the Siegfried Line to seize Udenbreth and the ridge extending south.

This attack was the most arduous in the Division's history and, at its end, probably the most bitterly fought, but the Division once again entered Germany and the seizure of Udenbreth placed the First U.S. Army in a position to attack down ridge lines all the way to Bonn.

From here the Division moved to the Hurtgen sector where, as a member of XVIII Corps (Airborne) and later III Corps, it participated in the advance to the Roer River. Except for extensive minefields, extremely difficult road conditions and hostile artillery fire, the operation was not too difficult. The Division arrived on the Roer River and had completed detailed plans for a river crossing and the seizure of Nideggen east of the river when it was withdrawn on February 17th and returned to the Sissonne-Suippes, France, area.

# Section III – Chronology

1. AFTER-ACTION REPORT FOR DECEMBER 1944
2. AFTER-ACTION REPORT FOR JANUARY 1945
3. AFTER-ACTION REPORT FOR FEBRUARY 1945

## Narrative

### 17 DECEMBER 1944

The Division, engaged in normal training activities near RHEIMS, FRANCE, was alerted at 1900 hours to move into combat the following day. At 2100 hours a movement order was received directing the Division to move by motor at 180900 from base camps and to concentrate in the vicinity of BASTOGNE, BELGIUM, where further instructions would be forth-coming. From general information available then, there appeared to be a serious GERMAN penetration in the VIII Corps sector.

### 18 DECEMBER 1944

The Division's leading serials left the base camps at SISSONNE and SUIPPES, FRANCE, at 0900 hours. Combat team component march units met at SEDAN and proceeded toward BASTOGNE. At SPIRIMONT, BELGIUM, the head of the Division column was directed to proceed to WERBOMONT. Higher headquarters had then decided that the Division would hold the North flank of the penetration and the 101st Airborne Division, the South flank at BASTOGNE. Roads were clogged with vehicles and refugees. The location of the German advance break-through elements was uncertain. A screening force from the 119th Infantry was deployed in the vicinity of HABLEMONT to cover the assembly of the Division. The leading serial arrived at WERBOMONT at 1730 hours. Defensive positions were organized without delay by each unit upon its arrival. Security and reconnaissance measures were established at once.

### 19 DECEMBER 1944

The Division closed in the WERBOMONT area by 1000 hours. Defensive positions were improved progressively.

325th Glider Infantry – The 3rd Battalion established road blocks in the vicinity of BARVAUX. "F" Company occupied GRAND-MENIL and MANHAY.
504th Parachute Infantry – Occupied RAHIER and relieved elements of the 119th Infantry in its sector.
505th Parachute Infantry – Occupied BASSE BODEUX and relieved elements of the 119th Infantry in its sector.
508th Parachute Infantry – "H" Company occupied crossroad just North of FLORET.

### 20 DECEMBER 1944

325th Glider Infantry – The 1st Battalion occupied a defensive position in the vicinity of BRA. The 3rd Battalion was relieved in the BARVAUX area by elements of the 3rd Armored Division. The 2nd Battalion, less "F" Company, in Division Reserve. "F" Company continued to occupy GRANDMENIL and MANHAY.
504th Parachute Infantry – The 1st Battalion (less "A" Company) attacked CHENEUX at 1400. A heavy engagement ensued with a battalion of the 1st SS Panzer Division supported by tanks, flak wagons, and artillery. "A" Company took positions in the vicinity of BRUME.
505th Parachute Infantry – Pushed out to the SALM River along the line TROIS PONTS-COURNAIMONT, South of GRAND HALLEUX and relieved elements of the 51st Combat Engineers at TROIS PONTS. One Company held the bridge at HOURT. One platoon crossed the river near TROIS PONTS. Another platoon crossed at LA TOUR.
508th Parachute Infantry – Began moving by foot and by motor to the vicinity of GORONNE.

### 21 DECEMBER 1944

Division completely occupied line TROIS PONTS-SALMCHATEAU-HEBRONVAL and made contact with 7th Armored Division, 106th Infantry Division, 28th Infantry Division (112th Infantry), and CCB, 9th Armored Division.

<u>325th Glider Infantry</u> – Closed in the area Southwest of LIERNEUX and occupied sector SART – HEBRONVAL. One platoon Company "F" occupied REGNE. Patrols advanced as far South as BIHAIN.

<u>504th Parachute Infantry</u> – 1st Battalion (less "A" Company), had cleared CHENEUX by mid-morning capturing 14 flak wagons, 6 half-tracks, 4 trucks, 4 105mm Howitzers, and one Mark VI. 3rd Battalion, less "G" Company, attacked and captured MONCEAU against strong enemy resistance and assisted 1st Battalion by swinging North of CHENEUX. The 1st Battalion, plus "G" Company, consolidated positions in CHENEUX and then with the 3rd Battalion attacked and drove the enemy across the L'AMBLEVE River and established positions on the South bank of the River.

<u>505th Parachute Infantry</u> – Two Companies of the 2nd Battalion crossed the SALM River at TROIS PONTS and established a bridgehead.

<u>508th Parachute Infantry</u> – Closed in its area Southeast of GORONNE and occupied sector VIELSALM-GRAND SART.

## 22 DECEMBER 1944

Troops of the 7th Armored Division, the 106th Infantry Division, the 28th Infantry Division, and CCB of the 9th Armored Division began to withdraw through the Division's lines.

<u>325th Glider Infantry</u> – 2nd Battalion occupied FRAITURE. "F" Company occupied the main crossroad Southeast of MANHAY and contacted 3rd Armored Division. Five enemy tanks and two enemy patrols were repelled in the vicinity of JOUBIEVAL by artillery. 125 enemy vehicles, including armor, were reported in OTTRE. Friendly artillery fired on town. Two enemy infantry attempts to form up for attack were both stopped by 155 mm fire. OTTRE was a mass of smoldering ruins.

<u>504th Parachute Infantry</u> – The 2nd Battalion relieved the 1st Battalion. Contact with 119th Infantry was established.

<u>505th Parachute Infantry</u> – 2nd Battalion bridgehead across the SALM River at TROIS PONTS was attacked by a Battalion of the 1st SS Panzer Division, supported by armor and artillery. 2nd Battalion forces were withdrawn and the bridge was blown. Two enemy squads infiltrated into TROIS PONTS but were driven back across the SALM River. 3rd Battalion repulsed an enemy platoon attempt to cross the SALM River at LA TOUR and another two platoon effort in the "G" Company sector. 1st and 3rd Battalion bridgeheads at GRAND HALLEUX and LA NEUVILLE were established.

<u>508th Parachute Infantry</u> – Organized defensive positions from VIELSALM to SALMCHATEAU to GRAND SART. The 1st Battalion was placed in Division Reserve. Patrols reported German columns moving in a steady stream through PETITE LANGLIR towards OTTRE.

<u>307th Airborne Engineer Battalion</u> – Blew the bridge at ROCHELINVAL. An officer patrol dispatched to PETITE LANGLIR blew a vital bridge over the RONCE stream which was being used by the enemy.

## 23 DECEMBER 1944

Troops and vehicles of the 7th Armored Division, the 106th Infantry Division, the 28th Infantry Division, and CCB of the 9th Armored Division continued to withdraw through Division lines.

<u>325th Glider Infantry</u> – The 2nd Battalion drove back several enemy probing attacks. A composite force consisting of "F" Company, 325th Glider Infantry, and tanks of the 3rd Armored Division was attacked by a strong enemy force at the main crossroad Southeast of MANHAY. Two platoons of the 509th Parachute Infantry Battalion joined the composite force. At 1630 hours, after a very effective mortar and artillery preparation, an estimated infantry battalion with tanks of the 2nd SS Panzer Division attacked. Enemy tanks shelled the crossroad with deadly effect. Enemy infantry and armor overran the defenders. "F" Company was forced to withdraw. 1st Battalion lost and reestablished an outpost in JOUBIEVAL. The 3rd Battalion captured an enemy document in OTTRE that contained plans for the attack to LIEGE.

<u>504th Parachute Infantry</u> – The 2nd Battalion, relieved by the 1st Battalion, moved into position as Division Reserve in the vicinity of LIERNEUX and latter was moved Southwest of MALEMPRE to meet an enemy threat. The 1st Battalion took over the sectors of the 2nd Battalion, 504th Parachute Infantry and the 2nd Battalion, 505th Parachute Infantry.

<u>505th Parachute Infantry</u> – Regiment continued to defend SALM River line against determined, well supported attacks of the German 1st SS Panzer Division. Except for patrols, all elements of the Regiment were located on the West bank of the river.

508th Parachute Infantry – Repulsed an enemy attack directed towards SLAMCHATEAU from the STE MAIRE-PROVEDROUX area. Enemy forces were estimated as a battalion of infantry supported by Mark III tanks. The three bridges at SALMCHATEAU and the railroad bridge at VIELSALM were blown. The 1st Battalion reverted to Regimental control. The 3rd Battalion, 112th Infantry was attached.

307th Airborne Engineer Battalion – Executed demolition of stone culvert 1-1/2 miles South of SALMCHATEAU after the last vehicle of the 7th Armored Division had passed.

14th Tank Battalion of CCB, 9th Armored Division – Attached to Division. Company "C" established a road block at the MANHAY crossroads.

## 24 DECEMBER 1944

The last elements of the 7th Armored Division were withdrawn through Division lines. Division was ordered by XVIII Corps (Airborne) to withdraw under cover of darkness to a defense line extending from TROIS PONTS-BASSE BODEUX-BERGIFAZ-TRI-LE-CHESLIANG. Regiments were ordered to delay enemy until 0400 December 25th with a covering shell.

325th Glider Infantry – 2nd Battalion with strong enemy pressure on both flanks withdrew from FRAITURE and took up a position in BOIS HOUBY after killing at least fifty enemy and routing the remainder. One platoon, holding REGNE, was overrun by enemy infantry and armor. "B" Company, supported by a tank company of the 14th Tank Battalion, recaptured the town and ejected the enemy.

504th Parachute Infantry – The 3rd Battalion, less "G" Company, moved into position Southwest of LIERNEUX and there repulsed a strong enemy attack.

505th Parachute Infantry – The 2nd Battalion moved North to intercept an enemy force estimated at 800 enemy reported to be attempting a crossing of the SALM River toward the East. "I" Company was attacked by an estimated enemy company who were trying to withdraw across the river. Most of the enemy was destroyed. Initiated withdrawal as per plan.

508th Parachute Infantry – The highway bridge at VIELSALM was blown. The covering shell was attacked by an enemy battalion, strongly supported by artillery and mortar fire.

307th Airborne Engineer Battalion – Upon receipt of the withdrawal order prepared extensive obstacles on the defense line, mined approaches, and prepared bridges and culverts on the withdrawal routes for demolitions.

14th Tank Battalion – "C" Company was relieved at the MANHAY road block by elements of 7th Armored Division. The enemy attacked in force and captured MANHAY.

## 25 DECEMBER 1944

All units successfully broke contact with the enemy and withdrew to the new defense line.

325th Glider Infantry – The 1st Battalion filled the gap between the 504th Parachute Infantry and the 7th Armored Division by occupying TRI-LE-CHESLIANG and VAUX CHAVANNE. At 2200 hours an enemy infantry attack was repulsed. The 2nd Battalion as Division Reserve and the 3rd Battalion as Regimental Reserve occupied positions near AU HETRE.

504th Parachute Infantry – The 2nd and 3rd Battalions occupied new positions along the line BERGIFAZ-BRA-VAUX CHAVANNE. The 1st Battalion, in Regimental Reserve, located vicinity of BRA.

505th Parachute Infantry – The 2nd and 3rd Battalions occupied new defensive positions between TROIS PONTS and BASSE BODEUX. The 1st Battalion occupied a position 3000 yards north of BASSE BODEUX as Regimental Reserve.

508th Parachute Infantry – Occupied new defensive positions along line HAUTE BODEUX-BERGIFAZ with all battalions on MLR. The 3rd Battalion, 112th Infantry was relieved of attachment to the 508th Parachute Infantry.

307th Airborne Engineer Battalion – Laid minefields, constructed abatis, and blew bridges to form a barrier along the Division front.

Company "B", 86th Chemical Battalion, Company "A", 703rd TD Battalion, and 551st Parachute Infantry Battalion were attached to the Division. Company "C", 563rd AAA AW Battalion was relieved of attachment to the Division.

## 26 DECEMBER 1944

325th Glider Infantry – At 0630 hour one battalion of the 2nd SS Panzer Division attacked and succeeded in over-running a portion of the sector. Company "B" and Company "C" promptly counterattacked and restored all positions, inflicting heavy casualties on the enemy. The 1st Battalion was relieved by the 23rd Armored Infantry Battalion, 7th Armored Division, and moved to an area Northeast of TRI-LE-CHESLIANG.

504th Parachute Infantry – The 2nd Battalion broke up two enemy attacks launched by the 9th SS Panzer Division from the vicinity of FLORET.

505th Parachute Infantry – Patrolled aggressively. Sector was generally quiet.

508th Parachute Infantry – 2nd Battalion repulsed attack near Road Junction West of REHARMONT by an estimated two companies of infantry supported by four half-tracks. The 3rd Battalion outposts repulsed attack by enemy infantry.

## 27 DECEMBER 1944

325th Glider Infantry – The 2nd Battalion, Division reserve, moved to a position approximately 1,000 yards South of MONCHENOUL.

504th Parachute Infantry – The 3rd Battalion extended MLR slightly to the Southeast. The 2nd Battalion knocked out an enemy flak wagon near BERGIFAZ.

505th Parachute Infantry – The 3rd Battalion received heavy artillery fire throughout the day. Company "A" and Company "B" moved to new areas in the rear of the 3rd Battalion.

508th Parachute Infantry – "F" Company and "G" Company attacked by an estimated two battalions of infantry of the 9th SS Panzer Division at 0120. "G" Company partially overrun. Enemy infiltrated to ERRIA. "I" Company (less) committed to aid "G" Company in destroying and ejecting the enemy. "E" Company (less one platoon) mopped up the town of ERRIA and the entire sector was cleared by 0430. Enemy casualties were heavy.

551st Parachute Battalion – Attacked at 2300 towards limited objectives ODRIMONT and AMCOMONT.

## 28 DECEMBER 1944

325th Glider Infantry – Improved defensive positions.

504th Parachute Infantry – The 3rd Battalion broke up an attack by an estimated 60 enemy and inflicted heavy casualties. The 2nd Battalion fired on by enemy tanks. Artillery and 4.2 mortar fire forced tanks to withdraw.

505th Parachute Infantry – Improved defensive positions. The 3rd Battalion captured an entire five man enemy patrol.

508th Parachute Infantry – Improved defensive positions.

551st Parachute Battalion – Reached NOIRFONTAINE, killed an estimated thirty enemy and captured five. Battalion sustained very light losses.

## 29 DECEMBER 1944

There were no major attacks along any of the regimental fronts. All units improved their defensive positions and patrolled aggressively to the front. The 307th Airborne Engineer Battalion placed additional minefields. The 740th Tank Battalion was attached.

## 30 DECEMBER 1944

There was very little enemy activity along the Division front. All units maintained and strengthened their defensive positions and patrolled vigorously to the front.

The Division Artillery fired on enemy concentrations. The 2nd Battalion, 325th Glider Infantry closed into new positions East of TROU-DE-BRA. The 307th Airborne Engineer Battalion continued to place minefields. The 1st Battalion, 505th Parachute Infantry conducted combined infantry-tank-tank destroyer-engineer training in the vicinity of CHENEUX.

## 31 DECEMBER 1944

Enemy activity was again very light along the Division front. The regiments patrolled vigorously to the front and contacted the enemy in the vicinity of FLORET and XHOUT-SI-PLOUX.

The 505th Parachute Infantry continued their combined infantry-tank-tank destroyer-engineer training. The 740th Tank Battalion sent two patrols, each consisting of three tanks and Division Reconnaissance platoon men, to reconnoiter South of TRI-LE-CHESLIANG, ERRIA, and TROIS PONTS. Two enemy soldiers were killed and nine captured.

Enemy material captured 19 December 1944 to 31 December 1944, inclusive

1 armored car
3 half-tracks (a)
5 other vehicles (b)
3 artillery pieces (c)
6 machine pistols
35 Panzerfausts
800 Jerricans
800 88 mm rounds
1 anti-tank rifle
1 German BC scope
2 Bull dozers (U.S.)
1 8-Ton trailer (U.S.)

Enemy material knocked out or destroyed 19 December 1944 to 31 December 1944, inclusive

8 tanks (1 MK IV, 1 MK III, 6 unidentified) (d)
4 armored cars
14 half-tracks (a)
9 other vehicles (b)
3 SP guns (c)
6 anti-tank guns (c)
2 artillery pieces (c)
15 machine pistols
15 machine guns
3 motorcycles (1 with sidecar)
1 radio

The figures are necessarily incomplete because of the following factors:

a. Rapidity of our movement over a large area in the attack which, coupled with our move from the area, left little time for thorough surveys.
b. Snowstorms which covered much material before it could be salvaged.
c. Inaccessibility to transportation of some of the area, making salvage and evacuation impracticable.

Notes (a) Includes flakwagons. At least 3 mounted 75 mm guns.
(b) Includes all other types, also U.S., British and German models.
(c) Includes all calibers.
(d) Includes only observed fire and only material known definitely to have been destroyed.

## Casualties
### (Inclusive 31 December 1944)

|  | OFFICERS | EM |
|---|---|---|
| BATTLE CASUALTIES |  |  |
| Division Organic Units | 53 | 946 |
| Attached Units | 2 | 5 |
| TOTAL | 55 | 951 |
|  |  |  |
| NON-BATTLE CASUALTIES |  |  |
| Division Organic Units | 21 | 659 |
| Attached Units | 0 | 8 |
| TOTAL | 21 | 667 |
|  |  |  |
| TOTAL CASUALTIES |  |  |
| Division Organic Units | 74 | 1605 |
| Attached Units | 2 | 13 |
| GRAND TOTAL | 76 | 1618 |

**Prisoners of War**

Total captured (inclusive 31 December 1944)          185

## Narrative

### 1 and 2 JANUARY 1945

The Division (517th Parachute Infantry attached) regrouped in preparation for an attack to protect left flank of VII Corps.

The 504th, 508th and 517th Parachute Infantry assumed responsibility for entire Division front. Patrolled aggressively to South and Southeast. Maintained contact with enemy.

The 325th Glider Infantry and 505th Parachute Infantry closed in forward assembly areas in preparation for attack.

The 628th Tank Destroyer Battalion attached to Division, relieved 703rd Tank Destroyer Battalion which passed to Corps control.

The 75th Infantry Division assumed tactical control 504th Parachute Infantry.

### 3 JANUARY 1945

Division attacked at 0830 with 517th Parachute Infantry, 505th Parachute Infantry and 325th Glider Infantry abreast. Division Artillery, 80th Airborne Anti-aircraft Battalion and 307th Airborne Engineer Battalion supported the Division advance.

325th Glider Infantry – On the right attacked through the 508th Parachute Infantry, seized HEID DE HEIRLOT and the town of AMCOMONT. Organized high ground East and West of AMCOMONT. Further advance limited to patrolling pending advance of VII Corps.

504th Parachute Infantry – Reverted to tactical control 82nd Airborne Division and prepared to move to area DERRIERE LE TRIER.

505th Parachute Infantry – In the center with Company "A", 740th Tank Battalion attached, captured REHARMONT and FOSSE and continued the attack to positions approximately 1100 yards South thereof.

508th Parachute Infantry – Maintained positions in the vicinity of the Division LD. At 1645 hours the 2nd Battalion was attached to the 505th Parachute Infantry and moved to vicinity FOSSE.

517th Parachute Infantry – On the left with 551st Parachute Battalion attached, gained the village TROIS PONTS and high ground vicinity HERISPECHE and ST JACQUES.

## 4 JANUARY 1945

The Division consolidated its gains of 3 January, seized limited objectives, and prepared to continue the attack pending further advance of VII Corps.

325th Glider Infantry – Captured HIERLOT and ODRIMONT, established contact with adjacent units and consolidated positions.

504th Parachute Infantry – Assumed responsibility for a portion of 517th Parachute Infantry sector and attacked to take the high ground Southeast of FOSSE. The accomplishment of this mission would permit the Division to dominate all crossings of the SALM River in vicinity of GRAND HALLEUX.

505th Parachute Infantry – Continued to attack, seized high ground and woods North and Northeast of ABREFONTAINE and consolidated positions.

508th Parachute Infantry – Assembled in Division Reserve area, vicinity HAUTE BODEUX. 2nd Battalion reverted to Regimental control in REHARMONT area.

517th Parachute Infantry – Continued to attack, captured St JACQUES, HERGEVAL and MONT DE FOSSE, and patrolled to SALM River.

## 5 JANUARY 1945

325th Glider Infantry – Seized the high ground between ABREFONTAINE and LIERNEUX and consolidated positions already taken.

504th Parachute Infantry – Succeeded in taking high ground overlooking GRAND HALLEUX and immediately organized for defense.

505th Parachute Infantry – Took ABREFONTAINE and occupied the high ground 1000 yards to the Southeast.

508th Parachute Infantry – Remained in Division Reserve

517th Parachute Infantry – Cleared all remaining enemy from sector, repulsed strong enemy counterattacks vicinity BERGEVAL, and liberated DAIROMONT.

## 6 JANUARY 1945

Division and attached units consolidated and improved positions, patrolled aggressively to front, maintained contact with adjacent units, prepared plans to continue advance in conjunction with VII Corps. The 551st Parachute Infantry Battalion detached from 517th Parachute Infantry and attached 504th Parachute Infantry in place.

## 7 JANUARY 1945

The Division resumed the offensive with a vigorous attack at 0630 hours, with the mission of advancing to the line GRAND SART-SALM CHATEAU-VIELSALM-GRAND HALLEUX-TROIS PONTS.

325th Glider Infantry – Occupied GRAND SART and seized the high ground THIER DEL PREUX. Consolidated positions and repulsed strong counterattacks. Contact was established with VII Corps on the right.

504th Parachute Infantry, 551st Parachute Infantry Battalion attached – Seized FARNIERES, MONT and ROCHELINVAL, established and consolidated positions on West bank of SALM River.

505th Parachute Infantry – Captured the town of GORONNE, established front line along West bank of SALM River North of RENCHEUX, and West of town in Southern portion of their sector.

508th Parachute Infantry – Attacked through the 325th Glider Infantry, gained and consolidated positions on THIER DU MONT against severe resistance.

517th Parachute Infantry, less 3rd Battalion – Was placed in Division Reserve in assembly area Northeast of ABREFONTAINE. The 3rd Battalion assumed responsibility of SALM River line from TROIS PONTS to a point Northeast of LA NEUVILLE.

Company "B", 643rd Tank Destroyer Battalion was attached to the Division. Company "C", 643rd Tank Destroyer Battalion was placed in support of Division.

Division Artillery, 307th Airborne Engineer Battalion, 80th Airborne Anti-aircraft Battalion, 628th Tank Destroyer Battalion, and Company "B", 86th Chemical Battalion continued in support of the Division.

### 8 & 9 JANUARY 1945

The Division consolidated positions along the Salm River from TROIS PONTS to SALMCHATEAU, thence West to GRAND SART and eliminated enemy pockets at PETIT HALLEUX and RENCHEUX. Town of COMTE was taken. Occupied STE MAIRE to contact 3rd Armored Division. Road blocks were established vicinity of VIELSALM bridges. Units patrolled East of the Salm River to GRAND HALLEUX and SALMCHATEAU.

### 10 JANUARY 1945

The Division maintained defensive positions. The 3rd Battalion 517th Parachute Infantry established bridgehead across Salm River, vicinity GRAND HALLEUX. Relief of Division by 75th Infantry Division commenced.

### 11 JANUARY 1945

Relief of the Division by 75th Infantry Division completed and Division moved to Corps Reserve area bounded by WAIMES, SHROFAIX, MALMEDY, and BOUGHEZ.

517th Parachute Infantry – was detached from Division and attached to 75th Infantry Division in place.
    During the period January 3-11, the Division captured 2,571 prisoners and killed an estimated 2,250 enemy.

### 12 to 20 JANUARY 1945

The Division, in Corps Reserve, reorganized, re-equipped and conducted intensive training. Special emphasis was placed on combined infantry-tank training, the use of the German Panzerfaust, and zeroing of weapons.

### 21 and 22 JANUARY 1945

The Division, less 508th Parachute Infantry, remained in Corps Reserve and continued training.

508th Parachute Infantry (319th Glider Field Artillery Battalion, Company "D", 307th Airborne Engineer Battalion and Company "B", 80th Airborne Anti-aircraft Battalion attached), was attached to 7th Armored Division, moved to DIEDENBURG area relieved 2nd Battalion, 23rd Infantry and elements of Combat Command "A" of the 7th Armored Division.

### 23 and 24 JANUARY 1945

The Division, less 508th Parachute Infantry; No change.

517th Parachute Infantry, less 2nd Battalion, was attached to the Division.
508th Parachute Infantry reinforced – was relieved by 7th Armored Division, reverted to control of the Division, and moved to the TROIS PONTS-BASSE BODEUX area.

### 25 JANUARY 1945

The 643rd Tank Destroyer Battalion, Company "A", 87th Chemical Battalion, 400th Armored Field Artillery Battalion (105 Howitzer) and 254th Field Artillery Battalion (155 Howitzer) were attached to the Division.

517th Parachute Infantry less 2nd Battalion – was detached from Division and reverted to control XVIII Corps (Airborne).

### 26 and 27 JANUARY 1945

Orders were received for the Division to attack through the 7th Armored Division to the Northeast with the mission of piercing the SIEGFRIED Line. All elements of the Division moved to forward assembly areas vicinity BORN, WALLERODE, MONTENAU and ST VITH.

**28 JANUARY 1945**

The Division attacked through the 7th Armored Division at 0600 hours with the 325th Glider Infantry on the left (North), the 504th Parachute Infantry on the right (South) and the 505th Parachute Infantry and the 508th Parachute Infantry in reserve. The 32nd Cavalry Reconnaissance Squadron was attached to the Division at 0850 hours. Progress of the attack was hindered by waist deep snow, intense cold and well organized enemy strong points.

325th Glider Infantry – Attacked to the South from the line of BORN-AMBLEVE road, passed South of MEDELL, pivoted to the East and North of MEYERODE, and by 2030 hours were on the high ground West of, and overlooking WERETH. Gains were consolidated and contact established with flank units.

504th Parachute Infantry – Advanced 7000 yards, captured HERRESBACH and in this engagement killed 65 and captured 201 of the enemy without suffering any casualties. Consolidated gains and repelled 3 counterattacks.

505th Parachute Infantry – Moved to an assembly area vicinity of MEYERODE, prepared to attack through the 325th Glider Infantry.

508th Parachute Infantry – Moved to an assembly area vicinity ALLERODE prepared to attack through 504th Parachute Infantry.

307th Airborne Engineer Battalion – Constructed and opened paths and roads to assist the Division's advance.

740th Tank Battalion, 643rd Tank Destroyer Battalion and Division Artillery actively supported the advance.

Division Reconnaissance Platoon protected Division's South flank between WALLERODE and HERRESBACH.

**29 JANUARY 1945**

The Division continued its attack to the Northeast. Advanced more than 2000 yards and maintained contact with the 1st Division on the North flank.

325th Glider Infantry – Continued its advance by attacking to the North at 0330 hours. Seized WERETH, pushed on to the high ground EAST of the town and patrolled to the North. Regiment assembled in area 2000 yards Southeast of VALENDER at 1800 hours.

504th Parachute Infantry – Maintained defensive positions and assisted in the protection of the South flank of Division.

505th Parachute Infantry – Attacked through the 325th Glider Infantry at 0500 hours, advanced more than 2000 yards to the high ground 1500 yards Southwest of HONSFELD. Established defensive positions and patrolled vigorously to the North and East. Maintained contact with 1st Division on the North.

508th Parachute Infantry – Attacked through the 504th Parachute Infantry at 0400 hours. By the end of the day they had taken HOLZHEIM and MEDENDORF, and had occupied the high ground Southwest of EIMERSHEID.

307th Airborne Engineer Battalion – Continued to maintain improve and clear roads for use of attacking elements of the Division.

32nd Cavalry Reconnaissance Squadron – relieved Division Reconnaissance Platoon, established outposts and maintained patrols along the Southern flank of the Division.

**30 JANUARY 1945**

325th Glider Infantry – Attacked to the Northeast at 0500 hours. By 1500 hours had occupied the line of the HONSFELD-LOSHEIM railway for a distance of 200 yards East and West of BUCHHOLTZ. Sent patrols Northeast into Germany.

504th Parachute Infantry – Attacked at 0500 hours, seized the high ground 1300 yards Southeast of HOLZHEIM, captured EIMERSCHEID, relieved elements of the 508th Parachute Infantry in MEDENDORF and were relieved by 32nd Cavalry Reconnaissance Squadron in HERRESBACH.

505th Parachute Infantry – Maintained and strengthened their positions. Made preparations to continue the attack to the Northeast by passing through the 325th Glider Infantry.

508th Parachute Infantry – Continued the attack to the East, captured LANZERATH and the high ground North of the town. The Regiment consolidated positions and sent patrols Northeast into GERMANY.

32nd Cavalry Reconnaissance Squadron – relieved elements of the 504th Parachute Infantry in HERNESBACH. Maintained screening position along Southern flank of the Division.

## 31 JANUARY 1945

325th Glider Infantry – Remained in Battalion assembly areas as Division Reserve. Sent contact patrols to screen Left flank of 505th Parachute Infantry and to contact 1st Division on the North.

504th Parachute Infantry – Maintained and improved defensive positions. Relieved elements of 508th Parachute Infantry in LANZERATH. Established roadblocks within area.

505th Parachute Infantry – Attacked through the 325th Glider Infantry at 0430 hours, captured LOSHEIMERGRABEN against moderate resistance and occupied a line extending 4,000 yards North of that town East of the HOLLERATH-LANZERATH highway. Established contact with 1st Infantry Division on the North and the 508th Parachute Infantry on the South. Patrolled vigorously to the Northeast.

508th Parachute Infantry – Repulsed enemy attack vicinity LANZERATH, attacked to the Northeast at 0500 hours, seized, organized and maintained defensive positions on high ground overlooking LOSHEIM and MANDERFELD. Patrolled aggressively to the front.

The 629th Tank Destroyer Battalion (SP) attached to Division, to move into area 1 February 1945.

ENEMY MATERIAL CAPTURED 1 JANUARY 1945 to 31 JANUARY 1945

1 Mark IV tank
3 Half tracks
29 Other vehicles
1 SP gun
1 AT gun
9 Pieces, other artillery
7 81mm Mortars
90 Machine guns
161 Machine Pistols
333 Panzerfausts
5 Motorcycles
7 Radios
3 Binoculars
6 Bicycles
370 Rifles
40 Automatic Weapons
24 Flame throwers
1,830 Hand grenades
1,000 Rifle grenades
5 Ammunition dumps

ENEMY MATERIAL KNOCKED OUT OR DESTROYED 1 JANUARY 1945 TO 31 JANUARY INCLUSIVE

2 King Tiger Tanks
3 Mark VI Tanks
6 Mark IV Tanks
2 Mark III Tanks
8 Half Tracks
93 Other Vehicles
6 SP guns
27 AT guns
20 Pieces, other artillery
1 35mm gun
24 81mm Mortar
71 Machine guns
102 Machine Pistols

Notes:

(1) Figures include only material definitely known to have been destroyed.

(2) The following factors make these figures necessarily incomplete:

    (a) While attached, 517th Parachute Infantry did not maintain records of captured or destroyed small arms and automatic weapons.

    (b) Rapidity of our movement over a large area.

    (c) Snowstorms.

    (d) Inaccessibility of transportation to the area, making salvage and evacuatio impractical.

## CASUALTIES
(Inclusive 1 January to 31 January 1945)

| Division Battle Casualties | Officers | EM's |
|---|---|---|
| Division Organic Units | 110 | 1648 |
| Attached Units | 97 | 1169 |
| Total | 207 | 2817 |

| Division Non-Battle Casualties | | |
|---|---|---|
| Division Organic Units | 79 | 867 |
| Attached Units | 44 | 501 |
| Total | 123 | 1368 |

| Total Casualties | | |
|---|---|---|
| Division Organic Units | 189 | 2515 |
| Attached Units | 141 | 1670 |
| Grand Total | 330 | 4185 |

Known Enemy Casualties

Total Captured ................. 2445

Total Killed (est.) ............ 3635

Grand Total .................... 6080

**Narrative**

**1 FEBRUARY 1945**

The Division maintained and improved positions, reconnoitered and patrolled to the Siegfried Line, maintained contact with adjacent units and prepared to continue the attack to penetrate the Siegfried Line.

2nd Battalion, 504th Parachute Infantry was relieved by elements 32nd Cavalry Reconnaissance Squadron and moved to an assembly area in rear of 505th Parachute Infantry positions.

517th Parachute Infantry was attached to the Division and prepared to move into the Division Zone

**2 FEBRUARY 1945**

Against intense opposition the Division advanced and breached the Siegfried Line from UDENBRETH to NEUHOF to HERTESROTT HEIGHTS. Positions were consolidated and numerous counterattacks repulsed.

325th Glider Infantry attacked through the 505th Parachute Infantry Regiment and after severe fighting, seized NEUHOF and UDENBRETH; organized for defense and repelled strong counterattacks of infantry supported by tanks.

504th Parachute Infantry – 1st and 3rd Battalions relieved by elements 32nd Cavalry Reconnaissance Squadron and

1st Battalion, 508th Parachute Infantry respectively. All battalions assembled in area in rear of 505th Parachute Infantry and immediately passed through the 505th Parachute Infantry, attacking to the East. Regiment advanced 6000 yards and seized HERTESROTT HEIGHTS, organized positions and repulsed extremely heavy enemy counterattacks.

505th Parachute Infantry attacked to the Southeast, made advances up to 4000 yards and established defense positions.

508th Parachute Infantry patrolled actively to the Southeast and maintained and improved defensive positions. 1st Battalion relieved 3rd Battalion, 504th Parachute Infantry.

517th Parachute Infantry closed in Division area and moved the 3rd Battalion forward to support the 325th glider Infantry. The 1st Battalion established road block on main road running North out of Division area. 2nd Battalion remained in Division reserve.

### 3 FEBRUARY 1945

The Division strengthened and consolidated defensive positions; eliminated scattered groups of enemy remaining in rear areas; repulsed strong counterattacks and inflicted heavy casualties on the enemy.

505th Parachute Infantry was relieved in place by the 508th Parachute Infantry and moved to Division reserve area.

508th Parachute Infantry was relieved by 32nd Cavalry Reconnaissance Squadron in area Northeast of HASENVENN and in turn relieved 505th Parachute Infantry in area Northeast of LOSHEIM.

### 4 FEBRUARY 1945

The Division maintained defensive positions and patrolled aggressively to the East. The 99th Infantry Division commenced relief of front line units of the Division.

505th Parachute Infantry moved by truck to assembly area vicinity VIELSALM.

517th Infantry moved by truck to vicinity RAEREN. Passed to command V Corps.

### 5 & 6 FEBRUARY 1945

The Division was relieved by the 99th Infantry Division and moved to the VIELSALM area; reorganized, refitted, and prepared to move to vicinity ROTT, Germany.

Task Force "A", composed of 505th Regimental Combat Team was organized under command of the Assistant Division Commander with the mission of moving to vicinity of BERGSTEIN, Germany to relieve elements of the 8th Infantry Division.

### 7 FEBRUARY 1945

The Division, less Task Force "A" – No Change.

Task Force "A" reached BERGSTEIN area, passed to operational control of V Corps. 517th Regimental Combat Team was attached in place.

505th Regimental Combat Team less 1st Battalion, commenced relief of elements of 8th Infantry Division vicinity VOSSENACK. 1st Battalion, 505th Regimental Combat Team in Task Force "A" reserve 2000 yards Northwest of BRANDENBERG.

517th Regimental Combat Team made reconnaissance in force to a point 1500 yards Southeast of BERGSTEIN, encountered intense resistance from enemy strong points, found dense enemy minefields, and returned to BERGSTEIN area.

### 8 FEBRUARY 1945

The Division, less Task Force "A", moved from area VIELSALM, closed in assembly area vicinity SCHMIDTHOF, GERMANY. Established Division Command Post at ROTT and assumed command of sector held by Task Force "A".

505th Parachute Infantry advanced 2500 yards to the Southeast against light opposition to vicinity KOMMERSCHEIDT and there contacted elements of 78th Infantry Division.

508th Parachute Infantry moved to vicinity KLEINHAU with mission of relieving 517th Regimental Combat Team and elements of the 505th Parachute Infantry during the night 8-9 February.

## 9 FEBRUARY 1945

The remainder of the Division closed in the SCHMIDTHOF area. Committed units of the Division advanced approximately 1600 yards through extremely dense minefields, organized and consolidated defensive positions.

505th Parachute Infantry advanced to the high ground 1500 yards East of ZU HARSCHEIDT, established contact with adjacent units, patrolled aggressively to the East and made preparations to continue the attack.

517th Parachute Infantry was completely relieved by the 508th Parachute Infantry and moved to assembly area vicinity HURTGEN.

## 10 FEBRUARY 1945

The Division attacked to the East and gained the high ground dominating the West bank of the ROER River, consolidated gains and improved defensive positions. Opposition to the advance was light but extensive minefields prohibited rapid progress.

505th Parachute Infantry gained the high ground overlooking ABENDEN and the ROER River, consolidated positions, established contact with adjacent units, and patrolled the West bank of the ROER River.

508th Parachute Infantry advanced to the high ground overlooking ZERKALL, HETZINGERHOF, and the ROER River, established roadblocks on roads leading West from the ROER River, consolidated positions and patrolled the West bank of the river.

517th Parachute Infantry relieved from attachment and left Division area.

## 11 & 12 FEBRUARY 1945

505th Parachute Infantry and 508th Parachute Infantry maintained and strengthened positions dominating West bank of the ROER River, patrolled actively and maintained contact with adjacent Divisions. Remainder of the Division remained in the SCHMIDTHOF area, refitted, reorganized and prepared for future operations.

## 13 & 14 FEBRUARY 1945

The Division conducted assault boat training and continued preparations to force a crossing of the ROER River.

504th Parachute Infantry – 1st Battalion relieved 1st Battalion, 508th Parachute Infantry in the area 1800 yards Southeast of BERGSTEIN, 3rd Battalion closed in assembly area West of BERGSTEIN, 2nd Battalion remained in SCHMIDTHOF area.

508th Parachute Infantry – 1st Battalion was relieved by 1st Battalion, 504th Parachute Infantry and moved to assembly area vicinity BRANDENBERG. Remainder of Regiment – No change.

## 15, 16, 17 FEBRUARY 1945

The Division maintained positions commanding the ROER River, continued preparations to attack across the river and actively patrolled the West bank of the river. One patrol succeeded in crossing the river the night of 17 February 1945 and returned without meeting enemy opposition.

325th Glider Infantry closed in forward assembly area vicinity HARSCHEIDT.

2nd Battalion, 504th Parachute Infantry closed in forward assembly area vicinity BRENDENBERG.

## 18 FEBRUARY 1945

9th Division relieved the Division of its sector of responsibility. The Division, less artillery elements, started movement to rear assembly areas vicinity WALHEIM and prepared for further movement to base camps in the REIMS, FRANCE area.

**19, 20, 21 FEBRUARY 1945**

All elements of the Division were relieved by the 9th Infantry Division, assembled in the WALHEIM area and from there commenced to move to base camps, vicinity REIMS, FRANCE. All units, less organic transportation, moved to base camps by rail. Organic transportation moved by road. All elements closed in REIMS area by 25 February 1945.

*Major General James M. Gavin visiting the 508th PIR near Erria, Belgium, after an attack from the 9th SS Panzer Division, December 1944.*

Above: Major General James M. Gavin at the Division Command Post in Werbermont, Belgium, December 1944.

Right: Major General James M. Gavin talks to a paratrooper of the 3rd Battalion, 508th PIR in the Ardennes Forest, Belgium, December 1944.

*An 81mm mortar of the 2nd Battalion, 505th PIR in the Ardennes, December 1944.*

*A 57mm antitank gun of the 80th AA Battalion in action during fighting in the Ardennes, December 1944.*

*An armored gun jeep of the 82nd Reconnaissance Platoon in the Ardennes, 1944-1945.*

*Troopers of the 504th PIR pass a 57mm antitank gun of the 80th AA Battalion as they enter Cheneux, Belgium, December 1944.*

*Paratroopers of the 551st PIB move into Stavelot, Belgium, 24 December 1944.*

*Above: Parachute field artillerymen load a 75mm pack howitzer for action in the Ardennes, Belgium, December 1944.*

*Left: SGT "Tex" Crownover (left) with Captain Wesley Harris (right) of C Company, 307th Engineer Battalion in Bra, Belgium, 25 December 1944. (Courtesy Al Nemeth)*

*Below: A lone paratrooper from the 504th PIR moves out for a patrol between Bra and Fraiture, Belgium, 24 December 1944.*

*Moving out for a patrol in the Ardennes Forest, Belgium, December 1944.*

*Paratroopers in defensive position in the snow of the Ardennes Forest, Belgium, December 1944.*

*Chaplain Joseph P. Kenny, 508th PIR, celebrates mass on 6 January 1945 for men of the 3rd Battalion before they begin an offensive near Haute, Belgium, 1945.*

*PFC Vernon Haught, 325th GIR, coming off guard duty in Ordimont, Belgium, 6 January 1945.*

*SSGT Marible and PFC Jenkins of the 325th GIR man a .30 cal. Machinegun in Ordimont, Belgium, 6 January 1945.*

*The 1st Platoon of Headquarters Company, 3rd Battalion, 508th PIR, takes a break during movement to an assembly area. La Avenanterrs, Belgium, 6 January 1945.*

*Paratroopers from 1st Battalion, 505th PIR go out on patrol near Garonne, Belgium, 8 January 1945.*

*A German King Tiger tank knocked out by the 505th PIR in Goronne, Belgium, 8 January 1945.*

*Paratroopers of the 517th PIR take cover along the sides of a snow-covered road in the Ardennes Forest, Belgium, January 1945.*

Troopers of the 307th Engineer Battalion watch a German soldier remove a booby trap from a German 88mm antitank gun in the Ardennes, 1945.

A bulldozer operated by an engineer of the 307th clears a road in the Ardennes, Belgium, January-February 1945.

Armored gun jeeps of the Division Recon Platoon in the Ardennes, Belgium, January 1945.

*Troops prepare to move out on patrol in the Ardennes Forest, Belgium, January 1945.*

*Troops move towards Herresbach, Belgium, 28 January 1945.*

*Left: Major General James M. Gavin uses an EE-8 field telephone to direct troops near Herresbach, Belgium, 28 January 1945.*

*Below: Soldiers of the 1st Battalion, 325th GIR move through the snow in Herresbach, Belgium, 28 January 1945.*

*Gliderman of the 1st Battalion, 325th GIR take a break during the advance to Herresbach, Belgium, 28 January 1945.*

*A bazookaman from A Company, 1st Battalion, 325th GIR in waist deep snow during the advance to Herresbach, Belgium, 28 January 1945.*

*The 1st Battalion, 325th GIR advances toward Herresbach, Belgium, on 28 January 1945 pulling sleds.*

*Paratroopers of the 3rd Battalion, 504th PIR advance with a tank of the 740th Tank Battalion near Herresbach, Belgium, 28 January 1945.*

Paratroopers of the 504th PIR advance atop a tank of the 740th Tank Battalion near Herresbach, Belgium, 28 January 1945.

Above: An M-29 Weasel evacuates a wounded 504th trooper near Herresbach, Belgium, 29 January 1945. It was the only vehicle with great mobility in the rough, snow-covered terrain encountered by the 82nd.

Right: The STARS AND STRIPES reaches the 505th PIR at Weneck, Belgium, 29 January 1945.

*MPs of the 82nd Military Police Platoon guard prisoners taken during the advance on Herresbach, Belgium, 29 January 1945.*

*First Sergeant Leonard Funk, Medal of Honor recipient, C Company, 1st Battalion, 508th PIR.*

*The Siegfried Line in the Hurtgen Forest, Germany, is reached by the 82nd. Note the warning for mines. February 1945.*

*Above: The Siegfried Line near Schmitthof, Germany, February 1945.*

*Above*
*Top: The 325th GIR moving through Schmidt, Germany, 17 February 1945.*

*Below: A trooper looks down into the Kall River Valley in the Hurtgen Forest, Germany, February 1945.*

# CHAPTER SIX

# Germany:
# The 82nd Airborne Division in Central Europe
*April-May 1945*

Part One: ACTION ON THE RHINE
Part Two: ACTION EAST OF THE ELBE
Part Three: MISCELLANEOUS INFORMATION AND MAPS

Maps: GSGS 4414, GERMANY, 1/25,000, Sheets 2630, 2730; GSGS 4416, GERMANY, 1/100,000, Sheets R1, S1, S2, L5, L6, M5, M6; National Geographic Society Map, "Germany and Its Approaches", 1/1,500,000, dated July 1944

## Part One
## Action on the Rhine

Note: See Part Three for charts accompanying Part One.

### SECTION I – PREFACE

In late March, 1945, the 82nd Airborne Division was engaged in training activities at its base camps at SISSONE, SUIPPES and LAON, France. Reorganization under a new Table of Organization was under way and a schedule of intensive airborne training was being carried out. Experiments also were being conducted with new equipment, including the recoilless 57mm gun. Several tentative airborne missions were in the planning stage at Division Headquarters at SISSONE.

Late in the afternoon of 30 March, the Division Commander, Major General James M. Gavin was called to XVIII Corps (Airborne) Headquarters at EPERNAY, France. Here he received instructions to the effect that the 82nd and 101st Airborne Divisions were to concentrate Southwest of BONN, Germany. On 31 March the 82nd Airborne Division was attached to the Fifteenth U.S. Army at 1400 and given the mission to patrol a section of the West bank of the Rhine River. This river was the western boundary of a huge "pocket" of German resistance in the Ruhr area. Aside from patrols the Division probably would not cross the river. Movement of the Division to the new area would begin on or about 3 April.

## SECTION II – NARRATIVE

### 1. Action on the Rhine

1 APRIL: The Division Commander, G-1, G-3 and a small group of staff officers and key enlisted men departed for the new Division area by plane during the day. General Gavin reported first to the Commanding General, Fifteenth Army, and then to the Commanding General XXII Corps. He also conferred with the Commanding General, 86th Infantry Division which the 82nd Airborne Division was to relieve on the West bank of the Rhine River on or about the night of 4-5 April.

At base camps plans were completed for the movement of the Division which, it was learned during the day, would begin 2 April.

2 APRIL: Movement of the Division by rail and motor began at 0500. Eight trains left SISSONE, SUIPPES and LAON between 0701 and 0807. Most of the motor echelons closed into new areas by 2400. Division Headquarters was established at WEIDEN, GERMANY, a few miles from COLOGNE.

3 APRIL: The process of closing into the new area was handicapped by the fact only one train at a time could be unloaded at the railhead at STOLBERG, GERMANY, there being only one siding. However, before 2400 a majority of the units had closed and relief of the 86th Infantry Division had begun. 82nd Airborne Division Field Order No.19 was published giving details of effecting relief of the 86th in the sector from WORRINGEN, inclusive, eight miles North of COLOGNE, to GRAU-RHEINDORG, inclusive, 13 miles South of COLOGNE, a total river front of about 32 miles.

The 325th Glider Infantry began relieving 343rd Infantry at 2000, with exception of 3rd Battalion, 325th, which became Division Reserve. The 504th Parachute Infantry began relieving the 342nd Infantry at 2045, the 1st Battalion completing its relief at 2345 or less than 40 hours after it had entrained at LAON, FRANCE.

4 APRIL: The 82nd Airborne Division officially relieved the 86th Infantry Division at 0829. The 325th Glider Infantry completed relief of 342nd Infantry at 0159, the 504th Parachute Infantry completed relief of 343rd Infantry at 0530, and 82nd Airborne Division Artillery relieved 86th Infantry Division Artillery at 0400. The 341st Infantry, 86th Infantry Division, came under control of 82nd Airborne Division from 0729 until 2330 when its relief by the 505th Parachute Infantry was completed.

The Division improved defensive positions. Artillery fired a total of 478 rounds of harassing and interdiction fire.

Field Artillery dispositions, made under provisions of Field Order No.19, were as follows: 319th Glider Field Artillery Battalion in general support, 320th Glider Field Artillery Battalion in direct support of 325th Glider Infantry, 376th Parachute Field Artillery Battalion in direct support of 504th Parachute Infantry, 456th Parachute Field Artillery Battalion in direct support of 505th Parachute Infantry.

A XXII Corps letter, dated 1 April, 1945, had directed that patrolling along the Corps front would be "intensified beginning night 2-3 April to the extent of not less than one patrol per front line battalion per night." Operations Instructions No.2, 82nd Airborne Division, added that "Within the discretion of the Regimental Commander, up to one rifle company may be left on the far bank of the Rhine River to screen, observe, and report on enemy activity."

5 APRIL: The Division continued to improve its defensive sector. Two patrols of 325th Glider Infantry and four patrols of 504th Parachute Infantry crossed the Rhine River during the night of 4-5 April and made contact with enemy troops. One prisoner was taken. Artillery fired 104 missions, 2,215 rounds.

6 APRIL: The Division continued active patrolling and also improved its defensive sector. Three patrols, exclusive of a company-sized patrol of the 504th Parachute Infantry, captured two prisoner during the night of 5-6 April.

Company A, 504th Parachute Infantry, crossed the Rhine River during the night of 5-6 April and seized HITDORF (4273) as a base for further patrol action. Company A, 504th Parachute Infantry, was cited by the War Department as follows:

"Company A", 504th Parachute Infantry, is cited for outstanding performance of duty in armed conflict against the enemy in Germany on 6-7 April 1945. This Company crossed the Rhine River at 0230 hours, 6 April 1945, and seized the mile-long town of HITDORF on the eastern shore, with the mission of providing a base for further patrolling, and to cause the German High Command to commit disproportionate forces against them in the belief that it was to be a major river crossing. The enemy immediately counter-attacked, but their assault groups were met with great vigor, and virtually destroyed to a man. Apparently under the impression that a strong American bridgehead had been established overnight, the Germans assembled and directed a considerable portion of two divisions to the mission of containing and annihilating this formidable thrust. In mid-afternoon the entire area was subjected to a withering and devastating artillery barrage for two hours, after which counter-attacking forces in overwhelming strength, with tanks in support, assaulted the defending troopers from every direction and penetrated to the heart of the town. The troopers of Company "A" doggedly stood their ground, fought at close quarters and at point-blank range, and inflicted terrible casualties on the masses of the enemy. Fighting with relentless ferocity throughout the afternoon and night, this gallant company held its ground and carried out its mission until it was finally ordered (By XXII Corps) to withdraw to the west bank of the Rhine on the night of 6-7 April. Fighting was bitter and at close quarters. The German armor committed was destroyed with hand weapons, Most of the troopers using captured German panzerfausts. The Company fought its way back step by step during the hours of darkness to their boats. The courageous and skillful efforts of the Officers and men of this brave group, although outnumbered numerically at least eight to one, is reflected in the total number of casualties inflicted on the German forces during the day's fighting. Eighty prisoners were taken and evacuated, and conservative estimates indicate that 150 of the enemy were killed and 250 wounded. The conduct of Company "A" reflects great credit on the Airborne Forces of the United States Army."

Artillery fired 111 missions, 1919 rounds.

7 APRIL: While the Division continued its active defense, withdrawal of Company A, 504th Parachute Infantry, was completed during the night of 6-7 April. Two platoons of Company "I" assisted in covering the withdrawal. Casualties received by the company were: Six killed in action, 14 wounded or injured in action, 26 missing in action.

A patrol from 505th Parachute Infantry received 12 casualties when it became entangled in a minefield.

Artillery fired 128 missions, 2,357 rounds.

8-16 APRIL: No additional large patrols were sent across the Rhine River, due in part to strict rationing of artillery and mortar ammunition allotments, but the Division continued to improve its defenses and to send small patrols across the river until its positions were masked by the attack from the South by XVIII Corps (Airborne) on the East side of the Rhine River.

8 APRIL: Practice smoke screens were laid down along the river banks. Four successful patrols reconnoitered the East bank. Artillery fired 76 missions, 1,065 rounds.

9 APRIL: Despite adverse wind conditions, practice smoke screens were laid in sections of the Division area. Mortar and machine gun fire was placed on observed enemy positions. There were two patrols. The Division relieved the 761st Field Artillery Battalion of responsibility of guarding bridges on the Erft Canal at 2300 hours. Artillery fired fifty-seven missions, 704 rounds.

10 APRIL: The Division continued to maintain its defensive positions, sending one reconnaissance patrol to the East bank of the Rhine River. One practice smoke screen was laid. Artillery fired ninety-one missions, 1,543 rounds, part of the fire being at request of XVIII Corps (Airborne) Artillery on a reported location of the Command Post, German 3rd Parachute Division.

11 APRIL: Aggressive defense of the West river bank was maintained and four patrols crossed the river. Ten casualties resulted in a 325th Glider Infantry patrol when a hand grenade exploded in a boat. Artillery fired sixty-eight missions, 1,053 rounds.

Operations Instructions No.3 was issued in the nature of a warning order, listing areas in which units of the division would carry out occupational duties. The Division Military Police and Reconnaissance Platoons were instructed to begin a through search of rear areas.

12 APRIL: Liaison was maintained with the 13th Armored Division which was advancing to the North on the East side of the Rhine River. Surrender propaganda was broadcast to German troops. Military government was enforced in the Division area. Artillery fired thirty-four missions, 913 rounds.

13 APRIL: Active defense of the West bank of the Rhine River was maintained, and, in addition, 505th Parachute Infantry obtained letters of surrender from mayors of LUISDORF (4984), LANGEL (4850), NIEDERKASSEL (4846), and ZUNDORF (5155) on the East bank. Two reconnaissance patrols were sent across the river. Artillery fired thirty-eight missions, 849 rounds, Artillery organic to the Division did not fire and other fire was in support of XVIII Corps (Airborne) advance.

Operations Instruction No.4 (amended slightly on 16 April) was issued. It outlined occupational areas and plans for conducting thorough searches for caches of arms, ammunition, explosives and for enemy soldiers.

14 APRIL: The 325th Glider Infantry and 505th Parachute Infantry continued to outpost the river line but began assembling in Battalion areas. The 746th Field Artillery Battalion was relieved from the 417th Field Artillery Group, converted to Special Guards and attached to the 82nd Airborne Division. It assumed responsibility for guarding bridges over the ERFT CANAL and Displaced Persons camps at 1800. Artillery fired sixteen missions, 475 rounds.

15 APRIL: Patrol contact was established with the 97th Infantry Division on the East bank of the river. The 746th Field Artillery Battalion (Converted) relieved organic units of the Division of responsibility for security of utilities installations in the Division zone. Attached artillery fired twenty-four missions, 572 rounds.

16 APRIL: Friendly troops advancing along the East bank of the RHINE RIVER masked the last of the 82nd Airborne Division's positions during the day. The 504th Parachute Infantry was relieved of its mission of active defense of the West bank at 1800. The 417th Field Artillery Group fired six missions, 288 rounds, at request of the 13th Armored Division, before being relieved from attachment to the 82nd Airborne Division at 1200 hours.

17 APRIL: Reallocation of troops within the Division area was made in order to secure and enforce military government in the sector. Preparations were made to carry out provisions of 82nd Airborne Division Operations Instructions No.4.

## 2. Military Government in COLOGNE, Germany Area

From 18 April until its relief 25 April, the 82nd Airborne Division carried on occupational duties in the COLOGNE, Germany Area. A thorough search was made of the area by sectors to locate prisoners of war and caches of arms, ammunition and explosives. Guards and administrative personnel were provided for Displaced Persons Camps. Bridges and ammunition dumps were guarded and minefields were located and marked.

Operations Instructions No.8 were published 18 April amplifying duties of organic and attached units. As amended under date of 23 April, these instructions provided that 80th Airborne Anti-Aircraft Battalion would first search its own area and then assist the 505th Parachute Infantry. The 319th and 320th Glider Field Artillery Battalions would search COLOGNE after completing work in their own area.

A temporary boundary was established for XXII and XXIII Corps pending the time XXIII Corps became operative. The 942d Field Artillery Battalion was assigned control of the area between the permanent and temporary corps' boundaries.

A total of 653 prisoners were taken during the search. Many of these had changed into civilian clothing.

## SECTION III – INTELLIGENCE

When the 82nd Airborne Division moved into the COLOGNE, Germany area, the German 353rd Infantry Division, having held a sector on the East bank of the Rhine River between COLOGNE and BONN, was reported in the process of moving to the SOEST area Northeast of the RUHR area. Elements of the enemy 3rd Parachute Division were shown to be occupying the defenses facing us on our right flank. The disposition of enemy troops at this time was vague. In the MULHEIM area, east of COLOGNE, Auxiliary police units and Army security troops were reported to be tied in with the tactical troops defending the industrial area. Identifications on hand to the North showed the probability of the presence of the 338th Infantry Division and elements of the 176th Infantry Division. In the central part of the 82nd Airborne Division front identifications had been made of the 12th Volksgrenadier Division, but it was believed only one regiment of the Division remained in this area.

After two nights of successful patrolling, daylight observations and interrogations of prisoners on our part, the following facts were established: Elements of the 3rd Parachute Division, comprising the 8th Parachute Regiment on the right and the 5th Parachute Regiment on the left, were defending the East bank of the river from PORZ to the South, to include the defenses of the SIEG river on the North. The 2nd Company and 3rd Company of the 8th Parachute Regiment were identified opposite the COLOGNE-PORZ sector. Later identifications placed the 5th Parachute Assault Company in the vicinity of LUISDORF (475480). To the North in the vicinity of LEVERKUSEN, prisoners from 6th Company identified the 1220th Regiment of the 176th Infantry Division on the night of April 4-5. However, identification of 176th Division's 1218th and 1219th Grenadier Regiments in the vicinity of WARBURG, outside of the pocket, made the presence of the entire 1220th Regiment in our sector questionable.

North of PORZ, to include MULHEIM, there were numerous flak batteries and miscellaneous Volksturm and supply troops. Identifications were made of the 419th Flak Battalion and the 314th Mixed Flak Battalion. From MULHEIM to the North across the Division's front, it was established by a successful Company raid by the 504th Parachute Infantry that the 330th Grenadier Regiment defended the river in the vicinity of HITDORF. Forty prisoners were captured from the Regiment's 5th Company and thirteen were taken from the 8th Company. Later the capture of additional prisoners, ten in number, proved the presence of the 8th Company in support of the 5th, 6th, and 7th Companies of this Regiment and placed the entire 2nd Battalion, 330th Regiment in the Northern part of the 82nd Airborne Division sector and the Southern part of the 101st Airborne Division sector. Elements of the 13th Infantry Howitzer Company of the 330th Regiment were believed to have supported the 2nd Battalion, 330th Regiment.

The enemy's first line of defense in the Division sector was the Rhine River, and he immediately availed himself of it by blowing all bridges. Following a familiar pattern, the villages along the East bank from MANHEIM in the north to MONDORF in the South became the strong points of his defensive line, with particularly heavy concentrations of men and weapons in HITDORF, LEVERKUSEN, STAMMHEIM, WESTHOVEN, ZUNDORF, LANGEL, NIEDERKASSEL and RHEIDT. Machine guns formed the backbone of his defenses, reinforced by light AA in a ground role. The use of flak guns was particularly noticeable in the Northern part of the sector, and searchlights were often brought into play at night, making patrol crossings difficult.

A few self-propelled guns and tanks were drawn into the HITDORF area about 7 April, following a threatened bridgehead executed as a company raid of Company A, 504th Parachute Infantry. The enemy reacted violently through the use of his local reserves to contain our effort.

Announcement followed over a German radio station that night that "the 82nd Airborne Division had established a bridgehead, strength of one battalion, but efforts to expand it were repulsed and the enemy were thrown back".

Trenches, weapon pits, and minefields in the most inviting beach area, together with wire at some points made up the bulk of the enemy's defensive system. Many of the emplacements were located almost at the water's edge and were occupied only at night. Artillery was concentrated mainly at the northern end of the sector. Except for a few heavy concentrations, artillery fire ordinarily was light and of a harassing nature.

## SECTION IV – SUPPLY

Movement of troops from base camps to the COLOGNE area during the first week of April was completed successfully despite difficulties caused by the distance of the railhead at STOLBERG from final assembly areas, changing location of the railhead, advancing the closing dates for troops to close in new areas, and the mechanical difficulties of current continental rail movements.

As the Division was in a static situation, there were no great problems of supply or evacuation. The Medical Company was fortunate in being able to occupy part of a large civilian hospital building.

During the military government phase of the period spent in the COLOGNE area the A.C. of S, G-4, was responsible for the supervising the vast quantities of lost and abandoned American and enemy equipment and supplies in the area. Salvage dumps for the collection of such material were established in different sections of the Division's area. It was impossible to make a complete inventory of the items collected in the time the Division spent in the COLOGNE area, but among them were fifty-one German trucks, 156 guns of various calibers, one complete German searchlight battery, one trainload of assault boats, thirty-two tanks, forty-six other armored vehicles, seven nebelwerfers, and 2,500 tons of ammunition.

## V – SIGNAL

While at base camps prior to operations in April, signal equipment had been overhauled, shortages had been filled wherever possible, and a limited amount of training was held. The Division Signal Officer conducted a series of tests to determine the status of signal training of the various units and found that the outstanding delinquencies were that units had allowed their CW radio operators to become "stale". The Division Signal Company had not received personnel and equipment to fill its new Tables of Organization and Equipment.

Despite the fact that the advance echelon of the Signal Company was found to be too small for the work load initially in the COLOGNE area, exchange of telephone circuits from the 86th Infantry Division was relatively simple as our units took up the same Command Post locations as units of the relieved Division. This was not the case, however, in respect to the Division Artillery units, which found it necessary to employ approximately 100 miles of additional wire.

## VI – MILITARY GOVERNMENT

Military government resources were employed to the full during a major portion of the month as the Division's mission was occupational as well as tactical. Military government duties in the COLOGNE area were taken over from the 86th Infantry Division at 050730 April, and on 060900 April the Division Commander appointed Col. W.M. Griffith, Division artillery executive, to carry out the military government phase while the Division also was engaged in a tactical role.

Contacts were made with all Military Government Detachments in the area. The situation was reviewed and policies of the Division explained to the detachments.

The 82nd Airborne Division assumed responsibility on 8 April 1945 for three Displaced Persons Camps, one at BRAUWEILER for "Westerners", one at OSSENDORF for Russians, and one at ETZEL for Polish Nationals. A field grade officer was appointed at each camp as camp supervisor and furnished three officers and up to five enlisted men as a staff.

The condition of the camps was particularly bad when the Division assumed control. Within a week conditions of poor sanitation and lack of coordinated administration was rectified as far as possible. A maximum of 25,000 Displaced Persons were cared for during the course of any one day, although the transitory situation of the BRAUNWEILER Camp precluded an exact or accurate count. The camps were located in former Luftwaffe or Wehrmacht barracks areas.

Proclamations, ordinances and enactments of Military Government were posted in every Stadkreis and Gemeinde in the entire Division area. The number of violations of the ordinances was not large and the Military Government Courts, established in COLOGNE, tried all cases. Most of the violations were of a minor nature such as violations of restrictions, travel, curfew and the like. There were a few cases of looting and sabotage, however, and the offenders received sentences up to 15 years of imprisonment.

The former Gestapo prison, KLINGLEPUTZ, was used in carrying out all sentences of confinement.

Duties of Military Government carried out by the 82nd Airborne Division in the COLOGNE area included the following:

Search and seizure.
Check of every individual in the Division area.
Collection of Wehrmacht weapons, ammunition and articles of war.
Apprehension of Wehrmacht deserters and other Army personnel.

Apprehension of Nazi officials and War Criminals.

Enforcement of laws and ordinances and General supervision of the German administration.

## VII – CASUALTIES

1. Casualties within the Division and within Company A, 504th Parachute Infantry, during the period 3-17 April 1945 were as follows:

|  | Division Total | | Company A, 504 | |
| --- | --- | --- | --- | --- |
|  | O | EM | O | EM |
| Killed in Action | 2 | 11 | 1 | 5 |
| Wounded or Injured in Action | 5 | 102 | 1 | 13 |
| Missing in Action | 9 | 94 | 1 | 25 |

2. Casualties within the Division during the entire action on the Rhine River, including the period of Military Government, were as follows:

|  | O | EM | Total |
| --- | --- | --- | --- |
| Killed in Action | 3 | 20 | 23 |
| Wounded or Injured in Action | 5 | 109 | 114 |
| Missing in Action | 9 | 94 | 103 |
| Total | 17 | 223 | 240 |

# Part Two
# Action East of the Elbe River

## I – Narrative

Speed and boldness were the requisites in the General Allied Military picture when the 82nd Airborne Division began arriving at the Elbe River, and it was decided to force a crossing of the river during the night of April 29-30. Only one regiment, the 505th Parachute, had arrived at the time.

Patrols from the Division Reconnaissance Platoon and 8th U.S. Infantry Division probed enemy defenses East of the river the night of 28-29 April, and the 505th forced a crossing the following night. Rain and snow kept the enemy in his fox holes, and opposition to the crossing was moderate except for heavy artillery fire.

By nightfall, April 30, 1945, the 82nd Airborne Division had established a small bridgehead East of the Elbe River in the vicinity of BLECKEDE, Germany. This bridgehead had been established by the 505th Parachute Infantry in a splendid example of coordination and river crossing technique by a veteran regiment.

During the night of April 30 – May 1, the plan was to build up sufficient forces from the 504th Parachute Infantry, which was arriving by train approximately five hours from the Elbe River, so as to attack out of the bridgehead with that regiment by daylight. One battalion of this regiment arrived at the bridgehead by 0430 hours and with a full appreciation of the value of time it jumped off at 0500 hours, the regiment being reinforced during the day by the later arrival of its other battalions. Troops completing the 4-6 day train trip from the Cologne area were immediately entrucked and taken into the bridgehead. Then, after being briefed and issued ammunition, they were committed to the attack. It was obvious that the German was disintegrating rapidly and it was of the utmost importance that regardless of the physical condition of our troops, the momentum of our drive be maintained until the enemy was completely destroyed or overrun.

With characteristic speed and courage, the 504th Parachute Infantry arrived at its objective by mid-morning and shortly after noon had reached the Forst Correnzien. On its left the 505th Parachute Infantry, despite the fact that it had been constantly moving for almost a week, drove ahead and reached its objective, the Forst Correnzien, by mid-afternoon of May 1. Speed was the keynote, and the pressure was kept on the enemy during the night of May 1-2. The Division Reconnaissance Platoon seized the very important bridges at Suckau and Rosien and held them until relieved by advancing forces the following morning. Reconnaissance was pushed eastward by all units, the 504 engaging its armor with some enemy in the Forst Leussow at approximately 2100 hours, May 1.

The 325th Glider Infantry had been brought up during the night of May 1-2 briefed and prepared for commitment. With the 504th it jumped off before daylight after a short night of reorganizing and preparation, and advanced with the mission of seizing the line Ludwigslust-Doenitz, some twenty-five miles distant. Sufficient tanks and trucks were made available to the 504 to motorize a battalion. Combat Command "B", of the 7th Armored Division, was to be used with the 325 after the initial breakthrough and the seizure of Lubtheen. The troops had been driving hard for some time and all the units were going to the maximum of their ability. The German resistance in spots was intense, bitter, costly in lives. In other places none existed.

Overall, it appeared that our plan of attack was justified. The developments of May 2 confirmed this, although in the form they took they were surprising. Jumping off at 0500 hours, May 2, all units moved ahead aggressively. Resistance was spotty to negligible. By mid-morning units arriving generally east of Forst Loussow found themselves overrunning groups of bewildered enemy with hardly any will to resist, who thought that we were still at the ELBE while they were fighting what appeared to be a retrograde action with the Russians. By noon Combat Command "B" and the 325 had captured Ludwigslust and the 504 had captured Doenitz. Both units immediately moved to gain contact at Eldena.

Many units of the German 21st Army were being cut off and surrounded. The hospitals and rear installations of the 21st German army were apparently endeavoring to continue functioning. Many German service units, hindered by thousands of refugees found themselves within our positions. With very few exceptions they surrendered without resistance. For the division after more than two years of intense and, at times, very costly fighting with the German Army, the spectacle that began to unfold itself was an unbelievable one. German command and control became completely paralyzed and entire units were being captured intact.

By late afternoon a group of staff officers of the German 21st Army, representing Lt. Gen. Tippelskirch, commanding that army, arrived at the 82nd Airborne Division's CP at Ludwigslust and endeavored to arrange the surrender of their casualties, allied prisoners, and some service units. Since these had already been captured, the offer was ridiculous on its face, and they were told so. They were further told that the attack would be continued and their army would be destroyed when we gained contact with our advancing Russian allies. At this time the Russian forces were approximately ten to twenty miles to the east.

They then offered, in the name of the commander of the German 21st Army, the surrender of the army to our forces, but not to the Russians. They were told that this too was impossible, that since the Russians were our Allies they would surrender unconditionally to both of us, and they were again told that there was to be no delay since we were continuing the attack with the purpose of destroying the army. The staff departed stating that they would transmit this information to General Tippelskirch. During the late afternoon and early evening German units continued to be overrun. Many came into our lines to surrender. There appeared to be no control of the German forces within their own ranks, except in small formations.

At about 2100 hours Lt. General Tippelskirch arrived at the CP in Ludwigslust and after some discussion unconditionally surrendered his army to the 82nd Airborne Division. He too desired to stipulate that his army would surrender on the ground where it was and that upon cessation of hostilities this division would accept his troops as their prisoners. This was rejected and he was told that his army would be destroyed by ours in conjunction with our Russian allies and that his unconditional surrender would be valid when his troops were physically within our lines and not until then. An added paragraph stipulating this was added to the unconditional surrender, which was signed at about 2200 hours.

This ended for this division approximately two years of very hard and costly combat, combat in which many lessons were learned, lessons that were applied and paid handsome dividends in the closing days of the fighting. The combat discipline of the units of the division, their appreciation of the need to drive ahead and their willingness to drive ahead, regardless of their physical condition, particularly in the infantry regiments, was never more apparent. Once his initial covering forces along the Elbe River were overrun, the German was never given an opportunity to offer an organized defense, and the lives saved and complete victory achieved were far beyond any measure of value in terms of sweat and labor.

Combat Command "B", under the command of Colonel Haskell, participated brilliantly in the final day of attack. Throughout the entire three-day attack, the division was very ably supported by Squadron "A" of the 4th Royals which provided 25 "Buffaloes" to assist in the crossing at BLECKEDE.

## II – Chronology

The Division was alerted on 23 April for possible movement and later received orders to move by rail and motor to the Elbe River Northeast of HANOVER, GERMANY, where it was to operate under XVIII Corps (Airborne). The Corps was to be attached tactically to the British Second Army and administratively to the Ninth United States Army.

On 251200 April the 82nd Airborne Division was relieved in the COLOGNE area by the 417th Field Artillery Group and began movement to UELZEN area on 26 April.

26-28 April: Major elements of the Division were en route by rail and motor to the new area. The railhead was established at LEHRTE (x5222) and the truckhead at WEYHAUSEN. An overnight staging area for the truck movement was established at WIEDENBRUCK. The Division Command Post opened at HOHENZETHEN (Y0799) at 271200 April.

Operations Instructions No.6, issued 28 April, provided that the 505th Parachute Infantry and 13th Infantry (8th U.S. Infantry Division), attached, would relieve elements of the Fifth British Division along the Elbe River. The 505th also would attack across the ELBE River and seize a limited bridgehead.

29 April: The 505th Parachute Infantry closed at 1700, but elements of the Regiments effected relief of the 13th Brigade, 5th British Division, by 1315 hours. The 13th Infantry had relieved the 17th Brigade, 5th British Division, at 0200 hours.

Three patrols from the Division Reconnaissance Platoon, each patrol made up of one officer and eight enlisted men, and one patrol from the 13th Infantry, crossed to the North bank of the Elbe River during the night of 28-29 April. Three patrols met little opposition, but one patrol from Division Reconnaissance Platoon encountered stiff resistance when it landed on the North bank. One officer and five enlisted men were missing.

The Division Command Post moved from HOHENZETHEN to BLECKEDE at 1000 hours.

30 April: The 505th Parachute Infantry forced crossings of the ELBE River at four points and established a limited bridgehead along the general line 053253 – 058305 – 036322 – 005315. Resistance was moderate and this permitted construction of a class 36 bridge by Corps Engineers which was completed by 2000 hours at 004268. Crossings were made in "Buffaloes" of the British 4th Royals, by assault and storm boats, manned by the 307th Airborne Engineers.

The 504th Parachute Infantry had not closed completely, but the 2nd Battalion was preparing to cross the ELBE as the day ended. The 13th Infantry, less 3rd Battalion, was relieved from attachment to the Division. The 121st Infantry (8th Infantry Division) was attached at 1900 with other components of its combat team, and, with the 3rd Battalion of the 13th, was in the process of relieving 2nd Battalion, 505th, as the period and month closed.

Other major elements of the Division, including the 325th Glider Infantry were still en route. Mortar elements of organic artillery fired thirteen missions, 221 rounds, and attached artillery fired ninety-two missions, 1,832 rounds.

A total of 588 prisoners were received at the Division Prisoner of War cage during the day, bringing the total for the ELBE River area to 606.

1 May: The attack moved from right to left, the 504th Parachute Infantry jumping off at 0500, the 505th at 0552 and the 121st (Reinforced) at 0600. The attack gained up to nine miles in an easterly direction against light opposition, and the Division front at the end of the day was along the general line SUCKAU-160278-150240-STAPEL-ZEITZE PRIVELACK. The Division Reconnaissance Platoon captured ROSIEN (1527), and kept contact with the British 6th Airborne Division at 013356 at 0630 hours, the 121st Regimental Combat Team (Reinforced) was relieved from attachment to the 82nd and reverted to control of the 8th Infantry Division.

The Division Command Post moved from BLECKEDE to NEUHAUS (1325). By the close of the day all remaining elements of the Division had detrained and were en route to forward assembly areas. Corps engineers completed a bridge at DARCHA (112203) by 1830 hours, and 82nd Airborne Division traffic was diverted to that bridge. Artillery fired twenty missions, 1,128 rounds during the day. A total of 696 prisoners were counted during the period.

Operations Instructions No.9, issued during the day, provided that the attack continue on 2 May with the 325th Glider Infantry passing through the 505th Parachute Infantry. Combat Command "D", attached from the 7th armored Division was to prepare for offensive action in the 325th Sector.

2 May: The attack was continued at 0500, and both the 325th Glider Infantry and 504th Parachute Infantry reached initial objectives by 0815. With 2nd Battalion, 325th, attached, Combat Command "B" (Task Force Haskell) attacked at 1000 along the main road toward LUDWIGSLUST (5132) and seized the city by 1210. The Division Reconnaissance Platoon suffered some casualties but succeeded in clearing the RAMM, QUAST and LEUSSOW Forest areas of enemy. The Division established a general line along the NEUE ELDE Canal North to 500370 and prepared to link up with Russian forces as contemplated in Operations Instructions No.10, issued 020830 May. The Division Forward Command Post moved to LUDWIGSLUST.

The Commanding General, 82nd Airborne Division, accepted the unconditional surrender of the Twenty-First German Army at 2130 from Lt. Gen. Von Tippelskirch. The surrender terms were signed at LUDWIGSLUST (See Annex No.3).

A total of 1,420 prisoners were counted during the day, but the mass movement of the German Twenty-First Army through the lines had begun before the period ended. Because of the rapid advance, few artillery rounds were fired during the day. The remainder of the organic artillery closed with the forward elements by the end of the day.

The task of handling the large numbers of prisoners and of displaced persons began with establishment of the DELLIEN and ZEETZE Camps under control of 505th Parachute Infantry as outlined in Operations Instructions No.11 issued at 02240 hours.

3 May: Firm contact with advancing Russian forces was made during the day. First contact were made by Troop B, 87th Cavalry Squadron, attached, with the 191st Russian Infantry Division at REPPTIN (9946) at 0925 and by the 82nd Abn Div Reconnaissance Platoon with the 8th Brigade of the 8th Russian Mechanized Corps at GRABOW (5526) at 1025 hours. A conference was held late in the day between Commanding General 82nd Airborne Division and General Firstovich, Commanding General 8th Mechanized Corps. The Division Command Post was consolidated at LUDWIGSLUST.

The Division's main activity during the day was the direction of prisoners and displaced persons to the rear. No count of prisoners taken was possible, but it was estimated that the surrendered German Twenty-First Army totaled approximately 144,000 men. (For brief discussion of the Twenty-First Army, see Section III, INTELLIGENCE PHASES, and for summary of captured material, see Section V, SUPPLY AND EVACUATION.) Operations Instructions No.12 established the front line and a cleared area between the American and Russian Forces.

4-19 May: Operations Instructions No.13, issued 4 May, divided the Division area into sectors of responsibility, and systematic searches of the area to "screen" all personnel were begun. Normal military governmental duties were carried out. A Division Memorandum dated 7 May provided for establishment of additional Displaced Persons Centers. (See Annex No.6 for locations of Prisoner of War and Displaced Persons camps.) These camps were closed one by one as their usefulness ended.

Minor changes were made in the Division front and the cleared area between the American and Russian lines through consultation of commanders concerned. These changes are reflected in Annexes Nos.6 and 7.

Among events during the period were the following:

a. Public funeral services on 7 May in LUDWIGSLUST for 200 of the approximately 1,000 bodies found in a concentration camp near LUDWIGSLUST. German civilians performed the necessary labor, and citizens of the city were ordered to attend the services which were held by American Army chaplains. (See Annex No.4.)

b. Formal meeting at 82nd Airborne Division Headquarters on 7 May of General DEMPSEY, commander of the British Second Army and General GRESHIN, Commander of the Russian Forty-Ninth Army.

c. A formal exchange of visits at American and Russian Headquarters, including dinners at the 82nd Airborne Division Headquarters on 17 May for the Commanding General of the Russian Fifth Guards Cossack Division and his staff and on 18 May for the Commanding General of the Russian 385th Infantry Division and his staff.

19 May – 011200 June: The 82nd Airborne Division relieved the 8th Infantry and 7th Armored Divisions of part of their occupational areas late on 19 May. Operations Instructions No.14, issued 18 May, divided the divisional area into new sectors of unit responsibility. The changes involved some movement of unit Command Posts.

During this period the Division Commander presented Legions of Merit and Bronze Stars to a number of Russian officers and enlisted men, and Russian commanders presented Soviet decorations to several 82nd Airborne Division officers and men. The Division's first quota of personnel to be redeployed to the United States left for base camp during May, and a second quota left the Division on 1 June.

Evacuation of prisoners of war remaining in the Division's stockade began on 27 May. Approximately 22,000 were evacuated daily by train and truck to British Second Army prisoner of war enclosures during a four-day period 27-30 May, after which slightly more than 4,000 prisoners remained in the Division enclosures.

The 82nd Airborne Division was alerted late in the month for movement back to its base areas near RHEIMS, France. Advance parties were sent out, and movement of the Division's main body began by rail and truck on 1 June. The 82nd Airborne Division was relieved of responsibility for its area by the 5th British Division at 011200 June 1945.

## III – Intelligence

When the 82nd Airborne Division moved up to the Elbe River in the vicinity BLECKEDE, British troops already had located the II Naval Battalion, the I Police Battalion and the CELLE School Troops, a unit of battalion size. Known to be in the area but unlocated was Battle Group RERIK, which was believed to be composed of Regiments WUSCHNER and JANTZEN. Subsequent patrols by the Division Reconnaissance Platoon confirmed the presence of the Police Battalion and the CELLE School Troops.

The whole enemy Order of Battle in the area became crystal clear as our attack across the ELBE River began on 30 April. Large numbers of talkative prisoners swarmed into the prisoner of war cage and from their statements the jigsaw puzzle of regiment and Battle group became sorted and the following picture resulted:

Battle Group RERIK had been reshuffled and bobbed up now as Brigade WALTERS consisting of Regiments WUSCHNER and BAUER, with a brigade of artillery, JANTZEN attached. The latter was armed only with flak guns. The German habit of renaming already existing groups appeared when Regiment WUSCHNER received itself into the II Naval Battalion operating as Battle Group KLOSE and the I Police Battalion masquerading as Battle Group AHRENS.

Among units identified on 1 May was Regiment Bauer, composed of Battle Groups KRUSE and KLEVE, and the 1020th Landeschutzen Battalion.

As the advance progressed, rear elements of the Twenty-First Army were encountered and overpowered, identifications including the 5th Jaeger Division, the 4th SS Panzergrenadier Division "Polizei" and the 606th Infantry Division. Enemy units were inclined to offer little resistance to our advance, and the end was reached with the surrender of the entire Twenty-First Army by Lieutenant General von Tipplelskirch at 2130 hours 2 May 1945 at LUDWIGSLUST, Germany, ninety-five miles Northwest of BERLIN, to Major General James M. Gavin, commander of the 82nd Airborne Division.

Troops surrendered by the Twenty-First Army represented an almost inseparable conglomeration of over 2,000 different units. The Army formerly had been the Fourth and was made up of remnants of the Ninth and Twelfth German Armies. The main units included the 5th Jaeger Division, the 4th SS Panzergrenadier Division "Polizei", SS Battle Group Solar, and the 606th Infantry Division, all making up the III Panzer Corps. Also surrendered were elements of XVII Corps Oder consisting of a Parachute Division, the 1st Naval Division, and SS Division Langemark.

In and around these units was a heterogeneous mass of station complements, supply troops, cadres, naval personnel, and a large number of units that may be classified only under the heading of "miscellaneous".

Interesting enough, the commander of the Twenty-First Army and his ranking staff officers were poorly informed as to the total troops to be surrendered was reduced to 144,000 by 82nd Airborne Division estimates.

Among the ranking Officers who surrendered were the following:

• Lieutenant General von TIPPLESKIRCH, CG Twenty-First Army, and his staff
• Brigadier General von BIEDERMANN, CG of a group of straggler and equipment collecting points.
• General Theodor PETSCH, CG Wehkrais IX (Kassel)
• Major General Rudolf SCHUBERT, Former CG of Wehkreis XVII (Vienna)
• Brigadier General Kurt KEYSER, CG of HAMBURG and CG of sector "Lower Elbe" as far as DOENITZ
• Brigadier General Franz Joseph GROBHOLZ, CG of Wehrmacht Ordnungstruppen (PM) of Twelfth Army
• Brigadier General ROSSKOFF, CG of 606th Infantry Division
• Brigadier General Dr. CONRAD, JA, Twelfth Army
• Brigadier General LUSCHNIG, CG of Engineers, Twenty-First Army
• Brigadier General WAGNER, CG, Twenty-First Army Artillery
• Colonel MULLER, Chief of Staff, 606th Infantry Division.
• Colonel von GARDECKER, CO of Division Z.B.V.

With the cessation of hostilities on the Division front, intelligence activities were concentrated on the problem of security. CIC and IPW teams concentrated on the task of "Screening" prisoners of war, displaced persons and civilians, segregating SS personnel and investigating war criminals. The CIC and IPW teams were stationed at or near the different camps to facilitate these activities. A total of approximately 15,000 prisoners of war, displaced persons and civilians all told, were "screened".

Close liaison was maintained between intelligence teams and the Military Government detachment. The Nazi Party organization was eliminated in the area, and the higher party officials in each town were evacuated to the British Second Army for further investigation.

In each town within the Division area the police force was subject to special scrutiny. The Mayors of LUBTHEEN and NEUHAUS were removed. The Mayor of LUDWIGSLUST committed suicide.

There were no cases of subversive activities and no proved cases of sabotage. So-called Werewolf activity was not in evidence.

## IV – Personnel

Aside from the normal routine of G-1 activities, the G-1 Section was concerned primarily with the problems incident to the capture of many thousands of German prisoners of war, and the evacuation of displaced Allied nationals.

A minimum estimate of the number of German prisoners of war who surrendered to the 82nd Airborne Division has been set at 144,000, during the period subsequent to the crossing of the Elbe River and the rapid advance to junction with the Russian forces between LUDWIGSLUST and GRABOW, Germany. The climatic disintegration of German formations in the area of Division responsibility presented an unparalleled situation. The surrender of enemy units was so rapid that it was impossible to concentrate the defeated foe in Division Collecting Points without seriously depleting its outnumbered strength to provide sufficient men to control and process the tens of thousands of Germans.

Prisoners were disarmed and returned to the rear to the XVIII Corps (Airborne) PW Cage, vicinity of BEVENSON and HIMBURG, Germany on foot and in such German military vehicles as would run. During the first two days, these vehicles traversed the roads from LUDWIGSLUST to NEUHAUS over the pontoon bridge at BLECKEDE and on to the Cage in an apparently endless stream, bumper to bumper, and loaded to overflowing with the bedraggled remnants of the German Army. The concentrations at the PW Collecting Point at HIMBURG were incredible. In single fields, more than 10,000 enemy soldiers stood shoulder to shoulder awaiting disposition. When traffic across the ELBE River was frozen and the areas of Division responsibility were finally delineated, tens of thousands of prisoners taken by the 82nd Airborne Division remained. These within the Division area were immediately segregated in numerous PW Camps and counted. The total on hand was found to be in excess of 44,000. This number was increased to exceed 69,000 when the 82nd took over part of the area of the 8th Infantry Division.

These Camps were organized and operated by Divisional units. Evacuation was organized by the G-1 Section in liaison with 8th Corps (British), and commenced on 27 May with rail movements which were completed by 30 May. Arrangements for this grand-scale evacuation were effected by the G-1 Section.

More than 10,000 liberated Allied prisoners of war were processed through Division Collecting Points to American and British Army points at LUNEBERG, HILDESCHEIM and HAGENOW.

More than 20,000 displaced nationals, both Eastern and Western, from co-belligerent and conquered countries, were processed through Division "DP" Camps. These persons were assembled by "freezing" all those who lacked transportation, and by arrangement with the Russians. In the Camps they were segregated by national groups, quartered, fed and de-loused. At the earliest opportunity, they were moved to various Second British Army Distribution Points at LUNEBERG, CELLE, HAGENOW, SOLINGEN or SALTAU, from which Centers they were dispatched toward their homelands.

The segregation and transfer of Displaced Persons within the Division area and from the Division area was accomplished with minimum use of Division transportation although often numbers in excess of 1500 were moved in a single day. G-1 maintained liaison with British-Russian Liaison Groups and Contact Points at SCHWERIN, NEUSTAT, and LUDWIGSLUST and GRABOW. All British transport conveying Russian nationals to the Russian lines was reported to G-1 with advice as to the number of lorries expected to return empty. "DP" camp commanders had their camps organized so that groups of any nationality could be assembled for movement on an hour's empties to any designated Camp, receive their loads and clearance papers to cross the ELBE, and move these people to designated Reception Centers. When the 82nd Airborne relinquished control of the area to the 5th British Division, all Displaced persons were concentrated at TREBS. Of the 2,000 remaining, 1,800 were Italians no facilities having been arranged by high or headquarters for the evacuation of Italians.

The sudden and dramatic termination of the war was further emphasized by almost immediate implementation of the Army Readjustment and Redeployment program. Six officers and 344 enlisted men were selected from among those with high adjusted service rating scores. Although instructions did not require it, the Inspector General cooperated with G-1 to inspect records prior to departure on only twenty-four hour's notice. This initial group was moved from LUDWIGSLUST, Germany to Base Camps in the REIMS area by truck and then to the Reception Depot near Lehavre by train.

A few days before the Division was scheduled to move from the LUDWIGSLUST area to base, a second Readjustment and Redeployment quota of two officers and 295 enlisted men was received. Allotment was made to units in accord with their ratios of high ASR Scores to the Division total in the priority groups of scores. Units were given forty-eight hours in which to accomplish the processing of administrative records. The imminence of the move precluded allotment of trucks to move this personnel to Base, and the entire group was moved in three days by air. All details, from movement schedules to preparation of passenger manifests and the loading of the aircraft were supervised directly by officers of the G-1 Section.

Division casualties during operations in the ELBE River Sector were as follows:

| | Officers | Enlisted Men | Totals |
|---|---|---|---|
| Killed in Action | 1 | 20 | 21 |
| Wounded or Injured in Action | 3 | 119 | 122 |
| Missing in Action | 0 | 11 | 11 |
| Totals: | 4 | 150 | 154 |

## V – Supply and Evacuation

Movement of the Division to the Elbe River in the BLECKEDE area also was handicapped by long motor shuttles to the railheads at each end of the journey and by railway mechanical difficulties.

During the first week of May, 1945, the Assistant Chief of Staff, G-4, and related agencies continued to support the Division during its tactical operations East of the Elbe River, those operations having commenced with a crossing of the river on 30 April. G-4 controlled traffic over the Elbe River bridge at BLECKEDE during the first 72 hours after the crossing.

Following the surrender of German forces, troops of the 82nd Airborne Division made a systematic, thorough search of the Division area, and all salvageable enemy equipment was collected in a number of dumps established throughout the section. This equipment consisted in the main of large numbers of assorted vehicles, vast stores of ammunition and innumerable minor items. All such equipment was inventoried carefully and complete records were maintained and later turned over to the British 5th Division which relieved the 82nd.

Approximately 300 enemy vehicles were registered with G-4 and utilized by the troops in servicing the thousands of prisoners of war and displaced persons quartered within the Division area.

The task of rationing, billeting and moving prisoners of war and displaced persons within the area was largely a G-4 problem. Special rations were issued to the various nationalities of displaced persons, and special reduced rations were issued to prisoners of war.

At the close of the month G-4 was completing arrangements for moving the Division from the LUDWIGSLUST area back to its base camps in the SISSONE-LAON area.

The following major items were among equipment and supplies collected in the Division salvage dumps:

| | |
|---|---|
| Assorted trucks and passenger cars | 1,911 |
| Half-trucks | 81 |
| Tanks | 11 |
| Motorcycles | 145 |
| Flak Wagons | 21 |
| Artillery pieces, all calibers | 35 |
| Guns, 88 mm | 11 |
| Guns, AT, 37 mm | 655 |
| Guns, AA | 972 |
| Mortars, 60mm | 17 |
| Mortars, 81mm | 402 |
| Guns, Machine, MG34 | 537 |
| Bazookas | 49 |
| Rifles | 10,111 |
| Artillery Ammunition | 247,705 rds |
| Panzerfausts | 16,081 |
| Small Arms Ammunition | 10,546,055 rds |
| Grenades, all types | 16,266 |
| Radios, transmitting | 117 |
| Radios, receiving | 50 |
| Generators | 57 |
| Wire | 175 miles |
| Kitchens | 7 |
| Buses | 77 |
| Locomotives | 15 |
| Tractors | 5 |
| Detonators | 3,000 |

NOTE: The above figures do not include a large number of vehicles and much equipment evacuated across the Elbe River and out of the Division area immediately after surrender of the German Twenty-First Army.

## VI – Signal

The advance echelon of the Signal Company reinforced for the move to the Elbe River found it necessary, due to tactical requirements, to install two complete command post installations and prepare a wire net for a river crossing, all within the space of a few days. The main body of the Signal Company did not arrive in the area until five hours before the River crossing operation began.

At the beginning of May it was felt that the axis of communication would be toward LEUSSOU or LOSSEN and wire teams began laying field wire in that direction but available open wire was surveyed when the Division Command Post was located at LUDWIGSLUST. It was found that by making a number of repairs the commercial overhead open wire could be used for the twenty-five mile Division main axis of communications.

A switchboard was left at NEUHAUS and served the Division units in that area for the rest of the month. This installation was called the "Champion Switch" and later handled telephone calls to the two bridges over the ELBE River, "A" at DACHAU and "B" at BLECKEDE for which the Division was later responsible.

The commercial telephone exchange was rendered inoperative upon the Division arrival at LUDWIGSLUST. A survey of the commercial telephone system in the area showed that the following underground cables existed:

One 98 pair cable to Berlin
(This cable went through a repeater station at Perelburg)

One 98 pair cable to Hamburg
(This cable went through a repeater station at Vallahn)

One 8 pair cable to Vallahn
One 98 pair cable from the Railway Station in Ludwigslust to the Railway station at Hagenow.

In addition to the long underground cables, most of the towns in the immediate vicinity were served by overhead open wire. The LUDWIGSLUST local switchboard was Local Automatic and the trunks were served manually.

On the 16th of May, upon request of the Military Government, a few local phones for the town of LUDWIGSLUST were installed. Telephones were installed for doctors, dairies, food stores, fire stations, and the like at the time.

Two pairs in the underground cable to Hamburg were used to connect Champion switchboard into the Hamburg local switchboard. HAMBURG was a large switching central, and this gave the Division an outlet into the main communication system of the Western Front.

In performing an occupational mission, the Division was again spread over an area much larger than its tables of equipment were able to handle. By repairing and utilizing commercial open wire and using commercial underground cable the normal division system was soon installed. A total of 375 miles of open wire was maintained to accomplish this.

Two telephone lines were put in to Headquarters of Soviet units, including line to the 121st Russian Corps and one to the 284th Russian Division.

XVIII Corps (Airborne) left the area on 22 May 1945, and the Corps' communication responsibilities were transferred to the 82nd Airborne Division. A Radio Link was established to the Ninth Army (US) and the Second Army (Br). Wire lines were established with the Ninth Army and the 8th Infantry Division. The British sent a radio team to the Division to enter the Second Army (Br) net, and the 82nd also entered one of the Ninth Army Radio Command Nets.

## VII – Military Government

On 1 May 1945, Military Government office was located in BLECKEDE, Kreis of LUNEBERG. On 1 May 1945, Military Government moved with the Division across the ELBE River, and at 031800 May was in LUDWIGSLUST, the objective of the Division. Here began a phase of Military Government which ran the gamut of operations. Initially, Military Government was set up in LUDWIGSLUST and the entire area on a tactical basis. Law and Order was the immediate need. This was attained by the appointment of 51 police to control the civilian disorder and uncertainty that prevailed.

The job that faced Military Government was an imposing one complicated by the presence of thousands of displaced persons and prisoners of war in the Division area. From this chaos developed organization, administration, law and Order, and a semblance of economic normalcy within a period of ten days.

An early discovery of a concentration camp at WOBBELIN was made and prompt action was taken. Sick and under-nourished were moved to a newly established hospital in LUDWIGSLUST where they were given care, medical treatment, and proper nourishment. This Division Military Government Section initiated mass burials of the atrocity victims, holding ceremonies on 7 May 1945 in LUDWIGSLUST at an especially dedicated cemetery located on the grounds of the Duke of MECKLENBURG. Two hundred of these victims were buried, with services performed by American Army Chaplains of all religious faiths, and attended by the entire population of the community, General Gavin and his staff, and all available military personnel.

During the month more than 60,000 "Western" displaced persons were started on their journey home, being processed through displaced persons camps established by the Division at TREBS, MALLISS, and the Luftwaffe Field in LUDWIGSLUST. As the month closed, there remained only ninety-one "Western" displaced persons in the entire Division area. The Military Government Section initiated arrangements with Russian forces for movement of Eastern German refugees back to their homes. Approximately 5,000 such refugees were moved through the Russian lines by mutual agreement with the Soviet forces.

All the essentials of Military Government were accomplished. These included establishment of law and Order, removal and appointment of officials, re-establishment of the economic life in the area to include food rationing, labor, communication, public utilities, public welfare, and the establishment and operation of Military Government Courts supervising the civil administration and operation of more than 150 gemeinden.

Initially, upon occupation, immediate surveys of captured enemy food and medical supplies were made, such supplies being frozen in warehouses established by the G-4 Section. Demands were made upon the communities for food stuffs, clothing, medical supplies, operation and administrative necessities for the operation and administration of camps for displaced persons. Bakeries were reestablished and put into maximum production, necessitating procurement of labor, raw food stuffs, fuel, and power. The entire productive facilities were placed at the disposal of the DP camps. A survey of the electric power for the area indicated that the sources were in the hands of our Russian Allies. Notwithstanding, separate sources of supply of power were developed, such supplies being rationed for essential military and civilian needs.

In the course of the month, "V-E" Day occurred and Military Government's transition from operation under SHAEF's directives from "prior to defeat and surrender" to "after defeat and surrender" was accomplished in a routine manner.

# Part Three
# Miscellaneous Information and Maps

I Miscellaneous Information:
1. Unit Commanders and Ranking Staff Officers.
2. Schedule of Attachments.
3. Surrender of the German Twenty-First Army.
4. Burial of Atrocity Victims.

II Maps:
1. Routes of March, Base Camps to Cologne Area, Cologne to Elbe River.
2. Rhine River Defense.
3. Military Government Areas in Cologne Sector.
4. Elbe River Crossing.
5. Operations 1-3 May 1945.
6. Military Occupation Area 3-19 May 1945.
7. Military Occupation Area 20 May – 1 June 1945.

## UNIT COMMANDERS AND RANKING STAFF OFFICERS

| | |
|---|---|
| Commanding General | Major Gen. JAMES M. GAVIN |
| Assistant Division Commander | Brig. Gen. IRA P. SWIFT |
| Division Artillery Commander | Brig. Gen. FRANCIS A. MARCH |
| Chief of Staff | Col. ROBERT H. WIENECKE |
| G-1 | Lt. Col. ALFRED W. IRELAND |
| G-2 | Lt. Col. WALTER W. WINTON, JR. |
| G-3 | Lt. Col. JOHN NORTON |
| G-4 | Lt. Col. ALBERT G. MARIN |
| Adjutant General | Lt. Col. MAURICE E. STUART |
| Chemical Officer | Lt. Col. JOHN P. GEIGER |
| Chaplain | Major GEORGE B. WOODS |
| Finance Officer | Lt. Col. WILLIAM E. JOHNSON |
| Headquarters Commandant | Capt. GEORGE J. CLAUSSEN |
| Inspector General | Capt. WILLIAM E. JONES |
| Judge Advocate General | Lt. Col. NICHOLAS E. ALLEN |
| Ordnance Officer | Lt. Col. MAYO S. SILVEY |
| Provost Marshall | Major FREDERICK G. McCOLLUM |
| | Major PAUL E. VAUPEL (fr 23 May) |
| | |
| Quartermaster | Lt. Col. JOHN W. MOHRMAN |
| Signal Officer | Lt. Col. ROBERT E. FURMAN |
| Surgeon | Lt. Col. WILLIAM C. LINDSTROM |
| CO, 325 Glider Infantry | Col. CHARLES E. BILLINGSLEA |
| CO, 504 Parachute Infantry | Col. REUBEN H. TUCKER |
| CO, 505 Parachute Infantry | Col. WILLIAM E. EKMAN |
| Executive Officer, Division Artillery | Col. WILBUR M. GRIFFITH |
| CO, 319th Glider FA Battalion | Lt. Col. JAMES C. TODD |
| CO, 320th Glider FA Battalion | Lt. Col. PAUL E. WRIGHT |
| CO, 376th Parachute FA Battalion | Lt. Col. ROBERT W. NEPTUNE |
| CO, 456th Parachute FA Battalion | Lt. Col. WAGNER J. D'ALLESSIO |
| CO, 80th Airborne Anti-Aircraft Battalion | Lt. Col. RAYMOND E. SINGLETON |
| CO, 307th Airborne Engineer Battalion | Lt. Col. EDWIN A. BEDELL |
| CO, 82d Airborne Signal Company | Capt. RICHARD E. NERF |
| CO, 307th Airborne Medical Company | Major JERRY J. BELDEN |
| CO, 407th Airborne Quartermaster Co. | Major SAMUEL M. MAYS |
| CO, 782nd Airborne Ord. Maintenance Co. | Capt. JEFF DAVIS, JR. |
| CO, 82nd Parachute Maintenance Co. | Capt. WYLIE COOPER |
| CO, Division Headquarters Company | Capt. ROBERT B. PATTERSON |
| CO, Headquarters Battery, Div. Artillery | Capt. TONY J. RABIL |
| CO, Special Troops | Major WILLIAM H. JOHNSON |
| CO, Division Reconnaissance Platoon | 1st Lt. JOSEPH V. DIMASI |
| CO, Division Military Police Platoon | Major FREDERICK G. McCOLLUM |
| | Major PAUL E. VAUPEL (From 23 May) |

**Schedule of Attachments**
**Cologne Phase**

| UNIT ATCHD SUB A FROM DIV | DATE SUB A | SUB-ATTACHMENTS RELIEF | DATE OF RELIEF | DATE OF | DATE OF |
|---|---|---|---|---|---|
| (Organic Units) | | | | | |
| 307 Abn Engr Bn | — | Co A to 325 G.I. | 4 Apr | 141200 | |
| | | Co C to 504 4 Apr | 141200 | | |
| | | Co B to 505 | 4 Apr | 132400 | |
| 80 Abn AA Bn | — | Btry E to 325 | 4 Apr | 141200 | |
| | | Btrys C & D to 504 | 4 Apr | 141200 | |
| | | Btrys A & F to 505 | 4 Apr | 141200 | |
| 3rd Bn 325 G.I. | — | To Div Res. 81 mm | 4 Apr | 17 Apr | |
| | | Mort Plat to 504 | 061945 | 071100 | |
| 319 G. FA Bn | — | To 320 G. FA Bn | 170800 | 251200 | |
| 376 P. FA Bn | — | To 504 P.I. | 170800 | 251200 | |
| 456 P. FA Bn | — | To 505 P.I. | 170800 | 242215 | |
| 80 Abn AA Bn | — | To 505 P.I. | 220800 | 242215 | |
| | | (Non-Organic Units) | | | |
| 666 QM Trk Co | — | — | | | |
| 341 Inf | 040829 | | | | 042330 |
| 417 FA Gp | 040829 | General Support | | | 161200 |
| 746 FA Gp (8" How) | 040829 | General Support | | 040829 | 141800* |
| 672 FA Bn (155 How) | 040829 | General Support | | | 142400** |
| 541 FA Bn (155 Gun) | 121745 | General Support | | | 161200 |
| 805 FA Bn (155 How) | 040829 | General Support | | | 161200 |
| 546 FA Bn | 110130 | General Support | | | 161200 |
| 790 FA Bn | 102200 | General Support | | | 140330** |
| 74 Chem. Gen Co | 041500 | 3d Sec to 504 | 4 Apr | 141200 | 210800 |
| | | 1st Sec, 2 Sqds 4 Sec to 505 | 6 Apr | 132400 | |
| | | 2d Sec, 2 Sqds 4 Sec to 325 | 6 Apr | 141200 | |
| | | 2 Sqds 4 Sec to 504 | 6 Apr | 141200 | |
| 417 FA Gp | | 417 FA Gp | 181200 | 251200 | |
| 746 FA Bn | | 417 FA Gp | 251200 | | |
| 74 FA Bn | 181200 | 417 FA Gp | 251200 | | |
| 541 FA BN | 181200 | 417 FA Gp | 251200 | | |
| 12 TD Gp | 181200 | 417 FA Gp | 241200 | 251200 | |
| 661 FA Bn | 181200 | 12 TD Gp | 181200 | 241200 | 251200 |
| 942 FA Bn | 181200 | 12 TD Gp | 181200 | 231200 | 251200 |
| 3rd Co, 22 Belg. Fus. Bn. | 210800 | 661 FA Bn | 210800 | 251200 | |
| 294 FA Obs Bn | 250600 | For movement to new area | | 251800 | |
| 1130 Combat Engr Bn | 250600 | For movement to new area | | 261900 | |

Elbe River Phase

(Organic)

| Unit | | Assignment | | | | |
|---|---|---|---|---|---|---|
| 80 Abn | | Btrys A, E, F to 505 | 291730 | 040815 | | |
| AA Bn | | Btry C to 504 | 302300 | 040815 | | |
| 307 Abn | | Co B to 505 | 290600 | 040815 | | |
| Engr Bn | | 1 plat Co C to 504 | 302300 | 040815 | | |
| 2nd Bn 325 G.I. | | CCB 7 Armd Div | 021000 | 022400 | | |

(Non-Organic)

| Unit | | Assignment | | | | |
|---|---|---|---|---|---|---|
| 666 QM Trk Co | | | | | | |
| 280 FA Bn | 27 Apr | Div Arty | 27 Apr | 170700 | 170700 | |
| 580 AAA | 271930 | Btrys B & D to 505 | 290600 | 300130 | 021000 | |
| Bn | 23 May | Div Arty | 24 May | 05 June | 05 June | |
| 13 Inf | 281200 | | | 302400 | | |
| (8 Div) | | Co M to 505 | 291830 | | | |
| | | 3d Bn to Div Res | 29 Apr | 301900 | | |
| | | 3d Bn to 121 Inf | | 301900 | 011205 | |
| 43 FA Bn | 281200 | 13th Inf | | 281200 | 302300 | |
| | | 121 Inf | | 302300 | 011205 | |
| 605 TD Bn | 281820 | Co A to 505 | 012330 | 020830 | 151500 | |
| | | Co B to 325 | 020830 | 040815 | | |
| | | Co C to 504 | 020830 | 040815 | | |
| | | Bn to 307 Engr | 042300 | 151500 | | |
| 4 Royals (Br) | | | | | | |
| Sqdn A | 291200 | Direct Supt 505 | 021200 | | | |
| 740 Tk Bn | 291700 | Co A to 505 | 302300 | 012100 | 012100 | |
| | | Co C to 504 | 302300 | 012100 | | |
| | | Co B to 121 | 302300 | —— | | |
| 644 TD Bn | 291700 | 1 plat, Co A to 504 | 302300 | 012100 | 012100 | |
| | | 1 plat, Co A to 505 | 302300 | 012100 | | |
| Co A, 89 | 291800 | To 505 | 291800 | 302300 | 090800 | |
| Chem. Bn. | | To 504 | 302300 | 090800 | | |
| 121 Inf | 301900 | 011205 | | | | |
| 56 FA Bn | 301900 | To 121 Inf | 301900 | 011205 | | |
| Co C, 89 | 301900 | To 121 Inf | 301900 | 011205 | | |
| Chem. Bn. | | | | | | |
| CCB, 7 Armd | 01 May | Co C, 814 TD Bn to 325 02 May | | 031030 | 041200 | |
| | | Co D, 31 Tk Bn to 504 02 May | | 031830 | | |
| 205 FA Gp | 031200 | To Div Arty | 042300 | 170700 | 170700 | |
| 207 FA Bn | 031200 | To Div Arty | 042300 | 170700 | 170700 | |
| 768 FA Bn | 031200 | To Div Arty | 042300 | 170700 | 170700 | |

\* Relieved from attachment to 417th FA Group 141800, converted to Special Guards, attached to 82nd Abn. Div.
\*\* Relieved attachment 417th FA Group as well as from 82nd Abn. Div.

**Record Of The Unconditional Surrender Of The German 21st Army
To The 82d Airborne Division, 022130 May 1945**
Headquarters 82d Airborne Division
Office of the Division Commander

Ludwigslust, Germany
2 May 1945

I, Lieutenant General von Tippelskirch, Commanding General of 21st German Army, hereby unconditionally surrender the 21st German Army, and all of its attachments, and equipment and appurtenances thereto, to the Commanding General of the 82nd Airborne Division, United States Army. This unconditional capitulation is valid only for those troops of 21st Army which pass through the America lines.

Ludwigslust, Germany
2 May 1945

Ich, General der Infantrie von Tippelskirch, kommanderender General der 21. deutschen Armee, usbergebe hiermit bedingungslos die aete and deten Zubehoe an den kimmandierenden General der 82. Fallschirmjaeger Division, Vereinigete Staaten Armee. Diese bedingungslose Kapitulation gilt nur fuer diejenigen Truppen der 21. Armee velche die amerikanischen Linien passieren.

/s/ von Tippelskirch
von Tippelskirch
General der Infantrie
Ludwigslust, Germany
Accepted.
/s/ James M. Gavin
James M. Gavin
Major General, U.S. Army

Burial of Atrocity Victims

Funeral services were held on the morning of 7 May at LUDWIGSLUST for 200 of the approximately 1,000 men whose bodies were found at a German concentration camp at WOBBELIN. German civilians of every social strata and occupation in LUDWIGSLUST removed the bodies from the concentration camp and prepared them for burial, dug the graves, and filled the graves after the services. The rites were attended by citizens of the city, a representative group of captured German army officers, and several hundred officers and men of the 82nd Airborne Division. The following purpose of the services was read by Major (Chaplain) George Wood, Division Chaplain:

"We are assembled here today before God and in the sight of men to give a proper and decent burial to the victims of atrocities committed by armed forces in the name and by the Order of the German Government. These 200 bodies were found by the American army in a concentration camp four miles north of the city of LUDWIGSLUST.

"The crimes here committed in the name of the German people and by their acquiescence were minor compared to those to be found in concentration camps elsewhere in Germany. Here there were no gas chambers, no crematoria; these men of Holland, Russia, Poland, Czechoslovakia, and France were simply allowed to starve to death. Within four miles of your comfortable homes 4,000 men were forced to live like animals, deprived even of the food you would give your dogs. In three weeks 1,000 of these men were starved to death; 800 of them were buried in pits in the nearby woods. These 200 who lie before us in these graves were found piled four and five feet high in one building and lying with the sick and dying in other buildings.

"The world has long been horrified at the crimes of the German nation; these crimes were never clearly brought to light until the armies of the United Nations overran Germany. This is not war as conducted by international rules of warfare. This is murder such as is not even known among savages.

"Though you claim no knowledge of these acts you are still individually and collectively responsible for these atrocities, for they were committed by a government elected to office by yourselves in 1933 and continued in office by your indifference to organized brutality. It should be the firm resolve of the German people that never again should any leader or party bring them to such moral degradation as is exhibited here.

"It is the custom of the United States Army through its Chaplain's Corps to insure a proper and decent burial to any deceased person whether he be civilian or soldier, friend or foe, according to religious preference. The Supreme Commander of the Allied Forces has ordered that all atrocity victims be buried in a public place, and that the cemetery be given the same personal care that is given to all military cemeteries. Crosses will be placed at the heads of the graves of Christians and Stars of David at the heads of the graves of Jews; a stone monument will be set up in memory of those deceased. Protestant, Catholic, and Jewish prayers will be said by Chaplain Woods, Hannan and Wall of the 82nd Airborne Division for these victims as we lay them to rest and commit them into the hands of our Heavenly Father in the hope that the world will not again be faced with such barbarity."

*Left: Private Alexander S. Nemeth, C Company, 307th Airborne Engineer Battalion at the wishing well in Sissone, France, 8 March 1945. Nemeth served with the 82nd from Anzio to Berlin. He was in the first assault boat across the Waal River on 20 September 1944 at Nijmegen, Holland. (Courtesy Al Nemeth)*

*Opposite*
*Top: A maintenance specialist inspects the experimental 57mm self-propelled antitank gun of the 80th Airborne Antiaircraft Battalion in Camp Suippes, France, March 1945.*

*Bottom: The self-propelled 57mm antitank gun of the 80th Airborne Antiaircraft Battalion showing the right side with barrel support in use at Camp Suippes, France, 7 March 1945.*

Left: A clear view of the breech of the self-propelled 57mm antitank of the 80th Airborne Antiaircraft Battalion at Camp Suippes, France, 7 March 1945.

Below: BG Francis A. March, Division Artillery Commander, inspects the new self-propelled 57mm antitank gun of the 80th Airborne Antiaircraft Battalion at Camp Suippes, France, 7 March 1945.

Opposite
Top: BG Francis A. March, Division Artillery Commander, is shown the new self-propelled 57mm antitank gun of the 80th Airborne Antiaircraft Battalion at Camp Suippes, France, on 7 March 1945.

Bottom: The self-propelled 57mm antitank gun ready to be fired on a range at Camp Suippes, France, 7 March 1945.

Above: Troopers of the 80th Airborne Antiaircraft Battalion prepare the self-propelled 57mm antitank gun for firing on a range at Camp Suippes, France, 7 March 1945.

Left: A clear view of the open breech of the self-propelled 57mm antitank gun on a range at Camp Suippes, France, 7 March 1945.

Opposite
Top: A crewmember prepares the self-propelled 57mm antitank gun for firing on a range at Camp Suippes, France, 7 March 1945.

Bottom: Should I pull the lanyard? A gunner of the 80th Airborne Antiaircraft Battalion prepares to fire the self-propelled 57mm antitank gun on a range at Camp Suippes, France, 7 March 1945.

*Left: 1SG Lemkowitz of Headquarters Company, 505th PIR, raises the U.S. flag on a castle near Cologne, Germany, on 12 April 1945.*

*Above: 82nd MPs conduct a mounted patrol in Cologne, Germany, April 1945. Examples of the stripe around the helmet have been seen in white and yellow.*

*Below: Trucks of the 666th Quartermaster Truck Company deliver troops of the 505th PIR to the railhead at Duren, Germany, for transportation by rail to Bleckede for the Elbe River crossing. Duren, Germany, 26 April 1945.*

*Right: Paratroopers aboard trucks of the 666th Quartermaster Truck Company get doughnuts from an American Red Cross volunteer. The 666th was an all Black unit attached to the 82nd. Germany 1945.*

*Below: Last combat action for the 82nd in World War II – Assault crossing of the Elbe River near Bleckede, Germany, 30 April 1945.*

*Bottom: Assault crossing of the Elbe River – Paratroopers of the 82nd aboard LVT-4 Buffaloes operated by the British 4th Royals near Bleckede, Germany, 30 April 1945.*

*Above: Engineers of the 307th Airborne Engineer Battalion diffuse a German anti-shipping mine along a road just east of the Elbe River, May 1945. Most members wear the red and white diamond helmet marking of the 307th.*

*Below: American and Soviet soldiers atop a Soviet T-34 tank in Ludwigslust, Germany, May 1945.*

*Above: Lieutenant General von Tippelskirch leaves Mecklenburg Castle after surrendering his 21st Army to the 82nd Airborne Division at Ludwigslust, Germany, 2 May 1945.*

*Below: A few of the nearly 150,000 soldiers of the German 21st Army that surrendered to the 82nd at Ludwigslust on 2 May 1945.*

*Mecklenburg Castle in Ludwigslust, Germany – Command Post for the 82nd in May 1945.*

*The Liberation of Wobbelin Concentration Camp, 2 May 1945, near Ludwigslust, Germany. Former prisoners walk to freedom.*

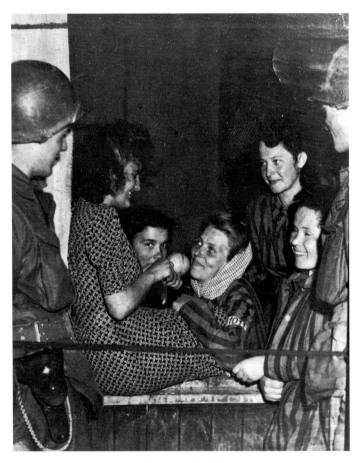

*Former prisoners with their liberators. Wobbelin Concentration Camp near Ludwigslust, Germany, May 1945.*

*Wobbelin Concentration Camp – the living and the dead, May 1945.*

*Former prisoners of Wobbelin help each other to freedom after liberation by the 82nd Airborne Division, 2 May 1945.*

272

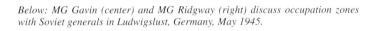

*Above: German citizens rebury the victims of Wobbelin Concentration Camp while officers of the 82nd Airborne Division supervise. Ludwigslust, Germany, May 1945.*

*Right: Reburial of Wobbelin victims. Local citizens view the corpses in Ludwigslust, Germany, May 1945.*

*Below: MG Gavin (center) and MG Ridgway (right) discuss occupation zones with Soviet generals in Ludwigslust, Germany, May 1945.*

# Epilogue

After twenty-two months of combat, the war had finally ended for the 82nd in May 1945. The Division, or elements of the Division, had participated in seven campaigns, four parachute assaults, two glider assaults, and several river crossings and amphibious operations. It had seen intense fighting in mountains, hedgerows, and urban terrain. Its record was one for all its veterans to be proud.

There was talk in the ranks about being shipped to the Pacific Theater to continue the war against Japan or inactivation. Neither came to pass. Because of its outstanding combat record, the 82nd would remain on active duty and be chosen for a high honor – to represent the United States in Berlin, the capital of our former enemy. Word was received of the mission in July as the 82nd was camped at Epinal, France. General Gavin, in his typical fashion, mounted the hood of his jeep to address the Division about the news. By 1 August 1945, the 82nd was in place in Berlin as an occupation force. It was there that the battle-hardened airborne soldiers earned another distinction for the Division. The honorific title of "America's Guard of Honor" was bestowed upon the 82nd by General George S. Patton as he reviewed the Division Honor Guard during a V-J Day celebration. Patton proclaimed:

> "In all my years in the Army and of all the honor guards I've ever seen, the 82nd Berlin Honor Guard is the best."

The city was in ruins and the combat veterans had to restore order as well as receive a host of dignitaries. The 82nd set about its new mission with as much vigor as it had done with its combat assignments. By December the Division had been relieved of occupation duty in Berlin and was preparing to return to the U.S.

The Division sailed upon the Queen Mary, departing Southampton England on 29 December 1945 and arriving in New York City on 3 January 1946. The biggest day came on 12 January as the 82nd led the victory parade as millions cheered them. General Gavin himself led the Division. When asked if he would ride Gavin stated he had walked allover Europe with the Division and he wasn't going to ride now. Gavin led the parade on foot as the 82nd marched down Fifth Avenue and through the Washington Arch. The Division, which had just created history, marched into the future as it prepared to be a contingency force for the U.S. in the uncertain days of the Cold War.

*Above: America's Guard of Honor at the Allied Flag Raising Ceremony in Berlin, Germany, 1945. Flags being raised are U.S., England, France, and USSR.*

*Below: The Honor Guard parading through the Brandenburg Gate in Berlin, Germany, 1945.*

*Above: 82nd Airborne Division Honor Guard in Berlin, Germany, 1945 – America's Guard of Honor.*

*Right: MG James M. Gavin with General George S. Patton during a review of the 82nd in Berlin, Germany, 1945. Patton's remarks gave the 82nd the nickname "America's Guard of Honor".*

*Armored jeeps of the 82nd Recon Platoon in Berlin, Germany, during occupation duty, 1945.*

*Above: The 307th Airborne Engineer Battalion Command Post sign in Berlin, Germany, 1945.*

*Top right: Certificate of passage aboard the Queen Mary on 29 December 1945. The Queen Mary brought the 82nd home.*

*Right: Reviewing Stand ticket for the Victory Parade in New York City, 12 January 1946.*

*Below: MG James M. Gavin salutes as he passes the reviewing stand in the World War II victory parade in New York City on 12 January 1945.*

*Jeeps towing 57mm antitank guns pass the reviewing stand during the Victory Parade in New York City, 12 January 1946.*

*The 82nd Honor Guard stands at parade rest as jeeps towing 57mm antitank guns pass the reviewing stand in the New York City Victory Parade on 12 January 1946.*

*Paratroopers marching in the World War II victory parade in New York City on 12 January 1946. The 82nd was chosen to lead the parade.*

*The 82nd Airborne Division passes under the Washington Arch in New York City during the World War II victory parade on 12 January 1946.*

*Opposite: MG James M. Gavin leads the 82nd Airborne Division through the Washington Arch in New York City during the victory parade on 12 January 1946.*

# Special Photographic Sections

# Helmet Markings and Insignia

*Colonel Charles Billingslea, Commander of the 325th GIR, presents awards to officers of the regiment. Note the Cross of Lorraine insignia, taken from the coat of arms, representing service in France during World War I.*

*Soldiers in the center of the photograph display good examples of the 325th GIR helmet marking. Circa March 1945.*

*Another example of the Cross of Lorraine insignia.*

*An American Red Cross worker serves hot soup to soldiers returning from the Ardennes. France, February 1945. Note the cross of Lorraine insignia, M-1944 equipment, and M-1943 combat "buckle" boots.*

*General Brereton, First Allied Airborne Army Commander, decorates Major Julian Cook, 3/504th PIR, for his role in the Waal River Crossing on 20 September 1944. Cook displays the skull and cross bones of the 504th. To his left is Captain Wesley Harris of the 307th Airborne Engineer Battalion. Belgium, 20 January 1945.*

*Major General James M. Gavin decorates a corporal of the 504th PIR who displays the skull and cross bones on his helmet. Note the tanker jacket issued to the 504th while in Italy. December 1944 - January 1945.*

*Major General James M. Gavin decorates a lieutenant of the 504th PIR who wears the skull and cross bones insignia on his helmet, 1945.*

*Captain Adam A. Komosa, D Company 2nd Battalion, 504th PIR, displays the late war shield (blue) with flaming sword used by the 504th. Berlin, Germany, 1945.*

*Typical equipment of a paratrooper rifleman. Note the rampant lion helmet marking of the 505th PIR. Kairouan, Tunisia, July 1943.*

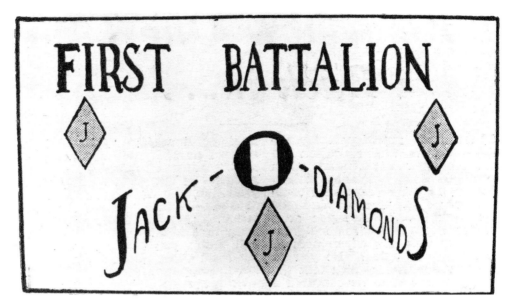

*STATIC LINE, 505th PIR newspaper, header for the 1st Battalion "Jack-O-Diamonds" news. The header shows the battalion helmet marking.*

*STATIC LINE, 505th PIR newspaper, header for the 2nd Battalion "Spearhead" news. The header shows the battalion helmet marking.*

*STATIC LINE, 505th PIR newspaper, header for the 3rd Battalion "Cannonball" news. The header shows the battalion helmet marking. LTC Krause, the battalion commander, was known as "Cannonball".*

*Above: Paratroopers from the 1st Battalion 505th PIR prepare for a jump in Berlin, 1945. They wear the "Jack-O-Diamonds" insignia of the 1/505th. It was a black outline with a read diamond and a black upper case "J" in the center.*

*Opposite*
*Top: Paratroopers of the 505th PIR rig for a jump in Berlin, Germany, 1945. The trooper rigging under the wing tip wears the "Spearhead" marking of the 2nd Battalion. In the center is a trooper of the 1st Battalion with the "Jack-O-Diamonds". The battalion insignia of the 505th were adopted prior to Normandy.*

*Bottom: Another view of helmet markings of the 1st and 2nd Battalions of the 505th PIR in Berlin, Germany, 1945.*

*Left: A lieutenant of the 505th PIR receiving the Silver Star Medal. He wears the "Cannonball" insignia of the 3rd Battalion. England December 1943 - February 1944.*

*Below: A bulldozer operated by engineers of the 307th Airborne Engineer Battalion in a town in Belgium, December 1944 - January 1945. The trooper to the right wears the late war 505th PIR helmet marking of a shooting star.*

*Opposite*
*Top: Major General James. M. Gavin, assisted by a paratrooper of the 505th PIR wearing the "shooting star" marking, prepares to demonstrate the T-7 parachute with combat equipment. Berlin, Germany, 1945.*

*Bottom: Major General James M. Gavin demonstrates how the T-7 parachute deploys to Soviet officers in Berlin, Germany, 1945. His assistant wears the "shooting star" of the 505th PIR on his helmet.*

*DEVIL'S DIGEST, 508th PIR newspaper, header for the 1st Battalion "Fighting 1st" news. The header shows the battalion helmet marking.*

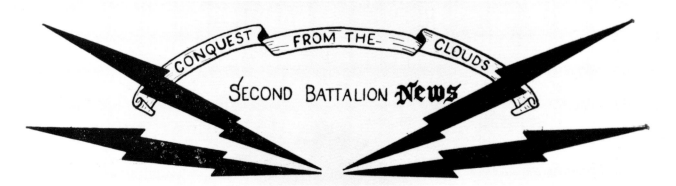

*DEVIL'S DIGEST, 508th PIR newspaper, header for the 2nd Battalion "Conquest from the Clouds" news. The header shows the battalion helmet marking of the double lightning bolts.*

*DEVIL'S DIGEST, 508th PIR newspaper, header for the 3rd Battalion "Free-Bold-Rapid" news. The header shows the winged foot helmet marking of the battalion.*

*Right: Captain Woodrow W. Millsaps, B Company, 1/508th PIR, receives a Silver Star Medal from Major General James. M. Gavin, 1945. Millsaps wears a helmet bearing the "Fighting First" insignia.*

*Below: Major General James M. Gavin decorates troopers of the 508th PIR, 1945. The two troopers to the left wear the double, white lightning bolts of the 2nd Battalion, "Conquest from the Clouds". The trooper to the right wears the winged foot of the 3rd Battalion, "Free-Bold-Rapid".*

*Bottom right: Another view of helmet markings of the 2nd and 3rd battalions of the 508th PIR, 1945.*

*Left: A captain of the 456th PFAB receives an award in Berlin, Germany, 1945. The commander displays a helmet marking consisting of white jump wings above a white 75mm pack howitzer on a red shield. The captain wears green leadership tabs on his epaulets.*

*Above: 82nd MPs prepare to move out on their WLA motorcycles in Germany, 1945.*

*Below: An 82nd MP with Dutch civilians, September 1944.*

*Above: An 82nd MP searching a German POW, 1944.*

*Top right: A corporal of the 456th PFAB receives a Bronze Star Medal. Berlin, Germany, 1945. The commander wears the battalion helmet marking.*

*Right: Lieutenant Michael Sabia, C Company, 307th Airborne Engineer Battalion, receives an award from MG Gavin, Holland, 1944. He wears the M-1944 suspenders. The troopers to his left display the red and white diamond helmet marking of the 307th. The red always faced forward.*

*Below: Paratroopers of the 376th PFAB near Sissone, France, 1944. Three of the troopers wear the circle insignia of the battalion on the front of their helmets.*

*Lieutenant McLeod of C Company, 307th Airborne Engineer Battalion, receives an award from MG Gavin, Holland 1944. McLeod wears a good example of the 307th helmet marking. He also wears the M-1944 field suspenders.*

*Captain Wesley D. "Spike" Harris, C Company, 307th Airborne Engineer Battalion, receives the DSC from LTG Brereton, First Allied Airborne Army, Belgium, 20 January 1945. Harris wears the red and white diamond helmet marking of the 307th. The award was for his role in the Waal River crossing on 20 September 1944.*

*A SFC receives a Silver Star Medal from General Gavin for actions in Normandy. Note the angle of the Pathfinder insignia varies from the one worn by the lieutenant in the previous photo. To the left can be seen the "Skull and Crossbones" marking of the 504th PIR.*

*A lieutenant of the Pathfinders receives a Silver Star Medal from General Gavin. Note the location of the Pathfinder insignia.*

*Right: A Pathfinder private receives an award from General Parks, First Allied Airborne Army, in Berlin, Germany, 1945.*

*Right: A Pathfinder Staff Sergeant receives an award from General Parks in Berlin, Germany, 1945.*

*Below: A rare example of a bazooka patch worn on a dress uniform by a paratrooper of the 505th PIR in England, around May 1944.*

*Bottom: Piper L-4 A Grasshoppers of the Division Artillery. The unit marking was the number "57". Ten of these aircraft were operated for artillery observation. The 82nd insignia was painted on the tail.*

# Ephemera

*A Christmas Service Program for the 505th PIR, 25 December 1942.*

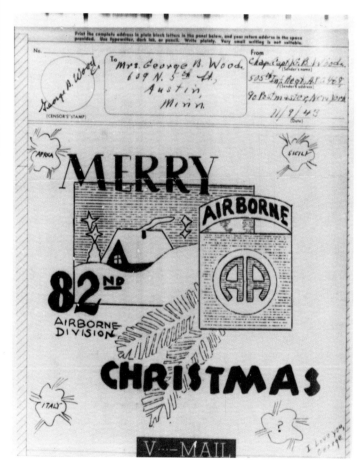

*A V-Mail from Chaplain George B. Wood of the 505th PIR, 9 November 1943. V (Victory) Mail was designed to reduce the weight of mail being sent overseas. It was photographed, the film shipped overseas, and printed and distributed.*

Top left: *An unused Christmas V-Mail from the 505th PIR, 1943.*

Above: *The 82nd Christmas card, 1944.*

Left: *The 82nd Christmas card, Berlin, Germany, 1945.*

Below: *Glider Qualification Certificate, 1944.*

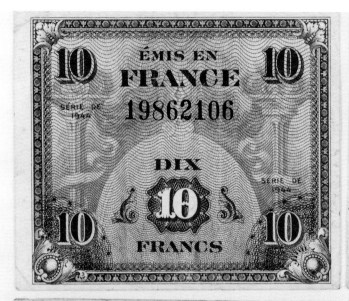

*Above: Allied Military Currency (AMC) known as invasion money; it was issued to troops prior to an invasion for use on the local economy.*

*Right: Certificate of Service for the 307th Airborne Engineer Battalion. Courtesy Al Nemeth.*

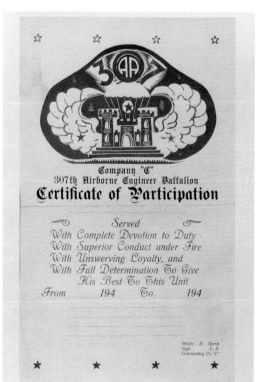

Pages 298-299: THE CLIQUESMAN, newsletter of the 82nd Parachute Maintenance Company.

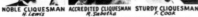

# The American Red Cross with
# the 82nd Airborne Division

*Harry Smith, American Red Cross Field Director for the 82nd in England, 1944.*

*A 504th paratrooper receives a doughnut and cup of coffee from an American Red Cross worker upon rejoining the 82nd in England, May 1944.*

*American Red Cross workers serve coffee and doughnuts from a Club Mobile to paratroopers of the 504th rejoining the Division in England after fighting in the Anzio Beachhead. May 1944.*

*Three paratroopers of the 504th Combat Team raise their canteen up in a toast to rejoining the 82nd after fighting at Anzio. England, May 1944.*

*Troopers of the 504th Combat Team line up at a Red Cross Club Mobile for coffee and doughnuts as they rejoin the Division in England, May 1944.*

*Troopers of the 504th Combat Team enjoy coffee and doughnuts from a Red Cross Club Mobile in England, May 1944.*

*MG Ridgway speaking at a ceremony to recognize the work of the American Red Cross in England, 1944.*

*Colonel Eaton, Chief of Staff, standing in a formation during a ceremony to recognize Red Cross workers, England, 1944.*

*MG Ridgway congratulating Red Cross workers in England, 1944.*

*An American Red Cross Representative congratulating Red Cross workers in England, 1944.*

MG Ridgway and a Red Cross representative inspect a new Club Mobile for the 82nd in England, 1944.

Red Cross workers show MG Ridgway a new Club Mobile for the 82nd in England, 1944.

Generals Ridgway and Gavin at a Red Cross Club Mobile, England, 1944. The "Springfield" and "Dayton" Club Mobiles were modified 2 1/2 ton trucks.

MG Ridgway enjoying a cup of coffee from a Red Cross Club Mobile in England, 1944.

A trooper getting a doughnut from a Red Cross Club Mobile in England, 1944.

Colonel Edson Raff, Executive Officer of the 2nd Airborne Brigade, enjoying coffee and doughnuts from a Red Cross Club Mobile in England on 7 August 1944. Raff led an armored task force, Task Force Raff, on D-Day.

*BG Gavin, Assistant Division Commander, confers with Colonel Eaton, Chief of Staff, by a Club Mobile in England, 1944.*

*Paratroopers file by Red Cross Club Mobiles for coffee and doughnuts. The "Nebraska" and "Buffalo" were modified British buses. England 1944.*

*Officers confer over coffee and doughnuts at the Red Cross Club Mobile "Springfield" in England, 1944.*

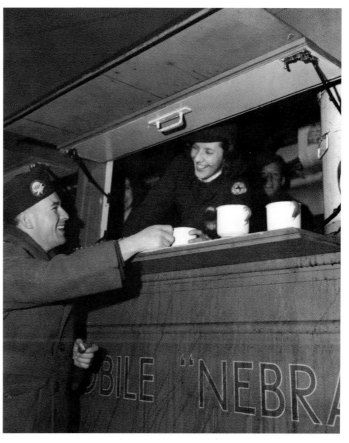

*An officer gets a cup of coffee and doughnut from the Red Cross Club Mobile "Nebraska" in England, 1944.*

*Left: Troops get hot coffee and doughnuts at a Red Cross club, 1944.*

*Louise Shepard and Dotie Davis, American Red Cross, in France, 1944.*

*Louise Shepard and Dotie Davis, American Red Cross, greet 82nd troopers returing from Holland. France, November 1944.*

*82nd troopers converse with Louise Shepard and Dotie Davis of the American Red Cross in France, November 1944.*

*Troops returing from Holland are greeted with hot coffee and doughnuts from the American Red Cross in France, November 1944.*

*Left: An American Red Cross worker waves goodbye to 82nd troopers truck-bound for camps in France, November 1944.*

*Evelyn Stevens with paratroopers of the 505th PIR in the Ardennes, Belgium, December 1944.*

*Evelyn Stevens, American Red Cross, with Captain Robert Piper, 505th PIR, in Belgium, January 1945. They were engaged in February and married at Epinal, France, in June 1945. "Stevie", as she was known by the 505th troopers, received a Bronze Star Medal in 1947 for her work on the front lines.*

*A 325th trooper receives hot coffee from a Red Cross worker after fighting in the Ardennes and Hurtgen Forests. France, March 1945. Note the Staff Sergeant wears the M-1944 field equipment and has the Cross of Lorraine insignia on his helmet.*

*An American Red Cross worker assigned to the 82nd gives out doughnuts to troops returning from the front, 1945. Note she wears jump wings, an oval, and an 82nd patch. The ARC workers were highly respected in the 82nd for their dedication to the troopers and their front-line service.*

*Right: A Red Cross worker gives doughnuts to troops aboard a train in Germany, 1945.*

*A Red Cross worker gives out doughnuts to troops as they board trains in Germany, 1945.*

*Troops on a train talk with an ARC worker while waiting to move out by train. Germany 1945.*

*A Red Cross worker greets truck-mounted 82nd troopers with a box of doughnuts. Germany 1945.*

*82nd troopers talk with Red Cross workers in Germany, April 1945.*

*82nd troopers pose for a photo with an American Red Cross worker in Germany, 1945.*

*An 82nd Red Cross worker at a memorial service in Nijmegen, Holland, September 1945.*

*An 82nd trooper and Red Cross worker in front of the 504th Red Cross Club in Berlin, Germany, 1945.*

*Troops returing from fighting in the Ardennes and Hurtgen Forests receive hot coffee from American Red Cross workers in France, March 1945. Note the troops are wearing the M-1944 field equipment.*

# Color Section

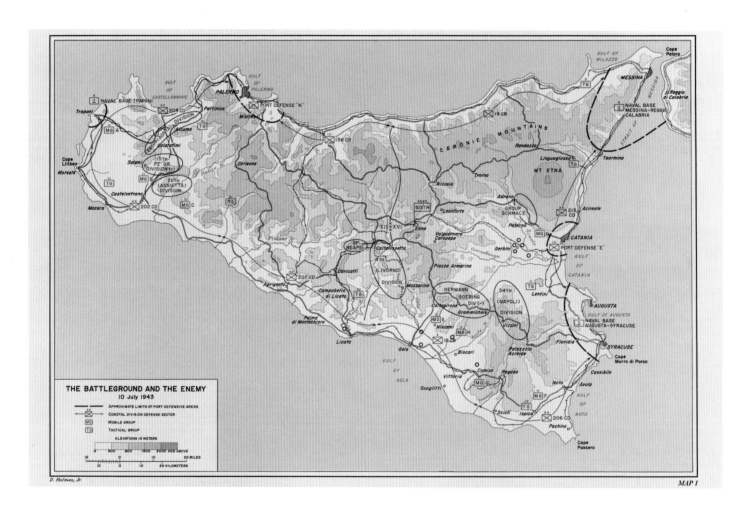

THE BATTLEGROUND AND THE ENEMY
10 July 1943

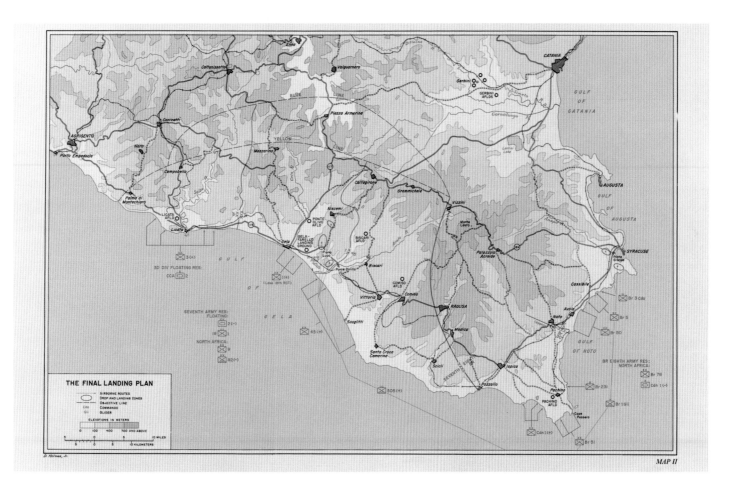

THE FINAL LANDING PLAN

MAP II

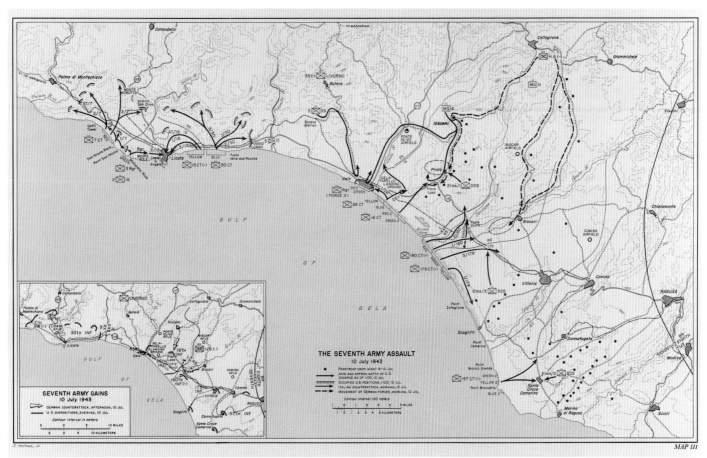

THE SEVENTH ARMY ASSAULT
10 July 1943

SEVENTH ARMY GAINS
10 July 1943

MAP III

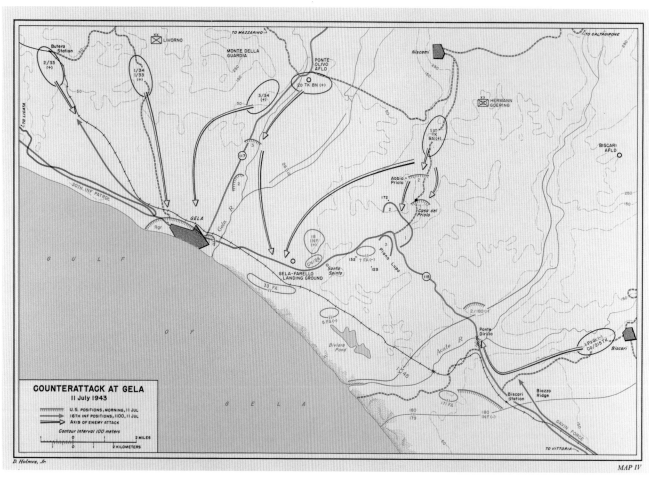

### COUNTERATTACK AT GELA
#### 11 July 1943

| | |
|---|---|
| (serrated line) | U.S. POSITIONS, MORNING, 11 JUL |
| (arrow line) | 16TH INF POSITIONS, 1100, 11 JUL |
| (bold arrow) | AXIS OF ENEMY ATTACK |

Contour Interval 100 meters

2 MILES
2 KILOMETERS

D. Holmes, Jr.

MAP IV

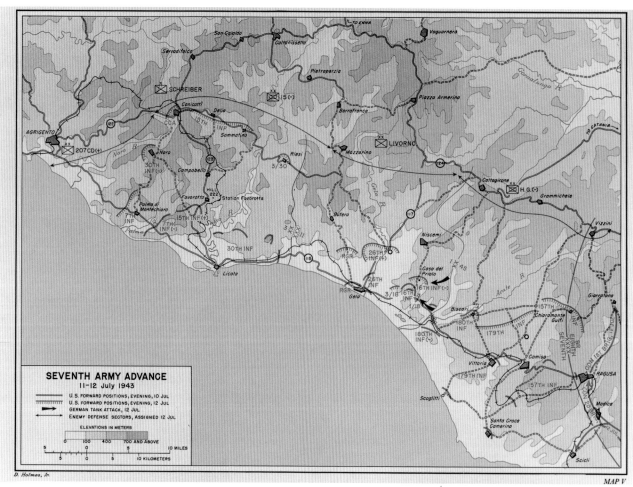

### SEVENTH ARMY ADVANCE
#### 11–12 July 1943

| | |
|---|---|
| (line) | U.S. FORWARD POSITIONS, EVENING, 10 JUL |
| (barbed line) | U.S. FORWARD POSITIONS, EVENING, 12 JUL |
| (bold arrow) | GERMAN TANK ATTACK, 12 JUL |
| (arrow) | ENEMY DEFENSE SECTORS, ASSIGNED 12 JUL |

ELEVATIONS IN METERS

0   100   400   700 AND ABOVE

10 MILES
10 KILOMETERS

D. Holmes, Jr.

MAP V

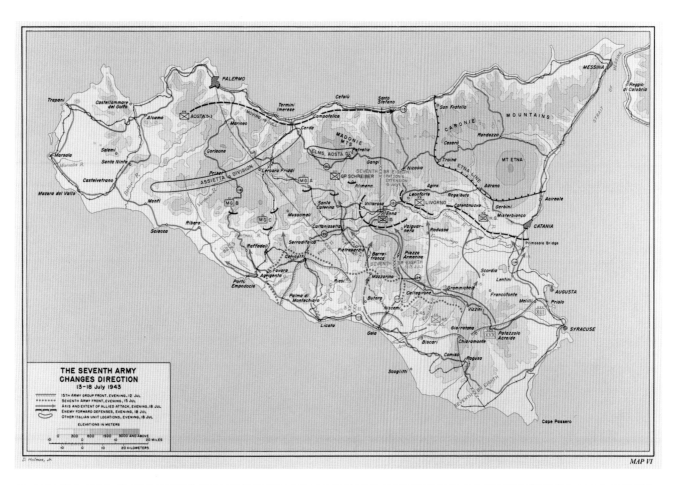

### THE SEVENTH ARMY
### CHANGES DIRECTION
#### 13–18 July 1943

MAP VI

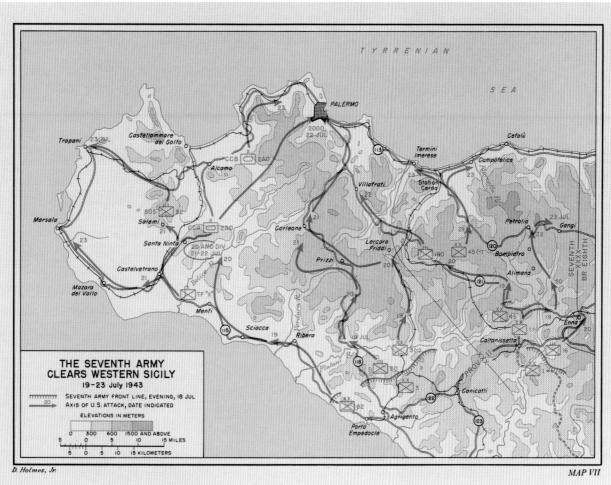

### THE SEVENTH ARMY
### CLEARS WESTERN SICILY
#### 19–23 July 1943

MAP VII

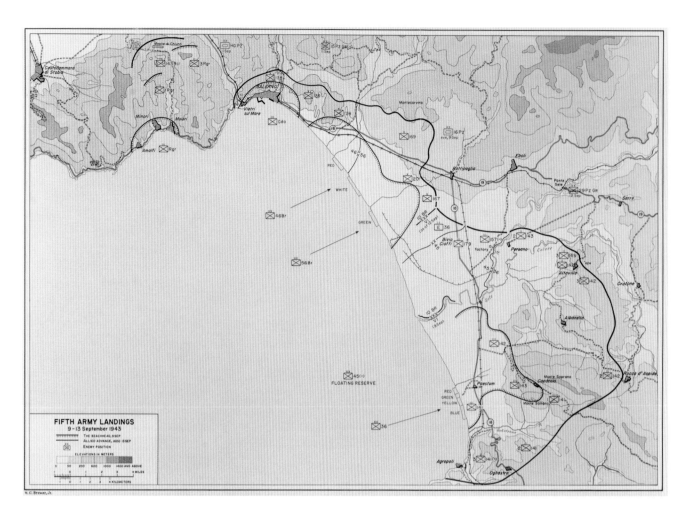

**FIFTH ARMY LANDINGS**
9–13 September 1943

THE BEACHES AT, 9 SEP
ALLIED ADVANCE, 1600 13 SEP
ENEMY POSITION

ELEVATIONS IN METERS

0   50   200   600   1000   1400 AND ABOVE

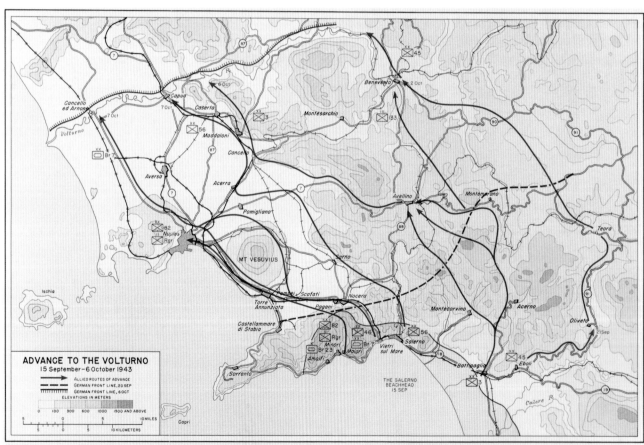

**ADVANCE TO THE VOLTURNO**
15 September–6 October 1943

ALLIED ROUTES OF ADVANCE
GERMAN FRONT LINE, 20 SEP
GERMAN FRONT LINE, 6 OCT
ELEVATIONS IN METERS

0   100   300   600   1000   1500 AND ABOVE

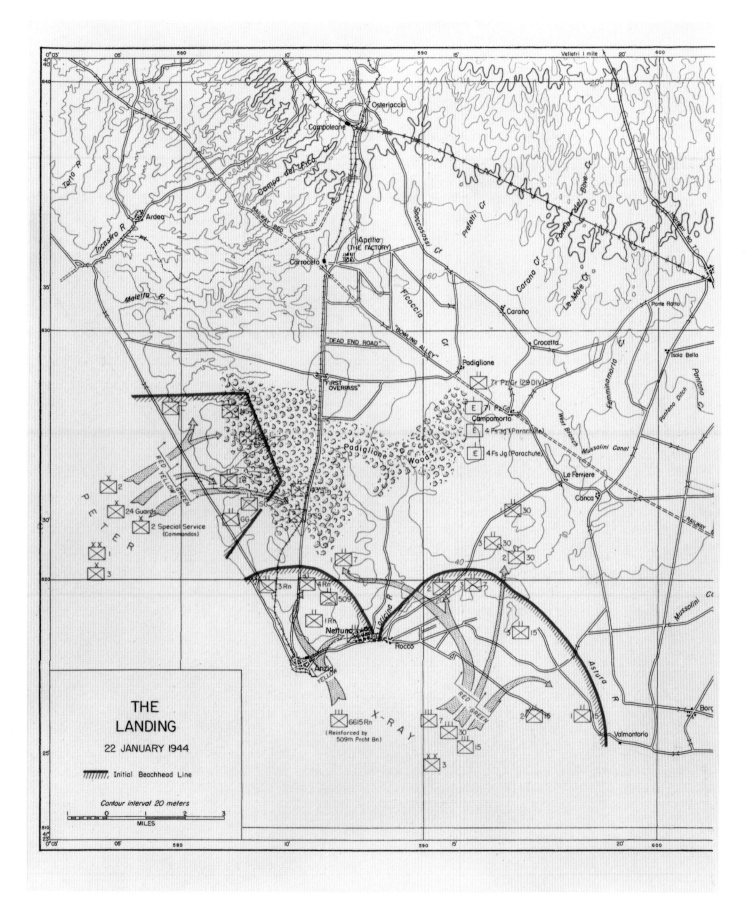

THE
LANDING

22 JANUARY 1944

///////. Initial Beachhead Line

Contour interval 20 meters

MILES

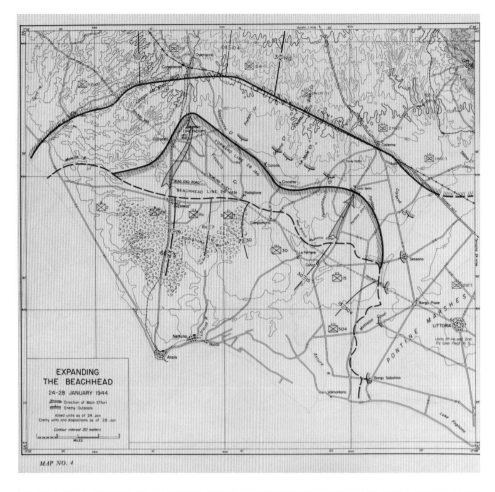

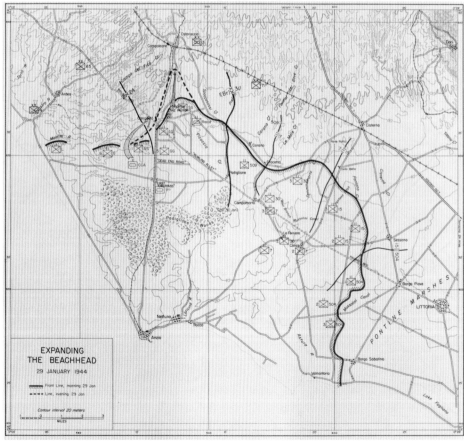

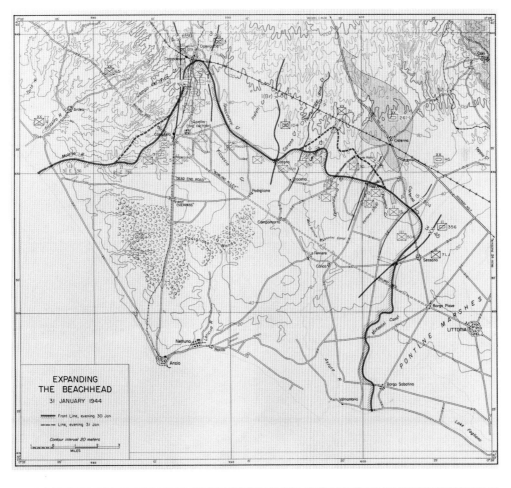

EXPANDING
THE BEACHHEAD
31 JANUARY 1944

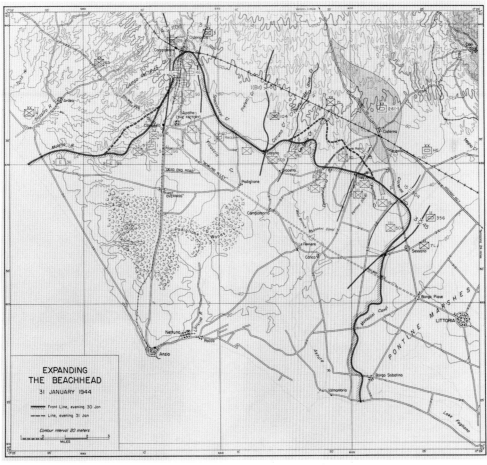

EXPANDING
THE BEACHHEAD
31 JANUARY 1944

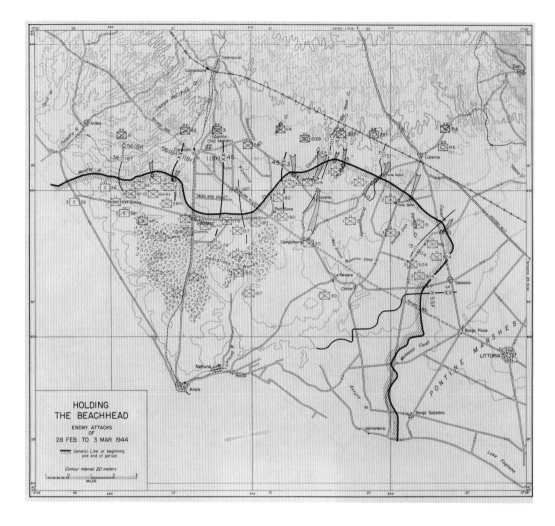

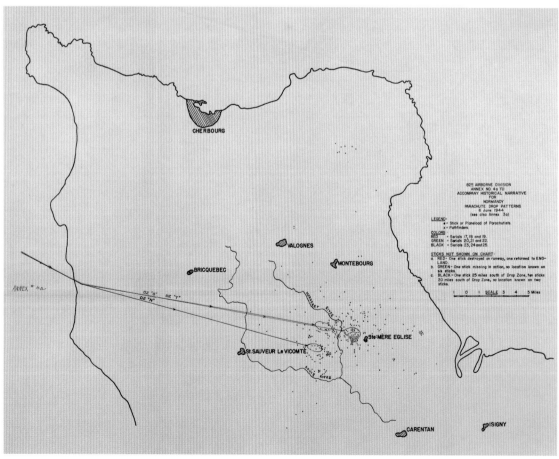

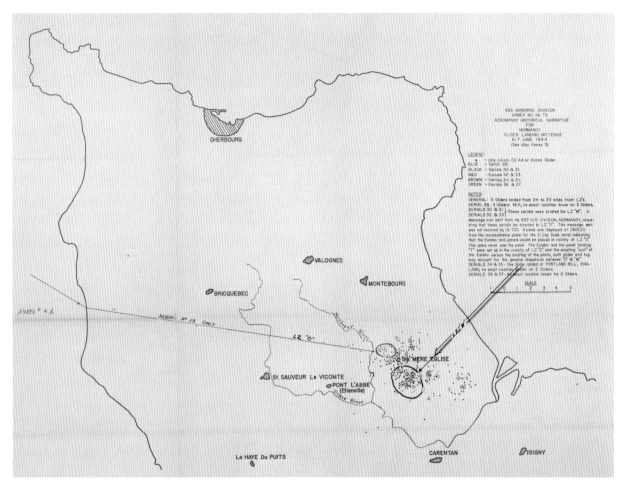

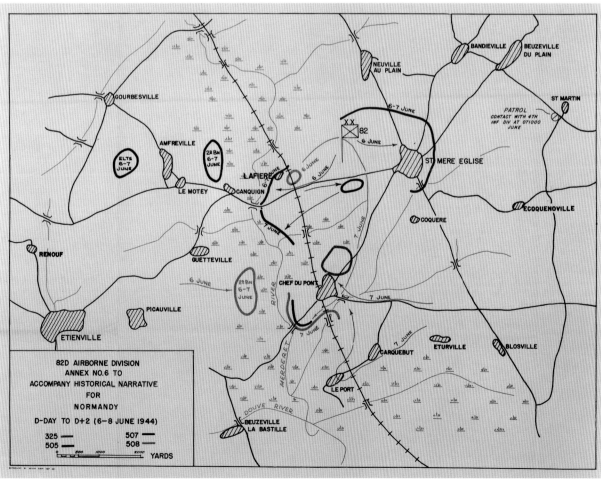

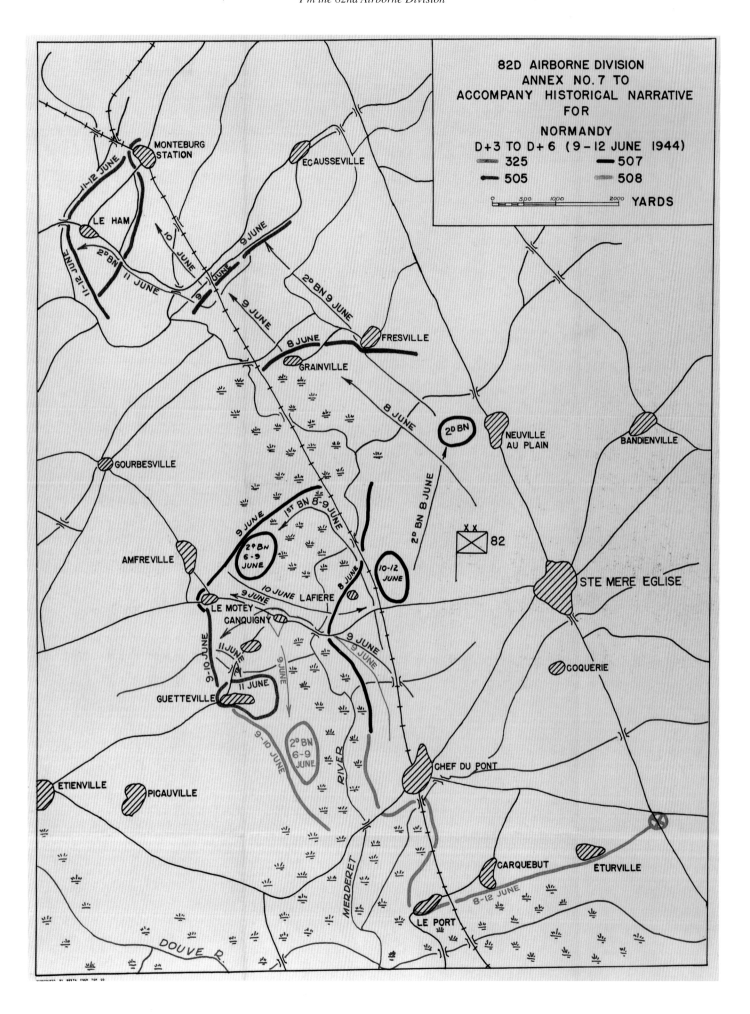

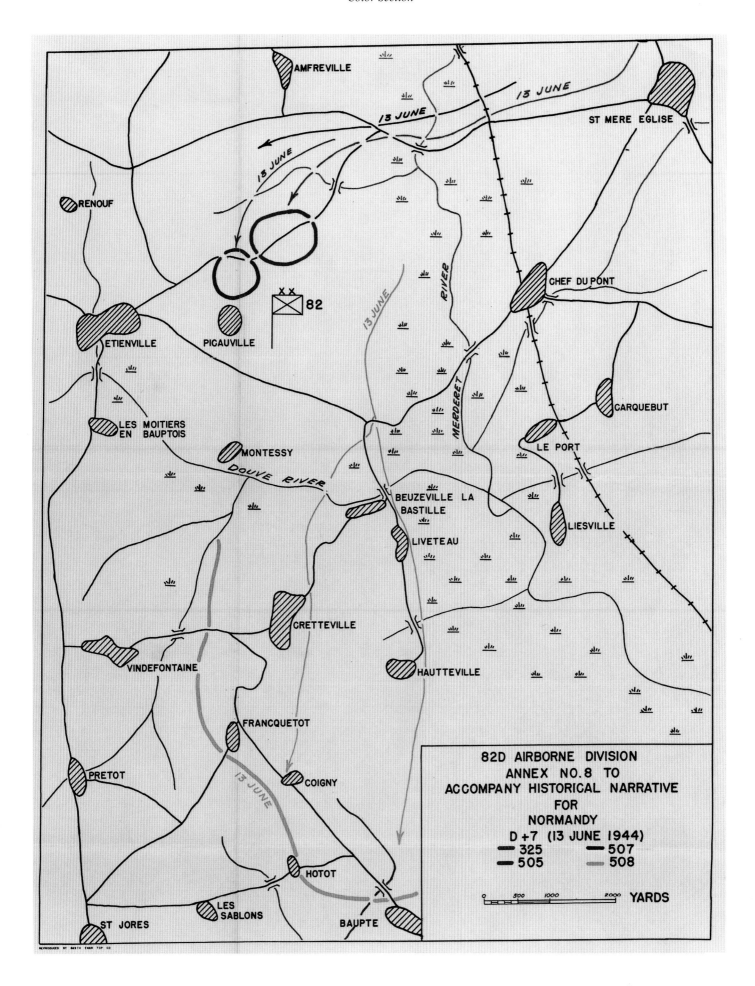

AMFREVILLE

13 JUNE

13 JUNE

13 JUNE

ST MERE EGLISE

RENOUF

XX 82

ETIENVILLE

PICAUVILLE

CHEF DU PONT

RIVER

13 JUNE

CARQUEBUT

LES MOITIERS
EN BAUPTOIS

MERDERET

LE PORT

MONTESSY

DOUVE RIVER

BEUZEVILLE LA
BASTILLE

LIESVILLE

LIVETEAU

CRETTEVILLE

VINDEFONTAINE

HAUTTEVILLE

FRANCQUETOT

13 JUNE

PRETOT

COIGNY

**82D AIRBORNE DIVISION
ANNEX NO. 8 TO
ACCOMPANY HISTORICAL NARRATIVE
FOR
NORMANDY**
D+7 (13 JUNE 1944)
━━ 325   ━━ 507
━━ 505   ━━ 508

HOTOT

LES
SABLONS

0   500   1000   2000  **YARDS**

ST JORES

BAUPTE

REPRODUCED BY 663TH ENGR TOP CO

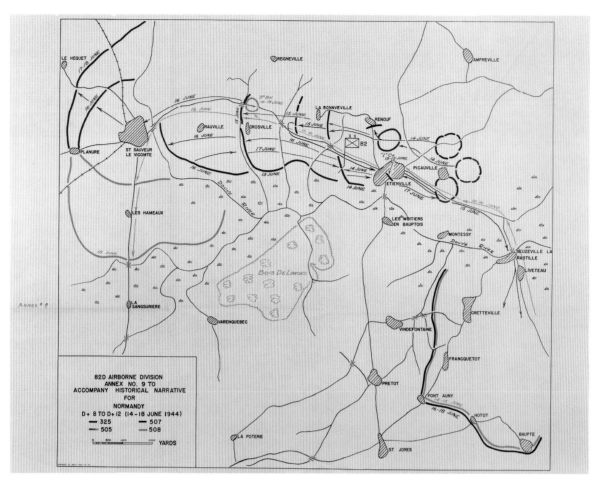

82D AIRBORNE DIVISION
ANNEX NO. 9 TO
ACCOMPANY HISTORICAL NARRATIVE
FOR
NORMANDY
D+ 8 TO D+ 12 (14-18 JUNE 1944)

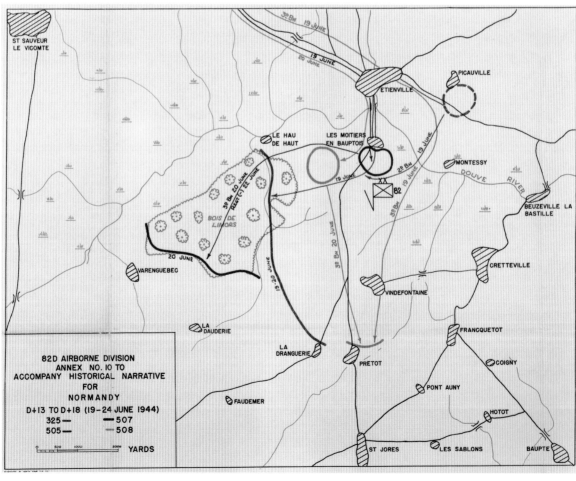

82D AIRBORNE DIVISION
ANNEX NO. 10 TO
ACCOMPANY HISTORICAL NARRATIVE
FOR
NORMANDY
D+13 TO D+18 (19-24 JUNE 1944)

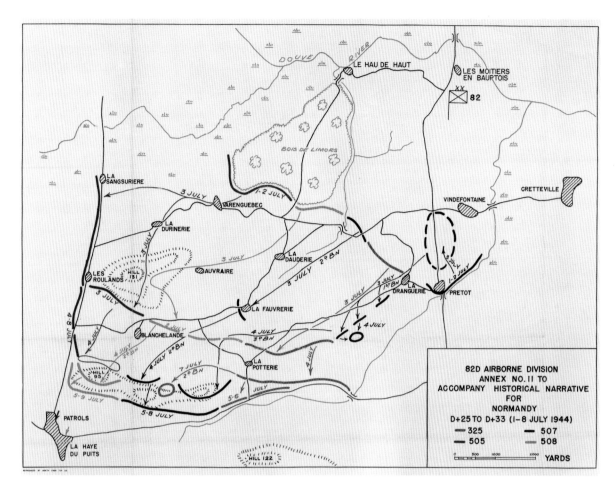

*Troopers of C Company, 307th Airborne Engineer Battalion. (L to R) Looker, Blount, Schnitski, and Corbin. Holland, October-November 1944) (Courtesy Al Nemeth)*

*1SG Kratch, C Company, 307th Airborne Engineer Battalion, salutes Captain Harris in Holland, October-November 1944. (Courtesy Al Nemeth)*

*"Old Men" in C Company, 307th Airborne Engineer Battalion, Holland, October-November 1944. (Courtesy Al Nemeth)*

*The 1st Platoon, C Company, 307th Airborne Engineer Battalion, in Holland, October-November 1944. (Courtesy Al Nemeth)*

*The 2nd Platoon, C Company, 307th Airborne Engineer Battalion in Holland, October-November 1944. (Courtesy Al Nemeth)*

*"Old Men" of 2nd Platoon, C Company, 307th Airborne Engineer Battalion, Holland, October-November 1944. (Courtesy Al Nemeth)*

*The 2nd Platoon, C Company, 307th Airborne Engineer Battalion prepare to board trucks in Holland, October-November 1944. (Courtesy Al Nemeth)*

*The 3rd Platoon, C Company, 307th Airborne Engineer Battalion, Holland, October-November 1944. (Courtesy Al Nemeth)*

*Troopers of the 307th Airborne Engineer Battalion in Holland, October-November 1944. (Courtesy Al Nemeth)*

*The Band plays while troopers of the 307th Airborne Engineer Battalion relax in the background. Holland, November 1944. (Courtesy Al Nemeth)*

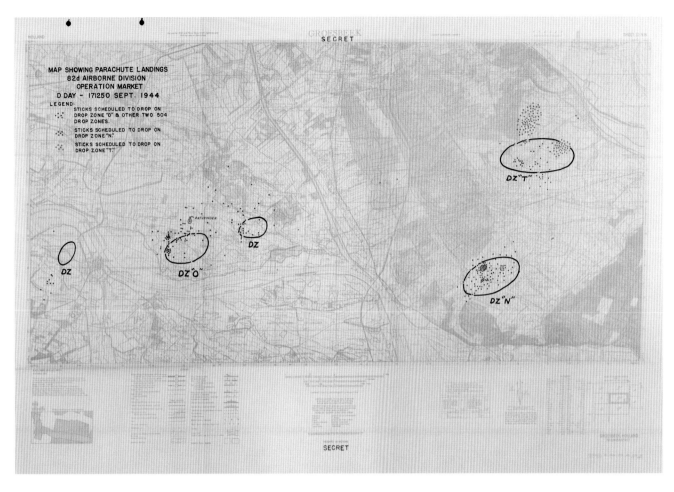

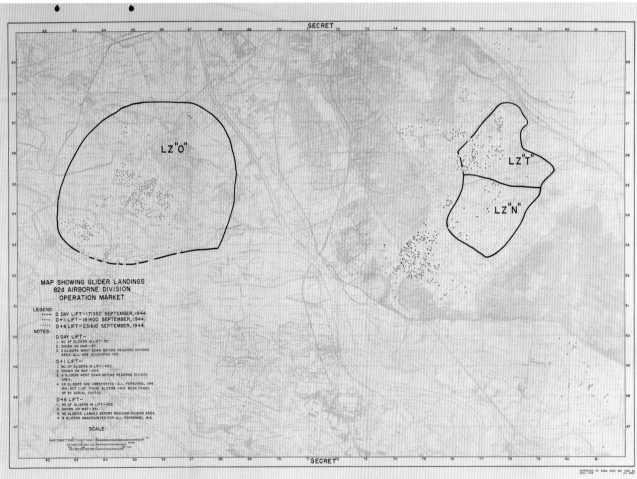

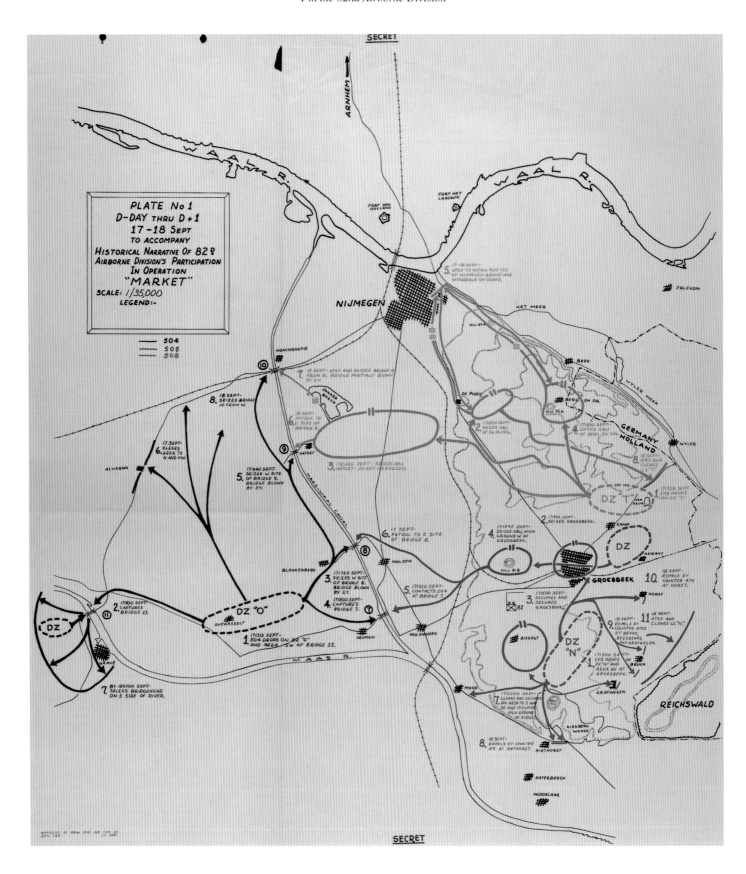

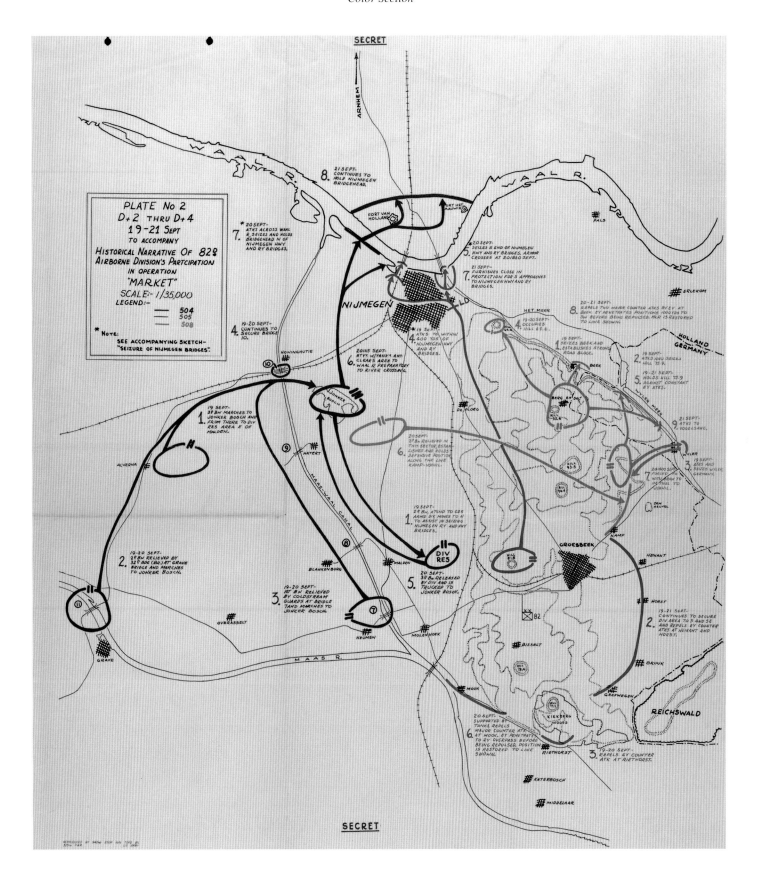

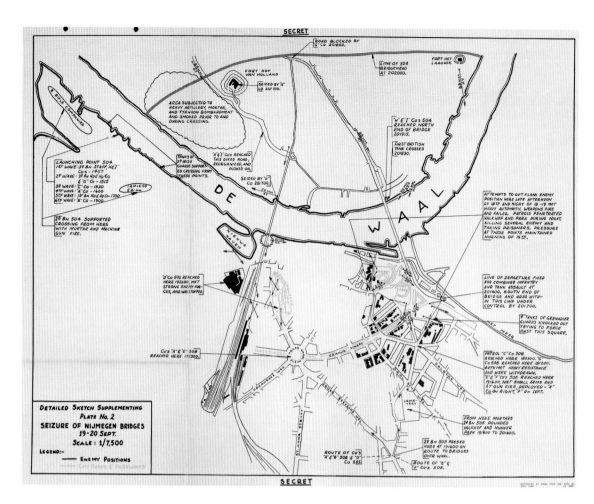

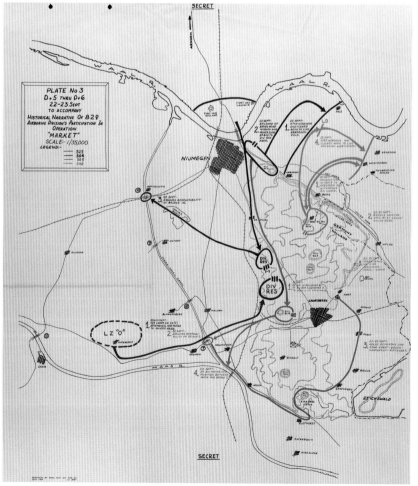

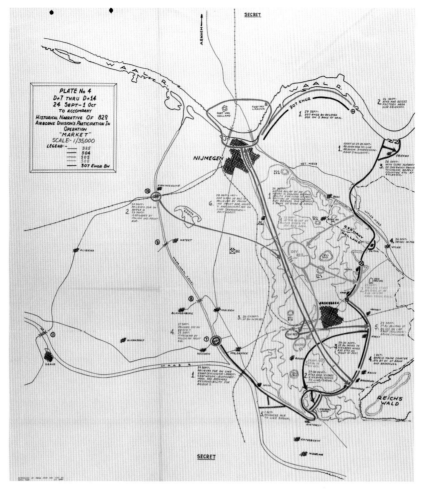

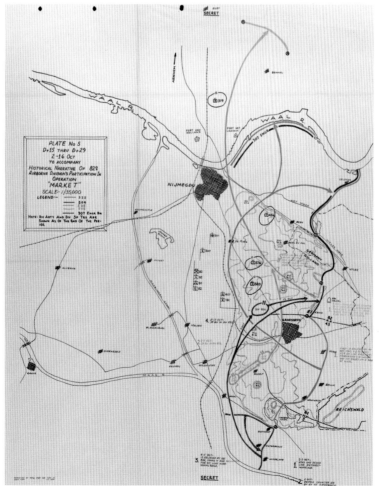

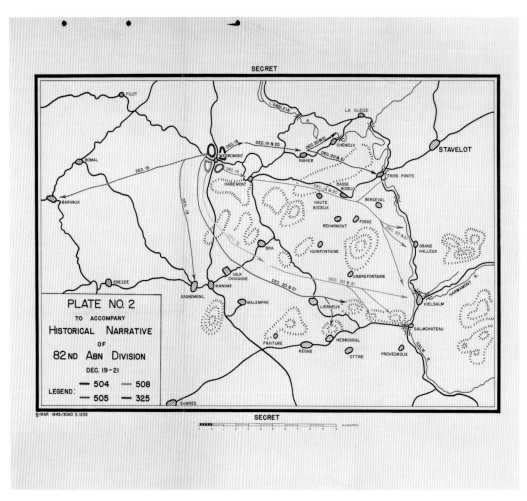

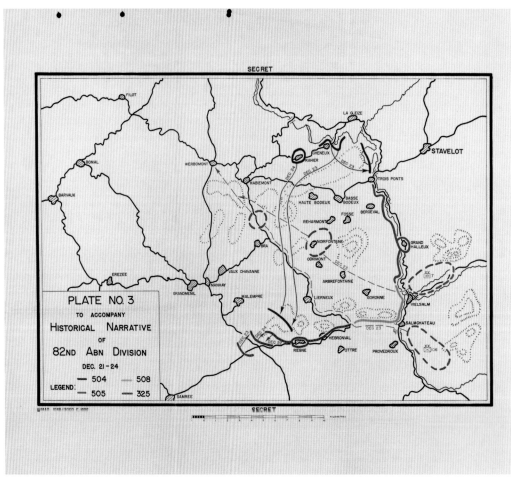

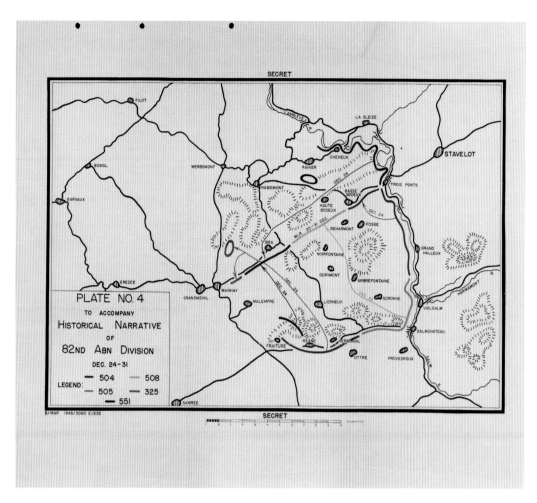

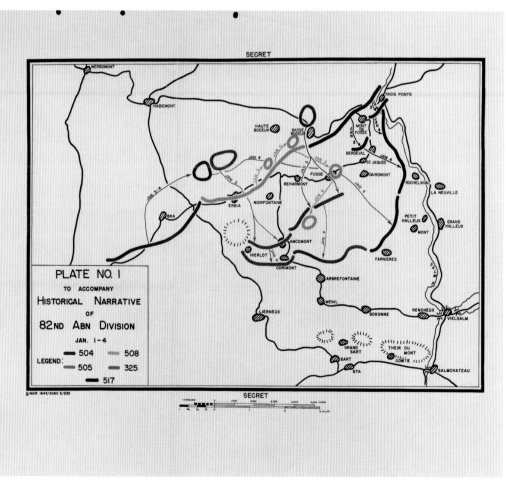

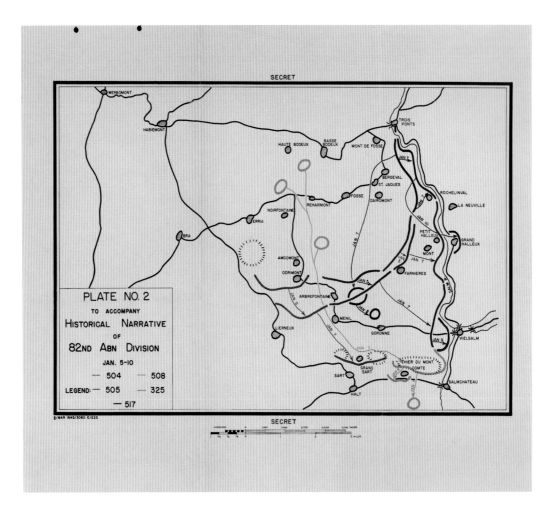

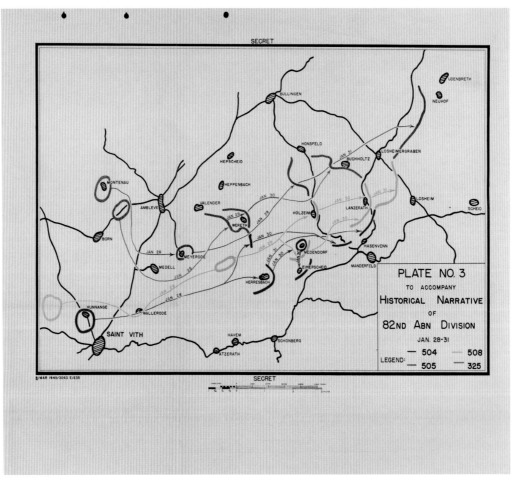

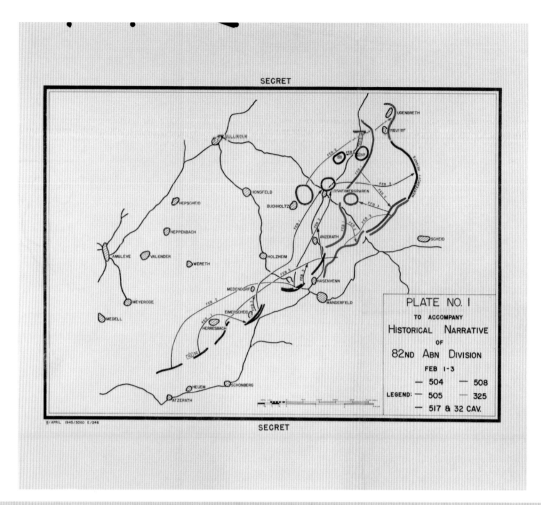

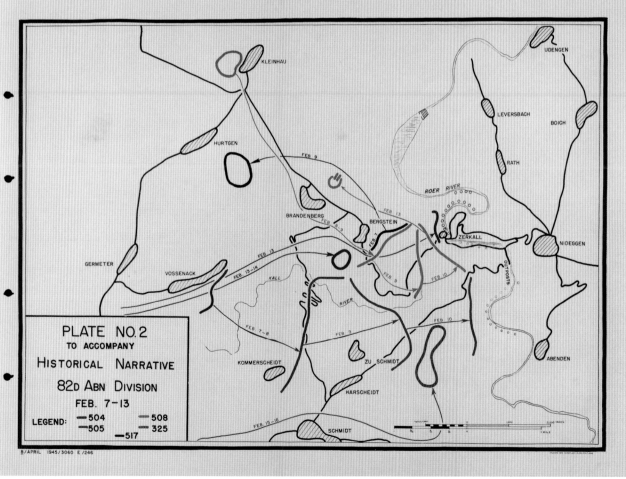

Left: *Victory edition of the 82nd Airborne Division newspaper.*

Right: *Lieutenant John Holabird, C Company, 307th Airborne Engineer Battalion near Ludwigslust, Germany, May 1945. (Courtesy Al Nemeth)*

Opposite
Top: *Troopers of the 307th Airborne Engineer Battalion with Soviet troops near Ludwigslust, Germany, May 1945. Note the battalion helmet marking with jump wings below the windshield.*

Bottom: *POWs of the German 21st Army at Ludwigslust, Germany, 2 May 1945.*

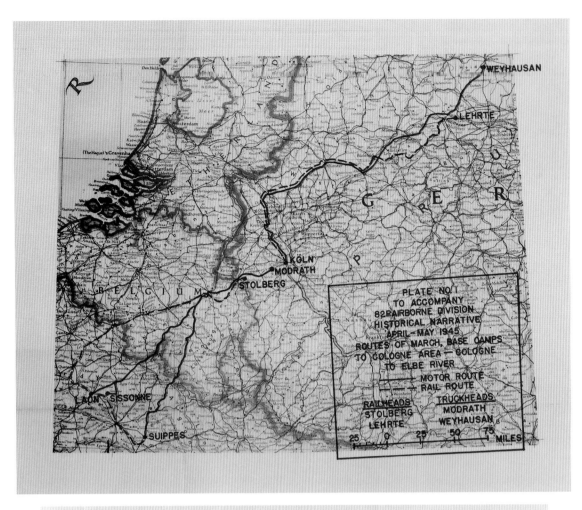

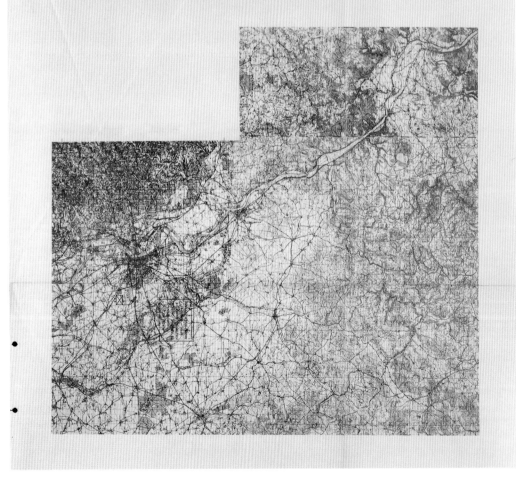

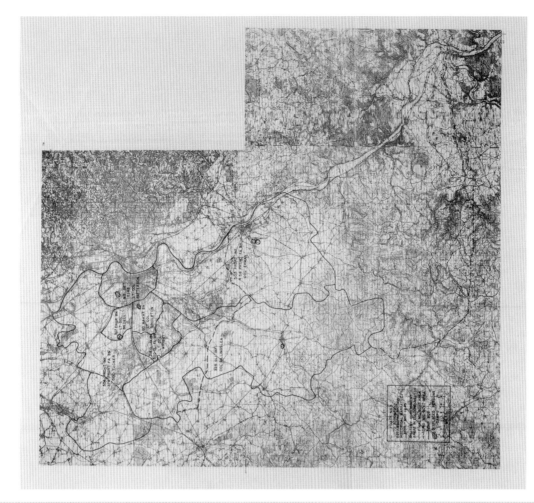

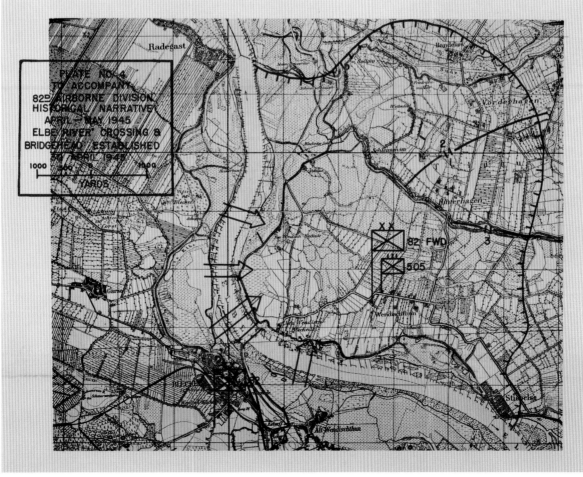

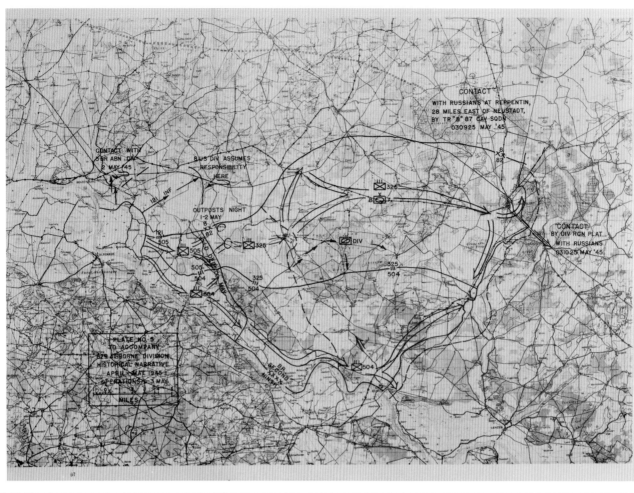

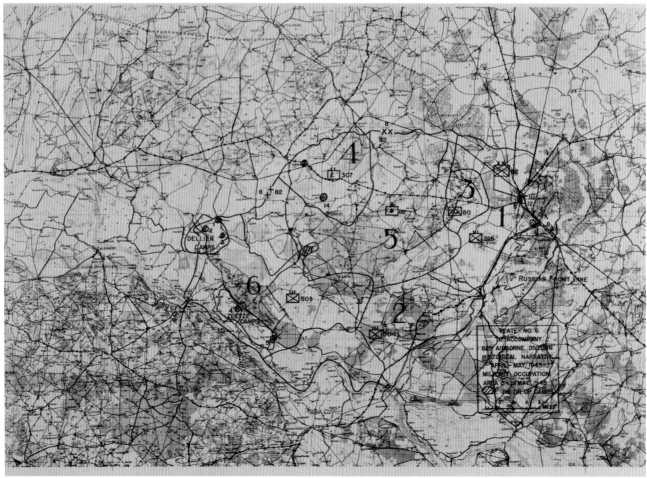

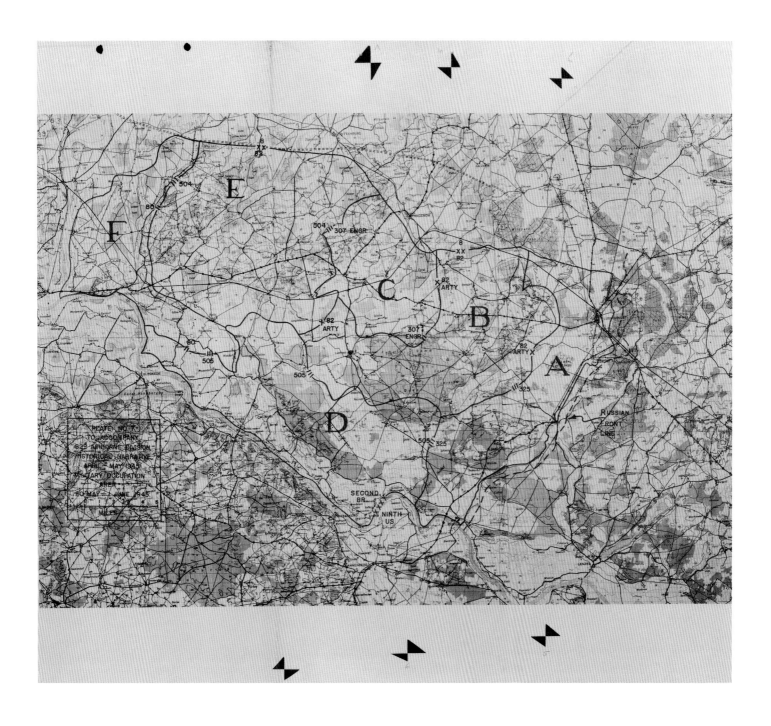

# Appendices

**Appendix 1: Appointment of a Committee to Study Airborne Tactics, Technique, and Training**

HEADQUARTERS 82ND AIRBORNE DIVISION
Office of the Division Commander

Camp Claiborne, Louisiana
September 4, 1942

SUBJECT: Appointment of a Committee to Study Airborne Tactics, Technique, and Training.

TO: Commanding General, Airborne Command, Ft. Bragg, N.C.

1. Much has yet to be done in the preparation of field manuals, and in the establishment of tactical doctrine and methods for the employment of airborne troops. FM31-30 "Tactics and Technique of Airborne Troops" is extremely brief and contains little regarding the use of glider troops. Part 2 of that manual covers the technique of parachute troops quite thoroughly, but leaves much to be desired regarding the tactical employment of such troops.

2. It is believed that studies should be initiated with minimum delay in the preparation of written instructions covering tactics, technique, and training of airborne divisions. This text should be complete and thorough, and should cover the technique and employment of all the various units in the airborne division down to and including squads. Initially, these texts might well be published in the form of training memorandums.

3. It is recommended that a Board of Officers be appointed by the Commanding General, Airborne Command for the purpose of studying and codifying the tactics, technique, and training of airborne divisions; that this Board be composed of one officer from the Airborne Command, one from each of the Airborne Divisions, and an officer from the Army Air Forces; and that this Board be convened at Ft. Bragg, North Carolina, subsequent to the transfer of the Airborne Divisions to that station. Officers recommended to represent the Divisions; for the 82nd Airborne Division, Brigadier General William M. Miley; for the 101st Airborne Division, Brigadier General Don Pratt.

4. The Commanding General of the 101st Airborne Division concurs in this letter.

M.B. Ridgway
Major General, U.S. Army,
Commanding.

The above memorandum, created only three weeks after the designation of the 82nd as an airborne division, shows the beginning of the growth of the airborne effort. Shortly, a number of charts and training memorandums were published by Airborne Command. It demonstrates the impact Ridgway was to have upon the airborne forces.

**Appendix 2: The All American Soldier by SGT Carl Sigman**

*We're All-American*
*And Proud to be*
*For We're the soldiers of Liberty*
*Some ride the gliders through the enemy*
*Others are sky paratroopers*

*We're All-American*
*And fight we will*
*Till all the guns of the foe are still*
*Airborne from skies of blue*
*We're coming through*
*Make your jumps, take your bumps*
*Let's Go!*

*Put on boots – your parachutes*
*Get all those gliders ready to attack today*
*For we'll be gone*
*Into the dawn*
*To fight 'em all the Eighty-Second way. Yes.*

### Appendix 3: A Paratrooper's Prayer

*Almighty God, Our Heavenly Father; Who art above us and beneath us, within us and around us; Drive from the minds of our paratroops any fear of the space in which Thou art ever present. Give them confidence in the strength of Thine Everlasting arms to uphold them. Endue them with clear minds and pure hearts that they may participate worthily in the victory which this nation must achieve in Thy name and through Thy will. Make them hardy soldiers of our country as well as of Thy Son, Our Savior, Jesus Christ, Amen.*

Chaplain George B. Wood
England, June 1944

### Appendix 4: Report of Loss of Aircraft to Friendly Fire over Sicily

HEADQUARTERS 82D AIRBORNE DIVISION
Office of the Division Commander

A.P.O. 469, U.S. Army Forces
August 2, 1943

SUBJECT: Reported Loss of Transport Planes and Personnel due to
Friendly Fire.

1. One hundred forty-four planes, C-47 type, of the 52nd Wing, Troop Carrier Command, loaded Combat Team 504 (less Third Battalion, 504th Parachute Infantry) and took off from the KAIROUAN area for a drop zone on the emergency landing field near GELA, SICILY, on the night of July 11/12, 1943. Twenty-three of these planes failed to return. Of these 23, the wreckage of the majority has since been identified. The others are still missing.

2. Investigations still continuing have disclosed beyond question that some of these losses were the result of fire delivered upon the planes by Allied Forces, both ground and sea. Evidence not yet evaluated indicates that some were destroyed by hostile aircraft, which were operating in the destination area of these C-47's at the time of their arrival therein. An attack by hostile bombers against our naval vessels just off the beaches was actually in progress at that time.

3. The loss of life is not yet accurately known. A few individuals continue to report in who either jumped before their plane crashed, or survived the crash. These deplorable losses demand the most searching investigation, in part to fix responsibility, but of much greater importance, to determine causes and prevent any possibility of recurrence.

4. The problem of eliminating the possibility of aircraft in flight and personnel after landing being fired upon by friendly forces was early recognized, and the following measures taken in an effort to solve it.

a. In early June, more than a month prior to the operation, the matter was presented to Major General BROWING, British Army, then acting as Airborne Advisor both to the Commander-in-Chief, Allied Forces, and to the Commanding General, Force 141. Presentation was made jointly by Brigadier General P.L. WILLIAMS, commanding the Troop Carrier Command, Colonel H.L. CLARK, commanding the 52nd Wing, and me. We were informed that the Navy would give no assurance that fire would not be delivered upon aircraft approaching within range of its vessels at night, the reason stated being that while fire from men-of-war could be controlled, fire from many miscellaneous merchant vessels and small craft included in the various convoys was impossible to control.

(1.) In spite of this reply, the matter was repeatedly represented.

(2.) One of these occasions was a meeting in the office of Air Commodore FOSTER, on the day following the conference at Headquarters, Force 141, at which General EISENHOWER presided. The date was June 22, 1943. Again, the reply was that the matter had been presented to the Navy, with the same result. The morning of the day following the conference alluded to above, I presented a note in longhand to Major General KEYES, Chief of Staff, Force 343, inviting attention to this situation and Stating that unless satisfactory assurances were obtained from the Navy, I would recommend against the dispatch of airborne troop movements. General KEYES at once initiated action on this memorandum, and a day or two later I was informed that the Naval Commander-In-Chief, MEDITERRANEAN, had given instructions in the sense desired.

(3.) Shortly before this time, Major General J.M. SWING was designated by the Commander-in-Chief, Allied Forces, as a special advisor to him on airborne matters, and this question of preventing the possibility of fire of friendly forces was at once presented to him by me.

(4.) Due largely to General SWING's energetic and prompt action, an agreement was reached with the Naval authorities concerned whereby they undertook to insure that if our air transport movements followed certain designated routes the fire of friendly forces would be withheld.

(5.) There still being some uncertainty on this matter, I personally mentioned it to the Allied Commander-in-Chief, General EISENHOWER, and to the Commanding General, Northwest African Air Force, Lieutenant General SPAATZ, on the afternoon of 2 July 1943, when they visited the KAIROUAN area where my Division was then assembled around its departure airfields. The Commander-in Chief made instant reply that he thought the desired action could be taken.

(6.) As a result of all of the foregoing efforts, categorical instructions, a copy of which is appended and marked annex A, were broadcast to all participating Naval Forces by radio by Allied Force Headquarters on 6 July 1943.

b. Identical instructions were ordered disseminated by the Commanding General, Force 343, on the same date, to ground forces participating in the assault, and the same instructions were repeated at least once between the time radio silence was broken, just prior to the assault, and 11 July 1943. A copy of the orders issued by the Commanding General, Seventh Army, is attached, marked annex B, and a copy of an order again directing attention to these instructions is attached, marked annex C.

c. At least six weeks prior to this operation the danger of our parachutists being fired upon by friendly forces upon landing was recognized. The problem was then discussed with the staff of the First Infantry Division, in whose zone it was contemplated our parachute elements would drop. Detachments of our parachute elements in their jump uniforms were sent to the First Division, and great care was taken with the Third Infantry Division and the Forty-Fifth Infantry Division, whose zones of action had been selected as a possible alternate operation area for our parachute units.

d. The Commanding General of anti-aircraft units to participate in this operation was early informed, and requested to insure that his troops were able to identify the C-47 plane and the CG 4-A glider. He requested silhouettes and was informed that the 82d Airborne Division had none, but that the C-47 was contained in training manuals.

e. On the afternoon of 11 July 1943, four to five hours prior to the scheduled arrival of the airborne movement, to which this memorandom relates, I personally went to the gun crews of at least six pairs of coast artillery ant-aircraft weapons, a few hundred yards from the beach in the vicinity of the Command Post of the First Infantry Division, to ask whether or not warning had been received of the approach that night of aircraft bearing friendly parachute troops. In all but one case the reply was affirmative. I then contacted an officer of the 103d Coast Artillery Ant-Aircraft, who told me there was a conference of the officers of anti-aircraft units in that area scheduled to be held shortly, and that he would see that the commanders concerned were once more duly warned.

5. Captain HARRISON, 504th Parachute Infantry, who rode in the lead plane of the lead serial on the night of 11 July 1943, reports his formation as on course and unmolested until it had crossed the coastline of SICILY and had been flying overland for about one minute. In substance his evidence then states that he saw one gun open fire on the formation, and that this seemed to be the signal for many others to open fire, both from the beach and from ships offshore. The evidence further shows that each succeeding serial received heavier fire that those preceding it. The last, the one bearing the 376th Parachute Field Artillery, received the heaviest fire, and suffered the greatest losses.

6. I was present on the edge of the designated drop zone, the emergency landing field at FARELLO, three miles east of GELA, when the C-47's began coming over. I personally saw fire directed upon these ships, red tracers being used, but could not, because of the intervening hills, determine whether they came from sea or land. As parachutists jumped and began landing, I went out on the field and shortly met the Combat Team Commander, Colonel R. H. TUCKER, 504th Parachute Infantry.

7. Later evidence shows that not only was friendly fire the cause of the destruction of many of our transport planes with loss of life, but that such fire was delivered from the ground upon descending parachutists, who were killed before or upon landing. Positive evidence also indicates that elements of the Forty-Fifth Infantry Division had a different countersign from that officillay furnished our parachute personnel. This, too, I verified from Colonel TUCKER within a few minutes of his landing, for he then had the same countersign (ULYSSES GRANT) as I. It was incorrect. At this time in the operation each Division ashore was authorized to designate and actually did designate its own sign and countersign.

8. Captain DYER, United States Navy, with whom I talked at Seventh Army Headquarters two or three days after this occurrence, in the presence of Lieutenant General O. N. BRADLEY, stated that Naval Forces off LICATA had shot down at least two of our transports because they had flown directly into the illuminated area of naval flares during actual attack by hostile bombers.

9. In this same meeting Lieutenant General BRADLEY informed me that his investigation up to that time had disclosed that enemy action had accounted for some of our planes, and that evidence indicated that some of our parachutists had been fired upon and killed by Quartermaster Troops of the Forty-Fifth Infantry Division.

10. <u>Conclusion.</u>

a. The danger of having friendly fire delivered upon our Airborne Forces was recognized, and strenuous efforts were made to eliminate it long before the operation was to take place.

b. The critical nature of the problem was early recognized by both Troop Carrier Command and the 82d Airborne Division.

c. The views of these two elements were not shared by Higher Echelons, particularly in the Naval Command.

d. The possibility, which later became a fact, that the Troop Carrier Command would disperse our parachutist over the zones of action of all three infantry divisions; that friendly fire, as delivered, would result in breaking up the transport plane formations and force them out of the designated safety lane; and that the sign and countersign, as a means of recognition once they were on the ground, might be changed too late for parachutists to be informed, were not visualized.

e. Neither was there visualized the possibility of the arrival of the troop carrier formations in their destination zone at the time of the actual attacks on our forces there by hostile aircraft.

f. The delivery of friendly fire upon our own aircraft, in the light of all this and all other past experience, can be guaranteed only by positive orders that during the anticipated hours of airborne movements fire of all kinds against all aircraft must be prohibited in a zone sufficiently large to insure that even planes that go astray shall not be subjected to this hazard.

g. The responsibility for loss of life and material resulting from this operation is so divided, so difficult to fix with impartial justice, and so questionable of ultimate value to the service because of the acrimonious debates which would follow efforts to hold responseble persons or services to account, that disciplinary action is of doubtful wisdom.

h. Deplorable as is the loss of life which occurred, I believe that the lessons now learned could have been driven home in no other way, and that these lessons provide a sound basis for the belief that recurrence can be avoided.

i. The losses are part of the inevitable price of war in human life.

M.B. RIDGWAY
Major General, U.S. Army,
Commanding.
3 Inclosures.

## Appendix 5: Surrender of the Hungarian Cavalry, Twenty-First German Army

The following is a copy of the original letter, written in both Hungarian and English, presented to Major General James M. Gavin on May 2, 1945:

We are on the side of the Americans since the 2nd of April. Till this time we were disarmed in German captivity. We want to give all our help to America. I have 600 men and 250 horses. We have with us our saved clothing, Hungarian women and children. We haven't any food, this was also taken from us by the Germans. As till now, the Americans handled us differently as the Germans, I ask removed for the same. The troupe is disciplined, so we offer our services and all given orders will be done. We ask for the transport over the Elbe as soon as possible, to get into ordered circumstances after a long period of suffrences. I ask to keep our cause in good will because we have been waiting 5 years for the moment to be united you. God may help America and England.

Commander of the Hungarian Cavalry.

## Appendix 6: Unit Call Signs

82nd Airborne Division – CHAMPION
505th PIR – CHALLENGE
504th PIR – CIDER
325th GIR – CHESTNUT
Division Artillery – CHANNEL
319th GFAB – CHOPSTICK
320th GFAB – CHARCOAL
376th PFAB – CIRCLE
456th PFAB – CHECKER
80th AA Bn. – CLASSIC

82nd Abn. Signal Co. – CHAMPAGNE
307th Abn. Engineer Bn. CLOVER
307th Abn. Medical Co. – CHEERFUL
407th Abn. QM Co. – CLOCKER
782nd Abn. Ordnance Co. CHINA

2nd Airborne Brigade – HADDOCK
507th PIR – HARDWARE
508th PIR – HARNESS

## Appendix 7: WWII Medal of Honor Recipients

**Private First Class Charles N. DeGlopper, Company C, 325th Glider Infantry**
*Merderet River at la Fiere, France, 9 June 1944*
He was a member of Company C, 325th Glider Infantry, on 9 June 1944 advancing with the forward platoon to secure a bridgehead across the Merderet River at la Fiere, France. At dawn the platoon had penetrated an outer line of machine guns and riflemen, but in so doing had become cut off from the rest of the company. Vastly superior forces began a decimation of the stricken unit and put in motion a flanking maneuver which would have completely exposed the American platoon in a shallow roadside ditch where it had taken cover. Detecting this danger, Private DeGlopper volunteered to support his comrades by fire from his automatic rifle while they attempted a withdrawal through a break in a hedgerow forty yards to the rear. Scorning a concentration of enemy automatic weapons and rifle fire, he walked from the ditch onto the road in full view of the Germans, and sprayed the hostile positions with assault fire. He was wounded, but continued firing. Struck again, he started to fall; and yet his grim determination and valiant fighting spirit could not be broken. Kneeling in the roadway, weakened by his grievous wounds, he leveled his heavy weapon against the enemy and fired burst after burst until killed outright. He was successful in drawing the enemy action away from his fellow soldiers, who continued the fight from a more advantageous position and established the first bridgehead over the Mederet. In the area where he made his intrepid stand his comrades later found the ground strewn with dead Germans and many machineguns and automatic weapons which he had knocked out of action. Private DeGlopper's gallant sacrifice and unflinching heroism while facing unsurmountable [sic.] odds were in great measure responsible for a highly important tactical victory in the Normandy Campaign.

**Private John R. Towle, Company C, 504th Parachute Infantry**
*Near Oosterhout, Holland, 21 September 1944*
For conspicuous gallantry and intrepidity at the risk of his life above and beyond the call of duty on 21 September 1944, near Oosterhout, Holland. The rifle company in which Private Towle served as a rocket launcher gunner was occupying a defensive position in the west sector of the recently established Nijmegen bridgehead when a strong enemy force of approximately one hundred infantry supported by two tanks and a half-track formed for a counter attack. With full knowledge of the diastous consequence resulting not only to his company but to the entire bridgehead by an enemy breakthrough, Private Towle immediately and without orders left his fox hole and moved two hundred yards in the face of intense small-arms fire to a position on an exposed dike roadbed. From this precarious position Private Towle fired his rocket launcher at and hit both tanks to his immediate front. Armored skirting on both tanks prevented penetration by the projectile, but both vehicles withdrew slightly damaged. Still under intense fire and fully exposed to the enemy, Private Towle the engaged a nearby house which nine Germans had entered and were using as a strong point, and with one round killed all nine. Hurriedly replenishing his supply of ammunition, Private Towle, motivated only by his high conception of duty which called for the destruction of the enemy at any cost, then rushed approximately one hundred and twenty-five yards through grazing enemy fire to an exposed position from which he could engage the enemy half-track with his rocket launcher. While in a kneeling position preparatory to firing on the enemy vehicle, Private Towle was mortally wounded by a mortar shell. By his heroic tenacity, at the price of his life, Private Towle saved the lives of many of his comrades and was directly instrumental in breaking up the enemy counterattack.

**First Sergeant Leonard A. Funk, Jr., Company C, 508th Parachute Infantry**
*Holzheim, Belgium, 29 January 1945*
Citation: He distinguished himself by gallant, intrepid actions against the enemy. After advancing fifteen miles in a driving snowstorm, the American force prepared to attack through waist-deep drifts. The company executive officer became a casualty, and Sergeant Funk immediately assumed his duties, forming headquarters soldiers into a combat unit for an assault in the face of direct artillery shelling and harassing fire from the right flank. Under his skillful and courageous leadership, this miscellaneous group and the Third Platoon attacked fifteen houses, cleared them and took thirty prisoners without suffering a casualty. The fierce drive of Company C quickly overran Holzheim, netting some eighty prisoners, who were placed under a four-man guard, all that could be spared, while the rest of the under-strength unit went about mopping up isolated points of resistance. An enemy patrol, by means of a ruse, succeeded in capturing the guards and freeing the prisoners, and had begun preparations to attack Company C from the rear when Sergeant Funk walked around the building and into their midst. He was ordered to surrender by a German officer who pushed a machine pistol into his stomach. Although overwhelmingly outnumbered and facing almost certain death, Sergeant Funk, pretending to comply with the order, began slowly to unsling his submachine gun from his shoulder and then, with lightening motion, brought the muzzle into line and riddled the German officer. He turned upon the other Germans, firing and shouting to the other Americans to seize the enemy's weapons. In the ensuing fight twenty-one Germans were killed, many wounded, and the remainder captured. Sergeant Funk's bold action and heroic disregard for his own safety were directly responsible for the recapture of a vastly superior enemy force, which, if allowed to remain free, could have taken the widespread units of Company C by surprise and endangered the entire attack plan.

## Appendix 8:Letter from MG Parks

U.S. Headquarters
Berlin District

Dear Gen. Gavin:
It is with pleasure that I welcome you and your splendid division to Berlin.

The officers and men of the Berlin District and First Airborne Army are delighted with General Eisenhower's decision to post your division in Berlin. There is a difficult job to be done here. No division is better qualified than the 82nd Airborne Division to do that job.

Personally, I think that your assignment to Berlin is a signal honor – an honor to be added to the division's illustrious battle record. The 82nd is well known as an outstanding combat division. All the world will be impressed with its conduct as the combat force representing the United States in the capital of defeated Germany

Again, welcome to the 82nd Airborne Division. We are happy to have it as a member of the garrison of Berlin.

Sincerely,
/s/t/ F.L.Parks,
Major General, USA,
Commanding.

## Appendix 9: Summary of Days in Combat Areas

(Note: The term "front line positions" is used below as any period of time in which a regimental combat team or larger group of the Division, whether or not detached from the Division, was in direct contact with enemy troops.)

| OPERATION | FRONT LINE POSITIONS | CORPS RESERVE | ARMY RESERVE | TOTAL |
|---|---|---|---|---|
| SICILY (HUSKY) | | | | 41 |
| (1) 10-14 July '43 | 5 | | | |
| 15-16 July '43 | | 2 | | |
| 17-24 July '43 | 8 | | | |
| (a) 25 July - 19 Aug. '43 | | | 26 | |
| Sub-Totals | (13) | (2) | (26) | (41) |
| ITALY | | | | 163 |
| Naples-Foggia (Avalanche Giant) | | | | |
| Rome-Arno (Shingle) | | | | |
| (2) 14-18 Sept. '43 | 5 | | | |
| (3) 16-25 Sept. '43 | 10 | | | |
| (4) 18-24 Sept. '43 | 7 | | | |
| (5) 25 Sept. - 2 Oct. '43 | 7 | | | |
| (6) 4 - 7 Oct. '43 | 4 | | | |
| (7) 27 Oct. - 25 Nov. '43 | 30 | | | |
| (8) 6 Dec. '43 - 1 Jan.'44 | 27 | | | |
| 9) 22 Jan. - 23 Mar. '44 | 62 | | | |
| (10)(b) 3 Oct. -19Nov.'43 | (net) | | 21 | |
| Net Sub-Totals | (142) | | (21) | (163) |
| NORMANDY (NEPTIUNE) | | | | 38 |
| 6 June - 8 July '44 | 33 | | | |
| 9 - 11 July '44 | | 3 | 2 | |
| 12 - 13 July '44 | | | | |
| Sub-Totals | (33) | (3) | (2) | (38) |

| OPERATION | FRONT LINE POSITIONS | CORPS RESERVE | ARMY RESERVE | TOTAL |
|---|---|---|---|---|
| HOLLAND (MARKET) | | | | 58 |
| (Rhineland) | | | | |
| 17 Sept. - 13 Nov. '44 | 58 | | | |
| | — | | | |
| | | | | |
| ARDENNES | | | | 63 |
| 18 Dec. '44 - 11 Jan. '45 | 25 | | | |
| 12 - 27 Jan. '45 | | 16 | | |
| 28 Jan. - 4 Feb. '45 | 8 | | | |
| 5 Feb. '45 | | 1 | | |
| 6 - 18 Feb. '45 | 13 | | | |
| | | | | |
| Sub-Totals | (46) | (17) | | (63) |
| | — | | | |
| | | | | |
| CENTRAL EUROPE | | | | |
| 4 -16 April '45 | 13 | | | 59 |
| (c) 17 - 25 April '45 | | 9 | | |
| 26 - 27 April '45 | | | 2 | |
| 28 April - 8 May '45 | 11 | | | |
| (d) 9 May - 1 June '45 | | 24 | | |
| | | | | |
| Sub-Totals | (24) | (33) | (2) | (59) |
| | | | | |
| GRAND TOTALS | 316 | 55 | 51 | 422 |

TOTALS DAYS IN COMBAT AREA - BY YEAR:
1943 — 141
1944 — 173
1945 — 108
TOTAL 422

TOTAL DAYS IN COMBAT AREA AS A RESULT OF

| AIRBORNE DEPLOYMENT | | GROUND DEPLOYMENT | |
|---|---|---|---|
| SICILY | 41 | ITALY | 143 |
| ITALY | 20 | ARDENNES | 63 |
| NORMANDY | 38 | CENTRAL | |
| HOLLAND | 58 | EUROPE | 59 |
| TOTAL | 157 | TOTAL | 265 |

NOTES
1. 505, 504 Prcht RCTs
2. 504, 505 Prcht RCTs3. 325 Gli RCT
4. Div on right flank of Fifth Army
5. Div on Sorrento Ridge and Naples Plain
6. 505 Prcht RCT on Volturno River.
7. 504 Prcht RCT in Isernia Sector.
8. 504 Prcht RCT in Venafro Sector.
9. 504 Prcht RCT on Anzio Beachhead.
10. Net, does not include periods 4-7 Oct '43 or 27 Oct. - 25 Nov. '43
a. Also occupational duty in Western Sicily.
b. Also occupational duty in Naples. Does not include periods 504 Prcht RCT was in Corps or Army reserve after Div proper left Italy.
c. Also occupational duty in Cologne, Germany, area.

"On the first day of the year of final victory in Europe, the Battalion was relieved of the attachment to VII Corps, 3rd Armored Division, and attached to XVIII Corps (Airborne), 82nd Airborne Division. These were truly fighting men. A squad of the 82nd Airborne Division Company will take on a German Battalion, and to assign any unit of the 82nd Airborne Division an objective is to know that the objective will be taken and held." (Excerpt from "Victory TD", the unit history of the 628th Tank Destroyer Battalion)

**Appendix 10: Casulties**

a. Average casualty rate: The 82nd Airborne Division occupied front line positions for a total of 316 days and suffered a total of 19,586 casualties of all types, an average of 61.98 casualties for each day, on the basis of computations made 28 May 1945.
1. An average of 4.85 men were missing in action, each day
2. An average of 39.88 men were wounded each day.
3. An average of 8.8. men were injured each day.
4. An average of 8.43 men were killed in action or died of wounds each day.

b. Casualties by campaign: Figures available as of 25 October 1945 show that only 106 individuals of the 82nd Airborne Division are still listed as "Missing in Action", all others listed earlier as "Missing" having been liberated from prison camps or legally declared dead. A tabulation of casualties on this basis, however, would not present a true picture of the Division's status during the particular campaign, and two sets of computations therefore are given below.

CAMPAIGN

| | MISSING IN ACTION | WOUNDED IN ACTION Not Rtd | Rtd | INJURED IN ACTION Not Rtd | Rtd | KILLED IN ACTION DIED OF WOUNDS |
|---|---|---|---|---|---|---|
| * SICILY | 48 | 474 | 336 | x | x | 197 |
| * ITALY | 73 | 1140 | 779 | x | x | 309 |
| * NORMANDY | 661 | 2373 | 1554 | 704 | 502 | 1142 |
| * HOLLAND | 622 | 1796 | 821 | 327 | 196 | 535 |
| **ARDENNES & RHINELAND | 101 | 2073 | 1036 | 609 | 364 | 440 |
| **CENTRAL EUROPE | 30 | 160 | 34 | 49 | 31 | 42 |
| TOTALS | 1535 | 8024 12,604 | 4580 | 1689 2,782 | 1093 | 2665 |

\* - Corrected to 12 December 1944
\*\* - Corrected to 28 May 1945
x - Figures not kept for these campaigns
Not Rtd - Did not return to Division
RTD - Returned to Division

Computations corrected on the basis of official reports received to 25 October 1945;

| CAMPAIGN | MISSING IN ACTION | KILLED IN ACTION OR DIED OF WOUNDS |
|---|---|---|
| SICILY | 12 | 206 |
| ITALY | 2 | 327 |
| NORMANDY | 0 | 1,282 |
| HOLLAND | 80 | 658 |
| ARDENNES & RHINELAND | 7 | 670 |
| CENTRAL EUROPE | 5 | 75 |
| TOTALS | 106 | 3,228 |

On the last day of its last campaign the 82nd Airborne Division liberated five of its soldiers who had been captured in Sicily and later had been "hired out" to German farmers as farm hands.

c. Casualties by unit (correct to 28 May 1945):

| UNIT | MIA | WOUNDED Not Rtd | Rtd | INJURED Not Rtd | Rtd | KIA or DOW |
|---|---|---|---|---|---|---|
| Div Hq | 4 | 11 | 11 | 9 | 4 | 4 |
| Div Hq Co | 1 | 15 | 10 | 9 | 7 | 17 |
| 82 Abn MP Plat | 5 | 4 | 2 | | | 1 |
| 325 Gli Inf | 190 | 1256 | 731 | 291 | 181 | 380 |

| | | | | | |
|---|---|---|---|---|---|
| 504 Prcht Inf | 208 | 1850 | 1122 | 125 | 85 | 522 |
| 505 Prcht Inf | 146 | 1760 | 1081 | 357 | 263 | 465 |
| 507 Prcht Inf | 337 | 526 | 270 | 96 | 56 | 251 |
| 508 Prcht Inf | 312 | 1280 | 665 | 446 | 284 | 551 |
| 2 Bn 401 Gli Inf | 165 | 630 | 274 | 109 | 56 | 141 |
| Hq & Hq Btry Div Arty | 44 | 15 | 9 | 2 | 2 | 1 |
| 319 Gli FA Bn | 44 | 75 | 45 | 51 | 37 | 36 |
| 320 Gli FA Bn | 49 | 48 | 30 | 37 | 24 | 33 |
| 376 Prcht FA Bn | 7 | 97 | 56 | 12 | 6 | 62 |
| 456 Prcht FA Bn | 1 | 104 | 65 | 16 | 8 | 44 |
| 80 Abn AA Bn | 17 | 91 | 57 | 46 | 40 | 42 |
| 307 Abn Engr Bn | 34 | 235 | 140 | 21 | 14 | 94 |
| 407 Abn QM Co | | 9 | 3 | | | |
| 307 Abn Med Co | 1 | 12 | 6 | 13 | 7 | 7 |
| 82 Abn Sig Co | 9 | 5 | 2 | 22 | 16 | 11 |
| 782 Abn Ord Maint Co | | 1 | 1 | 1 | 1 | |
| 82 Abn Rcn Plat | 5 | | | 6 | 2 | 3 |
| TOTALS | 1535 | 8024 | 4580 | 1689 | 1093 | 2665 |

NOTES:
1. The 507th Parachute Infantry was attached for the NORMANDY Campaign.
2. The 508th Parachute Infantry was attached for the NORMANDY, HOLLAND, ARDENNES & RHINELAND Campaigns.
3. The 2nd Battalion, 401st Glider Infantry, was attached to the 325th Glider Infantry (to give the 325th a total of three battalions) in the NORMANDY, HOLLAND, ARDENNES & RHINELAND Campaigns and was absorbed by the 325th on 1 March 1945.
4. Figures for the 82nd Parachute Maintenance Company (Provisional) are included in those for other Parachute units.

## Appendix 11: Awards and Decoration

### INDIVIDUAL DECORATIONS OF THE UNITED STATES OF AMERICA
### CONGRESSIONAL MEDAL OF HONOR

Private First Class Charles N. DeGlopper          325th Glider Infantry
  (Posthumously. Gallantry in Action in Normandy)
Private John R. Towle                        504th Parachute Infantry
  (Posthumously. Gallantry in Action in Holland)
First Sergeant Leonard A. Funk               508th Parachute Infantry
  (Gallantry in Action in the Ardennes)

### DISTINGUISHED SERVICE CROSS
*Denotes Oak Leaf Cluster also awarded

| NAME | RANK | UNIT |
|---|---|---|
| Atcheson, Robert B. | Major | 504th Parachute Infantry |
| Baldwin, Lewis N. | Cpl. | 456th Parachute Field Artillery Battalion |
| Bednarz, Walter J. | Cpl. | 508th Parachute Infantry |
| *Billingslea, Charles E. | Col. | 325th Glider Infantry |
| Clarke, James F. | 2d Lt. | 507th Parachute Infantry |
| Cook, Julian A. | Lt. Col. | 504th Parachute Infantry |
| Cynerys, Charles F. | Cpl. | 505th Parachute Infantry |
| Del Grippo, Daniel T. | Pfc. | 504th Parachute Infantry |
| Doerfler, Eugene A. | 1st Lt. | 505th Parachute Infantry |

| | | |
|---|---|---|
| Dunham, Don E. | Major | 504th Parachute Infantry |
| Dustin, Shelton W. | Sgt. | 504th Parachute Infantry |
| Fessler, John H. | S/Sgt. | 507th Parachute Infantry |
| Foley, John P. | 1st Lt. | 508th Parachute Infantry |
| Funk, Leonard A. | 1st Sgt. | 508th Parachute Infantry |
| *Gavin, James M. | Major Gen. | 505th Parachute Infantry |
| Gilbert, Emmil P. | T/5 | 507th Parachute Infantry |
| Gordon, Oscar L. | 2d Lt. | 505th Parachute Infantry |
| Gorham, Arthur F. | Lt. Col. | 505th Parachute Infantry |
| Grenado, John | Cpl. | 504th Parachute Infantry |
| Gushue, Charles A. | Sgt. | 508th Parachute Infantry |
| Hanna, Roy M. | 1st Lt. | 504th Parachute Infantry |
| Harper, Lee W. | Pvt. | 456th Parachute Field Artillery Battalion |
| Harris, Wesley O. | Capt. | 307th Airborne Engineer Battalion |
| Harrison, Willard | Major | 504th Parachute Infantry |
| Henderson, Alvin H. | S/Sgt. | 508th Parachute Infantry |
| Holstoi, Raymond S. | Pfc. | 504th Parachute Infantry |
| Hord, Shelby R. | Pvt. | 504th Parachute Infantry |
| Huempfner, Milo C. | Pfc. | Division Headquarters Company |
| Hughes, John A. | 1st Lt. | 507th Parachute Infantry |
| Jusek, Joseph | Cpl. | 504th Parachute Infantry |
| Kaiser, James L. | Lt. Col. | 505th Parachute Infantry |
| Karnap, Bernard E. | 2d Lt. | 504th Parachute Infantry |
| Kolley, Charles B. | Pvt. | 507th Parachute Infantry |
| Kellogg, William M. | Capt. | 307th Airborne Engineer Battalion |
| Kero, William E. | Sgt. | 307th Airborne Engineer Battalion |
| Kiernan, James R. | 1st Lt. | 504th Parachute Infantry |
| Kinsey, Paul S. | 1st Lt. | 325th Glider Infantry |
| Kirbey, Yarcel | T/5 | 507th Parachute Infantry |
| Koss, Joseph M. | Pfc. | 504th Parachute Infantry |
| Krause, Edward C. | Lt. Col. | 505th Parachute Infantry |
| Kumler, Lyle K. | Sgt. | 508th Parachute Infantry |
| Larnin, George D. | 1st Lt. | 508th Parachute Infantry |
| Lanseadel, William G. | Pfc. | 504th Parachute Infantry |
| Lockwood, John A. | Pvt. | 508th Parachute Infantry |
| Madlock, Hy F. | Pvt. | 507th Parachute Infantry |
| Magellas, James | 1st Lt. | 504th Parachute Infantry |
| Mendez, Louis G. | Lt. Col. | 508th Parachute Infantry |
| Myers, Joseph F. | 1st Lt. | 325th Glider Infantry |
| Muzvnski, Walter J. | Pfc. | 504th Parachute Infantry |
| Nau, Charles E. | Cpl. | 504th Parachute Infantry |
| Ostberg, E. J. | Lt. Col. | 507th Parachute Infantry |
| Parris, Harold L. | Pfc. | 508th Parachute Infantry |
| Polette, Lloyd L. | 1st Lt. | 508th Parachute Infantry |
| Prager, Clarence | S/Sgt. | 505th Parachute Infantry |
| Prager, Leonard A. | 1st Sgt. | 508th Parachute Infantry |
| *Ridgway, Matthew B. | Major General | Division Headquarters |
| Roberts, Ernest T. | Cpl. | 508th Parachute Infantry |
| Rutledge, James A. | T/Sgt. | 508th Parachute Infantry |
| Sanford, Teddy A. | Lt. Col. | 325th Glider Infantry |
| Sayre, Edwin M. | Capt. | 505th Parachute Infantry |
| Shanley, Thomas J. | Lt. Col. | 508th Parachute Infantry |
| Sirovica, Frank L. | S/Sgt. | 508th Parachute Infantry |
| Sprinkle, John I. | 1st Lt. | 505th Parachute Infantry |
| Stevens, Stanley E. | S/Sgt. | 508th Parachute Infantry |
| Swenson, John H. | Lt. Col. | 325th Glider Infantry |
| Taylor, Stokes M. | Cpl. | 80th Airborne Anti-aircraft Battalion |
| Terry, Dewitt S. | Sgt. | 325th Glider Infantry |
| *Tucker, Reuben H. | Col. | 504th Parachute Infantry |
| *Vandervoort, Benjamin H. | Lt. Col. | 505th Parachute Infantry |
| Walsh, William P. | S/Sgt. | 504th Parachute Infantry |
| Wason, Donald B. | 2d Lt. | 325th Glider Infantry |
| Werlich, Jake L. | 1st Lt. | 508th Parachute Infantry |
| Ziegler, Harvey | 1st Lt. | 505th Parachute Infantry |
| Zwingman, Otto K. | Pvt. | 508th Parachute Infantry |

## SUMMARY OF DECORATIONS OF UNITED STATES OF AMERICA
## BY CAMPAIGN

NOTE: Compilations listed below include decorations awarded through 12 October 1945. Approximately 140 recommendations for decorations were being processed at that time.

| CAMPAIGN | MofH | DSC | LofM | SS | BS |
|---|---|---|---|---|---|
| SICILY 9 July 43 - 19 Aug 43 | | 10 | 9 | 102 | 5 |
| ITALY 12 Sept 43 - 19 Nov 43 *22 Mar 44 | | 4 | 2 | 58 | 59 |
| NORMANDY 6 June 44 - 12 July 44 | 1 | 32 | 11 | 271 | 925 |
| HOLLAND 17 Sept 44 - 12 Nov 44 | 1 | 20 | 3 | 209 | 709 |
| BELGIUM 18 Dec 44 - 17 Feb 45 | 1 | 11 | 5 | 169 | 396 |
| GERMANY 2 Apr 45 | | 2 | 2 | 85 | 384 |
| TOTAL | 3 | 79 | 32 | 894 | 2478 |

*504th Parachute Infantry

### BY UNIT

| UNIT | MofH | DSC | Lof M | Silver Star | Bronze Star |
|---|---|---|---|---|---|
| Hq. 82nd Abn Div | | 4 | 12 | 11 | 108 |
| MP Platoon | | | 1 | 1 | 5 |
| Prcht Maint Co | | | 1 | | 4 |
| 307th Abn Med Co | | | 1 | 9 | 53 |
| 82nd Abn Sig Co | | | 3 | 1 | 9 |
| 407th Abn QM Co | | | | | 5 |
| 782nd Abn Ord Maint Co | | | 2 | | 17 |
| Recon Platoon | | | | 4 | 9 |
| 307th Abn Engr Bn | | 3 | 2 | 20 | 100 |
| 325th Gli Inf | 1 | 10 | 2 | 95 | 266 |
| 80th Abn AA Bn | | 1 | | 4 | 45 |
| 319th Gli FA Bn | | | | 8 | 45 |
| Hq. Div Arty | | | 1 | 5 | 22 |
| 320th Gli FA Bn | | | | 10 | 54 |
| 456th Prcht FA Bn | | 2 | | 24 | 25 |
| 376th Prcht FA Bn | | | | 7 | 44 |
| 504th Prcht Inf | 1 | 20 | 2 | 200 | 428 |
| 505th Prcht Inf | | 12 | 4 | 275 | 596 |
| Other | 1 | 26 | 1 | 220 | 641 |
| TOTAL | 3 | 78 | 32 | 894 | 2478 |

## SUMMARY OF DECORATIONS OF ALLIED GOVERNMENTS

| AWARD | NUMBER PRESENTED |
|---|---|
| **FRENCH** | |
| Croix De Guerre A L'Ordre De L'Armee (Army Level) | 7 |
| Croix De Guerre L'Ordre De La Division (Division Level) | 3 |
| Croix De Guerre A L'Ordre Du Regiment (Regimental Level) | 16 |
| Croix De Guerre Certificates | 27 |
| | 53 |
| **BRITISH** | |
| Military Cross | 6 |
| Military Medal | 11 |
| Distinguished Service Order | 2 |
| Distinguished Conduct Medal | 23 |
| | 42 |
| **RUSSIAN** | |
| Order of Alexander Nevsky | 1 |
| Order of the Peoples War, 1st Degree | 2 |
| Order of the Peoples War, 2nd Degree | 4 |
| Medal of Valor | 4 |
| Medal for Combat Service | 3 |
| | 14 |
| **HOLLAND** | |
| ORANGE NASSAU IN | |
| Degree of Grand Officer | 1 |
| Degree of Commander | 1 |
| Degree of Officer | 5 |

Military Willems Order          10
Bronze Lion          42
Bronze Cross          <u>14</u>
         73

Appendix 12: Citations of the 82nd Airborne Division

France – FOURRAGERE, 1939-1945 For gallantry in action in NORMANDY. (See Appendix 12c)

THE NETHERLANDS - MILITAIRE WILLEMS ORDE, DEGREE OF KNIGHT OF THE FOURTH CLASS. Awarded for gallantry in action in the NETHERLANDS during the period 17 September 1944 - 4 October 1944. (See Annex 12d)

BELGIUM - THE FOURRAGERE 1940. Awarded for gallantry in action in BELGIUM in December 1944 and January and February 1945 in the ARDENNES, the 82nd Airborne Division having been cited twice in the Order of the Day of the Belgian Army. (See Annex 12e)

## Appendix 12a
## PRESIDENTIAL CITATIONS OF UNITS OF THE 82ND AIRBORNE DIVISION

| UNIT | CAMPAIGN |
|---|---|
| Division Headquarters and Headquarters Company | Normandy |
| 325th Glider Infantry | Normandy |
| 1st Battalion, 504th Parachute Infantry (Less Company A) | Ardennes |
| Company A, 504th Parachute Infantry | Central Europe |
| 3rd Battalion, 504th Parachute Infantry | Rome-Arno (Anzio) |
| 505th Parachute Infantry | Normandy |
| 507th Parachute Infantry (Attached) | Normandy |
| 508th Parachute Infantry (Attached) | Normandy |
| Headquarters and Headquarters Battery, 82nd Airborne Division Artillery | Normandy |
| 319th Glider Field Artillery Battalion | Normandy |
| 320th Glider Field Artillery Battalion | Normandy |
| 82nd Airborne Signal Company | Normandy |
| 307th Airborne Medical Company | Normandy |
| Headquarters and Batteries A,B, and C, 80th Airborne Antiaircraft Battalion | Normandy |
| Companies A and B, 307th Airborne Engineer Battalion | Normandy |

## Appendix 12b
## MERITORIOUS SERVICE PLAQUES AWARDED UNITS

407th Airborne Quartermaster Company
307th Airborne Medical Company
782nd Airborne Ordnance Maintenance Company
82nd Parachute Maintenance Company
666th Quartermaster Truck Company (Attached)

## Appendix 12c: Award of the French Croix de Guerre with Palm and Fourargere

Decision No. 159
The President of the provisional Government of the French Republic:
Cities in the Orders of the Army

Elite units of the 82nd Airborne Division which so magnificently distinguished themselves by parachuting into France during the night of 5 to 6 June 1944.

    Through the military skill and heroism of their fighting men, they succeeded in seizing the important objective of Ste. Mere Eglise with very severe losses against stubborn resistance by the enemy, thus permitting the successful beach landing in force of the allied troops of liberation.

    This citation carries the attribution of the Croix de Guerre with Palm.

Decision No. 160
The President of the Provisional Government of the French Republic:
Cites in the Orders of the Army

These magnificent units, famed for their heroism and the spirit of sacrifice of their fighting men, gave further proof of their superior military quality in the course of the Battle of Normandy.

Comprising that part of the 82nd Airborne Division which had seized the roadlet and waterways commanding access to the landing beaches of the Cotentin Peninsula, they sacrificed themselves without regard to the cost on the Merderet and Douve Rivers, at Saint-Saveur Le Vicomte and Etienville, from the 6th to the 20th of June 1944 in containing German reinforcements which were infinitely superior in numbers and firepower, forcing them to remain on the defensive and thus permit the arrival of the main force of the Allies.

This citation carries the attribution of the Croix de Guerre with Palm.

Decision No.161
WHEREAS Decision No. 159 of 6 April 1946 attributes the Croix de Guerre with Palm to named units of the 82nd Airborne Division, and WHEREAS Decision No. 160 of 6 April 1946 attributes the Croix de Guerre with Palm to named units of the 82nd Airborne Division:

The President of the Provisional Government of the French Republic cites the following units, being part of the 82nd Airborne Division.

They are authorized to carry the Fourragere in the colors of the Croix de Guerre, 1939-1945.

Appendix 12d: Award of the Military Order of William and Orange Lanyard

HEADQUARTERS 82ND AIRBORNE DIVISION
Office of the Division Commander

APO 469 U.S. Army
12 October 1945

GENERAL ORDERS :)

:

NUMBER 125 )                                                    SECTION

NETHERLANDS DECREE, DATED 8 OCT 1945, AWARD OF THE "MILITAIRE WILLEMS ORDE"  I
MINISTERIAL DECREE, NETHERLANDS GOVERNMENT,
        8 Oct 1945. WEARING OF THE ORANGE LANYARD,
        ROYAL NETHERLANDS ARMY  II

I – NETHERLANDS DECREE:
Announcement is made of the Netherlands award of the "Militaire Willems Orde", degree of Knight of the fourth class, to the 82nd Airborne Division. The Netherlands Decree, dated 8 October 1945, is hereby quoted:

"WE WILHELMINA, by the Grace of God, Queen of Netherlands, Princess of Orange-Nassau, etc., etc., etc.

On the recommendation of Our Ministers of War and for Foreign Affairs, dated October 3, 1945, Secret Nr.Y.22;

In accordance with the provisions of the amended Act of April 30, 1815 Nr. 5 (Statue-Book Nr. 33);

In view of the clause 18 of the Regulations of administration and discipline for the "Militaire Willems Orde", as laid down in the Royal Decree of June 25, 1815, Nr. 10;

Considering that the 82nd Airborne Division of the United States Army during, the airborne operations and the ensuing fighting actions in the central part of the Netherlands in the period from September 17 to October 4, 1944, excelled in performing the tasks, allotted to it, with tact, coupled with superior gallantry, self-sacrifice and loyalty;

Considering also, that the actions, fought by the aforesaid Division, took place in the area of NIJMEGEN:

HAVE APPROVED AND ORDERED:
1.      To decree, that the Divisional Colours of the 82nd Airborne Division of the United States army shall be decorated with the "MILITAIRE WILLEMS ORDE", degree of Knight of the fourth class;
2.      To authorize the Division to carry in its Divisional Colours the name of the town of
NIJMEGEN 1944

Our Ministers of War and for Foreign Affairs are, each for his own part, in charge of the execution of this Decree, copy of which shall be sent to the Chancellor of the Netherlands Orders of Knighthood.

THE HAGUE, October 8, 1945
(sgd.) WILHELMINA

THE MINISTER OF WAR
(sgd.) J. MELJNEN
THE MINISTER OF FOREIGN AFFAIRS,
(sgd.) VAN KLEFFENS

II - MINISTERIAL DECREE, NETHERLANDS GOVERNMENT:

Ministerial Decree of the Netherlands Minister of War, dated 8 October 1945, granting the personnel of the 82nd Airborne Division, who participated in operations during the period of 17 September to 4 October 1944, authority to wear the ORANGE LANYARD of the Royal Netherlands Army is quoted:

"MINISTERIAL DECREE OF THE NETHERLANDS MINISTER OF WAR, dated October 8, 1945, Section III A, Secret No-X 25.

The Minister of War considering, that the outstanding performance of duty of the 82nd Airborne Division, United States Army, during the airborne operations and the ensuing fighting actions in the central part of the NETHERLANDS in the period from September 17 to October 4, 1944, have induced HER MAJESTY THE QUEEN to decorate its Divisional Colours with the "MILITAIRE WILLEMS-ORDE" degree of Knight of the fourth class; CONSIDERING also, that it is desirable for each member of the Division, who took part in the afore-said operations, to possess a lasting memento of this glorious struggle;

DECREES: That each member of the personnel of the 82D AIRBORNE DIVISION, UNITED STATES ARMY, who took part in the operations in the area of NIJMEGEN in the period from September 17 to October 4, 1944, is allowed to wear the ORANGE LANYARD, as laid down in article 123g of the Clothing Regulations/1944, of the Royal Netherlands Army.

THE HAGUE, OCTOBER 8, 1945
THE MINISTER OF WAR
(Minister van Oorlog)

## Appendix 12e. Award of Belgian Fourragere

HEADQUARTERS 82D AIRBORNE DIVISION
Office of the Division Commander

APO 469, U.S. Army
8 October 1945

GENERAL ORDERS )
NUMBER 123 )

*Belgium Citation*

Pursuant to authority contained in the Belgium Ministry of National Defense Decree Number 1034, dated 4 October 1945, announcement is made of the award of the Fourragere 1940 to the 82nd Airborne Division and the 508th Parachute Infantry Regiment. Appropriate portions from the Decree are hereby quoted:

"At the proposal of the Minister of National Defense, we have decreed and we order:

Article 1: The 82nd Airborne Division with the 508th Parachute Infantry Regiment attached is cited twice in the Order of the Day of the Belgian Army and is herewith given the Fourragere 1940, for:

1. This elite Division which has gone with the great elan through the campaigns of Tunisia, Sicily, Italy, Holland and France, has distinguished itself particularly in the Battle of the Ardennes from December 17 to December 31, 1944. Called upon as a reinforcement by the Allied High Command in the evening of the 17 December, at a time when the division was in the vicinity of Reims, the Division was able to take up combat positions in the region of Werbomont only twenty-four hours later and this under very severe climatic conditions. Progressing towards Ambleve and the Salm, the Division opened and maintained a corridor for the elements of four American Divisions which were surrounded in the vicinity of St. Vith, thus giving new courage to the engaged units. The Division had prevented the enemy from piercing the north flank of the pocket created by the offensive of Von Rundstedt and thusly succeeded in saving the city of Liege and its surroundings from a second occupation by the Germans.

2. After having excelled in defensive warfare at the banks of the Salm and the Ambleve and after having repelled successfully the repeated attacks of the best German shocktroops, the 82nd Airborne Division with the 508th Parachute Infantry Regiment attached, in spite of extreme cold and excessively deep snow, went on the offensive themselves and advanced to the German border, capturing 2500 German prisoners, including five battalion commanders. This fighting was extremely valorous as the organic composition of the Division handicapped the unit considerably, not having at their disposal, as any other Infantry Division would have, heavy weapons to support their attack. During twenty-three days, under most painful and adverse conditions, the veterans of the 82nd Airborne Division did not cease to give a wonderful example of courage and heroism, exemplifying their fighting spirit by several remarkably brilliant actions. By its valor, the Division wrote another page in heroic annals of Allied Airborne troops and rendered an important service to Belgium and to the Allied cause by establishing the necessary basis for the new pursuit of the enemy towards the Rhine River.

Article 2: The Minister of National Defense is herewith ordered to execute the decree.

For the Regent:
The Minister of National Defense
signed: L. Mundeleer."

## Appendix 13: Prisoners of War Captured by the 82nd Airborne Division

| CAMPAIGN | NO. OF PW'S |
|---|---|
| SICILY | 23,191 |
| ITALY | 74 |
| NORMANDY | 2,159 |
| HOLLAND | 2,995 |
| ARDENNES | 4,529 |
| CENTRAL EUROPE | 148,152* |
| TOTAL | 181,100 |

NOTES: Figures include only prisoners of war processed through the Division Prisoner of War Cage and do not include any prisoners captured by units of the Division while such units were detached from the Division. The above figures thus do not include prisoners taken by the 505th Parachute RCT in the early days of SICILY, the 325th, 504th and 505th RCTs on the SALERNO BEACHHEAD or much of the CHIUNZI PASS sector, the 505th RCT on the VOLTURNO, or the 504th RCT in the USERNIA, VENAFRO or ANZIO sectors.

The figure of 148,152 prisoners captured in the CENTRAL EUROPE Campaign includes an estimated 144,000 captured when the German Twenty-First Army surrendered to the 82nd Airborne Division at LUDWIGSLUST, Germany.

### Appendix 14: Command and Staff 82nd Infantry Division and 82nd Airborne Division
### 25 March 1942 - 25 October 1945

NOTE: Dates shown for promotion are dates of rank unless shown with an asterisk (*). If shown with an asterisk the dates are dates of acceptance of promotion. "End of War" indicates Berlin, 1945, when these statistics were compiled.

| COMMANDING GENERALS | FROM | TO |
|---|---|---|
| Major Gen. Omar N. Bradley | 25 March '42 | 25 June '42 |
| Brig. Gen. Matthew B. Ridgway | 26 June '42 | 5 August '42 |
| Major Gen. Matthew B. Ridgway | 7 August '42 | 27 August '44 |
| Brig. Gen. James M. Gavin | 28 August '44 | 19 October '44 |
| Major Gen. James M. Gavin | 20 October '44 | End of War |

| ASSISTANT DIVISION COMMANDERS | | |
|---|---|---|
| Brig. Gen. Matthew B. Ridgway | 25 March '42 | 25 June '42 |
| Col. Don F. Pratt | 3 July '42 | 15 August '42 |
| Brig. Gen. William M. Wiley | 18 August '42 | 15 January '43 |
| Col. Charles L. Keerans, Jr. | 17 January '43 | 6 February '43 |
| Brig. Gen. Charles L. Keerans, Jr. | 7 February '43 (MIA) | 11 July '43 |
| Col. James M. Gavin | 4 October '43 | 6 October '43 |
| Brig. Gen. James M. Gavin | *7 October '43 | 27 August '44 |
| Col. Ira P. Swift | 13 December '44 | 19 March '45 |
| Brig. Gen. Ira P. Swift | 20 March '45 | 2 September '45 |

| COMMANDING GENERALS, DIVISION ARTILLERY | | |
|---|---|---|
| Brig. Gen. Joseph M. Swing | 25 March '42 | 11 December '42 |
| Brig. Gen. Maxwell D. Taylor | *12 December '42 | 5 October '43 |
| Col. Francis A. March | 6 October '43 | 6 February '44 |
| Brig. Gen. Maxwell D. Taylor | 7 February '44 | 21 February '44 |
| Col. Francis A. March | 22 February '44 | 7 May '44 |
| Col. Lemuel Mathewson | 8 May '44 | 21 May '44 |
| Col. Francis A. March | 22 May '44 | 15 November '44 |
| Brig. Gen. Francis A. March | 16 November '44 | End of War |

| CHIEFS OF STAFF | | |
|---|---|---|
| Col. George Van W. Pope | 25 March '42 | 5 July '42 |
| Col. Maxwell D . Taylor | 6 July '42 | 11 December '42 |
| Lt. Col. Ralph P. Eaton | 12 December '42 | 4 January '43 |
| Col. Ralph P. Eaton | 5 January '43 | 27 August '44 |
| Lt. Col. Robert H. Wienecke | 28 August '44 | 28 October '44 |
| Col. Robert H. Wienecke | 29 October '44 | End of War |

| ASSISTANT CHIEF OF STAFF, G-1 | FROM | TO |
|---|---|---|
| Lt. Col. Ralph P. Eaton (Acting) | 25 March '42 | 2 May '42 |
| Major Ralph C. Cooper | 3 May '42 | 21 June '42 |
| Capt. Frederick M. Schellhammer | 22 June '42 | 13 August '42 |
| Major Frederick M. Schellhammer | 14 August '42 | 17 December '42 |
| Capt. Thomas B. Ketterson (Acting) | 9 September '42 | 16 December '42 |
| Capt. Thomas B. Ketterson | 17 December '42 | 29 January '43 |
| Major Thomas B. Ketterson | 30 January '43 | 27 March '43 |
| Major Frederick M. Schellhammer | 28 March '43 | 11 April '43 |
| Lt. Col. Frederick M. Schellhammer | 12 April '43 | 27 August '44 |
| Major Alfred W. Ireland | 28 August '44 | 5 November '44 |
| Lt. Col. Alfred W. Ireland | 6 November '44 | End of War |

| ASSISTANT CHIEF OF STAFF, G-2 | | |
|---|---|---|
| Major George E. Lynch | 25 March '42 | 3 April '42 |
| Lt. Col. George E. Lynch | *4 April '42 | 26 September '43 |
| Lt. Col. Whitfield Jack | 2 October '43 | 27 August '44 |
| Lt. Col. Walter W. Winton, Jr. | 28 August '44 | 20 June '45 |
| Major Michael K. Berkut (Acting) | 1 July '45 | 18 July '45 |
| Major Paul E. Vaupel | 19 July '45 | End of War |

ASSISTANT CHIEF OF STAFF, G-3

| | | |
|---|---|---|
| Major Willis S. Matthews | 25 March '42 | 3 April '42 |
| Lt. Col. Willis S. Matthews | *4 April '42 | 5 July '42 |
| Major Richard K. Boyd | 6 July '42 | 7 October '42 |
| Lt. Col. Richard K. Boyd | 8 October '42 | 19 August '43 |
| Lt. Col. Whitfield Jack | 20 August '43 | 1 October '43 |
| Lt. Col. Paul L. Turner, Jr. | 2 October '43 | 16 February '44 |
| Lt. Col. Robert H. Wienecke | 17 February '44 | 27 August '44 |
| Major John Norton | 28 August '44 | 25 October '44 |
| Lt. Col. John Norton | 26 October '44 | End of War |

ASSISTANT CHIEF OF STAFF, G-4

| | | |
|---|---|---|
| Lt. Col. Truman C. Thorson | 25 March '42 | 16 August '42 |
| Major Robert H. Wienecke | 19 August '42 | 31 January '43 |
| Lt. Col. Robert H. Wienecke | 1 February '43 | 16 February '44 |
| Major Bennie A. Zinn | 17 February '44 | 31 May '44 |
| Lt. Col. Bennie A. Zinn | 1 June '44 | 16 June '44 |
| Lt. Col. Frank W. Moorman | 17 July '44 | 27 August '44 |
| Major Albert G. Marin | 28 August '44 | 10 November '44 |
| Lt. Col. Albert G. Marin | 11 November '44 | End of War |

ASSISTANT CHIEF OF STAFF, G-5 (See also Military Government Officer)

| | | |
|---|---|---|
| Major Arthur W. Seward, Jr. | 13 August '45 | 17 October '45 |

ADJUTANT GENERAL

| | | |
|---|---|---|
| Lt. Col. Ralph P. Eaton | 25 March '42 | 11 December '42 |
| Captain Raymond M. Britton | 12 December '42 | 29 January '43 |
| Major Raymond M. Britton | 30 January '43 | 16 February '43 |
| Major John Poole | 17 February '43 | 12 March '43 |
| Major Raymond M. Britton | 13 March '43 | 31 January '44 |
| Lt. Col. Raymond M. Britton | 1 February '44 | 21 February '45 |
| Major Maurice E. Stuart (Acting) | 2 February '45 | 21 February '45 |
| Major Maurice E. Stuart | 22 February '45 | 15 May '45 |
| Lt. Col. Maurice E. Stuart | 16 May '45 | 30 June '45 |
| Major John D. Gray | 1 July '45 | End of War |

CHAPLAIN

| | | |
|---|---|---|
| 1st Lt. Garner D. Noland | 25 March '42 | 29 March '42 |
| Major Charles W. Lovin | 30 March '42 | 8 February '43 |
| Capt. George L. Riddle | 9 February '43 | 1 March '43 |
| Major George L. Riddle | 1 March '43 | 3 January '44 |
| Lt. Col. George L. Riddle | 1 February '44 | 12 November '44 |
| Captain George B. Wood | 13 November '44 | 21 January '45 |
| Major George B. Wood | 22 January '45 | End of War |

CHEMICAL OFFICER

| | | |
|---|---|---|
| Major John P. Geiger | 25 March '42 | 7 April '42 |
| Lt. Col. John P. Geiger | *8 April '42 | End of War |

FINANCE OFFICER

| | | |
|---|---|---|
| Major William E. Johnson | 25 March '42 | 2 August '42 |
| Lt. Col. William E. Johnson | 3 August '42 | End of War |

HEADQUARTERS COMMANDANT

| | | |
|---|---|---|
| Capt. Jean G. Callahan | 25 March '42 | 7 April '42 |
| Major Jean G. Callahan | *8 April '42 | 13 August '42 |
| Capt. John H. Swenson | 14 August '42 | 13 September '42 |
| Major John H. Swenson | 14 September '42 | 20 February '43 |
| Capt. William C. Shreve | 21 February '43 | 2 August '43 |
| Capt. Walter H. Chandler, Jr. | 21 August '43 | 17 January '44 |
| Capt. Don C. Faith, Jr. | 18 January '44 | 9 May '44 |
| Major Don C. Faith, Jr. | 10 May '44 | 23 August '44 |
| Capt. William H. Johnson | 24 August '44 | 6 October '44 |
| Major William H. Johnson | 7 October '44 | 28 February '45 |
| Capt. George J. Calussen | 1 March '45 | 30 June '45 |
| Major Lawrence L. Lynch | 1 July '45 | End of War |

INSPECTOR GENERAL

| | | |
|---|---|---|
| Lt. Col. Willard S. Wadelton | 25 March '42 | 8 September '42 |
| Lt. Col. Charles F. Barrett, Jr. | 9 September '42 | 27 August '44 |
| Lt. Col. Frank P. Dunnington | 28 August '44 | 16 March '45 |

Capt. William F. Jones | 17 March '45 | 30 June '45
Lt. Col. Edward S. Nelson, Jr. | 1 July '45 | End of War

## JUDGE ADVOCATE GENERAL

| | | |
|---|---|---|
| Major Eugene G. Cushing | 25 March '42 | 8 July '42 |
| Lt. Col. Eugene G. Cushing | 9 July '42 | 14 August '42 |
| Capt. Cassimir D. Moss | 15 August '42 | 6 September '42 |
| Major Cassimir D. Moss | 7 September '42 | 2 April '43 |
| Lt. Col. Cassimir D. Moss | 3 April '43 | 27 August '44 |
| Major Nicholas E. Allen | 28 August '44 | 6 December '44 |
| | | |
| Lt. Col. Nicholas E. Allen | 7 December '44 | 16 October '45 |
| Major Robert F. H. Pollock | 17 October '45 | End of War |

## ORDNANCE OFFICER

| | | |
|---|---|---|
| Capt. Joshua A. Finkel | 25 March '42 | 3 April '42 |
| Major Joshua A. Finkel | 4 April '42 | 29 November '42 |
| Lt. Col. Joshua A. Finkel | 30 November '42 | 12 December '44 |
| Major Mayo S. Silvey | 13 December '44 | 19 March '45 |
| Lt. Col. Mayo S. Silvey | 20 March '45 | 30 June '45 |
| Lt. Col. Raymond W. Smith | 1 July '45 | End of War |

## PROVOST MARSHAL

| | | |
|---|---|---|
| Major John C. Callahan | 25 March '42 | 13 August '42 |
| Capt. John H. Swenson | 14 August '42 | 13 September '42 |
| Major John H. Swenson | 13 September '42 | 19 October '42 |
| Capt. William P. Bowden | 20 October '42 | 29 January '43 |
| Major William P. Bowden | 30 January '43 | 6 January '44 |
| Major Frederick G. McCollum | 7 January '44 | 22 May '45 |
| Major Paul E. Vaupel | 23 May '45 | 18 July '45 |
| Capt. Robert B. Patterson | 19 July '45 | End of War |

## QUARTERMASTER

| | | |
|---|---|---|
| Lt. Col. Samuel H. Baker | 25 March '42 | 14 August '42 |
| Major Erle H. Landers | 15 August '42 | 29 November '42 |
| Lt. Col. Erle H. Landers | 30 November '42 | 16 March '43 |
| 1st Lt. Harvey M. Lifsot | 19 March '43 | 23 March '43 |
| Major John W. Mohrman | 24 March '43 | 18 November '43 |
| Lt. Col. John W. Mohrman | 19 November '43 | 30 June '45 |
| Lt. Col. Raymond H. Tiffany | 1 July '45 | 20 September '45 |
| Major Samuel M. Mays | 21 September '45 | End of War |

## SIGNAL OFFICER

| | | |
|---|---|---|
| Capt. Frank W. Moorman | 25 March '42 | 3 April '42 |
| Major Frank W. Moorman | *4 April '42 | 7 October '42 |
| Lt. Col. Frank W. Moorman | 8 October '42 | 16 July '44 |
| Capt. Robert E. Furman | 17 July '44 | 7 September '44 |
| Major Robert E. Furman | 8 September '44 | 28 February '45 |
| Lt. Col. Robert E. Furman | 1 March '45 | 30 June '45 |
| Lt. Col. Joseph P. Ahern | 1 July '45 | End of War |

## SPECIAL SERVICE OFFICER

| | | |
|---|---|---|
| 1st Lt. Harold A. Shebeck | 25 March '42 | 3 August '42 |
| Capt. Harold A. Shebeck | 4 August '42 | 20 December '42 |
| 1st Lt. Shirley H. Dix | 21 December '42 | 2 March '43 |
| Capt. Frederick G. McCollum | 3 March '43 | 18 September '43 |
| Major Frederick G. McCollum | 19 September '43 | 6 January '44 |
| Capt. Rudrick R. Otto | 7 January '44 | 31 August '44 |
| Major Rudrick R. Otto | 1 September '44 | 30 June '45 |
| Major Samuel H. Mays | 1 July '45 | 20 September '45 |
| Capt. John T. Elliott | 21 September '45 | End of War |

## SURGEON

| | | |
|---|---|---|
| Lt. Col. Clifford Bost | 25 March '42 | 21 January '43 |
| Major Woolcott L. Etienne | 30 January '43 | 2 March '43 |
| Lt. Col. Woolcott L. Etienne | 3 March '43 | 27 August '44 |
| Major William C. Lindstrom | 28 August '44 | 7 September '44 |
| Lt. Col. William C. Lindstrom | 8 September '44 | End of War |

## MILITARY GOVERNMENT (See Also G-5)

| | | |
|---|---|---|
| Capt. Peter Shouvaloff | 22 May '44 | 26 December '44 |
| Capt. Arthur Seward, Jr. (Acting) | 16 December '44 | 25 December '44 |

| | | |
|---|---|---|
| Capt. Arthur Seward, Jr. | 26 December '44 | 11 February '45 |
| Major Arthur Seward, Jr. | 11 February '45 | 12 August '45 |

PARACHUTE MAINTENANCE OFFICER (Authorized 1 March '45)

| | | |
|---|---|---|
| Capt. James E. Griffin | 1 March '45 | 30 April '45 |
| Major James E. Griffin | 1 May '45 | End of War |

COMMANDING OFFICER, 325TH INFANTRY (Redesignated 325TH Glider Infantry on 15 August 1942)

| | | |
|---|---|---|
| Col. Claudius M. Easley | 25 March '42 | 27 July '42 |
| Lt. Col. Jean D. Scott | 28 July '42 | 13 August '42 |
| Lt. Col. Harry L. Lewis | 14 August '42 | 21 August '44 |
| Lt. Col. Charles E. Billingslea | 22 August '44 | 28 October '44 |
| Col. Charles E. Billingslea | 29 October '44 | End of War |

COMMANDING OFFICER, 326TH INFANTRY (Redesignated 326TH Glider Infantry on 15 August 1942). TRANSFERRED FROM DIVISION ON 10 FEBRUARY 1943)

| | | |
|---|---|---|
| Col. Stuart Cutler | 25 March '42 | 10 February '43 |

COMMANDING OFFICER, 327TH INFANTRY (TRANSFERRED FROM DIVISION ON 15 AUGUST 1942)

| | | |
|---|---|---|
| Col. George S. Wear | 25 March '42 | 15 August '42 |

COMMANDING OFFICER, 504TH PARACHUTE INFANTRY (ASSIGNED TO DIVISION ON 15 AUGUST 1942).

| | | |
|---|---|---|
| Col. Theodore L. Dunn | 15 August '42 | 16 December '42 |
| | (Date Regt assigned to Division) | |
| Lt. Col. Reuben H. Tucker (Acting) | 1 December '42 | 15 December '42 |
| Lt. Col. Reuben H. Tucker | 16 December '42 | 28 May '43 |
| Col. Reuben H. Tucker | 29 May '43 | End of War |

COMMANDING OFFICER, 505TH PARACHUTE INFANTRY (ASSIGNED TO DIVISION ON 10 FEBRUARY 1943).

| | | |
|---|---|---|
| Col. James M. Gavin | 6 July '42 | 4 October '43 |
| Lt. Col. Herbert F. Batchelor | 3 October '43 | 21 March '44 |
| Lt. Col. William E. Ekman | 22 March '44 | 21 July '44 |
| Col. William E. Ekman | 22 July '44 | End of War |

EXECUTIVE OFFICER, DIVISION ARTILLERY

| | | |
|---|---|---|
| Col. Sidney F. Dunn | 25 March '42 | 5 January '43 |
| Lt. Col. Francis A. March | 6 January '43 | 15 January '43 |
| Col. Francis A. March | 16 January '43 | 5 October '43 |
| Lt. Col. William H. Bertsch | 6 October '43 | 6 February '44 |
| Col. Francis A. March | 7 February '44 | 21 February '44 |
| Lt. Col. William H. Bertsch | 21 February '44 | 9 June '44 |
| Col. William H. Bertsch | 10 June '44 | 24 September '44 |
| Lt. Col. Wilbur M. Griffith | 25 September '44 | 15 February '45 |
| Col. Wilbur M. Griffith | 16 February '45 | End of War |

COMMANDING OFFICER, 319TH FIELD ARTILLERY BATTALION (REDESIGNATED 319TH GLIDER FIELD ARTILLERY BATTALION ON 15 AUGUST 1942.)

| | | |
|---|---|---|
| Lt. Col. William H. Bertsch | 25 March '42 | 5 October '43 |
| Major James C. Todd | 6 October '43 | 6 February '44 |
| Major James C. Todd | 21 February '44 | 29 June '44 |
| Lt. Col. James C. Todd | 30 June '44 | 30 June '45 |
| Lt. Col. Joseph W. Keating | 1 July '45 | 16 October '45 |
| Major Dantes A. York | 17 October '45 | End of War |

COMMANDING OFFICER, 320TH FIELD ARTILLERY BATTALION (REDESIGNATED 320TH GLIDER FIELD ARTILLERY BATTALION ON 15 AUGUST 1942.)

| | | |
|---|---|---|
| Lt. Col. Francis A. March | 25 March '42 | 5 January '43 |
| Major Paul E. Wright | 6 January '43 | 9 April '43 |
| Lt. Col. Paul E. Wright | 10 April '43 | End of War |

COMMANDING OFFICER, 321ST FIELD ARTILLERY BATTALION (TRANSFERRED FROM DIVISION ON 15 AUGUST 1942.)

| | | |
|---|---|---|
| Lt. Col. John W. Works | 25 March '42 | 15 August '42 |

COMMANDING OFFICER, 907TH FIELD ARTILLERY BATTALION (TRANSFERRED FROM DIVISION ON 15 AUGUST 1942.)

| | | |
|---|---|---|
| Lt. Col. John E. Ray | 25 March '42 | 19 June '42 |
| Major Ephraim H. McLemore | 20 June '42 | 14 July '42 |
| Lt. Col. Ephraim H. McLemore | 15 July '42 | 15 August '42 |

COMMANDING OFFICER, 376TH PARACHUTE FIELD ARTILLERY BATTALION (ACTIVATED AND ASSIGNED TO DIVISION, 15 AUGUST '42.)

| | | |
|---|---|---|
| Capt. Paul E. Wright | 16 August '42 | 17 August '42 |
| Major Paul E. Wright | 18 August '42 | 20 October '42 |
| Capt. Robert W. Neptune (Acting) | 21 October '42 | 3 January '43 |
| Major Wilbur M. Griffith | 4 January '43 | 8 March '43 |
| Lt. Col. Wilbur M. Griffith | 9 March '43 | 24 September '44 |
| Major Robert W. Neptune | 25 September '44 | 10 November '44 |
| Lt. Col. Robert W. Neptune | 11 November '44 | 30 June '45 |
| Major Herbert H. Champlin | 1 July '45 | End of War |

COMMANDING OFFICER, 456TH FIELD ARTILLERY BATTALION (ASSIGNED TO DIVISION ON 10 FEBRUARY '43.)

| FROM | TO | |
|---|---|---|
| Lt. Col. Harrison B. Harden, Jr. | 10 February '43 | 2 August '43 |
| Major Hugh A Neal | 3 August '43 | 27 February '44 |
| Major Wagner J. D'Allessio | 23 February '44 | 29 June '44 |
| Lt. Col. Wagner J. D'Allessio | 30 June '44 | 30 June '45 |
| Major Frederick J. Silvey | 1 July '45 | End of War |

COMMANDING OFFICER, 80TH AIRBORNE ANTIAIRCRAFT BATTALION (ACTIVATED AND ASSIGNED TO DIVISION 3 SEPTEMBER '42.)

| | | |
|---|---|---|
| Major Whitfield Jack | 5 September '42 | 29 November '42 |
| Lt. Col. Whitfield Jack | 30 November '42 | 19 August '43 |
| Major Raymond E. Singleton (Acting) | 1 July '43 | 19 August '43 |
| Major Raymond E. Singleton | 20 August '43 | 31 January '44 |
| Lt. Col. Raymond E. Singleton | 1 February '44 | 30 June '45 |
| Lt. Col. John W. Paddock | 1 July '45 | 15 October '45 |
| Major Choice R. Rucker | 16 October '45 | End of War |

COMMANDING OFFICER, 307TH ENGINEER BATTALION (REDESIGNATED 307TH AIRBORNE ENGINEER BATTALION ON 15 AUGUST 1942.)

| | | |
|---|---|---|
| Lt. Col. Peter E. Bermel | 25 March '42 | 13 July '42 |
| Major Robert S. Palmer | 14 July '42 | 29 November '42 |
| Lt. Col. Robert S. Palmer | 30 November '42 | 6 June '44 |
| Major Edwin A. Bedell | 7 June '44 | 26 November '44 |
| Lt. Col. Edwin A. Bedell | 27 November '44 | End of War |

COMMANDING OFFICER, 307th MEDICAL BATTALION (REDESIGNATED 307TH AIRBORNE MEDICAL COMPANY ON 15 AUGUST 1942.)

| | | |
|---|---|---|
| Major Clifford Best | 25 March '42 | 3 April '42 |
| Lt. Col. Clifford Best | 4 April '42 | 20 May '42 |
| Major William E. Williams | 21 May '42 | 6 July '42 |
| Lt. Col. William E. Williams | 7 July '42 | 14 August '42 |
| Major Wolcott L. Etienne | 15 August '42 | 29 January '43 |
| Capt. William H. Houston | 30 January '43 | 2 March '43 |
| Major William H. Houston | 3 March '43 | 6 June '44 (KIA) |
| Capt. Jerry J. Belden | 7 June '44 | 30 June '44 |
| Major Jerry J. Belden | 1 July '44 | 30 June '45 |
| Capt. Hubert C. Stewart | 1 July '45 | End of War |

COMMANDING OFFICER, 407TH QUARTERMASTER BATTALION (REDESIGNATED 407TH AIRBORNE QUARTERMASTER COMPANY ON 15 AUGUST 1942.)

| | | |
|---|---|---|
| Capt. Harold E. Rose | 15 August '42 | 25 November '42 |
| 1st Lt. Samuel H. Mayes | 26 November '42 | 24 March '43 |
| Capt. Samuel H. Mayes | 25 March '43 | 28 February '45 |
| Capt. Edgar F. Brooks | 1 March '45 | 23 June '45 |
| Capt. Harold O. Karberly | 24 June '45 | End of War |

COMMANDING OFFICER, 782ND AIRBORNE ORDNANCE MAINTENANCE COMPANY (ACTIVATED ON 6 OCTOBER '42.)

| | | |
|---|---|---|
| 1st Lt. Lee B. Catlin | 6 October '42 | 31 October '42 |
| 1st Lt. Howard W. Crusey | 1 November '42 | 22 November '42 |
| 1st Lt. William B. McGuire | 22 November '42 | 20 January '43 |
| Capt. William B. McGuire | 21 January '43 | 8 May '43 |
| 1st Lt. Jeff Davis, Jr. | 9 May '43 | 21 June '43 |
| Capt. Jeff Davis, Jr. | 22 June '43 | 16 April '45 |
| 1st Lt. John D. Leonard | 17 April '45 | 30 June '45 |
| 1st Lt. Robert L. Feinsod | 1 July '45 | End of War |

COMMANDING OFFICER, 82ND RECONNAISSANCE TROOP (INACTIVATED ON 15 AUGUST 1942.)

| | | |
|---|---|---|
| Capt. John H. Swenson | 25 March '42 | 14 August '42 |

## COMMANDING OFFICER, 82ND AIRBORNE DIVISION RECONNAISSANCE PLATOON (PROVISIONAL)

| | | |
|---|---|---|
| 1st Lt. William C. Shreve | 15 August '42 | 21 December '42 |
| Capt. William C. Shreve | 22 December '42 | 20 February '42 |
| 1st Lt. Roland M. Hudson | 21 February '42 | 8 August '43 |
| 2d Lt. Joseph V. DeMasi | 25 August '43 | 21 November '43 |
| 1st Lt. Joseph V. DeMasi | 22 November '43 | 28 February '45 |

## COMMANDING OFFICER, 82ND AIRBORNE RECONNAISSANCE PLATOON (ACTIVATED ON 1 MARCH '45.)

| | | |
|---|---|---|
| 1st Lt. Joseph V. DeMasi | 1 March '45 | 30 June '45 |
| 1st Lt. Roland M. Hudson | 1 July '45 | End of War |

## COMMANDING OFFICER, 82ND SIGNAL COMPANY (REDESIGNATED 82ND AIRBORNE SIGNAL COMPANY ON 15 AUGUST 1942.)

| | | |
|---|---|---|
| 1st Lt. Lester H. Clark | 25 March '42 | 9 April '42 |
| Capt. Lester H. Clark | 10 April '42 | 5 August '42 |
| 1st Lt. Robert E. Furman | 6 August '42 | 12 April '43 |
| Capt. Robert E. Furman | 13 April '43 | 16 July '44 |
| 1st Lt. Richard E. Nerf | 17 July '44 | 16 October '44 |
| Capt. Richard E. Nerf | 17 October '44 | 30 June '45 |
| 1st Lt. Theodore M. Shema | 1 July '45 | End of War |

## COMMANDING OFFICER, HEADQUARTERS COMPANY, 82ND DIVISION (REDESIGNATED HEADQUARTERS COMPANY, 82ND AIRBORNE DIVISION, ON 15 AUGUST 1942.)

| | | |
|---|---|---|
| Capt. Jean G. Callahan | 25 March '42 | 7 April '42 |
| Major Jean G. Callahan | 8 April '42 | 13 August '42 |
| Capt. John H. Swenson | 14 August '42 | 13 September '42 |
| Major John H. Swenson | 14 September '42 | 20 February '43 |
| Capt. William C. Shreve | 21 February '43 | 2 August '43 |
| Capt. Walter H. Chandler, Jr. | 21 August '43 | 17 January '44 |
| 1st Lt. George J. Claussen | 18 January '44 | 31 May '44 |
| Capt. George J. Claussen | 1 June '44 | 28 February '45 |
| Capt. Robert B. Patterson | 1 March '45 | 18 July '45 |
| 1st Lt. William L. Stanley | 19 July '45 | 20 August '45 |
| 1st Lt. George C. Roberts | 21 August '45 | End of War |

## COMMANDING OFFICER, HEADQUARTERS AND HEADQUARTERS BATTERY, 82ND DIVISION ARTILLERY (REDESIGNATED HEADQUARTERS AND HEADQUARTERS BATTERY, 82ND AIRBORNE DIVISION ARTILLERY ON 15 AUGUST 1942.)

| | | |
|---|---|---|
| Capt. John W. Smiley | 25 March '42 | 6 June '42 |
| 1st Lt. Tony J. Raibl | 7 June '42 | 6 July '42 |
| Capt. Tony J. Raibl | 7 July '42 | 30 June '45 |
| Capt. James Lewis | 1 July '45 | End of War |

## COMMANDING OFFICER, 82ND MILITARY POLICE PLATOON (PART OF DIVISION HEADQUARTERS COMPANY UNTIL ACTIVATED AS MILITARY POLICE PLATOON, 82ND INFANTRY DIVISION ON 24 MAY '42. DISBANDED 15 AUGUST '42. ACTIVATED AS MILITARY POLICE PLATOON 82ND AIRBORNE DIVISION ON 8 SEPTEMBER '42.)

| | | |
|---|---|---|
| Capt. William P. Bowden | 25 March '42 | 20 October '42 |
| 1st Lt. Harod M. McLeod (Acting) | 16 September '42 | 10 December '42 |
| 1st Lt. George E. Bankston | 21 October '42 | 20 May '43 |
| 2d Lt. Jacob H. Sneiderman | 21 May '43 | 16 November '43 |
| 1st Lt. Jacob H. Sneiderman | 17 November '43 | 20 July '44 |
| 2d Lt. John J. McGillivary | 21 July '44 | 10 November '44 |
| 1st Lt. John J. McGillivary | 11 November '44 | 30 June '45 |
| 1st Lt. James P. Logan | 1 July '45 | End of War |

## COMMANDING OFFICER, PARACHUTE MAINTENANCE COMPANY (PROVISIONAL)

| | | |
|---|---|---|
| Capt. Albert G. Marin | 1 November '43 | 1 June '44 |
| Capt. James E. Griffin | 2 June '44 | 28 February '45 |

## COMMANDING OFFICER, 82ND PARACHUTE MAINTENANCE COMPANY (ACTIVATED 1 MARCH '45.)

| | | |
|---|---|---|
| Capt. Wylie Cooper | 1 March '45 | End of War |

## COMMANDING OFFICER, SPECIAL TROOPS, 82ND AIRBORNE DIVISION (ACTIVATED 1 MARCH '45.)

| | | |
|---|---|---|
| Major William H. Johnson | 1 March '45 | 30 June '45 |
| Lt. Col. Robert W. Johnson | 1 July '45 | End of War |

## COMMANDING OFFICER, 82ND INFANTRY DIVISION INFANTRY BAND (ACTIVATED 27 APRIL '42. REDESIGNATED 82ND AIRBORNE DIVISION INFANTRY BAND 15 AUGUST '42. REDESIGNATED 504TH PARACHUTE INFANTRY REGIMENT BAND 6 JANUARY '43. INACTIVATED 1 MARCH '45.)

| | | |
|---|---|---|
| WO (JG) Carl A. Moldenhauer | 26 August '42 | 25 February '43 |
| CWO Carl A. Moldenhauer | 26 February '43 | 28 February '45 |

COMMANDING OFFICER, 82ND INFANTRY DIVISION ARTILLERY BAND (ACTIVATED 27 APRIL '42. REDESIGNATED 82ND AIRBORNE DIVISION ARTILLERY BAND 15 AUGUST '42. INACTIVATED 1 MARCH '45.)

| | | |
|---|---|---|
| S/Sgt. Ricardo Sodero | 27 April '42 | 20 October '42 |
| WO (JG) Wilbur H. Hall | 21 October '42 | 19 March '44 |
| CWO Wilbur H. Hall | 20 March '44 | 28 February '45 |

COMMANDING OFFICER: 82ND AIRBORNE DIVISION BAND
(ACTIVATED 1 MARCH '45)

| | | |
|---|---|---|
| CWO Carl A Holdenhauer | 1 March '45 | 30 June '45 |
| CWO John T Venettozzi | 1 July '45 | End of War |

The Division Medical Supply Officer, 1st Lt. Arthur R. McAlpine, was supervising the storage of medical supplies at OUDJA, French Morocco, when he noticed a box that did not seem to belong with his supplies. Prying off the top, Lieutenant McAlpine discovered $1,000,000 worth of 1,000-franc notes issued by a French bank in DAKAR. Several months later another box containing $1,000,000 in francs was found among reserve Division supplies in BIZERTE, Tunisia.

The two boxes were part of a huge shipment of new banknotes that were being shipped by an American banknote company to the French bank. Somehow a total of 19 of the boxes became mixed with American military supplies being shipped to CASABLANCA. All were ultimately recovered.


## Appendix 15: Assignments, Attachments and Detachments

### Appendix15a: ASSIGNMENTS AND ATTACHMENTS OF DIVISION OR UNITS TO HIGHER HEADQUARTERS

THEATERS OF OPERATIONS

North African Theater of Operations (NATOUSA)
European Theater of Operations (ETOUSA)

ARMY GROUPS

| ARMY GROUP | CAMPAIGNS |
|---|---|
| 12th Army Group (U.S.) | Ardennes and Central Europe |
| 15th Army Group (U.S. & Br.) | Sicily, Italy (Naples-Foggia and Rome-Arno) |
| 21st Army Group | Normandy, Holland, Ardennes, Central Europe |

ARMIES

| ARMY | CAMPAIGN OR LOCATION |
|---|---|
| First (U.S.) | Normandy, Ardennes |
| First Allied Airborne | England, France |
| First (Canadian) | Holland |
| Second (U.S.) | U.S.A. |
| Second (Br.) | Holland, Central Europe |
| Third (U.S.) | U.S.A. |
| Fifth (U.S.) | North Africa, Italy |
| Seventh (U.S.) | Sicily |
| Ninth (U.S.) | England, Central Europe (For Administration) |
| Fifteenth (U.S.) | Rhineland |

CORPS

| CORPS | CAMPAIGN OR LOCATION |
|---|---|
| I Armored Corps (U.S.) | North Africa |
| 1st Airborne Corps (Br.) | Holland |
| II Corps (U.S.) | Sicily |
| Provisional Corps | Sicily |
| 2nd Corps (Canadian) | Holland |
| III Corps | Rhineland |
| IV Corps | U.S.A. |
| V Corps | Ardennes and Rhineland |
| VI Corps | Italy |
| VII Corps | Normandy |
| VIII Corps | Normandy, Ardennes |
| 10th Corps (Br.) | Italy |
| 12th Corps (Br.) | Central Europe |
| XV Corps (U.S.) | North Ireland |
| XVI Corps (U.S.) | France |
| XVIII Corps (Airborne) (U.S.) | Ardennes, Central Europe |
| XIX Corps (U.S.) | North Ireland |
| XXII Corps (U.S.) | Rhineland |
| 30th Corps (Br.) | Holland |

## Appendix 15a: UNITS OF DIVISION ATTACHED TO OTHER HEADQUARTERS

SICILY    505th Parachute RCT to 1st Infantry Division (U.S.)

ITALY    325th Glider RCT, 504th and 505th Parachute RCTs to
36th Infantry Division (U.S.) on Salerno Beachhead.
325th Glider RCT, 504th Parachute RCT, 319th Glider
Field Artillery Battalion, and the Batteries B, D, and F,
80th Airborne Antiaircraft Battalion, to Ranger Task
Force in Chiunzi Pass Sector.
505th Parachute RCT to 23rd Armored Brigade (Br.)
South of Naples.
505th Parachute RCT to 23rd Armored Brigade (Br.) In
Volturno River Sector.
504th Parachute RCT to 34th Infantry Division (U.S.)
and II Corps (U.S.) In Isernia and Venafro Sectors.
504th Parachute RCT to 3rd Infantry Divison (U.S.) on
Anzio Beachhead.

HOLLAND    508th Parachute RCT to 7th Armored North of Waal River.

BELGIUM    505th Parachute RCT to V Corps in Hurtgen Area.


## Appendix 15b: UNITS ATTACHED TO TIIE 82ND AIRBORNE DIVISION

NORTH AFRICA
(Complete records of attachments in North Africa are not currently available)
    2nd Battalion, 509th Parachute Infantry
    Engineer Co. (Cam)
    334th Quartermaster Company (Depot)

SICILY
(Complete records of attachments in Sicily are not currently available)
    39th Regimental Combat Team
    26th Field Artillery Battalion
    34th Field Artillery Battalion
    62nd Field Artillery Battalion
    77th Field Artillery Battalion
    20th Engineer Battalion (C)
    83rd Chemical Battalion (4.2" Mortar)

ITALY
(Complete records of attachments in Italy are not currently available)
    3rd Ranger Battalion (to 504th Parachute RCT)
    Ghurka Battalion, British (to 504th Parachute RCT)
    Quartermaster Truck Company

UNITED KINGDOM
    Headquarters and Headquarters Company, 2nd Airborne Brigade
    (From 20 January 1944 to 27 August 1944)
    507th Parachute Infantry
    (From 20 January 1944 to 27 August 1944)
    508th Parachute Infantry
    (From 20 January 1944 to 30 March 1945)

NORMANDY

| UNIT | FROM | TO |
|---|---|---|
| Troop B, 4th Cav Rcn Sqdn | 1 June 1944 | 23 June 1944 |
| 87th Armd FA Bn | 1 June 1944 | 8 June 1944 |
|  | 14 June 1944 | 8 July 1944 |
| Co C, 746th Tk Bn | 1 June 1944 | 11 June 1944 |
| Co A, 746th Tk Bn | 13 June 1944 | 21 June 1944 |
| Co A, 712th Tk Bn | 1 July 1944 | 8 July 1944 |
| 188th FA Bn | 12 June 1944 | 8 July 1944 |
| 172d FA Bn | 16 June 1944 | 19 June 1944 |
| Co C, 899th TD Bn | 1 June 1944 | 19 June 1944 |
| Co A, 607th TD Bn | 19 June 1944 | 4 July 1944 |
| 801 TD Bn | 30 June 1944 | 1 July 1944 |
| 803 TD Bn | 1 July 1944 | 8 July 1944 |
| Co B, 87th Chem Mortar Bn | 15 June 1944 | 21 June 1944 |
| Co D, 86th Chem Mortar Bn | 1 July 1944 | 4 July 1944 |

3809 QM Trk Co
3810 QM Trk Co
1st Plat, 603d QM Gr Co
1 Plat, 464th Amb Co, 31st Med Bn
493d Collecting Co, 179th Med Bn
374th Collecting Co, 50th Med Bn
429th Litter Bearing Platoon
591st Collecting Co

### HOLLAND

| UNIT | FROM | TO |
|---|---|---|
| Unit A, 50th Field Hosp. | 17 September 1944 | |
| 666th QM Trk. Co. | 19 September 1944 | |
| 1st Coldstream Gds. Armd. Bn (Br.) | 19 September 1944 | 22 September 1944 |
| 5th Coldstream Gds. Inf. Bn (Br.) | 19 September 1944 | 22 September 1944 |
| 2nd Irish Gds. Bn (Br.) | 19 September 1944 | 22 September 1944 |
| Sherwood Rangers Yeomanry (Br.) | 19 September 1944 | 10 October 1944 |
| Royals Recce Bn (Br.) | 10 September 1944 | 9 October 1944 |
| Polish Parachute Brigade | 25 September 1944 | 30 September 1944 |
| 231st Brigade (Br.) | 30 September 1944 | 1 October 1944 |
| 3d Gds. Brigade (Br.) | 30 September 1944 | 1 October 1944 |
| 5th Coldstream Gds. Inf. Bn (Br.) | 30 September 1944 | 10 October 1944 |
| 79th FA Regt. (Br.) | 30 September 1944 | 2 October 1944 |
| 304th AT Btry. (Br.) | 30 September 1944 | 3 October 1944 |
| 506th Prcht Inf. | 1 October 1944 | 3 October 1944 |
| 502d Prcht Inf. | 3 October 1944 | 4 October 1944 |
| 130th Inf. Brigade (Br.) | 5 October 1944 | 6 October 1944 |
| 2nd Gren Gds. Bn (Br.) | 6 October 1944 | 7 October 1944 |
| 13/18 Hussars | 10 October 1944 | 10 November 1944 |

### ARDENNES

| UNIT | FROM | TO |
|---|---|---|
| Unit A, 50th Field Hosp. | | |
| 666th QM Trk. Co. | | |
| Co C, 563d AAA AW Bn | 18 December 1944 | 25 December 1944 |
| CC "B", 9th Armd. Div. | 23 December 1944 | 24 December 1944 |
| Co B, 86th Cml Bn | 25 December 1944 | 11 January 1945 |
| 254th FA Bn | 20 December 1944 | 18 February 1945 |
| 551st Prcht Inf. Bn | 25 December 1944 | 12 January 1945 |
| 703d TD Bn | 20 December 1944 | 1 January 1945 |
| 591st FA Bn | 20 December 1944 | 11 January 1945 |
| 740th Tk Bn | 29 December 1944 | 11 January 1945 |
| | 27 January 1945 | 5 February 1945 |
| 628th TD Bn | 1 January 1945 | 11 January 1945 |
| 517th Prcht Inf. | 1 January 1945 | 11 January 1945 |
| | 1 February 1945 | 4 February 1945 |
| 634th AAA Bn | 5 February 1945 | 18 February 1945 |
| 887th Abn Engr Co | 25 December 1944 | 12 January 1945 |
| Co A, 87th Cml Bn | 25 January 1945 | 5 February 1945 |
| 643rd TD Bn | 25 January 1945 | 31 January 1945 |
| 400th Armd FA Bn | 25 January 1945 | 18 February 1945 |
| 32nd Cav Rcn Sqdn | 28 January 1945 | 5 February 1945 |
| 629th TD Bn | 31 January 1945 | 18 February 1945 |

### CENTRAL EUROPE

| UNIT | FROM | TO |
|---|---|---|
| 341st Inf. | 4 April 1945 | 4 April 1945 |
| 417th FA Gp | 4 April 1945 | 25 April 1945 |
| 746th FA Bn | 4 April 1945 | 25 April 1945 |
| 672nd FA Bn | 4 April 1945 | 14 April 1945 |
| 541st FA Bn | 4 April 1945 | 25 April 1945 |
| 805th FA Bn | 4 April 1945 | 16 April 1945 |
| 546th FA Bn | 11 April 1945 | 16 April 1945 |
| 790th FA Bn | 10 April 1945 | 14 April 1945 |
| 74th Cal Gen Co | 4 April 1945 | 21 April 1945 |
| 74th FA Bn | 18 April 1945 | 25 April 1945 |
| 12th TD Gp (Hq only) | 18 April 1945 | 25 April 1945 |
| 661st FA Bn | 18 April 1945 | 25 April 1945 |
| 942d FA Bn | 18 April 1945 | 25 April 1945 |
| 3rd Co, 22d Belgium Fus Bn | 21 April 1945 | 25 April 1945 |
| 294th FA Obs Bn | 25 April 1945 | 25 April 1945 |
| 1130th Engr C Bn | 25 April 1945 | 26 April 1945 |
| 280th FA Bn | 27 April 1945 | 17 May 1045 |
| 580th AAA AW Bn | 26 April 1945 | 2 May 1945 |
| | 23 May 1945 | 5 June 1945 |

| | | |
|---|---|---|
| 13th Infantry | 28 April 1945 | 1 May 1945 |
| 43rd FA Bn | 28 April 1945 | 1 May 1945 |
| 604th TD Bn | 26 April 1945 | 15 May 1945 |
| Sqdn A, 4th Royals (Br.) | 29 April 1945 | 2 May 1945 |
| 740th TK Bn | 29 April 1945 | 1 May 1945 |
| 644th TD Bn | 29 April 1945 | 1 May 1945 |
| Co. A, 98th Cml Bn | 29 April 1945 | 9 May 1945 |
| 121st Inf. | 30 April 1945 | 1 May 1945 |
| 56th FA Bn | 30 April 1945 | 1 May 1945 |
| Co. C, 99th Cml Bn | 30 April 1945 | 1 May 1945 |
| CC "B", 7th Armd Div | 1 May 1945 | 4 May 1945 |
| 205th FA Gp | 3 May 1945 | 17 May 1945 |
| 207th FA Bn | 3 May 1945 | 17 May 1945 |
| 768th FA Bn | 3 May 1945 | 17 May 1945 |

MILITARY INTELLIGENCE TEAMS ATTACHED IN ETOUSA
82nd Counter Intelligence Corps Detachment
Interrogator Prisoner of War Team No. 40
Interrogator Prisoner of War Team No. 43
Interrogator Prisoner of War Team No. 45
Interrogator Prisoner of War Team No. 47
Military Intelligence Interpreter Team No. 412
Order of Battle Team No. 16
Photo Interpretation Team No. 3
Photo Interpretation Team No. 11

## Appendix 16: Command Post Locations of the 82nd Airborne Division

| Date CP Opened | Place | Country |
|---|---|---|
| 25 March '42 | Camp Claiborne, Louisiana | United States |
| 02 October '42 | Fort Bragg, North Carolina | United States |
| 20 April '43 | Camp Edwards, Massachusetts | United States |
| 28 April '43 | U.S. Transport George Washington, Staten Island, New York | United States |
| 29 April '43 | U.S. Transport George Washington | At Sea |
| **NORTH AFRICA** | | |
| 10 May '43 | Camp Don B. Passage Casablanca | French Morocco |
| 12 May '43 | Oudja (Part of Division camped in Algeria) | French Morocco |
| 25 June '43 | Kairouan | Tunisia |
| **SICILY** | | |
| 6 July '43 | (Fwd) Aboard S.S. Monrovia | |
| 10 July '43 | (Fwd) Gela | Sicily |
| 17 July '43 | (Fwd) East of Agrigento | Sicily |
| 18 July '43 | (Fwd) Near Port Empedocle | Sicily |
| 19 July '43 | (Fwd) West of Montellegro | Sicily |
| 19 July '43 | (Fwd) West of Ribera | Sicily |
| 20 July '43 | (Fwd) Northeast of Sciacca | Sicily |
| 21 July '43 | (Fwd) S. Margherita | Sicily |
| 23 July '43 | (Fwd) Trapani | Sicily |
| 19 August '43 | Kairouan | Tunisia |
| (During period Forward CP was in Sicily the rear CP remained at Kairouan) | | |
| 02 September '43 | Bizerte | Tunisia |
| 05 September '43 | (Fwd) Licata | Sicily |
| 18 September '43 | (Fwd) Paestum | Italy |
| | (Rear) Termini | Sicily |
| | (Base) Comiso | Sicily |
| | (Rear) Base No. 1) Bizerte | Tunisia |
| | (Rear) Base No. 2) Kairouan | Tunisia |
| 22 September '43 | (Fwd) West of Castelcivita | Italy |
| 26 September '43 | Amalfi | Italy |
| 27 September '43 | (Fwd) Chiunzi Pass | Italy |
| 29 September '43 | Castellammare | Italy |
| 1 October '43 | Naples | Italy |
| 19 November '43 | U.S. Transport Funston | At Sea |

UNITED KINGDOM

| 9 December '43 | Castle Dawson | North Ireland |
| 14 February '44 | Braunstone Park, Leicester | England |
| 6 June '44 | (Fwd) West of Ste. Mere Eglise | France |
| | (Base) Leicester | England |

NORMANDY

| 14 June '44 | (Fwd) Near Picauville | France |
| 15 June '44 | (Fwd) North of Etienville | France |
| | (Rear) West of Etienville | France |
| 17 June '44 | (Fwd) East of St. Sauveur Le Vicomte France | |
| | (Rear) West of Etienville | France |
| 20 June '44 | (Fwd & Rear) South of Etienville | France |
| 2 July '44 | (Fwd) Southwest of Etienville | France |
| | (Rear) South of Etienville | France |
| 5 July '44 | (Fwd) Auvrairie | France |
| 12 July '44 | (Fwd & Rear) South of Etienville | France |
| 13 July '44 | Braunstone Park, Leicester | England |

HOLLAND

| 17 September '44 | (Fwd) West of Groesbeek | Netherlands |
| 24 September '44 | (Fwd) South of Nijmegen | Netherlands |
| 14 November '44 | (Fwd & Base) Camp Sissonne | France |

ARDENNES

| 18 December '44 | (Fwd) Werbomont | Belgium |
| 19 December '44 | (Fwd) Habiemont | Belgium |
| | (Rear) Werbomont | Belgium |
| 21 December '44 | (Fwd) Lierneux | Belgium |
| 22 December '44 | (Fwd & Rear) Bra | Belgium |
| 24 December '44 | (Fwd) Habiemont | Belgium |
| | (Rear) Chateau de Ville | Belgium |
| 27 December '44 | (Rear) Chevron | Belgium |
| 29 December '44 | (Fwd & Rear) Chevron | Belgium |
| 3 January '45 | (Fwd) Bassebodeux | Belgium |
| 5 January '45 | (Fwd) Abrefontaine | Belgium |
| 10 January '45 | (Rear) Nonceveux | Belgium |
| 11 January '45 | (Fwd & Rear) Nonceveux | Belgium |
| 25 January '45 | (Fwd & Rear) Nonceveux | Belgium |
| | (Main) Stevelot | Belgium |
| 26 January '45 | (Fwd) Hunnage | Belgium |
| 28 January '45 | (Fwd) Medell | Belgium |
| 29 January '45 | (Fwd) Wereth | Belgium |
| | (Rear Fwd) Medell | Belgium |
| | (Rear & Main) Stavelot | Belgium |
| 30 January '45 | (Fwd) Holzheim | Belgium |
| 5 February '45 | (Fwd) Vielsalm | Belgium |
| | (Rear & Main) Stavelot | Belgium |
| 8 February '45 | (Fwd & Rear) Rott | Germany |
| | (Main) Stavelot | Belgium |
| 10 February '45 | (Fwd) Hurtgen | Germany |
| | (Rear) Rott | Germany |
| | (Main) Stavelot | Belgium |
| | (Base) Sissonne | France |
| 18 February '45 | (Fwd & Rear) Rott | Germany |
| 19 February '45 | (All CPs) Sissonne | France |

CENTRAL EUROPE

| 2 April '45 | (Fwd) Weiden | Germany |
| 27 April '45 | (Fwd) Hohenzethen | Germany |
| | (Main) Weiden | Germany |
| 29 April '45 | (Fwd) Bleckede | Germany |
| 30 April '45 | (Advance) Wendischthun | Germany |
| | (Fwd & Rear) Bleckede | Germany |
| 1 May '45 | (Fwd) Neuhaus | Germany |
| | (Rear) Bleckede | Germany |
| 2 May '45 | (Advance) Ludwigslust | Germany |
| | (Fwd) Neuhaus | Germany |
| | (Rear) Bleckede | Germany |
| | (Main) Weiden | Germany |
| | (Base) Sissonne | France |

| 3 May '45 | (Fwd) Ludwigslust | Germany |
| | (Main) Weiden | Germany |
| 15 May '45 | (Fwd & Main) Ludwigslust | Germany |

POST - HOSTILITIES

| 1 June '45 | Sissonne | France |
| 18 June '45 | Épinal | France |
| 1 August '45 | Berlin | Germany |

At one time after the Italian campaign started troops of the 82nd Airborne Division were fighting or camped at seventeen different points in Italy, Sicily, and North Africa. As late as 25 September 1943, troops of the Division were fighting or camped in the Calore River Valley and on Sele Beach, Sorrento Peninsula and the Isle D'Ischia in Italy; Termini and Comiso in Sicily, and Bizerte and Kairouan in North Africa.

## Appendix 17
### Individual Clothing and Equipment List and Basic Load of Ammunition
### For Operation NEPTUNE

Extracted from 505th PIR Adm. Order No. 1 (May 23, 1944)

*Clothing and Equipment*
A. Worn by troops upon departure from Camp Quorn:
1. Tags, identification, w/necklace.
2. Underwear, summer.
3. Socks, wool or cotton.
4. Boots, parachutist.
5. Coveralls (Wool, OD, for Seaborne).
6. Belt, pistol or B.A.R. w/suspenders and canteen (full), intrenching tool, trench knife, first aid pouch w/sulphadiazine, and bayonet for rifleman.
7. Individual weapon.
8. Helmet, steel, w/net.
9. Bag, filed w/1 "K" and 2 "D" Rations, toilet articles, basic load of ammunition, wool socks (2 pair), hand towels (2), halazone, insecticide, handkerchiefs, and shoe impregnate.
10. Mask, gas, assault, complete.
11. Pay cards and officers identification card.
12. Kit, first aid, parachutist.
13. Raincoat.

B. Each Individual will carry one barracks bag to the departure fields with the following items:
1. Wool, OD Uniform.
2. Jump suit, impregnated, w/Div. patch and American Flag.
3. Summer underwear (1 pair).
4. Wool underwear (1 pair).
5. Extra toilet articles.
6. Extra towel, hand or bath.
7. Mess Kit, complete.

*Basic Load of Ammunition*

| Weapon | Rounds per Weapon | Remarks |
| --- | --- | --- |
| Rifle, M-1 | 167 | AP 100% |
| Rifle, '03 | 100 | AP 100% |
| Carbine | 135 | Ball 100% |
| B.A.R. | 680 | AP 90%, TR. 10% |
| Pistol | 21 | Ball 100% |
| Thompson S.M.G. | 270 | Ball 100% |
| Light M.G. (.30 cal.) | 2,250 | Rifle Co./4,250 Bn. HQ. Co. AP 90%, TR 10% |
| Heavy M.G. (.50 cal.) | 5,000 | AP 90%, TR 10% |
| Mortar, 60mm | 100 | HE 90%, Illum. 10% |
| Mortar, 81mm | 64 | HE 75%, WP 25% |
| Launcher, Rocket (2.36") | 12 | HE 100% |
| Launcher, Grenade | 16 | HE M9A1 100% |
| Grenade, Fragmentation | 2 | Per Individual |
| Grenade, Gammon | 1 | Per Individual |
| Grenade, Smoke | TBA | Per Signal Op. Instr. |
| Signal, Ground | 10 | Per discharger, M9 |
| Mine, At, US | 1,000 | Per Regiment |

**Appendix 18**
**Air Re-Supply Identification**

Extracted from 505th PIR Admin. Order No. 1 (May 23, 1944)

| Class of Supply | Supply | Canopy Color | Bundle Marking |
| --- | --- | --- | --- |
| Class I | QM (Rations "K") | Rations, "K" Blue | White "K" |
| Class II | Medical | Assorted Medical White | White Cross |
| Class II | Signal | Assorted Signal White | White "SI" |
| Class III | QM (POL) Gasoline | Green | White "G" |
| Class V | Ordnance (Ammo.) 75mm | Red or Yellow | White "75" |
| | .30 cal. | Red or Yellow | White "30" |
| Class V | Ordnance  Spare Parts | Red or Yellow | White "ORD" |
| Class V | Engineer (Mines)  Mines | Red or Yellow | White "M" |

**Appendix 19**
**Signal Instructions (Mutual Recognition – Ground to Ground)**

Extracted from 505th PIR Field Order No.1, Annex 7 (28 May 1944)

1. Recognition employed by friendly ground troops:
 a. Patrols and individuals – Countersign.
 b. Platoons and companies – Countersign, smoke, pyrotechnics, panels, flags, and lights.
 c. Bn. and larger units –  As above, plus authentication by radio.
 d. Tanks, scout cars, and other armored vehicles – Shape, flags, or marking panels.
2. Signals for ALL ground troops:
 a. Orange or Yellow Smoke, single yellow star M-44,
   Flourescent Colored Panels (AP50A),
   Three dots or dashed by light,
   Three snaps of a cricket – Friendly Troops.
 b. Violet smoke,
   Single green star M-45 – Do not land here or Keep Away – Demolitions to be set.
3. Three "Snaps" of a "Cricket" will be recognized by all A/B troops as Friendly Troops.

**Appendix 20**
**Letter from MG Ridgway to Each Member of the 82nd Evacuated to the UK**

18 June 1944
1. The hazards of battle which we all must accept in action have resulted in your hospitalization as a combat casualty. Wounds or injuries may incapacitate some for further airborne duty with this Division. But because you fought superbly, I know you will carry the same espirit into the accomplishment of any future assignment within your physical capacity. You, more than most, appreciate this vital importance of fighting spirit and the will to do in the rear, as well as in the front lines of battle.

2. Many of you will be able to rejoin the Division in a short while. Instructions have been issued to assure and facilitate your prompt return to your unit as soon as you period of hospitalization is completed and your convalescence permits.

3. Words cannot express adequately my admiration for your battle achievements.

4. Many met the supreme call of Duty for Country. For them and for you there can be no greater Honor than the tribute which is theirs in the hearts of us, your comrades, who continue to fight. We will keep the faith.

5. I wish you a speedy and complete recovery and an early return to us.

You, who remain to carry on the fight, have already established an enviable record of skill, courage and stamina. You have fought from day to day with continued and outstanding success to enlarge the invasion bridgehead in Western Europe. The many months of hard training and exacting exercises have proven your ability to prepare for and master any situation. The enemy has shown himself to be a crafty, skilled antagonist, but you have proven that you are better men in every respect.

It is vain to imagine that the Hun can be easily beaten. There is still hard fighting ahead, but I have full confidence that your future achievements will bring still greater credit to you, to the All-American Division, and to the United States Army.

My respects and best wishes to you all.
M.B. Ridgway
Major General, U.S. Army
Commanding.

# 75 MM PACK HOWITZER • *Parachute Delivery*

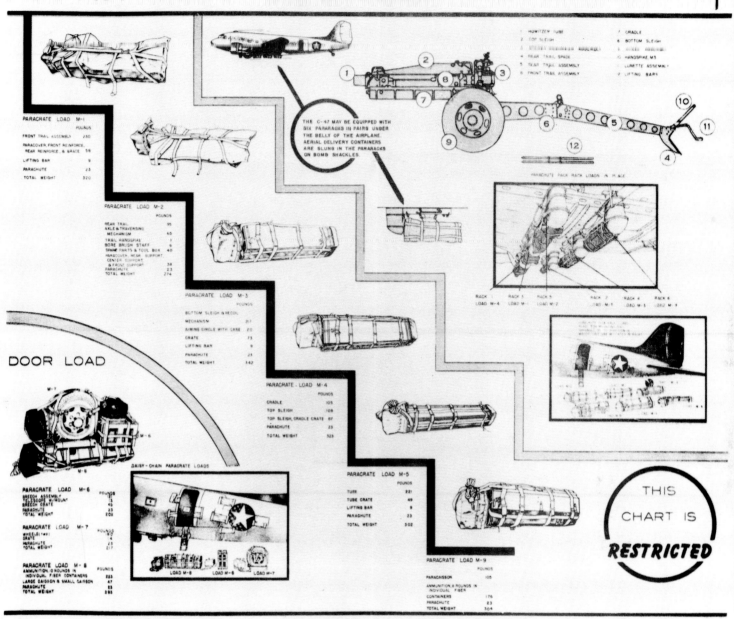

DOOR LOAD

**PARACRATE LOAD M-1**
POUNDS
FRONT TRAIL ASSEMBLY ... 230
PARACOVER, FRONT REINFORCE,
REAR REINFORCE & BRACE ... 58
LIFTING BAR ... 9
PARACHUTE ... 23
TOTAL WEIGHT ... 320

**PARACRATE LOAD M-2**
POUNDS
REAR TRAIL ... 95
AXLE & TRAVERSING
MECHANISM ... 65
TRAIL HANDSPIKE ... 1
BORE BRUSH STAFF ... 6
SPARE PARTS & TOOL BOX ... 40
PARACOVER, REAR SUPPORT
CENTER SUPPORT
& FRONT SUPPORT ... 38
PARACHUTE ... 23
TOTAL WEIGHT ... 274

**PARACRATE LOAD M-3**
POUNDS
BOTTOM SLEIGH & RECOIL
MECHANISM ... 217
AIMING CIRCLE WITH CASE ... 20
CRATE ... 73
LIFTING BAR ... 9
PARACHUTE ... 23
TOTAL WEIGHT ... 342

**PARACRATE LOAD M-4**
POUNDS
CRADLE ... 105
TOP SLEIGH ... 108
TOP SLEIGH, CRADLE CRATE ... 87
PARACHUTE ... 23
TOTAL WEIGHT ... 323

**PARACRATE LOAD M-5**
POUNDS
TUBE ... 221
TUBE CRATE ... 49
LIFTING BAR ... 9
PARACHUTE ... 23
TOTAL WEIGHT ... 302

**PARACRATE LOAD M-6**
POUNDS
BREECH ASSEMBLY
TELESCOPE W/MOUNT ... 31
BREECH CRATE ... 45
PARACHUTE ... 23
TOTAL WEIGHT ... 202

**PARACRATE LOAD M-7**
POUNDS
WHEELS (TWO) ... 180
CRATE ... 14
PARACHUTE ... 23
TOTAL WEIGHT ... 217

**PARACRATE LOAD M-8**
POUNDS
AMMUNITION, 9 ROUNDS IN
INDIVIDUAL FIBER CONTAINERS ... 223
LARGE CAISSON & SMALL CAISSON ... 47
PARACHUTE ... 23
TOTAL WEIGHT ... 293

**PARACRATE LOAD M-9**
POUNDS
PARACAISSON ... 105
AMMUNITION, 9 ROUNDS IN
INDIVIDUAL FIBER
CONTAINERS ... 176
PARACHUTE ... 23
TOTAL WEIGHT ... 304

THE C-47 MAY BE EQUIPPED WITH
SIX PARARACKS IN PAIRS UNDER
THE BELLY OF THE AIRPLANE.
AERIAL DELIVERY CONTAINERS
ARE SLUNG IN THE PARARACKS
ON BOMB SHACKLES.

1. HOWITZER TUBE
2. TOP SLEIGH
3. RECOIL MECHANISM ASSEMBLY
4. REAR TRAIL SPADE
5. REAR TRAIL ASSEMBLY
6. FRONT TRAIL ASSEMBLY
7. CRADLE
8. BOTTOM SLEIGH
9. WHEEL ASSEMBLY
10. HANDSPIKE M3
11. LUNETTE ASSEMBLY
12. LIFTING BARS

PARACHUTE PACK RACK LOADS IN PLACE

RACK 1 LOAD M-4   RACK 3 LOAD M-1   RACK 5 LOAD M-2   RACK 2 LOAD M-5   RACK 4 LOAD M-3   RACK 6 LOAD M-9

DAISY-CHAIN PARACRATE LOADS

LOAD M-8   LOAD M-6   LOAD M-7

THIS CHART IS **RESTRICTED**

AB CHART NO.9  15 AUGUST 1944

HQ AIRBORNE CENTER

# AERIAL DELIVERY CONTAINERS

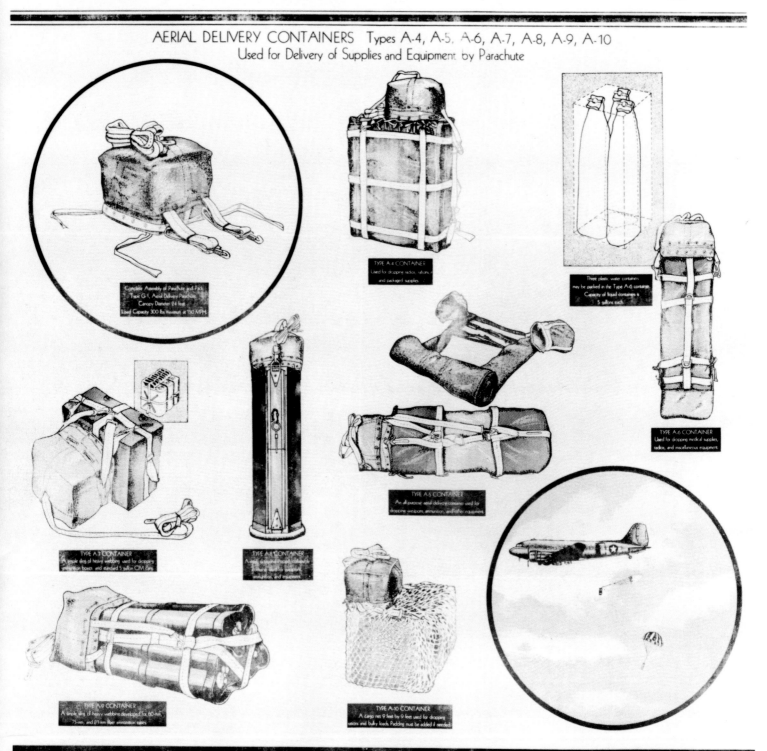

AERIAL DELIVERY CONTAINERS  Types A-4, A-5, A-6, A-7, A-8, A-9, A-10
Used for Delivery of Supplies and Equipment by Parachute

Complete Assembly of Parachute and Pack. Three G-1, Aerial Delivery Parachutes. Canopy Diameter 24 feet. Useful Capacity 300 lbs maximum at 150 MPH.

TYPE A-4 CONTAINER
Used for dropping radios, rations, and packaged supplies.

Three plastic water containers may be packed in the Type A-6 container. Capacity of liquid containers is 5 gallons each.

TYPE A-6 CONTAINER
Used for dropping medical supplies, radios, and miscellaneous equipment.

TYPE A-7 CONTAINER
A simple sling of heavy webbing used for dropping ammunition boxes and standard 5 gallon GM cans.

TYPE A-8 CONTAINER

TYPE A-5 CONTAINER
An all-purpose aerial delivery container used for dropping weapons, ammunition, and other equipment.

TYPE A-9 CONTAINER
A simple sling of heavy webbing developed for 60-mm, 75-mm, and 81-mm fiber ammunition cases.

TYPE A-10 CONTAINER
A cargo net 9 feet by 9 feet used for dropping rations and bulky loads. Padding must be added if needed.

Also See Training Film 31-1302, "Duties of the Parachute Rigger", and Film Strip 31-2 about Aerial Delivery Units.

# RADIO SETS IN AIRBORNE UNITS

NOTES

NOTES

NOTES

NOTES

NOTES

NOTES

NOTES

NOTES

## 82nd Airborne in Normandy
### A History in Period Photographs
Dominique François

On June 6, 1944, paratroops of the legendary 82nd Airborne Division jumped into Normandy with the mission of seizing the bridges over the Merderet River, Ste. Mere Eglise, and other surrounding villages. 82nd commander Major General Matthew Ridgway would later state about their exploits: "... thirty-three days of action without relief, without replacements. Every mission accomplished. No ground gained ever relinquished." This new, large-format book contains many first-person accounts from 82nd veterans, and more than 350 photographs and maps – most published here for the first time – as well as a selection of full-color photographs of World War II era airborne uniforms and equipment.
Size: 8½"x11" • 350+ b/w & color photos • 280 pp
ISBN: 0-7643-2057-2 • hard cover • $59.95

## The All American
### An Illustrated History of the 82nd Airborne Division
### 1917 – to the Present
Robert P. Anzuoni

This new book tells the complete story of the famous 82nd Airborne Division from its formation in 1917, through its legendary World War II campaigns (Sicily, Normandy and Holland), Vietnam, Grenada, Nicaragua, Operation Desert Storm to the present, and examines the many changes from a World War I infantry division to the rapid deployment organization it is today.
Size: 8½"x11" • over 230 b/w, color photographs • 176 pp.
ISBN: 0-7643-1321-5 • hard cover • $45.00

## Down to Earth
### The 507th Parachute Infantry Regiment
### in Normandy
Martin K.A. Morgan

In the early morning hours of D-Day, 2,004 paratroopers of the 507th Parachute Infantry Regiment jumped into Normandy as part of the famous 82nd Airborne Division. Out of the 2,004 men that jumped on June 6th, only 700 returned to England 35 days later. *Down To Earth* tells the story of those 35 days. Drawing on extensive oral history interviews with veterans of the regiment, *Down to Earth* focuses on the experiences of those who fought for the 507th during its baptism of fire.
Size: 8½"x11" • over 450 b/w and color photographs, maps • 256 pp
ISBN: 0-7643-2011-4 • hard cover • $69.95

## U.S. Army Rangers & Special Forces of World War II
### Their War in Photographs
Robert Todd Ross

This book tells the story of the U.S. Army's elite Rangers and Special Forces largely through pictures. Never before has such an expansive view of World War II elite forces been offered in one volume. An extensive search of public and private archives unearthed an astonishing number of rare and never before seen images, including color. Most notable are the nearly twenty exemplary photographs of Lieutenant Colonel William O. Darby's Ranger Force in Italy, taken by Robert Capa, considered by many to be the greatest combat photographer of all time. Complementing the period photographs are numerous color plates detailing the rare and often unique items of insignia, weapons, and equipment that marked the soldiers whose heavy task it was to "Lead the Way."
Size: 8½"x11" • over 250 black and white and color photographs • 216 pp.
ISBN: 0-7643-1682-6 • hard cover • $59.95

NOTES

## 82nd Airborne in Normandy
## A History in Period Photographs
Dominique François

On June 6, 1944, paratroops of the legendary 82nd Airborne Division jumped into Normandy with the mission of seizing the bridges over the Merderet River, Ste. Mere Eglise, and other surrounding villages. 82nd commander Major General Matthew Ridgway would later state about their exploits: "... thirty-three days of action without relief, without replacements. Every mission accomplished. No ground gained ever relinquished." This new, large-format book contains many first-person accounts from 82nd veterans, and more than 350 photographs and maps – most published here for the first time – as well as a selection of full-color photographs of World War II era airborne uniforms and equipment.
Size: 8 1/2"x11" • 350+ b/w & color photos • 280 pp
ISBN: 0-7643-2057-2 • hard cover • $59.95

## The All American
## An Illustrated History of the 82nd Airborne Division
## 1917 – to the Present
Robert P. Anzuoni

This new book tells the complete story of the famous 82nd Airborne Division from its formation in 1917, through its legendary World War II campaigns (Sicily, Normandy and Holland), Vietnam, Grenada, Nicaragua, Operation Desert Storm to the present, and examines the many changes from a World War I infantry division to the rapid deployment organization it is today.
Size: 8 1/2"x11" • over 230 b/w, color photographs • 176 pp.
ISBN: 0-7643-1321-5 • hard cover • $45.00

## Down to Earth
## The 507th Parachute Infantry Regiment
## in Normandy
Martin K.A. Morgan

In the early morning hours of D-Day, 2,004 paratroopers of the 507th Parachute Infantry Regiment jumped into Normandy as part of the famous 82nd Airborne Division. Out of the 2,004 men that jumped on June 6th, only 700 returned to England 35 days later. *Down To Earth* tells the story of those 35 days. Drawing on extensive oral history interviews with veterans of the regiment, *Down to Earth* focuses on the experiences of those who fought for the 507th during its baptism of fire.
Size: 8 1/2"x11" • over 450 b/w and color photographs, maps • 256 pp
ISBN: 0-7643-2011-4 • hard cover • $69.95

## U.S. Army Rangers & Special Forces of World War II
## Their War in Photographs
Robert Todd Ross

This book tells the story of the U.S. Army's elite Rangers and Special Forces largely through pictures. Never before has such an expansive view of World War II elite forces been offered in one volume. An extensive search of public and private archives unearthed an astonishing number of rare and never before seen images, including color. Most notable are the nearly twenty exemplary photographs of Lieutenant Colonel William O. Darby's Ranger Force in Italy, taken by Robert Capa, considered by many to be the greatest combat photographer of all time. Complementing the period photographs are numerous color plates detailing the rare and often unique items of insignia, weapons, and equipment that marked the soldiers whose heavy task it was to "Lead the Way."
Size: 8 1/2"x11" • over 250 black and white and color photographs • 216 pp.
ISBN: 0-7643-1682-6 • hard cover • $59.95

### The Supercommandos: First Special Service Force
### 1942-1944 – An Illustrated History
Robert Todd Ross

Chronicles the organization, training, and combat operations of the First Special Service Force during its brief but exhilarating history. Full-color maps, Order of Battle graphics, charts, and numerous noteworthy original Force documents are also included. Also shown are over eighty full-color images of authentic First Special Service Force uniforms, insignia, weapons and equipment. This book is an invaluable resource for any collector, reenactor, veteran, or historian.

Size: 8½"x11" • over 600 b/w photographs, over eighty color photographs, maps, documents • 320 pp
ISBN: 0-7643-1171-9 • hard cover • $59.95

### With the Black Devils
### A Soldier's World War II Account with the First Special Service Force and the 82nd Airborne
Mark J. Nelson

*With The Black Devils* offers readers a rare first-hand account of life with an elite group of American and Canadian World War II soldiers known as the First Special Service Force or "Black Devils". Based on the letters and diary entries of Sam Byrne, who served with the Force from the early days in Montana through the unit's inactivation in France, the book shares the thoughts and emotions of a front line soldier chronicling his activities as they take place. The book follows Sam's experiences after the Force's breakup, as he served in both the 504th and 507th Parachute Infantry Regiments. The author surrounds Sam's letters and diary entries with background information thereby placing Sam's words into a meaningful context for the reader. This book will appeal to anyone with an interest in World War II in general or the First Special Service Force specifically.

Size: 6"x9" • 30 b/w photographs • 176 pp
ISBN: 0-7643-2054-8 • hard cover • $29.95

### The Sky Men
### A Parachute Rifle Company's Story of the Battle of the Bulge and the Jump Across the Rhine
Kirk B. Ross

This is the story of F Company of the 513th Parachute Infantry Regiment, 17th U.S. Airborne Division. They were all volunteers to a new, dangerous, and elite corps – Airborne. Includes many never before used documents, with the personal accounts of nearly one hundred men of F Company and other associated organizations.

Size: 6"x9" • over 130 b/w photographs, documents, maps • 544 pp.
ISBN: 0-7643-1172-7 • hard cover • $35.00

### G-2: Intelligence for Patton
Brig.Gen. Oscar W. Koch with Robert G. Hays

The enigmatic science of military intelligence is examined in this personal record, written by Brig.Gen. Oscar W. Koch, who served during World War II as chief of intelligence for General George S. Patton, Jr. It traces the growth and development of the infant science through some of the most celebrated battles of the war. It is the exciting story of the operations behind the cloak and dagger illusions.

Size: 6"x9" • 168 pp.
ISBN: 0-7643-0800-9 • soft cover • $14.95

### Marine Pioneers
### The Unsung Heroes of World War II
Lt.Col. Kerry Lane

This book tells a powerful story that has never been told before and documents a rare look into a "Pioneer Unit," integrated with an infantry unit in the First Marine Division. Kerry Lane tells the riveting true story of his experiences as a Sergeant while serving with a Marine Pioneer Battalion during the Battle of Guadalcanal and the swamp battle known as "Suicide Creek." This book honors the many marine pioneers, their companies and battalion that contributed greatly to the victory that changed the course of the Pacific war.

Size: 6"x9" • over 100 b/w photos • 272 pp.
ISBN: 0-7643-0227-2 • hard cover • $29.95

**Forgotten Heroes**
**131 Men of the Korean War Awarded the Medal of Honor**
**1950-1953**
Kenneth N. Jordan, Sr.

*Forgotten Heroes* contains all 131 Medal of Honor citations. Also included are the official communiqués for that day and newspaper accounts of various battles.
Size: 6"x9" • b/w photographs • 352 pp.
ISBN: 0-88740-807-9 • hard cover • $24.95

**Heroes of Our Time**
**239 Men of the Vietnam War Awarded the Medal of Honor 1964-1972**
Kenneth N. Jordan, Sr.

*Heroes of Our Time* contains all 239 Medal of Honor citations such as this excerpt: "... His rifle ammunition expended, he seized two grenades and, in an act of unsurpassed heroism, charged toward the entrenched enemy weapon ... he marshalled his fleeting physical strength and hurled the two grenades, thus destroying the enemy position, as he fell dead upon the battlefield ..." Along with the citations are newspaper accounts of various battles.
Size: 6"x9" • 16 pp. of photographs • 368 pp.
ISBN: 0-88740-741-2 • hard cover • $24.95

**Men of Honor**
**Thirty-Eight Highly Decorated Marines of World War II, Korea and Vietnam**
Kenneth N. Jordan, Sr.

*Men of Honor* contains more than 100 official citations for bravery above and beyond the call of duty along with several eyewitness accounts. There are short biographies of all thirty-eight men, newspaper articles, and photographs.
Size: 6"x9" • 48 b/w photographs • 320 pp.
ISBN: 0-7643-0247-7 • hard cover • $29.95

**Palace Gate**
**Under Siege in Hue City: Tet January 1968**
Richard L. Brown

USAF Lt.Col. Richard Brown lived in the Hue MACV compound and remained in the city during the first seventeen days of the battle. These are his memoirs.
Size: 6" x9" • over 70 b/w photographs • 224 pp.
ISBN: 0-88740-745-5 • hard cover • $24.95

**The Advisor**
**The Phoenix Program in Vietnam**
Lt.Col. John L. Cook (USA, Ret.)

From his arrival in war-torn Vietnam in 1968 to his reluctant departure twenty-five months later, John Cook served as an advisor in the district of Di An and took part in the systematic operations of the Phoenix Program to destroy the Infrastructure, the political organization of the Viet Cong and North Vietnamese forces. The Advisor tells how one man came to see the Vietnam War as his war, how he became involved in the district villagers' struggle for their freedom from terrorism, and how he learned the true costs of that freedom.
Size: 6"x9" • 70 color and b/w photographs, 3 maps • 352 pp.
ISBN: 0-7643-0137-3 • hard cover • $35.00